D0463224

INTEGRATED CME PROJECT

Mathematics I

PEARSON

The Center for Mathematics Education Project was developed at Education Development Center, Inc. (EDC) within the Center for Mathematics Education (CME), with partial support from the National Science Foundation.

 Education Development Center, Inc.
Center for Mathematics Education
Newton, Massachusetts

 This material is based upon work supported by the National Science Foundation under Grant No. ESI-0242476, Grant No. MDR-9252952, and Grant No. ESI-9617369. Any opinions, findings, and conclusions or recommendations expressed in this material are those of the author(s) and do not necessarily reflect the views of the National Science Foundation.

Cover Art: Courtesy of Pearson Education, Inc.

Taken from:
CME Project: Geometry, Algebra 2, Algebra 1, Precalculus
By the CME Project Development Team
Copyright © 2009 by Education Development Center, Inc.
Published by Pearson Education, Inc.
Upper Saddle River, New Jersey 07458

CME Common Core Additional Lessons: Geometry, Precalculus, Algebra 2, Algebra 1
By the CME Project Development Team
Copyright © 2012 by Education Development Center, Inc.
Published by Pearson Education, Inc.
Upper Saddle River, New Jersey 07458

CME Project Development Team

Lead Developers: Al Cuoco and Bowen Kerins

Core Development Team: Anna Baccaglini-Frank, Jean Benson, Nancy Antonellis D'Amato, Daniel Erman, Brian Harvey, Wayne Harvey, Doreen Kilday, Ryota Matsuura, Stephen Maurer, Sarah Sword, Audrey Ting, Kevin Waterman. **Others who contributed include:** Elena Kaczorowski, Matt McLeod, Joe Obrycki, Carrie Abrams Ott, and William Thill.

Pearson Learning Solutions, 501 Boylston Street, Suite 900, Boston, MA 02116

A Pearson Education Company
www.pearsoned.com

Printed in the United States of America

4 5 6 7 8 9 10 V011 17 16 15 14 13

000200010271656490

MD  33380005815283

PEARSON   ISBN 10: 1-256-69465-7
ISBN 13: 978-1-256-69465-6

Contents in Brief

Introduction to the CME Project

CME PROJECT

The CME Project, developed by EDC's Center for Mathematics Education, is a new NSF-funded high school program, organized around the familiar courses of algebra 1, geometry, algebra 2, and precalculus. The CME Project provides teachers and schools with a third alternative to the choice between traditional texts driven by basic skill development and more progressive texts that have unfamiliar organizations. This program gives teachers the option of a problem-based, student-centered program, organized around the mathematical themes with which teachers and parents are familiar. Furthermore, the tremendous success of NSF-funded middle school programs has left a need for a high school program with similar rigor and pedagogy. The CME Project fills this need.

The goal of the CME Project is to help students acquire a deep understanding of mathematics. Therefore, the mathematics here is rigorous. We took great care to create lesson plans that, while challenging, will capture and engage students of all abilities and improve their mathematical achievement.

The Program's Approach

The organization of the CME Project provides students the time and focus they need to develop fundamental mathematical ways of thinking. Its primary goal is to develop in students robust mathematical proficiency.

- The program employs innovative instructional methods, developed over decades of classroom experience and informed by research, that help students master mathematical topics.

- One of the core tenets of the CME Project is to focus on developing students' Habits of Mind, or ways in which students approach and solve mathematical challenges.

- The program builds on lessons learned from high-performing countries: develop an idea thoroughly and then revisit it only to deepen it; organize ideas in a way that is faithful to how they are organized in mathematics; and reduce clutter and extraneous topics.

- It also employs the best American models that call for grappling with ideas and problems as preparation for instruction, moving from concrete problems to abstractions and general theories, and situating mathematics in engaging contexts.

- The CME Project is a comprehensive curriculum that meets the dual goals of mathematical rigor and accessibility for a broad range of students.

About CME

EDC's Center for Mathematics Education, led by mathematician and teacher **Al Cuoco**, brings together an eclectic staff of mathematicians, teachers, cognitive scientists, education researchers, curriculum developers, specialists in educational technology, and teacher educators, internationally known for leadership across the entire range of K–16 mathematics education. We aim to help students and teachers in this country experience the thrill of solving problems and building theories, understand the history of ideas behind the evolution of mathematical disciplines, and appreciate the standards of rigor that are central to mathematical culture.

Contributors to the CME Project

National Advisory Board The National Advisory Board met early in the project, providing critical feedback on the instructional design and the overall organization. Members include

Richard Askey, University of Wisconsin
Edward Barbeau, University of Toronto
Hyman Bass, University of Michigan
Carol Findell, Boston University
Arthur Heinricher, Worcester Polytechnic Institute
Roger Howe, Yale University
Barbara Janson, Janson Associates
Kenneth Levasseur, University of Massachusetts, Lowell
James Madden, Louisiana State University, Baton Rouge
Jacqueline Miller, Education Development Center
James Newton, University of Maryland
Robert Segall, Greater Hartford Academy of Mathematics and Science
Glenn Stevens, Boston University
Herbert Wilf, University of Pennsylvania
Hung-Hsi Wu, University of California, Berkeley

Core Mathematical Consultants

Dick Askey, Ed Barbeau, and **Roger Howe** have been involved in an even more substantial way, reviewing chapters and providing detailed and critical advice on every aspect of the program. Dick and Roger spent many hours reading and criticizing drafts, brainstorming with the writing team, and offering advice on everything from the logical organization to the actual numbers used in problems. We can't thank them enough.

Teacher Advisory Board

The Teacher Advisory Board for the CME Project was essential in helping us create an effective format for our lessons that embodies the philosophy and goals of the program. Their debates about pedagogical issues and how to develop mathematical topics helped to shape the distinguishing features of the curriculum so that our lessons work effectively in the classroom. The advisory board includes

> **Jayne Abbas, Richard Coffey,**
> **Charles Garabedian, Dennis Geller,**
> **Eileen Herlihy, Doreen Kilday,**
> **Gayle Masse, Hugh McLaughlin,**
> **Nancy McLaughlin, Allen Olsen,**
> **Kimberly Osborne, Brian Shoemaker,**
> and **Benjamin Sinwell**

Field-Test Teachers Our field-test teachers gave us the benefit of their classroom experience by teaching from our draft lessons and giving us extensive, critical feedback that shaped the drafts into realistic, teachable lessons. They shared their concerns, questions, challenges, and successes and kept us focused on the real world. Some of them even welcomed us into their classrooms as co-teachers to give us the direct experience with students that we needed to hone our lessons. Working with these expert professionals has been one of the most gratifying parts of the development—they are "highly qualified" in the most profound sense.

California Barney Martinez, Jefferson High School, Daly City; **Calvin Baylon** and **Jaime Lao,** Bell Junior High School, San Diego; **Colorado Rocky Cundiff,** Ignacio High School, Ignacio; **Illinois Jeremy Kahan, Tammy Nguyen,** and **Stephanie Pederson,** Ida Crown Jewish Academy, Chicago; **Massachusetts Carol Martignette, Chris Martino** and **Kent Werst,** Arlington High School, Arlington, **Larry Davidson,** Boston University Academy, Boston; **Joe Bishop** and **Carol Rosen,** Lawrence High School, Lawrence; **Maureen Mulryan,** Lowell High School, Lowell; **Felisa Honeyman,** Newton South High School, Newton Centre; **Jim Barnes** and **Carol Haney,** Revere High School, Revere; **New Hampshire Jayne Abbas** and **Terin Voisine,** Cawley Middle School, Hooksett; **New Mexico Mary Andrews,** Las Cruces High School, Las Cruces; **Ohio James Stallworth,** Hughes Center, Cincinnati; **Texas Arnell Crayton,** Bellaire High School, Bellaire; **Utah Troy Jones,** Waterford School, Sandy; **Washington Dale Erz, Kathy Greer, Karena Hanscom,** and **John Henry,** Port Angeles High School, Port Angeles; **Wisconsin Annette Roskam,** Rice Lake High School, Rice Lake.

Special thanks go to our colleagues at Pearson, most notably Elizabeth Lehnertz, Joe Will, and Stewart Wood. The program benefits from their expertise in every way, from the actual mathematics to the design of the printed page.

1 Arithmetic to Algebra

2 Expressions and Equations

3 Graphs

4 Lines

Contents

(5) Exponents and Functions

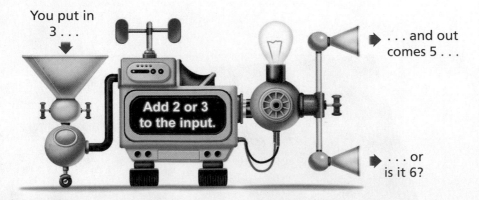

You put in 3 . . .

Add 2 or 3 to the input.

. . . and out comes 5 . . .

. . . or is it 6?

6 Statistics and Fitting Lines

Contents

7 Introduction to Geometry

8 Congruence and Transformations

Honors Appendix

CME Project
Student Handbook

What Makes CME Different

Welcome to the CME Project! The goal of this program is to help you develop a deep understanding of mathematics. Throughout this book, you will engage in many different activities to help you develop that deep understanding. Some of these instructional activities may be different from ones you are used to. Below is an overview of some of these elements and why they are an important part of the CME Project.

The Habits of Mind Experience

Mathematical Habits of Mind are the foundation for serious questioning, solid thinking, good problem solving, and critical analysis. These Habits of Mind are what will help you become a mathematical thinker. Throughout the CME Project, you will focus on developing and refining these Habits of Mind.

Lesson 1.0 is an introduction to Habits of Mind. This lesson consists of experiments that allow you to tinker with the mathematical ideas that you will formalize throughout the course.

Developing Habits of Mind

Develop thinking skills. This feature provides you with various methods and approaches to solving problems.

You will develop, use, and revisit specific Habits of Mind throughout the course. These include

- **Process** (how you work through problems)
- **Visualization** (how you "picture" problems)
- **Representation** (what you write down)
- **Patterns** (what you find)
- **Relationships** (what you find or use)

Developing good habits will help you as problems become more complicated.

Habits of Mind

Think. These special margin notes highlight key thinking skills and prompt you to apply your developing Habits of Mind.

Minds in Action

Discussion of mathematical ideas is an effective method of learning. The Minds in Action feature exposes you to ways of communicating about mathematics.

Join Sasha, Tony, Derman, and others as they think, calculate, predict, and discuss their way towards understanding.

Minds in Action

Sasha, Tony, and Derman have just skimmed through their Mathematics I book.

Sasha Did you notice the student dialogs throughout the book?

Derman Sure did!

Tony They talk and think just the way we do.

Sasha I know! And they even make mistakes sometimes, the way we do.

Tony But I like how they help each other to learn from those mistakes. I bet they use the Habits of Mind I saw all over the book, too.

Sasha That's great! They should help a lot.

Exploring Mathematics

Throughout the CME Project, you will engage in activities that extend your learning and allow you to explore the concepts you learn in greater depth. Two of these activities are In-Class Experiments and Chapter Projects.

In-Class Experiment

In-Class Experiments allow you to explore new concepts and apply the Habits of Mind.

You will explore math as mathematicians do. You start with a question and develop answers through experimentation.

Chapter Projects

Chapter Projects allow you to apply your Habits of Mind to the content of the chapter. These projects cover many different topics and allow you to explore and engage in greater depth.

Chapter Projects
Using Mathematical Habits

Here is a list of the Chapter Projects.

Using your CME Book

To help you make the most of your CME experience, we are providing the following overview of the organization of your book.

Focusing your Learning

In *Mathematics I*, there are 8 chapters, with each chapter devoted to a mathematical concept. With only 8 chapters, your class will be able to focus on these core concepts and develop a deep understanding of them.

Within each chapter, you will explore a series of Investigations. Each Investigation focuses on an important aspect of the mathematical concept for that chapter.

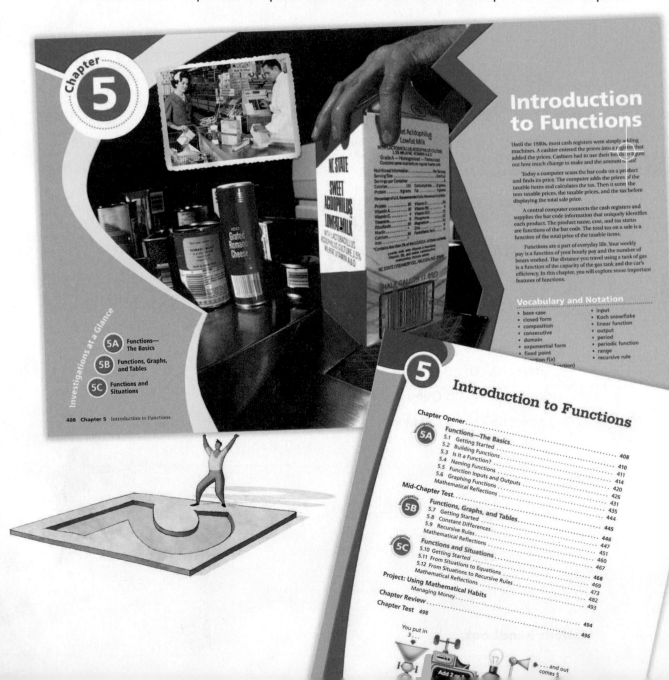

The CME Investigation

The goal of each mathematical Investigation is for you to formalize your understanding of the mathematics being taught. There are some common instructional features in each Investigation.

Getting Started

You will launch into each Investigation with a Getting Started lesson that activates prior knowledge and explores new ideas. This lesson provides you the opportunity to grapple with ideas and problems. The goal of these lessons is for you to explore—not all your questions will be answered in these lessons.

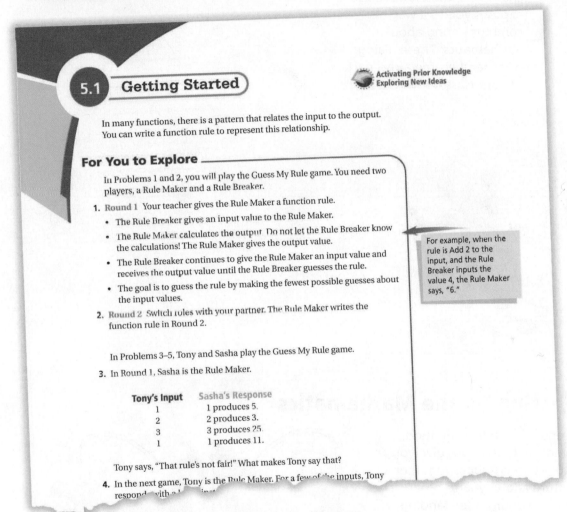

5.1 Getting Started

**Activating Prior Knowledge
Exploring New Ideas**

In many functions, there is a pattern that relates the input to the output. You can write a function rule to represent this relationship.

For You to Explore

In Problems 1 and 2, you will play the Guess My Rule game. You need two players, a Rule Maker and a Rule Breaker.

1. **Round 1** Your teacher gives the Rule Maker a function rule.
   - The Rule Breaker gives an input value to the Rule Maker.
   - The Rule Maker calculates the output. Do not let the Rule Breaker know the calculations! The Rule Maker gives the output value.
   - The Rule Breaker continues to give the Rule Maker an input value and receives the output value until the Rule Breaker guesses the rule.
   - The goal is to guess the rule by making the fewest possible guesses about the input values.

2. **Round 2** Switch roles with your partner. The Rule Maker writes the function rule in Round 2.

   In Problems 3–5, Tony and Sasha play the Guess My Rule game.

3. In Round 1, Sasha is the Rule Maker.

Tony's Input	Sasha's Response
1	1 produces 5.
2	2 produces 3.
3	3 produces 25.
1	1 produces 11.

   Tony says, "That rule's not fair!" What makes Tony say that?

4. In the next game, Tony is the Rule Maker. For a few of the inputs, Tony respond~ ~ith ~ ~

For example, when the rule is Add 2 to the input, and the Rule Breaker inputs the value 4, the Rule Maker says, "6."

Learning the Mathematics

You will engage in, learn, and practice the mathematics in a variety of ways. The types of learning elements you will find throughout this course include

- **Worked-Out Examples** that model how to solve problems
- **Definitions and Theorems** to summarize key concepts
- **In-Class Experiments** to explore the concepts
- **For You to Do** assignments to check your understanding
- **For Discussion** questions to encourage communication
- **Minds in Action** to model mathematical discussion

Communicating the Mathematics

Student dialogs

By featuring dialogs between characters, the CME Project exposes you to a way of communicating about mathematics. These dialogs will then become a real part of your classroom! •••••••

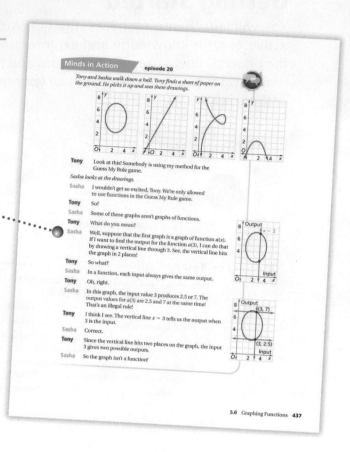

Reflecting on the Mathematics

At the end of each Investigation, Mathematical Reflections give you an opportunity to put ideas together. This feature allows you to demonstrate your understanding of the Investigation and reflect on what you learn.

Practice

The CME Project views extensive practice as a critical component of a mathematics curriculum. You will have daily opportunities to practice what you learn.

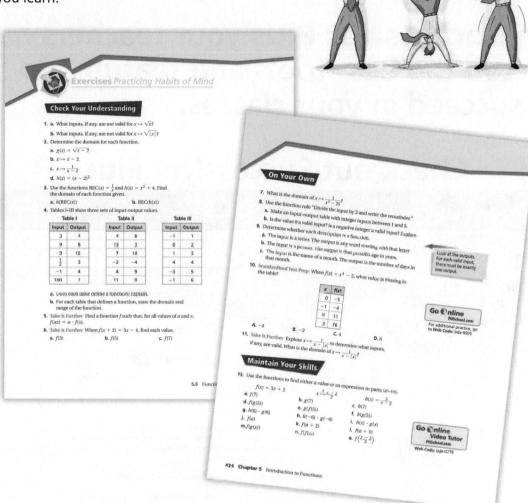

Check Your Understanding
Assess your readiness for independent practice by working through these problems in class.

On Your Own
Practice and continue developing the mathematical understanding you learn in each lesson.

Maintain Your Skills
Review and reinforce skills from previous lessons.

Also Available
An additional Practice Workbook is available separately.

Go Online

With SuccessNet Plus your teachers have selected the best tools and features to help you succeed in your classes.

Check out SuccessNet Plus

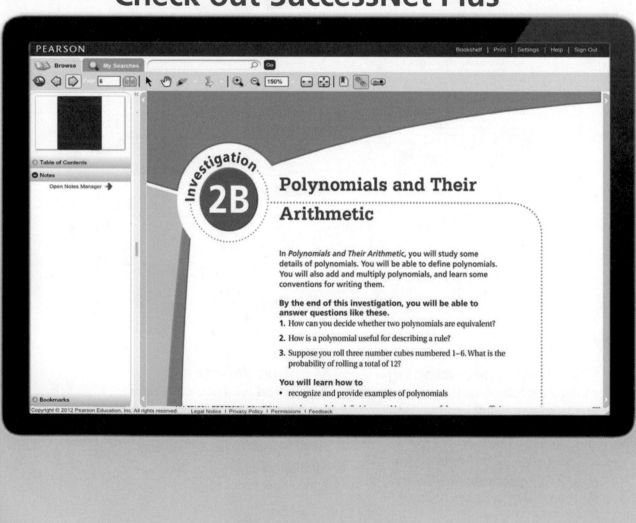

Log-in to www.successnetplus.com to find:

- an online Pearson eText version of your textbook

- extra practice and assessments

- worksheets and activities

- multimedia

Check out the TI-Nspire™ Technology Handbook on p. 788 for examples of how you can use handheld technology with your math learning!

Chapter 1

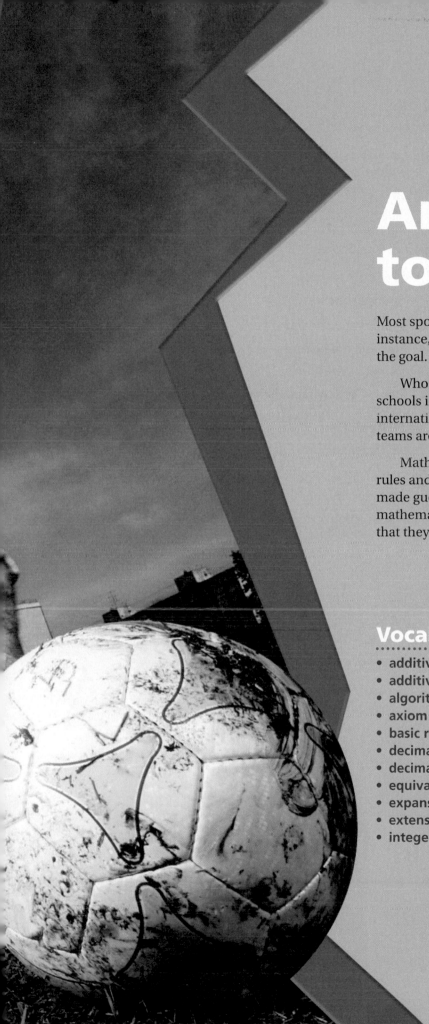

Arithmetic to Algebra

Most sports have very complicated rules. Soccer, for instance, seems like a simple game of kicking the ball into the goal. However, there are many rules.

Who developed the rules of soccer? In the 1600s, schools in England started making soccer rules. Today, an international organization maintains soccer rules so that teams around the world can use the same rules.

Mathematicians have agreed on a common set of rules and symbols. They have extended the rules and made guesses about the way numbers work. Finally, mathematicians have proved their guesses based on rules that they already knew.

Vocabulary and Notation

- additive identity
- additive inverse
- algorithm
- axiom
- basic rules of arithmetic
- decimal expansion
- decimal representation
- equivalent fractions
- expansion box
- extension of a rule
- integers
- least common denominator
- lowest terms
- multiplicative identity
- negative number
- number line
- opposites
- place-value part
- reciprocal
- square root
- · (multiplication)

Habits of Mind

Mathematical habits of mind are the most fundamental concepts and applications that you will take away from your mathematics courses. These habits are the bedrock for serious questioning, good problem solving, and critical analysis.

You will use each of the following behaviors beyond the world of mathematics. Sound habits of mind encourage and support your success in the world.

Be a pattern detective:

Build and see patterns.

Recognize a similar process.

Count without counting.

Look for relationships.

Be an experimenter:

Simplify the problem.

Find and repeat a process.

Try numerical cases.

Identify key characteristics.

Be a visualizer:

Imagine the result.

Model the situation.

"See" a proof.

Think proportionally.

Be an inventor:

Be systematic.

Cover the cases.

Consider the complement.

Reason about calculations.

Be a tinkerer:

Reverse the direction.

Investigate dynamic behavior.

Analyze continuous behavior.

Probe symmetric behavior.

Study extreme behavior.

Be a conjecturer:

Generalize to the nth value.

Generalize to higher dimensions.

Extend to general figure.

Find a counterexample.

Can you think of any other mathematical habits?

Try some of the following activities. As you proceed through the course, think about how you are thinking. Pay attention to your habits of mind!

Building mathematics and building a house require habits of mind that are surprisingly similar.

Be an Experimenter

You have developed the mathematical habits of mind you need to play Sudoku already. These habits are second nature.

1. Copy and play the easy game. Complete the table so that each row, column, and 3-by-3 square contains the numbers 1–9 with no repetition.

Easy

4	7	8	▣	▣	2	6	3	▣
2	3	6	4	7	▣	▣	5	8
9	1	▣	▣	▣	▣	▣	7	▣
3	▣	2	1	6	5	4	▣	▣
▣	6	▣	▣	▣	▣	▣	2	▣
▣	▣	▣	8	▣	9	3	1	▣
▣	5	9	▣	1	▣	7	▣	3
▣	▣	4	9	▣	▣	8	▣	5
▣	▣	▣	▣	5	▣	1	▣	2

Difficult

▣	▣	▣	B	▣	G	▣	A	▣
▣	▣	▣	H	D	F	▣	▣	C
D	▣	▣	▣	▣	▣	▣	G	▣
▣	▣	▣	▣	▣	▣	▣	▣	D
C	▣	▣	D	A	E	▣	▣	I
B	▣	▣	▣	▣	▣	▣	▣	▣
▣	F	▣	▣	▣	▣	▣	▣	H
A	▣	▣	G	I	C	▣	▣	▣
▣	E	▣	A	▣	H	▣	▣	▣

2. Copy and play the difficult game above. Explain how using letters instead of numbers changes how you play the game.

Be a Visualizer

Here is an equation that you solve by moving the given number of toothpicks to make a true equation. You do not remove toothpicks from the equation.

3. $VII + V = X$; one toothpick

4. $IX + I = VII$; one toothpick

5. $IV - II = V$; two toothpicks

6. a. Remove two toothpicks from the pattern of squares and leave two squares.

   b. Remove two toothpicks from the original pattern and leave three squares.

> **Remember...**
>
> Roman and Arabic Numerals
>
> | | | | |
> |---|---|---|---|
> | I | 1 | VI | 6 |
> | II | 2 | VII | 7 |
> | III | 3 | VIII | 8 |
> | IV | 4 | IX | 9 |
> | V | 5 | X | 10 |

Use the figure in Problem 6. You may cross the toothpicks to make squares.

7.

Number of Toothpicks to Move	2	2	3	4	4	4
Number of Squares to Make	6	7	3	2	3	10

Be an Inventor

In the early grades, you developed habits and skills with number operations.

8. Copy and complete the cross-sums table using the following rules. Pay attention to how you think about solving the puzzle. The first row and column are complete.

- The unshaded numbers in each row or partial row add up to the shaded number at the left of the row.

- The unshaded numbers in each column or partial column add up to the shaded number above the column.

- The addends for each sum are numbers from 1 to 9 without any repeated numbers.

9. Copy the blank cross-sums game. Make a cross-sums game to give to a classmate. Make an answer grid.

Be an Experimenter

In this game of "Dodgeball," you may combine the habits of mind by thinking ahead and considering the possibilities. If you do this, you know exactly what to expect.

10. Players A and B copy a table. Use these rules.

- Each player gets 6 turns. The symbols are always visible to both players.

- Player A fills Row 1 with X's and O's. Player B writes X or O in Cell 1.

- On each turn, Player A completes a row and Player B completes a cell.

- Player A wins if any of Player A's rows matches Player B's row. Otherwise, Player B wins.

11. Decide which player, A or B, has an advantage in this game. Explain.

Player A

Player B

In-Class Experiment

Be a Pattern Detective

Important habits of mind include looking for, finding, extending, and asking questions about patterns that you observe. Work in small groups. Study the look-and-say sequence at the right.

12. Find a pattern and write the next three strings of numbers. (*Hint:* To help find the pattern, try reading the numbers in each string aloud. As you read, look also at the preceding string.)

13. What other patterns can you find in the strings of numbers?

14. What questions can you ask about the number strings not yet listed?

1

11

21

1211

111221

312211

13112221

1113213211

31131211131221

13211311123113112211

In-Class Experiment

Be a Logical Thinker

In a row of six houses, each house is a different color. The house colors are blue, purple, red, white, green, and yellow. Pets live in five of the six houses. The pets are a dog, a cat, a bird, a fish, and a hamster.

- The blue house is fourth from the left.
- The cat lives in the white house.
- The yellow house is next to the white house.
- The blue house is between the yellow house and the green house.
- The cat does not live next to the dog, the bird, or the house with no pet.
- The hamster lives in the first (left-most) house.
- The white house is not next to the red house.
- The bird lives next to the house with no pet.

15. Which colors of houses could be second in the row?

16. Which colors of houses could be fifth in the row?

17. Which color of house does the fish live in?

18. Which pets could live in the blue house?

19. Also suppose the red house is first, the dog lives in the purple house, and the blue house has no pet. What is the order of the houses and pets?

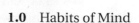

The Tables of Arithmetic

In *The Tables of Arithmetic,* you will learn about adding and multiplying integers using addition and multiplication tables. You will also learn about the basic rules of arithmetic.

By the end of this investigation, you will be able to answer questions like these.

1. How can you illustrate the properties of addition by using an addition table?

2. How can you illustrate the properties of multiplication by using a multiplication table?

3. Why is the sum of two negative numbers negative, and the product of two negative numbers positive?

You will learn how to

- identify, describe, and justify patterns in addition and multiplication tables

- perform integer addition and multiplication

- explain the rules for multiplying and adding negative integers

- subtract using integers, which is the same as to add the integer's opposite

- apply the basic rules of arithmetic to integers

You will develop these habits and skills:

- Identify, describe, and explain patterns.

- Gain a sense of how a mathematician works.

- Extend concepts and patterns to build mathematical knowledge.

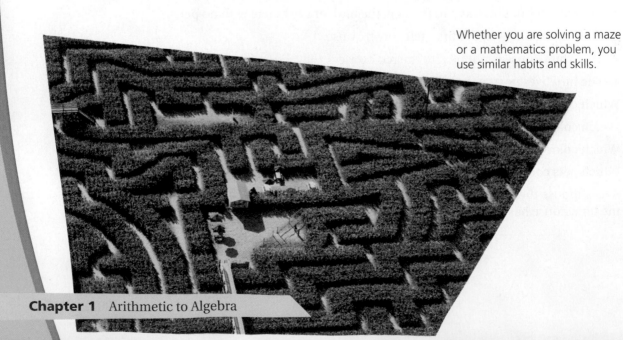

Whether you are solving a maze or a mathematics problem, you use similar habits and skills.

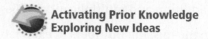

Activating Prior Knowledge
Exploring New Ideas

In multiplication and addition tables, you can find many number patterns.

For You to Explore

These parts of an addition table and a multiplication table may differ from tables you have seen, because they start in the lower left corner.

> Usually, addition and multiplication tables show smaller numbers in the upper left corner.

Addition Table

+	0	1	2	3	4	5	6	7	8	9	10	11	12
12	12	13	14		16	17	18	19	20	21	22	23	24
11	11	12	13			16	17	18	19	20	21	22	23
10	10	11	12		14		16	17	18	19	20	21	22
9	9	10	11		13	14		16	17	18	19	20	21
8	8	9	10		12	13	14		16	17	18	19	20
7	7	8	9		11	12	13	14		16	17	18	19
6	6	7	8		10	11	12	13	14		16	17	18
5	5	6	7		9	10	11	12	13	14		16	17
4	4	5	6		8	9	10	11	12	13	14		16
3	3	4	5		7	8	9	10	11	12	13	14	
2	2	3	4		6	7	8	9	10	11	12		14
1	1	2	3		5	6	7	8	9	10		12	13
0	0	1	2	3	4	5	6	7	8	9	10	11	12

Multiplication Table

×	0	1	2	3	4	5	6	7	8	9	10	11	12
12	0	12	24	36	48	60	72		96	108	120	132	144
11	0		22	33	44	55		77	88	99	110	121	132
10	0	10		30			60	70	80	90	100	110	120
9	0	9	18			45	54	63	72	81	90	99	108
8	0	8	16			40	48	56	64	72	80	88	96
7	0	7		21	28		42	49	56	63	70	77	84
6	0		12	18	24	30		42	48	54	60	66	72
5	0	5	10	15	20	25	30		40	45	50	55	60
4	0	4	8	12	16	20	24	28		36	40	44	48
3	0	3	6	9	12	15	18	21	24		30	33	36
2	0	2	4	6	8	10	12	14	16	18		22	24
1	0	1	2	3	4	5	6	7	8	9	10		12
0	0	0	0	0	0	0	0	0	0	0	0	0	0

Use the addition and multiplication tables.

1. What are the missing numbers in each table?

Exercise 1 gives you a few patterns.

2. Find and explain several patterns in the addition table.

3. Find and explain several patterns in the multiplication table.

4. Explain how values in the addition table change when you move in a direction given.

   a. up 1 row

   b. down 1 row

   c. right 1 column

   d. left 1 column

5. a. Copy a part of the multiplication table. Label each axis with factors from 0 to 7. Circle the even products. Describe the pattern.

   b. When you choose at random a product in the table, what is the probability that the product is even? Explain.

   c. **Take It Further** Does your result in Problem 5b change when you use a table with factors from 0 to 12? Explain.

Remember...

The number 0 is an even number.

Exercises *Practicing Habits of Mind*

On Your Own

6. How does each value in the addition table change when you move up one row and right one column? Explain.

7. Explain how each value in the addition table changes when you move up 5 rows and left 3 columns.

8. Illustrate the following arithmetic fact using an addition table. When you choose a number, add 5 and subtract 9 from the result, the result is 4 less than the number you chose.

9. a. Make a part of the addition table. Label each axis with summands from 0 to 7. Circle the even sums. Describe the pattern.

b. When you choose at random a sum in the table, what is the probability that the number is even? Explain.

c. Take It Further Does your result in Exercise 9b change when you use a table of summands from 0 to 12? Explain.

Remember...

A summand is either one of the two numbers that you add. For example, 5 and 8 are summands in $5 + 8 = 13$.

Maintain Your Skills

10. Find each sum.

a. $0 + 1 + 2 + 3 + 4$

b. $1 + 2 + 3 + 4 + 5$

c. $2 + 3 + 4 + 5 + 6$

d. $3 + 4 + 5 + 6 + 7$

e. $4 + 5 + 6 + 7 + 8$

f. What pattern in the sums do you find?

11. Find each sum.

a. $1 + 2 + 3 + 4 + 5 + 6 + 7 + 8$

b. $2 + 3 + 4 + 5 + 6 + 7 + 8 + 9$

c. $3 + 4 + 5 + 6 + 7 + 8 + 9 + 10$

d. $4 + 5 + 6 + 7 + 8 + 9 + 10 + 11$

e. $5 + 6 + 7 + 8 + 9 + 10 + 11 + 12$

f. What pattern in the sums do you find?

1.02 Thinking About Negative Numbers

The first number system you learned was the whole number system, {0, 1, 2, . . . }. The addition and multiplication tables in Lesson 1.01 use only the whole numbers.

When you first saw the subtraction 12 − 17, you probably started using **negative numbers.** Here are just a few ways that you can illustrate negative and positive numbers.

Temperature Whether you use a Fahrenheit or Celsius scale, thermometers measure temperatures "below zero." On the Celsius scale, water freezes at 0°. A negative Celsius temperature means that the temperature is below freezing. On the Fahrenheit scale, water freezes at 32°F.

What determines the point you choose for 0 on a thermometer's Celsius number line?

For You to Do

1. Use the photo. Find the temperature, in degrees Celsius, that is the same as −13°F.

Number Line A **number line** is like a scale on a thermometer. To make a number line, choose two points and label them 0 and 1. Then mark equal lengths in both directions. Label the marks with positive and negative numbers. The number line continues forever in both directions.

For You to Do

2. Suppose you start at 5 on the number line and move left 4 units. You will land on 1. So, moving left is similar to subtracting. Start at 5 on the number line below. Move left 4 units, right 1 unit, left 4 units, left 3 units, and right 2 units. On what number do you land?

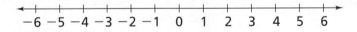

Money Balances When you have a checking account, you can get into trouble if you write checks for more money than you have, or overdraw your account. Many banks allow you to overdraw your account, leaving a negative balance in your account. For instance, suppose you have $45 in your account and you withdraw $145. Then your balance is −$100.

When keeping track of money, bookkeepers write profits in black ink and losses in red ink. The phrase *$100 in the red* means a balance of −$100.

For You to Do

3. Your checking account balance is −$100 and you deposit $85. What is your new balance? How much more do you need to deposit to have a balance of $75?

Subtraction Results When you first learned to subtract, you only subtracted a smaller number from a larger one. How do you evaluate an expression such as $15 - 17$?

Suppose $15 - 17$ represents a value. You know that subtracting 17 is the same as subtracting 15 and then subtracting 2. You can represent this idea using math symbols.

$$15 - 17 = 15 - 15 - 2$$

Since $15 - 15 = 0$, you can write $15 - 17$ this way.

$$15 - 15 - 2 = 0 - 2$$

What value does $0 - 2$ represent? It is the value that is 2 less than 0. The value must be -2.

For You to Do

4. What value do you find for $243 - 569$ by using the method described above? Is there a quicker way to find the difference?

Opposite of a Number The number 0 is special. When you add it to any number, you get the number itself. For example, $5 + 0 = 5$, $6 + 0 = 6$, and $0 + 0 = 0$.

To solve equations in algebra, you may need to add a value to another value to get 0. What value do you add to 5 to get 0? Since $5 + (-5) = 0$, you can think of -5 and 5 as **opposites.**

You can also use opposites to find the difference in subtraction. Suppose you think that $15 - 17$ equals -2. How do you explain your result? When you add 2 to $15 - 17$, the result is 0.

$$15 - 17 + 2 = 17 - 17 = 0$$

Since adding 2 to $15 - 17$ gives 0, then $15 - 17$ must be the opposite of 2. The opposite of 2 is -2.

So, $15 - 17 = -2$, just as you suspected.

For You to Do

5. Use opposites to calculate $115 - 300$. How does the subtraction $300 - 115$ help you find the difference $115 - 300$?

Remember...

Subtraction is the same as adding the opposite of a number. So, $5 + (-5)$ is the same as $5 - 5$.

Habits of Mind

Represent a number using words. Some mathematicians use *negative of a number*, instead of *opposite of a number*. So, the *negative* of 5 is -5. The *negative* of -3 is 3.

Exercises Practicing Habits of Mind

Check Your Understanding

1. Derman opens a checking account on June 14. He records his check withdrawals and deposits, but he does not calculate his balance for a week. On June 20, the bank tells Derman that he has overdrawn his account.

Number	Date	Purpose	Payment	✓	Deposit	Balance
	6/14	Deposit			$100	
001	6/16	Mulberry Comics	$40			
002	6/18	Jake's Joke Shop	$50			
003	6/18	Spica's Sports Equipment	$120			
004	6/19	On the Edge Books	$50			

   a. When did Derman first overdraw his account?

   b. How much money does he need to deposit to reach a positive balance?

   c. How could Derman have avoided overdrawing his account?

   Derman overdrew his account when he wrote a check for more than his bank balance. Banks do not like a checking account to have a negative balance.

2. In Detroit, Michigan, at 10 A.M., the temperature is 28°F. It drops 14°F by 2 P.M. Then suddenly, a cold front causes the temperature to drop 50°F in an hour. By 4 P.M., the temperature increases 25°F and stays the same for the rest of the day.

   a. What is the coldest temperature during the day?

   b. What is the temperature at the end of the day?

3. Start with each number given. Add 2, subtract 7, add 11, and subtract 15. Write each ending number.

	Starting Number	Ending Number
a.	12	▪
b.	23	▪
c.	6	▪
d.	8	▪

   e. Write a simple recipe explaining how to get from the starting number to the ending number.

   f. If the ending number is −4, what was the starting number?

   In this situation, a recipe gives directions for finding a result.

On Your Own

4. Start with the number given. For each number, subtract 1, add 5, add 2, and subtract 13. Write each ending number.

    a. 10   **b.** 6   **c.** 22   **d.** 2

    e. Write a simpler recipe explaining how to get from the starting number to the ending number.

5. Standardized Test Prep Maria plays a board game. On each turn, she moves her game piece forward or backward a number of spaces. In her first four moves, she moves forward 2 spaces, backward 3 spaces, backward 2 spaces, and forward 4 spaces. What is the ending position of Maria's game piece in relation to its starting position after all four moves?

    A. ahead 1 space   **B.** ahead 2 spaces

    C. back 1 space   **D.** back 2 spaces

6. Write About It Sasha says, "When I draw two diagonals in the addition table, I notice something interesting. On the first line, all the sums are 8. On the second line, all the sums are 17. It seems that on any diagonal line, the sums are the same. I can't explain why." Explain the pattern that Sasha notices.

Addition Table

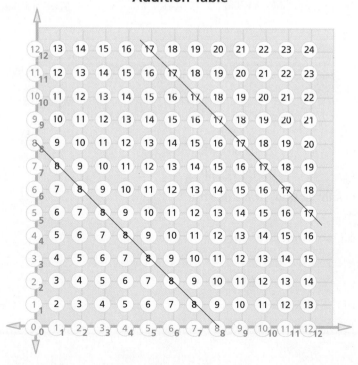

Go Online
www.successnetplus.com

7. Write About It Derman explains, "Draw a line through a row of numbers in the addition table. When you move up 1 row and left 1 column, you find the same row of numbers." Describe the pattern that Derman notices.

Addition Table

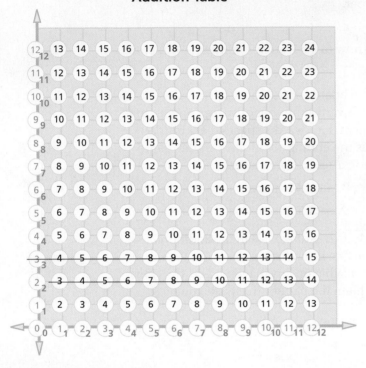

Maintain Your Skills

8. Find each difference.

   a. $313 - 189$ **b.** $189 - 313$ **c.** $1000 - 5$

   d. $5 - 1000$ **e.** $760 - 88$ **f.** $88 - 760$

   g. When you reverse the summands in subtraction, how does the result change?

9. Find each difference. Record the last digit of each difference.

   a. $62 - 38$ **b.** $62 - 48$ **c.** $62 - 58$

   d. $62 - 68$ **e.** $62 - 78$ **f.** $62 - 88$

   g. Identify a pattern in the last digits of the differences.

Extending the Addition Table

You may already know how to add and subtract negative numbers. In this lesson, you will learn why the rules of addition for negative numbers make sense.

Minds in Action

Tony and Sasha think about how to add negative and positive numbers.

Tony What we need to do is extend the addition table to the left and below each axis.

Addition Table

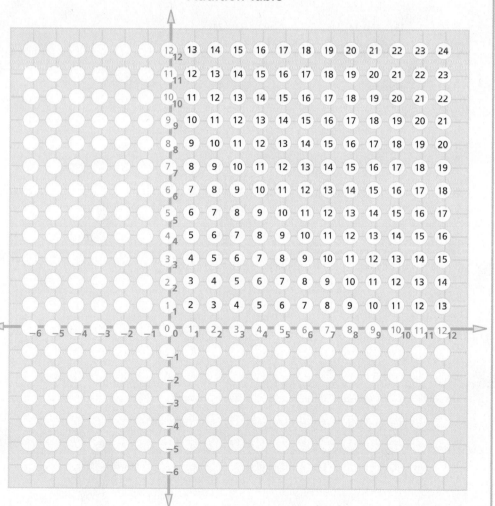

Sasha   I want to figure out what to write in all the blanks.

Tony and Sasha think for a moment.

Tony   It seems to me that we can fill in the blanks in any way that we want to. Let's just write a 5 in every blank. That's easy. What's wrong with that?

Sasha   Well, when you do that, you get things you don't want. You get $-3 + 3 = 5$. Don't you want $-3 + 3$ to equal 0? Why do we have $-2 + 1 = 5$ in the table? It doesn't make any sense. I think it's better if we try to extend some of the patterns in the table.

Tony and Sasha quietly think for a few moments.

Tony   I have an idea. Look at the row starting with 3.

Tony draws a line through the row starting with 3.

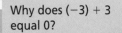

Why does $(-3) + 3$ equal 0?

Addition Table

	0	1	2	3	4	5	6	7	8	9	10	11	12
12		13	14	15	16	17	18	19	20	21	22	23	24
11		12	13	14	15	16	17	18	19	20	21	22	23
10		11	12	13	14	15	16	17	18	19	20	21	22
9		10	11	12	13	14	15	16	17	18	19	20	21
8		9	10	11	12	13	14	15	16	17	18	19	20
7		8	9	10	11	12	13	14	15	16	17	18	19
6		7	8	9	10	11	12	13	14	15	16	17	18
5		6	7	8	9	10	11	12	13	14	15	16	17
4		5	6	7	8	9	10	11	12	13	14	15	16
3		4	5	6	7	8	9	10	11	12	13	14	15
2		3	4	5	6	7	8	9	10	11	12	13	14
1		2	3	4	5	6	7	8	9	10	11	12	13

-6 -5 -4 -3 -2 -1 0 1 2 3 4 5 6 7 8 9 10 11 12

-1
-2
-3
-4
-5
-6

Tony   Sasha, in Lesson 1.01, you noticed that moving 1 entry to the left was the same as subtracting 1. Maybe we can use that idea to fill in the blanks in the third row. We just need to keep moving to the left.

Sasha   So, let's keep subtracting 1. We'll get something like this.

Addition Table

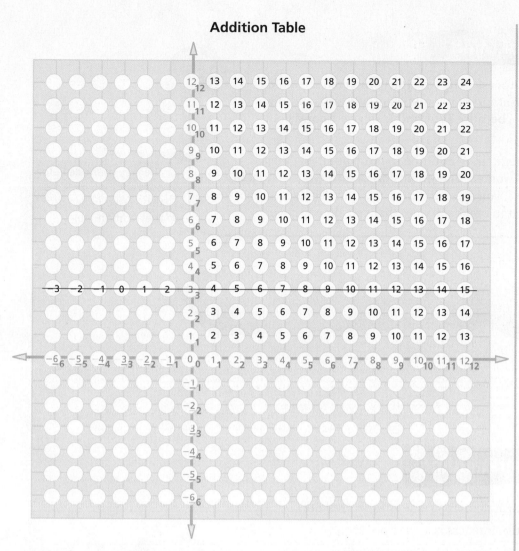

Tony   Wait, where did you get that −1 in the first entry to the left of zero on the horizontal axis?

Sasha   I just subtracted 1 from 0, or $0 - 1 = -1$.

Tony   Okay.

Sasha   This looks really good. We get $-3 + 3 = 0$, just as we want. The other entries make sense, too. Okay. Let's complete the table by extending the patterns in each row.

What does Sasha mean by saying, "The other entries make sense, too"?

For You to Do

1. On a copy of Tony and Sasha's table, fill in the missing numbers.

For Discussion

2. In the completed table, do all the patterns for positive numbers work?

Maintain a consistent process. The way you completed the table matches the way scientists and mathematicians add and multiply. Is this a coincidence? No, because Tony and Sasha were consistent and careful.

As they extended the operation of addition to more numbers, they made sure the rules still worked. The **extension of a rule** is essential in mathematics. In this case, you extended the rules from whole numbers to integers. You do not want to break the rules that you already have.

> The way your calculator does addition matches the way you filled out the addition table.

Exercises Practicing Habits of Mind

Check Your Understanding

1. Determine whether each statement is true or false. Explain.

   a. The sum of two positive integers is always positive.

   b. The sum of two negative integers is always negative.

   c. The sum of a negative integer and a positive integer is always negative.

   d. The sum of a negative integer and a positive integer is always positive.

2. Match each sum in column 1 with an equal sum in column 2.

Column 1	Column 2
3 + (−11)	2 + 8
(−23) + 13	(−4) + (−4)
20 + (−10)	16 + (−2)
32 + (−18)	1 + (−11)

3. Suppose you do not know the value of the subtraction 11 − 5. How can you use the addition table to find the difference?

4. Explain how you can use the addition table to find a difference.

5. Which of the following equations are true?

  a. $166 + (-117) \overset{?}{=} 166 - 117$

  b. $421 - (-29) \overset{?}{=} 421 - 29$

  c. $300 - (-92) \overset{?}{=} 300 + 92$

  d. $166 - (5 + 13) \overset{?}{=} 166 - 5 + 13$

  e. $421 - (17 + 43) \overset{?}{=} 421 - 17 - 43$

6. How many times does the number 143 appear in the entire addition table? Describe the location of each number 143 in the table.

On Your Own

7. Calculate each sum. Use the addition table.

a. $9 + (-3)$	**b.** $7 + (-3)$	**c.** $(-4) + (-3)$
d. $1 + (-4)$	**e.** $4 + (-4)$	**f.** $(-2) + (-4)$
g. $(-9) + (-8)$	**h.** $6 + (-11)$	

8. Complete the part of an addition table shown below.

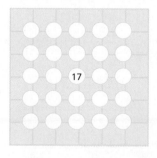

9. Find the product of each pair of numbers.

    a. a number and 0   **b.** a number and 1

    c. How can you illustrate your results from parts (a) and (b) by using the multiplication table?

For Exercises 10–12, use an addition table. Describe the location of the given number, or set of numbers, in the table. For each number, or set of numbers, describe the pattern in the table. (*Hint:* Zero is neither a positive nor a negative number.)

Addition Table

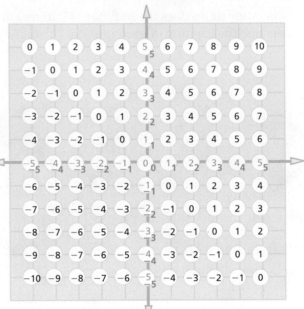

10. zeros

11. positive numbers

12. negative numbers

13. **Standardized Test Prep** In Calgary, Alberta, on Sunday, the low temperature forecast is 3°C. The low temperature will drop 4°C on Monday, 6°C on Tuesday, and 5°C on Wednesday. The low temperature will increase 2°C on Thursday and 1°C on Friday. What is the lowest temperature forecast?

    A. −18°C   **B.** −15°C

    C. −12°C   **D.** −9°C

Maintain Your Skills

For Exercises 14 and 15, find each sum.

14. **a.** $3 + 7 + 3 + 8 + 3 + (-8) + 3 + (-7)$

    b. $3 + 27 + 3 + 28 + 3 + (-28) + 3 + (-27)$

    c. $3 + 247 + 3 + 248 + 3 + (-248) + 3 + (-247)$

    d. What pattern can you use to find each sum?

15. **a.** $1 + 2 + 2 + 1$

    b. $1 + 2 + 3 + 3 + 2 + 1$

    c. $1 + 2 + 3 + 4 + 4 + 3 + 2 + 1$

    d. $1 + 2 + 3 + 4 + 5 + 5 + 4 + 3 + 2 + 1$

    e. $1 + 2 + 3 + 4 + 5 + 6 + 7 + 8 + 9 + 9 + 8 + 7 + 6 + 5 + 4 + 3 + 2 + 1$

    f. What pattern can you use to find each sum?

Extending the Multiplication Table

You can extend the multiplication table in the same way that Sasha and Tony extended the addition table. Then check that the extension is correct.

For You to Do

Explain how each value in the multiplication table changes when you move in each direction.

1. up 1 row
2. down 1 row
3. right 1 column
4. left 1 column

> Using the multiplication table may help.

The multiplication table below is partially complete. You can complete the table by extending patterns. You can start by extending the patterns for multiplying a negative number by 0 or 1.

Multiplication Table

row	1	2	3	4	5	6	7	8	9	10	11	12
12	12	24	36	48	60	72	84	96	108	120	132	144
11	11	22	33	44	55	66	77	88	99	110	121	132
10	10	20	30	40	50	60	70	80	90	100	110	120
9	9	18	27	36	45	54	63	72	81	90	99	108
8	8	16	24	32	40	48	56	64	72	80	88	96
7	7	14	21	28	35	42	49	56	63	70	77	84
6	6	12	18	24	30	36	42	48	54	60	66	72
5	5	10	15	20	25	30	35	40	45	50	55	60
4	4	8	12	16	20	24	28	32	36	40	44	48
3	3	6	9	12	15	18	21	24	27	30	33	36
2	2	4	6	8	10	12	14	16	18	20	22	24
1	1	2	3	4	5	6	7	8	9	10	11	12

Columns to the left are labeled −6, −5, −4, −3, −2, −1, 0. The row axis runs from −1 up through 12. The zero row and zero column entries are 0.

> Why does each entry in this row increase by 2 from left to right?

Look at the row starting with the number 2. As you move one entry to the right, you add 2 each time. As you move one entry to the left, you subtract 2 each time.

A similar pattern works for the row starting with 3. You add 3 for each move to the right, and you subtract 3 for each move to the left. You can find similar patterns in the columns, too. Using patterns, you can extend the table in all directions.

For You to Do

5. On a copy of an incomplete multiplication table, complete the table.

For Discussion

6. Sasha and Tony check their multiplication table by looking for more patterns. Tony says that 4 × 3 is the same as 4 + 4 + 4. He thinks that (−4) × 3 is the same as (−4) + (−4) + (−4). Does your multiplication table show this result?

Facts and Notation

In algebra, you can use a dot, ·, to show multiplication, instead of the × used in arithmetic. Instead of writing (−3) × 7 = −21, you can write (−3) · 7 = −21. When you need parentheses to show a calculation, you can sometimes remove the dot. For example, the quantity 3(5 + 2) means 3 times the quantity (5 + 2), or 3 · 7 = 21.

 **Exercises** *Practicing Habits of Mind*

Check Your Understanding

1. Find each product.

    a. 19 · 76
    b. (−19) · 76
    c. 19 · (−76)
    d. (−19) · (−76)
    e. −(19 · 76)
    f. (−76) · (−19)

2. Find each quotient.

    a. 76 ÷ 19
    b. (−76) ÷ (−19)
    c. (−76) ÷ 19
    d. 76 ÷ (−19)
    e. 19 ÷ 76
    f. 19 ÷ (−76)

3. What pair of numbers with sum 18 has the largest product?

4. Use the multiplication table. Explain why each fact is true.

   a. $4 \cdot (-3) = -12$ b. $-4 \cdot (-3) = 12$

5. How many times does the number 10 appear as an entry in the multiplication table? Explain.

6. Does 17, 24, 19, or 72 appear most frequently as an entry in the entire multiplication table?

7. **Take It Further** Use the multiplication table.

   a. Which numbers from 0 to 150 appear most frequently as entries in the multiplication table?

   b. Which numbers from 0 to 150 appear least frequently as entries in the multiplication table?

On Your Own

8. Determine whether each statement is true or false. Use examples to support your claim.

   a. The product of two positive integers is always positive.

   b. The product of two negative integers is always negative.

   c. The product of two negative integers is always positive.

   d. The product of a negative integer and a positive integer is always negative.

   e. The product of a negative integer and a positive integer is always positive.

9. Which pair of numbers with sum 8 has the largest product?

10. **Standardized Test Prep** A store displays watermelons in a rectangular space. Mrs. Burres wants the space to be 5 fence sections long and 4 fence sections wide. Mr. Chang prefers a length of 7 sections and a width of 2 sections. How much less storage area will there be in the 7 section-by-2 section space than in the 5 section-by-4 section space?

    A. 2 square sections   B. 3 square sections

    C. 6 square sections   D. 9 square sections

In a rectangular space, it is easier to display square watermelons than round watermelons.

For Exercises 11–13, use a multiplication table. Describe the location of the given number, or set of numbers, in the table. For each number, or set of numbers, describe the pattern in the table.

11. zeros

12. positive numbers

13. negative numbers

Multiplication Table

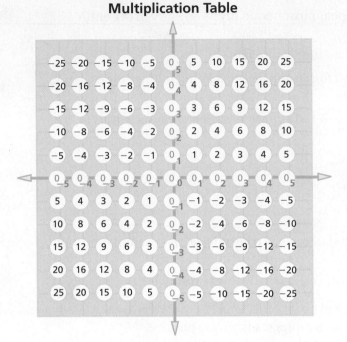

Remember...

Zero is neither a positive nor a negative number.

14. Find and describe patterns on the diagonal shown.

Multiplication Table

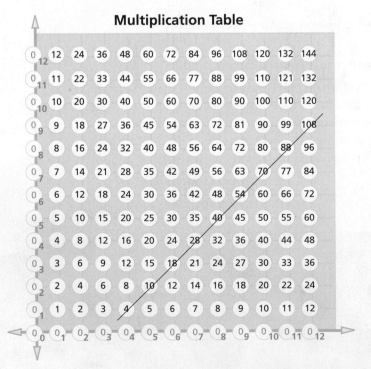

Maintain Your Skills

For Exercises 15 and 16, evaluate each expression or pair of expressions.

15. **a.** $(-1)^2$

b. $(-1)^3$

c. $(-1)^4$

d. $(-1)^5$

e. $(-1)^{347}$

f. What pattern do you find in the exponents and the results?

16. **a.** $5(3 + 7)$ and $5 \cdot 3 + 5 \cdot 7$

b. $(-5)(3 + 7)$ and $(-5) \cdot 3 + (-5) \cdot 7$

c. $5(3 + (-7))$ and $5 \cdot 3 + 5(-7)$

d. $5((-3) + (-7))$ and $5(-3) + 5(-7)$

e. $(-5)((-3) + (-7))$ and $(-5)(-3) + (-5)(-7)$

f. Make a conjecture about the values in each pair of calculations.

17. Given the fact that $1 + 2 + 3 + 4 + 5 + 6 + 7 + 8 + 9 + 10 = 55$, find each sum.

> A conjecture is what you believe is a true statement in general, based on specific examples.

a. $2 + 4 + 6 + 8 + 10 + 12 + 14 + 16 + 18 + 20$

b. $3 + 6 + 9 + 12 + 15 + 18 + 21 + 24 + 27 + 30$

c. $7 + 14 + 21 + 28 + 35 + 42 + 49 + 56 + 63 + 70$

d. $11 + 22 + 33 + 44 + 55 + 66 + 77 + 88 + 99 + 110$

e. $12 + 24 + 36 + 48 + 60 + 72 + 84 + 96 + 108 + 120$

f. What shortcut can you use?

> ### Habits of Mind
>
> **Speed up your process.** You can save time if you do not use a calculator and you look for shortcuts.

1.05 The Basic Rules of Arithmetic

The **basic rules of arithmetic** govern how addition and multiplication work for the set of integers. Studying the basic rules of arithmetic, or the properties of operations, is an important way that algebra differs from arithmetic. Studying number systems is another difference.

Facts and Notation

The capital letter $\mathbb{Z}$ stands for the set of **integers,**

$$\{ \ldots -5, -4, -3, -2, -1, 0, 1, 2, 3, 4, 5, 6, 7 \ldots \}$$

Zahl means "number" in German.

What are the basic rules, or properties, for $\mathbb{Z}$? Roughly speaking, order does not matter when you add or multiply.

Properties   *Any-Order, Any-Grouping in $\mathbb{Z}$*

Addition

- The order in which you add two numbers in a sum does not affect the result.

  $5 + 3 = 8$ $3 + 5 = 8$

- When you add more than two numbers, the way you group them does not matter.

  $5 + (3 + 7) = 15$ $(5 + 3) + 7 = 15$

Multiplication

- The order in which you multiply two numbers in a product does not affect the result.

  $5 \cdot (-3) = -15$ $-3 \cdot (5) = -15$

- When you multiply more than two numbers, the way you group them does not matter.

  $4 \cdot (3 \cdot 5) = 60$ $(4 \cdot 3) \cdot 5 = 60$

You call the first and third rules the commutative properties of addition and multiplication. You call the second and fourth rules the associative properties of addition and multiplication.

In this book, the letters AOAG stand for the any-order, any-grouping properties.

Understand the process. You have probably used AOAG before. You can just accept the properties as **axioms,** or basic facts, requiring no justification. Also, you can recall some processes you've seen before. If you insist on knowing why these properties are true, start thinking about the way you use positive integers to count. For example, suppose you line up some 5's in an array.

```
5  5  5  5
5  5  5  5
5  5  5  5
```

What sum do you find when you add the 5's? There are three processes you can use.

Process 1 There are three rows and four columns in the array, so there are 4 · 3, or twelve, 5's. The sum is the same as 12 · 5 = 60. You calculate the result to the following multiplication.

$$(4 \cdot 3) \cdot 5 = 60$$

Process 2 Each row contains four 5's, so the sum in each row is 4 · 5 = 20.

```
5  5  5  5 = 20
5  5  5  5 = 20
5  5  5  5 = 20
```

There are three rows, so the sum of the 5's is 3 · 20. You calculate the result by multiplying.

$$3 \cdot (4 \cdot 5) = 60$$

Process 3 Each column contains three 5's, so the sum in each column is 3 · 5 = 15.

```
 5   5   5   5
 5   5   5   5
 5   5   5   5
___ ___ ___ ___
15  15  15  15
```

There are four columns, so the sum of all the 5's is 4 · 15. You evaluate the following multiplication.

$$4 \cdot (3 \cdot 5) = 60$$

The product is 60, no matter what order you multiply the numbers.

$$(4 \cdot 3) \cdot 5 = 3 \cdot (4 \cdot 5) = 4 \cdot (3 \cdot 5) = 60$$

Habits of Mind

Understand the process. If you multiply 479 and 21 using paper and pencil, which number do you write first? Explain. Why can you choose which number to write first?

Rafts carrying 5 riders each can go through the rapids in any order. No matter what the order is, 12 of them will carry 60 people in all.

The next three basic rules for $\mathbb{Z}$ are about the special numbers 0 and 1.

Properties Identities and Inverses in $\mathbb{Z}$

- When you add 0 to any number, the result is the number itself. The number 0 is the **additive identity.**
- When you multiply 1 by any number, the result is the number itself. The number 1 is the **multiplicative identity.**
- When you add any number to its opposite, the result is 0. If the sum of two numbers is 0, each number is the opposite of the other. Every integer has a unique additive inverse. **Additive inverse** is another name for opposite.

Why do you use the word *the* in *the identity*? Is there a number besides 0 that you can add to another number that gives the second number as a result?

For You to Do

1. What is the result when you add 17, −5, 0, 5, 12, and −17? Find a shortcut to simplify your work. Explain.

Remember...

What is the opposite of 0?

Another basic rule of arithmetic summarizes how multiplication and addition work together. This is one of the most useful rules in algebra.

Property Distributive Property

Multiplying a number by a sum is the same as multiplying the number by each term in the sum and then adding the results.

An example of the Distributive Property follows.

$$4 \cdot (50 + 3) = 4 \cdot 50 + 4 \cdot 3$$
$$= 200 + 12$$
$$= 212$$

How can you use this property to calculate $5 \cdot 99$? You can rewrite 99 as $100 + (-1)$. Then you apply the Distributive Property.

$$5 \cdot (99) = 5 \cdot (100 + (-1))$$
$$= 5 \cdot 100 + 5 \cdot (-1)$$
$$= 500 + (-5)$$
$$= 495$$

Mentally, you can just multiply 5 times 100 and then add 5 times (−1). Many tricks for doing mental calculations rely on the Distributive Property.

For You to Do

2. Calculate $27 \cdot 102$ without using a calculator, or paper.

For Discussion

3. Use this array to show that $4 \cdot (50 + 3) = 4 \cdot 50 + 4 \cdot 3$.

50 50 50 50
 3   3   3   3

Exercises *Practicing Habits of Mind*

Check Your Understanding

1. Use the multiplication table to show that order does not matter in multiplication. For example, 5×3 is the same as 3×5.

2. Use the multiplication table to show that when you multiply a number by 1, you get the number itself. For example, $5 \times 1 = 5$.

3. What is the opposite of -5? Explain.

4. **Take It Further** Which of the basic rules of arithmetic are true when you restrict the number system to the positive integers?

On Your Own

5. Use the basic rules of arithmetic to rewrite each calculation more simply.

   a. $2 \cdot (473 \cdot 5)$ **b.** $12 \cdot 199$

   c. $42 \cdot 203$ **d.** $4 \cdot 27 \cdot 5 \cdot 3$

6. Find each result.

   a. $15 \cdot 3 + (-6)$ **b.** $15(3 + (-6))$ **c.** $15 + 3(-6)$

   d. $15 + (-6)3$ **e.** $15 + (-6)3 + (-15)$

Go Online
www.successnetplus.com

7. **Standardized Test Prep** Rosa finds the product of 32 and 96. She rewrites 96 as a sum or difference of two numbers and uses the Distributive Property. Which of the following could be a step in her computations?

   A. $32 \cdot 95 + 31$

   B. $30 \cdot 98$

   C. $2700 + 12$

   D. $3200 - 128$

8. **Take It Further** Use the basic rules of arithmetic to show that each statement is true.

   a. $(5 + 3)(5 - 3) = 5 \cdot 5 - 3 \cdot 3$

   b. $(4 + 5)(4 - 5) = 4 \cdot 4 - 5 \cdot 5$

Maintain Your Skills

For Exercises 9 and 10, find each result.

9. **a.** $10 \cdot 3 + 5$

   b. $10(10 \cdot 3 + 5) + 6$

   c. $10(10(10 \cdot 3 + 5) + 6) + 2$

   d. $10(10(10(10 \cdot 3 + 5) + 6) + 2) + 9$

   e. Find a pattern that you used to find each result.

10. **a.** $6 - 1 + 6 - 2 + 6 - 3 + 6 - 4$

    b. $5 - 1 + 5 - 2 + 5 - 3 + 5 - 4$

    c. $4 - 1 + 4 - 2 + 4 - 3 + 4 - 4$

    d. $3 - 1 + 3 - 2 + 3 - 3 + 3 - 4$

    e. $2 - 1 + 2 - 2 + 2 - 3 + 2 - 4$

Go Online
Video Tutor
www.successnetplus.com

Mathematical 1A Reflections

In this investigation, you learned to add and multiply integers. You also learned the basic rules of arithmetic. These questions will help you summarize what you have learned.

1. In an addition table, what is the total change in the values when you move as follows?

   a. up 2 rows and left 1 column   **b.** up 1 row and left 2 columns

2. Choose a number between 1 and 20. Add 3, subtract 4, and add 1. How is your result related to your starting number? Explain.

   Calculate each sum or product.

3. **a.** $8 + (-1)$ **b.** $(-8) + 5$ **c.** $(-8) + (-2)$ **d.** $8 + (-8)$

4. **a.** $4(5)$ **b.** $4(-5)$ **c.** $(-4)(5)$ **d.** $(-4)(-5)$

5. Tony asks Sasha to multiply 15 times 98. She calculates $1500 - 30 = 1470$. Is Sasha correct? Explain. What basic rule of arithmetic did she use?

6. How can you illustrate the properties of addition by using an addition table?

7. How can you illustrate the properties of multiplication by using a multiplication table?

8. Why is the sum of two negative numbers negative, and the product of two negative numbers positive?

Vocabulary and Notation

In this investigation, you learned these terms and symbols. Make sure you understand what each one means and how to use it.

- **additive identity**
- **additive inverse**
- **axiom**
- **basic rules of arithmetic**
- **extension of a rule**
- **integers, $\mathbb{Z}$**
- **multiplicative identity**
- **negative number**
- **number line**
- **opposites**
- **· (multiplication)**

Taking a different point of view can help you find a solution.

Investigation 1B

The Number Line

In *The Number Line,* you will order fractions and decimals on the number line. You will extend the basic rules of arithmetic to the set of real numbers.

By the end of this investigation, you will be able to answer questions like these.

1. How can you tell whether two fractions that look different represent the same number?

2. How do you add numbers on the number line?

3. Where is $\sqrt{2}$ located on the number line?

You will learn how to

- draw line segments with different endpoints and different scales

- represent fractions and real numbers as points on a number line

- represent a rational number in many different ways

- extend the basic rules of addition and multiplication from the integers to the real numbers

You will develop these habits and skills:

- Think of decimal representations as tools for locating points on the number line with any degree of precision.

- Choose the best representation of a number to solve a problem efficiently.

- Use the number line to visualize numbers and operations, such as addition and multiplication.

- Extend the basic rules to the set of real numbers.

This unusual-looking vertical number line has marks for 0 and one other number.

1.06 Getting Started

Activating Prior Knowledge
Exploring New Ideas

In Getting Started, you will review fractions on the number line.

For You to Explore

On graph paper, draw seven horizontal line segments that are 24 units in length. Label the endpoints 0 and 1.

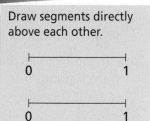

Draw segments directly above each other.

1. For parts (a)–(e), divide one segment into the given number of equal parts. Label each dividing point. Explain why the labels are appropriate.

   a. 2   **b.** 3   **c.** 4   **d.** 5   **e.** 6

   f. Which segment is the most difficult to divide equally? Explain why.

2. **a.** On the sixth line segment, label points for halves, thirds, fourths, and sixths. Which points have multiple labels? Explain.

   b. Using this line segment, order the following numbers from least to greatest: $\frac{1}{3}, \frac{4}{6}, \frac{3}{5}, \frac{1}{2}, \frac{1}{4}, \frac{5}{6}, \frac{2}{5}$.

3. **a.** Place each number on the seventh line segment.

   $$\frac{1}{12}, \frac{2}{12}, \frac{6}{24}, \frac{1}{8}, \frac{4}{8}, \frac{25}{100}, \frac{2}{10}, \frac{5}{10}, \frac{10}{60}, \frac{6}{12}, \frac{5}{8}, \frac{0}{13}, \frac{11}{11}, \frac{1,000,000}{2,000,000}$$

   b. Explain why some points have more than one label.

Exercises *Practicing Habits of Mind*

On Your Own

For Exercises 4 and 5, place a piece of paper next to this ruler. Copy the ruler's markings along one edge of the paper.

4. Label the ruler for each point given.

   a. $\frac{1}{2}$ inch   **b.** $\frac{1}{4}$ inch   **c.** $\frac{1}{8}$ inch

   d. $1\frac{1}{2}$ inches   **e.** $3\frac{1}{4}$ inches   **f.** $\frac{1}{3}$ foot

5. Mark a point on the ruler that is halfway between the two numbers in each pair below.

   a. 3 inches and 4 inches

   b. 2 inches and 4 inches

   c. 1 inch and 4 inches

   d. $\frac{1}{2}$ inch and 4 inches

6. On graph paper, draw a horizontal line segment that is 24 units long. Label the endpoints 0 and 72. Mark and label the points that divide the segment into the following equal parts.

   a. 3

   b. 8

Maintain Your Skills

7. In each list, the numbers increase by the same amount. Fill in the missing values.

   a. 0, 3, ■, ■, 12, ■   **b.** 0, ■, 20, ■, 40, ■

   c. 0, ■, ■, ■, 160, 200   **d.** 0, ■, ■, ■, ■, 35

   e. How does the second number in each list relate to the last number in each list?

For Exercises 8 and 9, points divide each line segment into five equal parts. Use the numbers shown for the first and sixth points. Label each of the remaining four points.

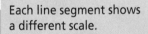
Each line segment shows a different scale.

8. a.

      0   100

   b. 0   35

   c. 0   0.5

   d. 0   0.1

   e. How is the first number you labeled related to the number at the right end of the line?

9. a.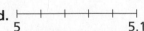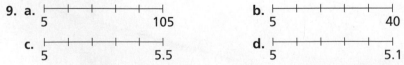

      5   105

   b. 5   40

   c. 5   5.5

   d. 5   5.1

   e. **Take It Further** How is the first number you labeled related to the numbers at both ends of the segment?

1.07 Numbers Besides the Integers—Fractions

A number line labeled with only integers has gaps between the integers.

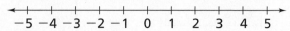

In each gap between two integers, there are many more numbers.
In Lesson 1.06, you located some numbers on the number line.

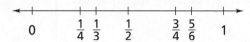

Fractions are numbers, just like integers, so they follow the basic rules of arithmetic. In this investigation, you will use the number line to extend arithmetic to fractions.

For You to Do

1. Plot each number on a number line.

$$\frac{1}{4}, \quad 0, \quad -1, \quad -\frac{2}{4}, \quad \frac{6}{4}, \quad \frac{3}{4}, \quad -\frac{6}{4}, \quad \frac{5}{4}$$

In Lesson 1.06, you learned that different fractions can refer to the same location on a number line. For example, $\frac{1}{2}$, $\frac{2}{4}$, and $\frac{3}{6}$ name the same point, because they represent the same number.

> Enter 1 ÷ 2 in a calculator. What is the result? What is the result when you enter 2 ÷ 4, or 3 ÷ 6?

$$\frac{1}{2} = \frac{2}{4} = \frac{3}{6}$$

For You to Do

2. Find an equivalent fraction for $\frac{1}{3}$.

> You can use the number line to define **equivalent fractions.** You can say that two fractions are equivalent when they refer to the same location on the number line.

Visualize fractions. Fractions with different denominators represent different units. A fraction with a denominator of 6 measures in sixths. *Measures in sixths* means divides the interval from 0 to 1 into six equal parts. A fraction with a denominator of 2 measures in halves.

one sixth

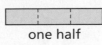
one half

Changing from halves to sixths is similar to changing from feet to inches. You are converting from one unit to another. You can describe the equation $\frac{1}{2} = \frac{3}{6}$ by saying, "There are 3 sixths in 1 half."

You can draw a picture to visualize the equation $\frac{2}{3} = \frac{4}{6}$.

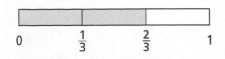

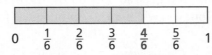

For Discussion

3. There is an arithmetic method for changing the denominator of a fraction. Suppose you want to find the number of sixths in $\frac{2}{3}$. You multiply the numerator and denominator of the fraction by 2.

$$\frac{2}{3} = \frac{2 \cdot 2}{3 \cdot 2} = \frac{4}{6}$$

Since $\frac{2}{3} = \frac{4}{6}$, $\frac{2}{3}$ and $\frac{4}{6}$ are equivalent fractions. Explain.

> What do *numerator* and *denominator* mean? Why did you multiply by 2?

Some important skills for working with fractions include

- finding equivalent fractions, especially for adding fractions
- writing fractions in lowest terms

You can say that $\frac{2}{3} + \frac{1}{12} = \frac{24}{36} + \frac{3}{36} = \frac{27}{36}$, but most of the time,

$\frac{3}{4}$ is clearer than $\frac{27}{36}$. To write $\frac{27}{36}$ in **lowest terms,** you can write

$\frac{(27 \div 3) \div 3}{(36 \div 3) \div 3} = \frac{3}{4}$, or $\frac{27 \div 9}{36 \div 9} = \frac{3}{4}$.

> A fraction is in lowest terms when the numerator and denominator do not have any common factor except 1. The fraction $\frac{84}{147}$ is not in lowest terms, because both 84 and 147 are divisible by 21.

For You to Do

Write each fraction in lowest terms.

4. $\frac{15}{20}$ 5. $\frac{72}{14}$ 6. $\frac{-5}{-15}$ 7. $\frac{3}{6}$ 8. $\frac{7}{31}$

Exercises *Practicing Habits of Mind*

Check Your Understanding

For Exercises 1–3, copy each number line on graph paper. Label the missing points.

1.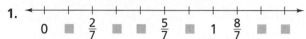

2.

3.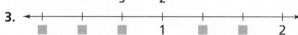

4. How many thirds are in each number?

   a. $\frac{8}{3}$ b. $\frac{25}{3}$ c. 3

   d. $\frac{14}{3}$ e. 17   f. $\frac{12}{6}$

   g. $\frac{5}{6}$ h. $\frac{60}{30}$ i. 11

5. **What's Wrong Here?** Rosa draws this number line incorrectly. Explain why this is not an accurate number line. Correct the number line.

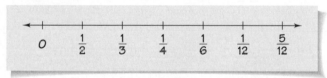

The vertical number line shows the height of the tide.

6. Place the following numbers on a number line.

   $\frac{3}{2}, \frac{4}{3}, \frac{5}{3}, \frac{5}{4}, \frac{6}{4}, \frac{7}{4}, \frac{7}{6}, \frac{8}{6}, \frac{9}{6}, \frac{10}{6}, \frac{11}{6}$

   a. Which fractions represent the same number, or are equivalent?

   b. What is the least number in this list?

7. Draw a picture that illustrates the equivalence $\frac{2}{5} = \frac{4}{10}$.

On Your Own

8. Find four different fractions equivalent to $\frac{7}{3}$.

9. A $\frac{3}{8}$-inch wrench is slightly too small to fit a bolt on your lawn mower. You have three more wrenches that measure $\frac{7}{16}$, $\frac{11}{16}$, and $\frac{5}{16}$ inches. Which wrench should you try next? Explain.

10. **Write About It** Travis says, "The number 12 is greater than 3. The number 17 is greater than 4. So, $\frac{12}{17} > \frac{3}{4}$." Explain to someone who knows nothing about fractions why Travis is wrong.

11. Match each number to a point on the number line.

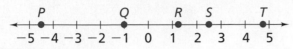

   a. -1 **b.** $\frac{5}{2}$ **c.** $-\frac{9}{2}$ **d.** $\frac{19}{4}$ **e.** $1\frac{1}{4}$

12. Plot each pair of numbers on a number line. Name a third number that is located between the pair of numbers.

   a. $\frac{7}{2}$ and $\frac{9}{2}$

   b. $-\frac{5}{2}$ and 0

   c. $\frac{7}{9}$ and 1

   d. $-\frac{8}{11}$ and $-\frac{9}{11}$

13. **Standardized Test Prep** Which number is between $\frac{27}{7}$ and $\frac{31}{8}$?

   A. $\frac{215}{56}$

   B. $\frac{35}{36}$

   C. $\frac{217}{56}$

   D. $\frac{433}{112}$

14. Use equivalent fractions. How many of each fractional part are in $\frac{1}{2}$?

   a. fourths

   b. eighths

   c. tenths

   d. hundredths

Maintain Your Skills

15. Identify the fractions equivalent to 7.

   a. $\frac{35}{5}$ **b.** $\frac{42}{7}$ **c.** $\frac{-42}{-6}$

   d. $\frac{17}{10}$ **e.** $\frac{7}{49}$ **f.** $\frac{81}{13}$

   g. Explain how you can decide whether a fraction is equivalent to 7.

16. Identify the fractions equivalent to -2.

   a. $\frac{8}{-4}$ **b.** $\frac{-6}{2}$

   c. $\frac{-20}{10}$ **d.** $\frac{-100}{20}$

   e. $\frac{-18}{-9}$ **f.** $\frac{12}{-6}$

   g. Explain how you can decide whether a fraction is equivalent to -2.

17. Identify the fractions equivalent to $\frac{3}{4}$.

   a. $\frac{6}{-8}$ **b.** $\frac{300}{400}$ **c.** $\frac{75}{200}$

   d. $\frac{-3}{-4}$ **e.** $\frac{60}{80}$ **f.** $\frac{36}{60}$

   g. Explain how you can decide whether a fraction is equivalent to $\frac{3}{4}$.

1.08 Decimals—Addresses on the Number Line

The decimal system locates numbers on a number line. The **decimal expansion** of a number is its address on the number line. For example, the decimal expansion for 1.63 is 1 unit + 6 tenths + 3 hundredths.

Example

Problem Locate 1.63 on a number line.

Solution $1.63 = 1 + 0.6 + 0.03$

$$= 1 + 6 \text{ tenths} + 3 \text{ hundredths}$$

The decimal expansion $1 + 6$ tenths $+ 3$ hundredths leads to the following recipe for locating 1.63 on a number line.

Step 1 Find the number 1.

Step 2 Add an additional 6 tenths to the number 1.

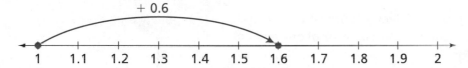

Step 3 Add an additional 3 hundredths to 1 and 6 tenths.

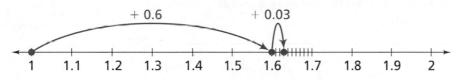

Decimal notation also provides the basis for a similar recipe for locating any number on a number line. The decimal expansion for 287.5 is as follows.

$$287.5 = 200 + 80 + 7 + 0.5$$

Here is a recipe for locating 287.5 on a number line.

Step 1 Locate 200 on a number line.

Step 2 Add an additional 80, or 8 tens.

Step 3 Add an additional 7, or 7 ones.

Step 4 Add an additional 0.5, or 5 tenths.

Sometimes it is useful to convert a fraction to a decimal. A fraction is just another way to write division. For example, $\frac{8}{2} = 8 \div 2$, $\frac{18}{3} = 18 \div 3$, and $\frac{3}{4} = 3 \div 4$.

$$\frac{3}{4} = 3 \div 4 = \begin{array}{r} 0.75 \\ 4\overline{)3.00} \\ \underline{-2.8} \\ 0.20 \\ \underline{-0.20} \\ 0 \end{array}$$

To convert the fraction $\frac{3}{4}$ into decimal notation, you perform long division as shown. The decimal representation of $\frac{3}{4}$ is 0.75.

Sometimes the long division does not end. Not every fraction has a simple **decimal representation,** because some decimals continue forever. A decimal representation can be useful for approximating the value of a number.

> The decimal representation of $\frac{1}{3}$ is 0.333 . . . The 3's repeat forever.

For You to Do

Label each number on a number line.

1. 1.81
2. $\frac{7}{4}$
3. $\frac{5}{3}$
4. Use your calculator to estimate $\sqrt{2}$ to 2 decimal places.

> The **square root** of 2, or $\sqrt{2}$, is the number that you multiply by itself to find the product 2. So, $\sqrt{2} \cdot \sqrt{2} = 2$.

Developing Habits of Mind

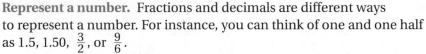

Represent a number. Fractions and decimals are different ways to represent a number. For instance, you can think of one and one half as 1.5, 1.50, $\frac{3}{2}$, or $\frac{9}{6}$.

What is the sum $\frac{3}{2} + \frac{1}{6}$? To find the sum, you can rewrite $\frac{3}{2}$ as $\frac{9}{6}$.

Is $\frac{3}{2}$ greater than 1.4? You can write $\frac{3}{2}$ as 1.5. The numbers $\frac{3}{2}$, $\frac{9}{6}$, and 1.5 are all representations of the same number.

For You to Do

Here are four different ways to represent the number $\frac{16}{25}$.

$$\frac{16}{25} \qquad 0.64 \qquad \frac{32}{50} \qquad \left(\frac{4}{5}\right)^2$$

For Problems 5–7, choose a representation above to help you find the answer. Explain each choice.

5. What is the sum $\frac{16}{25} + \frac{17}{50}$?
6. Is $\frac{16}{25}$ greater than 0.65?
7. Is there any number that you can multiply by itself to get $\frac{16}{25}$?

Exercises *Practicing Habits of Mind*

Check Your Understanding

1. Convert each fraction to a decimal with at most five decimal places.
   If the decimal repeats, write *repeating decimal*.

   a. $\frac{2}{5}$ **b.** $\frac{2}{3}$ **c.** $\frac{7}{8}$

   d. $\frac{9}{4}$ **e.** $\frac{5}{9}$ **f.** $\frac{7}{11}$

2. Convert each decimal to a fraction in lowest terms.

   a. 0.48   **b.** 2.47   **c.** 0.2

   d. 3.333   **e.** 3.8   **f.** −13.69

   g. Take It Further 0.88888 . . .   **h. Take It Further** 0.414141 . . .

3. Dana tells Andrew that, no matter what two points he names, she can
   always find a third point on the number line between those two points.

   Andrew replies, "I'm thinking of 0.99 and 1."

   Dana says, "That's easy! 0.997 is between those two numbers."

   Andrew says, "Okay, try 0.9999 and 1."

   Dana answers, "0.9999314 is between those two numbers."

   Is Dana correct? Can she always find a third point between any
   two points? Explain.

4. Hideki hears Dana tell Andrew that she can always find a number between
   two given numbers.

   Hideki says, "That's nothing, Dana. No matter what points you name, I can
   find *two* new points between your points."

   Show how Hideki can do this. Find two points between the
   two given numbers.

   a. 0.99 and 1   **b.** 0.9999 and 1   **c.** 0.999999 and 1

   d. Is Hideki correct? Can you always find two new points between any
   two points? Explain.

5. Draw a number line from 0 to 4. Plot each number.

    a. $\sqrt{2}$ **b.** $\frac{3}{2}$ **c.** $\sqrt{7}$ **d.** 2.3   **e.** $\sqrt{16}$

    f. 1.3   **g.** $\sqrt{3}$ **h.** 3.75   **i.** $\sqrt{8}$

> You can use a calculator to approximate the value of a square root.

6. **What's Wrong Here?** Derman labels a number line incorrectly.

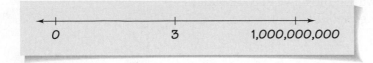

    a. Explain what is wrong with Derman's labels.

    b. Using graph paper, why is it difficult to draw a number line including 0, 3, and 1,000,000,000?

On Your Own

For Exercises 7 and 8, use graph paper. Copy each number line. Write the missing numbers.

7.

    0 0.03 ■ ■ ■ 0.15 ■ ■ ■ ■ 0.3

8.

    8.75 9 ■ ■ ■ ■ ■ 10.5 ■ 11 ■

9. Convert each decimal to a fraction in lowest terms.

    a. 1.63   **b.** 0.711   **c.** 14.75

    d. -11.5 **e.** -0.125 **f.** -0.001

10. **Standardized Test Prep** Choose the pair of numbers that makes the inequality ■ $< \sqrt{14} <$ ■ true.

    A. 2.5 and 3.0   **B.** 3.0 and 3.5

    C. 3.5 and 4.0   **D.** 4.0 and 4.5

11. Here are four representations of the number $\frac{7}{4}$.

    $\frac{7}{4}$ 1.75 $\frac{175}{100}$ $\frac{21}{12}$

For parts (a)–(d), choose one of the representations above to help you find the answer. Explain each choice.

    a. What is the sum of $\frac{7}{4} + \frac{3}{100}$?

    b. What number can you add to $\frac{7}{4}$ to get 3.86?

    c. What number can you add to $\frac{7}{4}$ to get $\frac{23}{12}$?

    d. **Take It Further** What number can you add to $\frac{7}{4}$ to get $\frac{7}{3}$?

Go Online
www.successnetplus.com

12. Order the numbers from least to greatest:

    3.009   3.08   3.7   3.18   3.5999

13. Which point is closest to -2 on the number line?

    a. $-\frac{1}{2}$ **b.** 2.3   **c.** $\frac{9}{2}$ **d.** -3 **e.** $-\frac{7}{2}$

Maintain Your Skills

14. Which numbers are between 1 and 2 on the number line?

    a. $\frac{7}{4}$ **b.** $\frac{5}{4}$ **c.** $\frac{7}{3}$ **d.** $\frac{5}{3}$ **e.** $\frac{13}{11}$

    f. $\frac{13}{17}$ **g.** $\frac{101}{121}$ **h.** $\frac{121}{101}$ **i.** $\frac{221}{101}$

    j. Explain how you can decide whether a fraction is between 1 and 2.

15. Find the number that is halfway between each pair of numbers.

    a. 2 and 8

    b. -3 and -6

    c. 3.2 and 3.8

    d. -2.3 and -2.34

    e. 0.5 and -2

    f. Sasha says, "I can find the number halfway between any two numbers by adding them together and then dividing by two." Does Sasha's method work? Explain.

    g. At about what time in the video clip below does Tara pick up her dog, Scruffy?

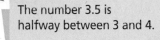

The number 3.5 is halfway between 3 and 4.

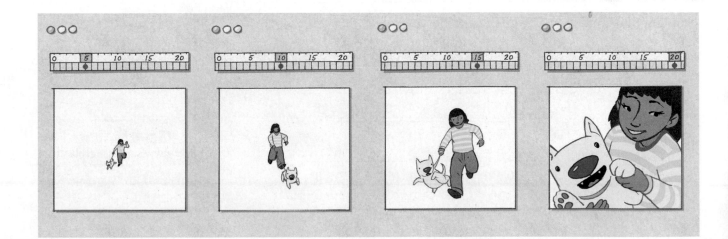

1.09 Number Line Addition

In Investigation 1A, you added integers using the addition table and learned the basic rules of arithmetic. You cannot use the addition table to add fractions. Instead, you can use the number line. To add using the number line, think about numbers as lengths that point in either a positive or negative direction.

Example 1

Problem Illustrate $4.5 + 3.5$ on the number line.

Solution First, illustrate both 4.5 and 3.5 as lengths on the number line.

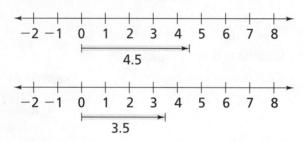

To add the lengths, line up the tail of the second arrow with the tip of the first arrow on a single number line. You can see that $4.5 + 3.5 = 8$.

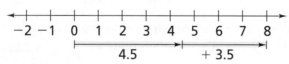

Example 2

Problem Illustrate $7 + (-2)$ on the number line.

Solution Use the solution method in Example 1. Note that (-2) points in a negative direction.

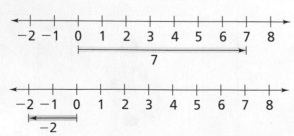

Line up the tail of the second arrow with the tip of the first arrow on the same number line. The sum of $7 + (-2)$ is 5.

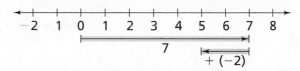

Why do you need to th ink about addition using the number line? You can add any two real numbers on the number line. For instance, you can add $\frac{31}{7}$ and $\sqrt{5}$.

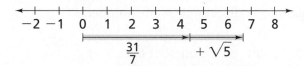

By using the number line, you preserve the rules of addition in Investigation 1A. Do you remember the following rule?

> The order in which you add two numbers in a sum does not affect the result.

This rule is still true when you think about addition on the number line. The number lines show that $\frac{31}{7} + \sqrt{5} = \sqrt{5} + \frac{31}{7}$.

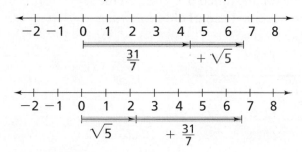

For Discussion

1. Illustrate the following rule using the number line: If you add 0 to any number, the result is the number itself.

Developing Habits of Mind

Recognize a similar process. The rules for adding real numbers on the number line are the same as the rules of addition that you learned for integers.

- You can add any two real numbers.
- You can extend the basic rules of addition that held for $\mathbb{Z}$.

Exercises Practicing Habits of Mind

Check Your Understanding

1 Illustrate each sum on a number line.

    a. $6 + (-3)$ **b.** $\frac{1}{2} + \frac{5}{2}$ **c.** $(-2) + \left(-\frac{3}{4}\right)$ **d.** $0 + 4$

2. Use the number line to illustrate the following addition rule: If any number is added to its opposite, the result is 0.

3. Copy the number line. A and B are the two points on the number line represented by open dots. Match each of the solid dots with one of the following labels.

    a. $-A$ **b.** $A + B$ **c.** $-B$ **d.** $\frac{1}{A}$

4. **What's Wrong Here?** Tony says, "Here's how I illustrated $5 + (-3)$ on the number line. The answer I got was 8 and not 2, so I know I did something wrong." What did Tony do wrong?

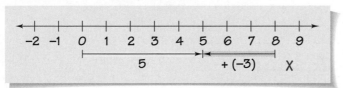

5. Find each sum.

    a. $\frac{1}{3} + \frac{7}{3}$ **b.** $\frac{1}{3} + \frac{1}{6}$ **c.** $\frac{11}{6} + \left(-\frac{3}{2}\right)$

    d. $\frac{3}{7} + \left(-\frac{4}{11}\right)$ **e.** $\frac{33}{11} + \left(-\frac{18}{6}\right)$

6. In each list, the numbers increase by the same amount each time. Fill in the blanks.

    Sample

    Fill in the blanks. $0, \frac{1}{3}, \blacksquare, \blacksquare, \blacksquare, \blacksquare$

    Solution $0, \frac{1}{3}, \frac{2}{3}, 1, \frac{4}{3}, \frac{5}{3}$

    a. $0, \frac{1}{2}, \blacksquare, \blacksquare, \blacksquare, \blacksquare, \blacksquare$ **b.** $0, \blacksquare, \frac{1}{2}, \blacksquare, \blacksquare, \blacksquare, \blacksquare$

    c. $0, \blacksquare, \frac{1}{4}, \blacksquare, \blacksquare, \blacksquare, \blacksquare$ **d.** $0, \blacksquare, \blacksquare, \blacksquare, \blacksquare, \blacksquare, \frac{2}{3}$

On Your Own

7 Copy the number line. Locate each point on the number line.

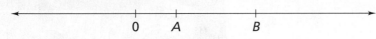

a. $-A$ **b.** $A + B$

c. $B - A$ **d.** $B + B$

Go Online
www.successnetplus.com

8. What's Wrong Here? Calvin draws the picture below to find $\frac{1}{2} + \frac{1}{4}$ on a number line.

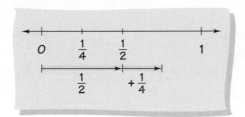

He explains, "To label the point $\frac{1}{2} + \frac{1}{4}$, I'll just add across the top and the bottom. So, $\frac{1}{2} + \frac{1}{4} = \frac{2}{6}$, which is the same as $\frac{1}{3}$." What is wrong with Calvin's reasoning?

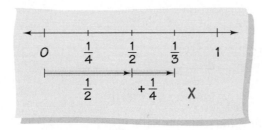

9. In each list, the numbers increase by the same amount each time. Fill in the blanks.

a. 0, 0.2, ■, ■, ■, ■, ■

b. 0, ■, 0.6, ■, ■, ■, ■,

c. 0, ■, 2.2, ■, ■, ■, ■

d. 0, ■, ■, ■, ■, ■, 3.6

10. Use a number line. Find the starting or ending number. Start at the number given. Move three units to the right, five units to the left, three units to the right, and four units to the left.

	Starting Number	Ending Number
a.	3	■
b.	−7	■
c.	11	■
d.	■	5
e.	■	0

11. **Standardized Test Prep** Choose the pair of numbers that makes the inequality $\blacksquare < (\sqrt{2} + \sqrt{3}) < \blacksquare$ true.

A. 1.5 and 2.0

B. 2.0 and 2.5

C. 2.5 and 3.0

D. 3.0 and 3.5

Maintain Your Skills

12. Fill in the blank with a number that makes the equation true.

a. $\frac{1}{3} + \blacksquare = 1$
b. $\frac{1}{4} + \blacksquare = 1$
c. $\frac{2}{5} + \blacksquare = 1$

d. $\frac{4}{3} + \blacksquare = 1$
e. $\frac{-3}{11} + \blacksquare = 1$
f. Identify a pattern.

13. For each value of point B on the number line, find the distance from point B to 10.

	Point B	Distance From Point B to 10
a.	2	■
b.	3	■
c.	4	■
d.	7.3	■
e.	$\frac{11}{3}$	■

f. In general, how is the distance from point B to 10 related to the value at point B?

Number Line Multiplication

In this lesson, you will use number lines to extend multiplication to all numbers. To show how to multiply 7 times 2, find 7 on the vertical number line and 2 on the horizontal number line. The product of 7 and 2 is the area of this rectangle.

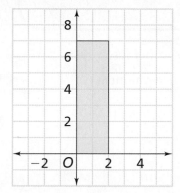

Using this method, you can show how to multiply *any* two positive numbers on the number lines. For instance, what is $\frac{7}{3}$ times $\sqrt{2}$? The number lines below illustrate the product.

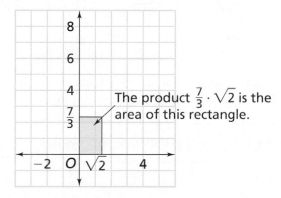

The product $\frac{7}{3} \cdot \sqrt{2}$ is the area of this rectangle.

You can extend the multiplication rules from Investigation 1A using the diagrams below. If you multiply a negative number and a positive number, the product is negative. If you multiply two negative numbers, the product is positive.

Multiplying Two Numbers With Different Signs

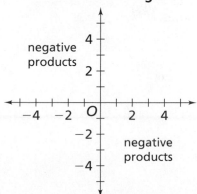

Multiplying Two Numbers With Same Signs

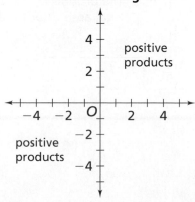

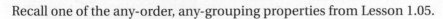

Visualize multiplication in a different way. It is impractical to draw two number lines every time you multiply. However, looking at a familiar process in a different way is sometimes helpful. When you use two number lines to multiply, you can understand why the basic rules for multiplication extend to all numbers.

Recall one of the any-order, any-grouping properties from Lesson 1.05.

> The order in which you multiply two numbers in a product does not affect the result.

This is the Commutative Property of Multiplication.

Here is how to use number lines to show $\frac{31}{7} \cdot \sqrt{5} = \sqrt{5} \cdot \frac{31}{7}$.

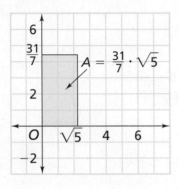
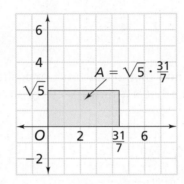

The Distributive Property in Investigation 1A states that multiplying a number by a sum is the same as multiplying the number by each term in the sum and then adding the results.

Here is an illustration of the Distributive Property. This illustration shows that $9 \cdot \left(\frac{1}{3} + 2 \right) = 9 \cdot \frac{1}{3} + 9 \cdot 2$.

The product $9 \cdot \frac{1}{3}$ is the area of the shaded rectangle.

The product $9 \cdot 2$ is the area of the unshaded rectangle.

The product $9\left(\frac{1}{3} + 2 \right)$ is the total area of both rectangles.

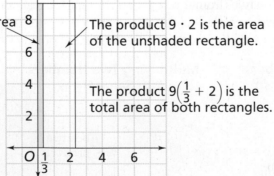

For You to Do

Find each product using the Distributive Property.

1. $9 \cdot \left(\frac{1}{3} + 2 \right)$ **2.** $12 \cdot \left(5 + \frac{1}{4} \right)$ **3.** $10 \cdot \left(5 - \frac{1}{10} \right)$

For Discussion

4. Using number lines and multiplication, explain why the following basic rule is true: If you multiply any number by 0, then the product is 0.

Exercises *Practicing Habits of Mind*

Check Your Understanding

1. Find each product using the Distributive Property.

  a. $15 \cdot \left(\frac{1}{3} + \frac{1}{5} \right)$

  b. $10 \cdot \left(\frac{1}{2} + \frac{1}{5} \right)$

  c. $25 \cdot \left(\frac{1}{5} + \frac{7}{25} \right)$

  d. $\frac{9}{4} \cdot \left(\frac{4}{3} + \frac{8}{9} \right)$

2. Sasha notices that if you move the negative sign in a multiplication problem, the change doesn't affect the product. For instance, $(-2) \cdot 5$ and $2 \cdot (-5)$ both equal -10. Using number line multiplication, explain Sasha's observation.

3. Every number except 0 has an inverse for multiplication. Why doesn't 0 have a multiplicative inverse?

4. Copy the number line. Points A and B are numbers represented by the open dots. Match each of the solid dots with one of the following labels.

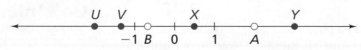

  a. $A \cdot B$ **b.** $\frac{3}{2}A$ **c.** $3B$ **d.** $\frac{1}{A}$

5. Fill in each blank with a number that makes the equation true.

a. $4 \cdot \left(\frac{1}{2} + \blacksquare \right) = 3$

b. $-\frac{1}{3} \cdot (8 + \blacksquare) = -\frac{10}{3}$

c. $\frac{1}{7} \cdot (18 + \blacksquare) = \frac{22}{7}$

d. $14 \cdot \left(\frac{3}{2} + \blacksquare \right) = 28$

e. $-5 \cdot \left(\frac{1}{9} + \blacksquare \right) = 0$

f. $24 \cdot \left(\frac{1}{2} + \blacksquare \right) = 4$

g. How did you find each missing number?

On Your Own

6. Find each product using the Distributive Property.

a. $20 \cdot \left(\frac{1}{10} + \frac{1}{5} \right)$ **b.** $12 \cdot \left(\frac{1}{2} + \frac{1}{3} \right)$

c. $35 \cdot \left(\frac{1}{5} + \frac{1}{7} \right)$ **d.** $\frac{1}{4} \cdot \left(\frac{4}{3} + \frac{4}{5} \right)$

7. **Standardized Test Prep** Evaluate $6 \cdot \left(\frac{5}{7} + \frac{4}{63} \right)$.

A. $\frac{54}{70}$

B. $\frac{14}{3}$

C. $\frac{4}{1}$

D. $\frac{49}{21}$

8. Copy the number line. Points A and B are numbers represented by the open dots. Match each of the solid dots with one of the following labels.

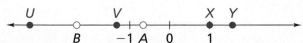

a. $2A$

b. $\frac{3}{2}B$

c. AB

d. $B \cdot \frac{1}{B}$

9. **Take It Further** Derman swims laps in a pool. After a few laps, he says, "I'm a quarter of the way there." After one more lap, he says, "Now I'm a third of the way there." How many laps does Derman intend to swim?

Maintain Your Skills

For Exercises 10–12, fill in the missing number to make each equation true.

10. a. $3 \cdot \blacksquare = 12$

　　b. $3 \cdot \blacksquare = 7$

　　c. $3 \cdot \blacksquare = -11$

　　d. $3 \cdot \blacksquare = 4$

　　e. $3 \cdot \blacksquare = -5$

　　f. How did you determine each missing number?

11. a. $7 \cdot \blacksquare = 1$

　　b. $\frac{2}{5} \cdot \blacksquare = 1$

　　c. $-\frac{5}{19} \cdot \blacksquare = 1$

　　d. $-3 \cdot \blacksquare = 1$

　　e. $\frac{22}{5} \cdot \blacksquare = 1$

　　f. $\frac{1}{7} \cdot \blacksquare = 1$

　　g. $\frac{88}{7} \cdot \blacksquare = 1$

　　h. How did you determine each missing number?

12. a. $7 \cdot \left(\frac{1}{7} + \blacksquare \right) = 3$　　**b.** $\frac{1}{5} \cdot (11 + \blacksquare) - \frac{14}{5}$

　　c. $\frac{1}{3} \cdot (8 + \blacksquare) = \frac{7}{3}$　　**d.** $-5 \cdot \left(\frac{1}{2} + \blacksquare \right) = -5$

　　e. $6 \cdot \left(\frac{1}{2} + \blacksquare \right) = 5$　　**f.** $-10 \cdot \left(\frac{1}{2} + \blacksquare \right) = 1$

　　g. How did you determine each missing number?

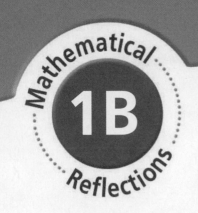

Mathematical 1B Reflections

In this investigation, you learned to locate fractions and decimals on the number line. You also used the number line to add and multiply real numbers. These questions will help you summarize what you have learned.

1. Draw a horizontal line segment about 2 inches long. Label the endpoints 0 and 1. Label points for $\frac{1}{2}$, $\frac{7}{8}$, $\frac{1}{4}$, and $\frac{3}{8}$. Which fraction is larger, $\frac{1}{4}$ or $\frac{1}{8}$? Explain.

2. Which of these fractions is NOT equal to the other fractions?

   A. $\frac{2}{3}$

   B. $\frac{8}{12}$

   C. $\frac{4}{5}$

   D. $\frac{10}{15}$

3. Find the sum $1.25 + \frac{1}{2}$ in the following two ways.

   a. Change $\frac{1}{2}$ to a decimal.

   b. Change 1.25 to a fraction.

4. Illustrate each sum using a number line.

   a. $6 + (-2)$

   b. $(-2) + 6$

   c. $(-3) + (-4)$

   d. $(-2) + 2$

5. Draw a number line. Label the number halfway between −1 and 0 point A. Point B is a number between 2 and 3. Mark the approximate location of each expression.

   a. point A

   b. point B

   c. $A \cdot B$

   d. $A + B$

6. How can you tell whether two fractions that look different represent the same number?

7. How do you add numbers on the number line?

8. Where is $\sqrt{2}$ located on the number line?

Vocabulary

In this investigation, you learned these terms. Make sure you understand what each one means and how to use it.

- **decimal expansion**
- **decimal representation**
- **equivalent fractions**
- **lowest terms**
- **square root**

Which girl can ride on the carnival attraction?

Investigation 1C

The Algorithms of Arithmetic

In *The Algorithms of Arithmetic,* you will learn why traditional methods work for the four operations.

By the end of this investigation, you will be able to answer questions like these.

1. Why do traditional ways to add and multiply numbers work?

2. Why do people say that dividing is the same as multiplying by the reciprocal?

3. How many weeks are in 1 billion seconds?

You will learn how to

- explain why the algorithms you commonly use for addition, subtraction, and multiplication work

- use nontraditional algorithms that can be faster in some cases

- become more familiar with the basic rules of arithmetic

- perform arithmetic with integers and fractions

You will develop these habits and skills:

- Find and justify new shortcuts for doing arithmetic.

- View algorithms and other mathematical processes not just as shortcuts for answering math questions, but also as ideas that mathematicians study.

1.11 Getting Started

**Activating Prior Knowledge
Exploring New Ideas**

In Getting Started, you will use the four operations and rational numbers. Unless stated otherwise, complete the exercises in this investigation without using a calculator.

For You to Explore

1. Perform each operation. Find shortcuts to simplify your work. Keep track of your steps.

   a. 48×5

   b. $2 + 55 + 31 + 45 + 98 + 9$

   c. $125 \cdot 13 \cdot 80$

   d. 2×98

   e. $\frac{1}{10} + \frac{37}{100} + \frac{243}{1000}$

   f.
   $$
   \begin{array}{r}
   0.1 \\
   0.37 \\
   + \ 0.243 \\
   \hline
   \end{array}
   $$

   g. $641 - 244$

   h. $\frac{1}{2} + \frac{3}{4} + \frac{5}{8}$

   i. $\frac{1}{2} \cdot \frac{2}{3} \cdot \frac{3}{4} \cdot \frac{4}{5}$

   j. $\frac{21}{83} \cdot \frac{77}{19} \cdot \frac{31}{21} \cdot \frac{19}{31} \cdot \frac{83}{77}$

   k. $\frac{14}{15} \cdot \frac{50}{28} \cdot \frac{11}{20} \cdot \frac{16}{22}$

   l. $\dfrac{\frac{10}{13}}{\frac{5}{13}}$

   m. $148 + 93 - 74 + 107 - 53 - 11$

   n. $81 - 72 + 63 - 54 + 45 - 36 + 27 - 18 + 9$

2. Explain any shortcuts you used in Problem 1.

Exercises *Practicing Habits of Mind*

For Exercises 3 and 4, each letter represents a single digit from 0 to 9.
Find all possible values of each digit that make the arithmetic exercise true.

3. Find all possible values for *A*, *B*, and *C*.

$$
\begin{array}{r}
AB \\
AB \\
AB \\
+\ AB \\
\hline
CA
\end{array}
$$

4. Find all possible values for *A*, *B*, and *C*.

$$
\begin{array}{r}
ABA \\
+\ BAB \\
\hline
CCC
\end{array}
$$

5. At a sports store, a water bottle cost \$7.99, a pair of shorts costs \$24.99, and a pair of shoes costs \$61.99.

   a. Without using a calculator, find the total cost of these items.

   b. Write About It Describe how to find the sum.

Maintain Your Skills

6. Find each sum.

   a. $1 + \frac{1}{2}$

   b. $1 + \frac{1}{2} + \frac{1}{4}$

   c. $1 + \frac{1}{2} + \frac{1}{4} + \frac{1}{8}$

   d. $1 + \frac{1}{2} + \frac{1}{4} + \frac{1}{8} + \frac{1}{16}$

   e. $1 + \frac{1}{2} + \frac{1}{4} + \frac{1}{8} + \frac{1}{16} + \frac{1}{32}$

   f. Describe a pattern that you can use to find the sum.

7. Find each result.

   a. $1 - \frac{1}{2}$

   b. $1 - \frac{1}{2} + \frac{1}{4}$

   c. $1 - \frac{1}{2} + \frac{1}{4} - \frac{1}{8}$

   d. $1 - \frac{1}{2} + \frac{1}{4} - \frac{1}{8} + \frac{1}{16}$

   e. $1 - \frac{1}{2} + \frac{1}{4} - \frac{1}{8} + \frac{1}{16} - \frac{1}{32}$

   f. Describe a pattern that you can use to find the result.

Addition and Subtraction Algorithms

This lesson focuses on addition and subtraction **algorithms.** An algorithm is a set of ordered steps for solving a problem. You will examine the algorithms to find why they work. Many of these algorithms are based on breaking up a number into place-value parts. In this lesson, you will review a number's place-value parts.

Facts and Notation

A **place-value part** is a number, such as 6000, 20, or 5 that has a single leading digit followed by some number of zeros. The number 270 is not a place-value part but is the sum of two place-value parts, 200 + 70.

For You to Do

Write each number as the sum of place-value parts.

1. 1982   2. 305   3. 39,150

Addition Using Columns The traditional addition algorithm follows these steps.

Step 1 Start with the column farthest to the right and add each number in the column.

Step 2 Write the sum of the ones digit column below the column.

Step 3 If the sum is 10 or greater, carry the tens to the top of the next column.

Step 4 Repeat a similar process with the next column, moving from right to left.

Here is an example.

$$
\begin{array}{r} 413 \\ 254 \\ +\ 91 \\ \hline \end{array}
\quad\rightarrow\quad
\begin{array}{r} 413 \\ 254 \\ +\ 91 \\ \hline 8 \end{array}
\quad\rightarrow\quad
\begin{array}{r} {}^{1}\,413 \\ 254 \\ +\ 91 \\ \hline 58 \end{array}
\quad\rightarrow\quad
\begin{array}{r} {}^{1}\,413 \\ 254 \\ +\ 91 \\ \hline 758 \end{array}
$$

          Step 1   **Step 2**   **Step 3**

Here are the steps you follow to find the sum above.

Step 1 Find the sum of 3, 4, and 1. Write the sum 8 below the ones column.

Step 2 Add 1, 5, and 9. The sum is 15. Write the digit 5 below the tens column. Write the other digits at the top of the next column.

Step 3 Add the carried digit 1 to 4 and 2. The sum is 7. The sum of 413 + 254 + 91 is 758.

Millions of people trust this algorithm. It gives the correct answer, but not many people ask why it works.

Example

Problem

a. Explain why addition using columns works.

b. When is this algorithm useful?

Solution

a. The algorithm uses the any-order, any-grouping properties of addition. To understand why this is true, look at the place-value parts in the addition algorithm.

$$413 + 254 + 91$$

Break each number into place-value parts. Then rearrange the place-value parts. Group the ones, tens, and hundreds together.

$$413 + 254 + 91 = (400 + 10 + 3) + (200 + 50 + 4) + (90 + 1)$$
$$= (400 + 200) + (10 + 50 + 90) + (3 + 4 + 1)$$

You can rearrange the numbers because the AOAG properties state that the order you use to add the numbers does not affect the result.

Adding by columns is the same as adding the place-value parts separately. First, add the ones digits. Next, add the tens digits. Finally, add the hundreds digits.

$$= (400 + 200) + (10 + 50 + 90) + 8$$
$$= (400 + 200) + 150 + 8$$
$$= 600 + 150 + 8$$

When you add $1 + 5 + 9$ in the tens column to get 15, you are actually adding $10 + 50 + 90$ to get 150. You need to carry, because 150 is not a place-value part. You need to split 150 into two place-value parts, $150 = 100 + 50$. You combine the number 100 with the other numbers in the next place value to the left.

$$(400 + 200) + 150 + 8 = (400 + 200) + (100 + 50) + 8$$
$$= (400 + 200 + 100) + 50 + 8$$
$$= 700 + 50 + 8$$
$$= 758$$

You can perform addition in any order and use any grouping, so $(400 + 200) + (100 + 50)$ is the same as $(400 + 200 + 100) + 50$, or $(50 + 400) + (100 + 200)$.

b. You can use this algorithm to add any numbers, so it is very useful. The only time that it is not useful is when you add larger numbers and do not have a pencil or paper.

Can a decimal such as 2.853 be broken up into place-value parts? Explain.

For Discussion

4. When adding by columns, you add the ones column before you add the digit in the tens column. Why do you add by columns moving from right to left?

Exercises *Practicing Habits of Mind*

Check Your Understanding

In a small group, you will discuss one or more algorithms and understand why each algorithm works.

For Exercises 1–7, answer these questions using sentences.

- How and why does the technique or algorithm work? Include the basic rules of arithmetic in your explanation, if possible.

- When is the technique or algorithm useful?

1. Add more and then subtract. Find the sum.

$$\begin{array}{r} \$17.99 \\ +\$19.99 \\ \end{array}$$

Think about $17.99 as $18 − $.01, and $19.99 as $20 − $.01. Then, add $18 and $20 and subtract $.02.

Here is how the calculation works.

$$\$17.99 + \$19.99 = (\$18 - \$.01) + (\$20 - \$.01)$$
$$= (\$18 + \$20) - \$.01 - \$.01$$
$$= \$38 - \$.02$$
$$= \$37.98$$

2. **Reorder the terms.** When you add many numbers, changing the order of the numbers can make finding a sum easier. How can you make this addition easier?

$$\begin{array}{r} 148 \\ 3 \\ 60 \\ 37 \\ + \ 152 \\ \hline \end{array}$$

Adding is easier if you can find numbers with a sum that equals a multiple of ten. For example, $3 + 37 = 40$, and adding 60 more equals 100. The other sum, $152 + 148$, equals 300. Finally, $100 + 300 = 400$.

3. **Subtract using columns.** The traditional subtraction algorithm uses columns. Instead of carrying, you "borrow" a unit. You borrow when a column shows a subtraction, such as $3 - 4$, that does not give a positive result.

For the subtraction $3 - 4$ in Step 2, you borrow 1 from the column at the left. You change 5 to 4 (column at the left) and 3 to 13 (Step 2). Then you find the difference $13 - 4$ in the second column. The last step is to subtract 3 from 5 in the column at the left.

$$\begin{array}{r} 537 \\ - \ 341 \\ \hline \end{array} \rightarrow \begin{array}{r} 537 \\ - \ 341 \\ \hline 6 \end{array} \rightarrow \begin{array}{r} {}^{4}\cancel{5}{}^{13}7 \\ - \ 341 \\ \hline 6 \end{array} \rightarrow \begin{array}{r} {}^{4}\cancel{5}{}^{13}7 \\ - \ 341 \\ \hline 96 \end{array} \rightarrow \begin{array}{r} {}^{4}\cancel{5}{}^{13}7 \\ - \ 341 \\ \hline 196 \end{array}$$

Step 1   **Step 2**   **Step 3**   **Step 4**

4. **Subtract some more.** Suppose you want to subtract 341 from 537. You can break up the number 341 into 337 and 4. Then you can subtract: $537 - 337 = 200$ and $200 - 4 = 196$.

$$\begin{array}{r} 537 \\ - \ 337 \\ - \quad 4 \\ \hline \end{array}$$

5. **Add from left to right.** Tyler has a method for adding numbers mentally. He explains his method this way.

"Look at the sum $42 + 37 + 55 + 96$.

Start with the largest place value. These are all 2-digit numbers, so the largest place value is the tens place. First, you add just the tens.

$$\overset{\overset{70}{\frown}\ \overset{120}{\frown}\ \overset{210}{\frown}}{42 + 37 + 55 + 96}$$

40 plus 30 is 70, 70 plus 50 is 120, and 120 plus 90 is 210. Next, take 210 and add the ones.

$$\overset{\overset{70}{\frown}\ \overset{120}{\frown}\ \overset{210}{\frown}}{\underset{\underset{212\quad 219\quad 224\quad 230}{}}{42 + 37 + 55 + 96}}$$

210 plus 2 is 212, 212 plus 7 is 219, 219 plus 5 is 224, and 224 plus 6 is 230. This is much easier!"

6. Subtract by counting up. To find the difference $1017 - 345$, start with 345 and add numbers until you reach 1017. Here is one way to do this.

$$345 + 600 = 945$$
$$945 + 60 = 1005$$
$$1005 + 10 = 1015$$
$$1015 + 2 = 1017$$

Because $345 + (600 + 60 + 10 + 2) = 1017$, $(600 + 60 + 10 + 2)$ is the difference $1017 - 345 = 672$.

Since the result is the sum of $600 + 60 + 10 + 2$, it is generally simpler to add place-value parts when you can.

7. Add consecutive integers. Here is a trick for adding a list of consecutive integers. Add the integers from 1 to 9. Then regroup the numbers so that many sums are the same.

$$1 + 2 + 3 + 4 + 5 + 6 + 7 + 8 + 9 = (1 + 9) + (2 + 8) + (3 + 7) + (4 + 6) + 5$$
$$= 10 + 10 + 10 + 10 + 5$$
$$= 45$$

On Your Own

Unless stated otherwise, complete Exercises 8 15 without using a calculator.

Go Online
www.successnetplus.com

8. Kye invents a subtraction method. Here is an example.

$$
\begin{array}{r}
73 \\
- 48 \\
\hline
-5 \\
30 \\
\hline
25
\end{array}
$$

Kye reasons that $3 - 8$ is -5, $70 - 40$ is 30, and $30 - 5$ is 25. Use Kye's method. Find the difference $47 - 59$.

9. Write About It Does Kye's method in Exercise 8 always work? Explain.

10. Find the sum $6312 + 2483$.

11. **Standardized Test Prep** Jason has his own method for subtraction. He rewrites $A - B = C$ as $B + C = A$. Then he starts at the left-most digit in the number B. He finds the greatest place-value part that he can add to B. He makes sure that this sum is no greater than the number A. Then Jason moves from left to right across B. He adds place-value parts until the sum of the place-value parts is the number A. Which of the following shows his method for finding $3964 - 2587$?

A. $2587 + 7 = 2594$

$2594 + 70 = 2664$

$2664 + 300 = 2964$

$2964 + 1000 = 3964$

$2587 + 1377 = 3964$

B. $2587 + 1400 = 3987$

$3987 - 30 = 3957$

$3987 + 7 = 3964$

$2587 + 1407 - 30 = 1377$

C. $2587 + 1000 = 3587$

$3587 + 300 = 3887$

$3887 + 70 = 3957$

$3957 + 7 = 3964$

$2587 + 1377 = 3964$

D. $3964 - 2587 = 300 + 7 + 1000 + 70$

$300 + 7 + 1000 + 70 = 1377$

12. Without adding, explain how you know that both sums are the same.

$$
\begin{array}{r}
413 \\
254 \\
+\ 91 \\
\end{array}
\qquad
\begin{array}{r}
294 \\
451 \\
+\ 13 \\
\end{array}
$$

13. A standard football field is 100 yards long from end zone to end zone. Vince measures a field and finds that it is five feet shorter than a standard field. How long is the shorter field?

14. A professional football field is 100 yards long from end zone to end zone and 160 feet wide.

    a. If you want to find the field's area, can you multiply 100 by 160?

    b. Find the area of the field in square feet.

    c. Find the area of the field in square yards.

    d. How many square feet are in a square yard?

Maintain Your Skills

15. a. How many $\frac{1}{6}$'s are in $\frac{1}{2}$?   b. How many $\frac{1}{6}$'s are in $\frac{2}{3}$?

    c. How many $\frac{1}{4}$'s are in $2\frac{1}{2}$?   d. How many 5's are in 37?

    e. Make a conjecture about the general rule that you can use to find each result.

Adding and Subtracting Fractions

In this lesson, you will learn to add and subtract fractions with like and unlike denominators.

Minds in Action

Tony and Sasha work on Exercise 13 from Lesson 1.12.

A standard football field is 100 yards long from end zone to end zone. Vince measures a field and finds that it is five feet shorter than a standard field. How long is the shorter field?

Tony I've got the answer. It's 295 feet.

Sasha Two hundred ninety-five? I got 95. That seems fine to me.

Tony No, the answer is definitely 295 feet.

Sasha How can the field be 295 feet long? The regular field is 100 yards. Oh, I see. You got 295 feet. Now I see what I did wrong.

To find the length of the shorter field, you can write this subtraction. When Sasha subtracts the numbers, the calculation does not make sense. The units are not the same!

$$\begin{array}{r} 100 \text{ yards} \\ - \quad 5 \text{ feet} \\ \hline \blacksquare \end{array}$$

There are two ways to change the units. You can convert 100 yards to feet, or convert 5 feet to yards. Converting yards to feet gives you this subtraction problem.

$$\begin{array}{r} 300 \text{ feet} \\ - \quad 5 \text{ feet} \\ \hline \blacksquare \text{ feet} \end{array}$$

There are three feet in a yard, so 100 yards equal 300 feet. You can also convert 5 feet to $\frac{5}{3}$ yards. Then subtract that amount from 100 yards. The result is in yards, instead of feet.

You can use this method to add and subtract fractions. For example, you can write the sum $\frac{2}{3} + \frac{1}{5}$ like this. You need to convert the denominators of both fractions to a common unit.

$$\begin{array}{r} 2 \text{ thirds} \\ + \quad 1 \text{ fifth} \\ \hline \blacksquare \end{array}$$

Here are some ways to write $\frac{2}{3}$ as an equivalent fraction.

$$\frac{2}{3} = \frac{4}{6} \qquad \frac{2}{3} = \frac{6}{9} \qquad \frac{2}{3} = \frac{8}{12} \qquad \frac{2}{3} = \frac{10}{15} \qquad \frac{2}{3} = \frac{12}{18}$$

Here are some equivalent fractions for $\frac{1}{5}$.

$$\frac{1}{5} = \frac{2}{10} \qquad \frac{1}{5} = \frac{3}{15} \qquad \frac{1}{5} = \frac{4}{20} \qquad \frac{1}{5} = \frac{5}{25}$$

In the list below there is a matching unit, fifteenths. Two thirds is equivalent to ten fifteenths, and one fifth is equivalent to three fifteenths. Now that you have a common unit, you can find the sum.

Fifteenths is the lowest possible match. So 15 is the least common denominator. What other matches are possible?

$$\begin{array}{r} 10 \text{ fifteenths} \\ + \quad 3 \text{ fifteenths} \\ \hline 13 \text{ fifteenths} \end{array}$$

$$\frac{2}{3} + \frac{1}{5} = \frac{10}{15} + \frac{3}{15}$$

$$= \frac{13}{15}$$

There is always a choice of common denominators for any two fractions. Using the lowest, or **least common denominator,** as the common unit is the most efficient. You can use the same idea when you subtract fractions. Since $\frac{5}{6}$ is equal to $\frac{10}{12}$, the result is $\frac{10}{12} - \frac{7}{12} = \frac{3}{12}$.

$$\begin{array}{r} 5 \text{ sixths} \\ - \ 7 \text{ twelfths} \\ \hline \blacksquare \end{array}$$

Even if you use the least common denominator, you can sometimes simplify the result of a calculation further.

$$\frac{3 \div 3}{12 \div 3} = \frac{1}{4}$$

The fraction $\frac{1}{4}$ is in lowest terms, which means that the numerator and denominator do not share a common factor greater than 1.

For You to Do

1. Find $\frac{11}{24} + \frac{3}{8}$ and $\frac{11}{24} - \frac{3}{8}$. Write each result in lowest terms.

For Discussion

2. Suppose you add $\frac{2}{3} + \frac{1}{5}$. How is the common denominator, 15, related to thirds and fifths? Is this always true?

Exercises *Practicing Habits of Mind*

Check Your Understanding

1. Find the sum of $\frac{1}{3} + \frac{1}{4} + \frac{1}{5} + \frac{1}{20} + \frac{1}{6}$ without a calculator.

> You can find this sum quickly and simply by adding the terms in a certain order.

2. The least common denominator for $\frac{2}{3}$ and $\frac{1}{5}$ is 15, and 15 is the product of 3 and 5.

   a. Find the least common denominator for each pair of fractions.

   $\frac{1}{3}$ and $\frac{1}{5}$ $\qquad$ $\frac{2}{3}$ and $\frac{4}{5}$

   b. Find the least common denominator for each pair of fractions.

   $\frac{3}{8}$ and $\frac{5}{16}$ $\qquad$ $\frac{3}{8}$ and $\frac{5}{7}$ $\qquad$ $\frac{3}{10}$ and $\frac{1}{12}$

c. When is the least common denominator of two fractions the product of the denominators?

d. Take It Further Is it possible for the least common denominator of two fractions to be greater than the product of the two denominators? Explain using examples.

3. Jill explains how she learned to add fractions using a crisscross style. She says, "You have $\frac{3}{5} + \frac{4}{7}$. I know the common denominator is 5 times 7, or 35, so I write that. The numerator, though, I get by doing a crisscross. I know that 3 times 7 is 21, and 5 times 4 is 20. I add those to get 41. The result of the addition is $\frac{41}{35}$. It works every time."

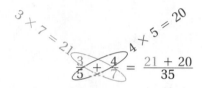

Use Jill's method to find each sum.

a. $\frac{3}{11} + \frac{1}{4}$ **b.** $\frac{1}{5} + \frac{3}{5}$

c. Take It Further Explain why Jill's method works.

d. Take It Further Can you apply Jill's method to subtracting fractions?

On Your Own

4. Find the product $24 \cdot \left(\frac{1}{3} + \frac{1}{4} + \frac{1}{8} + \frac{1}{6} \right)$ without using a calculator.

5. Find each sum or difference.

a. $\frac{1}{3} + \left(\frac{1}{11} - \frac{1}{3} \right)$ **b.** $-\frac{3}{7} + \left(\frac{1}{10} + \frac{3}{7} \right)$

c. $\left(\frac{1}{2} - \frac{7}{19} \right) + \left(\frac{7}{19} - \frac{1}{4} \right)$ **d.** $\left(\frac{2}{3} - \frac{1}{8} \right) - \left(\frac{1}{6} - \frac{1}{8} \right)$

6. Standardized Test Prep What is the sum $\frac{2}{9} + \frac{3}{18} + \frac{3}{27}$?

A. 1   **B.** $\frac{8}{27}$

C. $\frac{13}{27}$ **D.** $\frac{1}{2}$

Go Online
www.successnetplus.com

7. Write About It Write a step-by-step procedure for adding any two fractions for someone who does not know how to add fractions.

8. Find three distinct fractions having a sum that equals each number given.

   a. 1   **b.** −2   **c.** $\frac{1}{4}$

9. Fill in each missing number.

   a. ■ · (11) = $\frac{11}{5}$ **b.** ■ · $\frac{100}{7}$ = 1

   c. ■ · $\frac{4}{5}$ = 2   **d.** ■ · $\frac{7}{9}$ = −2

Maintain Your Skills

10. Find each sum. Write the result in lowest terms.

   a. $\frac{1}{3} + \frac{1}{6} + \frac{1}{9} + \frac{1}{18}$

   b. $\frac{1}{4} + \frac{1}{8} + \frac{1}{12} + \frac{1}{24}$

   c. $\frac{1}{10} + \frac{1}{20} + \frac{1}{30} + \frac{1}{60}$

   d. $\frac{1}{101} + \frac{1}{202} + \frac{1}{303} + \frac{1}{606}$

   e. Describe the pattern that you used to find each result.

11. Find each sum.

   a. $1 + \frac{1}{3}$

   b. $1 + \frac{1}{3} + \frac{1}{9}$

   c. $1 + \frac{1}{3} + \frac{1}{9} + \frac{1}{27}$

   d. $1 + \frac{1}{3} + \frac{1}{9} + \frac{1}{27} + \frac{1}{81}$

   e. $1 + \frac{1}{3} + \frac{1}{9} + \frac{1}{27} + \frac{1}{81} + \frac{1}{243}$

   f. Describe the pattern you used to find each result.

12. Find each result.

   a. $1 - \frac{1}{3}$

   b. $1 - \frac{1}{3} + \frac{1}{9}$

   c. $1 - \frac{1}{3} + \frac{1}{9} - \frac{1}{27}$

   d. $1 - \frac{1}{3} + \frac{1}{9} - \frac{1}{27} + \frac{1}{81}$

   e. $1 - \frac{1}{3} + \frac{1}{9} - \frac{1}{27} + \frac{1}{81} - \frac{1}{243}$

   f. Describe the pattern that you used to find each result.

Go Online
Video Tutor
www.successnetplus.com

1.14 Multiplication Algorithms

In this lesson, you will look at *why* multiplication algorithms work. You may already know a multiplication algorithm, but you may not know why it works.

In the traditional multiplication algorithm, you first place the greater number above the lesser number. Next, you multiply the number on top by the ones digit of the number on the bottom. Then, you multiply the number on top by the tens digit of the number on the bottom, and so on. Finally, you add these numbers in a column form, using the addition algorithm.

You can find the product 327×6 using these steps.

$$
\begin{array}{r} 327 \\ \times\ 6 \\ \hline \end{array}
\quad \rightarrow \quad
\begin{array}{r} \overset{4}{3}27 \\ \times\ 6 \\ \hline 2 \end{array}
\quad \rightarrow \quad
\begin{array}{r} \overset{1\,4}{3}27 \\ \times\ 6 \\ \hline 62 \end{array}
\quad \rightarrow \quad
\begin{array}{r} \overset{1\,4}{3}27 \\ \times\ 6 \\ \hline 1962 \end{array}
$$

$\qquad\qquad\qquad\qquad\qquad$ **Step 1** $\qquad\qquad$ **Step 2** $\qquad\qquad$ **Step 3**

Step 1 Multiply 6×7. The product equals 42. Write 2 below the line and carry 4.

Step 2 Multiply 6×2. The product equals 12. Add the 4 that you carried to get 16. Write 6 below the line. Carry 1.

Step 3 Multiply 6×3 and add 1 to get 19. Since you are done multiplying, you do not carry any more, and you write 19 below the line.

Look closely at what you are doing. As you did with addition, break down the greater number into its place-value parts.

$327 = 300 + 20 + 7$

You can rewrite the problem using place-value parts.

$327 \times 6 = (300 + 20 + 7) \times 6$

Then you can perform separate multiplications on each digit, starting with the ones digit and moving left. Remember that when you multiply 6×2 in the algorithm above, you are really multiplying 6×20.

$6 \times 7 = 42$

$6 \times 20 = 120$

$6 \times 300 = 1800$

$$327 \times 6 = \underbrace{(300 \times 6)}_{1800} + \underbrace{(20 \times 6)}_{120} + \underbrace{(7 \times 6)}_{42}$$

Then add the products. The product of 327 and 6 is 1962.

$1800 + 120 + 42 = 1962$

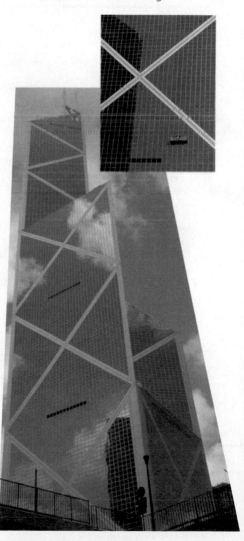

You can estimate the height of the Bank of China Tower when you know a few facts about the tower. It is 70 stories high, each story is 3 windows high, and each window is about 1.33 meters high.

Represent the multiplication process. You can use an **expansion box** to represent the equation $327 \times 6 = 1962$.

Write the place-value parts for 327 in the first column. Write the place-value parts for 6 in the first row. Each entry in the table is the product of its row and column. For example, $300 \times 6 = 1800$. The product 327 times 6 equals the sum of the numbers inside the box.

	6
300	1800
20	120
7	42

> You can add the numbers in any order using any grouping. How can you add them to model the usual multiplication algorithm?

You can find some shorter ways of multiplying other numbers using an expansion box. For example, you can represent 98 using place-value parts $90 + 8$. However, if you are multiplying a number by 98, a simpler representation might be $98 = (100 - 2)$. Compare the following expansion boxes. Which expansion box makes the calculations quicker?

	90	8
2	180	16

	100	−2
2	200	−4

You get the same result using either box: $180 + 16 = 196$ and $200 - 4 = 196$.

Exercises Practicing Habits of Mind

Check Your Understanding

1. **Traditional algorithm** In this lesson, you used the traditional algorithm to multiply a three-digit number (327) by a one-digit number (6). The Distributive Property is important in understanding why the algorithm works.

   a. Explain how to use the standard algorithm to multiply a three-digit number by a two-digit number.

   b. Using the Distributive Property, explain how the algorithm works.

   c. When is this algorithm useful?

2. Multiply by 5. To multiply a number by 5, halve the number. Then multiply by 10. For instance, to multiply 48×5, halve 48 to get 24. Then multiply by 10 to get 240.

   a. Using the basic rules of arithmetic, explain why this algorithm works.

   b. When is this algorithm useful?

   c. Invent a similar algorithm for multiplying by 25.

3. Multiply by closest place-value. You want to multiply a number by 99. For this algorithm, use the place-value amount closest to 99, which is 100, and the fact that $99 = 100 - 1$. For example, to evaluate $8 \cdot 99$, start with the product of 100 that is closer to $8 \cdot 99$, which is 800. Then subtract 8 from 800 to get 792.

   a. Using the basic rules of arithmetic, explain why this algorithm works.

   b. Can you think of a situation in which this algorithm will be useful?

   c. Invent a similar algorithm for multiplying by 98.

4. Russian method Here is an alternative algorithm for multiplying numbers. To find 21×5, make a table. Then you successively take half of one factor (throwing away any remainder) and double the other.

Half of 21 is not really 10. It is 10 with $\frac{1}{2}$ left over. So, you put a 10 under 21 and a * in the Save column to show that there is a remainder.

Multiplication Algorithm

Half	Double	Save
21	5	*
10	10	
5	20	*
2	40	
1	80	*

There is a * in each row where an odd number is in the Half column. Add the numbers in the Double column that have a * to their right: $5 + 20 + 80 = 105$. The product 21×5 is 105.

   a. Using the basic rules of arithmetic, explain why this algorithm works. (*Hint:* You can write every even number as a sum of powers of 2. You can write every odd number as a sum of 1 and powers of 2.)

   b. Can you think of a situation in which this algorithm will be useful?

5. Multiplication and division using lines To find a product or quotient, use graph paper and a slanted "multiplication line." Draw horizontal and vertical number lines. Label them using integers. At 1 on the vertical number line, draw a heavy horizontal line.

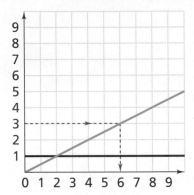

To multiply 2 and 3, draw a slanted multiplication line that starts at 0. The slanted line crosses the horizontal line at 2, since 2 is a factor. Draw a horizontal line at 3, since 3 is the other factor. Then move down to the horizontal number line to find the product 6.

a. Use the basic rules of arithmetic. Explain why this algorithm works.

b. When is this algorithm useful?

c. Make a grid on graph paper to find each product.

$$4 \times 3 \qquad 2 \times 7 \qquad 6 \times \frac{1}{2}$$

d. Describe a "division using lines" algorithm.

On Your Own

6. How many of each unit are in 1 million seconds? Use a calculator.

  a. minutes

  b. hours

  c. days to the nearest day

7. Take It Further You can measure speed in feet per second, in miles per hour, or in many other ways. A pitcher throws a baseball at 92 miles per hour. How many feet per second does the baseball travel? (*Hint:* There are 5280 feet in a mile.)

You can use radar to find the speed of a pitch in miles per hour.

8. Use expansion boxes. Find each product.

   a. 89×42

   b. 101×99

   c. 1989×37

   d. $4\frac{2}{3} \times 3\frac{1}{4}$

Remember...

There is more than one way to set up an expansion box. Are some boxes easier to use than others?

9. Each letter represents a single digit from 0 to 9. Find all possible values for A, B, C, D, and E. The digits 3 and 1 are given.

$$\begin{array}{r} 1ABCDE \\ \times 3 \\ \hline ABCDE1 \end{array}$$

10. Each letter represents a single digit from 0 to 9. Some digits are given.

$$\begin{array}{r} 2B3 \\ \times 327 \\ \hline 6CD5A \end{array}$$

What digit multiplied by 3 gives a product ending in 1? When you know the value of E, use it to find the value of D.

   a. What is the value of A? Explain.

   b. **Take It Further** Find the values of B, C, and D.

11. **Standardized Test Prep** Teresa makes a puzzle by assigning the letters A–E to the even-number digits. When she multiplies each number by each of the other numbers, she finds that she needs two more letters, J and K. They represent the tens place in the product. Here are Teresa's product pairs.

$A \cdot A = JA$	$A \cdot B = DB$	$A \cdot C = C$	$A \cdot D = KD$	$A \cdot E = BE$
	$B \cdot B = KA$	$B \cdot C = C$	$B \cdot D = E$	$B \cdot E = JD$
		$C \cdot C = C$	$C \cdot D = C$	$C \cdot E = C$
			$D \cdot D = B$	$D \cdot E = KA$
				$E \cdot E = AB$

Which of the following shows how Teresa assigned the letters?

   A. $A = 6$, $B = 4$, $C = 0$, $D = 2$, $E = 8$, $J = 1$, $K = 3$

   B. $A = 2$, $B = 4$, $C = 0$, $D = 6$, $E = 8$, $J = 3$, $K = 1$

   C. $A = 4$, $B = 2$, $C = 0$, $D = 8$, $E = 6$, $J = 1$, $K = 3$

   D. $A = 6$, $B = 4$, $C = 0$, $D = 2$, $E = 8$, $J = 3$, $K = 1$

Go Online
www.successnetplus.com

12. Use expansion boxes to find each product. Find more than one way to set up each expansion box.

    a. 103×97

    b. $3\frac{1}{3} \times 2\frac{2}{5}$

    c. 2.9×0.99

    d. 995×1.2

Maintain Your Skills

Find each product.

13. a. 107×109

    b. 1007×1009

    c. $10,007 \times 10,009$

    d. What is 17×19? How is this product related to the other products?

14. a. 17×102

    b. 18×102

    c. 42×102

    d. 35×102

    e. Describe the pattern that you used to find each product.

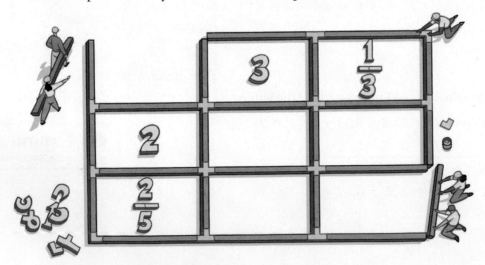

1.15 Multiplying and Dividing Fractions

Multiplying fractions is usually simpler than adding fractions. To find the product, you just multiply the numerators and multiply the denominators.

Developing Habits of Mind

Find relationships. To find the product $\frac{2}{3} \cdot \frac{5}{7}$, why do you multiply numerators and multiply denominators? This is not an easy question to answer. For now, you can use the following ideas and assumptions to understand why.

You can think of multiplication as repeated addition.

$$\frac{1}{3} \cdot 3 = \frac{1}{3} + \frac{1}{3} + \frac{1}{3} = \frac{3}{3} = 1$$

When you multiply $\frac{1}{3}$ by 3, you get 1. Is there any other number you can multiply by 3 to get 1? No, you can assume for now that the only number you can multiply by 3 to get 1 is $\frac{1}{3}$.

Because $\frac{2}{3} \cdot 3 = 2$, you can also assume that if you multiply a mystery number by 3 and get 2, then the mystery number is $\frac{2}{3}$.

You can assume that the any-order, any-grouping properties work for multiplication of real numbers, including fractions.

Why is $\frac{2}{3} \cdot \frac{5}{7} = \frac{10}{21}$? One way to explain this result is to multiply $\frac{2}{3} \cdot \frac{5}{7}$ by 21 and find whether the product is 10. To do that, rearrange the order of the calculations and use the assumptions above.

$$\left(\frac{2}{3} \cdot \frac{5}{7}\right) \cdot 21 = \left(\frac{2}{3} \cdot \frac{5}{7}\right) \cdot 7 \cdot 3$$

$$= \left(\frac{2}{3} \cdot 3\right) \cdot \left(\frac{5}{7} \cdot 7\right)$$

$$= 2 \cdot 5 = 10$$

Multiplying $\frac{2}{3} \cdot \frac{5}{7}$ by 21 gives a product 10. So, $\frac{2}{3} \cdot \frac{5}{7}$ is $\frac{10}{21}$.

> A common mistake is to apply the process for multiplication to addition of fractions. It is not true that $\frac{2}{3} + \frac{4}{5} = \frac{2+4}{3+5}$. Adding fractions usually involves converting to a common denominator.

To divide by a fraction, you can multiply by the reciprocal. What is a reciprocal? The reciprocal of 13 is a unit fraction, such as $\frac{1}{13}$. The reciprocal of $\frac{5}{3}$ is $\frac{3}{5}$. The **reciprocal** of a fraction is the result you get by flipping the numerator and denominator.

Notice something that both cases have in common. When you multiply a number by its reciprocal, the product is 1. For instance, $13 \cdot \frac{1}{13} = \frac{13}{13}$, or 1 and $\frac{5}{3} \cdot \frac{3}{5} = \frac{15}{15}$, or 1.

> The number 0 does not have a reciprocal. Explain.

Mathematicians use this property to write a more precise definition of a reciprocal. When you find the reciprocal of any number, you find another number that you can multiply times that number to get a product 1.

For You to Do

Find each reciprocal.

1. 99   **2.** $\frac{3}{11}$ **3.** $-\frac{8}{101}$ **4.** -5 **5.** -1

Dividing by a number is the same as multiplying by the number's reciprocal.

$$\frac{5}{3} \div \frac{5}{3} \stackrel{?}{=} \frac{5}{3} \cdot \frac{3}{5}$$

- You know from the rules of division that any number divided by itself equals 1. So, $\frac{5}{3} \div \frac{5}{3}$ equals 1.

- You also know about reciprocals. So, $\frac{5}{3} \cdot \frac{3}{5} = \frac{15}{15}$, or 1.

- Therefore, dividing by $\frac{5}{3}$ is the same as multiplying by $\frac{3}{5}$. The reciprocal of $\frac{5}{3}$ is $\frac{3}{5}$.

 **Exercises** *Practicing Habits of Mind*

Check Your Understanding

Describe an actual situation in which the given number is the practical result of dividing 17 by 4. For example, when you divide 17 soccer balls equally among 4 teams, each team gets 4 balls.

1. 5   **2.** 4.25

3. Sasha knows a trick for multiplying fractions. "Sometimes a number is in the numerator of one fraction and in the denominator of another fraction. So, the numbers cancel each other. Look at this example. The 21 is in the numerator and denominator. So, I can cancel the 21's. I can also cancel the 83's, 19's, and 77's."

$$\frac{\cancel{21}}{83} \cdot \frac{77}{19} \cdot \frac{31}{\cancel{21}} \cdot \frac{19}{31} \cdot \frac{83}{77}$$

Using Sasha's cancelling method, find each product.

a. $\frac{3}{8} \cdot \frac{7}{3} \cdot \frac{8}{10}$ **b.** $\frac{-2}{15} \cdot \frac{15}{3} \cdot \frac{9}{-2}$

c. $\frac{21}{83} \cdot \frac{77}{19} \cdot \frac{31}{21} \cdot \frac{19}{31} \cdot \frac{83}{77}$ **d.** $\frac{4}{5} \cdot \frac{25}{3} \cdot \frac{9}{40}$

e. Why does Sasha's cancelling method work?

4. Jill says that she can divide fractions using a method similar to the crisscross method in Lesson 1.13.

Jill explains, "I multiply the two numbers from the upper left, and that's the numerator. I multiply the two numbers from the lower left, and that's the denominator." Here is an example.

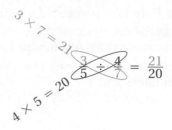

Use Jill's method to find each quotient.

a. $\frac{2}{3} \div \frac{4}{5}$ 　　　　　　　　　　**b.** $\frac{10}{13} \div \frac{5}{13}$

c. Explain how Jill's method relates to multiplying by the reciprocal.

5. You can think of division as a way of measuring. When you divide 35 by 5, you find how many 5 unit lengths are in 35. You can count seven 5's in 35.

$$5 + 5 + 5 + 5 + 5 + 5 + 5 = 35$$

This idea applies to fractions, too.

a. How many 5's are in 105? 　　　**b.** How many $\frac{1}{2}$'s are in 23?

c. How many $\frac{1}{4}$'s are in $\frac{11}{2}$? 　　　**d.** How many $\frac{1}{100}$'s are in $\frac{1}{4}$?

e. **Take It Further** How many $\frac{1}{7}$'s are in $\frac{1}{4}$?

On Your Own

6. Explain to someone who knows how to multiply fractions but doesn't know why the algorithm works, why $\frac{3}{5} \times \frac{4}{9} = \frac{12}{45}$.

7. Derman has a different way to divide fractions. He explains, "To divide fractions, I get a common denominator, just as when I add them. Then, I just divide the numerators.

$$\frac{\frac{5}{6}}{\frac{7}{8}} = \frac{5}{6} \div \frac{7}{8}$$

I get a common denominator for 6 and 8. It's 24. So

$$\frac{\frac{5}{6}}{\frac{7}{8}} = \frac{\frac{20}{24}}{\frac{21}{24}}$$

$$= \frac{20}{21}$$

I never use another method." Does Derman's method always work? Explain.

8. a. How many 9's are in 720? 　　　**b.** How many $\frac{1}{3}$'s are in $\frac{22}{3}$?

c. How many $\frac{1}{3}$'s are in 25? 　　　**d.** How many $\frac{1}{3}$'s are in $\frac{1}{6}$?

9. **Standardized Test Prep** Fifty-four percent of a high school senior class will attend a four-year college. Of the students going to a four-year college, two thirds have taken three or more years of a foreign language. What percent of the senior class have taken three or more years of a foreign language and will attend a four-year college?

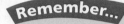

Remember...

You can write 54% as the fraction $\frac{54}{100}$.

A. 81%

B. 72%

C. 40%

D. 36%

10. Fill in each missing number.

a. $\blacksquare \cdot (11) = \frac{11}{5}$

b. $\blacksquare \cdot \frac{100}{7} = 1$

c. $\blacksquare \cdot \frac{4}{5} = 2$

d. $\blacksquare \cdot \frac{7}{9} = -2$

Maintain Your Skills

11. Find each product.

a. $\frac{1}{2} \times \frac{2}{3}$

b. $\frac{1}{2} \times \frac{2}{3} \times \frac{3}{4}$

c. $\frac{1}{2} \times \frac{2}{3} \times \frac{3}{4} \times \frac{4}{5}$

d. $\frac{1}{2} \times \frac{2}{3} \times \frac{3}{4} \times \frac{4}{5} \times \frac{5}{6}$

e. $\frac{1}{2} \times \frac{2}{3} \times \cdots \times \frac{8}{9} \times \frac{9}{10}$

f. Describe the pattern that you used to find these products.

12. Write each fraction in lowest terms.

a. $\dfrac{\frac{5}{13}}{\frac{10}{13}}$

b. $\dfrac{\frac{5}{19}}{\frac{10}{19}}$

c. $\dfrac{\frac{3}{4}}{\frac{7}{4}}$

d. $\dfrac{\frac{11}{3}}{\frac{7}{3}}$

e. $\dfrac{\frac{11}{100}}{\frac{43}{100}}$

f. Describe the pattern that you used to write these fractions in lowest terms.

In this investigation, you learned why addition, subtraction, and multiplication algorithms work. You applied each operation to fractions. These questions will help you summarize what you have learned.

1. Sasha buys a paperback novel for $6.99, a magazine for $1.99, and a cookbook for $22.99. Without using a calculator, find the total cost of these items.

2. You can add quickly $42 + 26 + 33 + 64 + 58 + 47$ without using a calculator by reordering the numbers. Find the sum. Explain how you reordered the numbers.

3. Find each sum. Write your result in lowest terms.

   a. $\frac{1}{3} + \frac{1}{8}$ b. $\frac{2}{3} + \frac{1}{8}$ c. $\frac{1}{2} + \left(\frac{2}{3} + \frac{5}{6} \right)$

4. Make two different expansion boxes to multiply $197 \cdot 3$.

5. Without using a calculator, find each product or quotient.

   a. $\frac{2}{5} \cdot \frac{3}{7}$ b. $\frac{2}{5} \div \frac{3}{7}$ c. $\frac{3}{5} \cdot 5$

   d. $\frac{3}{5} \div 5$ e. $\frac{3}{4} \cdot \frac{2}{5} \cdot \frac{5}{9}$

6. Why do traditional ways to add and multiply numbers work?

7. Why do some people say that dividing is the same as multiplying by the reciprocal?

8. How many weeks are in 1 billion seconds?

Vocabulary

In this investigation, you learned these terms. Make sure you understand what each one means and how to use it.

- algorithm
- expansion box
- least common denominator
- place-value part
- reciprocal

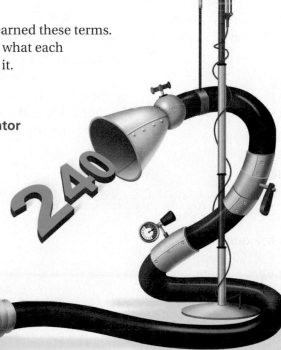

Project Using Mathematical Habits

Lo . . . ong Division

Division algorithms are some of the most complicated algorithms. In different parts of the world and at different times in history, people have used various methods for long division. In this project, you will learn how and why some different division algorithms work.

Traditional Division

1. Explain the steps you can use to perform this long division.

```
        14
216)3162
    216
   1002
    864
    138
```

Ladder Division

2. Some people arrange long division like this.

```
         4
        10
216)3162
    2160
   1002
    864
    138
```

They say,

- There are between 10 and 20 216's in 3162.

- Write 10 in the space for the quotient and then multiply: 10 × 216 = 2160. Subtract 2160 from 3162 to get 1002.

- There are between 4 and 5 216's in 1002.

- Write 4 in the space for the quotient (above the 10) and then multiply: 4 × 216 = 864. Subtract 864 from 1002 to get 138.

- 138 is smaller than 216, so 138 is the remainder.

- Find the quotient by adding: 10 + 4 = 14.

a. Does this method always work?

b. Is it easier or harder than the traditional method?

For Exercises 3–6, find each quotient using ladder division. Check your work using traditional division.

3. 6)2112

4. 27)1998

5. 41)2296

6. 113)6215

Division Using Subtraction

7. Around 300 B.C., Greek mathematicians counted how many of one length fit into a greater length. The number of the smaller lengths is the quotient, and any leftover part of the greater length is the remainder.

In modern notation, you repeatedly subtract the smaller length from the greater length to find the quotient.

In this algorithm, you subtract 216 a total of 14 times. You can count them! You can say, "216 goes into 3162 fourteen times with 138 left over." In other words, the quotient is 14, and the remainder is 138.

a. Does this method always work?

b. Is it easier or more difficult than the traditional method?

c. Why does the number 1002 appear in this algorithm and in Exercises 1 and 2?

For Exercises 8–10, divide using subtraction.

8. 54)650

9. 89)1224

10. 186)2215

11. Write About It Write a detailed explanation, including examples, to show why the method in Exercise 1 gives the correct answer.

```
 3162
  216
 2946
  216
 2730
  216
 2514
  216
 2298
  216
 2082
  216
 1866
  216
 1650
  216
 1434
  216
 1218
  216
 1002
  216
  786
  216
  570
  216
  354
  216
  138
```

Use any method to find each quotient.

12. 3372 ÷ 67

13. 59)4165

14. 2488 ÷ 31

15. 1005 ÷ 5

16. 3872 ÷ 17

As volunteers fill the sandbags, they subtract the same amount again and again from the pile of sand.

Review

Go Online
www.successnetplus.com

In **Investigation 1A,** you learned how to

- identify, describe, and justify patterns in arithmetic and in multiplication tables
- perform integer addition and multiplication
- explain the rules for multiplying and adding negative integers
- subtract using an integer, which is the same as using the integer's opposite to add
- apply the basic rules of arithmetic to whole numbers

The following questions will help you check your understanding.

1. In this part of the addition table, the number −4 is circled.

Addition Table

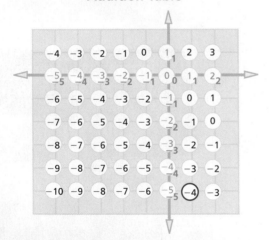

a. Write the addition problem that the table shows.

b. Find another entry of −4 and write the addition problem.

2. Use the multiplication table to find each product.

Multiplication Table

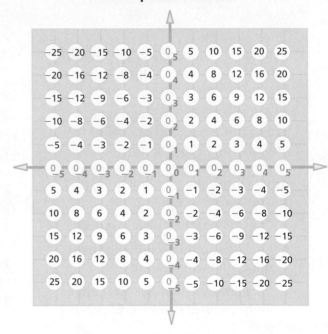

a. $(4)(-2)$

b. $(-4)(-2)$

c. $(-4)(0)$

d. $(-4)(2)$

e. Is it true that a negative number times a positive number is a negative number? Explain by using the table.

3. Use the basic rules of arithmetic to rewrite each calculation as an easier one. Find each product.

a. $8 \cdot 99$ **b.** $20 \cdot 18 \cdot 5$

In **Investigation 1B,** you learned how to

- draw line segments with different endpoints and scales
- think of fractions and real numbers as points on a number line
- represent a rational number in many different ways
- extend the basic rules of addition and multiplication from the integers to the real numbers

The following questions will help you check your understanding.

4. Place the numbers 2, $\frac{1}{3}$, $\frac{4}{5}$, $-\frac{4}{5}$, -1.1, and $\frac{8}{10}$ on a number line.

   a. Are any of these numbers equivalent? If so, which numbers are equivalent?

   b. Which positive number in the list is least?

5. Sasha starts at 0 on the number line. She moves 3 units to the right, 5 units to the left, 4 more units to the left, and 1 unit to the right.

   a. On what number on the number line does Sasha land?

   b. Write an addition problem to model Sasha's moves.

6. Find each product.

   a. $20 \cdot \left(\frac{1}{2} + \frac{4}{5} \right)$

   b. $\frac{1}{2} \cdot \left(\frac{2}{7} + \frac{4}{7} \right)$

   c. $\frac{2}{3} \cdot \left(\frac{3}{8} + \frac{3}{4} \right)$

In **Investigation 1C,** you learned how to

- explain why the algorithms you commonly use for addition, subtraction, and multiplication work
- use nontraditional algorithms that can be faster in some cases
- become more familiar with the basic rules of arithmetic
- perform arithmetic with integers and fractions

The following questions will help you check your understanding.

7. Without actually adding, explain how you know that both sums give the same answer.

   a. $212 + 18 + 35$

   b. $235 + 12 + 18$

8. What fraction do you add to each of the following to get a sum of 1?

   a. $\frac{2}{3}$

   b. $\frac{5}{8}$

   c. $\frac{1}{4} + \frac{1}{2}$

   d. $\frac{3}{4} + \frac{5}{8}$

9. Make an expansion box to find each product.

   a. $28 \cdot 31$

   b. $2\frac{2}{3} \cdot 3\frac{1}{4}$

Do not use a calculator.

Multiple Choice

1. How many tenths are in two fifths?

   A. $\frac{1}{2}$

   B. 1

   C. 4

   D. 100

2. Point X on the number line is between 1 and 2. Point Y on the number line is between -1 and 0. Which point could represent the product of X and Y?

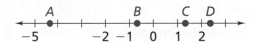

   A. point A

   B. point B

   C. point C

   D. point D

3. Which point is closest to -3 on the number line?

   A. $\frac{-20}{2}$

   B. $\frac{-20}{-2}$

   C. $\frac{-2}{-20}$

   D. $\frac{-2}{20}$

4. What is the opposite of $-\left(-\frac{4}{7}\right)$?

   A. $-\frac{7}{4}$

   B. $-\frac{4}{7}$

   C. $\frac{4}{7}$

   D. $\frac{7}{4}$

5. Which fraction is NOT equal to $\frac{8}{7}$?

   A. $\frac{16}{14}$

   B. $\frac{64}{49}$

   C. $\frac{32}{28}$

   D. $\frac{72}{63}$

6. Let $a = \frac{49}{54}$, $b = \frac{74}{81}$, and $c = \frac{11}{12}$. Which of the following is true?

   A. b is closer to a than it is to c.

   B. b is closer to c than it is to a.

   C. b is equally close to a and c.

   D. none of the above

7. Which of the following is NOT a valid way to compute $a \cdot b$ using a multiplication table? Assume $a < 0 < b$.

   A. Move down $-a$ spaces and then right b spaces.

   B. Move left $-a$ spaces and then up b spaces.

   C. Move right b spaces and then down $-a$ spaces.

   D. Move left $-a$ spaces and then down b spaces.

Open Response

8. Write an addition problem and two subtraction problems that you can illustrate using the addition table below.

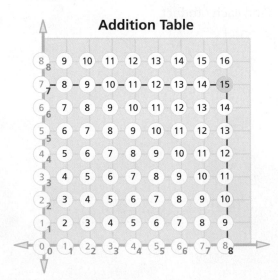

Addition Table

9. Write a multiplication problem and two division problems that you can illustrate using the multiplication table below.

Multiplication Table

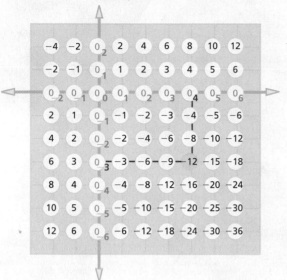

Use any method (except a calculator) to solve Exercises 10–23. Show your work.

10. $1 + 2 + 3 + \cdots + 48 + 49 + 50$

11. $2 + 4 + 6 + \cdots + 96 + 98 + 100$

12. $2 + 4 + 6 + \cdots + 86 + 88 + 90$

13. $-41 \cdot (152)$

14. $-105 \cdot (-112)$

15. $\frac{5}{6} + \frac{1}{8} + \frac{1}{6} + \frac{3}{8}$

16. $\frac{4}{9} \div \frac{8}{15}$

17. $\frac{4}{5} \cdot \left(\frac{3}{4} - \frac{5}{8} \right)$

18. $81 - 36 + 19 - 21 + 31 - 14$

19. $107 + 56 + 27 + 14 + 83$

20. $7 \div \frac{1}{5}$

21. $\dfrac{\frac{3}{4}}{2}$

22. $-\frac{1}{5} \cdot (-3) \cdot 4 \cdot \frac{3}{4} \cdot (-5)$

23. $\frac{5}{6} \div \frac{7}{9}$

24. Draw a number line from 0 to 1. Label $\frac{2}{8}, \frac{3}{5}, \frac{1}{3}$, and $\frac{3}{6}$ on the number line.

25. Draw a number line from -1 to 1. Label $\frac{1}{4}, -\frac{1}{4}$, $-\frac{3}{4}$, and $-\frac{7}{8}$ on the number line.

26. Draw a number line from 0 to 4. Label 1, 2, 3, $\sqrt{3}$, $\sqrt{8}$, and $\sqrt{11}$ on the number line.

27. Make a 2-by-2 expansion box to find the product $203 \cdot 197$.

28. Make a 2-by-2 expansion box to find the product of $2\frac{3}{4}$ and $-1\frac{1}{8}$.

29. Convert $\frac{5}{6}$ to a decimal.

For Exercises 30 and 31, convert each decimal to a fraction.

30. 0.8

31. 0.125

32. Explain why dividing a positive number by one half gives a result that is greater than the original number. For example, $6 \div \frac{1}{2} = 12$, and 12 is greater than 6.

Challenge Problem

33. A number plus its reciprocal equals $\frac{29}{10}$. Find both possible values for this number.

Expressions and Equations

Both dancers and mathematicians use symbolic language. Dancers read dance notation to learn their parts. Mathematicians use algebraic symbols to solve problems.

When you follow steps in mathematics, science, or the arts, you may find intriguing patterns. Here are some simple mathematical steps to follow.

- Choose a number.
- Add 4 to your number.
- Multiply the result by 2.
- Subtract 6.
- Find half of the result.
- Subtract your starting number.
- Add 3.
- Find half of the result.

Why is the result 2? To find out, you can represent each step using algebraic symbols and the basic rules of arithmetic.

You can also follow steps to solve word problems. You can represent a situation using algebraic symbols and the basic rules. In the last step, you will find the solution.

Vocabulary

- backtracking
- basic moves for solving equations
- evaluate
- expression
- guess-check-generalize method
- like terms
- linear equation
- reversible operation
- solution
- theorem
- variable

2A

Expressions

In *Expressions,* you will invent and perform number tricks. Using variable expressions, you will learn to describe a situation algebraically. Then, you will apply the basic rules of arithmetic to variable expressions.

By the end of this investigation, you will be able to answer questions like these.

1. Why are variables useful?

2. How can you invent a number trick that always gives the same ending number?

3. Use the following steps. Choose a number. Multiply by 5. Add 2. Multiply by 3. Subtract 8.

   a. Choose the number 4. What ending number do you get?

   b. Choose the variable x. What ending expression do you get?

You will learn how to

- state the need for variables and expressions

- determine the appropriate order for evaluating a numerical expression and explain why the order works

- express word problems using variables and mathematical notation

- evaluate numerical expressions involving parentheses, powers, and fraction bars

- write formulas using two or more variables

You will develop these habits and skills:

- Evaluate expressions using a variety of numbers such as integers, fractions, and decimals.

- Generalize patterns using words and algebraic methods.

- Consider the difference between evidence and proof and use variables to prove conjectures.

You can understand x, $5x$, $5x + 2$, . . . , regardless of the language you speak.

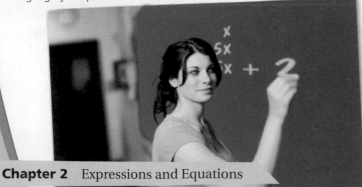

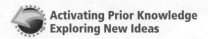

When you understand how a number trick works, you can have fun writing and performing your own. In this lesson, you will learn from Spiro the Spectacular and Maya the Magnificent, who specialize in number tricks.

For You to Explore

1. Here is one of Spiro the Spectacular's favorite number tricks.

   • Choose a number.

   • Add 6.

   • Multiply by 3.

   • Subtract 10.

   • Multiply by 2.

   • Add 50.

   • Divide by 6.

   Spiro says, "Now, tell me the result."
   Georgia replies, "17."
   Spiro exclaims, "Your starting number was 6!"
   Georgia replies, "You're right! How did you know that?"

   a. How did Spiro find Georgia's number?

   b. If Georgia's ending number is 13, what was her starting number?

   c. If Georgia's ending number is 6, what was her starting number?

2. Maya the Magnificent also does number tricks. Here is one of her favorites.

   • Choose a number.

   • Multiply by 3.

   • Subtract 4.

   • Multiply by 2.

   • Add 20.

   • Divide by 6.

   • Subtract your starting number.

   a. What is the trick?

   b. Explain why the trick always works.

3. **a.** Make up your own number trick.

   b. Find a partner. Perform your number tricks for each other. Try different starting numbers until you find how your partner's trick works.

Habits of Mind

Look for a pattern.
Try it with numbers!
Pick a number and see what you get. Do this a few times.

Exercises *Practicing Habits of Mind*

On Your Own

Do the number tricks in Exercises 4 and 5 work for all numbers? Explain.

4. Choose a number. Add 5. Multiply by 2. Subtract 7. Add 1. Divide by 2. Subtract 2. You get your starting number!

5. Choose a number. Add 3. Multiply by 2. Add 7. Subtract 15. Add 2. What is the result of the trick?

6. Ask someone you know who is older than you the following question: When you think about algebra, what do you think? Record the response.

7. Evaluate $\dfrac{17 \cdot 4 + 17 \cdot 3 + 17 \cdot 2 + 17 \cdot 1}{17}$.

> What happens if you label the starting number *x*? After the first step, you will have $x + 5$, then $2 \cdot (x + 5)$, and so on.

Maintain Your Skills

In Exercises 8 and 9, use the given number trick. Find the missing numbers.

8. Choose a number. Add 5. Subtract 3. Multiply by 2. Subtract 4.

	Starting Number	Ending Number
a.	2	■
b.	3	■
c.	7	■
d.	−2	■

 e. Is there a simpler way to get from the starting number to the ending number than by following each step?

9. Choose a number. Add 3. Multiply by 3. Subtract 3. Divide by 3.

	Starting Number	Ending Number
a.	2	■
b.	3	■
c.	7	■
d.	−2	■

 e. Is there a simpler way to get from the starting number to the ending number than by following each step?

Go Online
www.successnetplus.com

2.02 Modeling General Situations— Writing Expressions

You may hear that algebra is "full of *x*'s and *y*'s." Using letters to represent numbers lets you describe a general situation easily.

Example 1

Problem During a natural disaster, such as an earthquake or flood, many people must leave their homes and go to shelters. The table gives three situations. It shows how much food and how many beds a disaster relief group must provide.

Relief Camp Supplies

Number of People	Number of Beds	Amount of Food (lb)
1,000	1,010	3,000
5,000	5,010	15,000
10,000	10,010	30,000

The ten extra beds are for the relief workers.

Write expressions for how much food and how many beds you will need for any number of people.

Solution A disaster relief group can describe the general situation this way.

- (the number of people) + 10 beds
- 3 pounds of food per day · (the number of people)

There is a simper way to describe the situation. Let the **variable** *x* stand for the number of people needing food and shelter at a relief camp. Here is what the camp needs for *x* people.

- $(x + 10)$ beds
- $(3 \cdot x)$ pounds of food per day

The variable *x* stands for an unknown number. When the relief group knows the number of people at the camp, they can replace *x* with that number.

The letter *x* is a **variable**, or a placeholder for a number that you do not know. Mathematical phrases, such as $x + 10$ and $3 \cdot x$ are **expressions** that use operations to combine numbers and variables.

For Discussion

For each number of people, how many beds and how much food per day will a relief group need?

1. 15,000
2. 500
3. 8200

Example 2

Problem Ricardo has 3 fewer apples than Jeremy. Let j stand for the number of apples that Jeremy has. Write an expression for the number of apples that Ricardo has.

Solution Think about the steps you take to find how many apples Ricardo has.

Suppose Jeremy has 10 apples. Ricardo has 3 fewer apples than Jeremy, or $10 - 3$ equals 7 apples.

Suppose Jeremy has 15 apples. Ricardo has 3 fewer apples than Jeremy, and $15 - 3$ equals 12 apples.

Use j for the number of apples that Jeremy has. Suppose Jeremy has j apples. Ricardo has 3 fewer apples than Jeremy. The expression $j - 3$ equals the number of apples that Ricardo has.

For Discussion

4. Hideki says, "I chose a number. I multiplied it by 7. Then I subtracted 4." Let h stand for Hideki's starting number. Write an expression for Hideki's ending number.

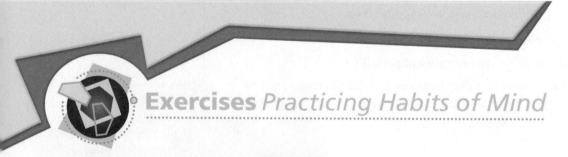

Exercises *Practicing Habits of Mind*

Check Your Understanding

1. Mary was born one year before Barbara. No matter how old they are, Mary will always be one year older than Barbara. Find the missing ages in years.

	Mary's Age	Barbara's Age
a.	11	■
b.	7	■
c.	53	■
d.	65	■
e.	m	■
f.	■	n

Shelter for 1000 Adults

Resource	Calculation	Total
Water	1000 ▪ 10	
Medical Kits	1000 ▪ 10	
Blankets	1000 ▪ 30	
Doctors	1000 ▪ 100	
Pillows	1000 ▪ 100	

2. A relief group can use expressions to plan for disasters.
At a relief camp, you need many kinds of supplies.

- For each adult, the camp needs 10 gallons of water per week.
- For every 10 adults, the camp needs one medical kit.
- The camp needs 30 more blankets than the number of adults.
- For every 100 adults, the camp needs one doctor.
- The camp needs 100 more pillows than the number of adults.

Let a equal the number of adults in the camp.
Match each expression to one of the five items above.
Explain your answers.

a. $\frac{a}{100}$ **b.** $10 \cdot a$ **c.** $\frac{a}{10}$

d. $a + 100$ **e.** $a + 30$

3. Match each expression below to a set of steps I–V.

a. $2 \cdot x - 2$ **b.** $3 \cdot (x + 5)$ **c.** $2 \cdot (x - 2)$

d. $5 \cdot (x + 3)$ **e.** $3x + 5$

I. Choose any number.   **II.** Choose any number.
   Subtract 2.   Multiply it by 2.
   Multiply it by 2.   Subtract 2.

III. Choose any number.   **IV.** Choose any number.
   Add 3.   Add 5.
   Multiply it by 5.   Multiply it by 3.

V. Choose any number.
   Multiply it by 3.
   Add 5.

4. For each expression, write a number trick.

a. $2 \cdot x + 1$ **b.** $-2 \cdot (x - 1)$

c. $5 \cdot (x + 2) - 2$ **d.** $7 \cdot (3 \cdot (x + 1) - 2) - 9$

5. Use the number x as your starting number. Write the expression resulting from following the steps.

- Choose a number.
- Add 5.
- Subtract 11.
- Multiply by 2.
- Add 3.

6. Jeremy has 3 more apples than Ricardo. Find the number of apples Jeremy has.

Number of Apples

	Ricardo	Jeremy
a.	2	▪
b.	13	▪
c.	107	▪
d.	r	▪

7. Match each expression below to a set of steps I–IV.

   a. $-7 \cdot x + 5$ **b.** $5 \cdot (x - 7)$

   c. $7 \cdot (x - 5)$ **d.** $7 \cdot x - 5$

   I. Choose any number.   **II.** Choose any number.
   Subtract 5.   Multiply by -7.
   Multiply by 7.   Add 5.

   III. Choose any number.   **IV.** Choose any number.
   Subtract 7.   Multiply by 7.
   Multiply by 5.   Subtract 5.

8. **What's Wrong Here?** Travis writes an expression using the following steps.

   • Start with x.

   • Subtract 3.

   • Multiply by 10.

   • Subtract 13.

   He writes the final expression $10x - 3 - 13$. Explain what he did wrong. Then find the correct expression.

9. **Standardized Test Prep** David counts the quarters in his change jar. He has 24 more quarters than his brother Rob. If r is the number of quarters Rob has, which expression represents the number of quarters that David and Rob have in all?

   A. $r + 24$ **B.** $2r - 24$ **C.** $2r$ **D.** none of these

10. A rectangle has length ℓ and width w. For a rectangle, write an expression for each of the following.

    a. area

    b. perimeter

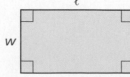

11. You overhear Mrs. Antonellis say, "During fifth period, I teach math. There are four other classes that meet during that period: computer, gym, history, and art. I notice some interesting things about the class sizes.

   - For every two students in my math class, there is one student in computer class.
   - For each student in math class, there are two students in gym class.
   - There are two more students in my math class than in the history class.
   - There are two more students in the art class than in my math class."

   Let x equal the number of students in Mrs. Antonellis' math class. Using x, write an expression for the number of students in each class.

   a. computer   **b.** gym   **c.** history   **d.** art

   e. Write an expression for the total number of students in the math, computer, gym, and history classes.

Maintain Your Skills

12. While in office, President Dwight D. Eisenhower standardized the proportions of United States flags. For every ten units of width, the flag must have nineteen units of length.

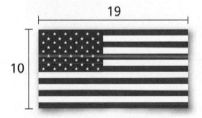

   Find a flag's length, in inches, for each given width.

   a. 20 inches   **b.** 5 inches

   c. 1 inch   **d.** x inches

13. A computer company wants to make computers with rectangular cases. The length of the longer side is four times the length of the shorter side.

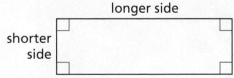

   Find the length of the longer side, in centimeters, for each given length of the shorter side.

   a. 20 cm   **b.** 25 cm   **c.** x cm

2.03 Evaluating Expressions

One type of expression that you will often use is a scientific formula. Using a formula to make calculations is an important skill.

Example

Problem If you drop an object, the object's speed after t seconds is $32t$ feet per second.

Suppose you drop a coin from a hot-air balloon over the desert. What is its speed after 1, 2, 3, 4, and 5 seconds?

Solution After 1 second, $t = 1$. To calculate the speed of the coin after 1 second, you substitute $t = 1$ into the expression $32t = 32 \cdot (1) = 32$.

You can use a table to arrange your answers.

Speed of a Coin

Time t (s)	Speed (ft/s)
1	$32 \cdot 1 = 32$
2	$32 \cdot 2 = 64$
3	$32 \cdot 3 = 96$
4	$32 \cdot 4 = 128$
5	$32 \cdot 5 = 160$

To **evaluate** an expression, replace the variable with the given number. Do the math to get a single number for your result. In this example, you evaluate $32t$ if $t = 1$ and get 32. If $t = 2$, you get 64, and so on.

For You to Do

1. How fast does the coin travel after 5.5 seconds? After $\frac{1}{8}$ of a second?

How does the height of the balloon affect the speed of an object that you drop from it?

Minds in Action

Sasha thinks she has discovered one of Spiro the Spectacular's many secrets.

Sasha   I can perform one of your tricks.

Spiro   Show me.

Sasha   Okay. Choose a number. Add 6. Multiply by 3. Subtract 10. What's your ending number?

Spiro   23.

Sasha turns away for a moment. She does some calculations on paper. After thirty seconds, she turns around.

Sasha   Your starting number was 5!

Spiro   That's right. How did you do it?

Sasha   Well, I called your starting number x. Then I wrote an expression for the ending number.

Choose a number.	x
Add 6.	$x + 6$
Multiply by 3.	$3 \cdot (x + 6)$
Subtract 10.	$3 \cdot (x + 6) - 10$

Spiro   Then what did you do?

Sasha   Then I substituted different numbers for x until I found your ending number. I kept track of the answers in a table.

Starting Number	Add 6	Multiply by 3	Subtract 10
1	7	21	11
2	8	24	14
3	9	27	17
4	10	30	20
5	11	33	**23**

Your ending number was 23, so your starting number was 5.

For Discussion

2. If Spiro chooses -2 as his starting number, what will his ending number be?

Exercises Practicing Habits of Mind

Check Your Understanding

1. A disaster relief group must provide beds, food, and water for a camp. It uses the following expressions for the quantities it needs. The expressions depend on two variables, the number of adults and the number of children. Let a = the number of adults. Let c = the number of children.

   • $a + c + 10$ beds

   • $5a + 2c$ pounds of food

   • $9a + 5c$ gallons of water

   How many beds and how much food and water are needed for 500 adults and 100 children? For 1000 adults and 300 children?

2. Evaluate $\frac{4x + 3x + 2x + x}{x}$ for each value of x.

   a. 3   **b.** 17   **c.** -2 **d.** 11

3. Maya says, "Choose a number. Subtract 1. Multiply by 3. Add 5." For each starting number given, what is your ending number?

   a. n **b.** 11   **c.** 1

4. Spiro says, "Choose a number. Multiply by 3. Subtract 2. Multiply by 5." For each starting number given, what is your ending number?

   a. n **b.** 4   **c.** $\frac{4}{3}$

5. A trapezoid is a shape with four sides that has one pair of parallel sides.

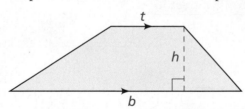

   You can find the area of a trapezoid using the three dimensions of the trapezoid labeled b, t, and h in the diagram. The expression for the area of a trapezoid is $\frac{(b + t)}{2} \cdot h$.

   Find the area of each trapezoid with the given dimensions.

   a. $b = 5, t = 3, h = 6$

   b. $b = 2, t = 3, h = 7$

   c. $b = \frac{3}{2}, t = \frac{1}{2}, h = \frac{7}{4}$

   d. $b = 8, t = 6, h = \frac{1}{4}$

> The variables b and t represent the lengths of the bottom and top parallel sides, respectively. The variable h represents the height of the trapezoid.

6. Insert parentheses to make each equation true.

> **Sample** $2 + 3 \cdot 7 \stackrel{?}{=} 35$
>
> **Solution** $(2 + 3) \cdot 7 = 35$

a. $3 \cdot 7 + 3 \stackrel{?}{=} 30$

b. $-3 + 3 \cdot 5 + 11 \stackrel{?}{=} 11$

c. $-3 + 3 \cdot 5 + 11 \stackrel{?}{=} 45$

d. $25 - 5 + 4 \cdot 5 \stackrel{?}{=} 0$

e. $25 - 5 + 4 \cdot 5 \stackrel{?}{=} -20$

On Your Own

7. Boyle's Law in chemistry states that when temperature is constant, the pressure of a gas is inversely proportional to its volume. Let p represent the pressure, and let V represent the volume of the gas. At a certain temperature, $V - \frac{\text{constant}}{p}$. By what factor does the volume of the gas change if the pressure changes by each given factor?

www.successnetplus.com

a. 2   **b.** 3

c. 4   **d.** 5

8. What's Wrong Here? Linda evaluates the expression $7 + 5x$ for $x = 3$ and $x = \frac{4}{5}$. When $x = 3$, she gets $7 + 5x = 7 + 5 \cdot (3) = 12 \cdot (3) = 36$.

When $x = \frac{4}{5}$, she gets $7 + 5x = 7 + 5 \cdot \left(\frac{4}{5}\right) = 12 \cdot \left(\frac{4}{5}\right) = \frac{48}{5}$.

What does Linda do wrong?

9. Evaluate the expression $5 + 3x$ for each value of x.

a. 3   **b.** -1

c. -5 **d.** 0

e. -11 **f.** -3

10. Evaluate the expression $(z + 3)^2 - 4$ for each value of z.

a. 3   **b.** -1

c. -5 **d.** 0

e. -11 **f.** -3

When you squeeze a balloon in one place, the increased pressure will force a bulge in another.

11. You can find a person's speed by dividing how far the person travels by the time spent traveling. The equation $r = \frac{d}{t}$ shows this relationship, where r is the rate (or speed), d is the distance, and t is the time.

a. Anh jogs 100 meters in 40 seconds. What is his rate in meters per second?

b. Isabel runs 50 yards in 25 seconds. What is her rate in yards per second?

c. Rosario jogs at a rate of 6 miles per hour. How far does she run in 30 minutes?

12. Standardized Test Prep Evaluate $14 - 6 + 32 \div 8 \cdot 2$.

A. 10   **B.** 6

C. 16   **D.** 12

Maintain Your Skills

13. Evaluate the expression $(x - 1) \cdot (x - 2) \cdot (x - 3) \cdot (x - 4) \cdot (x - 5)$ for each x value.

a. 1

b. 2

c. 3

d. 4

e. 5

f. What is similar about these five cases? Is there a sixth similar case? Explain.

14. Here are a complicated expression and a simple expression.

- $3x + (x - 1) \cdot (x - 2) \cdot (x - 3) \cdot (x - 4) \cdot (x - 5)$

- $3x$

Evaluate both expressions above for each x value.

a. 1

b. 2

c. 4

d. What are the x values that produce the same result in both expressions?

Go Online
Video Tutor
www.successnetplus.com

You can take an expression that looks complicated and make it simpler to use.

Minds in Action

Tony I think I know your secret, Maya. The key is to use variables.

Maya Show me what you mean.

Tony Well, look at this trick. Choose a number. Add 3. Multiply by 2. Subtract 6.

The ending number will always be twice as large as the starting number.

Maya How do you know that?

Tony Watch. If I start with x, I can follow these steps.

Choose a number.	x
Add 3.	$x + 3$
Multiply by 2.	$2 \cdot (x + 3)$
Subtract 6.	$2(x + 3) - 6$

Now watch this. You can simplify $2(x + 3)$. Use the Distributive Property and multiply: $2 \cdot (x + 3) = 2 \cdot x + 2 \cdot 3 = 2x + 6$.

Since $2(x + 3) = 2x + 6$, $2(x + 3) - 6 = 2x + 6 - 6 = 2x$. So the ending number is $2x$.

Maya Very good, Tony. Now can you figure out my other tricks?

For Discussion

1. Here is a number trick.
   - Choose any number.
   - Multiply by 2.
   - Add 7.
   - Multiply by 5.
   - Add 25.
   - Divide by 10.
   - Subtract 6.

   What is the trick? Use expressions to show that it always works.

In Lesson 1.05, you learned the basic rules of arithmetic. You can apply the rules to expressions and numbers. For instance, you can change the order of numbers and variables in a sum.

$$x + 7 = 7 + x$$

You can regroup the numbers and variables in a sum.

$$(a + 8) + z = a + (8 + z)$$

You can use the Distributive Property.

$$2(x + 3) = 2 \cdot (x + 3)$$
$$= 2 \cdot x + 2 \cdot 3$$
$$= 2x + 6$$

The identities are still true.

$$x \cdot 1 = x \text{ and } x + 0 = x$$

You can also use the Distributive Property *backward*. For instance, you can simplify $2x + 3x$ using the Distributive Property.

$$2x + 3x = 2 \cdot x + 3 \cdot x$$
$$= (2 + 3)x$$
$$= 5x$$

The expression $2x + 3x$ has two terms connected by the plus (+) sign. A term is an expression that only uses multiplication or division. When the variables are the same in both terms, you call them **like terms.** Grouping parts of an expression such as $2 + 3$ is called **combining like terms.**

Example

Problem Find a simpler way to write $3x + 7y + 8 + 4x + 2y - 10$.

Solution Rewrite the expression. Group the x terms together and the y terms together. Then group the numbers together.

$$3x + 4x + 7y + 2y + 8 - 10$$

Combine the like terms. Group the $3x$ and the $4x$ together to get $7x$ by using the Distributive Property backward.

$$3x + 4x = (3 + 4)x = x \cdot 7 = 7x$$

You can combine the y terms the same way. There are two terms with y, $7y$ and $2y$, that you can combine.

$$7y + 2y = (7 + 2) \cdot y = 9y$$

You can transform the expression this way.

$$3x + 7y + 8 + 4x + 2y - 10 = 3x + 4x + 7y + 2y + 8 - 10$$
$$= 7x + 9y + (-2)$$
$$= 7x + 9y - 2$$

You can simplify this expression using the any-order, any-grouping properties, but be careful of subtraction!

For Discussion

2. Use the Distributive Property to explain why $3x + 5x = 8x$. Then explain why $7y + (-2y) = 5y$.

Developing Habits of Mind

Visualize combining like terms. You can think about combining like terms using either math symbols or a length model. Using symbols, you can simplify $(2x + y) + (3x + 2y)$ by grouping the x terms.

$$2x + 3x = 5x$$

Then you can group the y terms.

$$y + 2y = 3y$$

The simplified expression looks like this.

$$(2x + y) + (3x + 2y) = (2x + 3x) + (y + 2y)$$
$$= 5x + 3y$$

You cannot combine $5x$ and $3y$, because they are not like terms.

You can use the Distributive Property to show why you can combine like terms. For instance, $2x + 3x = (2 + 3)x = 5x$, and $y + 2y = (1 + 2)y = 3y$. You cannot use the Distributive Property to combine unlike terms such as $5x$ and $3y$.

By using a model to visualize combining like terms, you can think of x and y as lengths.

—— ——————
x y

Here is a model of $2x + y + 3x + 2y$ using lengths for x and y.

— — + —————— + — — — + —————— ——————
$2x$ y $3x$ $2y$

You can arrange the lengths by grouping the x terms and the y terms. You can count the total number of x's and the total number of y's.

— — + — — — + —————— + —————— ——————
$2x$ $3x$ y $2y$

Go Online
www.successnetplus.com

Since x and y are different lengths, you cannot combine them.

For You to Do

Simplify each expression.

3. $3(x + 2) + 5x$

4. $2z + 7z - z + 5$

5. $3a + 4b + 5a + 6$

6. $4(x - 1) - 3(x + 2)$

Exercises *Practicing Habits of Mind*

Check Your Understanding

1. Here is a number trick similar to the trick in For Discussion Problem 1.

   • Choose any number.

   • Multiply by 2.

   • Add 7.

   • Multiply by 5.

   • Add 25.

   • Divide by 10.

   • Subtract your starting number.

   What is the trick? Will it work for any number? Explain by using expressions.

2. Here is a number trick with one missing step.

   • Choose any number.

   • Multiply by 2.

   • Add 7.

   • Multiply by 5.

   • ?

   • Divide by 10.

   • Subtract your starting number.

   • Your ending number is 7.

   What is the missing step?

3. Here is a number trick with the last step missing.

   • Choose any number.

   • Multiply by 3.

   • Add 5.

   • Multiply by 4.

   • Add 16.

   • Divide by 12.

   • ?

   For each result given below, what is the last step in the number trick?

   a. The ending number is the same as the starting number.

   b. The ending number is 3.

68 -166
-11 + -22 -33 -44 -55

4. Evaluate the expression $\dfrac{x + 2x + 3x + 4x + 5x}{x}$ for each x value given.

   a. 1   **b.** 2   **c.** 3   **d.** −3

   e. −11   **f.** $\frac{1}{2}$ **g.** 197

   h. Use the Distributive Property to simplify the expression.

5. The lengths and widths of four rectangles are given below. For each rectangle, find an expression for the area and an expression for the perimeter.

   a. length: $4x + 2$ width: 3

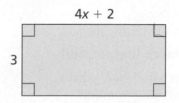

   b. length: 7   width: $x - 4$
   c. length: $6x - 8$ width: $\frac{1}{2}$
   d. length: $10 - 2x$ width: 9

On Your Own

6. Use the basic rules of arithmetic and what you know about like terms. Decide which expressions equal the expression $4x + 2y$. If an expression does not equal $4x + 2y$, explain why it does not.

   a. $4x + 6y + (-4y)$

   b. $4(x + y) - 2y$

   c. $6xy$

   d. $(4x)(2y)$

   e. $x + x + x + x + x + x - y - y - y - y + 2(3y - x)$

7. The lengths and widths of four rectangles are given below. For each rectangle, find an expression for the area and an expression for the perimeter.

   a. length: $5x + 9$ width: 2

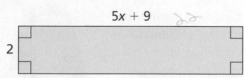

   b. length: 11   width: $x - 3$
   c. length: $2x + 9$ width: 2
   d. length: $8 - 3x$ width: 5

Go Online
www.successnetplus.com

8. Use the two number tricks.

Trick 1	**Trick 2**
• Choose a number.	• Choose a number.
• Add 6.	• Multiply by 2.
• Multiply by 3.	• Subtract 6.
• Subtract 4.	• Multiply by 5.
• Multiply by 2.	• Add 50.
• Add 2.	• Divide by 10.
• Divide by 6.	• Subtract your starting number.
• What is your ending number?	• What is your ending number?

a. Using one of these tricks, Spiro the Spectacular can find your starting number. Which trick can he use? How does he find your number?

b. Even Spiro the Spectacular cannot find your starting number using the other trick. Explain why not.

9. Evaluate the expression $2(3m + 5) - 5(m + 1) - 4$ for each value of m.

a. 3
b. 17
c. −2

d. 4
e. $\frac{1}{3}$
f. $-\frac{4}{11}$

g. Simplify the expression.

10. **Standardized Test Prep** Simplify the expression $7(6t + 2) + 3 - 5(t + 1)$.

A. 49
B. $37t + 12$

C. $42t + 17$
D. $47t + 22$

11. When Derman shops, he tries to buy all his clothes at the same store. Derman explains, "A store charges 6% sales tax on each purchase. Suppose you buy a shirt that costs s dollars at one store and a pair of pants that costs p dollars at another store. You pay $0.06 \cdot s$ in taxes for the shirt and $0.06 \cdot p$ in taxes for the pants. So you're paying taxes *twice*. If you buy them at the same store, you only pay the 6% once. So you're saving money."

Is Derman correct? Using expressions, explain.

12. Jabari's art club raises $300 to pay for a trip to a local museum. The bus costs $90, and admission is $6 per student. Jabari writes an expression for the amount the club has left based on the number of students who go to the museum. If x is the number of students who go to the museum, the amount remaining is $300 - 90 - 6x$.

a. What is the amount remaining after paying field trip expenses for 28 students? For 29 students? For 30 students?

b. What is the greatest number of students who can go on the field trip for $300?

In Exercise 12, suppose the student admission price changed to $8. How would this affect the expression $300 - 90 - 6x$?

13. Evaluate the expression $x \cdot (x + 1)$ for each value of x.

    a. 1   **b.** 2   **c.** 3   **d.** 4

    e. 11   **f.** −3   **g.** −7

    h. Explain why $x \cdot (x + 1)$ is always even if x is an integer.

14. Evaluate the expression $2 \cdot (x + 1)$ for each value of x.

    a. 1   **b.** 2   **c.** 3   **d.** 4

    e. 11   **f.** −3   **g.** −7

    h. Explain why $2 \cdot (x + 1)$ is always even if x is an integer.

    i. Explain why $2 \cdot x + 1$ is always odd if x is an integer.

15. Simplify each expression.

    a. $x + 2x + 3x + 4x + 5x - 12x$

    b. $x + 2x + 3x + 4x + 5x - 13x$

    c. $x + 2x + 3x + 4x + 5x - 14x$

    d. $x + 2x + 3x + 4x + 5x - 15x$

    e. $x + 2x + 3x + 4x + 5x - 16x$

    f. $x + 2x + 3x + 4x + 5x - 17x$

16. Evaluate the expression $\frac{1 - x^2}{1 - x}$ for each value of x.

    a. 2   **b.** 3

    c. −3   **d.** −11

    e. $\frac{1}{2}$ **f.** 197

    g. Identify a pattern in the results.

17. Evaluate the expression $(x + 1)^2 - x^2$ for each value of x.

    a. 2

    b. 3

    c. −3

    d. −11

    e. $\frac{1}{2}$

    f. 197

    g. Identify a pattern in the results.

2.05 Rephrasing the Basic Rules

You have applied the basic rules of arithmetic to expressions. Now you can use these expressions to write the basic rules concisely.

In-Class Experiment

Match each statement in List 1 with a statement in List 2 that has the same meaning.

List 1   Basic Rules of Arithmetic Using Words

1. The order in which you add numbers in a sum does not affect the result.

2. If you add more than two numbers, the order in which you group them does not matter.

3. The order in which you multiply two numbers in a product does not affect the result.

4. If you multiply more than two numbers, the order in which you group them does not matter.

5. Multiplying a number by a sum is the same as multiplying the number by each term in the sum and then adding the results.

6. When you add 0 to any number, the result is the number itself.

7. When you multiply 1 by any number, the result is the number itself.

8. When you add any number to its opposite, the result is 0. When the sum of two numbers is 0, each number is the opposite of the other.

9. When you multiply a nonzero number by its reciprocal, the result is 1. When the product of two numbers is 1, each number is the reciprocal of the other number.

List 2   Basic Rules of Arithmetic Using Symbols

A. For any three numbers a, b, and c, $a + (b + c) = (a + b) + c$.

B. For any two numbers a and b, $ab = ba$.

C. For any three numbers a, b, and c, $a(b + c) = ab + ac$.

D. For any number a, $a + 0 = a$.

E. For any three numbers a, b, and c, $a(bc) = (ab)c$.

F. For any two nonzero numbers a and b, $a \cdot \frac{1}{a} = 1$, and if $ab = 1$, $b = \frac{1}{a}$.

G. For any two numbers a and b, $a + b = b + a$.

H. For any number a, $a \cdot 1 = a = 1 \cdot a$.

I. For any two numbers a and b, $a + (-a) = 0$, and if $a + b = 0$, $b = -a$.

Facts and Notation

The list below gives four properties of arithmetic with names you will see in other math books. This book refers to these as the any-order, any-grouping properties.

- **Commutative Property of Addition** For any numbers *a* and *b*,

  $a + b = b + a$

- **Associative Property of Addition** For any numbers *a*, *b*, and *c*,

  $a + (b + c) = (a + b) + c$

- **Commutative Property of Multiplication** For any numbers *a* and *b*,

  $ab = ba$

- **Associative Property of Multiplication** For any numbers *a*, *b*, and *c*,

  $a(bc) = (ab)c$

You will also see the following names for the properties about identities and inverses.

- **Additive Identity** For any number *a*,

  $a + 0 = a$

- **Additive Inverse** For any number *a*,

  $a + (-a) = 0$

  If $a + b = 0$, then $b = -a$.

- **Multiplicative Identity** For any number *a*,

  $a \cdot 1 = a$

- **Multiplicative Inverse** For any nonzero number *a*,

  $a \cdot \frac{1}{a} = 1$

  If $ab = 1$, then $b = \frac{1}{a}$.

Finally, the Distributive Property relates addition and multiplication.

- **Distributive Property** For any numbers *a*, *b*, and *c*,

  $a(b + c) = ab + ac$

Exercises Practicing Habits of Mind

Check Your Understanding

1. Express each sentence using variables.

   a. Dividing is the same as multiplying by the reciprocal.

   b. Subtracting is the same as adding the opposite.

   c. If you have a product of two numbers, and you find the products of the opposites of the numbers, you get the same result.

   d. If you multiply two numbers together and the result is 1, then the numbers are reciprocals.

2. The Zero-Product Property states that if the product of two numbers is zero, then one of the numbers equals zero. You can write the property using symbols this way.

   If $ab = 0$, then $a = 0$ or $b = 0$.

   The steps show you a proof of this property. Start with the equation $ab = 0$.

   a. If $a = 0$, then you can stop doing the proof. Explain.

   b. Assume $a \neq 0$. Then a has a reciprocal. Explain.

   c. Since a has a reciprocal $\left(\frac{1}{a}\right)$, you can use a basic rule and multiply both sides of the equation by this reciprocal. What effect does this have on the left side of the equation? On the right side of the equation?

   d. Explain why these steps prove the Zero-Product Property.

> **Remember...**
>
> Sometimes you will see the term *negative* or *additive inverse* instead of *opposite*. They all mean the same thing.

On Your Own

3. The binary operation ♥ is defined by the following rule.

   $$x \heartsuit y = 3x + y$$

   a. Explain how to find $4 \heartsuit 6 = 18$.

   b. Evaluate $6 \heartsuit 4$.

   c. Is ♥ commutative? In other words, does ♥ have an any-order property?

4. The binary operation ♠ is defined by the rule $x \spadesuit y = -3(x + y)$.

   a. Is ♠ commutative? In other words, does ♠ have an any-order property? Explain.

   b. Is ♠ associative? In other words, does ♠ have an any-grouping property? Explain.

> The prefix *bi-* means "two." A **binary operation** takes two numbers and produces one number.

> **Go Online**
> www.successnetplus.com

5. Simplify.

    a. $2(x + 2) - (x + 2)$

    b. $2(x + 2) - (x + 2) + 4(x + 2) - 3(x + 2)$

    c. $2(x + 2) - (x + 2) + 4(x + 2) - 3(x + 2) + 6(x + 2) - 5(x + 2)$

    d. $2(x + 2) - (x + 2) + 4(x + 2) - 3(x + 2) + 6(x + 2) -$
       $5(x + 2) + 8(x + 2) - 7(x + 2)$

    e. $2(x + 2) - (x + 2) + 4(x + 2) - 3(x + 2) + 6(x + 2) -$
       $5(x + 2) + 8(x + 2) - 7(x + 2) + 10(x + 2) - 9(x + 2)$

    f. Evaluate each simplified expression for $x = -2$. What is the pattern in your results? Explain.

For Exercises 6 and 7, use the any-order, any-grouping properties and the Distributive Property to simplify each expression. Remember to combine like terms.

6. a. $4(x + 2) + 11$ **b.** $x + 2(5 + 2x)$

   c. $9(2x - 5) - 3$ **d.** $5(x - 1) + 8(x + 1)$

   e. $7(x + 1) + (7x + 7)$ **f.** $7(x + 1) + (-1)(7x + 7)$

7. a. $2(x + 4) + 7$ **b.** $13 + 3(1 + 2x)$

   c. $3(2x - 5) - 8$ **d.** $4(x + 3) + 7(x + 3)$

   e. $6(3 - 2x) - 3(x + 1)$ **f.** $4(x - 7) - 2(2 - 3x)$

8. Here is one of Maya the Magnificent's number tricks.

- Choose a number.
- Add 6.
- Multiply by 3.
- Subtract 10.
- Multiply by 2.
- Add 50.
- Divide by 6.

Maya says, "I take the ending number and subtract 11. That's your starting number."

    a. Let the starting number equal x. Write the result after each step. Simplify each expression after each step.

    b. Identify four places where you used a basic rule to simplify an expression.

    c. Explain why Maya only needs to subtract 11 to get the starting number.

9. **Standardized Test Prep** Define the binary operation $\otimes$ with the rule

$$a \otimes b = ab + a.$$

Which of the following statements is true?

A. The binary operation $\otimes$ is associative but not commutative.

B. The binary operation $\otimes$ is commutative but not associative.

C. The binary operation $\otimes$ is both associative and commutative.

D. The binary operation $\otimes$ is neither associative nor commutative.

10. **Take It Further** Tony buys CDs at a music store Web site. He says, "You get a great deal. You get 20% off the price of a CD. You still have to add 5% sales tax. But you find the sales tax after the discount. So you save money on taxes, too."

How much money does Tony save by getting the discount *before* adding the sales tax? Explain by using expressions.

> Start by writing an expression for the cost of a CD in which you calculate the sales tax after the discount.

Maintain Your Skills

Find each product. Look for patterns.

11. **a.** $(5 \times 4) \times 2$

b. $(5 \times 213) \times 2$

c. $(5 \times 91,827) \times 2$

d. Describe a pattern.

12. **a.** $(25 \times 17) \times 4$

b. $(25 \times 22) \times 4$

c. $(25 \times 197) \times 4$

d. Describe the pattern.

13. **a.** $\left(\frac{10}{13} \times 54\right) \times 13$

b. $\left(\frac{10}{13} \times 81\right) \times 13$

c. $\left(\frac{10}{13} \times 1113\right) \times 13$

d. Describe a pattern.

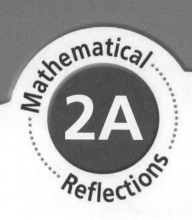

Mathematical 2A Reflections

In this investigation, you used and invented number tricks. You learned to write a variable expression to model a situation. Using the basic rules of arithmetic, you evaluated and simplified expressions. These questions will help you summarize what you have learned.

1. To build a rectangular dog pen, Cheng uses a wall of his house for one of the long sides. Let ℓ equal the length of the longer side. Let w equal the length of the shorter side.

   a. Write an expression for the amount of fencing Cheng needs to build the pen.

   b. How much fencing does Cheng need if he wants a width of 8 feet and a length of 12 feet?

   c. How much fencing does Cheng need if he wants a width of 5 feet and a length of 20 feet?

   d. Suppose the length is 9 feet more than the width. Use only *one* variable to write an expression for the amount of fencing Cheng needs.

2. Evaluate the expression $4(2x + 3) + 2(x + 1) - 7$ for each value of x.

   a. 1   b. 6   c. −2   d. $\frac{1}{2}$

   e. Simplify the expression. When you evaluate the simplified expression for $x = 1$ and $x = 6$, do you get the same results as in part (a) and part (b)? Do you get the same result for every value of x?

3. Why are variables useful?

4. How can you invent a number trick that always gives the same ending number?

5. Use the following steps.

   • Choose a number.

   • Multiply by 5.

   • Add 2.

   • Multiply by 3.

   • Subtract 8.

   a. Choose the number 4. What ending number do you get?

   b. Choose the variable x. What ending expression do you get?

Puedes comprender x, $5x$, $5x + 2$, . . . , sin importar la lengua que hables.

Vocabulary

In this investigation, you saw these terms. Make sure you understand what each one means and how to use it.

• **binary operation**
• **combining like terms**
• **evaluate**

• **expression**
• **like terms**
• **variable**

Investigation 2B

Equations

In *Equations,* you will develop techniques for solving equations using the language of algebra. To solve equations, you will learn how to reverse, or undo, an operation.

By the end of this investigation, you will be able to answer questions like these.

1. What is an equation?

2. What are some ways to solve an equation?

3. Breanna chooses a number, multiplies it by 3, and subtracts 8. The ending number is 7. What is Breanna's starting number?

You will learn how to

• reverse, or undo, a series of steps

• understand the relationship between an equation and its solutions

• use backtracking to solve a problem

You will develop these habits and skills:

• Find the reverse operation that undoes a particular operation.

• Use equations to solve a complex problem.

• Apply a standard formula, such as temperature conversion or velocity of falling objects, to solve a problem.

To reassemble the bike, recall the steps you took to disassemble it. Then backtrack.

You know the directions from your home to school. To go from school to your home, it may be possible to simply reverse the directions. Such a "backtracking" skill will be useful for solving equations.

For You to Explore

Kelly gives directions for walking from Cambridge, Massachusetts, to the Thomas P. O'Neill Federal Building in Boston.

- Walk across the Longfellow Bridge from Cambridge to Boston on Cambridge Street. Stay on the right side of Cambridge Street to avoid the construction.

- When you reach Staniford Street, turn left. Walk down the hill. Staniford Street becomes Causeway Street. You should see the O'Neill Federal Building on your left—it's gigantic! You can't miss it.

When you arrive at the O'Neill Federal Building, you see Justin. He asks you for directions to return to Cambridge.

1. Work in a group. Write directions for Justin.

2. Compare the directions you write to Kelly's directions. How do your directions differ from Kelly's? How are your directions the same as Kelly's?

3. Spiro the Spectacular asks you to choose a number, multiply it by 5, and then subtract 10. When you tell Spiro the ending number, which of the following methods can he use to find your starting number?

    a. Multiply the ending number by 5 and then subtract 10.

    b. Divide the ending number by 5 and then subtract 10.

    c. Divide the ending number by 5 and then add 10.

    d. Add 10 to the ending number and then divide by 5.

    e. Add 10 to the ending number, double it, and then divide by 10.

    f. Drop the last digit of the ending number and then add 10.

    g. Divide the ending number by 5 and then add 2.

    > More than one of these methods will work. Find them all.

4. Maya wants to be absolutely sure that she can undo any step, so that she can find the starting number without guessing. For each step, describe how to undo it, or explain why you cannot undo it.

    a. Add 5.   b. Divide by 10.   c. Multiply by 0.

    d. Multiply by 3 and then subtract 28.

    e. Find the sum of the digits of a number.

    f. Subtract 11 from a number six times in a row.

5. Spiro tells you to start with the number 3 and then add 5 as many times as you want. You tell him your ending number. Spiro tells you how many times you added 5. Explain.

Exercises *Practicing Habits of Mind*

On Your Own

6. Dae gives directions from the baseball field to her house.

   - You should be on Clark right now, heading south.
   - Turn right on Addison.
   - After about 4 blocks, turn left on Western.
   - At the next street, turn right on Belmont.
   - When you see a police station on the corner, turn right.
   - My house is the fourth building on the left.

   Write directions to return to the baseball field from Dae's house.

7. Use the Internet to find driving direction between two cities or towns. Record the directions. Then, write directions for the return trip. How do the directions compare?

   > Sometimes, you cannot simply backtrack. Explain.

8. Jamal describes the steps he uses to get each ending number. Find each starting number. If you cannot, explain why.

		Ending Number
a.	Multiply by 4.	36
b.	Subtract 18.	−14
c.	Double the number 3 times.	−48
d.	Divide the number by itself.	1
e.	Divide by 23 and then multiply by a favorite number.	12
f.	Subtract 4 and then multiply by a favorite number.	100
g.	Add 7, divide by 10, subtract 3, multiply by 4, and add 13.	37

   > The operation in part (b) looks like this picture.

9. Maya starts with a number and repeats an operation several times. Find the number of times she repeats the operation to get each ending number. If you cannot, explain why.

Starting Number	Repeated Operation	Ending Number
a. 8	Add 5.	93
b. 1	Multiply by 10.	1,000,000
c. 30	Subtract 2.	−100
d. 0	Multiply by 5.	0
e. 100	Divide by 2.	$3\frac{1}{8}$
f. 5	Multiply by −1.	−5
g. 10	Add 7.	more than 1000

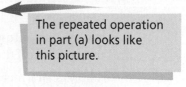

The repeated operation in part (a) looks like this picture.

10. **Write About It** Spiro asks you to choose a number, add 10, and then find the remainder when you divide by 7. When you tell him the ending number, can Spiro always find your starting number? Explain.

Maintain Your Skills

11. List the six sets of steps below in pairs. The steps in each pair must produce the same ending number when you use the same starting number.

I. Divide a number by three and then multiply by twelve.

II. Add three to a number and then add the original number.

III. Multiply a number by four.

IV. Divide a number by three, multiply by four, and then divide by eight.

V. Divide a number by six.

VI. Double a number and then add three.

2.07 Reversing Operations

You can reverse some actions. You cannot reverse others. Here are some reversible actions.

- You can reverse opening a window by closing the same window.
- To reverse setting a 12-hour clock forward by one hour, you can set the same clock back one hour, or set the clock forward another 11 hours.
- You can reverse putting on socks and then shoes by taking off the shoes and then taking off the socks.

Some examples of irreversible actions include sending an e-mail, compacting trash, and skydiving.

In mathematics, you can reverse some operations on a number and not others. An operation is a **reversible operation** if there is a second operation that always brings you back to the situation before the first operation. For example,

- You can reverse adding 5 to a number by subtracting 5 from the result.
- You can reverse multiplying a number by 3 by dividing the result by 3.
- You can reverse adding seven hours to the current time on a 12-hour clock by adding five more hours to the resulting time.

You cannot reverse other operations. For example,

- When you multiply a number by 0, it is impossible to find your starting number. Explain.
- You can't reverse adding the digits of a number together. Explain.

> *Reverse* in this lesson has the same meaning as *undo* in Lesson 2.06.

> If the starting number is n, you can write this expression as $n + 5$. Reversing the operation looks like $(n + 5) - 5$.

Developing Habits of Mind

Prove by counterexample. Here is one way to show that you cannot reverse a particular operation. Find *two* different starting numbers that produce the same ending number. There is no way to know from the ending number what the starting number was.

For example, think about the operation of adding the digits together. The starting numbers 17 and 26 both have a digit sum of 8. If you only know 8 is the digit sum, it is impossible to tell what the starting number was.

Takashi guesses what number Tom chose.

Tom Hey, I'll bet you can't guess my number!

Takashi Guessing again? Okay. Is it 246.3?

Tom No.

Takashi What about 137 and a quarter?

Tom No. I'll give you a big hint, but then you get only one guess. When you square my number, you get 169. Alright, so, what's my number?

Takashi gets out a calculator and fiddles with it for a moment.

Takashi I got it. It's 13.

Tom No! I fooled you.

For Discussion

1. What did Takashi do wrong? What number do you think Tom chose?

One way Takashi can be sure what number Tom chose is not to allow him to choose a negative number. Some operations are only reversible when the set of starting values does not include all numbers.

Now, you will learn a method called **backtracking,** which means reversing operations. Spiro and Maya use backtracking in their number tricks.

Example

Problem Find the value of x that solves the equation $3x - 14 = 37$.

Solution Use backtracking to solve $3x - 14 = 37$.

Step 1 Write the steps, in order, that show how to get from the input variable x to the output value 37.

- Multiply by 3.
- Subtract 14.

Here is a machine diagram showing the steps.

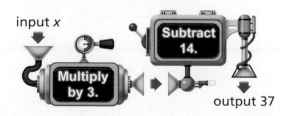

input *x*

output 37

> You read the equation as, "Three times some starting number, minus 14, is equal to 37." The equation is like one of Spiro's number tricks.

Step 2 Make a list that reverses the order of the first list and shows how to undo each operation.

- Add 14.
- Divide by 3.

Here is a machine diagram showing these steps.

Why is it important to keep track of the steps?

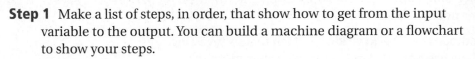

Step 3 Start with the output. Perform each step on the list of reverse steps to find the value of the input variable x. Start with output 37.

$37 + 14 = 51$ Add 14 to the output 37.

$51 \div 3 = 17$ Divide by 3 to find the value of the input variable, x.

$$x = 17$$

This process is the same as following 37 through the machine diagram above.

Developing Habits of Mind

Establish a process. Here is a method for performing good backtracking steps.

Step 1 Make a list of steps, in order, that show how to get from the input variable to the output. You can build a machine diagram or a flowchart to show your steps.

Step 2 Make a list that reverses the order of the steps in the first list and shows how to undo each operation.

Step 3 Start with the output. Perform each step on the list of reverse steps to find the value of the input variable.

For Discussion

2. Derman solves an equation such as $3x - 14 = 37$ by making a guess, checking it, and then making a better guess until he finds the solution. Compare Derman's method with the backtracking method. What advantages does backtracking have? Are there any disadvantages to backtracking?

Exercises *Practicing Habits of Mind*

Check Your Understanding

1. Getting into a car involves these steps.

   • Open the car door.

   • Sit down.

   • Close the car door.

   • Buckle the seat belt.

   Describe the steps you take in getting out of a car. How are they related to the steps involved in getting into a car?

2. Find a partner. Each person thinks of a number. Take your number and follow these steps.

   • Add 6.

   • Divide by 4.

   • Multiply by 8.

   • Add 7.

   • Multiply by 10.

   Take your partner's result and find the starting number. Describe your process.

   > **Remember...**
   > You perform each step starting with the result that you got from the step before it.

3. Write each algebraic expression as a statement of one or more operations. For each operation that is reversible, describe the operation that reverses it.

   a. $n + 13$

   b. $\frac{b}{-2}$

   c. $3(5m - 12)$

   d. $15m - 36$

   > Describe, in words, what each of these expressions tells you to do with the number.

4. Dana says, "I take a number, multiply it by 2, add 7, and then subtract 5. My final result is 22." What is Dana's starting number?

5. Hideki says, "I take a number, multiply it by 12, and then subtract 9. My final result is −5." What is Hideki's starting number?

6. Here is a table for the input and output of $y = x^2$, where x has integer values from -4 to 4. Some values of x^2 are missing.

Input, x	Output, x^2
-4	16
-3	■
-2	■
-1	■
0	■
1	■
2	■
3	9
4	■

A sky diver's jump from an airplane is not a reversible step.

a. Copy and complete the table.

b. From this table, how do you know that squaring is not a reversible operation?

c. Make a similar table for cubing the input. This means that if the input is x, the output is x^3. Use inputs from -4 to 4. Is this operation reversible?

d. Make tables for the outputs x^4, x^5, x^6, and x^7. Which powers produce reversible operations?

e. Why is the result $(-3)^4$ positive? What powers of -3 produce negative numbers?

On Your Own

7. Write each algebraic expression as a statement of one or more operations. For each operation that is reversible, describe the operation that reverses it. ◄

Describe, in words, what each of these expressions tells you to do with the number.

  a. $y^2 + 6$

  b. $3x - 28$

  c. $\dfrac{j - 8}{4}$

  d. $3x - 33 + 5$

8. Marty says, "I take a number, add 5, and then multiply by 8. My final result is 24." What is Marty's starting number?

9. Bianca says, "I take a number, multiply it by 4, and then add 11. My final result is 39." What is Bianca's starting number?

10. **Write About It** Describe how you can use backtracking to solve the equation $179x + 318 = 1429$. Describe your steps without solving the equation.

Go Online
www.successnetplus.com

11. Suppose each table represents the entire chart for an input-output operation. Which tables show a reversible operation?

Table A

Input	Output
−2	−3
−1	−3
0	−3
1	−3
2	7

Table B

Input	Output
0	1
1	3
2	5
3	7
4	9

Table C

Input	Output
1	4
2	0
3	0
4	0
5	12

Table D

Input	Output
0	1
1	2
2	4
3	8
4	16

12. **Standardized Test Prep** Which step can you use to undo the operation in the equation $\frac{5}{3}x = 10$? Give the most complete answer.

I. Multiply by $\frac{3}{5}$. **II.** Multiply by $\frac{5}{3}$.

III. Divide by $\frac{3}{5}$. **IV.** Divide by $\frac{5}{3}$.

A. I only **B.** III only **C.** II or III **D.** I or IV

13. **Take It Further** For each operation below, can you restrict the types of numbers you use as the input so that the operation is reversible? Explain.

a. Multiply your number by zero.

b. Find the sum of the digits of your number.

14. For each operation, find a number that produces itself as the output. This number is a fixed point for the operation. If you cannot find a fixed point, explain.

a. Take the average of your number and the number 5.

b. Add 6 to your number.

c. Take the square root of your number.

d. Multiply your number by 3 and then add 12.

e. **Take It Further** Square your number and then subtract 6.

Maintain Your Skills

Choose any number and perform the operations. Then take the result and repeat the operations. Repeat this process many times. Explain how the results change.

15. Add 3 and then divide that sum by 2.

16. Add 5 and divide by 2.

17. Add 1 and divide by 2.

2.08 Solving Equations by Backtracking

In Lesson 2.07, you learned the technique called backtracking. You can also use that technique to solve equations. You have seen arithmetic equations, such as $3 + 4 = 7$. In algebra, equations can include variables and complex expressions, but the idea of what an equation is remains essentially the same as in arithmetic.

Definition

An **equation** is a mathematical sentence that states that two quantities are equal.

The quantities can be any mathematical expression such as 12, $42x + 10$, or $3a^2b + 2ab^2 + 7c$.

The definition does not state that an equation must be true. It only states that it is a complete thought about numbers. The equation $3 + 4 = 7$ happens to be true. The statement $2 + 1 = 9$ is also an equation. It just happens to be false.

Here are some more examples of equations.

$2 + 5 = 7$	true
$3 + 8 = 10$	false
$x + y = y + x$	true
$x^2 = x \cdot x$	true
$x = x + 1$	false

Things can get a tricky when you start looking at equations with variables. You do not know what the values of the variables are. How do you know if the equation is true or false?

For Discussion

1. How do you know that $x + y = y + x$ is always true?

2. How do you know that $x^2 = x \cdot x$ is always true?

3. How do you know that $x = x + 1$ is always false?

Most of the time, an equation containing one or more variables is only true when those variables have certain values. For example, $x + 1 = 8$ is true only when x has a value of 7.

Definition

The values of the variables that make an equation true are **solutions** of the equation.

Example 1

Problem Why is the value 3 a solution to the equation $x + 4 = 7$?

Solution The value 3 is a solution to the equation $x + 4 = 7$, since 3 makes the equation true.

$$x + 4 = 7$$
$$3 + 4 = 7 \quad ✔ \text{ true}$$

Any other value of x makes the equation false, so 3 is the only solution.

Habits of Mind

Represent x with a number. Try replacing x with a number different from 3. What is your result?

Some equations have more than one solution. For instance, $x^2 = 9$ has two solutions, 3 and -3, since both numbers make it true. You use the term **solution set** for the collection of all solutions of an equation. The expression $x^2 = 9$ has the solution set $\{-3, 3\}$.

When an equation is always false, it has no solutions. For instance, the equation $x = x + 1$ has no solutions, so its solution set is the **empty set,** or the **null set.**

You can write the empty set as two braces with nothing inside { } or the null symbol ∅.

To find out if a number is a solution to an equation, just test it out! A variable such as x represents a number, so every time you see an x in an equation, replace it with the same number. If you get a true statement, that number is a solution.

Example 2

Problem Is the number 7 a solution to the equation $3x - 28 = 46$?

Solution No. Replace x with 7 and find whether the result is true.

$$3x - 28 = 46$$
$$3 \cdot 7 - 28 \stackrel{?}{=} 46$$
$$-7 \neq 46 \quad \text{✗ false}$$

For Discussion

4. Suppose you want to find the solution to $3x - 28 = 46$ by guessing. How can you do it?

5. Can you solve the equation $3x - 28 = 46$ by backtracking? Explain.

6. Suppose you want to find both solutions to $x^2 - x - 2 = 0$. How can you do this?

Example 3

Problem Solve the equation $81 = \frac{q}{3} + 76$ to find the value of q.

Solution Suppose you divide the starting number q by 3 and then add 76. Backtrack by reversing each step in the opposite order. To find q, start with the ending number, 81, and follow these steps.

- Subtract 76. $\quad\quad\quad\quad 81 - 76 = 5$
- Multiply by 3. $\quad\quad\quad 5 \cdot 3 = 15$

> Think: I have a number, add 76, and get 81. My number is $81 - 76$, or 5.

The starting value of q is 15. After the first backtracking step, what remains is $5 = \frac{q}{3}$. You find the value of q by multiplying.

Verify that $q = 15$ is a solution by replacing q with 15.

$$81 = \frac{q}{3} + 76$$

$$81 \stackrel{?}{=} \frac{15}{3} + 76$$

$$81 \stackrel{?}{=} 5 + 76$$

$$81 = 81 \quad\quad\quad ✔ \text{ true}$$

> Think: I have a number, divide it by 3, and get 5. My number is $3 \cdot 5$, or 15.

For Discussion

7. Solve the equation $3(a - 1) - 5 = 34$.

8. Explain *why* backtracking helps you solve the equation in Problem 7. Use the phrase "reversible operations."

Exercises *Practicing Habits of Mind*

Check Your Understanding

Use backtracking to find the solution of each equation in Exercises 1–6.

1. $7 + y = 3$

2. $2x - 7 = 110$

3. $10 = \frac{z}{12}$

4. $15 - 2w - 31$

5. $\dfrac{n - 13}{12} = 3.5$

6. $38 = 5n - 1$

Using a truck 11 ft high is not a solution for passing under this bridge.

7. The equation $3a + 6b = 75$ gives a relationship between the variables a and b.

a. If the value of a is 11, find the value of b.

b. If the value of b is 12, find the value of a.

c. Copy and complete this table relating a and b for different values of a.

d. Describe the relationship in the table between a and b.

a	b
0	■
1	■
2	■
3	■
4	■
5	■

8. a. Show that $x = 1$ and $x = 8$ are solutions to the equation $x^3 + 26x = 11x^2 + 16$.

b. Find two numbers that are *not* solutions.

c. **Take It Further** Find another number, besides 1 and 8, that is a solution.

> Another way to write the equation in Exercise 4 is $15 + (-2) \cdot w = 31$.

On Your Own

9. Tony and Sasha are trying to solve the equation $3(x + 2) - 11 = 26$.

Tony explains, "First I write the steps to get from the starting number to 26. Then I make a list of how to undo each operation in reverse order. Here is my list.

- Add 11.
- Divide by 3.
- Subtract 2.

Then I use those steps to find the starting number."

Sasha says, "I do it differently, Tony. First I simplify the expression on the left side of the equation.

$$3(x + 2) - 11 = 3x + 6 - 11$$
$$= 3x - 5$$

Then I have the equation $3x - 5 = 26$. To backtrack this equation, I follow the following steps.

- Add 5.
- Divide by 3."

Do both methods work?

10. **a.** Write the expression $3(a + 2) - 1$ as a set of steps describing the operations.

   b. Write the steps to reverse the operations.

11. Use your result from Exercise 10. Solve each equation.

   a. $3(a + 2) - 1 = 17$ **b.** $3(a + 2) - 1 = 8$

   c. $3(a + 2) - 1 = -19$ **d.** $3(a + 2) - 1 = 0$

12. Andrew explains, "I choose a number. I add 1 and multiply by -4. Then I add 2. My ending number is 22." What is Andrew's starting number?

13. **Standardized Test Prep** Joya adds 8 to her starting number and then multiplies by 3. She subtracts 15 from the result and multiplies by 2. The ending number is 6. What is Joya's starting number?

   A. -2 **B.** 2

   C. 10   **D.** none of these

14. In Exercise 8f from Lesson 2.06, Jamal chose a starting number, subtracted 4, and multiplied by his favorite number. His ending number was 100. Parts (a)–(d) refer to n as Jamal's starting number and f as Jamal's favorite number.

   a. Suppose Jamal's favorite number is 25. Find the starting number.

   b. Suppose Jamal's favorite number is 10. Find the starting number.

   c. Write an equation that tells you the starting number n in terms of Jamal's favorite number f.

   d. Are there any numbers Jamal cannot use as his favorite number in this situation?

The right side of the equation needs to have an f in it.

Maintain Your Skills

15. Solve each equation using backtracking.

   a. $-5x + 13 = 93$

   b. $13 - 5x = 93$

   c. $-7x + 12 = -45$

   d. $12 - 7x = -45$

   e. $-3x - 17 = 4$

   f. $-17 - 3x = 4$

Go Online
Video Tutor
www.successnetplus.com

16. Use backtracking to solve these equations. Write the steps in the correct order.

Go Online
www.successnetplus.com

  a. $10(x + 3) = 73$ **b.** $10x + 3 = 73$

  c. $73 = 10(x + 3)$ **d.** $73 = 10x + 3$

  e. $\dfrac{x + 3}{10} = 73$ **f.** $\dfrac{x}{10} + 3 = 73$

  g. $73 = \dfrac{x - 3}{10}$ **h.** $73(3x) = 10$

Historical Perspective
Temperature Scales

In the 1600s and early 1700s, scientists devised as many as 35 different temperature scales. The Fahrenheit and Celsius scales have survived as standard scales today.

In 1714, a German scientist, Daniel Fahrenheit, developed a more accurate thermometer than what existed. He used mercury encased in glass. The advantage of using mercury is that it expands at a nearly constant rate. This means that you can mark a scale on a thermometer similar to the way that you mark a scale on a ruler. In the Fahrenheit temperature scale, 32° is the freezing point of water and 212° is the boiling point of water.

Anders Celsius, a Swedish astronomer, developed the Celsius scale in 1742. He chose 0° as the boiling point of water and 100° as the freezing point of water. After Celsius died, 0°C became the freezing point, and 100°C became the boiling point.

The Celsius temperature scale (sometimes called centigrade) is the standard scale in most of the world outside the United States. *Centigrade*, derived from Latin, means "100 steps." It refers to dividing the interval between the freezing point and the boiling point of water into 100 equal parts. When you travel, you may want to convert between Celsius and Fahrenheit temperatures. You can use the conversion formula

$$F = \frac{9}{5}C + 32$$

where C is temperature in degrees Celsius (°C), and F is temperature in degrees Fahrenheit (°F).

Daniel Fahrenheit designed his thermometer at age 28.

Twenty-eight years after Fahrenheit designed his thermometer, Anders Celsius (above) described the scale that now uses his name.

Mathematical
2B
Reflections

In this investigation, you learned to reverse arithmetic operations. You defined an equation and its solutions. Using the backtracking method, you found the solution to an equation. These questions will help you summarize what you have learned.

1. Scientists often use the Kelvin temperature scale. You call the temperature 0 kelvins absolute zero. The formula for converting from degrees Celsius to kelvins is $K = C + 273.15$.

   a. Write a formula to convert kelvins to degrees Celsius.

   b. What is absolute zero in degrees Celsius?

   c. What is absolute zero in degrees Fahrenheit?

   d. **Take It Further** Write a formula to convert kelvins to degrees Fahrenheit.

> You name units in the Kelvin scale *kelvins*, not degrees Kelvin.

2. For each set of steps, describe how to undo the steps.

   a. Add 3 to your number.

   b. Subtract 6 from your number.

   c. Multiply your number by 2 and add 5.

   d. Add 2 to your number and divide by 3.

3. Use backtracking to find the solution to each equation.

   a. $2x + 5 = 11$ b. $3m - 4 = -7$

   c. $\frac{y}{3} + 1 = 5$ d. $\frac{y + 1}{3} = 5$

If the trail fails on a bike trip, you can backtrack.

4. a. Show that $w = 8$ is a solution to the equation $18 = 3(w - 2)$.

   b. Show that $x = 3$ and $x = -2$ are solutions to the equation $x^2 = x + 6$.

5. Show that $n = -4$ is not a solution to the equation $2(3n + 1) = 22$.

6. What is an equation?

7. What are some ways to solve an equation?

8. Breanna chooses a number, multiplies it by 3, and subtracts 8. The ending number is 7. What is Breanna's starting number?

Vocabulary

In this investigation, you saw these terms. Make sure you understand what each one means and how to use it.

- backtracking
- empty set
- equation
- null set
- reversible operation
- solution
- solution set

Investigation 2C

Solving Linear Equations

In *Solving Linear Equations,* you will evaluate and simplify an expression using the basic rules of arithmetic. Using basic moves, you will solve an equation that may have one solution, more than one solution, or even no solution.

By the end of this investigation, you will be able to answer questions like these.

1. How can you solve an equation for which backtracking does not work?

2. How can you visualize an equation using the number line?

3. Solve the equation $5x = x + 24$.

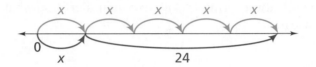

You will learn how to

- evaluate and simplify expressions using the basic rules

- solve equations using the basic moves

- understand that equations can have multiple solutions or no solutions

- solve an equation involving many variations of the Distributive Property

You will develop these habits and skills:

- Visualize solving an equation in a variety of ways.

- Understand why the basic moves do not change the solutions of an equation.

- Quickly solve linear equations.

- Check results to ensure that your algebraic steps are correct.

- Use expansion boxes to distribute expressions.

When an equation is true, the amounts on both sides of the = sign are the same.

2.09 Getting Started

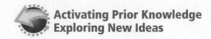

Activating Prior Knowledge
Exploring New Ideas

In Lesson 2.08, you used backtracking to find the starting number in a number trick. Can you always use backtracking to find your starting number? Here are some number tricks for you to explore.

For You to Explore

1. Sasha says, "I pick a number.
   - I multiply my number by 2.
   - I add 3.
   - I subtract 8.
   - My final result is 13."

   What is Sasha's starting number?

2. Tony says, "I pick a number.
   - I subtract 11 from my number.
   - I multiply by $\frac{1}{2}$.
   - I add 3.
   - My final result is 8."

   What is Tony's starting number?

3. Derman says, "I pick a number.
   - I add 4 to my number.
   - I multiply by −2.
   - I subtract 19.
   - My final result is −9."

   What is Derman's starting number?

4. Casey says, "I pick a number.
   - I multiply my number by 7.
   - I add 18.
   - My final result is ten times my starting number."

   What is Casey's starting number?

5. Anna says, "I pick a number.
   - I multiply my number by 3.
   - I subtract 4.
   - I subtract 3.
   - My final result is two times my starting number."

   What is Anna's starting number?

6. Sophie says, "I pick a number.
   - I multiply my number by 5.
   - I add 6.
   - My final result is my starting number times 3 plus 12."
   What is Sophie's starting number?

7. James says, "I pick a number.
   - I add 1 to my number.
   - I multiply by 4.
   - I subtract 11.
   - My final result is two times my starting number."
   What is James's number?

8. Emma says, "I pick a number.
   - I add 1 to my number.
   - I multiply by 6.
   - I add 1.
   - My final result is 18 more than my starting number."
   What is Emma's starting number?

9. Here is an arrangement of two rectangles placed side by side to form a larger rectangle. The smaller rectangles have the same width. Find an expression for the area of each of the two smaller rectangles. Find two expressions for the area of the larger rectangle.

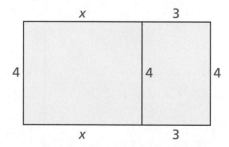

You can combine two photos that have the same height to make a panoramic scene.

Exercises *Practicing Habits of Mind*

On Your Own

10. Solve each equation using backtracking.

    a. $3a + 11 = 29$ **b.** $-2(p - 15) + 5 = -15$

11. **Write About It** You cannot solve the equation $3t + 12 = 5t + 6$ by using backtracking. Explain why.

12. **Take It Further** Solve the equation $3t + 12 = 5t + 6$. Explain your steps.

13. For each equation, determine whether $r = -2$ is a solution.

    a. $6r + 2 = 12 + r$ **b.** $3r + 2 + 10r = 7 + 7r + (-17)$

    c. $r + 11 - 3r = 15 + 2r$ **d.** $7(r + 2) + 8 = 4r + 16$

14. For each equation, determine whether $s = \frac{4}{3}$ is a solution.

    a. $4s = s + 4$ **b.** $9s - 2 = 5s + \frac{10}{3}$

    c. $5(s - 1) - 1 = 2s - \frac{2}{3}$ **d.** $2(s + 1) + 5 = 7s + \frac{1}{3}$

15. Colleen works on a number game. She says, "I'm thinking of a number. I do some things to it, and I end up with 27. The last step in my game is to add -7."

What is Colleen's ending number if she changes the last step of her game to each of the following?

    a. add 8   **b.** multiply by 2   **c.** subtract 7

16. Here is an arrangement of two small squares and two rectangles that form a large square. Find an expression for the area of each of the four smaller regions. Find *two* expressions for the area of the large square.

Maintain Your Skills

17. For each equation, find a value of x that makes the equation true.

    a. $8 \cdot x = 1$ **b.** $-19 \cdot x = 1$ **c.** $\frac{11}{13} \cdot x = 1$

    d. $\frac{10}{11} \cdot \frac{11}{13} \cdot x = 1$ **e.** $\frac{5}{7} \cdot \frac{11}{12} \cdot x = 1$

When Backtracking Does Not Work

As you saw in Lesson 2.09, you cannot solve all equations using backtracking. For instance, you cannot solve the equation $3t + 12 = 5t + 6$ from Exercise 6 by using backtracking because there is a t on both sides of the equation. You cannot write the equation as a process. Instead, you can look at this kind of equation in different ways.

Equality on the Number Line

To illustrate the equation $3t + 12 = 5t + 6$, you can draw t as an unknown length. Whatever length you choose for t, you cannot compare it to the length of 6 or 12, because you do not yet know the value of t. You do know that every t has the same length.

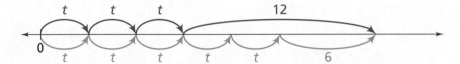

The symbols above the number line show $3t + 12$. The symbols below the number line show $5t + 6$. The equation $3t + 12 = 5t + 6$ tells you that the two expressions are equal. So, when you draw the two expressions, they can start and end at the same point on the number line.

Look at the $3t$'s on the left above and below the line.

3t is in each expression.

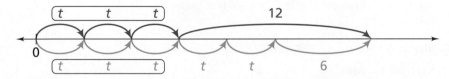

Suppose you ignore the $3t$'s on both the top and bottom. The 12 above the line and the $2t + 6$ below the line start and end at the same point on the number line. So they must be equal.

Ignoring the $3t$'s above and below the line is the same as subtracting $3t$ from both sides of the equation. Above the line, 12 units are left over, and below the line $2t + 6$ units are left over. Now you have an equation, $12 = 2t + 6$, that you can solve using bactracking.

For You to Do

1. Solve the equation $12 = 2t + 6$.

For Discussion

2. Solve the equation $7w + 8 = 4w + 23$.

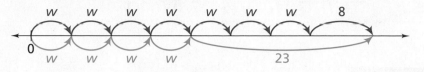

Keeping it Equal

You can represent equations by illustrating each number and variable. Each triangle represents a 1, and each square represents a t.

$$3t \quad + \quad 12 \quad = \quad 5t \quad + \quad 6$$

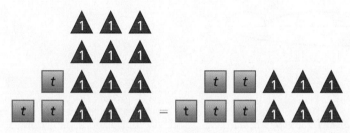

If you remove the same number from each side of the equation, the equation is still true. To begin, you can remove $3t$'s from each side.

Again, you get a simpler equation, $12 = 2t + 6$.

To finish solving the equation, you can remove 6 triangles from each side.

For Discussion

3. Solve the equation $2x + 4 = x + 8$.

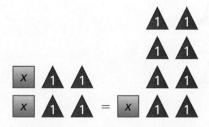

Check Your Understanding

Solve each equation.

1. $2\ell + 5 = 35$

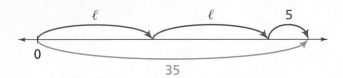

2. $7j = 5j + 10$

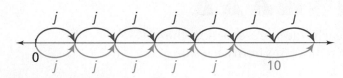

3. $4n + 7 = 2n + 10$

4. $6x + 2 = x + 10$

5. $3x = -15$

6. $2y + 11 = 27$

7. $2a + 5 = a + 8$

8. $4u - 5 = u + 16$

9. $11m + 1 = 8m + 28$

10. Each expression is the left side of an equation. Write an expression for the right side so that $x = 3$ is a solution of the equation.

a. $2(x + 1)$ b. $3x - 1$ c. $7x + 5 + 2(x - 1)$

d. 6   e. any expression

11. Solve each equation.

a. $5r + 11 = 95 - r$

b. $14 - 23x = 60x + 180$

c. $37a + 12 + 14a - 9 = 6a + 11 - 14 + 5a$

d. $s - 2s + 3s - 4s + 5s = s + 100$

On Your Own

Solve each equation.

12. $6r + 2 = r + 12$

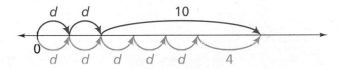

13. $2d + 10 = 5d + 4$

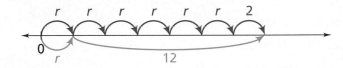

14. $3p = 36$

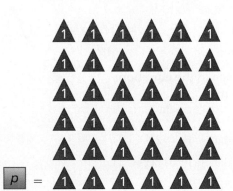

15. Solve the equation $7x - 8 = x + 16$.

16. Solve each equation.

a. $3x + 5 = 26$ b. $26 = 3(x - 1) + 5$

c. $26 = 3(x + 3) + 5$ d. $3(x - 7) + 5 = 26$

e. $26 = 3(2x + 1) + 5$ f. $3(5 - 2y) + 5 = 26$

Go Online
www.successnetplus.com

17. James says to his sister Emma, "I'm six years older than you. Two years from now, I'll be twice as old as you." Since you don't know Emma's or James's age, you can let x stand for Emma's age today.

    a. Write an expression for James's age today.

    b. Write an expression for Emma's age in two years.

    c. Write an expression for James's age in two years.

    d. In two years, James will be twice as old as Emma. Explain why the equation $x + 8 = 2(x + 2)$ represents this fact.

    e. Solve the equation in part (d). How old is James today? How old is Emma today?

18. **Standardized Test Prep** Shantell and Yahaira have the same amount of money to spend on shoes. Shantell purchases 7 pairs of shoes and has $17 left. Yahaira purchases 4 pairs of shoes and has $71 left. Each pair costs the same amount and there is no sales tax. What is the cost of a pair of shoes?

    A. $8   **B.** $17   **C.** $18   **D.** $22

19. Solve each equation.

    a. $5x - 7 = 2x + 2$ **b.** $3g - 8 = 5g - 20$

    c. $1 - 3b = 2b - 8$ **d.** $15 - 4k = 12 - 7k$

20. **Take It Further** Find all the solutions to the equation $5x^2 - 27 = 2x^2 + 48$.

Maintain Your Skills

21. Solve each equation.

    a. $3x + 1 = 19 + x$ **b.** $4x + 1 = 19 + x$ **c.** $5x + 1 = 19 + x$

    d. $6x + 1 = 19 + x$ **e.** $7x + 1 = 19 + x$

    f. Which steps are the same for solving each of the equations in parts (a)–(e)? Which steps are different?

22. Solve each equation.

    a. $3(x - 1) = 2(x + 1)$ **b.** $4(x - 1) = 2(x + 1)$

    c. $5(x - 1) = 2(x + 1)$ **d.** $6(x - 1) = 2(x + 1)$

    e. $7(x - 1) = 2(x + 1)$ **f.** $8(x - 1) = 2(x + 1)$

    g. Which steps are the same for solving each of the equations in parts (a)–(f)? Which steps are different?

2.11 The Basic Moves for Solving Equations

In this lesson, you will solve a one-variable equation using two basic moves for solving equations.

Minds in Action

Tony and Sasha solve the equation $7x - 8 = x + 16$.

Tony To solve this problem, I'd start by drawing a number line, and and then . . .

Sasha Don't bother with all of that, Tony. I've got a shortcut.

Tony Show me.

Sasha Well, whenever I solve an equation, the solution ends up being $x =$ some number. So, I make the equation look like that.

Tony How?

Sasha First I get rid of the x term on one side of the equation. To do that, I subtract x from each side of the equation.

$$
\begin{array}{rcl}
7x - 8 & = & x + 16 \\
-x & & -x \\
\hline
6x - 8 & = & 16
\end{array}
$$

See, no x term on the right. I'm almost done.

Tony This equation is like the ones we've solved before.

Sasha Exactly. Then, add 8 to each side.

$$
\begin{array}{rcl}
6x - 8 & = & + 16 \\
+ 8 & & + 8 \\
\hline
6x & = & 24
\end{array}
$$

Now we have $6x = 24$. Finally, I divide each side by 6 to get the answer.

$$\frac{6x}{6} = \frac{24}{6}$$

$$x = 4$$

Tony   Are you sure that's the correct answer?

Sasha   Let's check it.

Tony substitutes $x = 4$ into the equation $7x - 8 = x + 16$.

$$7x - 8 = x + 16$$
$$7(4) - 8 = (4) + 16$$
$$28 - 8 = 20$$
$$20 = 20 \quad ✔ \text{ true}$$

Tony $x = 4$ works. Each side of the equation is 20.

Sasha   I use that method to solve all sorts of equations.

For Discussion

1. Use Sasha's method to solve the equation $3x - 5 = x + 7$.

2. Why does Sasha's method work?

Sasha's method will help you solve many equations. She adds the same value to each side of the equation, or she subtracts the same value from each side of the equation. Then, she does not change the solutions of the equation. There is a special name for moves that never change the solutions of an equation—the **basic moves for solving equations.**

Assumption   *The Basic Moves for Solving Equations*

1.   If you start with an equation and add the same number to each side, you do not change the solutions of that equation.

   In symbols, for any three numbers a, b, and c,
   $a = b$ if, and only if, $a + c = b + c$.

2.   If you start with an equation and multiply each side of the equation by the same nonzero number, you do not change the solutions of that equation.

   In symbols, for any three numbers a, b, and c, where $c \neq 0$,
   $a = b$ if, and only if, $ac = bc$.

Habits of Mind

Represent a variable with a number. Why is $c \neq 0$? Try replacing the variables a and b with different numbers.

For Discussion

3. You can also use the following two basic moves.

   • If you start with an equation and subtract the same number from each side, you do not change the solutions of that equation.

   • If you start with an equation and divide each side of the equation by the same number (unless that number is zero), you do not change the solutions of that equation.

   These rules are both correct, but they are not in the list of basic moves. Why do you think these rules are not in the list of basic moves?

For You to Do

4. Use the basic moves to solve the equation $3s - 5 = s + 7$.

5. Explain which basic move you used at each step.

Example

Problem Solve $4x + 3 = 7x + 15$.

Solution First, subtract $4x$ from each side of the equation. This step removes $4x$ from the left side, leaving only one side with an x variable.

$$\begin{array}{rrl} 4x + 3 - & 7x & + 15 \\ \underline{-4x \quad\quad} & \underline{-4x} & \\ 3 = & 3x & + 15 \end{array}$$

Next, subtract 15 from each side.

$$\begin{array}{rl} 3 = & 3x + 15 \\ \underline{-15} & \underline{\quad- 15} \\ -12 = & 3x \end{array}$$

By subtracting, you isolate $3x$ on the right side. To make the equation look like "some number $= x$," divide each side by 3.

$$\frac{-12}{3} = \frac{3x}{3}$$
$$-4 = x$$

The result is $x = -4$. Finally, check your result by plugging it into the starting equation.

$$\begin{array}{rl} 4x + 3 =& 7x + 15 \\ 4(-4) + 3 =& 7(-4) + 15 \\ -16 + 3 =& -28 + 15 \\ -13 =& -13 \quad ✔ \quad \text{true} \end{array}$$

The correct solution is $x = -4$.

Habits of Mind

Look for relationships. Subtract 15. Then divide by 3. These steps look a lot like backtracking.

Exercises *Practicing Habits of Mind*

Check Your Understanding

1. Solve each equation.

   a. $6x + 12 = 11x - 33$ **b.** $8x + 13 = -4x + 11$

   c. $13 + 8x = 11 - 4x$ **d.** $6(a + 2) = 11(a - 3)$

   e. $2z + 9z = 4z + 45 + 2z$ **f.** $3n + 13 = 3n + 13$

2. Suppose that you teach a robot to do your algebra homework. Give the steps for solving the equation $73x - 15 = 48x + 99$.

> Something is different about the equation in part (f).

3. Sasha says, "I'm thinking of a number. I do some things to it, and I end up with 13. The last step is adding 10. What will I get if everything stays the same except for the last step, which becomes adding 8?"

4. Describe one basic move you can use to transform the equation $3t + 13 = 5t + 6$ into each equation.

   a. $3t + 7 = 5t$ **b.** $2t + 13 = 4t + 6$

   c. $3t + 113 = 5t + 106$ **d.** $13 = 2t + 6$

   e. $-2t + 13 = 6$ **f.** $15t + 65 = 25t + 30$

5. Choose three equations from Exercise 4. Solve each equation. Explain your results.

6. **a.** Solve the equation $4(x - 7) + 13 = 27$ using backtracking. Show all your steps.

   b. Solve the equation $4(x - 7) + 13 = 27$ using basic moves.

   c. In parts (a) and (b), how are the steps similar? How are they different?

7. So far, most equations you have solved have only one solution. However, not all equations have exactly one solution. Match one equation to each number of solutions. Explain.

   $$3s + 12 = 3(s + 3) + 3 \qquad 2x + 2 = 2x + 7 \qquad 4z + 2 = z - 4$$

   a. one solution   **b.** no solutions   **c.** infinitely many solutions

On Your Own

For Exercises 8–10, solve each equation.

8. $7f - 19 = 4f + 41$

9. $4r + 6 = 2r - 17$

10. $4a + 1 = 11a + 8$

Go Online
www.successnetplus.com

11. Describe the one basic move you need to change the equation $2x + 17 = 36$ into each equation.

a. $2x + 13 = 32$ **b.** $2x - 12 = 7$

c. $2x = 19$ **d.** $6x + 51 = 108$

e. $x + 8.5 = 18$ **f.** $5x + 17 = 3x + 36$

g. $2x - 19 = 0$ **h.** $x + 17 = 36 - x$

12. Choose three of the equations in Exercise 11. Solve for x. Explain your results.

13. Here is one of Maya the Magnificent's number tricks.

Choose any number. Multiply by 3. Add 5. Multiply by 4. Add 16. Divide by 12. Subtract your starting number.

Maya says, "I know what your final answer is!"

a. Let your starting number equal x. Record the result and simplify the expression after each step.

b. Does Maya know for sure what your final answer is? Explain.

14. a. For which numbers n is $(5n + 12)$ equal to $(5n + 13)$? Explain.

b. Solve the equation $5x + 12 = 5x + 13$. What are your results? What does the resulting equation tell you about the solutions to the starting equation?

15. Standardized Test Prep Solve the equation $17 - (5 - p) = 2(5p - 16)$. What is the value of p?

A. $\frac{28}{11}$ **B.** 4 **C.** $\frac{44}{9}$ **D.** 5

16. a. For which numbers n is $(3n - 7)$ equal to $(3n - 7)$?

b. Try to solve the equation $3x - 7 = 3x - 7$. What are your results? What does the resulting equation tell you about the solutions to the starting equation?

Maintain Your Skills

17. Solve each equation.

a. $3x + 2 = 22 - x$ **b.** $(3x + 2) + 1 = (22 - x) + 1$

c. $(3x + 2) + 2 = (22 - x) + 2$ **d.** $(3x + 2) + 5 = (22 - x) + 5$

e. $(3x + 2) - 11 = (22 - x) - 11$ **f.** $(3x + 2) + \frac{99}{7} = (22 - x) + \frac{99}{7}$

g. What do these equations have in common? Explain.

You have already extended the basic rules of arithmetic to include numbers and variables. You can also use the basic rules as a starting point for deriving new rules. Then you can use derived rules in the same way that you use basic rules.

The difference between basic rules and derived rules is that derived rules are not assumptions. You call derived rules of mathematics *theorems*. Later, you will prove many theorems starting from basic assumptions. The first few theorems below are concepts that you may already accept. However, now you can use the basic rules to make certain that the theorems are true.

A **theorem** is a fact that follows logically from other known facts. For example, you know that San Diego is in California, and that Tony lives in San Diego. Based on these assumptions, you can derive and prove the theorem that Tony lives in California.

Theorem 2.1

If a is any real number, then $a \cdot 0 = 0 \cdot a = 0$.

Theorem 2.2

The number 0 does not have a reciprocal.

Theorem 2.3

For all real numbers a and b, $a - b = a + (-b)$.

Remember...

You can define the expression $a - b$ as the number that, if you add it to b, you get a.

For Discussion

1. How can you use the basic rules and Theorem 2.1 to derive Theorem 2.2?
2. **Take It Further** How can you use just the basic rules to derive Theorem 2.1?
3. **Take It Further** How can you use the basic rules and the definition of subtraction to derive Theorem 2.3?

The real power of Theorem 2.3 is that now you have a way to apply the any-order, any-grouping properties to subtraction. For example, you know that

$$5 - 3 \neq 3 - 5$$

because you cannot subtract in any order. If you change the statement using Theorem 2.3, you get a true statement.

$$5 + (-3) = (-3) + 5$$

You will use this theorem over and over again when simplifying and solving equations.

For Discussion

4. Sasha tried solving the equation $3x + 2 = 2x + x + 7$ using the basic moves.

$$3x + 2 = 2x + x + 7$$
$$3x + 2 = 3x + 7$$
$$3x + 2 - 3x = 3x + 7 - 3x$$
$$2 \overset{?}{=} 7$$

Did Sasha do something incorrectly? Why did Sasha get $2 \overset{?}{=} 7$ on the last line?

For You to Do

5. What results do you get when you try to solve the equation $4(x + 1) = 4x + 4$?

In this lesson, you are using linear equations. A **linear equation** is any equation in which the variable terms are not raised to a power. For example,

- $3t + 2 = 4t - 1$ is a linear equation.
- $3t^2 + 5t = 9$ is not a linear equation because it has a t^2 term.

There are only three possibilities for the solutions of a linear equation.

- A linear equation can have no solutions. For example,
  $$3x + 2 = 3x + 7$$
- A linear equation can have one solution. For example,
  $$6x - 3 = 4x + 13$$
- Every real number can be a solution to the linear equation. For example,
  $$4(x + 1) = 4x + 4$$

  is true for every real number x.

For You to Do

Determine whether each equation has no solutions, one solution, or every real number as a solution.

6. $10a - 2 = 10(a + 1) - 8$ 7. $7 - 2z = 5 - 2z$

8. $2p + 3p = p + 6$ 9. $-5k + 10 = 5(2 - k)$

10. $3(j + 2) = 3j + 2$

For Discussion

11. Write 5 equations that have no solutions.

12. Write 5 equations that have one solution.

13. Write 5 equations that have every real number as a solution.

Check Your Understanding

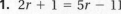

Solve each equation. (*Hint:* Some equations may not have a solution. Others may have infinitely many solutions.)

1. $2r + 1 = 5r - 11$

2. $4 - w = 3w + 1$

3. $16t + 9 = 2(8t + 1)$

4. $5u + 8 = 40 - 2u$

5. $\frac{3}{2}r + 4 = 10$

6. $4 + 11e = 2 + 5e + (2 + 6e)$

7. **a.** Write an equation that has $x = 3$ as a solution.

   b. Write an equation that has a variable on both sides and $x = 5$ as a solution.

   c. Write an equation that has a variable on both sides and $x = -11$ as a solution.

   d. Write an equation that has a variable on both sides and $x = \frac{5}{3}$ as a solution.

   e. Write an equation that has a variable on both sides but does not have any solutions.

8. Explain how you can use the basic moves to transform the equation $6x + 2y = 15$ into each of the following equations.

   a. $6x + 2y - 15 = 0$

   b. $0 = 15 - 6x - 2y$

   c. $2y = 15 - 6x$

   d. $y = \frac{15}{2} - 3x$

9. If $10(7a + 5) = 90$, what is $(7a + 15)$?

10. Tony says, "I'm thinking of a number. I do some things to it, and I end up with 36. The last two steps are add 11 and then multiply by 3. What do I get if the last two steps change to each of the following, and everything else stays the same?"

    a. Add 8 and then multiply by 8.

    b. Multiply by 5 and then subtract 20.

    c. Add 19 and then multiply by 5.

11. Suppose you know that the equation $x + y = 7$ is true. Which of these must be true also? Which must be false? Which might be true or false?

    a. $x + y + 6 = 12$ **b.** $x + y - 4 = 3$

    c. $3(x + y) = 28$ **d.** $xy = 12$

    e. $\dfrac{x + y}{7} = 1$ **f.** $7 = x + y$

    g. $x - y = 3$ **h.** $y = 7 - x$

    i. $x < 7$

On Your Own

Solve each equation. (*Hint:* Some equations may not have a solution. Some equations may have infinitely many solutions.)

12. $2a + 1 = 6a + 11$

13. $11 - 2(d - 1) = -2d + 13$

14. $4(n - 1) = 6n - 12$

15. Solve each equation.

    a. $25 = 3x + 5$ **b.** $3(x - 1) + 5 = 25$

    c. $3(x + 3) + 5 = 25$ **d.** $25 = 3(x - 7) + 5$

    e. $3(2x + 1) + 5 = 25$ **f.** $25 = 3(5 - 2y) + 5$

16. If you know that $3r + 2 = 9$, which of these must also be true? Which must be false? Which might be true or false?

    a. $2(3r + 2) = 18$ **b.** $3r + 22 = 20$

    c. $3r + 22 = 29$ **d.** $-9 = -2 - 3r$

    e. $3r - 9 = 0$ **f.** $6r + 4 = 18$

    g. $3r = 7$ **h.** $r = -4$

17. **Standardized Test Prep** What is the number of solutions for each of the following equations?

Go Online
www.successnetplus.com

I. $4s - 4 = 3(s - 3) + 5 + s$

II. $-3(t + 2) = 8(t + 1) - 11(t - 2)$

III. $5(t - 1) = -5(t + 4) + 15$

A. I has 0 solutions.

   II has 1 solution.

   III has more than 1 solution.

B. I has more than 1 solution.

   II has 1 solution.

   III has 1 solution.

C. I has 1 solution.

   II has more than 1 solution.

   III has 0 solutions.

D. I has more than 1 solution.

   II has 0 solutions.

   III has 1 solution.

Maintain Your Skills

18. Solve each equation.

   a. $5d - 2 = 2d + 10$

   b. $5d - 2 = 3d + 10$

   c. $5d - 2 = 4d + 10$

   d. $5d - 2 = 5d + 10$

   e. $5d - 2 = 6d + 10$

   f. $5d - 2 = 7d + 10$

   g. $5d - 2 = 8d + 10$

   h. Which equation has a different number of solutions than the other equations? Explain.

   i. Describe another pattern in the solutions.

19. Solve each equation.

   a. $4c + 2 = 4c - 1$

   b. $4c + 2 = 4c$

   c. $4c + 2 = 4c + 1$

   d. $4c + 2 = 4c + 2$

   e. $4c + 2 = 4c + 3$

   f. Which equation has a different number of solutions than the other equations? Explain.

Learning to use the Distributive Property is especially important when solving equations. It helps you avoid losing a negative sign somewhere and finding an incorrect result.

For You to Do

1. **What's Wrong Here?** Rebecca, Anna, and Jenna tried to solve the equation $40 - 4(x + 3) = 7x - 5$. They got three different results.

Rebecca

$40 - 4(x + 3) = 7x - 5$

$40 - 4x + 12 = 7x - 5$

$52 - 4x = 7x - 5$

$52 - 4x + 5 = 7x - 5 + 5$

$57 - 4x = 7x$

$57 - 4x + 4x = 7x + 4x$

$57 = 11x$

$\frac{57}{11} = x$

Anna

$40 - 4(x + 3) = 7x - 5$

$40 - 4x + 3 = 7x - 5$

$43 - 4x = 7x - 5$

$39x = 7x - 5$

$39x - 7x = 7x - 5 - 7x$

$32x = -5$

$x = -\frac{5}{32}$

Jenna

$40 - 4(x + 3) = 7x - 5$

$40 - 4x - 12 = 7x - 5$

$28 - 4x = 7x - 5$

$28 - 4x + 4x = 7x - 5 + 4x$

$28 = 11x - 5$

$28 + 5 = 11x - 5 + 5$

$33 = 11x$

$3 = x$

Who has the correct result? What mistakes did each of the others make?

Developing Habits of Mind

Repeat a familiar process. In Investigation 1C, you used an expansion box for multiplying numbers. Recall that to multiply $327 \cdot 6$, you made an expansion box similar to the one below.

	300	20	7
6	1800	120	42

Then you added all the numbers inside the box to get the product.

You can use an expansion box to apply the Distributive Property to expressions, too. Use an expansion box to multiply $7(3x - 4)$.

	$3x$	-4
7	$21x$	-28

So $7(3x - 4) = 21x + (-28) = 21x - 28$.

For You to Do

Expand each expression. It may be useful to use expansion boxes.

2. $3(16 - 2x)$

3. $7 - 5(y - 11)$

4. $2(3z + 1) - (z - 6)$

5. $11(a + 5b - 3c)$

As you get more comfortable with distributing expressions, it might seem unnecessary to set up expansion boxes every time you distribute an expression. They are a useful technique when you deal with more complicated expressions.

 **Exercises** *Practicing Habits of Mind*

Check Your Understanding

For Exercises 1–10, solve each equation.

1. $2(x + 3) = 15$

2. $5(j - 3) = 10(j - 2)$

3. $3(k - 4) + 6 = 2$

4. $-(x + 3) = 7$

5. $-(s + 2) = 4(s + 1)$

6. $-2(2w + 3) = 10$

7. $-(-3 - q) = -\frac{1}{2}(6q - 26)$

8. $4(e + 4) = 2(17 - 2e)$

9. $2(2x + 1) - 3(x - 5) = 18$

10. $-\left(z + \frac{2}{3}\right) = z$

11. **What's Wrong Here?** Using expansion boxes or some other method, show that $(a + b)^2$ does not necessarily equal $a^2 + b^2$.

12. Use this array to show that $4(a + b) = 4a + 4b$.

    $a\ a\ a\ a$
    $b\ b\ b\ b$

13. Use this array to show that $4(a + b + c) = 4a + 4b + 4c$.

    $a\ a\ a\ a$
    $b\ b\ b\ b$
    $c\ c\ c\ c$

14. Look at the arrays in Exercises 12 and 13. Make an array that illustrates this fact.

    $$7(x + y + z) = 7x + 7y + 7z$$

> The expression $(a + b)^2$ is equal to $(a + b)(a + b)$, since *squaring* means to multiply the expression by itself.

On Your Own

$5(4 + 5) = 5 \cdot 4 + 5 \cdot 5$

For Exercises 15–21, solve each equation.

15. $5(2a - 1) = 60$

16. $-(d - 4) = 13$

17. $15 = -5(x - 4)$

18. $3(x - 2) + 2(x - 2) = 40$

19. $28 - -7(2x - 3)$

20. $-4(p + 2) + 8 = 2(p - 1) - 7p + 15$

21. $2(5 - n) = 6 + 6n$

22. Use expansion boxes or another method to write each expression without parentheses.

    a. $12(2x - 7)$
    b. $3(4 - x)$
    c. $x(2x + 5)$
    d. $\frac{2}{3}(3x - 18)$
    e. $\frac{4}{7}(14x - 3)$
    f. $(-4)(3x - 6)$
    g. $(-3)(x^2 + 7x - 14)$
    h. $\left(-\frac{5}{6}\right)(12x + 18)$
    i. $\left(-\frac{1}{2}x\right)(7x^2 - 22)$

23. **Standardized Test Prep** Which expression equals $4z - 2az$?

    A. $-2z(2a - 2)$
    B. $-2(2z - az)$
    C. $-z(2a - 4)$
    D. $-z(-2a + 4)$

24. What's Wrong Here? Decide whether Jade solved each equation correctly. If Jade made a mistake, find the correct result. Explain her mistake.

Go Online
www.successnetplus.com

a. Problem $-(x - 3) = 13$

Jade's Solution

$$-(x - 3) = 13$$

$$-x - 3 = 13$$

$$-x = 16$$

$$x = -16$$

b. Problem $-\left(\dfrac{1}{4} - u\right) = 3u - \dfrac{17}{4}$

Jade's Solution

$$-\left(\dfrac{1}{4} - u\right) = 3u - \dfrac{17}{4}$$

$$-\dfrac{1}{4} + u = 3u - \dfrac{17}{4}$$

$$-\dfrac{1}{4} = 2u - \dfrac{17}{4}$$

$$-\dfrac{1}{4} + \dfrac{17}{4} = 2u$$

$$\dfrac{16}{4} = 2u$$

$$4 = 2u$$

$$2 = u$$

c. Problem $-3(v - 8) = 5(v + 1)$

Jade's Solution

$$-3(v - 8) = 5(v + 1)$$

$$-3v - 24 = 5v + 5$$

$$-24 = 8v + 5$$

$$-29 = 8v$$

$$-\dfrac{29}{8} = v$$

Maintain Your Skills

25. Solve each equation.

a. $5x = 2x + 21$

b. $5(x - 100) = 2(x - 100) + 21$

c. $5(x - 40) = 2(x - 40) + 21$

d. $5(x - 90) = 2(x - 90) + 21$

e. $5(x - 8) = 2(x - 8) + 21$

f. $5(x + 100) = 2(x + 100) + 21$

g. Find a pattern in the relationship between the calculations and the result.

Mathematical 2C Reflections

In this investigation, you learned the basic moves for solving an equation. An equation may have only one solution, more than one solution, or no solution. These questions will help you summarize what you have learned.

1. Give an example of an equation that has no solution. Give an example of an equation that has infinitely many solutions.

2. For each equation, determine whether $x = -3$ is a solution.

   a. $4x + 1 = 2x - 5$ **b.** $x - 4 = -2x$

   c. $2(x + 1) + 5 = x + 2$ **d.** $2x + 3 - 4x = -3x$

3. Solve each equation.

   a. $6x + 3 = 2x + 7$ **b.** $4m - 3 = m + 12$

4. Solve each equation. (*Hint:* Some equations may not have a solution. Other equations may have infinitely many solutions.)

   a. $5x - 6 = 3x + 4$ **b.** $x + 2 + 3x = 4(x - 1)$

   c. $2(3x + 4) + 2 = 6x + 10$ **d.** $3 - x = 2x + 9$

5. Solve the equation $2(m + 3) - 4(2m + 1) = m - 3(2 + m)$.

6. How can you solve an equation for which backtracking does not work?

7. How can you visualize an equation using the number line?

8. Solve the equation $5x = x + 24$.

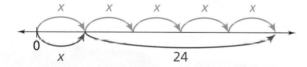

When you add to one side of an equation, you must add the same amount to the other side, or the solutions will change.

Vocabulary

In this investigation, you saw these terms. Make sure you understand what each one means and how to use it.

- **basic moves for solving equations**
- **linear equation**
- **theorem**

Investigation 2D

Word Problems

In *Word Problems,* you will learn to write an equation to represent a situation. Then you will use the basic moves to solve the equation, and thus solve the word problem.

By the end of this investigation, you will be able to answer questions like these.

1. How can you use the guess-check-generalize method to solve a word problem?

2. How do you solve for y in a two-variable equation?

3. What number plus one fourth of itself equals 560?

You will learn how to

• use the guess-check-generalize method for solving word problems

• solve a two-variable equation

• build an equation from a mathematical situation

You will develop these habits and skills:

• Use the guess-check-generalize method to solve a mathematical problem.

• Interpret a situation and represent it mathematically.

Diagrams and symbols can help you solve a problem.

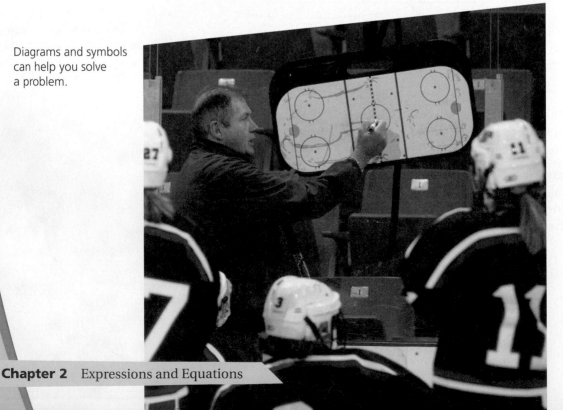

2.14 Getting Started

**Activating Prior Knowledge
Exploring New Ideas**

You can solve a number puzzle using any method that works. Later in this investigation, you will learn a systematic method that you can use with any puzzle.

For You to Explore

1. Chiko says, "There's an amazing fact about the number I'm thinking of. I call this fact the four 4's. Using my number, you can get four different answers if you add 4, subtract 4, multiply by 4, or divide by 4. That's not impressive, but if you add all the answers, you get 60."

   a. Is Chiko's number 12?

   b. Is Chiko's number 8?

   c. Find Chiko's number. Describe how to find it.

2. Find the number with four 5's (add 5, subtract 5, multiply by 5, and divide by 5) that have a sum of 144.

3. This problem is from a collection of puzzles made around A.D. 500. The puzzle is about the Greek mathematician Diophantus, who lived around A.D. 250.

   > His childhood lasted one sixth of his life; he grew a beard after one twelfth more; one seventh later, he was married. Five years later, he had a son. The son lived exactly half as long as his father. Four years later, Diophantus died. How old was he?

   a. Guess how old Diophantus was when he died. Check your guess. Do not worry about making a good guess!

   b. Make another guess. Write the steps you use to find whether your guess is correct.

   c. Suppose your guess is a number n. How can you check whether n is the correct result?

   d. Find the correct result without guessing.

4. Cameron tells about his trip to the Big Books store. "How awful! They want me to join their club to get 10% off. It costs $15 to join the club. It costs $8 more to buy my books if I join the club than if I don't!" How much do Cameron's books cost without joining the club?

Diophantus' age is an integer.

Habits of Mind

Look for a relationship. These steps are the same ones you follow in checking numerical guesses.

Exercises *Practicing Habits of Mind*

On Your Own

5. Is each statement true for all, some, or no numbers?
   If it is true for all or no numbers, explain.

   Equations are statements about numbers. They can be true for all, some, or no numbers.

   a. Adding 6 to a number gives the same result as multiplying that number by 3.

   b. $n + 6 = 3n$

   c. Subtracting 3 from a number gives the same result as adding 3 to that number.

   d. $5n - 6 = 3n + 34$

   e. $2n - 6 = 34$

   f. Doubling a number and then adding 6 gives the same result as adding 3 to a number and then doubling the result.

   g. $n - 3 = n + 3$

   h. $2n + 6 = 2(n + 3)$

   i. Subtracting 5 from a number and then squaring the result gives the result 16.

6. Vanessa works 32 hours per week at her job. Her boss offers her a full-time position (40 hours per week) and a $2-per-hour raise. She says, "This is great! Now I'll make $200 more per week!" What is Vanessa's hourly wage before the raise?

In Exercise 6, you can guess Vanessa's pre-raise wage and then check your guess. An easy wage to begin with is $10 per hour.

7. For each statement in Exercise 5 that is true for some numbers, find what numbers make the statement true.

8. a. Write About It Explain why the equation $5n + 8 = 3n + 22$ has the same solution as the equation $5n + 8 - 3n = 22$.

  b. Solve the equation $7n - 13 = 4n + 35$ by using basic moves.

  c. Solve the equation $13(n - 1) = 5(2n + 7)$ by using the Distributive Property and basic moves.

Maintain Your Skills

9. Solve each equation.

  a. $3x - 7 = 13 - x$

  b. $3(a + 2) - 7 = 13 - (a + 2)$

  c. $3(5b) - 7 - 13 - (5b)$

  d. $3(8 - c) - 7 = 13 - (8 - c)$

  e. $3(12 + 2d) - 7 = 13 - (12 + 2d)$

  f. How can you solve each equation without using the Distributive Property?

Habits of Mind

Look for relationships. Does your solution to part (a) help you solve parts (b)–(f)? Explain.

10. Solve each equation.

  a. $5x - 3 = x + 14$

  b. $7a - 3 = 3a + 14$

  c. $5m - 19 = m - 2$

  d. $-2q - 6 = -6q + 11$

  e. What pattern do you find when you solve these equations? How does the pattern relate to Exercise 9?

  f. Write another equation that fits the pattern in this exercise.

Go Online
Video Tutor
www.successnetplus.com

2.15 Building Equations

Many students are good equation solvers. Sometimes the hardest part is setting up the equation when you are solving a word problem. In this lesson, you will learn the **guess-check-generalize method** to find an equation for a word problem.

Remember...

To *solve* an equation, you find all the numbers that make the equation true.

Example

Problem Vanessa works 32 hours per week at her job. Her boss offers her a full-time position (40 hours per week) and a $2-per-hour raise. She says, "This is great! Now I'll make $200 more per week!" What is Vanessa's hourly wage before the raise?

Solution Use the guess-check-generalize method to write an equation. Here is how the method works.

First, guess what Vanessa's hourly wage was before the raise. The point of this method is not to guess the correct answer, but to learn how to check a guess. Suppose you guess $10 per hour.

Next, check your guess. It is important to keep track of the steps.

	Check	Step
1	If Vanessa made $10 per hour before her raise, she makes $10 + $2, or $12, per hour after her raise.	Add $2 to her wage before the raise.
2	Before her raise, she made $320 per week.	Multiply her wage before her raise by 32.
3	After her raise, she makes $480 per week.	Multiply her wage after her raise by 40.
4	If the guess $10 is correct, she makes $320 plus $200, or $520, after her raise.	Add 200 to the result of step 2.
5	This $520 should equal the amount in step 3. It doesn't, so $10 is incorrect. That's okay.	Compare this sum to the result in step 3.

You can draw lines between each step in the check to help you keep track of the steps.

Repeat the process until the steps become automatic. The crucial point is that you understand how you can check whether any guess is correct. Suppose your second guess is that Vanessa's wage before her raise was $13 per hour.

	Check	Step
1	Now Vanessa makes $13 + $2, or $15, per hour.	Add $2 to her wage before the raise.
2	Before, she made 32 • $13 = $416 per week.	Multiply her wage before her raise by 32.
3	Today, she makes 40 • $15 = $600 per week.	Multiply her wage after her raise by 40.
4	If the guess $13 is correct, then she makes $416 plus $200, or $616, after her raise.	Add 200 to the result of step 2.
5	This $616 should equal the $600 in step 3. It doesn't, so $13 is incorrect.	Compare this sum to the result in step 3.

Finally, generalize by making your guess a variable. Let w equal Vanessa's wage before the raise. Apply the same steps shown above to w:

	Check	Step
1	Now Vanessa makes $w + 2$ dollars per hour.	Add $2 to her wage before the raise.
2	Before, she made $32 \cdot w = 32w$ dollars per week.	Multiply her wage before her raise by 32.
3	Today, she makes $40 \cdot (w + 2) = 40(w + 2)$ dollars per week.	Multiply her wage after her raise by 40.
4	The sum $32w + 200$ should equal $40(w + 2)$. The correct equation is $32w + 200 = 40(w + 2)$.	Add 200 to the result of step 2. The sum should equal the product in step 3.

The last line of the check gives you the equation $32w + 200 = 40(w + 2)$. Many algebra students like this method. Try it!

For You to Do

1. Solve the equation $32w + 200 = 40(w + 2)$.

2. What is Vanessa's wage before her raise? After her raise?

3. Recheck your result.

Exercises *Practicing Habits of Mind*

Check Your Understanding

1. Ancient Egyptian mathematicians used the concept of *false position* to solve equations. You guess a convenient answer and then adjust it to find the correct answer. Here's an example.

   A number plus one fourth of itself equals 210. What is the number?

   a. A convenient guess is 4. Why is 4 a convenient guess?

   b. Suppose you guess 4. What is the result of the calculation a number plus one fourth of itself?

   c. Suppose you guess 12. What is the result of the calculation a number plus one fourth of itself? How is that result related to the result of guessing 4?

   d. Use the guess-check-generalize method to solve this exercise.

> You call this method *false position* since you assume an incorrect answer is correct. You check the incorrect result to find the correct one.

2. Last summer, Katie mowed lawns to earn money. She mowed 35 lawns per week and charged $6 per lawn. This summer, Katie wants to earn an additional $150 per week. She will raise her price to $8 and find more customers.

   a. If Katie finds 4 new customers and still keeps her former customers, will she earn an additional $150 per week?

   b. If Katie finds 13 new customers, will she earn an additional $150 per week?

   c. If Katie finds 8 new customers, will she earn an additional $150 per week?

   d. Use the guess-check-generalize method to build an equation for finding the number of new customers Katie needs to earn an additional $150.

   e. Solve your equation.

3. Suppose Katie charges $9 per lawn. How many new customers will she need to find to earn an additional $150 per week?

4. Tony has a $100 gift certificate at a music store Web site. The store offers a 15% discount off the retail price of CDs. Tony must also pay $12 for shipping per order. Find whether Tony can buy each order given.

   a. 6 CDs for $15.99 each

   b. 7 CDs for $15.99 each

   c. 2 CDs for $15.99 each and 5 CDs for $11.99 each

   d. Tony wants to spend exactly $100 including the discount and shipping cost. What is the greatest total retail price he can afford?

5. In 36 years, Anna will be five times as old as she is today. How old is Anna? Use the guess-check-generalize method.

> Katie hopes all her customers still want to hire her after she raises the price.

On Your Own

6. Derman says, "I'm halfway through reading my book. If I read another 84 pages, I'll be two thirds of the way through my book." How many pages are in Derman's book?

7. Seventeen years ago, Arnold was $\frac{2}{3}$ as old as he is now. How old is Arnold?

> Start by making a guess.

8. **Standardized Test Prep** Use a calculator. Five years ago, Allen was two years older than $\frac{5}{6}$ of his age today. What is his age today?

   A. 35

   B. 37

   C. 42

   D. cannot be determined

9. If Cameron pays $15 to join the Big Books club, he gets 10% off the price of each book. He wants to decide whether to join the club. For each amount given that he spends on books, will he save money by joining the club?

   a. $70

   b. $250

   c. $100

   d. How much money does Cameron need to spend so that the cost of his books is the same whether he joins the club or not?

Go Online
www.successnetplus.com

10. **What's Wrong Here?** Travis solved the equation below incorrectly. Here are his steps.

$$x + 5 - \frac{1}{10}x = 12 + \frac{1}{2}x$$

$$\frac{11}{10}x + 5 = 12 + \frac{1}{2}x$$

$$\frac{11}{10}x + 5 - \frac{1}{2}x = 12 + \frac{1}{2}x - \frac{1}{2}x$$

$$\frac{6}{10}x + 5 - 5 = 12 - 5$$

$$\frac{6}{10}x = 7$$

$$x = \frac{70}{6}$$

$$= \frac{35}{3}$$

a. Show that Travis found the incorrect result.

b. Explain what Travis did wrong.

c. Solve the equation correctly.

11. Mr. Rodriquez comments on a recent test. "Well, the class average on that test is exactly 83. If I take away the best score, the average is exactly 82. Fine work, Anya." If there are 16 students in the class, what is the best score?

12. Taylor gets a $100 gift certificate to a music store for her birthday. She buys seven CDs and has $16 left on her gift certificate. The CDs cost the same amount of money. How much does each CD cost?

Maintain Your Skills

13. Find the value of x that makes each equation true.

a. $5x - 3 = x + 15$

b. $6x - 3 = x + 15$

c. $10x - 3 = x + 15$

d. $99x - 3 = x + 15$

e. $181x - 3 = x + 15$

f. These equations have the form $Ax - 3 = x + 15$. How does the solution x change as A increases?

g. **Take It Further** Solve $Ax - 3 = x + 15$ to find an expression in terms of A.

To solve *in terms of* A means to find the solution in which x equals some expression that may have A in it.

2.16 Solving Word Problems

In this lesson, you will solve more advanced word problems. You will combine an ability to set up equations and an ability to work with percentages or fractions. The guess-check-generalize method can help you find the correct equation.

For You to Do

1. **What's Wrong Here?** Tony solved the following problem incorrectly using the guess-check-generalize method.

   Mr. Corrado buys 60 bagels. He gets a 25% discount on bagels. The total cost of the bagels with the discount is $24.75. How much does a bagel cost without the discount?

   Tony explains, "First, I guess that a bagel costs $1. I check this guess and keep track of my steps in this table."

	Check	Step
1	If a bagel costs $1, then 60 bagels cost $60 \cdot 1 = 60$.	Multiply the cost of a bagel by 60.
2	Next I find the discount. It's a 25% discount, so that's $60 \cdot (0.25) = 15$.	Multiply the cost of the bagels by 0.25.
3	I check whether this is the correct cost: $15 \stackrel{?}{=} 24.75$.	Compare with 24.75.
4	It's not correct, so I'll make another guess.	

   "For my second guess, I try $2 and apply the same steps."

	Check	Step
1	$60 \cdot 2 = 120$	Multiply the cost of a bagel by 60.
2	$120 \cdot (0.25) = 30$	Multiply the cost of the bagels by 0.25.
3	$30 \stackrel{?}{=} 24.75$	Compare with 24.75.
4	It's not correct.	

"I know what the steps are, so I try using a variable *b* to stand for the cost of the bagels."

	Check	Step
1	$60 \cdot b = 60b$	Multiply the cost of a bagel by 60.
2	$60b \cdot (0.25) = 15b$	Multiply the cost of the bagels by 0.25.
3	I check whether this is the correct cost: $15b \stackrel{?}{=} 24.75$.	Compare with 24.75.
4	That's my equation.	

"Finally, I solve that equation."

$$15b = 24.75$$
$$b = 1.65$$

"So, one bagel costs $1.65."

What is wrong with Tony's steps? Find the correct result.

For Discussion

2. Use the guess-check-generalize method to write an equation for this situation.

   Al drives from Boston to Washington, D.C., and then returns. On his trip to Washington, he travels 60 miles per hour. On his return trip, he travels 50 miles per hour. His trip to Boston takes an hour and a half longer than his trip to Washington. How far apart are Washington and Boston?

Exercises *Practicing Habits of Mind*

Check Your Understanding

1. Ms. Ramirez buys school supplies for her students. She gets a $12 bulk discount. The new cost of supplies is 80% of the original cost.

   a. If d is the cost of the school supplies, explain why you can use the equation $\frac{d - 12}{d} = \frac{8}{10}$ to represent Ms. Ramirez's purchase. What is the significance of $\frac{8}{10}$ in this equation?

   b. Explain why the value of d cannot be zero in the equation given.

   c. Multiply each side of the equation by d (a basic move). Write the resulting equation.

   d. Multiply each side by 10 (another basic move) to remove all fractions from the equation.

   e. Find the value of d by solving the equation.

   > You can multiply by d, because you know that d is not zero. The supplies are not free!

   For Exercises 2–4, find each probability. **Probability** describes the likelihood that a specific event will happen. For example, the probability that today is Thursday is $\frac{1}{7}$, since there are 7 days in each week, and only 1 day is Thursday. You can represent a probability as a fraction or a decimal. 100% becomes 1 when written as a decimal, and 50% becomes 0.5.

2. a. On Monday, a meteorologist says that there is 30% chance of rain. What is the probability that it will rain on Monday?

   b. What is the probability that it will not rain on Monday?

   c. On Tuesday, the meteorologist says that there is 0.1 probability that it will rain. What is the probability that it will not rain on Tuesday?

   d. Suppose the probability that it will rain today is p. Find the probability that it will not rain today, in terms of p.

3. A meteorologist says that there is a 50% greater chance of rain than no rain on Wednesday. What is the probability that it will rain on Wednesday?

4. A meteorologist says that there is a 50% chance of rain on Saturday and a 50% chance of rain on Sunday. He concludes that it will definitely rain at least once next weekend. Does his conclusion sound reasonable?

5. Heidi tries to qualify for a gymnastics team. Qualifying is based on the average of six event scores. Heidi knows she needs at least a 7.5 average in the six events to make the team. Her scores for the first five events are 6.4, 8.0, 8.1, 6.5, and 8.2.

> *Average* in the events refers to the mean, not the median.

   a. What is Heidi's mean event score for five events? What is her median score?

   b. Suppose Heidi scores a 7.6 in the final event. Will she make the team? Show your steps.

   c. Make another guess about the minimum score Heidi needs to make the team. Check your guess. Keep track of your steps.

   d. Use the guess-check-generalize method to find an equation for the minimum score Heidi needs to make the team.

   e. Solve your equation.

6. **Take it Further** Use Exercise 5.

   a. The rules change so that you exclude the highest and lowest scores before finding the average. What score does Heidi now need to make the team?

   b. Suppose you exclude the highest and lowest scores. What is the highest possible average Heidi can get? What is the lowest possible average?

On Your Own

7. Ms. Meyer remarks, "Isn't it great? This theater usually charges $9 per student. On Student Night, I can bring 47 more students for the same cost!" How many students can Ms. Meyer bring to the theater in the photo on the right?

8. Chi has a big pile of nickels. He says, "Even if I use 100 of these nickels, I'll still have 95% of my original pile." How many nickels does Chi have?

9. Eight years from now, Bianca will be 50% older than she is now. How old is Bianca?

10. A round trip from Seattle, Washington, to Orlando, Florida, is one of the longest flight paths in the continental United States. The jet stream that blows from west to east affects the flight's average speed. A plane flying nonstop from Seattle to Orlando can fly at an average speed of 523 miles per hour. The same plane flying from Orlando to Seattle travels at an average speed of 415 miles per hour. The full round trip takes exactly 11 hours. To the nearest mile, how far is Seattle from Orlando?

Go Online
www.successnetplus.com

11. **Standardized Test Prep** Eduardo goes to a restaurant for lunch. He orders a turkey sandwich for $6.75 and a fruit smoothie for $3.95. Eduardo must also pay a sales tax and a tip. The sales tax is 8%. The tip is 15% of the pretax cost of the meal. Which expression shows how Eduardo computes his final bill?

A. $6.75 + 3.95(0.23)$

B. $(6.75 + 3.95)(0.23)$

C. $6.75 + 3.95 + (6.75 + 3.95)(0.23)$

D. $6.75 + 3.95 + (6.75 + 3.95)(0.08) + (6.75 + 3.95)(0.08)(0.15)$

12. **What's Wrong Here?** Derman tried to solve the equation $20 - 3(x - 2) = 9x - 4$.

$$20 - 3(x - 2) = 9x - 4$$
$$20 - 3x - 6 = 9x - 4$$
$$14 \quad 3x = 9x \quad 4$$
$$14 - 3x + 4 = 9x - 4 + 4$$
$$18 - 3x + 3x = 9x + 3x$$
$$18 = 12x$$
$$\frac{18}{12} = x$$
$$\frac{3}{2} = x$$

a. Show that Derman found the incorrect result.

b. Explain what Derman did wrong.

c. Solve the equation correctly.

Maintain Your Skills

For Exercises 13 and 14, you do not need to solve the equations. Determine which equation in each set of three equations has no solution. Explain.

13. $2x + 5 = 3x + 11$

$2x + 5 = 19x + 11$

$2x + 5 = 2x + 11$

14. $-11k + 14 = -3k - 25$

$-11k + 14 = -11k - 25$

$-11k + 14 = 14k - 11$

More Than One Variable

Many equations relate variables to each other. Equations with more than one variable, such as $3x + 4y = 12$, often have more than one solution.

Example 1

Problem High-definition television screens are different sizes. However, they all have the same proportions. If you divide the width of an HDTV screen by its height, the result is $\frac{16}{9}$. If you label the height h and the width w, then every HDTV screen satisfies the two-variable equation.

$$\frac{w}{h} = \frac{16}{9}$$

Find the width of each HDTV screen for the height given in inches.

HDTV means high-definition television.

a. 18

b. 36

c. 30

Solution For parts (a)–(c), use a single equation, $\frac{w}{h} = \frac{16}{9}$, instead of setting up three separate equations.

Use the basic move of multiplying each side by the same quantity. Multiply each side by h.

$$\frac{w}{h} \cdot h = \frac{16}{9} \cdot h$$

$$w = \frac{16h}{9}$$

You can "eyeball" different-sized HDTV screens and see that they are all proportional.

What is the importance of this? You have solved the equation for w. For any value of h, you can find w. Here are the results for each problem using the equation solved for w.

a. Find w. Let height h equal 18.

$$w = \frac{16 \cdot 18}{9}$$

$$= 32$$

b. Find w. Let height h equal 36.

$$w = \frac{16 \cdot 36}{9}$$

$$= 64$$

c. Find w. Let height h equal 30.

$$w = \frac{16 \cdot 30}{9}$$

$$= \frac{480}{9}$$

$$= \frac{160}{3}$$

Developing Habits of Mind

Represent the solution with a variable. The previous example illustrates solving for one variable. When you solve for w, you get w on one side of the equation by itself. The equation $w = \frac{16h}{9}$ is correctly solved for w, but the equation $w = \frac{16h}{9} + 3w$ is not solved for w, since there is a w term on both sides.

One way to think about these equations is to treat any variable you are not solving for as a number that you cannot combine with other numbers. Solving $3x + 4y = 12$ is just like solving $3(176) + 4y = 12$. You follow the same steps. However, you will not get an equation like this.

$y =$ some number

Instead, you will get an equation like this.

$y =$ some expression involving x

Example 2

Problem Solve the equation $7y - 13 = 2x + 3y$ for y.

Solution To solve for y, use basic moves to get the variable y by itself on the left side of the equation. Since there are y terms on each side of the equation, you can subtract $3y$ from each side.

$$7y - 13 = 2x + 3y$$
$$7y - 13 - 3y = 2x + 3y - 3y$$
$$4y - 13 = 2x$$

You want only y on the left side. So you add 13 to each side.

$$4y - 13 = 2x$$
$$4y - 13 + 13 = 2x + 13$$
$$4y = 2x + 13$$

Finally, divide each side by 4.

$$4y = 2x + 13$$
$$\frac{4y}{4} = \frac{2x + 13}{4}$$
$$y = \frac{2x + 13}{4}$$

To check this equation, you can try an "easy" value of x, such as 10, in the final equation and find y. Do these values work in the original equation?

> **Remember...**
>
> *Solve for y* means that the final equation must have the variable y by itself on one side of the equation, and no y's are on the other side!

> You can say that you solved the equation $y = \frac{2x + 13}{4}$ for y *in terms of x*. The phrase *in terms of x* means the solution may have x in it.

For Discussion

1. Solve the equation $3x + y + 15 = 2(x + 1) - 5$ for y.

Exercises *Practicing Habits of Mind*

Check Your Understanding

1. Solve the equation $6x + 3y = 5x - 13 + 2y$ for y.

2. Example 2 shows that the equation $7y - 13 = 2x + 3y$ is equivalent to the equation $y = \frac{2x + 13}{4}$.

   The first basic move is to subtract $3y$ from each side of the equation.

   a. Suppose x is 0. Use either equation to find the value of y. Think about which equation might be easier to use.

   b. Suppose x is 10. Use either equation to find the value of y.

   c. Suppose y is 0. Use either equation to find the value of x.

   d. Is the pair (20, 13) a solution to the equation $2x + 3y = 7y - 13$? Explain.

   e. Is the pair (20, 13) a solution to the equation $y = \frac{1}{2}x + 3\frac{1}{4}$? Explain.

   Remember...

   The notation (20, 13) means that $x = 20$ and $y = 13$.

3. If w is the width of a standard television set, and h is the height, then w and h satisfy the equation $\frac{w}{h} = \frac{4}{3}$.

   a. Solve for w.

   b. Solve for h.

   c. What is the height of a standard TV set that is 15 inches wide?

   d. How wide is a standard TV set that is 21 inches high?

   e. Stores advertise TV sizes by giving the corner-to-corner diagonal length of the screen. If a TV screen is 21 inches high, how long is its diagonal?

4. The equation $5x + 6y = 90$ relates x and y.

   a. Suppose x is 10 and y is 6. Do these values make the equation true? Explain.

   b. Suppose x is 9. Find a value of y that makes the equation true. Find two values of y that make it false.

   c. Find four pairs of points (x, y) that make the equation true.

   d. **Take It Further** Locate the points you found in part (c) on a coordinate grid. Are they related?

5. In the Range Game, a player guesses the price of an object. The player wins the object if the guess is no more than $75 from the actual value.

   a. If you win with a guess of $2599, what is the range of the actual price?

   b. If the actual price is $4599, what is the range of possible guesses that allows you to win?

   c. If g is the amount you guess, and p is the actual price of the object, describe the situation in terms of g and p.

6. **Take It Further** Javan manages a picture framing shop. When he frames a photograph, he mats it on a piece of cardboard. He allows 2 inches of cardboard on each side of the photo.

   Javan realizes that he can use an equation to determine whether a piece of cardboard is the appropriate size for matting a photograph. He says, "If h is the height of the cardboard, and w is the width, then a piece of cardboard will be the right size if it satisfies the equation $\frac{w-4}{h-4} = \frac{4}{3}$."

   Javan typically trims the photographs so that the ratio of the width to height is 4 : 3.

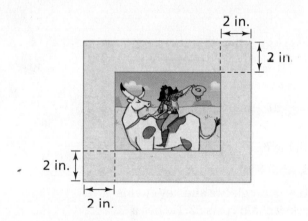

   a. Explain how Javan found the equation.

   b. Solve the equation for w.

   c. If the piece of cardboard is 12 inches high, how wide is it?

   d. If the piece of cardboard is 15 inches high, how wide is it?

   e. If the piece of cardboard is 20 inches high, how wide is it?

7. Chi has nickels and dimes. He has a total of 90 cents. Let n stand for the number of nickels that Chi has. Let d stand for the number of dimes that Chi has.

   a. Can Chi have 4 nickels and 8 dimes? Explain.

   b. Can Chi have 6 nickels and 4 dimes? Explain.

   c. Write an equation using n and d to find how much money Chi has.

   d. Solve your equation for d.

   e. **Take It Further** Can Chi have an odd number of nickels? Explain.

8. Which of these statements are true for all numbers? Not true for all numbers? If a statement is not true for all numbers, change the statement to make it true for all numbers.

Go Online
www.successnetplus.com

    a. If $y = 2x + 4$, then $5y = 5(2x + 4) = 10x + 4$.

    b. 25% of a number n is $0.25n$.

    c. For any numbers a and b, $3a + 4b$ is the same as $7(a + b)$.

    d. For any numbers a and b, $3a \cdot 4b$ is the same as $12ab$.

    e. For any number m, $0.9m - 2m$ is the same as $-2.9m$.

    f. The expression $-4(d + 6)$ means the same as the expression $-4d + 24$.

    g. The fraction $\frac{10x}{10y}$ has the same value as the fraction $\frac{x}{y}$.

    h. The fraction $\frac{x + 3}{3}$ is the same as x.

9. The perimeter of a rectangle is 10 centimeters more than four times the difference between its length and width.

    a. If the rectangle's length is ℓ and its width is w, what is its perimeter?

    b. Explain why the equation $2\ell + 2w = 10 + 4(\ell - w)$ is true for the rectangle.

    c. Solve the equation in part (b) for the variable ℓ.

    d. If the rectangle's width is 10 centimeters, what is the length?

10. **Standardized Test Prep** Nathan wants to buy snow globes and key chains for his friends. A snow globe costs $3, and a key chain costs $2. He has a total of $15 to spend. If Nathan wants to buy two snow globes, what is the greatest number of key chains he can buy?

    A. 3   **B.** 4   **C.** 5   **D.** 6

    For Exercises 11 and 12, use the following information. Corey needs at least $2.10 in postage. She has $.41 letter stamps and $.26 postcard stamps. Let ℓ equal the number of letter stamps and p equal the number of postcard stamps. The amount of postage is exact when $41\ell + 26p = 210$.

11. **a.** If Corey has 3 letter stamps, can she make exactly $2.10 in postage by adding postcard stamps?

    b. If Corey has 3 letter stamps, what is the least number of postcard stamps she needs?

    c. If $\ell = 3$, find the value of p that makes the equation $41\ell + 26p = 210$ true. How can you use this equation for part (b)?

12. a. Solve the equation $41\ell + 26p = 210$ for the variable p. Write the equation in the form $p =$ an expression.

b. Copy and complete the table to show the minimum number of postcard stamps Corey needs when she has different numbers of letter stamps.

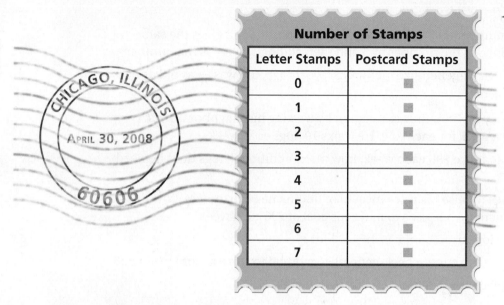

Number of Stamps

Letter Stamps	Postcard Stamps
0	■
1	■
2	■
3	■
4	■
5	■
6	■
7	■

Even though the equation gives a decimal answer, Corey cannot split up the postcard stamps. How can she round the answer correctly? What is the result when there is enough postage using only the letter stamps?

c. Take It Further What is the least expensive choice Corey can make using letter and postcard stamps?

Maintain Your Skills

13. Solve for y in each equation. Write the equation in the form y equals an expression. Then solve for x.

a. $5x + 6y = 90$

b. $11x + 13y = 150$

14. Solve for each variable in the equation $5x + 6y + 7z = 90$.

a. x

b. y

c. z

d. How are the results in parts (a)–(c) related?

Mathematical 2D Reflections

In this investigation, you learned to the use the guess-check-generalize method to solve word problems. For two-variable equations, you learned to solve for either variable. These questions will help you summarize what you have learned.

1. Adding 5 to a number and then multiplying the number by 2 gives the same result as multiplying the number by 5 and then adding 1. What is the number?

2. Use the guess-check-generalize method. Six years ago, Bill was $\frac{1}{4}$ as old as he is now. How old is Bill?

3. Jim raises money for his summer vacation by walking his neighbors' dogs. He charges $8 a week for each dog. He walks 10 dogs each week.

   a. If he wants to make $96 each week, how many additional dogs does he need to walk?

   b. If Jim decides to raise his price instead of finding new customers, how much should he increase his price to make his goal of $96 each week?

4. Solve the equation $2x + 3y = x - 4y + 10$ for y.

5. How can you use the guess-check-generalize method to solve a word problem?

6. How do you solve for y in a two-variable equation?

7. What number plus one fourth of itself equals 560?

Vocabulary

In this investigation, you saw these terms. Make sure you understand what each one means and how to use it.

- **guess-check-generalize method**
- **probability**

She scores a goal! Her team solved a problem.

Project: Using Mathematical Habits

Good Questions About Perfect Squares

Mathematicians ask questions about numbers to understand the underlying structure of numbers. In this project, you will answer some questions about the sums of perfect squares. A perfect square is an integer that is the square of another integer. For example, each of the following numbers is a perfect square.

$$1 = 1^2 \qquad 4 = 2^2 \qquad 9 = 3^2$$

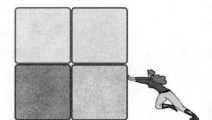

Finding Perfect-Square Sums

Paulo writes a few sums of two perfect squares.

$$1^2 + 1^2 = 2$$
$$1^2 + 2^2 = 5$$

Based on these examples, he asks this good question about positive integers. Is every integer the sum of two nonzero perfect squares?

1. Can you write every integer as the sum of two nonzero perfect squares? If you can, tell how to find the two perfect squares for a given integer. If not, find an integer that cannot be written as the sum of two nonzero perfect squares.

   A table similar to an addition table can help you find all possible sums of two perfect squares. Use an addition table with the squares 1, 4, 9, 16, 25, 36, 49, 64, 81, and 100 along each axis to answer Exercises 2 and 3.

2. Find two perfect squares that are both the sum of two perfect squares.

3. Are there any integers you can write as the sum of two nonzero squares in two different ways? Explain. Note that

   $$5 = 1^2 + 2^2 \text{ and } 5 = 2^2 + 1^2$$

   do *not* represent two different ways to write 5 as the sum of two perfect squares.

Asking Good Questions

An important habit is asking a good question. Paulo based his question on two examples. The following exercises show three more ways to come up with good questions.

For Exercises 4–6, start with each question given. Replace each italicized word with another word. Do you think your question is a good one? Explain.

4. Is every integer the sum of two nonzero perfect *squares*?

5. Is every integer the *sum* of two nonzero perfect squares?

6. Is every integer the sum of *two* nonzero perfect squares? Write a question different from any you wrote in Exercises 4 and 5.

7. You can ask a good question by extending an idea. Paulo's question is about positive integers only. Does it suggest a good question you could ask about negative integers? Explain.

8. Good answers to good questions can lead to more good questions. Write a good question that Exercise 2 suggests. Do you already know the answer to your question?

In **Investigation 2A,** you learned how to

- state the need for variables and expressions
- determine the appropriate order for evaluating a numerical expression and explain why the order works
- express word problems using variables and mathematical notation
- write formulas using two or more variables

The following questions will help you check your understanding.

1. Use the variable x as your starting number. Write the expression you get by following the steps. Simplify the expression.
   - Choose a number.
   - Multiply by 3.
   - Add 4.
   - Multiply by 5.
   - Subtract 2.

2. Evaluate $2(3x + 5) + x$ for each value of x.
   a. 2
   b. 5
   c. -3
   d. Simplify the expression. Then evaluate the expression for $x = 2$.

3. Name the property that each equation illustrates.
   a. $5 + 4 = 4 + 5$
   b. $(c \cdot 7) \cdot 8 = c \cdot (7 \cdot 8)$
   c. $w = w + 0$
   d. $9 \cdot \frac{1}{9} = 1$
   e. $2(8 + 3) = 2(8) + 2(3)$

4. Use the any-order, any-grouping properties and the Distributive Property. Simplify each expression. Remember to combine like terms.
   a. $3(x + 5) + 8$
   b. $2(4x - 3) + 7(x + 2)$
   c. $3(2x - 8) - 4(x - 5)$
   d. $2(3x - 4) - (2x - 1)$

In **Investigation 2B,** you learned how to

- reverse, or undo, a series of steps
- understand the relationship between an equation and its solutions
- use backtracking to solve a problem

The following questions will help you check your understanding.

5. Describe how to undo each instruction, if possible. If not possible, explain.
   a. Add 3.
   b. Multiply by 5.
   c. Find the sum of the digits.
   d. Divide by 10.

6. Write each algebraic expression as a statement of an operation.
   a. $x^2 + 15$ b. $\frac{y + 9}{7}$
   c. $5(8b + 2)$ d. $7a - 12 + 4$

7. Use backtracking to find the solution to each equation.
   a. $2x + 4 = 10$ b. $3x - 2 = 8$
   c. $\frac{x}{4} + 1 = 7$ d. $\frac{x + 2}{5} = -1$

In **Investigation 2C,** you learned how to

- evaluate and simplify expressions using the basic rules
- solve equations using the basic moves
- understand that equations can have multiple solutions or no solutions
- solve an equation involving many variations of the Distributive Property

The following questions will help you check your understanding.

8. For each equation, determine whether $x = -3$ is a solution.

   a. $2x + 7 = x + 2$

   b. $x - 4 + 3x = 8 - x$

   c. $2(x - 1) = x - 5$

   d. $(x - 4) - (3 - x) = 5x + 2$

9. What equation does each model represent?

   a.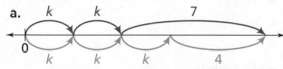

   b.

10. Solve each equation.

    a. $3x + 2 = x - 12$

    b. $x + 2(3x - 5) = 5x - 6$

    c. $2(x + 1) + 3(2x - 5) = 4(2x + 3)$

11. Determine whether each equation has no solutions, one solution, or every real number as a solution.

    a. $7(a + 2) - 5 = 7a + 9$

    b. $11 - 3t = 8 - 3t$

    c. $6(x + 7) = 6x + 7$

    d. $7q + 8q = q + 12$

In **Investigation 2D,** you learned how to

- use the guess-check-generalize method to solve word problems
- solve a two-variable equation
- build an equation from a mathematical situation

The following questions will help you check your understanding.

12. Solve each equation for x.

    a. $y = 8x$

    b. $y = 8x - 3$

    c. $y = 8(x - 3)$

    d. $y = 8(x - 3) + 7$

13. Sue scores 90, 85, and 83 on her first three math tests.

    a. What is Sue's average?

    b. If Sue scores 90 on the fourth test, what will her average be?

    c. If Sue wants an average of 90, what score does she need on the fourth test?

14. Henry shoveled snow during the last snowstorm. He charged $5 for a sidewalk and $12 for a driveway. He earned $80. Let x equal the number of sidewalks and y equal the number of driveways.

    a. Write an equation to model the situation.

    b. Solve for y.

Chapter 2 Test

Go Online
www.successnetplus.com

Multiple Choice

1. Which number is NOT a solution to the equation $(x - 3)(x - 5)(x + 7) = 0$?

   A. -7 **B.** 3

   C. 5   **D.** 7

2. Which expression is NOT equal to the other expressions?

   A. $-5(t + 4)$

   B. $-5(t - 4)$

   C. $5(4 - t)$

   D. $-(5t - 20)$

3. Which expression is a simplified version of the expression $3(2x - 4) - 2(5x - 1)$?

   A. $16x - 14$

   B. $-4x - 14$

   C. $-4x - 10$

   D. $-4x - 5$

4. Which equation can you NOT solve by backtracking?

   A. $28 = \frac{t}{6} + 4$

   B. $5(b - 3) + 4 = 39$

   C. $7x + 2 = 5x - 8$

   D. $12 = \frac{p}{3}$

5. Which equation can you use to represent the following model?

   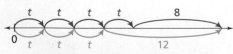

   A. $7t = 20$

   B. $4t + 8 = 3t + 12$

   C. $t = 4$

   D. cannot be determined

6. Find the solution of the equation $3(b - 2) = 2(b + 1)$.

   A. 3   **B.** 4   **C.** 7   **D.** 8

7. Which equation is $2x + 3y = 5x + 6$ correctly solved for x?

   A. $x = \frac{5x - 3y + 6}{2}$ **B.** $x = 3$

   C. $x = y - 2$ **D.** $x = \frac{3x - 6}{7}$

Open Response

8. Use the number y as your starting number. Write the expression you get by following the steps. Simplify the expression.

   • Choose a number.

   • Add 7.

   • Multiply by 3.

   • Subtract 8.

   • Multiply by 2.

9. Use an expansion box or another method to write the expression $-4(3x + 2y - 6)$ without parentheses.

10. Explain why the expression $\frac{r + 2r + 3r + 4r}{r}$ always has the same value, no matter what number other than zero you choose for r.

11. Define the binary operation ♣ in the following way.

    $$x \clubsuit y = 5(x - y)$$

    a. Find $5 \clubsuit 15$.

    b. Find x if $x \clubsuit 3 = 20$.

    c. Find y if $3 \clubsuit y = 20$.

    d. Is the ♣ operation commutative? Explain.

12. For each equation, determine whether $x = 4$ is a solution.

    a. $2x + 7 = x + 11$

    b. $x - 4 + 3x = 8 + x$

    c. $x^2 = 36$

    d. $3(x - 2) = x + 7$

13. Use the basic rules and moves to solve the equation $5(2x - 3) - 6x = 0.5(4x - 10)$. Show your work.

14. Sarah has two coupons for pizza. Coupon A offers the pizza at 15% off. Coupon B offers the pizza for $2 off.

    a. If the pizza without the discount costs x dollars, write an expression for the pizza's cost with each coupon.

    b. What price of a pizza makes Coupon A and Coupon B worth the same amount? Build and solve an equation to find the price to the nearest cent.

15. Find three ways to rewrite the expression $4(2z - 12)$ without changing its value. For example, rewriting the expression as $8z - 12$ is incorrect, since $8z - 12$ is not equal to $4(2z - 12)$.

16. Write a number trick that results in each of the following expressions.

    a. $3 \cdot x - 5$

    b. $3 \cdot (x - 5)$

    c. $2 \cdot (x + 1) + 6$

    d. $4 \cdot (2 \cdot (3 \cdot x + 6) - 7)$

17. Use the any-order, any-grouping properties and the Distributive Property to simplify each expression. Remember to combine like terms.

    a. $5(2x - 1) - 9$

    b. $4(3x + 1) + 2x$

    c. $3(2x - 5) + 2(5x + 8)$

    d. $3 + 2(4x - 5)$

    e. $2(x - 3) - (x + 4)$

    f. $5x - 3(2x - 6)$

18. Here is a number trick with the final step missing.

    • Choose any number.

    • Add 10.

    • Multiply by 4.

    • Subtract 8.

    • Divide by 2.

    • Subtract 2.

    • Divide by 2.

    • ?

    a. What is the final step if you want the ending number to be the same as the starting number?

    b. What is the final step if you want to end with the same number, no matter what the starting number is?

19. Use the conversion formula $F = \frac{9}{5}C + 32$, where F is a temperature in degrees Fahrenheit and C is a temperature in degrees Celsius.

    a. Convert $100°$ C to degrees Fahrenheit.

    b. The temperature of a healthy human body is $98.6°$ F. Use backtracking to find this temperature in degrees Celsius.

    c. Solve the equation $F = \frac{9}{5}C + 32$ for C.

    d. Use the equation you found in part (c) to convert $68°$ F to degrees Celsius.

20. Ashlee makes beaded jewelry. She charges $6 for a bracelet and $12 for a necklace. She earned $168. Let a equal the number of bracelets and b equal the number of necklaces.

    a. Write an equation to model the situation.

    b. Solve for b.

Challenge Problem

21. Write an equation that has $x = 3$ and $x = 7$ as its only solutions.

Chapter

3

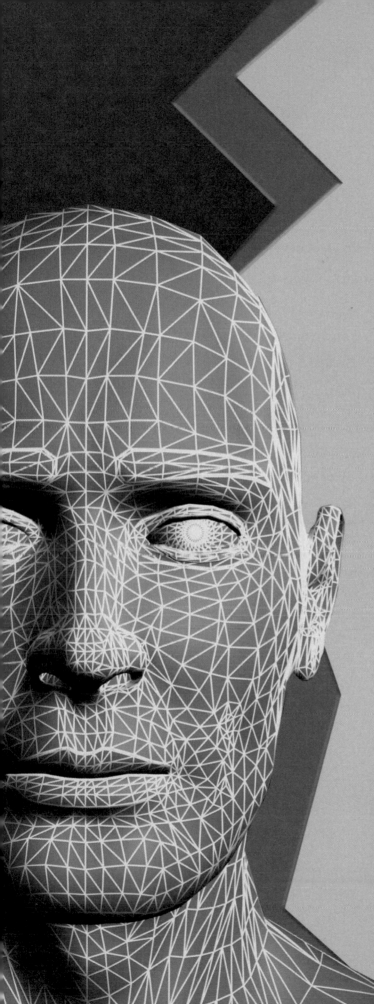

Graphs

Both video games and movies rely on amazing graphic images that computers produce. Animators make these images by representing the desired shape as a collection of polygons. A polygon is a closed shape with edges that are line segments, such as a square, a rectangle, a triangle, or a hexagon. The computer draws line segments connecting the polygons' corners to form a "wire frame" version of the shape.

Various mathematical techniques bring the images to life. They describe movement and color and simulate light that shines on the image.

You are not going to make computer animations yet, but you will explore the idea at the heart of computer graphics. You will connect algebraic ideas about numbers with the geometric representation of those ideas in visual form.

Vocabulary and Notation

- collinear points
- direct variation
- graph of an equation
- intersection point
- inverse variation
- point tester
- quadrant
- rise
- run
- slope
- speed
- subscript
- transformation

Equations and Their Graphs

In *Equations and Their Graphs*, you will focus on graphs of algebraic equations. You will use graphs to represent data and to draw pictures. Graphs can help you understand complicated data.

By the end of this investigation, you will be able to answer questions like these.

1. How are equations and graphs related?

2. How can you tell if a point is on a graph?

3. Do the graphs of $4y = (x - 3)^2$ and $3x - y = 14$ intersect at (5, 1)? Explain.

You will learn how to

• test a point to determine whether it is on the graph of an equation

• graph an equation by plotting points

• write the equation of a vertical or horizontal line given its graph or a point on its graph

• read a graph to identify points that are solutions to an equation

• find the intersection point of two graphs and understand its meaning

You will develop these habits and skills:

• Substitute values for variables.

• Write an equation that corresponds to a graph.

• Identify different graphs as belonging to the same family of graphs.

Security compares eye-scan data against a database in order to grant access.

In this lesson, you will explore some properties of graphs in the coordinate plane.

For You to Explore

1. Each point in the following table satisfies the equation $x + y = 5$.

   a. Complete the table.

   b. Graph the (x, y) coordinates that satisfy the equation $x + y = 5$.

   c. What shape is the graph?

x	y	(x, y)
1	4	(1, 4)
2	▨	▨
−3	▨	▨
▨	0	▨
$\frac{1}{2}$	▨	▨
▨	−2	▨
▨	$\frac{11}{3}$	▨

> **Remember...**
> If a point's coordinates make an equation true, the point "satisfies the equation."

2. On a coordinate plane, draw a vertical line that passes through (5, 3).

   a. List six points that are on your line.

   b. List six points that are not on your line.

   c. How do you tell whether a point is on your line by looking at its coordinates?

3. You can draw the tree below by connecting, in order, the following points.

   (1, 1) (2.5, 3) (2, 3) (3.5, 5) (3, 5) (4, 7)

   (5, 5) (4.5, 5) (6, 3) (5.5, 3) (7, 1) (1, 1)

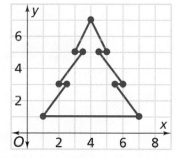

   a. For each point in the tree, add 2 to the x-coordinate. For instance, (1, 1) becomes (3, 1). Connect the resulting points to draw another picture.

   b. Describe the similarities and differences between the first picture and the second picture.

4. Use the equation $2x + 3y = 12$.

   a. Find five points that satisfy the equation.

   b. Find five points that do not satisfy the equation.

5. Sketch a graph of all the (x, y) coordinates that satisfy the equation $y - x^2 = -1$. What shape is the graph?

> **Go Online**
> www.successnetplus.com

> **Habits of Mind**
> **Experiment.** Choose values for x and find the y values. Then plot those points.

Exercises *Practicing Habits of Mind*

On Your Own

For Exercises 6 and 7, sketch a graph of the (x, y) coordinates that satisfy the equation. Describe the shape of each graph.

6. $(y - 3) = -1(x - 2)$

7. $y = |x|$

8. On a coordinate plane, draw a horizontal line that passes through $(5, 3)$. List six points that fit each description.

   a. on the line

   b. not on the line

   c. How can you tell whether a point is on the line by looking at its coordinates?

Maintain Your Skills

For Exercises 9–11, sketch a graph of the (x, y) coordinates that satisfy the equation. What shape is each graph?

9. $x + y = 0$

10. $x + y = 1$

11. $x + y = 2$

12. How are the graphs in Exercises 9–11 similar?

In Lesson 3.01, you found the coordinates for the graph of this pine tree shape by adding 2 to each *x*-coordinate. You drew a tree that looked like this.

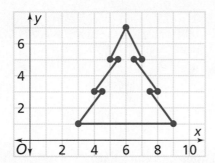

A rule that takes a set of points and produces another set of points is a **transformation.** The rule tells you to take every point (*x*, *y*) and replace it with (*x* + 2, *y*). The result of applying the rule is a set of points. When you connect the points, you draw a tree with the same shape and size as the tree above, but your tree is 2 units to the right of the tree shown here. You transform the tree by shifting it 2 units to the right.

For You to Do

1. How does the picture of the tree above change when you subtract 4 from each *y*-coordinate?

Facts and Notation

Sometimes a transformation uses a combination of operations (addition, subtraction, multiplication, or division) that you perform on each point. A transformation transforms, or maps, the original point to another point.

You use the symbol $\mapsto$ to describe a transformation. The symbol means "maps to." When you read the transformation (*x*, *y*) $\mapsto$ (*x* + 3, *y*), you say, " (*x*, *y*) maps to (*x* + 3, *y*)." The rule tells you to add three to the *x*-coordinate of each point and leave the *y*-coordinate of each point unchanged.

For example, if you perform the transformation (*x*, *y*) $\mapsto$ (*x* + 3, *y*) on the point (5, 12), the result is (8, 12). You say, "(5, 12) maps to (8, 12)." You can also say, "(5, 12) is transformed to (8, 12)."

What do you see from the stands when all the band members march 10 yards to the left?

Sasha and Tony plot three points on a coordinate plane and connect them to form a triangle.

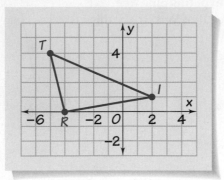

Sasha Let's apply a rule to the coordinates of the triangle and see what happens to it.

Tony Okay! How about if we use $(x, y) \mapsto (x + 3, y)$?

Sasha Well, that means that we add 3 to the *x*-coordinates. The *y*-coordinates stay the same.

Tony Wait! I need some way to label the new points. Then I can remember whether points are old or new.

Sasha I've seen it done like this.

T (−5, 4)	T′ (−2, 4)
R (−4, 0)	R′ (−1, 0)
I (2, 1)	I′ (5, 1)

In an ordered pair, order is important.

Tony Good idea, Sasha! That little mark after the letter means the point is a transformed point. Let's plot the new points so we can see what happens to the triangle.

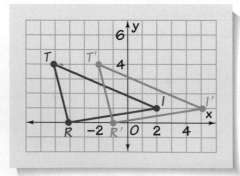

For You to Do

Describe the relationship between the original triangle *TRI* and the triangle that each transformation produces.

2. $(x, y) \mapsto (x - 3, y)$

3. $(x, y) \mapsto (2x, y)$

4. $(x, y) \mapsto (2x, 2y)$

5. $(x, y) \mapsto (-x, y)$

The *x*- and *y*-axes divide the coordinate plane into four parts, or **quadrants.**

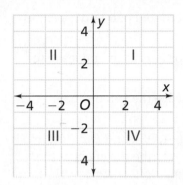

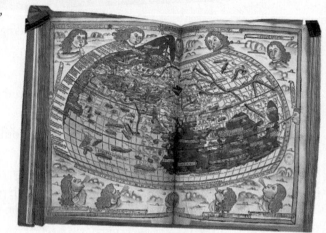

Ptolemy made maps with grids and quadrants about A.D. 150.

Here are some examples of points in each quadrant.

Quadrant I	(1, 1)	(3, 2)	$\left(\frac{1}{12}, \frac{1}{17}\right)$	(200, 468)
Quadrant II	(−1, 1)	$\left(-1.8, \frac{4}{3}\right)$	$\left(-7, \frac{3}{2}\right)$	(−4, 1003)
Quadrant III	(−1, −1)	(−3, −2)	$\left(-\frac{1}{12}, -\frac{1}{17}\right)$	(−200, −468)
Quadrant IV	(3, −2)	(6, −5)	(9.3, −1)	(0.07, −0.001)

For Discussion

6. How can you tell what quadrant a point is in just by looking at its coordinates?

7. In what direction are the quadrants numbered?

For You to Do

The tree in Lesson 3.01 is in the first quadrant. Describe a transformation that places the tree entirely in each quadrant given.

8. second quadrant

9. third quadrant

10. fourth quadrant

Exercises *Practicing Habits of Mind*

Check Your Understanding

1. Describe how a point's location changes after each transformation.

   a. Add a positive value to the x-coordinate of an ordered pair and leave the y-coordinate the same.

   b. Add a positive value to the y-coordinate of an ordered pair and leave the x-coordinate the same.

   c. Add a negative value to the x-coordinate and leave the y-coordinate the same.

2. Draw the square with corners $A(1, 3)$, $B(-3, 1)$, $C(-1, -3)$, and $D(3, -1)$. Transform all four points using each rule given. Describe the effect of the transformation on each point and on each square.

   a. $(x, y) \mapsto (x + 1, y)$

   b. $(x, y) \mapsto (x + 5, y + 2)$

   c. $(x, y) \mapsto (x - 2, y + 1)$

3. **a.** Is there a transformation that locates square $ABCD$ from Exercise 2 entirely in the first quadrant? If so, describe the transformation.

   b. **Take It Further** Is there a transformation that locates three corners of square $ABCD$ in the fourth quadrant and one corner in the first quadrant? If so, describe the transformation.

4. Draw a square with corners $S(1, 1)$, $T(-1, 1)$, $U(-1, -1)$, and $V(1, -1)$. Transform each point using the rule given. Describe the effect of the transformation on each point and on the square.

   a. $(x, y) \mapsto (x, 2y)$

   b. $(x, y) \mapsto (2x, y)$

   c. $(x, y) \mapsto (2x, 2y)$

   d. **Take It Further** $(x, y) \mapsto (-y, x)$

5. **Take It Further** Sometimes a transformation rearranges the points in a figure but leaves the overall figure looking the same. Find at least two transformations that leave the square in Exercise 4 looking the same.

A transformation like this "fixes" the figure.

6. Apply each transformation to the number 23 in the coordinate plane. Make a sketch of each result.

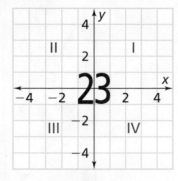

a. $(x, y) \mapsto (x, 2y)$ **b.** $(x, y) \mapsto (2x, y)$ **c.** $(x, y) \mapsto (2x, 2y)$

7. **Write About It** Is there any slanted line that passes through only two quadrants and does not pass through the origin? Explain.

On Your Own

8. Describe how the position of a point changes with each transformation given.

     a. Change the sign of its x-coordinate, but keep the sign of the y-coordinate the same.

     b. Change the sign of its y-coordinate, but keep the sign of the x-coordinate the same.

     c. Change the sign of both coordinates.

9. For each part, draw a set of coordinate axes. Shade the quadrants with points that match each description.

     a. negative x-coordinates

     b. positive y-coordinates

     c. negative x-coordinates and positive y-coordinates

10. On graph paper, draw a set of coordinate axes.

     a. Shade the region where $5 \leq x \leq 8$.

     b. Shade the region where $-3 \leq y \leq 6$.

     c. Is there any overlap of the shaded regions? If so, what shape is the intersection of the shaded regions? What is its area in square units?

     d. Rewrite the instructions in parts (a) and (b) to make the shaded intersection in the shape of a square. What is the area of your square?

Habits of Mind

Experiment. Try it with points! Choose points from different quadrants.

Go Online
www.successnetplus.com

There is more than one possible result.

11. **Write About It** Is it possible for a line to pass through only one quadrant? To pass through all four quadrants? Explain.

12. **Standardized Test Prep** The transformation
$$(x, y) \mapsto (-x, y)$$
maps points in the second quadrant to points in another quadrant. To which quadrant does the transformation map points of the second quadrant?

   A. first

   B. second

   C. third

   D. fourth

13. Follow the recipe for drawing a picture.

   • Draw a square with corners $(1, 1)$, $(4, 1)$, $(1, 4)$, and $(4, 4)$.

   • Transform this square using the rule $(x, y) \mapsto (x + 2, y + 2)$. Draw the resulting square on the same coordinate plane as the starting square.

   • Connect each corner of the original square to its matching corner in the transformed square. What does your picture look like?

> The *matching corner* means the location of the corner point after the transformation. Another name for the matching corner is the *image* of the corner.

Maintain Your Skills

For Exercises 14–16, apply the transformation to each shape given. Draw a sketch for each transformation.

   • triangle A with corners $(-4, 2)$, $(0, 2)$, and $(-3, 4)$

   • triangle B with corners $(1, 1)$, $(6, 1)$, and $(1, 3)$

   • a rectangle with corners $(5, 3)$, $(7, 3)$, $(5, 7)$, and $(7, 7)$

14. $(x, y) \mapsto (x - 4, y + 2)$

   a. triangle A   **b.** triangle B   **c.** rectangle

   d. Describe how far and in what direction the transformation moves each point.

15. $(x, y) \mapsto (2x, y)$

   a. triangle A   **b.** triangle B   **c.** rectangle

   d. Describe how the transformation changes each shape.

16. $(x, y) \mapsto (y, -x)$

   a. triangle A   **b.** triangle B   **c.** rectangle

   d. Describe how the transformation moves each shape.

3.03 Equations as Point-Testers

In Lesson 3.01, you sketched graphs of equations. For each equation, some (x, y) pairs make the equation true. If you plot on a coordinate plane each pair that satisfies the equation, the result is a graph of the equation.

You can test whether a coordinate pair is part of the graph of an equation by plugging the coordinates into the equation. For instance, suppose you want to find whether the point $(6, 0)$ is part of the graph of the equation $2x + 3y = 12$. You can just plug $x = 6$ and $y = 0$ into the equation.

$$2x + 3y = 12$$
$$2 \cdot (6) + 3 \cdot (0) \overset{?}{=} 12$$
$$12 + 0 \overset{?}{=} 12$$
$$12 = 12 ✔$$

Since $12 = 12$ is true, the point $(6, 0)$ satisfies the equation.

There are (x, y) pairs that do not satisfy the equation. For instance, test the point $(-1, 8)$. You plug $x = -1$ and $y = 8$ into the equation.

$$2x + 3y = 12$$
$$2 \cdot (-1) + 3 \cdot (8) \overset{?}{=} 12$$
$$-2 + 24 \overset{?}{=} 12$$
$$22 \neq 12 ✗$$

Since $22 = 12$ is false, the point $(-1, 8)$ does not satisfy the equation.

> In fact, there are many more pairs that do not satisfy the equation.

For You to Do

1. Find two additional points that make the equation $2x + 3y = 12$ true. Then find two additional points that make the equation false.

The graph of the equation $2x + 3y = 12$ is a line.

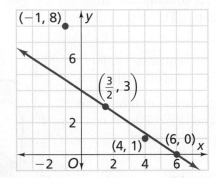

Each point that makes the equation true is on this line. Each point on the line makes the equation true. Notice that $(6, 0)$ is on the line, but $(-1, 8)$ is not on the line.

> Does $\left(\frac{3}{2}, 3\right)$ satisfy the equation? Does $(4, 1)$ satisfy the equation?

You can use the equation $2x + 3y = 12$ as a **point-tester.** Some points, such as (6, 0), pass the test. Other points, such as (−1, 8), fail. Points that pass the test are part of the graph. Points that fail are not part of the graph. Using this method, you can draw a graph of all points that satisfy an equation.

A recurring theme in algebra is that equations are point-testers.

- Any point that is on the graph of the equation makes the equation true.
- Any point that makes the equation true is part of the graph of the equation.

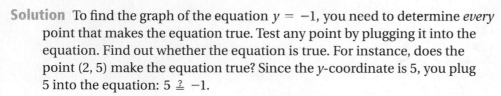

A point satisfies an equation if its coordinates make the equation true.

Definition

The **graph of an equation** is the collection of all points with coordinates that make the equation true.

Example

Problem In the coordinate plane, draw the graph of the equation $y = -1$.

Solution To find the graph of the equation $y = -1$, you need to determine *every* point that makes the equation true. Test any point by plugging it into the equation. Find out whether the equation is true. For instance, does the point (2, 5) make the equation true? Since the y-coordinate is 5, you plug 5 into the equation: $5 \stackrel{?}{=} -1$.

The equation is false, so (2, 5) is *not* on the graph.

Does the point (2, −1) make the equation true? Plug the y-coordinate −1 into the equation: $-1 \stackrel{?}{=} -1$.

The equation is true, so (2, −1) is on the graph of the equation $y = -1$.

What other points make the equation true? Usually, when you test a point, you substitute two numbers (x-coordinate and y-coordinate) into an equation. In this case, the x-coordinate doesn't matter. The answer depends only on the y-coordinate.

A point makes the equation true if the y-coordinate is equal to −1. For example, points such as (1, −1), (5, −1), and (0, −1) satisfy the equation.

If the y-coordinate equals −1, the x-coordinate can be any number. The graph of the equation $y = -1$ extends to the left and right of the y-axis. The graph of the equation $y = -1$ is a horizontal line one unit below the x-axis.

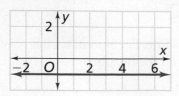

Developing Habits of Mind

Represent a solution. Equations can have different types of solutions, depending on the context. If the equation has one variable, a solution is a number that satisfies the equation when you use it in place of the variable. $x = 2$ is a solution of $3x + 7 = 13$.

In this chapter, you will look for points (pairs of numbers) that satisfy an equation with two variables. The solutions to the equation $3x + 7y = 13$ are a collection of points that include $(2, 1)$ and $(-5, 4)$. There are infinitely many other points that satisfy $3x + 7y = 13$. You cannot list them all. Instead, you can represent the solutions as a graph in the coordinate plane.

Exercises *Practicing Habits of Mind*

Check Your Understanding

1. **a.** Name and plot six points that are on the graph of $y = 4$.

   b. Describe the graph of $y = 4$. Draw the graph.

2. Line m is horizontal and passes through $(3, 7)$.

   a. Draw a graph of m.

   b. Find the coordinates of six points that are on m.

   c. Find the coordinates of six points that are *not* on m.

   d. How can you tell whether a point is on m by looking at its coordinates?

   e. Write an equation for m.

3. Line ℓ is vertical and passes through $(3, 7)$.

   a. Draw a graph of ℓ.

   b. Find the coordinates of six points that are on ℓ.

   c. Find the coordinates of six points that are *not* on ℓ.

   d. How can you tell whether a point is on ℓ by looking at its coordinates?

   e. Write an equation for ℓ.

4. Some graphs have more complicated equations. The graph of the equation $x^2 + y^2 = 25$ is a circle.

  a. Determine whether $(5, 0)$, $(-3, 0)$, and $(-3, 4)$ are on the graph.

  b. Find four more points that are on the circle. (Or, find four more points that satisfy the equation.)

5. a. Find five points that are on the graph of the equation $y = x$.

  b. Find five points that are not on the graph of the equation $y = x$.

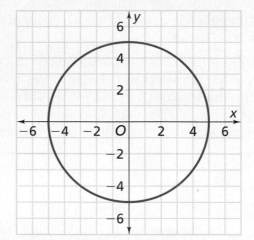

  c. What does the graph of the equation look like? Draw the graph and explain why the graph is correct.

6. Draw a coordinate plane.

  a. Name and plot six points with a first coordinate that is the opposite of the second coordinate.

  b. A graph shows every point with a first coordinate that is the opposite of the second. What shape is the graph?

  c. Which of the following equations describes this graph? Explain.

   A. $y = x$ **B.** $x + y = 5$ **C.** $|x| = y$ **D.** $y = -x$

On Your Own

7. Let $P = (-2, 4)$.

  a. Line r is horizontal and passes through P. Write an equation for r.

  b. Line s is vertical and passes through P. Write an equation for s.

8. Use your equations from Exercise 7 to determine whether each of the following points is on r, s, neither r nor s, or on both r and s.

  a. $(1, 1)$ **b.** $(-2, 1)$ **c.** $(4, -2)$ **d.** $(4, 4)$

  e. $(-2, -2)$ **f.** $(3, -2)$ **g.** $(1, 4)$ **h.** $(-1, -3)$

9. Apply the transformation $(x, y) \mapsto (x + 3, y - 2)$ to the graph in Exercise 4.

  a. Sketch the resulting graph.

  b. **Take It Further** Find the equation of the resulting graph.

10. Line h is horizontal and passes through (5, 2).

 a. Find four points on h.

 b. Write a point-tester equation for h.

 c. Draw a graph of h.

11. Line v is vertical and passes through (−4, 3).

 a. Find four points on v.

 b. Write a point-tester equation for v.

 c. Draw a graph of v.

12. Find the point that is on both lines h and v from Exercises 10 and 11. Explain.

13. **Write About It** Is there any vertical line that contains both (0, 2) and (2, 0)? Explain.

All points of a horizontal line are the same distance above the horizontal floor.

14. a. Find five points that satisfy the equation $2y - 4x = 24$.

 b. Find five points that do not satisfy the equation $2y - 4x = 24$.

15. Add $4x$ to both sides of the equation $2y - 4x = 24$. Divide both sides by 2.

$$2y - 4x = 24$$
$$2y - 4x + 4x = 24 + 4x$$
$$2y = 24 + 4x$$
$$y = 12 + 2x$$

The result is the equation $y = 12 + 2x$.

 a. Find five points that satisfy this equation.

 b. Find five points that do not satisfy this equation.

 c. Compare your points in this exercise with the points in Exercise 14. How are they similar? Explain.

16. **Standardized Test Prep** Which point is NOT on the graph of $5x + 6y = -42$?

 A. (6, −12) **B.** (−12, 3) **C.** (−9, 0.5) **D.** (4, −10)

Maintain Your Skills

17. Graph each equation.

 a. $y = x$ b. $(y - 1) = x$ c. $(y - 2) = x$

 d. $(y - 3) = x$ e. $(y - 4) = x$ f. $(y - 5) = x$

 g. Describe the pattern. How do the equations change? How does the change affect the graphs?

3.04 Graphing by Plotting

To draw a graph, you might start by plotting several points.

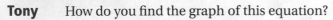

Minds in Action

Sasha is working through her algebra homework. Tony walks over to ask for some help.

Tony How do you find the graph of this equation?

Tony points to the equation $y = x^2 - 4x + 3$.

Sasha Plug in different values of x. Try $x = 0$.

$$y = x^2 - 4x + 3$$
$$y = (0)^2 - 4 \cdot (0) + 3$$

> When Sasha says *plug in,* she means "substitute."

Tony 0 is a good one to start with. All those zeros go away, since $(0)^2 = 0$, and $-4 \cdot (0) = 0$.

Sasha Right, and we get this.

$$y = (0)^2 - 4 \cdot (0) + 3$$
$$y = 0 - 0 + 3$$
$$y = 3$$

Tony $y = 3$? Now what do I do with the 3?

Sasha Remember, we started by saying $x = 0$ and found that if $x = 0$, then $y = 3$. The point $(0, 3)$ is on our graph.

Sasha plots the point $(0, 3)$ on a coordinate plane.

Sasha Now you try one.

Tony Okay, so if $x = -1$, then we get this.

$$y = x^2 - 4x + 3$$
$$y = (-1)^2 - 4 \cdot (-1) + 3$$
$$y = 1 - (-4) + 3$$
$$y = 8$$

> $(-1)^2 = 1$, not -1.
> $1 - (-4) = 1 + 4$.

Tony We now know that the point $(-1, 8)$ satisfies our equation. It's also on our graph.

Sasha Exactly.

Sasha draws the point $(-1, 8)$ *on the coordinate plane.*

Sasha   Let's find some more points on the graph. We can figure out what the whole graph looks like. Here, you try $x = 1$, $x = 2$, and $x = 3$. I'll try $x = 4$ and $x = 5$.

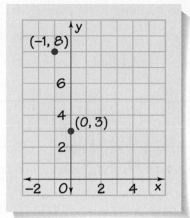

Sasha and Tony both start working on their points.

Tony   Okay, I've found the points $(1, 0)$, $(2, -1)$ and $(3, 0)$.

Sasha   I've found the points $(4, 3)$ and $(5, 8)$.

Sasha plots all of the points on a coordinate plane.

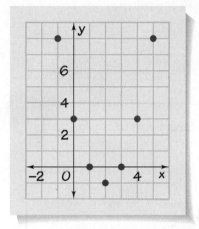

Tony   Oh, I can tell the shape of the graph. It looks like a big smile.

Sasha   That seems right. Now we can connect the dots, and that's our graph.

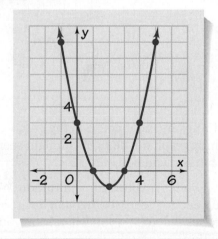

For You to Do

Use the graph from Minds in Action.

1. Guess what values of x make $y = 0$. Check your guesses in the equation.

2. Guess what values of x make $y = 3$. How can you be sure that your guesses are correct?

For Discussion

3. At the end of Minds in Action, Sasha says, "Now we can connect the dots." Do you agree? Explain.

4. If you plug $x = 2.5$ into the equation $y = x^2 - 4x + 3$, what is the result? Can you use Sasha's graph to approximate this result?

5. Give an equation with a graph that has the shape of a big frown.

Developing Habits of Mind

Consider more than one strategy. In the Example, Sasha and Tony plot five points. Then they connect the dots. There is more than one way that they can connect the dots.

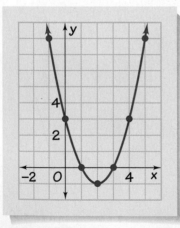
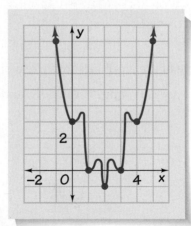

Is it possible that Sasha and Tony are incorrect? Can the graph of $y = x^2 - 4x + 3$ be the bumpy graph on the right? It might seem that the correct graph is on the left, but can you be sure?

For now, graphing by plotting points involves some intuition. When solving an unfamiliar equation, you need to judge whether you have plotted enough points. For the exercises that follow, you will rely on your own judgment to solve each equation.

There is never any harm in plotting a few additional points.

Exercises *Practicing Habits of Mind*

Check Your Understanding

1. These four equations may look different, but three of them have the same graph. Which graph is different? Explain.

   A. $y = \frac{3}{2}x + 2$

   B. $2y + 3x = 4$

   C. $(y - 5) = \frac{3}{2}(x - 2)$

   D. $2y - 3x = 4$

2. Use the equation $2y + 5x = 10$. For each point, find the value of k that satisfies the equation. Then plot the point.

   a. $(0, k)$ **b.** $(1, k)$

   c. $(-3, k)$ **d.** $\left(\frac{1}{5}, k\right)$

   e. $(3, k)$ **f.** $(-4, k)$

   g. Using the plotted points, draw the graph of the equation $2y + 5x = 10$.

3. Look at the graphs of the equations $y = |x - 3|$ and $(y - 3) = |x|$. Which graph corresponds to each equation? Explain.

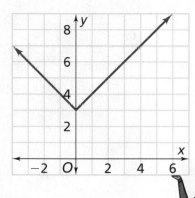 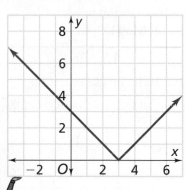

4. Match each equation with a graph. Explain each choice.

a. $2x - y = -1$ b. $x = 2$

c. $y = x^2 + 1$ d. $(y - 1) = 2(x - 3)$

I.
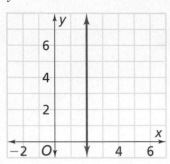

II.
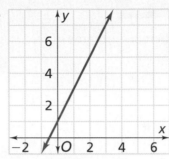

III.
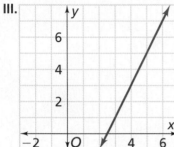

IV.
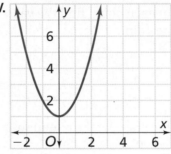

The Leaning Tower of Pisa stands about 183 ft high. Since $0 = 183 - 16(3.38)^2$, it takes about 3 s for a grape to reach the ground from the top of the tower.

For Exercises 5 and 6, use what Molly has learned in science about calculating the height of a falling object. If the initial height is h_0, then after t seconds, the object is at the following height.

$$h = h_0 - 16t^2$$

5. Molly drops grapes from her balcony to test the height equation.

a. Molly's balcony is 160 feet above the ground. Rewrite the equation using 160 feet as the initial height.

b. Use the equation to find the grape's height after 0 seconds ($t = 0$).

c. How high is the grape after 1 second? After 2 seconds? After 3 seconds?

d. How long does it take the grape to reach the ground? Round your result to the nearest tenth of a second.

e. Use the points you have calculated. Sketch a graph by hand or with a calculator. Plot the grape's height against time.

f. Sketch a picture of the grape's path.

6. Molly's friend Aya lives on a floor that is 320 feet above the ground. Molly goes to Aya's balcony to test the height equation using a different initial height.

a. Rewrite the height equation using 320 feet for the initial height.

b. According to the equation, how high is the grape after 0 seconds ($t = 0$)?

c. How high is the grape after 1 second? After 2 seconds? After 3 seconds? After 4 seconds?

d. Molly says, "I'm dropping the grape from 320 feet. It should take twice as long to hit the ground as it does if I drop it from 160 feet." Is she correct? Explain.

e. Sketch a graph of the grape's height against time.

> This graph is not a picture of the path of the grape.

On Your Own

7. Use the equation $\frac{2}{3}y - x = 2$. For each point, find the value of h so that the point satisfies the equation. Plot the point.

a. $(h, 3)$ **b.** $(h, -3)$ **c.** $(h, 0)$

d. $(h, 1)$ **e.** $(h, 9)$ **f.** $(h, -2)$

g. Using the plotted points, draw the graph of $\frac{2}{3}y - x = 2$.

8. Match each equation with a graph. Explain your choice.

a. $y = -2$ **b.** $x + y = -2$

c. $y = (x + 1)^2$ **d.** $x = -2$

I.

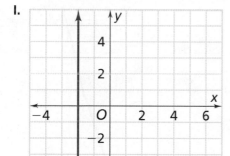

II.

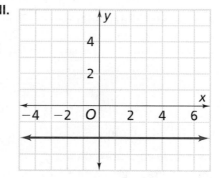

III.

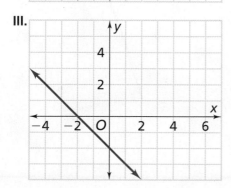

IV.

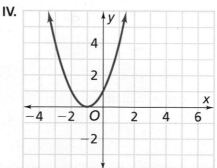

> **Go** **online**
> www.successnetplus.com

For Exercises 9 and 10, graph the equation.

9. $(y - 1) = 2x$

10. $(y - 4) = 2(x - 2)$

11. **Take It Further** Use the equation $x^2 - xy + y^2 = 1$.

  a. Find four points on the graph of the equation.

  b. Show that if (a, b) is on the graph, then $(-a, -b)$ is also on the graph.

  c. Sketch the graph.

12. **Standardized Test Prep** Which point is NOT on the graph of $y = x^2 - 5x + 4$?

  A. $(0, 4)$

  B. $(4, 0)$

  C. $(3, 2)$

  D. $(1, 0)$

Maintain Your Skills

13. Graph each equation on the same coordinate plane.

  a. $y = x$

  b. $y = 2x$

  c. $y = 3x$

  d. $y = 4x$

  e. $y = 5x$

  f. Describe the pattern. How do the equations change? How does the change affect the graphs?

14. Graph each equation on the same coordinate plane.

    a. $y = x$

    b. $2y = x$

    c. $3y = x$

    d. $4y = x$

    e. $5y = x$

    f. Describe the pattern. How do the equations change?
       How does this change affect the graphs?

15. Plot points to graph each equation on the same coordinate plane.

    a. $y = x^2$

    b. $(y - 1) = x^2$

    c. $(y - 2) = x^2$

    d. $(y - 3) = x^2$

    e. Describe the pattern. How do the equations change?
       How does this change affect the graphs?

Go Online
Video Tutor
www.successnetplus.com

3.05 Graphing Related Quantities

You can use *x*- and *y*-coordinate axes to represent a variety of numerical relationships. For instance, let the horizontal axis represent free throws attempted in a basketball game. Let the vertical axis represent free throws made. Look at the following points.

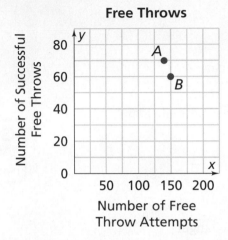

Point *A* (140, 70) represents a person who attempts 140 free throws and makes 70 of them. Point *B* (150, 60) represents a person who attempts 150 free throws and makes 60 of them.

Now, change the meaning of the axes. Let the horizontal axis represent the weight in pounds of a person. Let the vertical axis represent the person's height in inches.

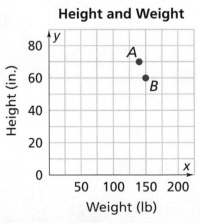

Point *A* (140, 70) represents a person who weighs 140 pounds and is 70 inches tall. Point *B* (150, 60) represents a person who weighs 150 pounds and is 60 inches tall. Person B is shorter and heavier than Person A.

The numerical values of points *A* and *B* stay the same. However, the axes represent entirely different quantities. The first graph shows free throws made against free throws attempted. The second graph shows height against weight.

Habits of Mind

Visualize. Which person has a better free-throw percentage?

In general, you can graph any numerical value against any other numerical value.

Example

Problem Invent a story that the graph illustrates.

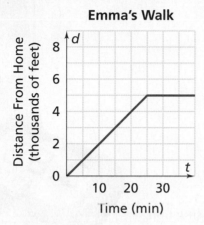

Emma's Walk

Solution In the graph, the horizontal axis represents time. The vertical axis represents distance from home. Time and distance increase as you move to the right from the origin. After 25 minutes, time increases, but distance from home stays the same.

You can use this information to write a story about Emma.

Emma leaves home at the point (0, 0). While she walks at a constant rate to the basketball court, the graph slants upward. After 25 minutes, she arrives at the basketball court, at the point (25, 5000).

When she gets to the court, Emma plays basketball for 15 minutes. During the time she plays, the *y*-coordinate, or her distance from home, remains the same. So the graph is flat from (25, 5000) to (40, 5000).

For Discussion

Emma's story is unfinished. For each ending, draw a graph of the complete story.

1. Emma walks home at the same speed as she walked to the basketball court. She arrives home in 25 minutes.

2. Emma realizes she will be late for dinner, so she runs home. She takes 10 minutes to get home.

3. Emma gets a ride home from a friend. She takes 5 minutes to get home.

For You to Do

What's Wrong Here? Adam makes a graph to represent the following situation. Jen walks to school. When she is halfway to school, Jen realizes that she has forgotten her lunch. She turns around and walks home. Jen realizes she will be late, so she runs to school.

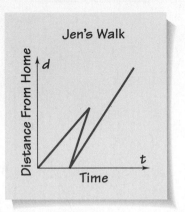

Jen's Walk

4. Explain what is wrong with Adam's graph.

5. Make a graph that more accurately represents the situation.

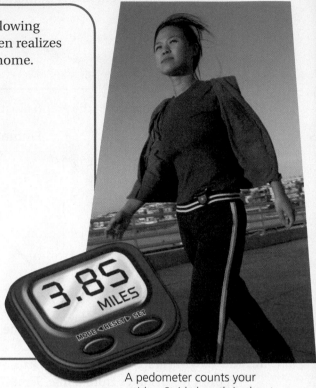

A pedometer counts your strides. Stride length is about 0.4 times your height. Distance you walk = stride count × stride length.

Exercises *Practicing Habits of Mind*

Check Your Understanding

1. Write a sentence that can explain this graph when the axes have the following labels.

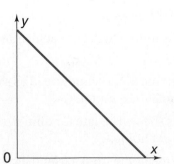

Horizontal Axis	Vertical Axis
a. Time	Distance From Home
b. Price of Movie Tickets	Number of Tickets Sold
c. Distance Driven	Amount of Gas in Tank

2. George and Martha leave their house in Washington at the same time in separate cars. The graph represents their trips.

Assume they travel a straight road from their house.

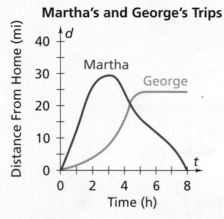

Martha's and George's Trips

a. Write a story about George's trip that matches the graph.

b. Write a story about Martha's trip that matches the graph.

c. What happens in each trip at the point where the graphs cross?

d. What does the horizontal part of George's graph represent?

e. About how many miles does Martha travel during her trip?

f. About how many miles does George travel during his trip?

3. Write About It Suppose you have an empty bucket. The cross section of the bucket is in the shape of a rectangle. You fill the bucket with water that runs at a constant rate from a faucet. The height of the water in the bucket rises at a constant rate. Explain why the graph represents this situation.

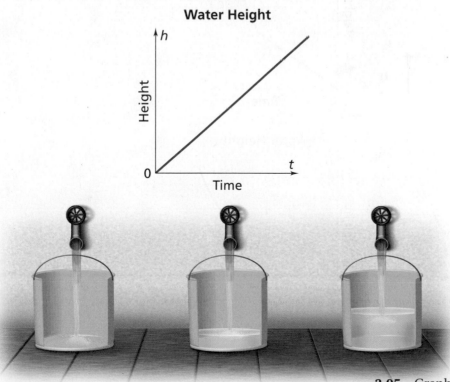

Water Height

4. Each diagram represents a cross section of a bucket.

I. II. III.

IV. V. VI.

Water flows into the bucket at a constant rate. Match each graph to the corresponding bucket. Explain each choice.

A. **Water Height**

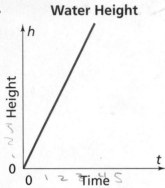

B. **Water Height**

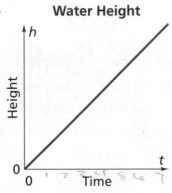

C. **Water Height**

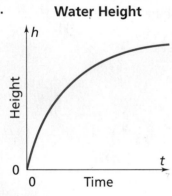

D. **Water Height**

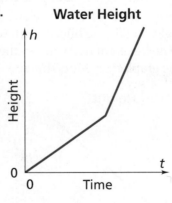

E. **Water Height**

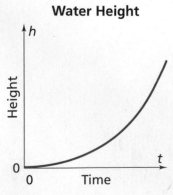

F. **Water Height**

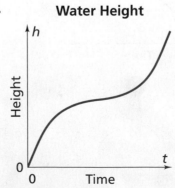

5. Every day, Mr. Hayashi walks his dog. This graph illustrates his walk.

 a. Which two points on the graph show Mr. Hayashi at his house?

 b. In the middle of the graph, there is a sharp angle. What does Mr. Hayashi do at this point in his walk?

Mr. Hayashi's Walk

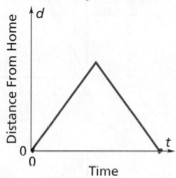

6. Francesca and Demitri run a race. Francesca is faster than Demitri, so she reaches the finish line first. Make a graph that illustrates this situation by graphing distance against time.

> There is not enough information in Exercise 6 to draw a precise graph. You can draw a graph that illustrates the basic idea.

7. Draw a graph of each situation.

 a. To make the race more even, Demitri starts the race 10 feet closer to the finish line. Francesca catches up to him and still reaches the finish line first.

 b. Francesca gives Demitri a 5-second head start. Francesca never catches up, and Demitri wins the race.

8. Ruth runs a 100-meter race. For parts (a)–(c), make a graph that illustrates each situation.

 a. Ruth's official time is 14 seconds.

 b. Ruth trips and falls at the beginning of the race. She loses five seconds, so her official time is 19 seconds.

 c. Ruth starts running two seconds before the starting gun. Nobody notices, and her official time is 12 seconds.

 d. Fill in the blank. To get from the graph in part (a) to the graph in part (b), you can apply the rule $(x, y) \mapsto (x + \blacksquare, y)$.

 e. Fill in the blank. To get from the graph in part (a) to the graph in part (c), you can apply the transformation $(x, y) \mapsto (x + \blacksquare, y)$.

Go Online
www.successnetplus.com

9. **Standardized Test Prep** Jamar walks quickly to the store, buys a newspaper, and then walks slowly home. Which graph best describes his walk?

A.
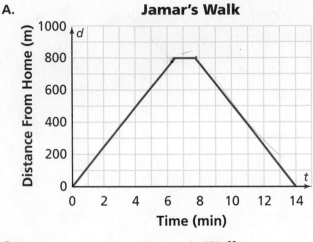

B.
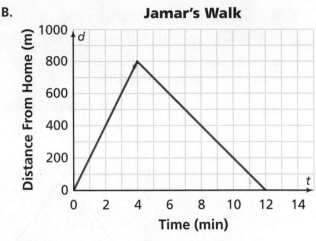

C.
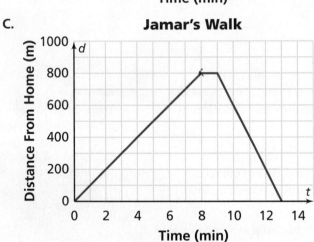

D.
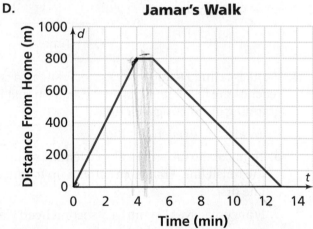

Maintain Your Skills

10. Adam makes a table showing the number of factors the number *n* has. Adam writes the number of factors in the second column. Adam says, "The number 6 has four factors: 1, 2, 3, and 6. I write 6 in the first column and 4 in the second column."

    a. Make a graph of the number of factors of *n* against the number *n*. Label the horizontal axis *n*. Label the vertical axis Number of Factors of *n*. For instance, (6, 4) is a point on this graph because the number 6 has 4 factors. Does it make sense to connect the dots on this graph?

    b. What do the points on the horizontal line passing through (3, 2) have in common?

Adam's Table

n	Number of Factors
1	1
2	2
3	2
4	3
5	2
6	4
7	2

Intersection of Graphs

Look at the graphs of the equations $y = x^2 - 1$ and $y = 3$ on two different coordinate planes.

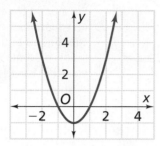

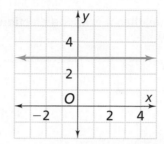

Each point on this graph satisfies the equation $y = x^2 - 1$.

Each point on this graph satisfies the equation $y = 3$.

Notice the result when you draw both graphs on the same coordinate plane.

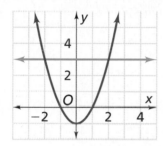

The graphs intersect at two points, $(2, 3)$ and $(-2, 3)$.

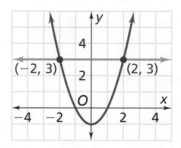

The points where two graphs cross are **intersection points.** Since the intersection points are on both graphs, they must satisfy both equations.

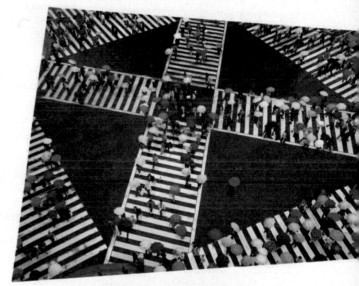

Can you describe six intersections suggested by this picture?

For Discussion

1. Use the equations of the two graphs above. Show that the graphs intersect at $(2, 3)$ and $(-2, 3)$.

Developing Habits of Mind

Find a relationship. There is a relationship between an intersection point of two graphs and the corresponding equations.

- An intersection point of two graphs satisfies both of the corresponding equations.

- If a point makes two equations true, then it is an intersection point of the corresponding graphs.

> For a point to satisfy an equation, the coordinates of the points must make the equation true.

Exercises *Practicing Habits of Mind*

Check Your Understanding

1. Use the graphs of the equations $y = x$ and $y = 1000 - x$. These graphs intersect at one point. Explain why each point is not the intersection of the two graphs.

   a. $(100, 25)$

   b. $(-25, -25)$

   c. $(1000, 1000)$

   d. $(1000, 500)$

   e. Explain why the point $(500, 500)$ is an intersection of the two graphs.

2. Find two equations with graphs that intersect at $(3, -1)$. Show that $(3, -1)$ makes both equations true.

3. **a.** Does the graph of the equation $y = 3x - 2$ intersect the graph of the equation $y = 3x + 2$? Explain.

   b. Describe the result you find when you solve the equation $3x - 2 = 3x + 2$.

4. **a.** Find two equations with graphs that never intersect.

   b. **Take It Further** Explain why the graphs of the equations in part (a) do not intersect. In addition to drawing the graphs, explain how you can be certain that the graphs do not intersect.

5. The graphs of the equations $x^2 + y^2 = 25$ and $16x^2 + 9y^2 = 288$ are on the same coordinate plane.

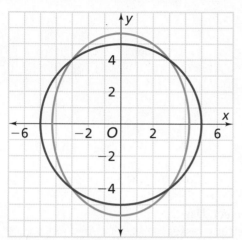

> The shapes are a circle and an ellipse. An ellipse is an oval shape that has some unique properties.

a. Match each graph with its equation.

b. Use the graphs to estimate the points where the graphs intersect. Use the equations to show that your guesses are correct or to find better guesses.

On Your Own

6. Graph the equations $y = x^2$ and $y = 3x - 2$. Where do these graphs intersect?

7. Find two equations with graphs that intersect at the point $(-5, 4)$. Show that the point $(-5, 4)$ makes both equations true.

8. Standardized Test Prep Which point is the intersection of the graphs of $y = 3$ and $y = -2x + 5$?

A. $(0, 3)$

B. $(4, 3)$

C. $(3, 4)$

D. $(1, 3)$

The paths of the planets are ellipses.

Go Online
www.successnetplus.com

9. Look at the graphs of the equations
$x^2 + 16y^2 = 25$ and $y = \frac{1}{4}(x + 5)$.

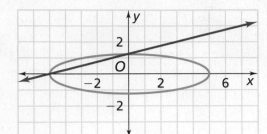

a. Match each graph with its equation.

b. Use the graphs to estimate the points where the graphs intersect. Use the
equations to show that your guesses are correct or to find better guesses.

Maintain Your Skills

10. Find the intersection of the graph of $y = -2$ and the graph of
each equation.

a. $x = 0$

b. $x = 1$

c. $x = 2$

d. $x = 3$

e. $x = 4$

f. What is the pattern of the graphs?

11. Find the intersection of the graph of $x = -1$ and the graph of
each equation.

a. $(y - 3) = 2(x + 1)$

b. $(y - 3) = 13(x + 1)$

c. $(y - 3) = -4(x + 1)$

d. $(y - 3) = \frac{(x + 1)}{5}$

e. $(y - 3) = -99(x + 1)$

f. What is the pattern of the graphs?

Mathematical 3A Reflections

In this investigation, you related an equation to a graph. You learned to find an intersection point of two equations. These questions will help you summarize what you have learned.

1. **a.** Find five points that satisfy the equation $5y + 3x = -13$.

   b. Find five points that do not satisfy the equation $5y + 3x = -13$.

2. Match each equation with a graph. Explain each choice.

   a. $y = 3$ **b.** $y + 3 = x$ **c.** $y = x + 3$ **d.** $y + 3 = x^2$

   I. 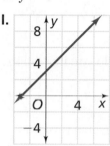   **II.** 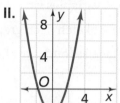   **III.** 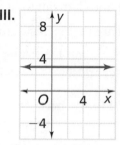   **IV.**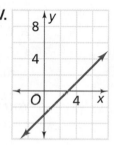

3. Graph the equations $y + 2x = 0$ and $x + 2y = 0$. Where do these graphs intersect?

4. For each point, find the value of h such that the point satisfies the equation $y^2 = x + 4$.

   a. $(h, 0)$ **b.** $(h, 1)$ **c.** $(h, 2)$

   d. $(h, 3)$ **e.** $(h, -1)$ **f.** $(h, -2)$

   g. Draw the graph of the equation $y^2 = x + 4$ by plotting the points in parts (a)–(f).

5. How are equations and graphs related?

6. How can you tell if a point is on a graph?

7. Do the graphs of $4y = (x - 3)^2$ and $3x - y = 14$ intersect at $(5, 1)$? Explain.

Vocabulary

In this investigation, you learned these terms. Make sure you understand what each one means and how to use it.

- **graph of an equation**
- **intersection point**
- **point-tester**

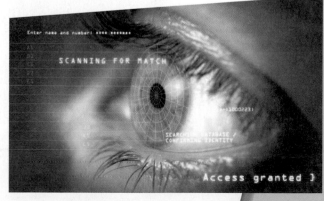

Access granted.

Investigation 3B

Basic Graphs and Translations

In *Basic Graphs and Translations,* you will look at six basic graph shapes for common equations. Knowing the key features of each shape will enable you to sketch many graphs quickly and easily.

By the end of the investigation, you will be able to answer questions like these.

1. What does it mean to say two variables vary directly or inversely?

2. What are the six basic graphs? Sketch each graph.

3. If you free fall 4.9 meters in one second, how far do you free fall in four seconds?

You will learn how to

- decide whether a situation represents direct or inverse variation

- sketch the graphs of the equations
  $y = x$, $xy = 1$, $y = x^2$, $y = x^3$, $y = \sqrt{x}$, $y = |x|$,
  and variations of these equations

- recognize the distinguishing features of the basic graphs, such as their general shape, and the points and quadrants that they pass through

You will develop these habits and skills:

- Use an equation as a point-tester for a graph.

- Quickly sketch the graph of a basic equation.

- Recognize proportionality in direct and inverse variation.

- Find similarities and differences between scatter plots and continuous graphs.

The transformation
$(x, y) \mapsto (x, y + 10)$
takes you up 10 floors.

In this lesson, you will relate some simple equations to basic graph shapes. You will also observe how changing an equation changes a graph.

For You to Explore

In this experiment, you will build patterns using tiles and cubes.

1. Start building larger squares using smaller square tiles.

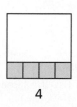

4

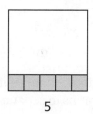

5

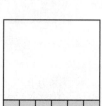

6

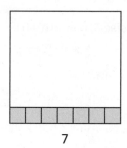

7

> Suppppose the number of tiles you need for a square is *n*, and the number of tiles in the bottom row is *t*. Write an equation that relates *n* and *t*.

Graph the number of tiles you need to complete each larger square against the number of tiles in the bottom row. If you continue to build larger squares, what will be the next five points on the graph?

2. Build larger cubes using smaller cubes. Record the *width* of each larger cube.

2

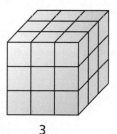

3

> Suppose the number of smaller cubes you need for a larger cube is *n*, and the width is *w*. Write an equation that relates *n* and *w*.

Graph the number of smaller cubes that you need to complete the larger cubes against the width of the bottom row. If you continue to build larger cubes, what are the next five points on the graph?

3. Graph the number of smaller cubes you need to complete the larger cubes against the number of smaller cubes in the bottom layer of each cube. If you continue to build larger cubes, what will be the next five points on the graph?

Exercises *Practicing Habits of Mind*

On Your Own

4. For each equation, find at least seven ordered pairs (x, y) that make the equation true.

   a. $y = x^2$ **b.** $y = (x - 5)^2$

   c. $y = (x + 3)^2$ **d.** $(y - 6) = x^2$

   e. $(y + 4) = x^2$ **f.** $(y - 8) = (x - 7)^2$

5. Use the points you found in Exercise 4, and additional points if needed, to graph each equation in Exercise 4. Draw the graphs in separate coordinate planes.

   Use the same scale on the x- and y-axes for all the graphs.

6. Describe how each graph you drew for Exercise 5, parts (b)–(f), is related to the graph of the equation $y = x^2$ that you drew for part (a).

7. Look at the graph of the equation $x^2 + y^2 = 25$.

   The graph is a circle. What is the center of the circle? What is the radius?

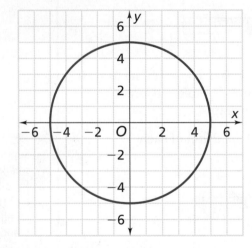

   Decide whether each point is on the graph.

   a. $(3, 4)$

   b. $(-3, -4)$

   c. $(4.9, 1)$

   d. $(-5, 0)$

   e. $(0, 0)$

   f. $(-2, -4.5)$

8. Look at the graph of the equation $x^2 + (y - 2)^2 = 25$.
Decide whether each point is on the graph.

  a. (3, 6)   **b.** (−3, −6)   **c.** (3, −2)

  d. (5, 4)   **e.** (0, −2)   **f.** (−5, 2)

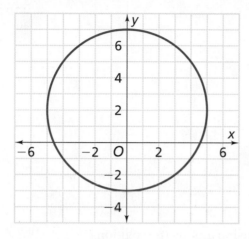

How can you get this graph from the graph in Exercise 7?

9. Suppose an object is in free fall, being pulled to the ground by Earth's gravity. The equation $v = 9.8t$ shows the relationship between the velocity v of the object, in meters per second, and the time t, in seconds, that it has been falling.

  a. If t is 0, what is v?

  b. Find v when t is 4, 8 and 16.

  c. If t doubles, how does v change?

  d. What is t if v is 100? If v is 300?
     Round to the nearest hundredth.

  e. If v triples, how must t have changed?

Habits of Mind

Establish a process.
You may find it useful to make a table to keep track of your results.

10. Katie earns $1000 by mowing lawns during the summer.

  a. If Katie charges $4 per lawn, how many lawns does she need to mow to earn $1000?

  b. If Katie charges $10 per lawn, how many lawns does she need to mow to earn $1000?

  c. If Katie can only mow 50 lawns during the summer, how much does she need to charge per lawn to earn $1000?

  d. Katie decides to double what she charged last year. If she wants to earn the same amount of money as last year, how does the number of lawns she needs to mow change?

  e. Write an equation that relates the amount c Katie charges per lawn and the number of lawns n she needs to mow to reach $1000.

You are in free fall for much of the time you spend jumping on a trampoline.

11. A rectangular piece of paper has an area of 80 square inches. Draw a graph that shows the possible lengths and widths of the paper.

Graph length against width, or width against length. Why don't you get much information if you graph area against width?

Maintain Your Skills

12. Find the solutions to each equation.

a. $7x - 3 = 2x + 17$

b. $7(x - 4) - 3 = 2(x - 4) + 17$

c. $7(x - 8) - 3 = 2(x - 8) + 17$

d. $7(x - 83) - 3 = 2(x - 83) + 17$

e. $7(x + 9) - 3 = 2(x + 9) + 17$

f. $7(x + 1) - 3 = 2(x + 1) + 17$

g. **Write About It** Explain in detail the relationship among the solutions in parts (a)–(f).

h. Without using any basic moves, find the solution to the equation $7(x - 13) - 3 = 2(x - 13) + 17$.

i. Without using any basic moves, find the solution to the equation $7(x + 13) - 3 = 2(x + 13) + 17$.

13. Find the number of intersections of the graphs for each pair of equations.

a. $y = 2x$ and $y = 10 - 3x$

b. $y = 2(x + 3)$ and $y = 10 - 3(x + 3)$

c. $y = 2(x - 5)$ and $y = 10 - 3(x - 5)$

d. $y = x^2$ and $y = 10 - 3x$

e. $y = (x - 5)^2$ and $y = 10 - 3(x - 5)$

f. $(y + 6) = x^2$ and $(y + 6) = 10 - 3x$

Two Basic Graphs: Direct and Inverse Variation

In Investigation 3A, you learned to sketch graphs by using equations as point testers.

There are several basic shapes for graphs. Knowing these basic shapes can help you sketch graphs more quickly than you can using the point-tester method.

For You to Do

1. A ride on a carousel costs $3 per person. Using at least six points, draw a scatter plot with the number of riders on the horizontal axis and the total cost for the riders on the vertical axis.

Direct Variation

A **direct variation** is the relation of two variables that are in a constant ratio. For example, you find the number of days in a given number of weeks by multiplying by 7. If d is the number of days and w is the number of weeks, then the equation

$$d = 7w$$

expresses the relationship between d and w. The ratio between the number of days and number of weeks is always 7. If the value of w doubles, then the value of d also doubles. If the value of d doubles, then the value of w doubles.

For You to Do

2. There are 98 days in 14 weeks. How many days are there in 140 weeks? In 42 weeks?

> **Habits of Mind**
>
> **Check your equation.** You may expect the equation to be $7d = w$, because you are thinking that there are 7 days in 1 week. When there is any doubt, you can check your equation by substituting. If you use 7 for d and 1 for w, which equation is true, $7d = w$ or $d = 7w$?

Example

Problem A ride on a carousel costs $3. Let the variable r stand for the number of rides. Let c stand for the cost of the rides. Then $c = 3r$, and c and r vary directly.

Draw a graph of the direct variation $c = 3r$ for all values of r from 0 to 8, including noninteger values. Label the horizontal axis r and the vertical axis c.

Solution The table shows some points of the graph. The relationship between c and r is almost the same as the relationship between the number of riders on the carousel and the total cost for the riders. But the graph below shows the difference. The graph of the direct variation $c = 3r$ is a continuous line instead of distinct points.

r	c
0	0
0.5	1.5
1	3
2	6
3	9
6	18

Direct Variation

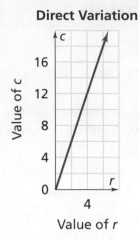

When you plot cost *c* against the number of riders *r*, the values of *r* and *c* are nonnegative integers. In the complete graph of $c = 3r$, both *r* and *c* represent all real numbers. When *r* can have both positive and negative values, what quadrants would contain the complete graph?

Developing Habits of Mind

Represent a direct variation. In direct variation, an increase in one variable means a proportional increase in the other variable. The ratio of the two numbers stays constant.

$$\frac{y}{x} = c$$

The standard equation for direct variation looks like this.

$$y = cx$$

The graph of the equation $y = cx$ is always a line that passes through the origin $(0, 0)$ and the point $(1, c)$. Here is the graph when $c = \frac{1}{2}$, along with a table of values for the graph.

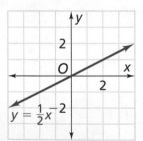

x	y
-2	-1
-1	$-\frac{1}{2}$
$-\frac{1}{2}$	$-\frac{1}{4}$
0	0
$\frac{1}{2}$	$\frac{1}{4}$
1	$\frac{1}{2}$
2	1

The variable *c* is a number (a constant), while *x* and *y* are variables, each representing any number. So $y = 5x$ is a direct variation equation in which $c = 5$.

The location of the graph depends on whether *c* is positive, negative, or zero. If *c* is positive, the graph passes through Quadrants I and III. If *c* is negative, the graph passes through Quadrants II and IV.

For Discussion

3. How do you know that the graph of $y = cx$ goes through $(0, 0)$, no matter what number c is?

4. What is the difference between the graph of $y = 3x$ and the graph of the carousel riders in this lesson?

Inverse Variation

An **inverse variation** is the relation between two variables that have a constant product.

Suppose, for example, that you have 100 grapes to share equally among your friends. Here are some ways that you can do this.

- 25 grapes to each of 4 friends
- 10 grapes to each of 10 friends
- 2 grapes to each of 50 friends

If g is the number of grapes that you give to each of f friends, the product of g and f must be 100.

$$g \cdot f = 100$$

The product of g and f is a constant. When the value of f doubles, the value of g is halved. When the value of g doubles, the value of f is halved. You can say that g and f vary inversely.

> What does the word *inverse* mean in everyday language?

For You to Do

5. Give an example using numbers for f and g to illustrate the sentence "When the value of f doubles, the value of g is halved."

Sasha and Tony work on Exercise 11 from Lesson 3.07.

11. *A rectangular piece of paper has an area of 80 square inches. Draw a graph that shows all the possible lengths and widths of the paper.*

Sasha   We need some points to graph. The paper could be 8 inches by 10 inches, so we should plot (8, 10). That area is 8×10, or 80 square inches.

Tony   So can we use any two numbers that multiply to 80? Okay. The paper could be 4 inches by 20 inches. It could be 5 inches by 16 inches. I'm just finding any number that divides 80 evenly.

Sasha   I'll graph these three points. They're all in the first quadrant.

Tony   That looks good, but I can't complete the graph from 3 points. It's not a line through the origin. We need more points. I can think of (1, 80) and (2, 40).

Sasha   Those help a little. We need to know what the graph is when the length is more than 8. What happens if the length is 10 inches?

Tony   Then the width is 8 inches! All the points show up again, reversed. That gives us a ton of points.

They plot all the points that fit and draw this graph.

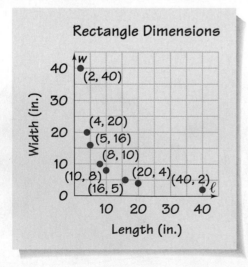

Tony   So, is that all? Did we get all the points?

Sasha   I'm not sure, but I think there might be more. This graph paper is $8\frac{1}{2}$ inches by 11 inches. Can we have a length of $8\frac{1}{2}$ inches and still get an area of 80 square inches?

Tony   Sure, that's like solving an equation. What number times $8\frac{1}{2}$ makes 80? I don't know exactly what it is, but I know there is one.

Sasha   What does that mean for our graph?

Tony   I think it means we need more points.

Sasha   A lot more! The length could be anything! We'll be plotting points forever.

Tony   Ah. It's not going to be a scatter plot, then. It's going to be like a line. I'll draw a curved line instead of a bunch of dots. I'll connect the points as smoothly as I can.

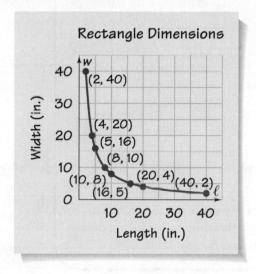

How are the points that correspond to (4, 20) and (20, 4) related?

Sasha   That looks great! I think it's perfect. Is there an equation for this thing?

For You to Do

6. Find an equation for Sasha and Tony's graph.

For Discussion

7. The point (800, 0.1) is not visible in the graph that Tony draws, but is the point part of the graph? Explain.

Developing Habits of Mind

Represent an inverse variation. In an equation representing inverse variation, the product of x and y is constant, or $xy = c$. You can also write the equation $xy = c$ as $y = \frac{c}{x}$. The equation shows that an increase in one variable means a proportional decrease in the other variable.

The graph of $y = \frac{c}{x}$ passes through $(1, c)$ and $(c, 1)$. This graph is the second basic graph shape. Here are the graph and a table of values for $c = 6$.

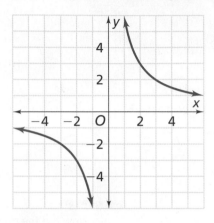

x	y
-6	-1
-3	-2
-1	-6
$-\frac{1}{2}$	-12
0	undefined
$\frac{1}{2}$	12
1	6
3	2
6	1

> The variable c is a number (a constant), while x and y are both variables that represent a number. So $xy = -5$ is an inverse variation equation, in which $c = -5$.

This graph is in two pieces! Since the value of x cannot be zero, the graph cannot cross the y-axis. If x is near zero, y is large in magnitude for both positive and negative values of x.

The location of the graph depends on whether the value of c is positive or negative. If c is positive, the graph goes through Quadrants I and III. If c is negative, the graph goes through Quadrants II and IV.

> Another term for *magnitude* is *absolute value*. The number -1000 is greater in magnitude than 16, although $-1000 < 16$.

San Francisco, 1906

San Francisco, 2006

The greater magnitudes possible for sway in modern structures make them less likely to be damaged in earthquakes. If you stand relaxed on a bumpy bus ride, it is easier to stay upright than if you rigidly brace yourself.

Exercises *Practicing Habits of Mind*

Check Your Understanding

1. Suppose a TV show offers a $1 million grand prize for a contest. If more than one person wins the contest, the winners split the prize.

   a. If five people win, how much money does each winner receive?

   b. Heidi wins and finds it shocking that her share of the grand prize is less than $50,000. Suppose each person receives less than $50,000. What is the least number of people who can split $1 million?

   c. Is this a case of direct variation or inverse variation? Explain.

   d. Describe this situation by defining variables and writing an equation.

2. Here is a graph for a direct variation situation.

   a. Is the point (16, 4) on the graph? Explain.

   b. The equation for direct variation is $y = cx$. Find c.

   c. **Write About It** Describe a situation that this graph represents. Define the variables x and y in the situation.

3. Decide whether each point is on the graph of $y = 3x$.

   a. $(-2, 6)$ **b.** $(3, 1)$ **c.** $(-2, -6)$

   d. $(2, 6)$ **e.** $(-4, -3)$ **f.** $(0, 0)$

4. Decide whether each point in Exercise 3 is on the graph of $xy = 12$.

5. As the value of x increases in the equation $xy = 6$, how does the value of y change? Can y equal zero?

6. What symmetries does the graph of $xy = 6$ have?

7. **a.** Find at least six ordered pairs (x, y) that are on the graph of $xy = -12$.

   b. What quadrants does the graph of $xy = -12$ pass through? Explain.

   c. Sketch the graph of the equation $xy = -12$, including the points you found in part (a).

8. How many points of intersection are on the graphs of $y = 3x$ and $xy = -12$?

9. **Take It Further** Suppose (a, b) is on the graph of $xy = 100$.

   a. Show that $(-a, -b)$ and (b, a) are also on the graph.

   b. What other points are on this graph?

On Your Own

10. A supermarket sells two cartons of milk for a total of $5.00.

    a. How much do you pay for 10 cartons?

    b. How much do you pay for one carton if each carton costs the same amount?

    c. Write a rule relating the number n of cartons to the total cost c.

    d. Is this situation an example of direct variation or inverse variation? Explain.

11. The distance a car travels at a constant speed varies directly with time. Suppose the car travels at 55 miles per hour.

    a. Find the amount of time it takes to travel 330 miles.

    b. How many miles does the car travel in 20 minutes?

    c. How many miles does the car travel in 40 minutes?

    d. Draw a graph of the number of miles traveled against the number of hours traveled.

    e. Find an equation relating distance d to time t.

12. Find a direct variation equation with a graph that contains each given point.

    a. $(3, 21)$

    b. $(21, 3)$

    c. $(-3, 21)$

    d. Find an inverse variation equation with a graph that contains the points $(3, 21)$ and $(21, 3)$.

13. The graphs of $y = 3x$ and $xy = 12$ intersect at two points.

    a. Explain why $(2, 6)$ and $(-2, -6)$ are intersection points.

    b. Sketch the graphs on graph paper. Show the location of the intersections.

Your distance from the lightning and the time it takes to hear the thunder are in direct variation.

Go Online
www.successnetplus.com

14. **Standardized Test Prep** Which of the following points is an intersection point of the graphs of $y = x$ and $y = \frac{16}{x}$?

   A. $(16, 1)$

   B. $(-4, -4)$

   C. $(-2, 8)$

   D. $(2, 2)$

15. **a.** Plot points and sketch the graph of $(x - 4) \cdot y = 12$.

   b. How does the graph in part (a) relate to the graph of $xy = 12$ in Exercise 13?

16. Suppose the equation $y = \frac{6}{x}$ is true.

   a. Are there any values that x cannot equal? Explain.

   b. Are there any values that y cannot equal? Explain.

Habits of Mind

Experiment. Try replacing x with numbers near 4. What pattern do you find in your results?

Maintain Your Skills

17. Graph each equation on the same coordinate plane.

   a. $y = x$

   b. $y = 2x$

   c. $y = 3x$

   d. $y = 4x$

   e. $y = 5x$

   f. Describe the pattern. How do the equations change? How does this change affect the graphs?

18. Graph each equation on the same coordinate plane.

   a. $y = x$

   b. $y = \frac{1}{2}x$

   c. $y = \frac{1}{3}x$

   d. $y = \frac{1}{4}x$

   e. $y = \frac{1}{5}x$

   f. Describe the pattern. How do the equations change? How does this change affect the graphs?

Go Online
Video Tutor
www.successnetplus.com

3.09 Four More Basic Graphs

The two basic graphs in Lesson 3.08 are graphs of the simple equations $y = cx$ and $xy = c$. You can represent the remaining four graphs using simple equations also. Becoming familiar with the location and shape of each graph is your goal for now.

The Equation $y = x^2$

In Lesson 3.07, you graphed the relationship between the side length and the area of a square. You can represent this relationship with the equation $y = x^2$, where x is the side length and y is the area.

The graph of this relationship is almost the same as the graph in Lesson 3.07 that relates the total number of tiles and the number of tiles in each row. The difference is that the area graph (at the right) is a smooth continuous curve that allows for all possible side lengths.

Even this graph is not the complete graph of $y = x^2$, because the side lengths include only positive numbers. The complete graph of $y = x^2$ allows for all real-number values of x. The complete graph lies in Quadrants I and II.

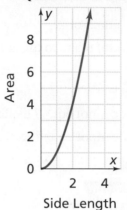

Quadratic Growth

Side Length / Area

$y = x^2$

x	y
−2	4
−1	1
$-\frac{1}{2}$	$\frac{1}{4}$
0	0
$\frac{1}{2}$	$\frac{1}{4}$
1	1
2	4

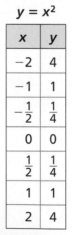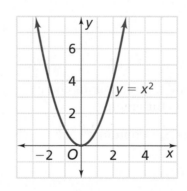

Habits of Mind

Experiment. To find points on the graph, substitute a value for x in the equation $y = x^2$. Then find y. Equations are point-testers, so if the value makes the equation true, the value is on the graph!

No matter what real number you choose for x, the value of x^2 is never negative. There are no negative y values on the graph.

Cross sections of these solar panels are quadratic curves.

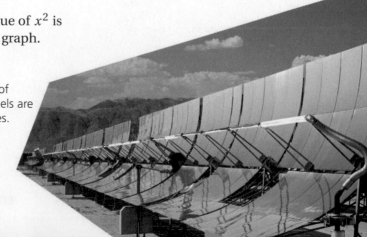

For Discussion

1. According to the graph of the equation $y = x^2$, how many values of x make $y = 9$?

2. Use only the graph of $y = x^2$ to find a close approximation of $\sqrt{5}$.

The Equation $y = x^3$

In Lesson 3.07, you graphed the relationship between the width of a cube on an edge and the number of smaller cubes in a larger cube. You used the equation

$$y = x^3$$

where x is the length of an edge and y is the volume of the cube. The graph of this relationship is the same as the graph in Lesson 3.07, showing the number of smaller cubes in a larger cube against the number of smaller cubes on an edge. The difference is that this graph is a smooth graph that includes all possible values of the side lengths.

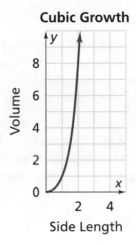

Cubic Growth

The complete graph of $y = x^3$ includes all the points on the above graph and the points where x is negative. When you cube a negative number, the result is also a negative number. For instance,

$$(-2)^3 = (-2) \cdot (-2) \cdot (-2) = -8$$

Unlike the graph of $y = x^2$, the other half of the graph of $y = x^3$ passes through Quadrant III.

$y = x^3$

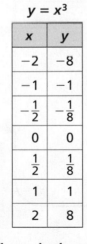

x	y
-2	-8
-1	-1
$-\frac{1}{2}$	$-\frac{1}{8}$
0	0
$\frac{1}{2}$	$\frac{1}{8}$
1	1
2	8

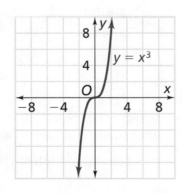

As the graph above shows, both x and y can be positive, negative, or zero.

3. According to the graph, between which two integers is the value of x for which $x^3 = -5$?

Developing Habits of Mind

Look for a relationship. The graph of $y = x^2$ and the graph of $y = x^3$ can look the same near the origin. Both graphs are nearly flat close to the origin, pass through the point (1, 1), and increase rapidly after that. Now, take a closer look.

When you square or cube a number between -1 and 1, the result is close to 0. However, the cube of a number between -1 and 1 is smaller in absolute value than the square of the number. This means that near zero the graph of $y = x^3$ is closer to the x-axis and flatter than the graph of $y = x^2$.

When you square or cube a number greater than 1 or less than -1, the absolute value of the result is greater than the original number. The cube of a positive number greater than 1 is greater than the square of the number. This means that in the graph of $y = x^3$ the values of y to the right of the intersection point (1, 1) increase more quickly than in the graph of $y = x^2$.

This sketch shows the two graphs on the same axes, when x is between -2 and 2.

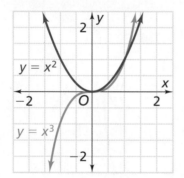

Notice that the two graphs intersect at two points, (0, 0) and (1, 1). These points of intersection occur since 0^3 equals 0^2, and 1^3 equals 1^2.

Notice that the graph of $y = x^3$ is below the graph of $y = x^2$ when x is between 0 and 1.

Habits of Mind

Experiment. Replace x in $y = x^2$ with numbers between -1 and 1. Then, replace x with numbers greater than 1 or less than -1. Compare how far the y-values are from 0. Repeat the experiment for $y = x^3$.

Equations are point-testers. Points (0, 0) and (1, 1) are on the graph of $y = x^2$, because $0^2 = 0$ and $1^2 = 1$. Also, (0, 0) and (1, 1) are on the graph of $y = x^3$ because $0^3 = 0$ and $1^3 = 1$. Why are there no other intersections?

The Equation $y = \sqrt{x}$

In Lesson 3.07, you graphed the relationship $y = x^2$ between a square's side length x and the square's area y.

You can look at the relationship between side length and area in another way. Suppose you need to change the area of a square and want to know the effect this would have on side length. You can represent the relationship with the equation $y = \sqrt{x}$, where x is the area and y is the side length.

Square Root

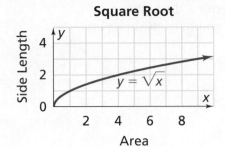

The graph of $y = \sqrt{x}$ looks like the graph of $y = x^2$, except the axes are reversed. There is, however, a big difference between the graphs of $y = x^2$ and $y = \sqrt{x}$. Part of the graph of $y = x^2$ lies in Quadrant II where the values of x are negative. For the equation $y = \sqrt{x}$, the value of x cannot be negative.

Turn your book 90° counterclockwise. Does this graph now look like the graph of $y = x^2$?

By convention, the square root of a number is always nonnegative, so the value of y cannot be negative, either. Since both x and y cannot be negative, the graph of $y = \sqrt{x}$ lies only in Quadrant I.

$y = \sqrt{x}$

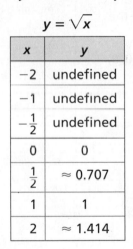

x	y
−2	undefined
−1	undefined
$-\frac{1}{2}$	undefined
0	0
$\frac{1}{2}$	≈ 0.707
1	1
2	≈ 1.414

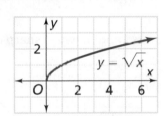

For You to Do

4. Is there a value for x that makes y greater than 100 on the graph of $y = \sqrt{x}$? Find a value if you can. If you cannot, explain.

The Equation $y = |x|$

Suppose you want to graph the relationship between a number and its distance from 0 on the number line. The absolute value of a number represents a number's distance from 0 on a number line. You can express this relationship with the equation $y = |x|$, where x is the number on the number line and y is its distance from 0. The graph below shows this relationship.

Absolute Value

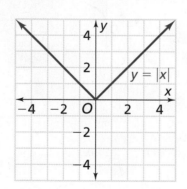

This graph resembles the graph of $y = x^2$ but has a sharp corner at the origin. Also, its sides are straight, not curved.

If you look at the graph as two pieces, each piece is a straight line, much like the direct-variation graphs. When x is positive, the graph looks just like the graph for the equation $y = x$. When x is negative, y is still positive since the absolute value of a number is never negative. The graph looks just like the graph of $y = -x$.

Breaking the graph into two pieces relates to the meaning of absolute value.

$$|x| = \begin{cases} x, & \text{if } x \geq 0 \\ -x, & \text{if } x < 0 \end{cases}$$

The complete graph lies in Quadrants I and II, with a sharp corner at (0, 0).

$y = |x|$

x	y
-2	2
-1	1
$-\frac{1}{2}$	$\frac{1}{2}$
0	0
$\frac{1}{2}$	$\frac{1}{2}$
1	1
2	2

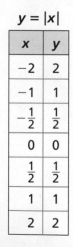

For Discussion

5. How does the graph change if y is the distance of x from 3 on the number line instead of from zero?

Exercises *Practicing Habits of Mind*

Check Your Understanding

Exercises 1–5 use the graphs of these six equations.

- $y = x$
- $y = x^2$
- $y = \sqrt{x}$
- $y = \frac{1}{x}$
- $y = x^3$
- $y = |x|$

1. Which of the six graphs pass through $(1, 1)$?

2. Which of the six graphs pass through $(-1, 1)$?

3. Which of the six graphs pass through Quadrant IV?

4. Each set of axes shows three (I–III) of the six graphs.
   Write the equation for each graph.

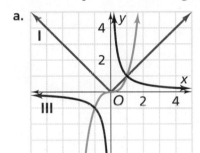   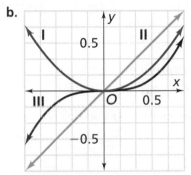

As the number of painters increases, the time that it takes to paint a mural decreases. Which basic graph does this suggest?

5. Name all of the six graphs that pass through each point.

   a. $(9, 3)$ b. $(-2, -8)$ c. $(-4, 4)$ d. $(-10, -10)$
   e. $(10, 10^2)$ f. $(-10, -0.1)$ g. $(10^2, 10^6)$ h. $(10^2, 10)$

6. Suppose x is a number greater than 1000. Order the values
   $|x|, \frac{1}{x}, x^3, x^2$, and $\sqrt{x}$ from least to greatest.

7. Sketch a graph of each equation. What are the possible values of x and y?
   a. $y = \sqrt{x - 4}$ b. **Take It Further** $y = \sqrt{-x}$

On Your Own

8. Suppose x is a positive number less than 1 and close to 0.
   Order the values $|x|, \frac{1}{x}, x^3, x^2$, and $\sqrt{x}$ from least to greatest.

9. Suppose x is a small-magnitude negative number greater than -1.
   Order the values $|x|, \frac{1}{x}, x^3, x^2$, and x from least to greatest.

10. Suppose x is a large-magnitude negative number less than -1000. Order the values $|x|$, $\frac{1}{x}$, x^3, x^2, and x from least to greatest.

11. **Standardized Test Prep** Choose the rule that shows the relationship between x and y in the table.

    A. $y = -3x + 4$ **B.** $y = 4x$

    C. $y = \sqrt{x}$ **D.** $y = x^2$

x	y
-4	16
-1	1
0	0
3	9
7	49

12. Find the number of points of intersection for the graph of each pair of equations.

    a. $y = x^2$ and $y = x^3$ **b.** $y = x$ and $y = x^3$

    c. $y = |x|$ and $y = \frac{1}{x}$ **d.** $y = x^2$ and $y = |x|$

13. **Take It Further** Recall the six equations listed before Exercise 1. Which two of these equations have graphs with more than three intersection points? How many intersection points do the two graphs have?

14. You can represent the relationship between time and distance for an object in free fall in Earth's gravity with the equation $d = 4.9t^2$. Here, d is the distance in meters and t is the time in seconds.

    a. If the value of t is 0, what is the value of d?

    b. Find the value of d when the value of t is 4, 8, and 16.

    c. If the value of t doubles, how does the value of d change?

    d. Draw a graph of the relationship between t and d.

    e. **Write About It** Describe the similarities and differences between the graph in part (d) and the basic graph of $y = x^2$.

15. **Take It Further** Use the equation $d = 4.9t^2$.

    a. What is the value of t when d is 100? When d is 300? Round to the nearest hundredth.

    b. If the value of d triples, how does the value of t change?

Go Online
www.successnetplus.com

Maintain Your Skills

16. Sketch the graph of each equation.

    a. $y = (x + 3)^2$ **b.** $y = (x + 3)^3$ **c.** $y = |x + 3|$

    d. $y = \sqrt{x + 3}$ **e.** $(y - 6) = x^2$ **f.** $(y - 6) = x^3$

    g. $(y - 6) = |x|$ **h.** $(y - 6) = \sqrt{x}$ **i.** $(y - 6) = (x + 3)^2$

    j. $(y - 6) = (x + 3)^3$ **k.** $(y - 6) = |x + 3|$ **l.** $(y - 6) = \sqrt{x + 3}$

    m. How are the graphs in parts (a)–(l) related to the basic graphs?

Habits of Mind

Look for a pattern. If you can find the pattern, you can sketch these graphs more quickly.

Mathematical 3B Reflections

In this investigation, you learned about six basic graphs and their equations. Two of the basic graphs show direct and inverse variation. These questions will help you summarize what you have learned.

1. Show that the points are on the graph of the given equation.

   a. (6, 13) and (−6, −13), $xy = 78$

   b. (12, 3) and (3, 12), $xy = 36$

2. Describe the relationship between the graphs of $y = x^2$ and $y + 4 = (x - 5)^2$.

3. What is the point that all six basic graphs pass through?

4. Sketch a graph of each equation.

   a. $y = (x + 2)^2$ **b.** $y - 3 = x^3$

   c. $y + 4 = |x - 2|$ **d.** $y = 5x$

   e. $xy = 5$ **f.** $y = 5x^2$

5. Sketch the basic graph of $y = x^2$.

6. What does it mean to say two variables vary directly or inversely?

7. What are the six basic graphs? Sketch each graph.

8. If you free fall 4.9 meters in one second, how far do you free fall in four seconds?

Vocabulary

In this investigation, you learned these terms. Make sure you understand what each one means and how to use it.

- **direct variation**
- **inverse variation**

The transformation $(x, y) \mapsto (x, y - 10)$ takes you down 10 floors.

Investigation 3C

All About Slope

In *All About Slope*, you will find the slope between two points. You will discover the relationship between the slope of a graph and the rate of change. You will also learn the meaning of collinear points.

By the end of this investigation, you will be able to answer questions like these.

1. How do people use linear equations and slope in different fields of work such as carpentry, engineering, and mathematics?

2. How can you use slopes to tell whether three points are collinear?

3. How can you use a point-tester to tell whether the point $(3, -2)$ is on the line through $A(2, -5)$ and $B(4, 3)$?

You will learn how to

• calculate the slope between two points

• calculate the average speed between two points on a distance-time graph

• find other points on a line when given a slope and a point

You will develop these habits and skills:

• Relate slope to the steepness of a graph.

• Calculate speed and other rates of change.

• Understand how the slope of a graph relates to a rate of change.

• Use slopes to determine whether three points are collinear.

Slope between points can be a large positive number.

Activating Prior Knowledge
Exploring New Ideas

You can describe the steepness of a line by comparing rise to run. Carpenters calculate the steepness of roofs and ramps. Mathematicians calculate the steepness of lines.

For You to Explore

1. Which roof is the steepest?

a.

b.

> Explain how you decided which roof is the steepest to a person who does not understand the word *steep*.

c.

d.

2. The gable end of a roof is the triangular part of the wall. It supports the peak of the roof at each end of the house. When building a gable end, a builder supports the roof with vertical boards. The builder spaces the boards 16 inches apart.

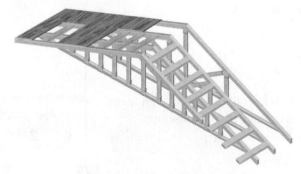

Diagram of a Gable End

The diagram shows half of the gable end of a house.

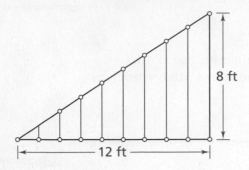

8 ft

12 ft

a. What are the rise and run of the gable end?

b. How many vertical boards are there? How are the vertical boards spaced?

c. How long is each of the vertical boards?

3. Tony makes a distance-time graph for a bike trip he took with Sasha.

Rise is the difference between the starting and ending points on a vertical number line. **Run** is the difference between the starting and ending points on a horizontal number line.

a. Who rode faster, Tony or Sasha? Explain.

b. What does the intersection of the lines represent?

c. How many miles did Sasha travel in an hour?

d. How many miles did Tony travel in an hour?

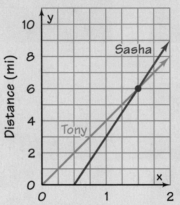

Distance From School

4. Use your graphing calculator. Which equations have a graph that is a line? What do the equations with graphs that are lines have in common?

a. $y = x$

b. $y = x^2$

c. $y = 5x + 2$

d. $y = \frac{1}{x}$

e. $y = x^3 - x^2 + 5$

f. $y = 4x - 13 + 2x - 7$

g. $y = x + 1$

h. $y = \sqrt{x} + 1$

i. $y = x^3 + 1$

j. $y = 2(13 - 7x)$

For Problems 5 and 6, plot the points given. Draw a straight line through them. Name three points that are on the same line as each given pair of points.

Points that lie on the same line are **collinear**.

5. (3, 1) and (7, 3)

6. (7, 1) and (12, −3)

On Your Own

7. Manny uses an extension ladder to paint the window shutters on his house. A safety label on the ladder states that you need to place the base of the ladder 1 foot from the wall for every 4 feet the ladder reaches up the wall. The diagram shows a ladder that reaches 8 feet up the wall. The base of the ladder is 2 feet from the wall.

> An extension ladder is a ladder with a length you can change.

8 ft.

2 ft.

a. How far away from the wall should Manny place the base of the ladder if he needs to paint window shutters 12 feet up the wall?

b. How far away from the wall should Manny place the base of the ladder if he needs to paint window shutters 10 feet up the wall?

c. How can Manny determine the ladder's safe distance from a wall if he knows how high he wants the top of the ladder?

8. a. What is an equation of the vertical line that contains the point (5, 7)?

b. What is an equation of the horizontal line that contains the point (2, −1)?

c. At what point do the two lines intersect?

9. Determine whether the three points are collinear. Explain.

a. $X(-3, 3)$, $Y(4, 3)$, $Z(100, 3)$

b. $P(-3, 8)$, $Q(-3, 2)$, $R(-3, -4)$

c. $A(-1, 3)$, $B(4, 15)$, $C(14, 39)$

d. $E(3, 5)$, $F(4, 6)$, $G(10, 13)$

> **Remember...**
> Points are collinear if they lie on the same straight line.

10. Maria rode her bike 8 miles in 1 hour. How fast did she travel in miles per hour?

11. Write About It The graph shows the distance Maria travels against the time she bikes.

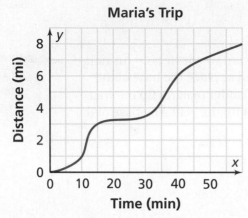

Maria's Trip

The vertical axis on this graph represents the actual distance Maria travels on her bike. It does not necessarily represent the exact distance she is from her starting point.

a. Why is this graph a better representation of Maria's trip than the description in Exercise 10?

b. Does Maria travel at a constant pace? Explain.

c. How does the pace you calculated in Exercise 10 relate to the graph?

Maintain Your Skills

Go Online
www.successnetplus.com

12. Use graph paper. Sketch each pair of equations.

   a. $y = x$ and $y = -x$

   b. $y = 2x$ and $y = -2x$

   c. $y = \frac{1}{2}x$ and $y = -\frac{1}{2}x$

   d. What do you notice about the pairs of graphs?

For Exercises 13 and 14, graph each equation on graph paper.
Look for a pattern.

13. a. $y = x$ **b.** $y = 2x$ **c.** $y = 3x$

    d. $y = 4x$ **e.** $y = 15x$ **f.** $y = 1000x$

    g. Describe the pattern.

14. a. $y = \frac{1}{2}x$ **b.** $y = \frac{1}{3}x$ **c.** $y = \frac{1}{4}x$

    d. $y = \frac{1}{5}x$ **e.** $y = \frac{1}{15}x$ **f.** $y = \frac{1}{1000}x$

    g. Describe the pattern.

Go Online
Video Tutor
www.successnetplus.com

3.11 Pitch and Slope

Builders describe the steepness of a roof using a number that they call the *pitch*. The pitch tells how many inches the roof rises vertically for every 12 inches of horizontal run.

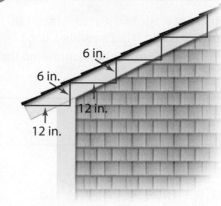

Suppose a roof rises 6 inches for every 12 inches of horizontal run. You can say that the roof has a "6 in 12 pitch," "6–12 pitch," or "6 pitch."

In mathematics, you use a number, or *slope*, to describe the steepness of a line between one point and another point in the Cartesian plane. Suppose the vertical rise from one point to another on a line is 6 units, and the horizontal run is 12 units. You can say that the line has a slope of $\frac{6}{12}$, or $\frac{1}{2}$.

> In carpentry, the custom is to write pitch as a number related to 12, because there are 12 inches in a foot. There is no such custom for slope. You can express slope as a fraction in simplest form.

Example 1

Problem Suppose a line connects points $A(5, 6)$ and $B(9, 13)$. Find the slope of the line between the points.

Solution $m(A, B) = \dfrac{\text{rise}}{\text{run}} = \dfrac{13 - 6}{9 - 5} = \dfrac{7}{4}$. The slope is $\dfrac{7}{4}$.

> It is common to use m to denote slope. The expression $m(A, B)$ represents the slope of a line between points A and B.

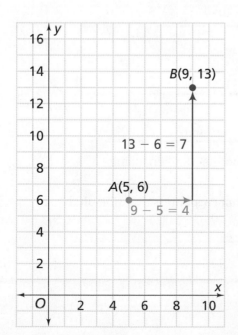

Represent slope. You can represent slope in different ways. For example, the slope between points A and B in Example 1 is $\frac{7}{4}$. You can also write $\frac{7}{4}$ as $1\frac{3}{4}$, $\frac{14}{8}$, 1.75, or any other expression that represents the same number as $\frac{7}{4}$.

For You to Do

Graph points A and B from Example 1.

1. Find two other points, S and T, such that $m(S, T) = \frac{7}{4}$ also.

2. Does $m(S, T) = m(T, S)$?

3. Given point $M(3, 15)$, plot 6 other points such that the slope from each of the points to M is $\frac{4}{3}$.

> Draw lines through points A and B and through points S and T.

Example 2

Problem Find the slope between the points $R(7, 2)$ and $S(10, 0)$.

Solution $m(R, S) = \frac{0-2}{10-7} = \frac{-2}{3} = -\frac{2}{3}$. The slope is $-\frac{2}{3}$.

> Is $m(S, R)$ also negative?

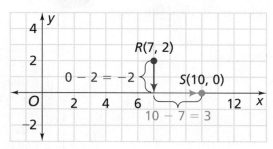

For Discussion

4. How can you calculate the slope between two points? Explain, using an example.

5. What are some differences between the ways that carpenters describe pitch and mathematicians describe slope?

Definition

In the Cartesian plane, the **slope** between two points with different x-coordinates is the change in their y-coordinates divided by the change in their x-coordinates.

For any two points $A(x_1, y_1)$ and $B(x_2, y_2)$,

$$m(A, B) = \frac{\text{rise}}{\text{run}} = \frac{\text{change in the } y\text{-coordinates}}{\text{change in the } x\text{-coordinates}} = \frac{\Delta y}{\Delta x} = \frac{y_2 - y_1}{x_2 - x_1}.$$

> If the x-coordinates are the same, slope is undefined. This happens when the two points are in line vertically.

Facts and Notation

- The Greek letter Δ, delta, means *change in*.
- The "1" and "2" in x_1 and x_2 are **subscripts**. The subscripts indicate that x_1 and x_2 represent different variables. Likewise, y_1 and y_2 are different variables.

> You can use different letters to represent the coordinates. However, using x_1 and x_2 makes it clear that they both represent x-coordinates. Similarly, y_1 and y_2 are both y-coordinates. The subscripts also help you keep track of relationships among variables.

For You to Do

6. **What's Wrong Here?** Sasha calculates the slope from $P(3, 4)$ to $Q(2, 6)$.

> The change in the y-coordinates is $4 - 6 = -2$.
>
> The change in the x-coordinates is $2 - 3 = -1$.
>
> The slope is $\frac{-2}{-1} = 2$.

Tony calculates the slope differently.

> The change in the y-coordinates is $6 - 4 = 2$.
>
> The change in the x-coordinates is $2 - 3 = -1$.
>
> The slope is $\frac{2}{-1} = -2$.

a. Who found the correct slope?

b. What can you say to help the person with the incorrect slope?

Exercises Practicing Habits of Mind

Check Your Understanding

1. Find the slope between each pair of points.

   a. (2, 1) and (6, 8)

   b. (6, 8) and (2, 1)

   c. (3, 10) and (12, 2)

   d. (3, 10) and $\left(\frac{15}{2}, 6\right)$

   e. $\left(\frac{15}{2}, 6\right)$ and (12, 2)

   f. (−4, 5) and (0, 0)

   g. (5, 4) and (0, 0)

   h. (−8, 10) and (0, 0)

   i. (−4, 5) and (12, 5)

   j. (5, 4) and (−20, 4)

   k. (3, 3) and (25, 25)

   l. (4, 5) and (4, −7)

2. For each of the following, graph points A and B. Find another point C such that $m(A, B) = m(A, C)$.

   a. $A(-2, 4), B(-1, 5)$

   b. $A(3, 4), B(-1, 5)$

   c. $A(0, 0), B(4, -12)$

   d. $A(-3, 1), B(0, 0)$

   e. What can you conclude about points A, B, and C when $m(A, B) = m(A, C)$?

> **Remember...**
>
> The slope is the rise over the run.

3. Find two points A and B that will make each statement true, if possible.

   a. $m(A, B) > 0$

   b. $m(A, B) < 0$

   c. $m(A, B) = 0$

   d. $m(A, B)$ does not exist.

4. Use tables to graph each equation. Choose three points on each graph to test for a constant slope. How do the graphs that have a constant slope differ from those that do not?

   a. $y = \frac{1}{2}x - 4$

   b. $y = x^2$

   c. $y = 5x$

   d. $y + 3 = 2(x - 4)$

   e. $y = 2^x$

   f. $y = 2x^2 + 1$

> Constant slope means that the slope between any two points on the graph is the same.

If the rise is the same and the runs are opposites, then the slopes are opposites.

5. **Write About It** What are some other situations in which you can describe and compare steepness?

6. **Take It Further** The slope between points $J(9, r)$ and $K(6, 3)$ is $-\frac{1}{3}$. What is the value of r?

On Your Own

7. Find the slope between each pair of points.

   Again, plot the points to find the slope.

   a. $(-6, 4)$ and $(0, 0)$ **b.** $(4, 6)$ and $(0, 0)$

   c. $\left(\frac{1}{2}, 13\right)$ and $\left(-2\frac{2}{3}, 13\right)$ **d.** $(27, -7.1)$ and $(27, 5.2)$

   e. $(-6, -1)$ and $(-1, 8)$ **f.** $(-6, -1)$ and $(4, 17)$

   g. $(4, 17)$ and $(-1, 8)$ **h.** $(3, 4)$ and $(5, 1)$

   i. $(5, 1)$ and $(3, 4)$

8. Given $A(5, 3)$ and $O(0, 0)$, find a point B that makes the following true.

   a. $m(A, B) - 3$ **b.** $m(A, B) = -3$ **c.** $m(A, B) = -\frac{1}{3}$

   d. $m(A, B) = 0$ **e.** $m(A, B) = m(O, B)$

   f. $m(A, B) = \frac{3}{4}$ and the distance between points A and B is 5.

9. How can you describe the relative positions of A and B in each situation?

   a. $m(A, B) > 0$ **b.** $m(A, B) < 0$

   c. $m(A, B) = 0$ **d.** $m(A, B)$ does not exist.

   Go Online
   www.successnetplus.com

10. **a.** What is $m(T, J)$?

    b. Choose another point P on $\overleftrightarrow{TJ}$. Calculate $m(T, P)$ and $m(P, J)$.

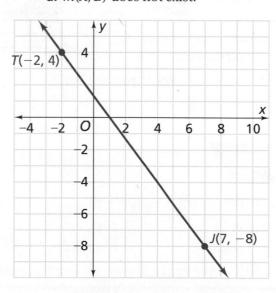

11. Jenna tests whether points $A(3, 4)$, $B(5, 7)$, and $C(9, 13)$ are on the same line. She plots the points. Then she draws triangles with sides parallel to the x- and y-axes.

She explains her test. "To go from A to B, I go over 2 and up 3. To go from B to C, I go over exactly twice as far and up exactly twice as far."

Try Jenna's test on Exercise 10. Does her method work? Explain. Use the word *slope* in your explanation.

12. Standardized Test Prep Lorna writes a computer game on a coordinate grid. The frog in her game can jump from one pair of integer coordinates to another pair. Point A is at $(4, 5)$ and $m(A, B) = -\frac{2}{3}$. Which of the following cannot be the coordinates of point B?

A. $(10, 1)$ **B.** $(7, 3)$ **C.** $(1, 7)$ **D.** $(2, 8)$

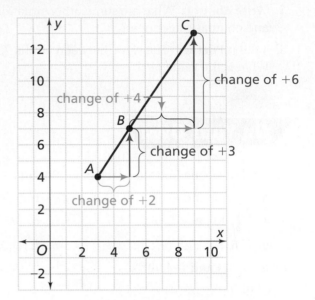

13. Take It Further The roof pitch for the house at the right is 6–12. The house is 28 feet wide.

a. What is the attic roof height h?

b. Steps are usually 8 inches high. The treads you step on are usually 12 inches from the front to the back of the tread. About how high above the ground is the front porch?

c. About how far from the porch foundation is the front of the bottom step?

d. About how high is the house? (*Hint:* Estimate the height between the porch and the attic.)

e. About how far from the house foundation do you need to place a ladder so that it safely reaches the peak of the house?

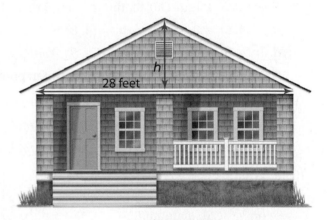

For safety, a ladder's base must be 1 foot from the wall for every 4 feet it extends up the wall.

Maintain Your Skills

14. Use graph paper. Sketch a roof with each given pitch.

a. 1–12   **b.** 3 in 12   **c.** 6 pitch

d. 2 in 12   **e.** 4 pitch   **f.** 12 in 12

15. Suppose each roof in Exercise 14 represents a line in the coordinate plane.

a. Write the pitch of each line as a fraction in lowest terms.

b. How does each fraction relate to the steepness of each roof?

In Lesson 3.05, you graphed one set of data against another. For instance, you used this graph to illustrate Emma walking to a basketball court.

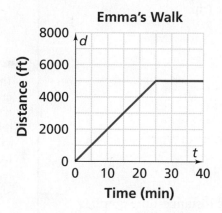

Emma's Walk

In that example, you focused on describing her distance from home at particular times. You can also use the graph to determine her average speed between two points on the graph.

Speed is the rate at which distance traveled changes. For example, Emma travels 5000 feet in 25 minutes. You can find her average speed using this formula.

$$\text{average speed} = \frac{\Delta \text{distance}}{\Delta \text{time}}$$

$$= \frac{5000 \text{ ft}}{25 \text{ min}}$$

$$= \frac{200 \text{ ft}}{1 \text{ min}}$$

Emma travels at 200 feet per minute (ft/min).

You can also calculate her speed by finding the slope between the two points $A(10, 2000)$ and $B(25, 5000)$.

$$m(A, B) = \frac{5000 \text{ ft} - 2000 \text{ ft}}{25 \text{ min} - 10 \text{ min}}$$

$$= \frac{3000 \text{ ft}}{15 \text{ min}}$$

$$= \frac{200 \text{ ft}}{1 \text{ min}}$$

Per implies division. *Percent* means "part of one hundred."

If Emma is not traveling at a constant speed, you can still calculate her average speed by finding the slope between two points.

Example

Problem The graph represents a trip Tia took. The labeled points on the graph have the coordinates $O(0, 0)$, $A(1, 75)$, $B(1.5, 7.5)$, and $C(2, 100)$.

What is Tia's average speed between the following points?

a. O and A

b. B and C

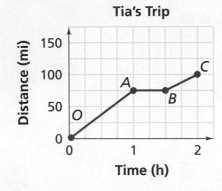

Tia's Trip

> The distance on this graph is the actual distance the car traveled. It is not necessarily the exact distance Tia is from home.

Solution The average speed between two points on a distance-time graph is the change in distance divided by the change in time. As you saw in Tia's case, the slope between these two points is the same as her average speed between the two points.

a. Calculate Tia's average speed from point O to point A.

$$m(O, A) = \frac{75\text{ mi} - 0\text{ mi}}{1\text{ h} - 0\text{ h}} = \frac{75\text{ mi}}{1\text{ h}} = 75\text{ mi per hour}$$

Her average speed is 75 miles per hour.

b. Calculate Tia's average speed from point B to point C.

$$m(B, C) = \frac{100\text{ mi} - 75\text{ mi}}{2\text{ h} - 1.5\text{ h}} = \frac{25\text{ mi}}{0.5\text{ h}} = 50\text{ mph}$$

Her average speed is 50 miles per hour.

> You can write abbreviations, such as mi for miles and h for hours. You can also write mph, or mi/h, for miles per hour.

For You to Do

1. What is Tia's average speed between point A and point B?

If you pick any two points on a distance-time graph, the slope between the two points is the same as the average speed of travel between those points. This statement is true because of the facts below.

- On a graph, you calculate the slope between two points as the vertical change divided by the horizontal change.
- On a distance-time graph, vertical change represents the distance traveled.
- On a distance-time graph, horizontal change represents the elapsed time.
- Therefore, the slope between two points on a distance-time graph is distance traveled divided by elapsed time. You can calculate average speed the same way.

Theorem 3.1

The slope between two points on a distance-time graph is the average speed of travel between those points.

For You to Do

2. Explain the theorem in your own words. Give an example.

Developing Habits of Mind

Visualize relationships. You can compute the average speed if you know the total change in position divided by the change in time. In these graphs, the total change in distance is 100 miles. The total change in time is 2 hours.

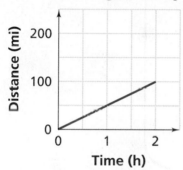

Moving Steadily

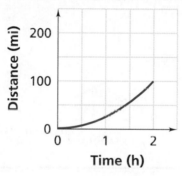

Speeding Up Gradually

The Moving Steadily graph is a line because the slope between any two points is the same.

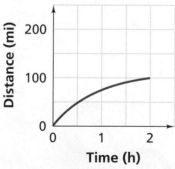

Slowing Down Gradually

In each case, the overall rate of change is 50 miles per hour. Remember that the average speed is the slope between the start and end points on a graph.

The graphs below show speed against time instead of distance against time for the same situations. In speed-time graphs, you view speed differently than in distance-time graphs. In distance-time graphs, you think of average speed as the change in distance over a large interval of time. In speed-time graphs, you can think of speed as the change in distance over a very small amount of time.

A car's speedometer shows average speed for a very small interval using this method.

Moving Steadily

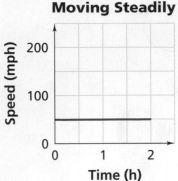

Speeding Up Gradually

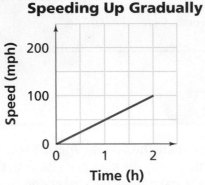

In a speed-time graph at $t = 1$, the plotted value of speed is approximately the change in distance from $t = 1$ to $t = 1.0001$ hours. The ratio may involve very small numbers, such as 0.005 mi/0.0001 h, or 50 mi/h. You can think of travelling 50 mi/h for a very short time interval.

Slowing Down Gradually

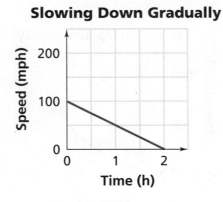

For You to Do

3. Write a story for another trip with an average rate of change of 50 mph. Illustrate this story with a graph different from the graphs above. Draw a distance-time graph and a speed-time graph for your story.

4. Explain how each of the speed graphs relates to the corresponding distance graph.

You have seen examples of rate of change that compare distance over time. In fact, rate of change problems can compare any two numerical quantities. For example, accountants measure rate of change by tracking money over time. Electric companies track the amount of electricity a customer uses over time. Exercise physiologists calculate the Calories a person burns for each minute of exercise.

Rates of change do not always involve time. The nutrition labels on food show the number of Calories per serving. Fabric shops and carpet stores charge for their goods by the square yard.

Exercises Practicing Habits of Mind

Check Your Understanding

1. The graph shows additional details of Tia's trip. As in the Example, the points on the graph are $O(0, 0)$, $A(1, 75)$, $B(1.5, 75)$, and $C(2, 100)$. The coordinates for points D and E are unknown.

   a. Compute the average speed between points D and A.

   b. Compute the average speed between points A and E.

   c. Estimate the coordinates of points D and E. Approximate the average speed between points D and E.

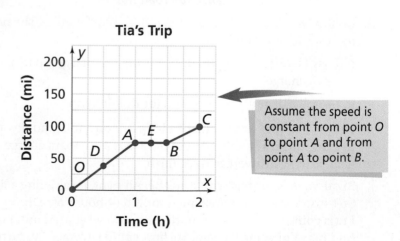

Assume the speed is constant from point O to point A and from point A to point B.

When entering a toll road, you take a ticket that shows your location. When leaving the toll road, you give the ticket to a toll-taker. The toll-taker reads the ticket to tell how far you have traveled and collects the correct toll.

Some toll road systems also time-stamp a ticket when you take it. A toll-taker can then tell how far you have traveled and the time you have taken. Using these two numbers, the toll-taker can calculate your average speed.

For Exercises 2–5, make the following assumptions.

- A toll ticket shows your location and the time that you entered a toll road.

- The toll is 3¢ per mile.

- A toll-taker charges an extra $100 if your average speed is between 65 mi/h and 80 mi/h.

- A toll-taker charges an extra $200 if your average speed is more than 80 mi/h.

2. Tanner enters a toll road at 3 P.M. He leaves the toll road at 6:30 P.M. He travels 200 miles.

   a. What is the toll for the distance he travels?

   b. What is his average speed? Is there an extra charge?

3. Tanner travels home on a toll road from 10 A.M. to 1 P.M. He travels 200 miles.

   a. What is the toll for the distance he travels?

   b. What is his average speed? Is there an extra charge?

   c. Tanner does not want to pay an extra charge. What is the shortest time that he could travel on a toll road home?

4. Kristin travels a toll road for 120 miles. After 70 miles, she notices that she has traveled for one hour.

   a. How fast should Kristin drive for the rest of the trip to avoid an extra charge?

   b. Sketch a distance-time graph for Kristin's trip.

5. **Take It Further** At the end of a long trip on a toll road, Ryota gives his ticket to a toll-taker. The toll-taker says, "There is an extra charge of $100. You were driving an average of 70 mi/h."

   Ryota replies, "What? That can't be. All right, I was going a little too fast. So I stopped at a rest area and took a half-hour nap. During that time, I was going zero miles per hour. Also, when I started out, I was going 0. And now I'm going 0 again. So, how could I average 70 mi/h?"

The astute toll-taker responds, "Well, take out the nap time and you averaged 80 mi/h."

Catching the drift, Ryota murmurs, "OK, so maybe I didn't take a nap."

a. How many miles was Ryota's trip? How long did it take, including the alleged nap?

b. Sketch two possible distance-time graphs for Ryota's trip. Include his nap in one graph but not in the other.

On Your Own

6. You can measure a car's fuel efficiency in miles per gallon. Compare the number of miles driven to the number of gallons of gasoline used. The graph shows examples of distance against gas used in highway driving for three car models.

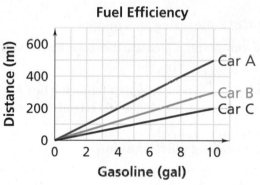

Fuel Efficiency

SUV

Sedan

Hybrid

a. Based on the type of car at the right, which graph do you think represents the fuel used by each car?

b. Find each car's rate of change in miles per gallon.

7. The time it takes to download files from the Internet varies depending on the type of connection. The rate of transfer is measured in kilobits per second (kbps).

A trailer for a new video game is available online. It is 6 megabytes, which is about 49,000 kilobits. How long does it take to download the trailer with the following connections?

a. cable modem running at 1200 kbps

b. DSL line running at 384 kbps

c. 56-kbps modem

d. 2400-baud modem (2.4 kbps)

> The first modems transferred data at a rate of 300 baud, or about 0.3 kbps. Today's modems are nearly 200 times as fast!

8. An advertisement claims a car can go from zero to 60 in five seconds.

a. What unit of measure is implied by 60?

b. Is it impressive that a car can go 60? Are there any cars that cannot go 60?

c. Draw a speed-time graph for a car that travels from zero to 60 in five seconds.

9. **Take It Further** Refer to Exercise 8.

   a. What is the rate of change of the car's speed?

   b. What word usually describes the rate of change of speed?

   c. Draw a distance-time graph for a car traveling from 0 to 60 in 5 seconds. How far does the car travel during those 5 seconds?

Go Online
www.successnetplus.com

For Exercises 10 and 11, assume Katie bikes at a rate of 230 yards per minute.

10. a. How far will she bike in 5 minutes?

    b. How long will it take her to bike the length of a football field? A football field is 100 yards long.

    c. Draw a distance-time graph of Katie biking for 5 minutes.

    d. Choose any two points on your graph. Calculate the slope between those two points.

11. One minute after Katie starts biking, two friends start following her. Nick bikes at a rate of 200 yards per minute. Lance bikes at a rate of 300 yards per minute.

    a. Will Nick catch Katie? If so, how long will it take him?

    b. Will Lance catch Katie? If so, how long will it take him?

12. **Standardized Test Prep** Tamara travels 1 mile at 60 miles per hour. She travels the next 1 mile at 30 miles per hour. How long is her trip, in minutes? What is her average speed, in miles per hour?

    A. 2 min; 45 mi/h

    B. 2 min; 40 mi/h

    C. 3 min; 40 mi/h

    D. 3 min; 45 mi/h

Competitive racers can travel at the rate of 900 yards per minute.

13. a. Between which pairs of points is the speed constant?

    b. Between which pair of points is the speed 0?

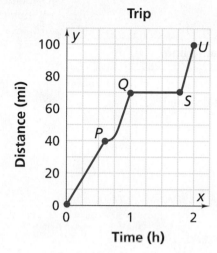

14. Take It Further Tony tosses a ball straight up. Sasha records its flight with a video camera. Later they graph the ball's height against time. Graph the ball's speed against time.

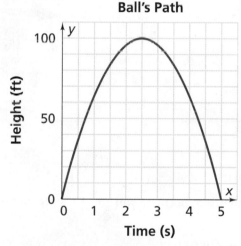

> If the ball travels straight up, why does the graph move up and across?

15. Write About It Kwata says, "I can use a car's speedometer to figure out my average speed between any two points. I note my speed at each point. Then I find the average of the speeds." Is Kwata correct? Explain.

Maintain Your Skills

16. Draw a distance-time graph for a three-hour trip at these steady speeds.

    a. 30 mph   **b.** 40 mph   **c.** 45 mph

    d. 50 mph   **e.** 60 mph

You can always draw a line that includes any two given points. However, you cannot always draw a single line that includes three or more points.

Sometimes, the three points form a triangle.

Definition

Points in a set are **collinear** if they all lie on the same line.

These points appear to form a triangle. They are not collinear.

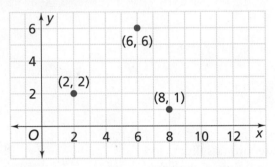

These points lie on a horizontal line. They are collinear.

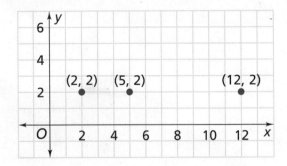

How can you tell whether points are on a horizontal line by looking at their coordinates?

Here are a few facts about points and collinearity:

• Any two points are always collinear with each other, because you can draw a line that contains them both.

• All the points on a line are collinear with each other.

• A point that is not on a line cannot be collinear with any pair of points on the line.

For Discussion

1. What are some possible ways to determine whether three points are collinear by looking at their coordinates? How can you tell if three points lie on a horizontal line? On a vertical line? On any line?

You can use slope between points to test for collinearity. In this lesson, you may already have made conjectures about pairs of points that have the same slope. As you work with equations of lines, these conjectures will be very important.

Assumption

Three points, *A*, *B*, and *C*, are collinear if and only if the slope between *A* and *B* is the same as the slope between *B* and *C*. That is,

A, *B*, and *C* are collinear $\Leftrightarrow$ $m(A, B) = m(B, C)$

> Read the symbol $\Leftrightarrow$ as *if and only if.*

In this diagram, $m(A, B) = m(B, C)$ so *A*, *B*, and *C* are collinear.

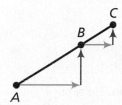

However, in this diagram, $m(A, B) \neq m(B, C)$ so *A*, *B*, and *C* are not collinear.

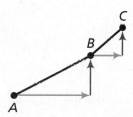

For You to Do

Suppose line ℓ contains the points $(1, -2)$ and $(7, 1)$.

2. What is the slope between the points given?

3. Explain why the point $(5, 0)$ is collinear with these two points.

4. Explain why the point $(13, 5)$ is not collinear with these two points.

5. Explain why the following fact proves that the point $(11, 3)$ is on the line ℓ.

$$\frac{3 - 1}{11 - 7} = \frac{1}{2}$$

6. **Take It Further** Suppose point (x, y), different from $(7, 1)$, is a point in the same plane as line ℓ.

Explain why the equation $\frac{y - 1}{x - 7} = \frac{1}{2}$ is true if and only if (x, y) is on line ℓ.

Exercises *Practicing Habits of Mind*

Check Your Understanding

1. Are the three points collinear?

   a. $A(-1, 3)$, $B(4, 15)$, $C(14, 39)$

   b. $X(-3, 3)$, $Y(4, 3)$, $Z(100, 3)$

   c. $P(-3, 8)$, $D(0, 2)$, $Q(3, -4)$

   d. $N(3, 5)$, $M(4, 6)$, $D(10, 13)$

2. Which three points lie on the same line? Explain.

   $A(-4, -1)$ $B(-1, 2)$ $C(2, 4)$ $D(3, 6)$

3. Derman is wondering about the assumption in this lesson. He says, "Why do they use $m(A, B) = m(B, C)$? Why not use $m(B, A) = m(A, C)$ or $m(A, C) = m(C, B)$?" How would you explain to Derman that these all work as well?

4. Name another point on the line containing X and Y.

   a. $X(3, -4)$, $Y(0, -4)$

   b. $X(-4, 2)$, $Y(-4, 8)$

   c. $X(0, 0)$, $Y(1, 2)$

5. Describe a point-tester to determine whether a point is on the line that contains $(2, 3)$ and $(12, -4)$.

   You can use words or write an equation.

On Your Own

6. Find three points on the graphs of each equation. Are they collinear?

   a. $y - 5 = 4(x - 2)$ **b.** $3x + 2y = 4$

   c. $y = x^2$ **d.** $y = -4x - 3$

   e. $y = 2^x + 1$

7. **Standardized Test Prep** In the morning, the temperature at the top of Mt. Washington in New Hampshire was $-10°$ Fahrenheit. Use the conversion formula $C = \frac{5}{9}(F - 32)$ to find the temperature to the nearest Celsius degree.

   Go Online
   www.successnetplus.com

   A. $-48°$ **B.** $-28°$ **C.** $-23°$ **D.** $-12°$

For Exercises 8–10, suppose ℓ is the line that contains the points $R(-2, 4)$ and $S(6, 2)$.

8. Which of the following points are on ℓ? Explain.

   a. $(1, 3)$ **b.** $\left(1, \frac{13}{4}\right)$ **c.** $\left(1, \frac{14}{3}\right)$

   d. $\left(2, \frac{13}{4}\right)$ **e.** $(2, 3)$ **f.** $\left(2, \frac{14}{3}\right)$

   g. $\left(4, \frac{13}{4}\right)$ **h.** $(4, 2.6)$ **i.** $\left(4, \frac{5}{2}\right)$

9. Find the missing numbers if these points are on ℓ.

   a. $(3, a)$ **b.** $(5, b)$ **c.** $(c, 8)$

   d. $(7, d)$ **e.** $(13, e)$ **f.** $(120, f)$

   g. $(x, -2)$ **h.** $(y, -5)$ **i.** $(z, 12)$

   j. $(v, v + 1)$ **k.** $(w, 1.5w)$ **l.** $(u, u + 14)$

10. What is an equation that you can use to determine whether a point is on line ℓ?

11. **Standardized Test Prep** Which equation describes the relationship between x and y in the table?

   A. $x + y = -2$

   B. $2x - 3y = -9$

   C. $2x + 3y = -3$

   D. $x + 3y = 0$

x	y
-3	1
-1	$2\frac{1}{3}$
1	$3\frac{2}{3}$
3	5
5	$6\frac{1}{3}$

12. Recall the house with a roof pitch of 6–12 from Lesson 3.11. Use graph paper. Draw the pitch on a Cartesian plane. The origin is in the lower left corner. Find each slope.

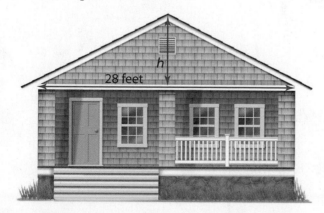

   a. left half of the roof

   b. right half of the roof

13. **Take It Further** Here is a picture of a castle. The attached building in front is a carriage house.

A shipbuilder designed this copper roof. Do you see any connection between the roof design and the builder's experience?

a. Where on the left side of the carriage house roof is the slope least?

b. Where is the slope greatest?

Maintain Your Skills

As you do these exercises, you may find a fast way to determine collinear points. Find a pattern and you may not need to find the slope between every pair of points.

When you are in doubt, calculate each slope.

For Exercises 14–16, points A, B, and C are collinear. Is point X collinear with points A, B, and C? Look for a pattern.

14. **a.** $A(7, 0)$, $B(2, 0)$, $C(-5, 0)$, $X\left(\frac{14}{9}, 0\right)$

   b. $A(3, 3)$, $B(-8, 3)$, $C(7, 3)$, $X(-2, -3)$

   c. $A(5, -2)$, $B\left(\frac{3}{7}, -2\right)$, $C(-\sqrt{3}, -2)$, $X(2, 3)$

   d. $A\left(17, \frac{14}{9}\right)$, $B\left(21, \frac{14}{9}\right)$, $C\left(2.4, \frac{14}{9}\right)$, $X\left(\frac{17}{9}, \frac{14}{9}\right)$

   e. Describe a pattern.

15. **a.** $A(4, 3)$, $B(4, 9)$, $C\left(4, -\frac{2}{3}\right)$, $X(4, 0)$

   b. $A(-\sqrt{7}, 7)$, $B(-\sqrt{7}, 5)$, $C(-\sqrt{7}, 3)$, $X(-\sqrt{7}, 0)$

   c. $A(0, 1)$, $B(0, 2)$, $C(0, 3)$, $X(4, 0)$

   d. $A\left(-\frac{14\pi}{23}, \pi\right)$, $B\left(-\frac{14\pi}{23}, -2.9801\right)$, $C\left(-\frac{14\pi}{23}, -1383\right)$, $X\left(-\frac{14\pi}{23}, 3\pi\sqrt{5}\right)$

   e. Describe a pattern.

16. **a.** $A(1, 2)$, $B(2, 4)$, $C(3, 6)$, $X(4, 8)$ **b.** $A(1, 3)$, $B(2, 6)$, $C(3, 9)$, $X(-4, -12)$

   c. $A(8, -1)$, $B(16, -2)$, $C(-24, 3)$, $X(64, 8)$ **d.** $A(-6, 2)$, $B(9, -3)$, $C(0, 0)$, $X(-3\sqrt{2}, \sqrt{2})$

   e. Describe a pattern.

In this investigation, you found the slope between two points. You also studied the similarity between pitch and slope. You have also learned how to determine if three or more points are collinear. These questions will help you summarize what you have learned.

1. How can you find the average speed of a car from its distance-time graph?

2. Are the three points collinear? Explain.

   a. $P(-1, 2)$, $Q(3, 2)$, $R(11, 2)$

   b. $D(4, 6)$, $E(3, 8)$, $F(5, 12)$

   c. $G(0, 3)$, $H(-1, 2)$, $I(2, 7)$

   d. $J(-5, 1)$, $K(-5, 5)$, $L(-5, -1)$

3. Given points $A(-4, 1)$ and $B(2, y)$, find the value of y such that the following are true.

   a. $m(A, B) = 2$

   b. $m(A, B) = -1$

   c. $m(A, B) = 0$

   d. $m(A, B)$ does not exist.

4. Chan leaves his house at 8:00 A.M. to walk $\frac{1}{2}$ mile to his grandmother's house. He arrives there at 8:15 A.M. He stays for 1 hour. Then he walks 3 miles to the park to meet his friends at 10:15 A.M. He stays there until noon.

   a. Draw a distance-time graph to represent this situation.

   b. Find Chan's average speed walking from his home to his grandmother's house.

   c. Find Chan's average speed walking from his grandmother's house to the park.

   d. Find Chan's average speed from 8:00 A.M. to 10:15 A.M.

5. Find three points on the graph of each equation. Are they collinear?

   a. $y = 3x - 2$

   b. $2x - y = 5$

   c. $y = 3x^2 + 1$

   d. $y - 2 = -(x + 1)$

6. How do people use linear equations and slope in different fields of work such as carpentry, engineering, and mathematics?

7. How can you use slopes to tell whether three points are collinear?

8. How can you use a point-tester to tell whether the point $(3, -2)$ is on the line through $A(2, -5)$ and $B(4, 3)$?

Slope between points can be a negative number close to zero.

Vocabulary

In this investigation, you learned these terms. Make sure you understand what each one means and how to use it.

- collinear points
- rise
- run
- slope
- speed
- subscript

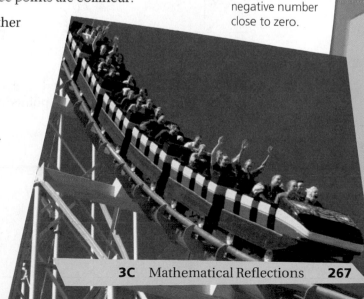

In **Investigation 3A,** you learned how to

- test a point to determine whether it is on the graph of an equation

- graph equations by plotting points

- write the equation of a vertical or horizontal line given its graph or a point on its graph

- read a graph to identify points that are solutions to an equation

- find the intersection point of two graphs and understand its meaning

The following questions will help you check your understanding.

1. The graph of $(x - 3)^2 + (y - 4)^2 = 25$ is a circle. Determine whether each point is on the circle. Explain.

   a. $A = (0, 8)$

   b. $B = (7, 7)$

   c. $C = (7.5, 2)$

   d. $D = (3, -1)$

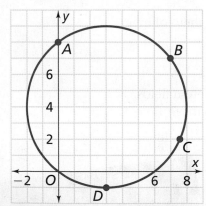

2. Graph the equations $y = (x - 3)^2$ and $x + y = 5$. What are the intersection points?

In **Investigation 3B,** you learned how to

- decide whether a situation represents a direct or inverse variation

- sketch the graphs of the equations $y = x$, $xy = 1$, $y = x^2$, $y = x^3$, $y = \sqrt{x}$, $y = |x|$, and variations of these equations

- recognize the distinguishing features of the basic graphs, such as their general shape, and the points and quadrants that they pass through

The following questions will help you check your understanding.

3. Sketch each graph.

   a. $y + 4 = |x - 3|$

   b. $y = \sqrt{x - 7}$

   c. $y = \frac{1}{3} x$

   d. $y - 3 = (x + 2)^3$

   e. $y = \frac{15}{x}$

   f. $y - 1 = -x^2$

4. The figure shows parts of four basic graphs.

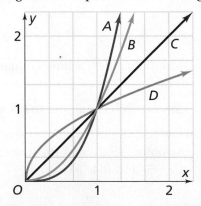

   a. Identify each graph.

   b. Which graph is part of two different basic graphs? Identify the two basic graphs.

   c. For each graph, name the quadrant that is not shown that the graph passes through.

In **Investigation 3C,** you learned how to

- calculate the slope between two points
- calculate the average speed between two points on a distance-time graph
- find other points on a line when given a slope and a point

The following questions will help you check your understanding.

5. Graph points A and B. Find another point C such that $m(A, B) = m(A, C)$.

   a. $A(0, -2)$ and $B(3, 1)$

   b. $A(4, 2)$ and $B(6, -2)$

   c. $A(-5, -1)$ and $B(-8, 3)$

   d. $A(-2, 3)$ and $B(5, 3)$

   e. What can you say about points A, B, and C?

6. On a recent car trip, Lily drove 180 miles on the highway in 3 hours. She stopped for $\frac{1}{2}$ hour to have lunch. She continued her trip on two-lane roads, traveling 60 miles in $1\frac{1}{2}$ hours.

   a. Draw a distance-time graph to represent Lily's trip.

   b. What was Lily's average speed on the highway?

   c. What was Lily's average speed on the two-lane roads?

   d. What was Lily's average speed for the entire trip?

7. Let ℓ be the line that passes through $P(4, -1)$ and $Q(6, 5)$.

   a. Is the point $R(5, 2)$ on ℓ?

   b. Find a if the point $A(-2, a)$ is on ℓ.

   c. Write an equation that can be used to test whether points are on ℓ.

Multiple Choice

1. Which equation has a graph that goes through points $(2, 3)$ and $(-1, -5)$?

   A. $3x - 4y = -6$

   B. $y = 3x^2 - 9$

   C. $8x - 3y = 7$

   D. $x^2 + y^2 = 26$

2. Which point is on the graph of $x^2 - 2y^2 = 1$?

   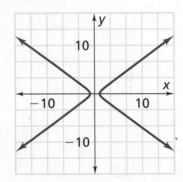

   A. $(7, 5)$ B. $(0, 0)$

   C. $(10, -7)$ D. $(-17, -12)$

3. Which is an intersection point of the graphs of $y = 4$ and $y = \sqrt{x}$?

   A. $(16, 4)$ B. $(4, 16)$

   C. $(4, 2)$ D. $(2, 4)$

4. Which quadrant does the graph of $(y + 3) = (x - 4)^2$ NOT pass through?

   A. I   B. II

   C. III   D. IV

5. How many intersection points are in the graphs of the equations $(y + 4) = |x|$ and $(y - 2) = \sqrt{x + 1}$?

   A. 0   B. 1

   C. 2   D. 3

6. Consider these lines.

   $\ell : y = 2x - 1$

   $m : 5x - 3y = -30$

   What is true about point $(-3, -5)$?

   A. It is on both lines.

   B. It is not on either line.

   C. It is on line ℓ only.

   D. It is on line m only.

7. The relationship between variables a and b is an inverse variation. When a equals 100, b equals 6. Which statement is true?

   A. If a equals 200, b equals 12.

   B. If a equals 5, b equals 120.

   C. If a equals 25, b equals 25.

   D. Variables a and b can never be equal.

8. Which list gives the values of the expressions, in order, from least to greatest when $x = -2$?

   A. $|x|, 1, x^2, x^3$

   B. $1, |x|, x^2, x^3$

   C. $x^3, 1, |x|, x^2$

   D. $x^3, x^2, 1, |x|$

Open Response

9. Write three different equations with graphs that contain the point $(3, 7)$. Explain how you know that each graph contains $(3, 7)$.

10. Sketch the graph of $y = x^2 - 5x + 6$.

11. Find the equation that has a graph that is different from the other graphs. Explain.

   A. $y = \frac{5}{3}x - 2$

   B. $3y = 5(x - 2)$

   C. $y - 5 = \frac{5}{3}(x - 3) - 2$

   D. $3y + 6 = 5x$

12. Find the coordinates of both intersection points for the graphs of $y = x^2$ and $y = \frac{1}{3}x$.

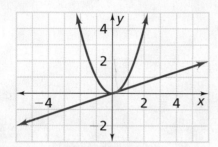

13. Colleen, James, and Violet ride their bikes on the same 4-mile path. They start at the same time and arrive at the end of the path 30 minutes later. Graph distance traveled against time on a graph using the following descriptions.

   • Colleen rides for 10 minutes and travels 2 miles. Then she rests for 10 minutes. Finally, she rides another 10 minutes to the end of the path.

   • James rides at a constant speed for 30 minutes.

   • Violet rides for 5 minutes and travels 1 mile. She rests 5 minutes. She rides for 10 minutes and travels $1\frac{1}{2}$ miles. She rests another 5 minutes. Finally, she rides for 5 minutes to the end of the path.

14. Sketch the graph of each equation.

   a. $x = 0$

   b. $(x - 7) = 0$

15. How are equations and graphs related? If two graphs intersect, what do you know about the equations?

Challenge Problem

16. A lattice point has integers for both coordinates. For example, $(-6, 3)$ is a lattice point, and $(0.5, -7)$ is not. Through how many lattice points does the graph of $x^2 + y^2 = 65$ pass?

Lines

You may stand in a line almost every day. For example, you may stand in line in a cafeteria, at a ticket booth, or on a hike. Lines have the property of being straight. You can look at the line ahead of you to find how much longer you will have to wait.

Lines are an important mathematical topic. They are the simplest graphs you can draw on the coordinate plane. Unlike many of the lines you see every day, geometric lines do not bend or curve. Another difference between geometric lines and lines of people is that geometric lines continue in both directions forever. Imagine standing in that line!

In the last chapter, you learned about basic graphs and their equations. Some graphs are lines, such as graphs of direct variations. Others are more complex. Before you solve more complex equations, you will develop algebraic techniques to solve linear equations.

Vocabulary and Notation

- cutoff point
- elimination method
- inequality
- parallel lines
- slope of a line
- substitution method
- system of equations
- *x*-intercept
- *y*-intercept

Linear Equations and Graphs

In *Linear Equations and Graphs*, you will find the relationship between a linear equation and its graph. To make this connection, you will use what you know about slope and point-testers. You will also look at distance-time graphs again.

By the end of this investigation, you will be able to answer questions like these.

1. How can you determine whether the graph of an equation is a line?

2. How can you use a distance-time graph to tell when one runner overtakes another in a race?

3. How can you write an equation of the line that connects points $(-3, 7)$ and $(4, 2)$?

You will learn how to

• write linear equations

• sketch graphs of linear equations

• determine the slope from its equation

• determine whether a runner will overtake another runner

You will develop these habits and skills:

• Use a point-tester to write a linear equation.

• Understand various ways of a constructing an equation, using the most efficient method based on the information given.

• Realize that you can use any two points on a line to graph the line.

• Calculate intersections in distance-time graphs.

After the first lap, a Nordic skier's distance-time graph can suggest a linear function.

In Investigation 3C, you found the slope between points. In this investigation, you will learn how to find the slope of a line. You will also use slope to write equations of lines.

For You to Explore

In Investigation 3B, you studied several basic graphs, such as $y = x$, $y = \frac{1}{x}$, $y = |x|$, and $y = x^2$. For Problems 1–4, you will calculate slopes between points on each graph.

1. The figure below shows a graph of the direct variation equation $y = 3x$.

   a. Choose two points on the graph. Calculate the slope between them.

   b. Choose two other points on the graph. Calculate the slope between them.

   c. How do the two slopes compare?

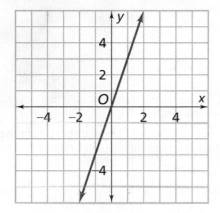

For Problems 2 and 3, answer parts (a)–(c) in Problem 1.

2. $y = \frac{5}{x}$

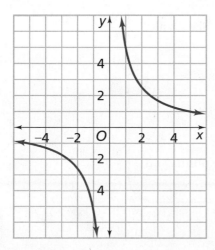

3. $y = 2x^2$

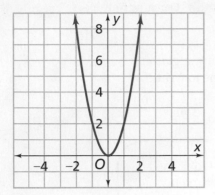

4. The figure below shows a graph of the equation $y = |4x|$.

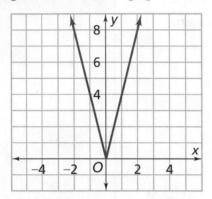

    a. Choose two points in the first quadrant on the graph. Calculate the slope between them.

    b. Choose two other points in the first quadrant on the graph. Calculate the slope between them.

    c. How do the two slopes compare?

    d. Choose two points in the second quadrant on the graph. Calculate the slope between them.

    e. How does this slope compare to the slope between points in the first quadrant?

5. For each pair of points, find three other points that are collinear. Sketch all five points on the same graph.

    a. $(5, 7)$ and $(1, 8)$

    b. $(7, 0)$ and $(0, 5)$

    c. $(-2, 3)$ and $(-3, -5)$

    d. $(1, -8)$ and $(4, 6)$

6. For each part in Problem 5, use a point-tester to see whether the points you chose are collinear with the two given points.

How does slope between points differ for the two types of water slides?

Exercises *Practicing Habits of Mind*

On Your Own

7. John leaves his house at 8:00 A.M. He rides his bike to school. He pedals at a constant rate of 15 ft/sec. How far has John biked at each of the following times?

   a. 8:10 A.M.

   b. 8:20 A.M.

   c. 8:45 A.M.

   d. t minutes after 8:00 A.M.

8. Pete, John's older brother, leaves their house 10 minutes after John. He rides at 20 ft/sec to the same school. At the times shown in parts (a)–(c), how far has Pete biked? Has he caught up with John?

   a. 8:10 A.M.

   b. 8:20 A.M.

   c. 8:45 A.M.

   d. At t minutes after 8:00 A.M., write an expression for how far Pete has ridden.

   e. How can you find the exact time when Pete catches up with John?

9. **What's Wrong Here?** Derman tests whether four points, $E(2, 4)$, $F(5, 6)$, $G(6, 7)$, and $H(9, 9)$, are collinear.

   Derman says, "To test whether points are collinear, I should find the slope between them and compare. The slope between E and F is $m(E, F) = \frac{6 - 4}{5 - 2} = \frac{2}{3}$. The slope between G and H is $m(G, H) = \frac{9 - 7}{9 - 6} = \frac{2}{3}$.

   The two slopes are equal, so all four points must be collinear."

   a. Sketch the four points to show they are not collinear.

   b. What is wrong with Derman's reasoning?

   c. What can you say about the line that contains E and F and the line that contains G and H?

10. Find three points such that the slope between each point and the given point is the given slope. Sketch all four points.

    a. point $(5, 0)$, slope $\frac{1}{2}$

    b. point $(0, 6)$, slope $\frac{3}{8}$

    c. point $(-1, 4)$, slope $\frac{9}{7}$

    d. point $(1, 4)$, slope $-\frac{3}{5}$

11. For each part in Exercise 10, use a point-tester. Determine whether the slope between the given point and some point $P(x, y)$ is the given slope.

12. Solve each equation for y. Simplify.

   a. $y + 3 = 2(x - 5)$

   b. $y - 2 = -\frac{1}{3}(x + 3)$

   c. $4x - 5y = 7$

   d. $\frac{y - 8}{x} = -3$

   e. $y + 6 = 2x + 1$

   f. $\frac{y - 2}{x - 1} = 5$

   g. $\frac{y + 7}{x - 3} = -\frac{11}{3}$

   h. $xy = 9$

Remember...

Solve for y means use the basic rules and moves to get y alone on one side of the equation. The other side of the equation will be an expression that does not include y.

Simplify means to combine or multiply terms where you can.

Maintain Your Skills

For Exercises 13 and 14, parts (a)–(f), find the slope between each pair of points. Sketch the two points and the line containing them. Then complete parts (g)–(i).

13. a. $(1, 2)$ and $(3, 3)$ **b.** $(2, 3)$ and $(4, 4)$

   c. $(3, 4)$ and $(5, 5)$ **d.** $(4, 5)$ and $(6, 6)$

   e. $(5, 6)$ and $(7, 7)$ **f.** $(6, 7)$ and $(8, 8)$

   g. Is there a pattern among the lines? Describe.

   h. What is the slope between $(1 + a, 2 + a)$ and $(3 + a, 3 + a)$? How does it relate to the slope in part (a)?

   i. Given $A(1, 2)$ and $B(3, 3)$, transform the points using the rule $(x, y) \mapsto (x + a, y + b)$, where a and b are any numbers. You will get two new points, A' and B'. How does $m(A', B')$ relate to $m(A, B)$?

14. a. $(1, 2)$ and $(3, 3)$ **b.** $(2, 4)$ and $(6, 6)$

   c. $(3, 6)$ and $(9, 9)$ **d.** $(4, 8)$ and $(12, 12)$

   e. $(5, 10)$ and $(15, 15)$ **f.** $(6, 12)$ and $(18, 18)$

   g. Is there a pattern among the lines? Describe.

   h. What is the slope between $(a, 2a)$ and $(3a, 3a)$? How does it relate to the slope in part (a)?

   i. Given $A(1, 2)$ and $B(3, 3)$, transform the points using the rule $(x, y) \mapsto (ax, by)$, where a and b are any numbers. You will get two new points, A' and B'. How does $m(A', B')$ relate to $m(A, B)$?

Go Online
Video Tutor
www.successnetplus.com

Equations of Lines

The Assumption in Lesson 3.13 is essential in developing a way to write the equation of a line. From that assumption comes the following theorem.

Theorem 4.1

The slope between any two points on a line is constant.

In other words, if the slope between two points on a line is m, then the slope between any two points on that line must be m.

For Discussion

1. Prove Theorem 4.1.

In the previous lessons, you defined slope as a measurement between two points. With Theorem 4.1, you can now describe the slope of a line.

Definition

The slope of a line is the slope between any two points on the line.

To find the equation of a line, you only need to know one point on the line and the slope of the line. Once you know these, the equation of the line is just a point-tester. You can verify that the slope between some arbitrary point on the line and the fixed point matches the slope of the line.

Minds in Action

Sasha and Tony are trying to find the equation of the line ℓ that goes through points $R(-2, 4)$ and $S(6, 2)$.

Sasha   To use a point-tester, we first need to find the slope between R and S.

Tony goes to the board and writes

$$m(R, S) = \frac{2 - 4}{6 - (-2)} = \frac{-2}{8} = -\frac{1}{4}.$$

Tony   It's $-\frac{1}{4}$.

Sasha   Okay. Now, we want to test some point, say P. We want to see whether the slope between that point and one of the first two, say R, is equal to $-\frac{1}{4}$. If it is, that point is on ℓ. So our test is $m(P, R) \overset{?}{=} -\frac{1}{4}$.

It doesn't matter which point you choose as the base point. Either point R or point S will work.

Tony Let's guess and check a point first, like $P(7, 2)$. Tell me everything you do so I can keep track of the steps.

Sasha Well, the slope between $P(7, 2)$ and $R(-2, 4)$ is $m(P, R) = \frac{2 - 4}{7 - (-2)} = \frac{-2}{9} = -\frac{2}{9}$. This slope is different, so P isn't on ℓ. Maybe we should use a variable point.

Tony How do we do that?

Sasha A point has two coordinates, right? So use two variables. Say P is (x, y).

Tony Then the slope from P to R is $m(P, R) = \frac{y - 4}{x - (-2)} = \frac{y - 4}{x + 2}$. The test is $\frac{y - 4}{x + 2} = -\frac{1}{4}$.

So, that must be the equation of the line ℓ.

> Notice how Sasha switches to letters. She uses x for point P's x-coordinate. She uses y for point P's y-coordinate.

Example 1

Problem **What's Wrong Here?** Tony and Sasha go back to check their work. They want to make sure both R and S work in their point-tester equation.

Sasha says, "Okay, let's try R."

Sasha writes the following on the board.

$$\frac{y - 4}{x + 2} = -\frac{1}{4}$$

$$\frac{4 - 4}{-2 + 2} \stackrel{?}{=} -\frac{1}{4}$$

$$\frac{0}{0} \stackrel{?}{=} -\frac{1}{4}$$

Tony states, "We can't divide by 0. Now what?" Why doesn't the point tester equation work for the point R?

Solution Sasha knows she has a problem, because she cannot divide by 0. The easiest way to eliminate that problem is to multiply the variable x out of the denominator. You can do this by multiplying each side by the denominator, $(x + 2)$.

$$\frac{y - 4}{x + 2} \cdot (x + 2) = -\frac{1}{4} \cdot (x + 2)$$

$$y - 4 = -\frac{1}{4}(x + 2)$$

> Multiplying each side of an equation by an expression containing a variable is *not* a basic move. The resulting equation may have more or fewer solutions than the original equation. Here, the resulting equation gains a solution, $(-2, 4)$. This is exactly the solution you were missing.

For You to Do

2. Test whether the points R and S satisfy the equation $y - 4 = -\frac{1}{4}(x + 2)$.

You can simplify and change the equation $y - 4 = -\frac{1}{4}(x + 2)$ with basic rules and moves. The different forms the equation can take highlight different information about the line. You will work with the different forms throughout the rest of this investigation.

You can use the basic rules and moves to change any form of an equation of a line to the form $ax + by = c$, where a, b, and c are constants.

Any such equation is a linear equation.

> It works the other way, too. The graph of any equation in the form $ax + by = c$ is a line.

Example 2

Problem Find the slope of the line with the equation $2x + y = 5$.

Solution Find two points on the line.

If $x = 0$, then $2(0) + y = 5$. So $y = 5$, and $(0, 5)$ is on the line.

If $x = 1$, then $2(1) + y = 5$. So $y = 3$, and $(1, 3)$ is on the line.

The slope between the points $(0, 5)$ and $(1, 3)$ is $\frac{5 - 3}{0 - 1} = \frac{2}{1} = -2$. The slope of the line is -2.

Exercises *Practicing Habits of Mind*

Check Your Understanding

1. Use Sasha and Tony's method to find an equation for line ℓ. This time, use point S as the base point. Do you get the same equation? Explain.

2. Try Sasha and Tony's method with two points of your own. Use your equation. Test some points to see if they are on your line.

For Exercises 3 and 4, write an equation for each line.

3. **a.** through $A(6, 7)$ and $B(12, 1)$ **b.** through $(5, 4)$ and $(-3, -4)$

   c. through the origin and $(9, 3)$

   d. through $(0, 10)$ and parallel to the line in part (c)

   e. through the origin and parallel to the line in part (a)

> Two lines in the same plane are **parallel** if they do not intersect.

4. a. a horizontal line that passes through $(6, 7)$

b. through $(5, 4)$ and $(5, -4)$

c. through the origin that splits the first and third quadrants in half

d. line through the origin and parallel to the line in part (a)

5. For each part:

- Decide whether the graph is a line. Explain.

- If the equation represents a line, find the slope and the points where the line crosses the x- and y-axes.

a. $y - 3 = \frac{3}{4}(x - 8)$ **b.** $xy = 12$ **c.** $y = \frac{3}{4}x - 3$

d. $y = 5x - 7$ **e.** $3x - 4y = 12$ **f.** $y = -\frac{5}{3}x - 9$

g. $x^2 + y^2 = 1$ **h.** $3x - 4y = 9$ **i.** $y = -\frac{5}{3}x + 8$

6. Prove that the slope between any two points on the line $3x - y = 7$ is 3.

You can use these hints to help you.
• Test a few points.
• Keep track of your steps!
• Develop a point-tester.
• Translate your point-tester into an equation.

On Your Own

7. Write About It Explain Sasha and Tony's method for finding the equation of a line as an algorithm. Be sure to include precise instructions and steps.

8. Write the equation of the line that includes each pair of points or matches each description. Write the equation in $y = ax + b$ form.

a. $(5, 2)$ and $(-3, -4)$ **b.** $(5, 4)$ and the origin

c. $(5, 5)$ and $(7, 7)$ **d.** includes $(5, 4)$ and has slope $\frac{2}{3}$

e. passes through the origin and is parallel to the line in part (a)

f. passes through the origin and is parallel to the line in part (d)

9. What is the slope of each line that has the description or equation given?

a. through $(-5, 6)$ and $(-3, -4)$ **b.** $y = \frac{3}{4}x + 7$

c. $2x + 4y = 8$ **d.** $2x + 4y = 15$

e. $5.1476x + 5.1476y = 15$ **f.** $y - 3 = \frac{7}{13}(x - 4)$

g. $y - 7.3591 = \frac{7}{13}(x - 4.0856)$

h. through the origin and parallel to the line in part (d)

What do the lines in parts (c) and (d) have in common?

10. a. What is the equation for the line containing points $J(3, -6)$ and $K(8, 4)$? Use J as the base point.

b. What is the equation through $J(3, -6)$ and $K(8, 4)$ if you use K as the base point?

c. Prove that the two equations in parts (a) and (b) describe the same graph. Use basic rules and moves.

11. Alejandra is selling candy bars for $.85 each.

    a. If she sells 20 candy bars, how much does she make?

    b. If she sells 50 candy bars, how much does she make?

    c. Let c be the number of candy bars Alejandra sells. Let s be her sales in dollars. Which equation represents the relationship between c and s?

       A. $c = 0.85(s)$ **B.** $s = 0.85(c)$

       C. $s = c + 0.85$ **D.** $s = c + 85$

12. **Standardized Test Prep** What is the slope of the line with equation $5x + 2y = 10$?

    A. $-\frac{2}{5}$ **B.** $-\frac{5}{2}$ **C.** $\frac{5}{2}$ **D.** $\frac{2}{5}$

13. **Write About It** Find an equation of the line that contains $(5, 3)$ and has a slope of -4. Can you find a point that satisfies your equation but is not on the line? Explain.

> How many lines pass through (5, 3) and have a slope of −4?

14. **Take It Further** Explain why the slope between any two points on the line $ax + y = b$ is constant.

15. **Take It Further** Given $A(5, 2)$, $B(3, 7)$, and $C(10, 4)$, find equations for the lines that form the sides of $\triangle ABC$.

Maintain Your Skills

16. Sketch each pair of equations. Do the lines intersect?

    a. $y - 2 = 2(x - 7)$ and $y - 2 = 5(x - 7)$

    b. $y + 4 = \frac{2}{3}(x - 1)$ and $y + 4 = \frac{3}{2}(x - 1)$

    c. $y - \frac{14}{23} = \frac{1}{7}\left(x + \frac{13}{23}\right)$ and $y - \frac{14}{23} = \frac{1}{6}\left(x + \frac{13}{23}\right)$

    d. $y - 5 = x - 10$ and $y - 5 = 3(x - 10)$

    e. What pattern do you notice in the line intersections?

17. a. Graph the family of equations.

       $2x - 3y = 0$

       $2x - 3y = 1$ $2x - 3y = -1$

       $2x - 3y = 2$ $2x - 3y = -2$

    b. What pattern do you notice among the graphs?

> You can use the term family to describe a collection, or a set. This family is the set of equations in the form $2x - 3y = k$, where k is any number.

18. a. Find equations for five distinct lines that include the point $(5, 1)$.

    b. Is there a pattern among the equations? Explain.

4.03 Jiffy Graphs: Lines

You can write the equation of a line in many different ways, and the equations are still equivalent. No matter what form of equation you use, you only need to find two points to graph a line. However, it may be very time-consuming to work with a linear equation like this one.

$$6x + 3(x + 2y) - 5y + 18 = 4(2y + 3) + 5(x + 3) - 4\left(y - \frac{1}{2}\right)$$

You can transform such an equation into a simpler form. You can use the simpler equation to find points and sketch a graph. Each of the following equations is equivalent to the equation above.

$$y - 3 = \frac{4}{3}(x - 5) \qquad 4x - 3y = 11 \qquad y = \frac{4}{3}x - \frac{11}{3}$$

Remember...

Two equations are equivalent if you can use the basic rules and moves to change one to the other.

For You to Do

1. Show that $y - 3 = \frac{4}{3}(x - 5)$, $4x - 3y = 11$, and $y = \frac{4}{3}x - \frac{11}{3}$ are equivalent.

Example

Problem Sketch the graph of the line whose equation is $4x - 3y = 11$.

Solution You have sketched a graph by finding enough points to determine the basic pattern before. In this case, you know the graph is a line, so you only need to find two points on the graph. Then you can draw the line that goes through them both.

To find two points, choose numbers that make the calculations as easy as possible. When you have an equation such as $4x - 3y = 11$, you can find one point easily by plugging in 0 for x and solving for y. Then you can plug in 0 for y and solve for x.

$$4x - 3y = 11 \qquad\qquad 4x - 3y = 11$$
$$4(0) - 3y = 11 \qquad\qquad 4x - 3(0) = 11$$
$$-3y = 11 \qquad\qquad 4x = 11$$
$$y = -\frac{11}{3} \qquad\qquad x = \frac{11}{4}$$

When you plug in 0 for x, you find the point where the line crosses the y-axis. That point is called the **y-intercept**. The point where a line crosses the x-axis is called the **x-intercept**.

The points $\left(0, -\frac{11}{3}\right)$ and $\left(\frac{11}{4}, 0\right)$ will both be on the graph. Draw the points and the line that contains them.

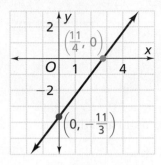

For Discussion

2. What numbers can you use to find points on the graph of $y = \frac{4}{3}x - \frac{11}{3}$? On the graph of $y - 3 = \frac{4}{3}(x - 5)$? Choose points that are easy to use.

3. How do you know the graphs of the equations $y = \frac{4}{3}x - \frac{11}{3}$ and $y - 3 = \frac{4}{3}(x - 5)$ will be the same as the graph of $4x - 3y = 11$?

Some equations have specific names. You can determine certain pieces of information just by looking at certain equations. Recognizing these forms helps you graph lines or write linear equations more quickly. If you forget how to work with these forms, remember that you can always rely on the point-tester to write an equation, and you need only two points to graph a line.

For You to Do

Let ℓ be the line with the equations $y = \frac{4}{3}x - \frac{11}{3}$, $4x - 3y = 11$, and $y - 3 = \frac{4}{3}(x - 5)$.

4. What is the slope of line ℓ?

5. Where does ℓ cross the y-axis? The x-axis?

6. Which equation for ℓ makes it easiest to see that the point (5, 3) is on the line? Explain.

For Discussion

7. Does the slope of line ℓ appear in any of its equations? Do the x- and y-intercepts appear?

Exercises *Practicing Habits of Mind*

Check Your Understanding

1. Write an equation for each line that contains the given point and that has the given slope m.

   a. $(4, 3)$; $m = -1$

   b. $(-2, 5)$; $m = \frac{1}{3}$

   c. $(7, -3)$; $m = \frac{4}{5}$

   d. $(-1, -5)$; $m = -\frac{11}{7}$

   e. $\left(-\frac{3}{2}, -\frac{1}{2}\right)$; $m = 2$

   f. $(14.6, -9.8)$; $m = -4.38$

   g. $(0, 12)$; $m = \frac{5}{6}$

   h. $(0, -3)$; $m = -\frac{2}{3}$

   i. $\left(0, -\frac{8}{5}\right)$; $m = \frac{5}{16}$

   j. $(0, 5)$; $m = \frac{21}{13}$

   k. $(3, 9)$; $m = 0$

   l. $(-8, 7)$; slope is undefined

> Try to find the quickest way to write an equation. You might decide it is easier to work with one particular form.

For Exercises 2 and 3, graph each equation.

2. a. $y - 2 = \frac{1}{2}(x + 4)$

   b. $y + 3 = -4(x + 1)$

   c. $y + 7 = \frac{5}{4}(x - 2)$

   d. $y - \frac{1}{2} = -\frac{9}{7}\left(x + \frac{2}{3}\right)$

   e. $y = -\frac{2}{3}(x - 6) + 6$

   f. $y = 18(x - 27) - 38$

   g. $y = -\frac{7}{5}\left(x - \frac{5}{7}\right) + 3$

   h. $y = \frac{4}{13}\left(x + \frac{1}{4}\right) - \frac{7}{4}$

3. a. $y = 4x - 3$

   b. $y = -2x + 1$

   c. $y = 7x + 5$

   d. $y = -4x - 6$

   e. $y = -\frac{1}{2}x + 4$

   f. $y = \frac{3}{7}x - 2$

   g. $y = -\frac{15}{4}x + \frac{9}{2}$

   h. $y = \frac{21}{17}x + \frac{5}{8}$

On Your Own

4. Use any of the three equations from For You To Do. Find the value of k such that $(100, k)$ is on line ℓ.

5. **Write About It** Use Exercises 1–3.

   a. Does it matter which form of an equation you use to graph a line? Explain.

   b. Do you prefer one form of an equation over another form? If so, which form do you prefer? Explain.

> Which equation makes your work easiest?

6. Alejandra is selling candy bars for $.85 each. She buys a box of 100 candy bars for $20.00. Let m be the amount of money she makes. Let c be the number of candy bars she sells. Notice that if Alejandra does not sell any candy bars ($c = 0$), then she will lose $20.00 ($m = -20$).

You answered a similar question about Alejandra in Lesson 4.02.

   a. Which equation represents the relationship between the amount of money Alejandra makes and the number of candy bars she sells?

   A. $c = 0.85(m) + 20$ **B.** $m = 0.85(c) - 20$

   C. $c = 0.85(m) - 20$ **D.** $m = 0.85(c) + 20$

   b. How many candy bars must Alejandra sell to break even?

7. **Standardized Test Prep** In which case is it possible to graph a linear equation by finding both its x- and y-intercepts?

   A. The graph goes through the origin.

   B. The graph has an undefined slope.

   C. The graph has a slope of zero.

   D. The coordinates of the x- and y-intercepts of the graph are all negative.

For Exercises 8–27, write an equation for the line through the given points or having the given slope and through the given point.

8. $(-3, -5)$ and $(1, 11)$

9. $(6, -7)$ with slope $\frac{7}{5}$

10. $(-5, 13)$ and $(4, -23)$

11. $(0, 13)$ with slope $\frac{11}{3}$

12. $\left(-\frac{1}{2}, -\frac{3}{2}\right)$ with slope $-\frac{2}{3}$

13. $(14, -1)$ with slope 3

14. $(0, 7)$ and $(-4, 9)$

15. $(4, 7)$ and $(4, -2)$

16. $(-6, 0)$ and $(2, -15)$

17. $(0, -2)$ with slope 5

18. $(-3, 0)$ and $(0, 11)$

19. $\left(0, -\frac{1}{2}\right)$ with slope $\frac{5}{4}$

20. $(-2, -4)$ with slope $3\frac{1}{3}$

21. $(8, -2)$ and $(2, -8)$

22. $(-7.5, 3.6)$ with slope -4.8

23. $(-5, 3)$ with slope $-\frac{7}{6}$

24. $(0, 2)$ and $(-4, 0)$

25. $(0, 0)$ and $(15, -12)$

26. $(5, 0)$ and $(-3, -1)$

27. $(10, -3)$ with slope 7

For Exercises 28–39, graph each equation.

28. $x + y = 3$

29. $y = \frac{1}{3}x + 3$

30. $x - 4y = 8$

31. $y - 7 = \frac{2}{3}(x - 9)$

32. $-5x + 3y = 15$

33. $y - 2 = -\frac{9}{4}(x - 3)$

34. $3(y - 3) = x$

35. $y = -\frac{2}{5}x - 4$

36. $y + 2 = -3(x + 1)$

37. $-2x - 3y = 6$

38. $-y = \frac{2}{3}x - 7$

39. $2(y - 4) = -\frac{2}{5}(x + 6)$

For Exercises 40–49, solve each equation for y.

40. $-6x + y = -1$

41. $9x + y = 4$

42. $2x - 3y = 15$

43. $-x - 4y = -20$

44. $3y + 7 = 4x - 7y + 9$

45. $\frac{1}{2}x + \frac{2}{3}y - \frac{11}{4} = \frac{1}{3}y - \frac{9}{2} - \frac{3}{8}x$

46. $4x - 3(y - 4) + 6 = 2x - y$

47. $y - (x - y) = 5$

48. $2(x + y) - 4(x + y) = 8(x + 2) - 8(y + 2)$

49. $2x + 3y - 4(x + 2y) = 13 - 2(3y - x) + y$

Maintain Your Skills

50. Write an equation of a line that contains each pair of points. Use the form $ax + by = c$.

   a. $(4, 0)$ and $(0, 5)$

   b. $(1, 0)$ and $(0, -2)$

   c. $(-15, 0)$ and $(0, -7)$

   d. $(-6, 0)$ and $(0, 4)$

   e. How do integers a, b, and c relate to the coordinates given?

51. **Take It Further** Write an equation of a line that passes through each pair of points in the form $ax + by = c$.

   a. $\left(\frac{1}{2}, 0\right)$ and $\left(0, -\frac{2}{3}\right)$

   b. $\left(-\frac{11}{7}, 0\right)$ and $\left(0, \frac{17}{4}\right)$

   c. $\left(\frac{5}{9}, 0\right)$ and $\left(0, \frac{10}{9}\right)$

   d. $\left(-\frac{3}{8}, 0\right)$ and $\left(0, \frac{1}{2}\right)$

   e. How do integers a, b, and c relate to the coordinates of the two points? How is this relationship different from Exercise 50?

52. For each linear equation, find the slope.

   a. $3x + y = 7$

   b. $3x + y = -3$

   c. $3x + 7y = \frac{42}{13}$

   d. $2x - 7y = 9$

   e. $2x - 7y = -11$

   f. $5x - 4y = 20$

   g. $3x - 4y = 15$

   h. $2x - 4y = 19$

   i. How is slope related to the coefficients of x and y?

4.04 Overtaking—Slope in Distance-Time Graphs

Tony and Sasha bike from their school to a nearby lake. Tony leaves at 2:00 P.M. He travels at 4 miles per hour. Sasha leaves at 2:30 P.M. She travels on the same bike path at 6 miles per hour. When she catches up with Tony, she waves and yells, "Too late to stop now," and continues to the lake. Later they meet at the lake and talk about what happened.

Minds in Action

Tony You were really moving!

Sasha I had to go faster than you to catch up.

Tony What time did you pass me? Around 3:00?

Sasha I'm not sure. Let's figure it out. Let's assume I passed you at 3:00. At 3:00, I had been riding for half an hour, so I'd biked 3 miles.

Tony I had been on the road for an hour, so I'd gone 4 miles. That means I was still ahead of you.

Sasha Maybe I passed you at 4:00. At 4:00, I'd biked for an hour and a half. So, I had ridden 9 miles. You were biking for 2 hours, so you had gone 8 miles. I was ahead of you at that point.

Tony I think an equation will help. If you biked for t hours when you passed me, you'd gone $6t$ miles. I biked 4 miles per hour, but for how many hours?

Sasha You started half an hour before me, so t plus a half.

Tony Nice. That means I biked for $4\left(t + \frac{1}{2}\right)$ hours, which is the same as $4t + 2$ hours.

Sasha Now, when I passed you, we'd gone the same distance. We need to solve the equation $6t = 4t + 2$.

Tony That's not very hard, it's $t = 1$. What time is that?

Sasha What did t represent? My time or yours?

> Sasha bikes at 6 miles per hour, so in a half hour, she travels 3 miles.

Habits of Mind

Represent a variable. Tony uses t instead of x, to remind himself that the time is unknown.

For You to Do

1. How did Tony get $t = 1$? What does t represent? At what time did Sasha pass Tony?

Minds in Action

Tony made a distance-time graph for their trip.

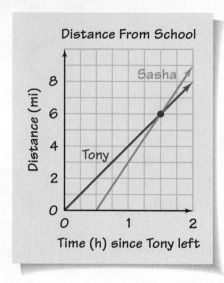

Sasha How did you draw this graph?

Tony On a distance-time graph, speed is the same as slope. Each of our graphs has a constant slope, which means they're lines. Your line has a slope of 6. My line has a slope of 4.

Sasha I understand. Also, since I started half an hour later than you, my graph doesn't start until time $\frac{1}{2}$.

Tony There is one thing I don't understand. We traveled on exactly the same bike path, but it looks like you went up a steeper hill than I did.

Sasha   The graph isn't a picture of our trip. That would look like this.

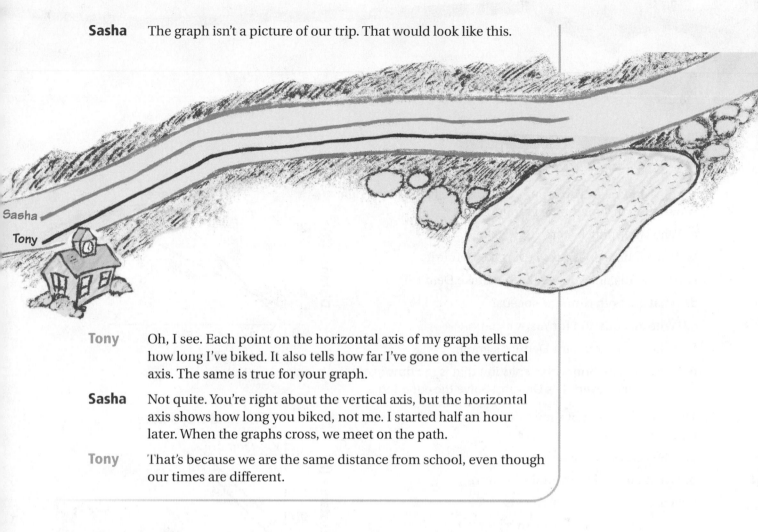

Tony   Oh, I see. Each point on the horizontal axis of my graph tells me how long I've biked. It also tells how far I've gone on the vertical axis. The same is true for your graph.

Sasha   Not quite. You're right about the vertical axis, but the horizontal axis shows how long you biked, not me. I started half an hour later. When the graphs cross, we meet on the path.

Tony   That's because we are the same distance from school, even though our times are different.

For You to Do

2. Write equations for Tony's line and for Sasha's line.

3. At what point do the lines intersect?

4. If the lake is 8 miles from school, what time did Sasha arrive? When did Tony arrive?

> Recall that Tony started biking at 2 P.M.

In Lesson 3.06, you learned that the point where two graphs intersect must satisfy the equations for both of the graphs. Similarly, the intersection point, where Sasha passed Tony, must satisfy both of the equations you found. In the next investigation, you will learn some algebraic strategies for finding the intersection points of lines without graphing.

Exercises *Practicing Habits of Mind*

Check Your Understanding

1. Demitri and Yakov run around a track. The figure at the right shows their distance-time graphs.

   a. Who is running faster?

   b. At what time does Yakov overtake Demitri?

   c. At what distance does Yakov overtake Demitri?

   d. What are both runners' speeds?

   e. Write an equation for Yakov's graph.

   f. Write an equation for Demitri's graph.

   g. Write an equation with a solution that is the time at which Yakov overtakes Demitri. Solve the equation.

2. The figure at the right shows their distance-time graphs for the next day.

   a. Who is running faster?

   b. When does Yakov overtake Demitri?

   c. What are the runners' speeds?

   d. Write an equation for Yakov's graph.

   e. Write an equation for Demitri's graph.

   f. Write and solve an equation with a solution that is the time at which Yakov overtakes Demitri.

3. The runners practice again on a third day.

   a. When does Yakov overtake Demitri in the race?

   b. Do the two graphs intersect? Explain.

   c. Approximately where would the lines of the two graphs intersect?

   d. Can two different lines intersect at more than one point?

First Day's Race

Second Day's Race

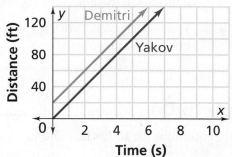
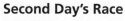

Third Day's Race

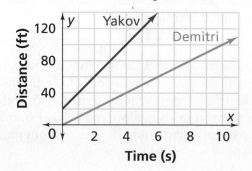

4. **Write About It** The next day, Demitri runs 500 feet per minute. Yakov runs 501 feet per minute. Demitri gets a 50-foot head start. Will Yakov eventually catch and pass Demitri? Explain.

5. Tony and Derman often run quarter-mile races. A quarter mile is about 440 yards. Derman's best time in the race is $1\frac{3}{8}$ minutes. Tony's best time is $1\frac{1}{2}$ minutes. Who has the best time?

   Exercises 6–8 are about a quarter-mile race that Derman and Tony ran. In this race, Tony had a 20-yard head start. Assume that both matched the speed of their best times given in Exercise 5.

6. Sketch a distance-time graph that shows Tony's and Derman's run on the same axes.

   > It may be helpful to use yards for distance and seconds for time.

7. Will Derman overtake Tony? If so, when? If not, why not?

8. How long does each runner take to run the race?

9. **Write About It** As you walk down the sidewalk, you see someone walking ahead of you. Although you do not know how fast either of you is walking, you realize that you are walking faster than the other person. If you both keep walking at the same speed, will you eventually catch up? Explain.

10. **Write About It** You see someone walking ahead of you on the sidewalk. This time, you are walking at exactly the same speed as the other person. If you both keep walking at the same speed, will you eventually catch up? Explain.

11. **Standardized Test Prep** Mrs. Merrill drives from Dallas to St. Louis. The length of the trip is 650 miles. She travels at 50 miles per hour. Her husband leaves two hours later and travels at 62.5 miles per hour. At what distance from Dallas will Mr. Merrill catch up with his wife?

    A. 500 miles   **B.** 600 miles   **C.** 625 miles

    D. Mrs. Merrill arrives in St. Louis before her husband.

Maintain Your Skills

12. For each equation, find the points that lie on both graphs.

    a. $y = 2x$ and $y = 3x$ **b.** $y = 2x + 1$ and $y = 3x + 1$

    c. $y = 2x - 1$ and $y = 3x - 1$ **d.** $y + 1 = 2x$ and $y + 1 = 3x$

    e. $y - 2 = 2x$ and $y - 2 = 3x$ **f.** $y - 2x = 2$ and $y - 3x = 2$

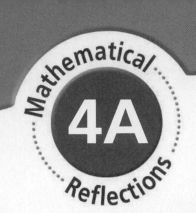

Mathematical 4A Reflections

In this investigation, you learned to find the slope of a line. You also wrote equations given a slope and a point. These questions will help you summarize what you have learned.

1. Name three points collinear with each pair. Sketch all five points.

   a. $(2, 5)$ and $(6, 13)$

   b. $(-1, 3)$ and $(5, 3)$

   c. $(1, -4)$ and $(3, -5)$

   d. $(-6, 7)$ and $(-6, 0)$

2. What is the equation of the line through each point and with the given slope? Write in $y = ax + b$ form.

   a. $A(1, 4)$ with slope $= \frac{1}{2}$

   b. $Q(1, -4)$ and $R = (0, 2)$

   c. $B(-2, 5)$ with slope $= 0$

   d. $B(-2, 5)$ with an undefined slope

   e. $B(-2, 5)$ and parallel to the line with equation $2x - 3y = 8$

3. Sketch the graph of each equation. Is the point $(4, 5)$ on the line?

   a. $y = 2x - 3$

   b. $y - 1 = \frac{1}{2}(x + 4)$

   c. $2x + 3y = 6$

   d. $3x - y = 7$

4. Solve each equation for y.

   a. $2x + y = 5$

   b. $3x - y = 4$

   c. $x + 2y = -6$

   d. $y - 4 = 3(x - 2)$

5. After soccer practice, Ling runs home at the rate of 6 miles per hour. Her sister, Akira, left soccer practice one half hour before Ling. She is walking the 4 miles home at 3 miles per hour.

   a. Sketch a distance-time graph that shows Ling's and Akira's walk home.

   b. When will Ling overtake Akira?

6. How can you determine whether the graph of an equation is a line?

7. How can you use a distance-time graph to tell when one runner overtakes another in a race?

8. How can you write an equation of the line that connects points $(-3, 7)$ and $(4, 2)$?

Vocabulary

In this investigation, you learned these terms. Make sure you understand what each one means and how to use it.

- **parallel lines**
- **slope of a line**
- **x-intercept**
- **y-intercept**

The slope of a Nordic skier's distance-time graph increases near the end of a race. Explain.

Intersections

In *Intersections*, you will interpret the meaning of the intersection of two lines in the coordinate plane. You will use algebra to find this point of intersection. You will also explore characteristics of parallel lines.

By the end of this investigation, you will be able to answer questions like these.

1. How can you find the intersection of two lines?

2. How can you determine from their equations whether two lines will intersect?

3. Are the graphs of $3x - 4y = 16$ and $y = \frac{3}{4}x - 1$ parallel? Explain.

You will learn how to

- solve systems of linear equations with two variables using substitution and elimination

- determine whether two lines are parallel or intersecting using the slope of each line

- write and solve word problems for systems of equations

You will develop these habits and skills:

- Understand the relationship between systems of equations and intersections of graphs.

- Interpret the intersection of two graphs as a solution to the corresponding system of equations, and vice versa.

- Use basic moves to build new problem solving techniques.

The ball and a teammate should meet where their paths intersect.

4.05) Getting Started

Activating Prior Knowledge
Exploring New Ideas

Knowing the slope of a line can help you solve many problems. You can use the slope of two lines to find where they intersect. Likewise, you can find the slope of two lines to find their common solution.

For You to Explore

1. Tuan wants to sell printed shirts to raise money for the school band. He spends $72.00 to buy a silk-screen machine and ink. He buys each shirt for $1.25. Tuan sells each printed shirt for $5.75. How many shirts does Tuan need to sell to break even?

2. What is the intersection point of the graphs of $y = 72 + 1.25x$ and $y = 5.75x$?

3. Tuan decides to buy a high-quality silk-screen machine and long-lasting inks, making his starting costs for printing shirts $130.00. The cost of the shirts and his selling price remain the same. How many shirts does Tuan need to sell to make a profit?

4. Nicole and Katy ride their bicycles. Nicole rides at 300 yards per minute. Katy rides at 375 yards per minute. Since Katy is a faster rider, she gives Nicole a head start of 125 yards.

   In the graph, the horizontal axis represents the time in minutes since Katy started. The vertical axis represents the distance in yards from where they start. The two lines show each rider's distance d against time t.

Bike Ride

   a. Which line corresponds to Nicole's ride? To Katy's ride?

   b. Write an equation for Katy's graph.

   c. Write an equation for Nicole's graph.

   d. In Lesson 3.06, you learned that the intersection point of two graphs satisfies both equations. In the distance-time graph, the two lines intersect. This shows that Katy catches up to Nicole. At what time and distance does this happen?

5. Conan waits at the train station for Courtney. Courtney gets off the train 217 feet away from where Conan is waiting on the platform. They start running toward each other. Conan runs 11 feet per second. Courtney runs 10 feet per second.

   a. How long will it take for them to meet?

   b. How far will Conan have run when they meet?

   c. Write an equation that can be used to find how long it will take for Conan and Courtney to meet.

   d. Suppose they had started 350 feet apart. Calculate how long it would take them to meet in this situation.

On Your Own

6. Write a problem similar to Problem 4. Decide the distance of the head start and the speed of each rider. Draw graphs that represent each bicyclist.

7. Graph ℓ and m. Are the given points on ℓ, m, both, or neither?

   a. ℓ: $y = 2x + 1$ and m: $y + 3x = 1$

      points: $A(0, 0)$, $B(0, 1)$, and $C\left(1, \frac{1}{3}\right)$

   b. ℓ: $y = x^2$ and m: $\frac{1}{2}y + x = 4$

      points: $A(-2, 4)$, $B(2, 4)$, and $C(0, 0)$

   c. ℓ: $y = \frac{1}{5}x - 1$ and m: $x = 5$

      points: $A(5, 0)$, $B(5, 3)$, and $C(-5, 2)$

   d. ℓ: $y = 2x$ and m: $y = \frac{3}{2}x + 1$

      points: $A(1, 2)$, $B(6, 10)$, and $C(2, 4)$

8. For each pair of lines, find each of the following:

   • a point on neither line

   • a point on one line but not the other

   • a point on both lines

   a. p: $y + 3 = x$ and q: $x + y = 3$

   b. p: $y = \frac{3}{5}x + 2$ and q: $y = -\frac{5}{3}x + 2$

   c. p: $2y + 10x = -8$ and q: $y - \frac{1}{5}x = -4$

9. Find the equations of two lines that intersect at $(2, -4)$. Check that the point $(2, -4)$ satisfies both equations.

10. In 2002, Town X had a population of 7250, and Town Y had a population of 9000. Since 1990, the population of Town X has been steadily decreasing by 120 people per year. The population of Town Y has been steadily increasing by 300 people per year. In what year did Town X and Town Y have the same population?

Maintain Your Skills

11. Graph each pair of linear equations. Name any points they have in common.

   a. $y = 2x + 1$ and $y + 3x = 1$

   b. $(y - 0) = \frac{1}{2}(x - 3)$ and $(y - 0) = -3(x - 3)$

   c. $(y + 1) = 2(x - 3)$ and $3y - 6x = 9$

   d. $y - \frac{5}{2}x - 1$ and $2\left(y - \frac{5}{2}\right) = 5(x + 1)$

   e. $y = \frac{3}{5}x + 1$ and $y = -\frac{5}{3}x + 1$

   f. When do the graphs of two lines intersect at one point?

   g. When do the graphs of two lines have no intersection points?

   Use slope for Exercises 11f and 11g.

In Lesson 4.04, you compared the graphs of two different lines. When the slopes, or rates of change, of the two graphs were different, the graphs eventually intersected. How can you find the intersection point directly from the equations?

Consider this pair of equations.

$$d = 375t$$

$$d = 300t + 125$$

If you graph the equations, the intersection point is at approximately $t = 1.5$.

> These equations describe Katy's and Nicole's bike ride in Lesson 4.05.

Bike Ride

Test whether $t = 1.5$ gives the same value for d in each equation.

Substitute $t = 1.5$ into the first equation.

$$d = 375t$$

$$d = 375(1.5)$$

$$d = 562.5$$

Substitute $t = 1.5$ into the second equation.

$$d = 300t + 125$$

$$d = 300(1.5) + 125$$

$$d = 575$$

The values of d are different, so $t = 1.5$ does not give the intersection point. But it is close. You could refine your guess, trying a value of t that is slightly greater.

The guess-and-check process will eventually give you the answer. However, there is a way to calculate the intersection exactly. Wherever the graphs cross, both variables must have the same values in the two equations. In other words, the values of both t and d are the same in both equations.

> If $t = 1.5$, Nicole has biked 575 yards and Katy has biked 562.5 yards. Since Katy bikes faster, she still has not passed Nicole. So the value of t must be greater than 1.5.

You are given the two equations $d = 375t$ and $d = 300t + 125$. If the values of d have to equal each other, then these expressions are also equivalent.

$$d = 375t$$

$$d = 300t + 125$$

$$375t = d = 300t + 125$$

$$375t = 300t + 125$$

You can use this equation to find the exact value of t at the intersection. Solve with the basic moves.

$$375t = 300t + 125$$

$$75t = 125$$

$$t = \frac{125}{75}$$

$$t = \frac{5}{3}$$

To find the d-value, substitute $t = \frac{5}{3}$ into either of the two original equations. The first equation seems simpler.

$$d = 375t$$

$$d = 375\left(\frac{5}{3}\right)$$

$$d = 625$$

The intersection point is $\left(\frac{5}{3}, 625\right)$. You can also write the coordinates as mixed numbers, $\left(1\frac{2}{3}, 625\right)$.

For You to Do

1. For what value of t is Katy leading the ride?
2. For what values of t is Nicole leading?
3. Who rides 1 mile first?

It is not a coincidence that both equations are in "$d =$" form. Situations often suggest describing one variable in terms of operations on another variable. It is less common for a situation to yield an equation like $2x + 3y = 87$.

Sometimes, you are given two equations that are in different forms, for example, $ax + by = c$ or $y - b = m(x - a)$. There are several ways you can find the intersection points of these lines. You can solve both equations for the same variable and then set the other sides equal to each other. You can also use the **substitution method.** First solve one of the equations for any variable. Then substitute this result for the variable in the other equation.

Example

Problem Find an ordered pair (x, y) that makes both equations true.

$$2x + 5y = 20$$

$$x - y = 3$$

Solution First solve one equation for a variable in terms of the other. Either variable in either equation can be selected. Typically, you want to select the one that requires the least work. In this example, it is easiest to solve the second equation for x.

$$x - y = 3 \qquad \text{Add } y \text{ to both sides.}$$

$$x - y + y = 3 + y \qquad \text{Simplify.}$$

$$x = 3 + y$$

Next you want to substitute the expression $3 + y$ for every x in the first equation.

$$2x + 5y = 20 \qquad \text{Substitute } 3 + y \text{ for } x.$$

$$2(3 + y) + 5y = 20$$

You now have an equation with only one variable. Solve using the basic moves.

$$2(3 + y) + 5y = 20$$

$$6 + 2y + 5y = 20$$

$$6 + 7y = 20$$

$$7y = 14$$

$$y = 2$$

The y-coordinate of the intersection point is 2. Substitute 2 for y in either equation to find the corresponding x-coordinate.

$$x - y = 3$$

$$x - (2) = 3$$

$$x = 5$$

The intersection point is $(5, 2)$. Check your work by substituting $x = 5$ and $y = 2$ into each equation.

$$2x + 5y = 20 \qquad\qquad x - y = 3$$

$$2(5) + 5(2) = 20 ✔ \qquad\qquad 5 - 2 = 3 ✔$$

The point $(5, 2)$ makes both equations true. It is the intersection point for the graphs of $2x + 5y = 20$ and $x - y = 3$.

> Don't forget the parentheses!

For Discussion

4. The point (5, 2) is an intersection of the graphs of $2x + 5y = 20$ and $x - y = 3$. Are there any others? Explain.

For You to Do

5. Find an ordered pair (a, b) that solves the equations $a = 15 - 2b$ and $3a - 5b = 15 - 2a$.

6. **What's Wrong Here?** Tony needs to find the intersection point of the graphs of $2x + 5y = 20$ and $y = x - 3$. He says, "Since the second equation is solved for y, I can substitute into the first equation. I just need to replace y with $x - 3$.

$$2x + 5y = 20$$
$$2x + 5x - 3 = 20$$
$$7x = 23$$
$$x = \frac{23}{7}$$

Now I plug this value of x in to find y in either equation. I'll pick the second one.

$$y = x - 3$$
$$y = \frac{23}{7} - 3$$
$$y = \frac{2}{7}$$

Let me check my work. I'll plug the point $\left(\frac{23}{7}, \frac{2}{7}\right)$ into the first equation.

$$2x + 5y = 20$$
$$2\left(\frac{23}{7}\right) + 5\left(\frac{2}{7}\right) \stackrel{?}{=} 20$$
$$\frac{46}{7} + \frac{10}{7} \stackrel{?}{=} 20$$
$$\frac{56}{7} \stackrel{?}{=} 20$$
$$8 \neq 20 \quad ✗$$

I must have done something wrong. I'm glad I checked the result. Now I know to look for a mistake."

What was Tony's mistake?

Use a different process to find the same result. As you have seen in this lesson, you can find the intersection of the graphs of two equations without sketching the graphs. You can find the points algebraically by solving a system of equations. A **system of equations** is a group of equations with the same variables. When you solve the system, you find a common solution to all the equations at once.

Exercises *Practicing Habits of Mind*

Check Your Understanding

1. At a lunch shop, Aisha buys 2 veggie wraps, 3 apples, and a drink. Her bill is $6.24. Jaime buys 3 veggie wraps, 2 apples, and a drink. His bill is $6.64. If drinks cost $.99, how much does a veggie wrap cost?

2. What is the intersection point of the graphs of these linear equations?

$$2v + 3a + 0.99 = 6.24$$

$$3v + 2a + 0.99 = 6.64$$

3. Many phone companies offer a "10-10" number that you can dial before a long-distance call to save money. If you dial 10-10 with BigPhone Company, you pay $.39 for the connection and $.03 per minute. If you dial 10-10 with LittlePhone Company, you pay $.25 for the connection and $.07 per minute. Assume you are charged for the exact time you use.

   a. How much does a 6-minute call cost with each company?

   b. For how much time do the two companies charge the same amount?

   c. Which company's plan is less expensive for a 10-minute call?

4. For each pair of equations, find any common solutions. Check that your result satisfies both equations.

  a. $y = 6x - 7$
     $y = -2x - 9$

  b. $m = 8n - 3$
     $m = -4n + 6$

  c. $y = 3x$
     $3x - 2y = 12$

  d. $(y - 5) = 3(x + 2)$
     $(y - 5) = 6(x + 2)$

  e. $y = 9x + 4$
     $y = 9x - \frac{2}{3}$

  f. $(y - 1) = \frac{2}{3}(x + 1)$
     $(y - 1) = 4\left(x - \frac{1}{4}\right)$

5. The Walton Taxi Company charges $2.25 for each trip plus $.19 for every $\frac{1}{10}$ mile. The Newtham Taxi Company charges $1.50 for each trip plus $.25 for each $\frac{1}{10}$ mile.

  a. How much will a $\frac{3}{10}$-mile ride cost with each company?

  b. How much will a 1-mile ride cost with each company?

  c. Use t for the total cost of the ride and m for each $\frac{1}{10}$ mile. Write an equation to describe each taxi company's fee schedule. Graph the two equations on the same set of axes.

  d. For what distance do the taxi companies charge the same amount?

  e. Which company charges less if you need to travel 6 miles?

  f. When is it less expensive to use the Walton Taxi Company?

Is this a Walton or a Newtham taxi meter?

6. What is the intersection point for each pair of lines?

a.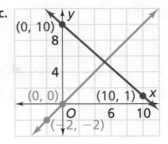
(−4, 6) (7, 6)
(2, 3)
(2, 0)

b. $\left(7, 5\frac{1}{2}\right)$
(−5, 3)   (8, 3)
(0, −2)

c. (0, 10)
(0, 0)   (10, 1)
(−2, −2)

Write About It Describe a situation that could make use of each given system.

7. system of two equations in two variables

8. system of three equations in two variables

On Your Own

9. Tyrell needs to call a plumber. RotoPlumb charges $75 for the first half hour of work and $30 for each additional half hour. Just Plumbing charges $45 for every half hour of work. Which plumbing company should Tyrell choose if the job takes the given amount of time?

   a. 1 hour

   b. 6 hours

   c. For what time will both companies charge the same amount?

10. Standardized Test Prep Each DVD club offers some DVDs for free and then charges a fixed price for other DVDs. If you join Club 1, you receive 4 free DVDs. You must purchase at least 4 DVDs at the club price. The club price for each DVD is $11.99. If you join Club 2, you receive 5 free DVDs. You must purchase at least 4 DVDs at the club price. The club price for each DVD is $13.99.

Total Number of DVDs	Total Cost	
	Club 1	Club 2
9	▪	▪
10	▪	▪
11	▪	▪
12	▪	▪

   a. You plan to get a total of nine DVDs including the free DVDs. What will be the total cost with Club 1? With Club 2?

   b. Copy and complete the table.

   c. Use the data from your completed table to draw a graph.

   d. Compare the two offers. Explain which is the most economical.

11. a. Use substitution to find the intersection point of the graphs of $y = 5 - 3x$ and $y + 3x = 1$. Explain what happens.

b. Graph each equation. What do the graphs suggest about the solution to the system of equations?

12. Take It Further Suppose k and ℓ are fixed numbers. Since the following are lines with different slopes, the graphs of the two lines $y = 18x + k$ and $y = 5x + \ell$ must always intersect somewhere. Find a formula, using k and ℓ, for the intersection point.

13. What is the solution to each system of equations? If there is not any solution, explain.

a. $y = 18x - 30$ and $y = 17.5x + 12$

b. $y = 18x - 30$ and $y = 18x + 12$

Go Online
www.successnetplus.com

Maintain Your Skills

14. Write equations for lines ℓ and m. Tell whether ℓ and m are parallel.

a. ℓ passes through $(-1, 5)$ and $(-3, 1)$; m passes through $(2, -2)$ and $(5, 4)$.

b. ℓ passes through $(10, 4)$ and $(-5, 1)$; m passes through $(5, 0)$ and $(15, 2)$.

c. ℓ passes through $\left(0, \frac{1}{2}\right)$ and $(3, -4)$; m passes through $(0, 5)$ with slope 2.

d. ℓ passes through $(7, 7)$ and $(-1, -1)$; m passes through $(0, -7)$ and $(7, 0)$.

e. ℓ passes through $(3, 7)$ and $(9, 11)$; m passes through $(3, 1)$ and $(-6, -4)$.

f. ℓ passes through $(-3, 12)$ and $(4, 5)$; m passes through $\left(\frac{1}{2}, 4\right)$ and $\left(\frac{3}{2}, 3\right)$.

g. ℓ passes through $(0, -9)$ and $(2, -1)$; m passes through $(0, 0)$ and $(4, 4)$.

h. How can you tell from the equations whether lines ℓ and m are parallel?

Go Online
Video Tutor
www.successnetplus.com

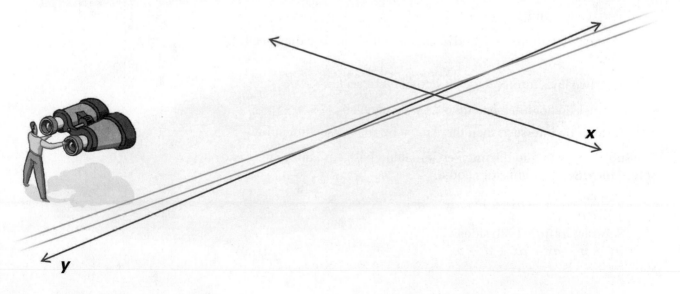

Slope and Parallel Lines

Slope is an important concept in understanding lines that do not intersect. You can determine if lines intersect by finding their slopes.

For You to Do

What is the slope of each line?

1. $3x - 2y = 7$ **2.** $y = 5x - 3$

3. $x = 3y + 2$ **4.** $(y - 4) = 7(x + 5)$

Throughout this chapter, you have encountered graphs of two lines that do not intersect. For example, when you sketch the distance-time graphs of two objects traveling at the same constant speed, the two lines never cross. Two lines that do not intersect are parallel.

How are parallel runways used?

Definition

Two lines in the same plane are parallel if they have no points in common.

You may have noticed in this investigation that if two different lines have the same slope, they are parallel. You can prove that this conjecture is true.

Theorem 4.2

If two distinct lines have the same slope, then they are parallel.

Distinct means "different." Distinct lines will not have the same graph.

Proof Consider two different lines with the same slope. Let a be the slope of the lines. Write equations for these lines.

$$y = ax + b \text{ and } y = ax + d$$

The two constant numbers, b and d, are not equal because the lines are different.

Either the two lines intersect, or they do not intersect.

- If the lines do not intersect, then they are parallel.
- If the lines do intersect, then there must be an intersection point.

Use substitution to find the intersection point. Both equations are already solved for y. Set the right sides equal.

$$\left.\begin{array}{l} y = ax + b \\ y = ax + d \end{array}\right\} \rightarrow ax + b = ax + d$$

Subtract ax from both sides.

$$ax + b - ax = ax + d - ax$$
$$b = d$$

But this contradicts the fact that $b \neq d$. Therefore, the two lines cannot intersect.

Thus, if two distinct lines have the same slope, then they are parallel.

For Discussion

Explain why the following sentences from the proof are true.

5. If the lines do not intersect, then they are parallel.

6. If $b = d$, then the two lines, $y = ax + b$ and $y = ax + d$ must be the same.

Different lines with the same slope are parallel. Can lines that do not have the same slope also be parallel? The next theorem states that they cannot.

Theorem 4.3

If two lines have different slopes, then they must intersect in exactly one point.

Proof Consider two lines, as in the previous proof. Let a be the slope of the first line and let c be the slope of the second line. Write equations for these lines where $a \neq c$, and b and d are two constant numbers that may or may not be equal.

$$y = ax + b \text{ and } y = cx + d$$

If there is a point of intersection, then the lines cannot be parallel. Use substitution to find the intersection.

$$\left.\begin{array}{l} y = ax + b \\ y = cx + d \end{array}\right\} \rightarrow ax + b = cx + d$$

Solve this equation for x.

$ax + b = cx + d$	Subtract cx from each side.
$ax - cx + b = d$	Subtract b from each side.
$ax - cx = d - b$	"Undistribute" the x.
$(a - c)x = d - b$	Divide each side by $a - c$.
$x = \frac{d - b}{a - c}$	

You also can find out that $y = \frac{ad - bc}{a - c}$. The intersection point is $\left(\frac{d - b}{a - c}, \frac{ad - bc}{a - c} \right)$.

> The fact that $a \neq c$ is important. If $a = c$ then $a \square c$ equals 0, and you cannot divide by 0.

For Discussion

Complete the proof by answering these questions.

7. You found an expression for the intersection point. How does this fact prove the theorem?

8. Can there be more than one intersection point?

You proved that parallel lines have the same slope and intersecting lines do not have the same slope. Therefore, the statements "two distinct lines are parallel" and "two distinct lines have the same slope" are equivalent. Logicians write equivalence statements such as the following:

Two different lines are parallel if and only if they have the same slope.

Exercises *Practicing Habits of Mind*

Check Your Understanding

1. Identify the graphs of each pair of equations as *parallel, intersecting,* or *identical.* Explain.

   a. $4x - y = 12$ and $y = 4x + 7$

   b. $y = \frac{5}{3}x + 9$ and $y = -\frac{3}{5}x + 200$

   c. $y = \frac{4}{12}x + 9$ and $y = \frac{1}{3}x - 3.7$

   d. $6x + 9y = 1$ and $9y - 1 = -6x$

   e. $x - 4y = 13$ and $2x + \frac{1}{2}y = \frac{3}{4}$

   f. $y - 5 = -2x - 6$ and $y - 2 = -x + 1$

2. In Lesson 4.06, you worked with BigPhone's plan. If you dial "10-10-B-I-G," you pay $.39 as a connection fee and $.03 per minute. Huge Phone offers a plan that has a connection fee of $10, but only charges $.01 per minute. Sasha thinks that Huge Phone will always be more expensive than BigPhone. Tony thinks that if you talk for a very long time, Huge Phone might be less expensive. Who is correct?

3. Describe a calling plan that is always more expensive than BigPhone's plan from Exercise 2. Justify your example.

4. Sasha graphs a line with the equation $2x + 3y = 7$. Then she multiplies both sides by 4 to get $8x + 12y = 28$. She graphs this equation. The graph is not another line. Explain.

On Your Own

For Exercises 5–9, write an equation of the line that contains the given point and is parallel to the line with the given equation.

> You may want to develop a point-tester.

5. $(10, 15)$; $y = -\frac{1}{5}x + 4$

6. $(-4, 3)$; $2x - 4y = 7$

7. $\left(13, -\frac{22}{7}\right)$; $y - 5 = \frac{22}{7}(x - 8)$

8. $(0, 0)$; $y = ax + b$ (a and b are constant numbers, and $b \neq 0$.)

9. a. $(5, -3)$; $y = 7$

   b. $(5, -3)$; $x = 7$

10. **Write About It** Meredith describes to Liza two purchases she made. "On Monday, I bought 39 books and 21 CDs for $396. On Tuesday, at the same prices, I bought 52 books and 28 CDs for $518."

    Liza thought about the numbers and said, "That's impossible!" Is Liza correct? Assume that all books cost the same amount and all CDs cost the same amount. Explain.

11. **Write About It** Tim tries to solve a system of two linear equations. He concludes that there is no solution. Explain what this means about the graphs.

> When you solve a system of linear equations, you find the point where the graphs of the lines intersect.

12. **Standardized Test Prep** Julia and Marcia buy identically priced cans of chili and identically priced jars of salsa.

    - Julia buys 3 cans of chili and 2 jars of salsa for $10.07.

    - Marcia buys 2 cans of chili and 4 jars of salsa for $12.98.

    Which system of equations can be used to find x, the cost of 1 can of chili, and y, the cost of 1 jar of salsa?

    A. $x + y = 10.07$
       $x + y = 12.98$

    B. $10.07x + 12.98y = 11$
       $x + y = 11$

    C. $2x + 4y = 10.07$
       $2x + 3y = 12.98$

    D. $3x + 2y = 10.07$
       $2x + 4y = 12.98$

13. **Write About It** Diego needs to solve this system.

$$2x + 3y = 7$$

$$4x - 3y = 5$$

He graphs each line to get an estimate of the solution. Next, he adds the equations. His result is $6x = 12$. Diego says, "What a great way to solve systems! I hope that adding the equations is a legal move."

a. If you use the equation $6x = 12$, what is the solution to the system?

b. Is Diego's move legal? Explain.

What does the graph of $6x = 12$ look like on the Cartesian plane?

Maintain Your Skills

14. What is the value of k such that the graph of the equation will pass through $(0, -5)$?

a. $y = 2x + k$

b. $y = 3x + k$

c. $y = 4x + k$

d. $y = 99x + k$

e. What pattern do you notice about the values of k?

15. What is the value of k such that the graph of the equation will pass through $(-5, 0)$?

a. $y = 2x + k$

b. $y = 3x + k$

c. $y = 4x + k$

d. $y = 99x + k$

e. What do you notice about the relationship between k and the slope?

Go Online
www.successnetplus.com

4.08 Solving Systems: Elimination

Recall the following basic move:

> If you start with any equation and add the same number to each side, you will not change the solutions to the equation.

For example, suppose $x = 5$ and $y = 6$. What is true about $x + y$? You can easily decide that $x + y$ is 11. You can also get this result using basic moves. Start with $x = 5$ and add 6 to each side.

$$x = 5$$

$$x + 6 = 5 + 6$$

Since $y = 6$, substitute y for 6 on the left side of the equation.

$$x + 6 = 5 + 6$$

$$x + y = 5 + 6$$

This is a great deal of work for such a simple problem. You can extend the basic rules so that you can say, "Add the same value (instead of number) to each side of an equation." *Value* can mean a variable, number, or any mathematical expression.

Theorem 4.4 *Additive Property of Equality*

If $X = A$ and $Y = B$, then $X + Y = A + B$, where A, B, X, and Y can be any mathematical expressions.

The proof of this theorem is exactly like the example above.

This theorem explains why Diego's idea in Lesson 4.07 works. It also points to another method for solving systems of equations. You can combine equations in ways that eliminate one of the variables. When you reduce the system to a simpler one, you can find the solution easily.

Example 1

Problem Find the intersection of the graphs of $x + y = 10$ and $x - y = 3$.

Solution Use the Additive Property of Equality. If $x + y$ is 10 and $x - y$ is 3, then their sum must be 13.

$$
\begin{array}{r}
x + y = 10 \\
(+) \quad x - y = 3 \\
\hline
(x + y) + (x - y) = 13
\end{array}
$$

Habits of Mind

Use a different process to get the same result. Draw the graph to estimate the solution.

When you use the **elimination method** , you use either addition or subtraction to remove a variable. For example, the result of adding $(x + y) + (x - y)$ is $2x$. You have eliminated the variable y.

In general, it is faster to add each variable separately. Write the two equations one under the other so that matching variables line up. Then, add each column. First add the x values. Then add the y values. Add the numbers last.

$$\begin{array}{r} x + y = 10 \\ (+)\underline{x - y = 3} \\ 2x - 0y = 13 \end{array}$$

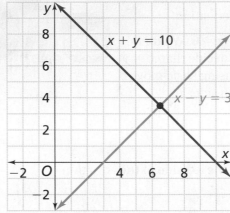

You can write the plus sign + in parentheses to indicate that it applies to all of the terms on both sides of the second equation.

The result is $2x = 13$, so x is $6\frac{1}{2}$.

Substitute the x value, $6\frac{1}{2}$, into one of the equations to find that $y = 3\frac{1}{2}$. The graphs of the equations intersect at $\left(6\frac{1}{2}, 3\frac{1}{2}\right)$.

For You to Do

1. Use the Additive Property of Equality. Solve the system of equations.

$$6y - 4x = 3$$
$$4x + 2y = 1$$

For Discussion

2. When you add these equations, you will not eliminate any variables.

$$3x + 2y = 11$$
$$3x - 5y = 25$$

Is it a legal move to subtract equations the same way you add them? If $X = A$ and $Y = B$, is it always true that $X - Y = A - B$? What is the solution to this system?

Try replacing A and B with numbers. Is the equation always true?

Elimination by adding or subtracting works whenever the coefficients of one variable are the opposite or the same, respectively, for both equations. Some systems of equations, like the one below, do not have a variable with the same coefficient.

$$5y - 2x = -15$$
$$12y + 3x = 3$$

You can still use elimination to solve these equations, but you will need some extra steps.

Example 2

Problem   What is the intersection of the graphs of $5y - 2x = -15$ and $12y + 3x = 3$?

Solution   Remember this basic move of equations.

If you multiply both sides of an equation by the same nonzero number, you will not change the solutions of that equation.

- Multiply both sides of the first equation by 3 to get $15y - 6x = -45$. The coefficient of x is now -6.

- Multiply both sides of the second equation by 2 to get $24y + 6x = 6$. The coefficient of x is now 6.

Now when you add the equations together, you eliminate the x term.

$$
\begin{array}{r}
15y - 6x = -45 \\
(+)\ 24y + 6x = 6 \\
\hline
39y = -39
\end{array}
$$

Divide both sides by 39 to solve the equation and get $y = -1$.

Plug this y value into either of the original equations. Find x at the intersection.

$$5y - 2x = -15$$
$$5(-1) - 2x = -15$$
$$-5 - 2x = -15$$
$$10 = 2x$$
$$5 = x$$

The intersection point is $(5, -1)$.

For Discussion

3. Why did you change both x coefficients to 6?
4. Can you solve this system by eliminating y instead? Explain.

Exercises Practicing Habits of Mind

1. Use elimination. Solve each system of equations. Check that your solution satisfies both equations.

   a. $x + y = 30$ and $x - y = 6$

   b. $-10a + 6b = 25$ and $10a + 5b = 30$

   c. $2x + y = 4$ and $x - y = 2$

   d. $2x - 3y = 17$ and $2x - 3y = 1$

   e. $4z - 5w = 15$ and $2w + 4z = -6$

   f. $y = 7x + 1$ and $y = 15$

2. At a snack bar, 2 granola bars and 2 drinks cost $3.50. Two granola bars and 4 drinks cost $6.00. What is the cost of each item? Assume items at the snack bar are tax-free.

3. Isabel solves the system of equations below. Explain each step.

   $$10x + 3y = 34$$
   $$5x + 4y = 37$$

   $$10x + 3y = 34$$
   $$\underline{(+) \ -10x + -8y = -74}$$
   $$-5y = -40$$
   $$y = 8$$

   $$5x + 4(8) = 37$$
   $$5x + 32 = 37$$
   $$5x = 5$$
   $$x = 1$$
   $$10(1) + 3(8) = 34 ✔$$
   $$5(1) + 4(8) = 37 ✔$$

4. a. Write the equation of the horizontal line that passes through the intersection of the graphs of $2x + 5y = 17$ and $3x - 2y = 16$.

   b. Write the equation of the vertical line that passes through the intersection in part (a).

   c. The sum of the equations in part (a) is $5x + 3y = 33$. How is the graph of this equation related to the graphs of the equations in part (a)?

5. **Take It Further** Solve this system of equations.

$$2x + 3y + 5z = 11$$
$$x - y + z = 1$$
$$3x - 4y - 5z = 16$$

6. **Take It Further** Prove that Theorem 4.5 gives the solution of any system of linear equations in two variables.

Theorem 4.5

Given the system $ax + by = e$ and $cx + dy = f$, where a, b, c, d, e, and f are known constants, the unique solution is $(x, y) = \left(\dfrac{de - bf}{ad - bc}, \dfrac{af - ce}{ad - bc} \right)$ when $ad - bc \neq 0$. If $ad - bc = 0$, the graphs of the two equations have the same slope, so they are either parallel (the system has no solutions) or the same (the system has infinitely many solutions).

On Your Own

7. **a.** Write the equations of two lines that do not intersect.

   b. Write the equations of two lines that intersect at $(1, -2)$.

8. Kenji bought 2 hats and an umbrella for $22.00. The next day, he bought 2 hats and 3 umbrellas for $33.00. The hats are identical, as are the umbrellas.

   a. What is the price of 2 umbrellas?

   b. What is the price of 1 umbrella?

   c. What is the price of 1 hat?

   d. What combination of hats and umbrellas, if any, would cost $77.00?

9. **Standardized Test Prep** Jeremy helps Madeline build a rectangular pen with a perimeter of 86 feet. Twice the pen's width is one more than three times its length. What is the width of the pen?

   A. $8\frac{3}{5}$ feet

   B. 17 feet

   C. 26 feet

   D. $33\frac{2}{5}$ feet

You can find the cost of two umbrellas in one step.

10. What is the point of intersection of each pair of graphs? Check that this point satisfies both equations.

   a. $y = -5x + 30$
      $3x - 4y = 41$

   b. $y = 2x - 1$
      $y = 9x + 6$

   c. $3x + 2y = 7$
      $-2x + 2y = -2$

   d. $5e - 2f = 30$
      $9e - 2f = 54$

   e. $27x + 5y = 30$
      $-3x - 2y = 1$

   f. $5j - 4k = 19$
      $-7j - 3k = 22$

11. Solve each system.

   a. $2x + 3y = 5$
      $3x - 2y = 14$

   b. $2x + 3y = 5$
      $6x - 4y = 28$

   c. $2x - 3y = 5$
      $3x + 2y = 14$

   d. $2x + 3y = 5$
      $6x + 9y = 18$

12. **Take It Further** Solve each system.

   a. $3x - 2y = 10$
      $4x + y = 5$
      $x + 3y = -7$

   b. $3x - 2y = 10$
      $4x + y = 5$
      $x + 3y = -6$

13. You can use graphs of the following equations to draw a triangle.

   $$y = \frac{3}{2}x$$
   $$y = -\frac{9}{4}x + \frac{15}{2}$$
   $$y = -\frac{3}{8}x - \frac{15}{4}$$

   Draw the graph of the triangle and list its vertices.

Maintain Your Skills

14. Which pairs of equations in the following list form a system with a solution that is $(1, 1)$? Justify your answer.

   $x + y = 2$

   $x + 2y = 3$

   $x + 3y = 4$

   $x + 4y = 5$

   $\vdots$

   $x + (n - 1)y = n$

   $x + ny = n + 1$

Mathematical 4B Reflections

In this investigation, you used slope to find the intersection of two lines. You also used slope to determine whether two lines were parallel. These questions will help you summarize what you have learned.

1. Graph the equations $y = 2x - 3$ and $x - y = 3$. Name a point that satisfies each description.

   a. on neither line   **b.** on only one line   **c.** on both lines

2. What are the equations of two lines that intersect at $(1, -3)$? Check that $(1, -3)$ satisfies both equations.

3. What is the intersection of each pair of linear equations? Sketch the graphs.

   a. $2x + 3y = 2$ **b.** $y - 2 = 3(x + 1)$ **c.** $y = 2x$

   $y = x - 1$ $x + y = 3$ $y = -x - 3$

4. Write an equation for each description.

   a. line parallel to $2x - y = 4$

   b. line intersecting $2x - y = 4$ at $(1, -2)$

5. Solve each system.

   a. $x - 2y = 5$ **b.** $2x - 3y = 15$

   $3x + 2y = -1$ $x + y = 10$

   c. $4x + 3y = 12$ **d.** $2x + 3y = 1$

   $8x + 6y = 8$ $4x - 2y = 10$

6. How can you find the intersection of two lines?

7. How can you determine from their equations whether two lines will intersect?

8. Are the graphs of $3x - 4y = 16$ and $y = \frac{3}{4}x - 1$ parallel? Explain.

Vocabulary

In this investigation, you learned these terms. Make sure you understand what each one means and how to use it.

- **elimination method**
- **substitution method**
- **system of equations**

An opponent anticipates where the ball and the receiver's paths should intersect.

Investigation 4C

Applications of Lines

In *Applications of Lines,* you will solve inequalities in one variable using graphs. You will also solve inequalities in the variables using graphs.

By the end of this investigation, you will be able to answer questions like these.

1. How do the solutions of inequalities relate to the solutions of equations?

2. How can you approximate data using a line of best fit?

3. One taxi charges $1.10 for the first mile and $1 for each additional mile. Another taxi charges $2.30 for the first mile and $.60 for each additional mile. For what distances will the first taxi be less expensive than the second?

You will learn how to

• solve inequalities algebraically and by using graphs

• graph the solution set of an inequality

You will develop these habits and skills:

• Use an equation as a point-tester for a graph.

• Graph lines and inequalities.

• Identify graphs, such as those for $y = x^2$ and $y = |x|$, by their shape.

• Estimate the intersection points of graphs.

Some shapes occur commonly and are easy to identify.

In this investigation, you will solve and graph inequalities with one variable. You will also determine fitting lines for scatter plots of data.

For You to Explore

1. Consider the equation $4x - 7 = -2x + 9$.

   a. Is the equation true or false when $x = 5$?

   b. What are the values of x that make the equation true?

   c. Describe the values of x that make the equation false.

   d. List five values of x that make $4x - 7 < -2x + 9$ true.

   e. List five values of x that make $4x - 7 > -2x + 9$ true.

   f. Write a rule that states whether a value of x makes $4x - 7 < -2x + 9$ or $4x - 7 > -2x + 9$ true. Test more values if necessary.

2. The local Big Games store is offering a special trade-in deal. When you buy a new game, Flat Tire Racing, you receive $6 for each used game you trade in. The game costs $49.99, plus 5% tax.

   a. How much does the game cost, including tax? Round to the nearest cent.

   b. Justin has $10 and 7 used games to trade. Can he afford the game?

   c. Jason has $20 and 15 used games to trade. Can he afford the game?

   d. If Jason has $20, what is the minimum number of used games he needs to trade to get the new game? Explain.

   e. How many different options does Jason have if he has $20? Explain.

3. Sketch the graphs of the equations $y = 4x - 7$ and $y = -2x + 9$. Find their intersection point.

4. Use the graph of $y = x^2 - 5$ and $y = x + 1$ at the right.

   a. Name all the solutions to the equation $x^2 - 5 = x + 1$.

   b. Draw a number line. Shade it with all the solutions of $x^2 - 5 > x + 1$.

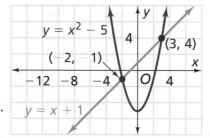

For part (a), find each x value for which $y = x^2 - 5$ and $y = x + 1$ have the same y value. Where do you see this on the graph?

5. Consider the equations $y = (x - 11)^2 - 5$ and $y = (x - 11) + 1$.

   a. List the solutions to $(x - 11)^2 - 5 = (x - 11) + 1$.

   b. Draw a number line. Shade it with all the solutions of $(x - 11)^2 - 5 < (x - 11) + 1$.

6. **a.** Find seven points that make the inequality $y > 2x - 5$ true. Plot them on a coordinate plane.

   b. Graph the points in the coordinate plane that make the inequality $y > 2x - 5$ true.

7. **Take It Further** Graph the points in the coordinate plane that make the inequality $y \le x^2$ true.

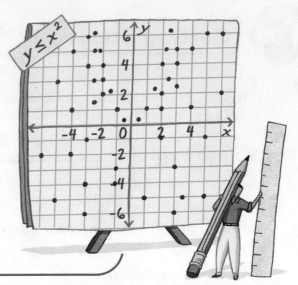

Exercises *Practicing Habits of Mind*

On Your Own

8. Consider the equation $(x - 3)^2 + 5 = 41$.

   a. Is the equation *true* or *false* when $x = 7$?

   b. Test whether -3 makes the equation true.

   c. What other number(s) make the equation true?

   d. Find five values of x that make $(x - 3)^2 + 5 < 41$ true.

   e. Find five values of x that make $(x - 3)^2 + 5 > 41$ true.

   f. Write a rule to determine whether a value of x makes $(x - 3)^2 + 5 < 41$ or $(x - 3)^2 + 5 > 41$ true. Test more values if necessary.

9. Draw a number line. Mark it with all the values of x that satisfy each inequality.

   a. $5x + 14 < 2x - 12$

   b. $5x + 14 \le 2x - 12$

   c. $(x - 3)^2 + 5 > 41$

10. Use the graph of $y = x^3 - 3x$ and $y = x$.

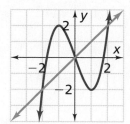

   a. At how many points do the graphs intersect?

   b. What are the exact coordinates of the intersection point(s)?

   c. What are the solutions to the equation $x^3 - 3x = x$?

   d. Describe the values of x that make $x^3 - 3x < x$ true.

11. Describe the numbers that make each statement true.

   a. $3a - 16 > 23$

   b. $3b - 16 \geq 23$

   c. $|d - 4| < 3$

   d. $|h - 4| \leq 3$

   e. $(d - 4)^2 < 9$

Maintain Your Skills

12. Suppose n is a number greater than 10. What do you know about the value of each of the following?

   a. $2n$ **b.** $n - 20$ **c.** $-n$

   d. $\frac{n}{2}$ **e.** $-3n + 7$

13. What is the intersection point for each pair of lines?

   a. $y = 3x - 5$ and $y = -2x + 10$

   b. $y = 3x - 8$ and $y = -2x + 7$

   c. $y = 3x + 5$ and $y = -2x + 20$

   d. $y = 3(x - 4) - 5$ and $y = -2(x - 4) + 10$

   e. What patterns do you notice in the graphs?

Solving by Graphing

In Investigation 4B, you learned several ways to solve systems of two equations and two variables similar to the following.

$$y = 3x - 4$$
$$y = -2x + 5$$

To solve this system using substitution, set the right sides of the two equations equal to each other.

$$3x - 4 = -2x + 5$$

From there, you can use the basic moves to find the value of x. Remember, the x-coordinate of the point of intersection of the two graphs is the same as the solution of the equation you made.

To solve the equation $x^2 - 5 = x + 1$. You would have to use the basic moves. You put everything on one side, leaving 0 on the other, and then factor.

Notice that the system of equations below includes the two sides of the original equation.

$$y = x^2 - 5 \qquad y = \text{(left side)}$$
$$y = x + 1 \qquad y = \text{(right side)}$$

The x-coordinate of the points of intersection of these graphs corresponds to a solution to the original equation. This graphing method is simply substitution. It takes two equations with two variables and builds a single equation with one variable.

Sasha and Tony are using the graphing method to solve an equation.

> You finish the exercise by substituting that value into either equation to find the y-coordinate.

Minds in Action

Tony teaches Sasha how to solve equations using a graphing calculator.

Tony You know, I love this graphing calculator.

Sasha Why's that?

Tony I don't have to do algebra anymore! I can solve an equation without algebra.

Sasha Good luck!

Tony Say I want to solve $x^3 + 5x = 7x^2 - 5$.

Sasha I already know how to do that. Move everything to one side and then factor. Oh, do we know how to factor a polynomial with a cubed term in it?

Tony	Not really, but watch this. I make two graphs on the same coordinate plane. The first one is $y = x^3 + 5x$ and the second one is $y = 7x^2 - 5$. Here's what it looks like on the calculator. I set the window for x from -2 to 2, and y from -10 to 15.

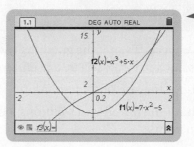

For help graphing the function and adjusting the window settings, see the TI-Nspire Handbook, p. 788.

And there's the answer.

Sasha	What do you mean, there's the answer? I just see graphs crossing.
Tony	Where they intersect, that x value makes both equations true, so it's the answer. And the y-value is what each side adds up to for that x.
Sasha	Okay, but how can I read the answer from the calculator?
Tony	You can zoom in on the intersection. You can change the window settings around it. You can trace along the graph. Some calculators can even find the intersection for you.
Sasha	That's a nice way to estimate, since I don't know if I can factor polynomials with a degree greater than 2.
Tony	This way will even show you how many answers there should be. Just look for how many times the graphs intersect.
Sasha	We have to be careful, though. You're never really sure that the calculator is giving you the exact right answer. Plus, the calculator could give some messy decimal when the exact answer is a fraction or something like the square root of 2. And you might have more intersections that aren't in your window.
Tony	Yes, you're right, but I think it's good to know many ways to do the same problem. You can check the calculator answer to make sure it's exactly right. And even when it isn't, it'll be really close.

For Discussion

1. Use Tony's method and a graphing calculator to find the solutions to $5x + 3 = 20 - 2x$ and $x^2 = 2x + 15$. What are the advantages and disadvantages of using the calculator to find the solutions?

For You to Do

2. Find an equation where the graphing method is easier than algebra.

3. Find another equation for which algebra is easier than the graphing method.

4.10 Solving by Graphing **325**

Developing Habits of Mind

Evaluate the graphing process. Even if the graphing method does not always lead to an exact solution, it can still be a useful tool.

- It gives you an idea about the size of each solution.

- It gives you an idea about the number of solutions, because you can count the intersection points.

- It gives you the ability to approximate each solution to any degree of accuracy, up to the limits of your calculator.

- As you will see in Lesson 4.12, it gives you the ability to decide what numbers make one side greater than the other. So it can be used to solve inequalities.

Exercises *Practicing Habits of Mind*

Check Your Understanding

1. Use Tony's method to find the number of solutions to the following equations.

   a. $x^2 = 9$ **b.** $x^2 = 0$ **c.** $x^2 = -9$

2. Find the number of solutions to each of these equations.

   a. $3x - 7 = 5x + 1$

   b. $3x - \frac{2}{3} = 3x + \frac{5}{4}$

   c. $(x + 1)^3 = \sqrt{x}$

   d. $x^2 = 15$

   e. $x^3 = 15$

   f. $\sqrt{x} = 15$

3. **a.** Describe the graph of the equation $y = 0$.

   b. Use the graphing method and a graphing calculator to find both solutions to the equation $x^2 + 3x - 10 = 0$.

   c. Find the values of x that make the inequality $x^2 + 3x - 10 < 0$ true.

4. Which of these equations have solutions?

a. $x^2 - 2x + 3 = 0$

b. $x^2 - 2x - 3 = 0$

c. $x^2 + 6x + 11 = 0$

d. $x^2 + 6x - 11 = 0$

e. $x^2 + 8x + 12 = 0$

f. $x^2 + 8x - 12 = 0$

5. Take It Further In Exercise 4, some equations in the form $x^2 + Bx + C = 0$ have solutions, and some do not. The solutions depend on the values given for B and C. (Either or both may be positive, negative, or zero.) Find a decision-making rule that shows whether the equation will have solutions.

> A rule might be that if $B + C$ is greater than 10, then the equation will have solutions. Otherwise, it will not. (This rule does not work.)

On Your Own

You apply basic moves to an equation in order to solve it. This produces other equations with the same solution(s). So, you end up with a string of equations that are all equivalent.

Consider these steps using the basic moves to solve the equation $7(x - 3) = 10x - 42$.

$$7(x - 3) = 10x - 42 \quad \text{Distribute the 7.}$$
$$7x - 21 = 10x - 42 \quad \text{Add 21 to each side.}$$
$$7x = 10x - 21 \quad \text{Subtract } 10x \text{ from each side.}$$
$$-3x = -21 \quad \text{Divide each side by } -3.$$
$$x = 7$$

For Exercises 6 and 7, use Tony's graphing method to solve each equation.

6. a. $7(x - 3) = 10x - 42$

b. $7x = 10x - 21$

c. $-3x = -21$

d. $x = 7$

e. What happens if you apply the graphing method to each of the steps?

7. a. $x^2 = 16$

b. $x^2 - 16 = 0$

c. $x^2 - 4x = 21$

d. $x^2 - 4x - 21 = 0$

e. $17x - x^2 = 52$

f. $x^2 - 17x + 52 = 0$

> Do not use the basic moves on these equations before you use Tony's method. After all, his method means you do not do any algebra, correct?

8. **Standardized Test Prep** How many solutions are there to the equation $4 = x^3 + 5x^2 + 4$?

   A. 0

   B. 1

   C. 2

   D. 3

Go Online
www.successnetplus.com

9. The figure below shows the graphs of $y = 2x^2 + x - 14$ and $y = 3x - 2$ on a graphing calculator (x and y both range from -10 to 10).

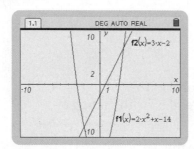

   a. According to the graph, how many solutions are there to the following equation?

   $$2x^2 + x - 14 = 3x - 2$$

   b. Use the graphs to find all values of x that make the equation true.

10. Suppose you know that $x < 4$ is true. Which of these must also be true? Which must be false? Which may be true or false?

   a. $x + 3 < 7$

   b. $2x > 8$

   c. $4 < x$

   d. $x \leq 3$

   e. $x < 5$

   f. $-5x < -20$

   g. $x^2 < 16$

   h. $|x| > 4$

   i. $-6x > -24$

Habits of Mind

Experiment. If you are not sure, try it with numbers. Do not forget that there are many possibilities for x that make $x < 4$ true.

Maintain Your Skills

11. Use the graphing method to solve each of these equations.

   a. $3x - 2 = -2x + 10$

   b. $3x - 5 = -2x + 7$

   c. $3x + 8 = -2x + 20$

   d. $3(x - 4) - 2 = -2(x - 4) + 10$

4.11 Inequalities With One Variable

Tony's parents are choosing a new long-distance phone plan.
Tony and Sasha try to determine which one is cheaper.

Minds in Action

Tony   The phone company offers two plans. With Plan 1, a long-distance call costs 43 cents plus 2 cents per minute. With Plan 2, a long-distance call costs 25 cents plus 4 cents per minute. My mom makes a lot of long calls, so she wants to know which plan is cheaper for longer calls.

Sasha   Let's write expressions for each plan first. If m is the number of minutes, then the cost for a phone call with Plan 1 is $43 + 2m$. A call with Plan 2 is $25 + 4m$. Let's try to figure out when Plan 1 is less than Plan 2. We can use the statement $43 + 2m < 25 + 4m$.

Tony   That's an inequality. I've seen those before, but I don't remember what to do with them.

> An **inequality** is a statement that compares two expressions. It is similar to an equation, but, rather than an equal sign, it has < (less than), ≤ (less than or equal to), > (greater than), or ≥ (greater than or equal to).

Sasha   We can write each of the two plans as a separate equation. Let's pick c for the cost of the call. The equation for Plan 1 is $c = 43 + 2m$. The equation for Plan 2 is $c = 25 + 4m$.

Tony   That looks like a system of equations. We know how to solve that.

Sasha   We do, but does that help with the inequality? What if we graph the two equations first?

Sasha graphs the two equations on her calculator.

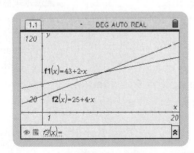

> Show the graph on the coordinate plane. See the TI-Nspire™ Handbook, p. 788.

Sasha   Judging by the graphs, the line $c = 25 + 4m$ is above the line $c = 43 + 2m$ to the right of the intersection point.

Tony   I see. We want to find where the Plan 2 line is higher than the Plan 1 line, for instance, where $m = 15$.

Sasha   So when m is greater than the m-value at the intersection, the call is cheaper using Plan 1.

Tony   The intersection looks like it's at about 9 minutes. We could estimate, but my mom likes me to be precise. Actually, where the two graphs intersect, it's the solution to the system of equations! I told you we should have solved that system.

Sasha   You're right, Tony. We also could just solve the equation $43 + 2m = 25 + 4m$. That's the inequality written as an equation.

$$43 + 2m = 25 + 4m \qquad \text{Subtract 25 from both sides.}$$
$$18 + 2m = 4m \qquad \text{Subtract } 2m \text{ from both sides.}$$
$$18 = 2m \qquad \text{Divide both sides by 2.}$$
$$m = 9$$

Tony   The result is 9. Plan 1 is less expensive for any call longer than 9 minutes. Plan 1 is a better choice since my mom talks with business clients on the phone for hours.

Tony and Sasha found that the solution to the inequality $43 + 2m < 25 + 4m$ is $m > 9$. Sometimes, when the inequality you start with has a less than sign, the result has a greater than sign. If you check the two graphs, the result is clear.

You can also express the solution set of an inequality by sketching a graph of the solutions on a number line. There is a conventional notation that indicates the differences in inequalities, such as $m > 9$ and $m \geq 9$.

Facts and Notation

On a number line, solutions to inequalities are displayed as shaded rays on intervals. A closed circle includes an endpoint. An open circle excludes it. The inequality $3 < x \leq 6$ would look like this.

Notice the circle at $x = 3$ is not filled in, while the circle at $x = 6$ is filled in.

The notation $3 < x \leq 6$ means that x is greater than 3 and less than or equal to 6.

For You to Do

1. Use a number line. Show the solution to $43 + 2m < 25 + 4m$.

You can also solve and graph more complicated inequalities.

Example

Problem Draw a number line. Show the solutions to $|x - 3| \leq \frac{1}{2}x$

Solution Graph the two equations $y = |x - 3|$ and $y = \frac{1}{2}x$ to estimate the solution set.

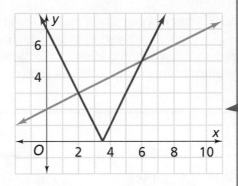

Notice that the y-values on the graph of $y = |x - 3|$ are below the y-values on the graph of $y = \frac{1}{2}x$ in the region between the two intersection points.

Find the intersection points. If $|x - 3|$ equals $\frac{1}{2}x$, then $x - 3$ must be $\frac{1}{2}x$ or $-\left(\frac{1}{2}x\right)$.

For help finding the intersection point(s) of two graphs, see the TI-Nspire Handbook, p. 788.

$$x - 3 = \frac{1}{2}x$$

$$x - 3 + 3 = \frac{1}{2}x + 3$$

$$x = \frac{1}{2}x + 3$$

$$x - \frac{1}{2}x = \frac{1}{2}x - \frac{1}{2}x + 3$$

$$\frac{1}{2}x = 3$$

$$\frac{2}{1}\left(\frac{1}{2}x\right) = \frac{2}{1}(3)$$

$$x = 6$$

$$x - 3 = -\frac{1}{2}x$$

$$x - 3 + 3 = -\frac{1}{2}x + 3$$

$$x = -\frac{1}{2}x + 3$$

$$x + \frac{1}{2}x = \frac{1}{2}x - \frac{1}{2}x + 3$$

$$\frac{3}{2}x = 3$$

$$\frac{2}{3}\left(\frac{3}{2}x\right) = \frac{2}{3}(3)$$

$$x = 2$$

When $x = 2$ and $x = 6$, the inequality is true. Draw closed circles at 2 and 6 on a number line.

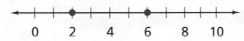

The two intersections divide the number line into three regions. Compare your number line with the original graph. Notice that the number line lines up exactly with the graph.

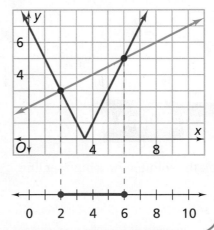

Shade the region on the number line that corresponds to where the graph of the line is above the absolute value graph.

The number line gives you the solution to the inequality. You can also write it as $2 \leq x \leq 6$.

Use a different process to get the same result. The intersections of the graphs act as **cutoff points.** The x-coordinates of the cutoff points split the number line into regions to check.

If you do not have your calculator or you cannot picture the graphs in your head, you can check one point from each region to see which graph is above the other. If one point from a region is above, then the whole region is above. Likewise, if one point from a region is below, then the whole region is below.

For You to Do

2. Use the graphs of $y = x^2 - 5$ and $y = x + 1$. On a number line, draw the solution to the inequality $x^2 - 5 > x + 1$.

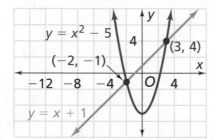

Exercises Practicing Habits of Mind

Check Your Understanding

1. For each inequality, graph the solution on a number line.

   a. $5x < 25$

   b. $3x + 7 \geq 19$

   c. $4x - 9 > 2x + 3$

   d. $14x + 13 \leq 6(2x + 4)$

2. Use algebra and a graphing calculator. Solve each inequality.

a. $5x - 23 > -2x + 50$

b. $|x - 4| < 3$

c. $3(x + 3)^2 > 192$

d. $(x - 3)^2 \leq 0.01$

e. $(x + 5)^2 \leq -0.01$

f. $7x - 23 > 50$

g. $x^2 \geq |x|$

For instructions on adjusting the window settings, see the TI-Inspire Handbook, p. 788.

3. a. Use algebra and testing intervals. Solve the inequality $-27.4x + 13 > -27.2x + 12$.

b. Use a graphing calculator. Plot $y = -27.4x + 13$ and $y = -27.2x + 12$ on the same axes. Is it more difficult or less difficult to use a graphing calculator to solve this exercise? Explain.

4. a. What is the solution set to the inequality $5x - 17 > 2x - 6$?

b. How can you most easily find the solution set to the inequality $5x - 17 < 2x - 6$?

c. What is the solution set to the inequality $5(x - 3) - 17 > 2(x - 3) - 6$?

d. Graph the solutions to parts (a) and (c) on number lines. Compare the solutions to the two parts.

e. Predict the solution set to $5(x - 11) - 17 > 2(x - 11) - 6$. Check your result.

f. Predict the solution set to $5(x + 8) - 17 > 2(x + 8) - 6$. Check your result.

5. Use a graphing calculator. Draw the graphs of $y = \frac{x + 4}{2}$ and $y = \sqrt{4x}$ on the same axes. Use the graphs to solve the inequality $\frac{x + 4}{2} > \sqrt{4x}$.

6. Take It Further Answer each question to solve the inequality $\frac{x - 5}{x + 3} \leq 2$.

Note that ">" does not include equality.

a. What value of x makes the equation undefined?

b. What is the solution of the corresponding equation?

c. Draw the two values for x from parts (a) and (b) on a number line. Remember to use a filled circle if the number is part of the solution to the inequality. Use an open circle if it is not.

d. Test a value in each chunk defined by these points. Solve the inequality.

e. Use a graphing calculator or computer software. Draw a graph of the equation $y = \frac{x - 5}{x + 3}$. How can you use this graph to solve the inequality?

7. Solve each inequality. Graph your solution on a number line.

   a. $2x > 18$

   b. $9x \leq 27$

   c. $-4x + 11 \geq 43$

   d. $17 - 9x > 2x - 16$

   e. $2(3x + 1) < x + 6$

   f. $4x - 5 \leq 23$

   g. $13 + x > 13 - x$

   h. $-2(3 - 2x) \geq 4x + 7$

8. **Write About It** Explain how you can use this graph to draw a number-line graph for the solutions to $x^2 - 3x - 4 > 0$.

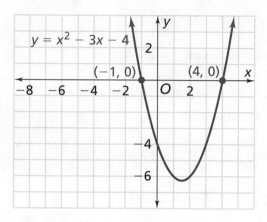

> What are the cutoff points for this inequality?

9. Use different methods to find all the values of x such that $x^3 > x$. Draw your solution set on a number line.

10. The equation $x^3 + 28x = 10x^2 + 24$ has two solutions, $x = 2$ and $x = 6$. Answer each question to find the graph of the solution set for $x^3 + 28x < 10x^2 + 24$ without graphing either side.

    a. Does the number 2.5 make $x^3 + 28x < 10x^2 + 24$ *true* or *false*?

    b. Try again with 3, 3.5, and 5. Do they make $x^3 + 28x < 10x^2 + 24$ *true* or *false*?

    c. Your answers to parts (a) and (b) should be the same. Explain why this would happen.

    d. The solutions $x = 2$ and $x = 6$ separate the number line into three parts. Test a value in each part. Draw the solution on a number line.

11. **a.** Draw a number line to represent $x > 3$.

    b. Draw a number line to represent $x \leq 10$.

    c. How can the number lines from parts (a) and (b) be combined to show a number line for $3 < x \leq 10$?

    d. What x values make $x > 3$, $x \leq 10$, or both true? How does that look on a number line?

12. Take It Further Consider the equation $\frac{6}{x-4} = 2$.

   a. Is the equation true or false when $x = 7$?

   b. Are there any values x cannot be? If so, what are they?

   c. What values of x make the equation true?

   d. Find the values of x that make the equation false.

   e. List five x values that make $\frac{6}{x-4} < 2$ true.

   f. List five x values that make $\frac{6}{x-4} > 2$ true.

   g. Graph the solution to $\frac{6}{x-4} \leq 2$ on a number line.

13. What's Wrong Here? Tony and Derman try to solve the inequality $2x - 4 \geq 3x + 11$.

Derman says, "Inequalities look almost like equations. Can I use the basic moves to solve them like equations?"

Tony replies, "I don't know. Let's try it out."

Tony writes the following:

$$2x - 4 \geq 3x + 11 \qquad \text{Add 4 to both sides.}$$
$$2x \geq 3x + 15 \qquad \text{Subtract 3x from both sides.}$$
$$-x \geq 15 \qquad \text{Divide both sides by } -1.$$
$$x \geq -15$$

Derman says, "That looks like a fine result."

Tony suggests, "We should make sure it's correct. Let's try $x = 0$."

Derman replies, "Zero is greater than -15, so it's in the solution set."

Tony argues, "But does $2(0) - 4 = 3(0) + 11$? Since -4 is not greater than or equal to 11, zero makes the first inequality false. Did we do something wrong? What happened?"

   a. Each step in Tony and Derman's solution shows a different inequality. Substitute 0 in each step. What are true inequalities?

   b. What basic move caused the result to be false? Explain.

14. In Chapter 2, you learned the two basic moves for equations. Determine whether each statement is *always true*, *sometimes true*, or *never true*. If your result is sometimes true, add a condition that makes the statement always true.

   a. For all real numbers a, b, and c, $a < b$ if and only if $a + c < b + c$.

   b. For all real numbers a, b, and c, $a < b$ if and only if $ac < bc$.

Habits of Mind

Check your work.
Do not just assume your conjectures work. Derman has the right idea to try extending the basic moves to cover inequalities. However, always make sure you test your conjecture with numbers.

The basic moves for equations:
For all real numbers a, b and c,
- $a = b$ if and only if $a + c = b + c$
- $a = b$ if and only if $ac = bc$ and $c \neq 0$

15. Standardized Test Prep Which inequality does the graph represent?

Go Online
www.successnetplus.com

A. $2 < n + 6 \leq 10$ **B.** $-12 \leq -3n < 12$

C. $-4 \leq 2n < 4$ **D.** $6 \geq 2 - n > -2$

Maintain Your Skills

16. For each inequality, graph the solution on a number line.

a. $x > 6$ b. $(x - 5) > 6$

c. $(x + 3) > 6$ d. $2x + 12 \leq 4$

e. $2(x - 1) + 12 \leq 4$ f. $2(x + 6) + 12 \leq 4$

17. For each inequality, graph the solution on a number line.

a. $x > 3$ b. $x > -3$

c. $-x > 3$ d. $-x > -3$

e. $2x < 9$ f. $-2x < 9$

g. $-x - 1 \geq 2$ h. $x + 1 \geq 2$

Go Online
Video Tutor
www.successnetplus.com

Inequalities With Two Variables

In Lesson 4.11, you looked at strategies for solving inequalities. Those strategies incorporated Tony's method from Lesson 4.10. They also provided a way to solve inequalities of all sorts, even daunting inequalities such as $2x^2 - 21x + 24 > -7\sqrt{2x + 3}$.

Solving such an inequality can be very tricky. You can use the graphing method. You may not find the exact solution, but you will get a good estimate for the solution.

For You to Do

1. Use the graphing method to solve the inequality
$2x^2 - 21x + 24 > -7\sqrt{2x + 3}$.

All of the inequalities you have studied so far have had only one variable. You can visualize the solution set of one-variable inequalities by graphing the solution on a number line.

To visualize the solution set of a two-variable inequality, you can graph it on the coordinate plane.

Example 1

Problem Graph the solution set to the inequality $y < 3x + 5$.

Solution First, you graph the corresponding equation, $y = 3x + 5$. Notice that the inequality is $<$, and not $\le$. So points along the line $y = 3x + 5$ will not be part of the solution set. You can indicate that the line is not in your solution set by drawing a dashed line.

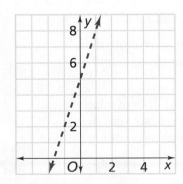

The dashed line in the graph of a two-variable inequality is similar to the open circle in a one-variable inequality.

Think of each point that is on the line as having coordinates of the form $(x, 3x + 5)$. You want all the points that satisfy $y < 3x + 5$. So for any x, you want the value of the y-coordinate to be less than $3x + 5$.

Try $x = 0$. The point on the line with x-coordinate 0 would be $(0, 5)$. Any point on the vertical line with equation $x = 0$ with y-coordinate less than 5 is part of the solution set.

Next, try $x = 5$. The point on the line with x-coordinate 5 is $(5, 20)$, and any point with x-coordinate 5 and y-coordinate less than 20 is part of the solution set.

It would take you forever to write out the situation for every possible value of x, but you can see that any point that is below the line is part of the solution set.

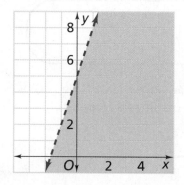

Just as you had systems of equations in Chapter 4, you can also have systems of inequalities. Tony's graphing method helps with these problems, too.

Tony and Sasha are having a conversation about a movie they showed to raise money for their school's highly successful math team.

Tony   What a turnout for the movie. Over 100 people showed up.

Sasha   Yes, that was great! We still didn't make it to our $500 goal, though.

Tony   Really? I can't believe that's possible. There were more than 100 people! We charged $8 per adult and $4 per student, and there were some of each.

Sasha   Here, make a graph of it. Let's say a is the number of adult tickets, and s is the number of student tickets. We want to see what the graph of $8a + 4s < 500$ looks like. Let's start by graphing the line with equation $8a + 4s = 500$.

Tony pulls out some graph paper and quickly sketches this graph.

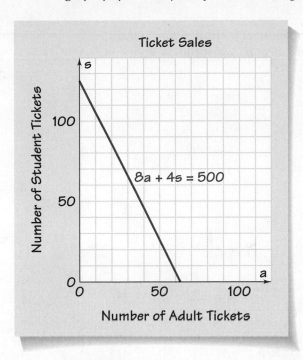

Sasha   Since we didn't make $500, we must be below that line.

Tony   How do you know that?

Sasha   Think about it. If we made $480, the line would have the equation $8a + 4s = 480$. If we made $200, the line would have the equation $8a + 4s = 200$. Here, I'll draw those lines.

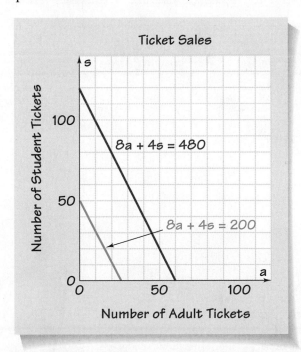

So the graph of $8a + 4s =$ anything less than $500 would be below that line.

Tony   Okay, I get it. But I still don't think we can be below that first line with over 100 people paying.

Sasha   Look, we had more than 100 people, so let's add $a + s > 100$ to the graph. Here's the line with equation $a + s = 100$.

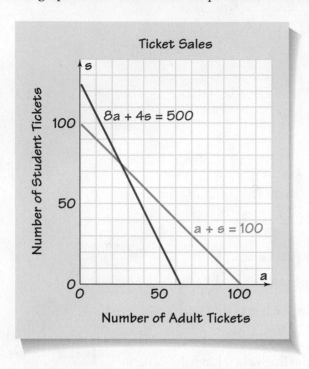

Since we had more than 100 people, we had to be above this line. And we know we're below the graph of $8a + 4s = 500$.

Sasha shades in the graph.

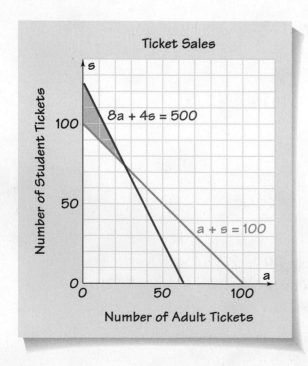

Sasha And see that little corner? Our sales must be somewhere in that shaded part. That's what happens when you let students in for half price.

Tony Maybe next year we should charge all of them five dollars.

For Discussion

2. Using algebra, find the intersection of the two lines that Sasha graphed.

3. Are there any other restrictions on the values of a and s?

> What kinds of numbers can a and s be?

As with inequalities of one variable, the solution set for Problem 2 includes more than one number. It is a portion (or portions) of the coordinate plane, instead of a portion of the number line. Graphs describe sets. A shaded region indicates that any point in that region satisfies the inequality. The boundaries of solution regions do not have to be straight lines.

Example 2

Problem Draw a graph with all points that are solutions to both inequalities.

$$y \geq x^2 \quad \text{and} \quad y < 6 - x$$

Solution Start by sketching the graphs of $y = x^2$ and $y = 6 - x$.

The y-coordinate of any point *above* the graph of $y \geq x^2$ is greater than the y-coordinate of the point *on* the graph with the same x-coordinate. So all the points on or above the graph are part of the solution set. Similarly, for $y < 6 - x$, any point *below* the line is part of the solution set.

To satisfy both inequalities, a point has to be on or above the graph of $y = x^2$ and below the graph of $y = 6 - x$.

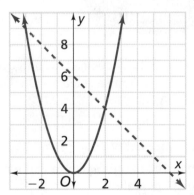

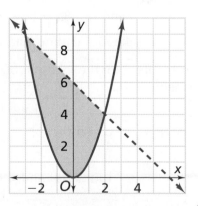

> The graph of $y = x^2$ is solid, because the inequality is $\leq$. A solid boundary indicates that points on the curve are included in the solution set. The graph of $y = 6 - x^2$ is dashed, because points on the line are not included.

For Discussion

4. What does the solution for this system of inequalities look like?

$$y \geq x^2 \qquad \text{and} \qquad y < -6 - x$$

For You to Do

5. Using your graphing calculator, sketch the solution set for this system of inequalities.

$$y \geq 2x^2 - 21x + 24 \qquad \text{and} \qquad y \leq -7\sqrt{2x + 3}$$

> For help graphing a system of inequalities, see the TI-Nspire Handbook, p. 788.

Exercises *Practicing Habits of Mind*

Check Your Understanding

1. For the next showing of a movie, Tony decides to charge $5 per student. Adults will still pay $8. His goal is to raise at least $500. The inequality $8a + 5s \geq 500$ describes this goal.

   a. Graph the line with equation $8a + 5s = 500$.

   b. Graph the solution to the inequality $8a + 5s \geq 500$.

2. Tony expects that more than 100 people will attend the next showing. Graph the solution to the system of inequalities.

   $$a + s > 100 \qquad \text{and} \qquad 8a + 5s \geq 500$$

   Can Tony be sure the movie will make $500 if more than 100 people attend?

3. Draw graphs in the coordinate plane for the solutions of each of these inequalities or systems of inequalities.

   a. $y \leq 5$

   b. $y \geq 0$ and $x \geq 0$

   c. $y > -3$ and $x \geq 4$

   d. $y > 2x - 5$

   e. $2x + 3y < 12$ and $2x + y < 8$

   f. $y \geq x^2$

   g. $y \geq x^2$ and $y \leq 4$

   h. $y \geq |x|$ and $y < -3$

4. Take It Further Graphing the inequality $\frac{y-4}{x-3} \geq 2$ is difficult, since x cannot be 3.

   a. Why can't x equal 3 in this inequality?

   b. Draw $\frac{y-4}{x-3} = 2$ and $x = 3$ on a coordinate plane. Use dashed lines for the parts of each graph that should not be in the graph of $\frac{y-4}{x-3} \geq 2$.

   c. Graph the solution set for the inequality.

5. Derman looks at Exercise 4 and says, "Hmm, this is the equation for slope. So it's telling me I want a line through (3, 4) that has a slope of at least 2. There are many lines like that."

   a. Draw a few lines that go through the point (3, 4) and have a slope of at least 2. A slope of at least 2 means that there are no negative slopes!

   b. How steep can these lines be? Is there a boundary?

   c. Take It Further What does the set of these lines look like?

Remember...

Use a solid line when the boundary is included in the solution. Use a dashed line when the boundary is not included.

On Your Own

6. a. On the same coordinate plane, graph the two lines $y = x + 1$ and $y = -2x + 11$.

   b. Find the value of x such that $x + 1 = -2x + 11$. What does this value of x represent?

   c. Find two points (x, y) such that $y > x + 1$ and $y < -2x + 11$. Where are these points located on the graph?

   d. Find two points (x, y) such that $y > x + 1$ and $y > -2x + 11$. Where are these points located on the graph?

   e. Shade the entire region where $y < x + 1$ and $y > -2x + 11$ are both true.

Exercises 7 and 8 refer to Exercise 3.

7. In Exercise 3e, you graphed an inequality involving lines with the following equations.

$$2x + 3y = 12$$

$$2x + y = 8$$

Use algebra to find the intersection of the two lines. Then check your result by testing the values of x and y in each equation.

Go Online
www.successnetplus.com

8. a. Sketch the solution set of these inequalities.

$$2(x - 3) + 3y < 12 \qquad \text{and} \qquad 2(x - 3) + y < 8$$

b. What is the intersection point of the graphs of the corresponding equations?

c. How is the graph in part (a) related to the graph in Exercise 3e?

d. Predict the intersection point of the graphs of $2(x - 8) + 3y = 12$ and $2(x - 8) + y = 8$. Then check your prediction.

e. Predict the intersection point of the graphs of $2(x + 8) + 3y = 12$ and $2(x + 8) + y = 8$. Then check your prediction.

f. Sketch the solution set of these inequalities.

$$2x + 3(y - 4) < 12 \qquad \text{and} \qquad 2x + (y - 4) < 8$$

Find the new intersection point.

g. Predict the intersection point of the graphs of $2(x - 4) + 3(y + 5) = 12$ and $2(x - 4) + (y + 5) = 8$. Then check your prediction.

Use a graphing calculator or computer software to make these graphs.

9. Standardized Test Prep Which point is NOT in the intersection of the graphs of $y > x^2 + 5x + 6$ and $y \leq 4$?

A. $(-4, 3)$ **B.** $(-3, 4)$ **C.** $(-2, 0)$ **D.** $(-1, 3)$

10. a. Graph $y > |x|$. Where is the shaded area relative to the graph of $y = |x|$?

b. Use the graph of $y = x^3 - x$ to draw a graph of $y \geq x^3 - x$.

c. If an inequality has the form $y > f(x)$, do you shade above or below the graph of the equation $y = f(x)$? Explain.

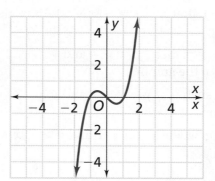

11. Take It Further Sketch the graph of each inequality. You might start by finding some points that make the inequality work, or by finding the boundaries.

a. $|x| + |y| \leq 2$ **b.** $|x + y| \leq 2$

c. $|x| - |y| \leq 1$ **d.** $\dfrac{|y|}{|x|} \geq 1$

What makes the graphs for parts (a) and (b) different?

Maintain Your Skills

12. Graph the solution set for each inequality.

a. $(y - 5) > 3(x + 2)$ **b.** $(y - 5) \geq 2(x + 2)$

c. $(y - 5) < \frac{1}{2}(x + 2)$ **d.** $(y - 5) \leq -\frac{1}{3}(x + 2)$

Go Online
Video Tutor
www.successnetplus.com

In this lesson, you will explore the connection between equations and inequalities, and learn a technique for sketching the graphs of linear inequalities.

Example

Problem Sketch the graph of the inequality $3x - 2y > 12$.

Solution The graph of the equation $3x - 2y = 12$ is a line. A point that solves $3x - 2y = 12$, such as $(6, 3)$, does *not* make the inequality true. The line is not part of the graph of the inequality. You indicate this by drawing a dashed line.

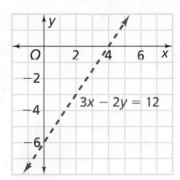

The graph of $3x - 2y \geq 12$ includes the boundary, so that would be drawn with a solid line. Points on the line make $3x - 2y \geq 12$ true.

So which points satisfy the inequality and are in the graph? One way to think about this is to consider a specific value of x. If $x = 6$, the inequality now has one variable and can be written as $18 - 2y > 12$. By comparing this one-variable inequality to the equation $18 - 2y = 12$ and point-testing, the solution is $y < 3$. Any point $(6, y)$ with $y < 3$ satisfies the inequality and is part of the graph. This gives an open ray of solutions below the point $(6, 3)$.

Remember...

A *ray* is a portion of a line that starts at one point and goes in one direction to infinity.

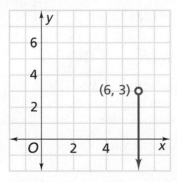

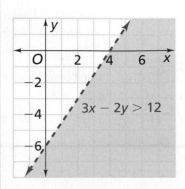

Similar vertical rays will come from any point on the graph of $3x - 2y = 12$. Any point below the line is part of the solution set. The graph of $3x - 2y > 12$ is the half-plane below the graph of $3x - 2y = 12$, shown at the right.

For You to Do

Sketch the graph of each inequality on a coordinate plane.

1. $3x - 2y < 12$

2. $y \leq 1$

3. $x + y > 5$

4. $x + y \leq 5$

In-Class Experiment

In Lesson 3.03 you learned how to graph the equation $2x + 3y = 12$ by using the equation as a point-tester. Use the same coordinate plane and four different colors for the following.

5. In green, plot four points that make the equation $2x + 3y = 12$ true.

6. In black, sketch the graph of $2x + 3y = 12$.

7. In blue, plot four points that make $2x + 3y > 12$ true.

8. In red, plot four points that make $2x + 3y < 12$ true.

Minds in Action

Derman In the experiment, all my blue points were on the same side of the line.

Tony Same for the red points. If that's always true, it gives us an easy way to graph one of these linear inequalities.

Derman Look at the example, $2x + 3y < 12$. I pick $(1, 1)$, and it works. So, does that mean the entire half of the coordinate plane containing $(1, 1)$ is the solution set?

Tony I think so. And I think the solutions to $2x + 3y > 12$ form the other half.

Derman Wow, that would save a lot of work. Is it always true?

Tony It has to be. It works the same way in the example with the rays—they all point to the same side. The ray concept can help explain why we can use half-planes. Using half-planes seems easier.

Derman I like easier. But what about inequalities with only one variable, like $x > 2$?

Tony That's a half-plane, too. Read it: *where is* x *bigger than 2?*

Derman Oh, it's to the right of the vertical line with equation $x = 2$.

> A linear inequality is one whose corresponding equation is linear. The graph of the equation is a line.

A line divides the coordinate plane into two *half-planes,* and you can test points to decide which half contains the solutions of the linear inequality. As with equations, the *graph of an inequality* is the collection of all points with coordinates that make the inequality true.

You can also say these points *satisfy* the inequality. The same is true for equations: a value or point *satisfies* an equation whenever it makes the equation true.

Theorem 4.6

The solution to a linear inequality is a half-plane whose boundary is the graph of the corresponding equation. If the inequality uses < or >, the solution *does not* include the boundary line. If the inequality uses ≤ or ≥, the solution *does* include the boundary line.

A system of linear inequalities can be graphed by sketching the graph of each inequality, and then looking for the intersection of the graphs.

Minds in Action

Sasha Let's sketch the graph of this system of inequalities:
$a + s > 100$ and $8a + 4s \geq 400$

Derman This looks familiar. Okay, the first one is a line that goes through $(80, 20)$ and $(70, 30)$ and $(60, 40)$ and…

Sasha Careful, you're talking about $a + s = 100$.

Derman Don't I have to graph the line anyway?

Sasha You do, but those points don't make $a + s > 100$ true. You need to draw a dashed line to make it clear the line isn't in the solution.

Derman Okay, here's my line:

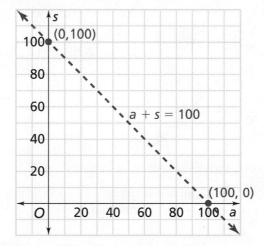

Derman Now what? Do I shade left, right, up, or down?

Sasha Shade one side of the line or the other, whichever makes the inequality true. Pick a point that isn't on the line and we'll test it to decide which way to shade.

Derman I'll pick my favorite point: $(0, 0)$.

Sasha   That would be your favorite. Actually, it's a great point to pick when you can. Does $(0, 0)$ make $a + s > 100$ true?

Derman   No! And that means we shade the other side of the line!

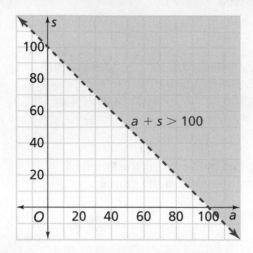

Sasha   Now we have to graph $8a + 4s \geq 400$ on the same coordinate plane. We can start by graphing the line $8a + 4s = 400$.

Derman   I think this one will be a solid line.

Sasha   You're right. It's solid because a point that makes $8a + 4s = 400$ true also makes the inequality true. Let's find the two intercepts…

Sasha and Derman graph the line…

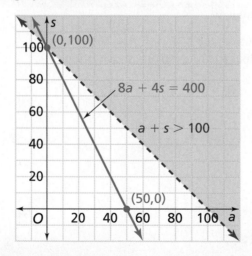

Derman   I'll test $(0, 0)$ again. It doesn't work, so we shouldn't shade that side.

Sasha   You can test a point on the other side of the line if you're ever unsure. $(100, 100)$ is on the other side and it does make $8a + 4s \geq 400$ true.

Derman   Cool. I'll use a different shading so we can find the intersection.

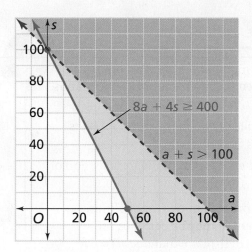

Sasha And see where the red shading and the blue shading combine to make a purple section? That's the intersection. You're right, this does look familiar.

For Discussion

9. Sasha says $(0, 0)$ is a great point to pick "when you can." When might you not be able to pick $(0, 0)$ to test?

10. The point $(0, 100)$ is the intersection of the two lines $a + s = 100$ and $8a + 4s - 400$. Is this point part of the solution to the system of inequalities? Explain.

11. How is the graph of this system of inequalities different from the graph in the Minds in Action from Lesson 4.12?

Find a relationship. As with one-variable inequalities graphed on a number line, there is a relationship between the intersections of the graphs of two linear inequalities.

- Any point in the intersection of the graphs of two inequalities satisfies both of the corresponding inequalities.

- If a point makes two inequalities true, then it is part of the intersection of the corresponding graphs.

Systems of inequalities frequently involve more than two inequalities. When more than two inequalities are present, it may be easier to see a complete intersection by "shading out" the half-plane that *doesn't* solve each inequality, instead of "shading in" the half-plane that does. The graph of the system of inequalities then becomes the portion of the plane that is completely unshaded.

For example, here is the graph of the system of inequalities $2x + 3y > 12$ and $2x + 3y < 24$ and $x \geq 0$ and $y \geq 0$:

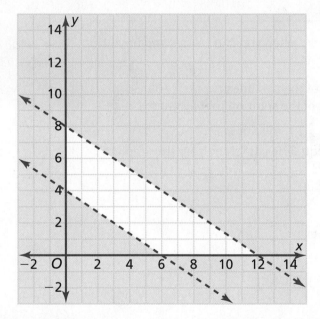

You can check by testing a point from the solution area in all of the inequalities. For example, the point $(4, 4)$ is in the solution area and makes all of the inequalities true.

Habits of Mind

Compare this to Lesson 3.06, in which you learned about the intersections of graphs of equations.

With normal shading, you have to find the portion of the plane shaded by *all* the inequalities, which may be difficult to determine.

Exercises *Practicing Habits of Mind*

Check Your Understanding

1. Graph each inequality.

    a. $x + 2y > 6$

    b. $x + 2y \geq 6$

    c. $x + 2y \leq 6$

    d. $x + 2y < 6$

2. Graph each system of inequalities.

    a. $\begin{cases} x + 2y > 6 \\ \quad x < 4 \end{cases}$

    b. $\begin{cases} x + 2y \leq 6 \\ \quad y > 1 \end{cases}$

    c. $\begin{cases} x + 2y \leq 6 \\ \quad y > 1 \\ \quad x \geq 2 \end{cases}$

3. Write a system of inequalities that is true for all points in Quadrant II but not true for any other points.

4. Graph each system of inequalities. Remember, a point in the intersection of two inequality graphs must make both inequalities true.

    a. $\begin{cases} x + 2y > 6 \\ x + 2y > 12 \end{cases}$

    b. $\begin{cases} x + 2y \leq 6 \\ x + 2y > 12 \end{cases}$

    c. $\begin{cases} x + 2y \geq 6 \\ x + 2y \leq 12 \end{cases}$

Remember...

One efficient way to graph a linear equation is to find its two intercepts.

Habits of Mind

Use point-testing. Based on its coordinates, how could you tell if a point is in Quadrant II?

Habits of Mind

Use lumping. What does each inequality say about the quantity $x + 2y$?

5. Three cities are located in the coordinate plane at $A(-8, 0)$, $B(4, 0)$, and $C(0, 8)$. The three lines drawn on the graph below indicate locations that are the same distance from each pair of cities.

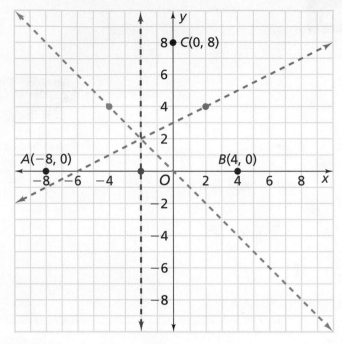

a. What is true about the point $(-2, 2)$ for the cities?

b. Using the graph, determine an equation for each of the three lines.

c. Write a system of inequalities that is true for all points where A is the closest city, and no others.

d. Write a system of inequalities that is true for all points where B is the closest city, and no others.

e. Write a system of inequalities that is true for all points where C is the closest city, and no others.

6. There are several types of cholesterol. HDL (high-density lipoprotein) is considered "good cholesterol" and LDL (low-density lipoprotein) is considered "bad cholesterol." On a cholesterol test, the ideal results are:

- HDL: 60 mg/dL and above

- LDL: less than 100 mg/dL

- Total cholesterol: less than 200 mg/dL

Sketch a graph showing the region where all three of these results are true, clearly labeling the axes.

7. **Take It Further** Sketch the graph of $x^2 + y^2 < 25$.

Habits of Mind

Connect equations and graphs. The point $(-2, 2)$ is on all three lines. What does that mean?

Total cholesterol includes other lipids, but for the purposes of this problem, consider it to be the total of HDL and LDL, which are measured in milligrams per deciliter.

On Your Own

8. Write a system of linear inequalities that has $(1, 3)$ as part of its solution set, but does not have $(3, 1)$ as part of its solution set. Then graph the system.

9. **Standardized Test Prep** This is the graph of which system of inequalities?

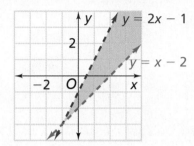

A. $\begin{cases} x - y > 2 \\ y < 2x - 1 \end{cases}$ B. $\begin{cases} x - y > 2 \\ y > 2x - 1 \end{cases}$ C. $\begin{cases} x - y < 2 \\ y > 2x - 1 \end{cases}$ D. $\begin{cases} x - y < 2 \\ y < 2x - 1 \end{cases}$

10. **What's Wrong Here** Jacob drew this graph of $x - 2y > 4$:

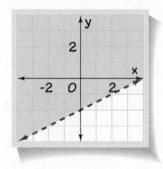

Jacob: I started by drawing the graph of the equation $x - 2y = 4$. It's a dotted line because points on the line don't make the inequality true. Then I shaded up because it's a *greater than* symbol.

Sketch the correct graph of $x - 2y > 4$. How might you convince Jacob that his method is incorrect?

11. Reflect and Write Describe the steps you take in graphing the inequality $4x - y < 6$.

12. Take It Further Sketch the graph of $|x + y| > 0$.

13. Write a system of three linear inequalities that defines this triangular region:

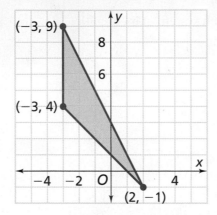

14. Write a system of inequalities you can use to define the rectangle with this boundary:

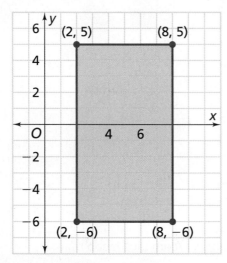

How many inequalities will you need?

Maintain Your Skills

15. Graph each system of inequalities.

a. $\begin{cases} x + y < 10 \\ x - y > 2 \end{cases}$ b. $\begin{cases} x + y < 10 \\ x > 2 \end{cases}$ c. $\begin{cases} x + y < 10 \\ x + y > 2 \end{cases}$ d. $\begin{cases} x + y < 10 \\ x + 2y > 2 \end{cases}$

Mathematical

4C

Reflections

In this investigation, you solved and graphed inequalities with one and two variables. These questions will help you summarize what you have learned.

1. Use a graphing calculator. Find the number of solutions to each equation.

   a. $3x + 7 = 5 - x$ **b.** $3x + 7 = x^2$

   c. $3x + 7 = 3x - 2$ **d.** $3x + 7 = -x^2$

2. Solve each inequality. Graph your solution on a number line.

   a. $3x - 5 > 1$ **b.** $x - 8 \geq 2x - 5$ **c.** $|x - 2| < 7$

3. Use algebra and a graphing calculator. Solve each inequality.

   a. $4x + 2 > 5x - 3$ **b.** $2x + 3 \leq 48$ **c.** $|2x + 1| < 5$

4. How do the solutions of inequalities relate to the solutions of equations?

5. One taxi charges $1.10 for the first mile and $1 for each additional mile. Another taxi charges $2.30 for the first mile and $.60 for each additional mile. For what distances will the first taxi be less expensive than the second?

Vocabulary and Notation

In this investigation, you learned these terms and symbols. Make sure you understand what each one means and how to use it.

- **cutoff point**
- **inequality**

A parabola is the graph of an equation containing x^2.

Go Online
www.successnetplus.com

In **Investigation 4A,** you learned how to

- write linear equations
- sketch graphs of linear equations
- determine the slope of a line from its equation
- determine whether a runner will overtake another runner

The following questions will help you check your understanding.

1. Write an equation for each line that passes through the given point and has the given slope.

   a. $(3, 7)$ with slope 2

   b. $(2, -4)$ and $(-1, 0)$

   c. $(-6, 4)$ with slope 0

   d. $(-6, 4)$ with undefined slope

2. Let ℓ be the line with equation $3x + 5y = -15$.

   a. What is the slope of line ℓ?

   b. Sketch the graph of line ℓ.

   c. Solve the equation for y.

3. Scott leaves home and walks 1.5 miles to school at a rate of 3 miles per hour. Fifteen minutes later, his brother leaves for school. He is riding his bike at a rate of 9 miles per hour.

   a. Draw a distance-time graph to represent this situation.

   b. When will Scott's brother overtake him?

   c. How far from home will they be when they meet?

In **Investigation 4B,** you learned how to

- solve systems of linear equations with two variables using substitution and elimination
- determine whether two lines are parallel or intersecting using the slope of each line
- write and solve word problems for systems of equations

The following questions will help you check your understanding.

4. Write the equations of two lines that intersect at the point $(-2, 3)$. Check that $(-2, 3)$ satisfies both equations.

5. Solve each system.

   a. $4x + y = 3$

      $3x - 2y - 5$

   b. $x - 3y = 11$

      $2x + y = 1$

6. Write an equation of the line through $(-1, -2)$ that is parallel to the line with equation $3x - 2y = 8$.

In **Investigation 4C,** you learned how to

- solve inequalities algebraically and by using graphs
- graph the solution set of an inequality
- sketch the solutions of inequalities of two variables and systems of inequalities of two variables

The following questions will help you check your understanding.

7. Solve each inequality. Graph your solution on a number line.

   a. $8x \leq 24$

   b. $3(x - 1) > 2x - 5$

   c. $4x - 3 < 7x + 9$

   d. $|x + 3| \geq 5$

8. Consider the following set of data points.
$(-2, 6)$, $(-1, 4.5)$, $(0, 5)$, $(1.5, 4)$, $(4.5, 3)$, $(5, 2.5)$, (a, b)

   a. Find a and b such that the balance point is $(2, 4)$.

   b. Graph the data points and the balance point.

   c. Will the slope of the line of best fit be positive or negative? Explain.

9. Draw graphs in the coordinate plane for the solutions of each of these inequalities or systems of inequalities.

   a. $y > 1$ and $x \leq 3$

   b. $y \geq -2x + 1$

   c. $x + y > 3$ and $2x - y < 4$

   d. $y > -x^2$

   e. $y \leq 2x^2$ and $y < x + 3$

Multiple Choice

1. The intersection of the two lines $y = 5x + 10$ and $y = 6x - 3$ is in which quadrant?

   A. I   **B.** II

   C. III   **D.** IV

2. Which pair of lines does NOT intersect?

   A. $y = 3x - 5$ and $y = -3x + 5$

   B. $(y + 7) = 2(x - 3)$ and $(y - 4) = 2(x + 5)$

   C. $2x - 3y = 12$ and $y = 4$

   D. $y = 2x - 1$ and $5x - 3y = -30$

3. Use the graphs of $y = 3 - x^2$ and $y = \frac{1}{2}x$.

   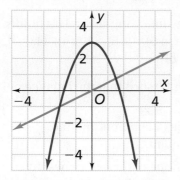

   What is the solution to the inequality $\frac{1}{2}x > 3 - x^2$?

   A. $-2 \le x \le 1.5$

   B. $x \le -2$ or $x \ge 1.5$

   C. $-2 < x < 1.5$

   D. $x < -2$ or $x > 1.5$

4. Suppose a is less than 10. Which of these must be true?

   A. $-a > 10$ **B.** $a \le 9$

   C. $3a + 7 < 40$ **D.** $|a| < 10$

5. Which system of inequalities describes the shaded region below?

   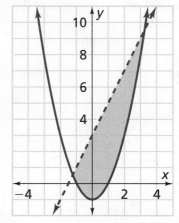

   A. $y \ge x^2 - 1$ and $y < 2x + 3$

   B. $y \le x^2 - 1$ and $y > 2x + 3$

   C. $y \ge x^2 - 1$ and $y > 2x + 3$

   D. $y \le x^2 - 1$ and $y < 2x + 3$

Open Response

6. Solve this system of equations. Show your work.

$$x + 2y = 17$$
$$5x - 2y = 16$$

7. At a store, six bottles of juice and two bags of nuts cost $11.50. Three bottles of juice and four bags of nuts cost $11.75. What is the cost of a single bottle of juice? Show your work.

8. Graph the two lines. Find the exact coordinates of their point of intersection.

$$5x - 3y = -30$$
$$y = -4x$$

9. Graph the solution set to the inequality $-3a + 15 > -3$.

10. How can you tell by their equations whether two lines will intersect?

Challenge Problem

11. Find three points M, N, and P such that $m(M, N) = \frac{1}{2}$, $m(M, P) = 5$, and $m(N, P) = -\frac{2}{3}$.

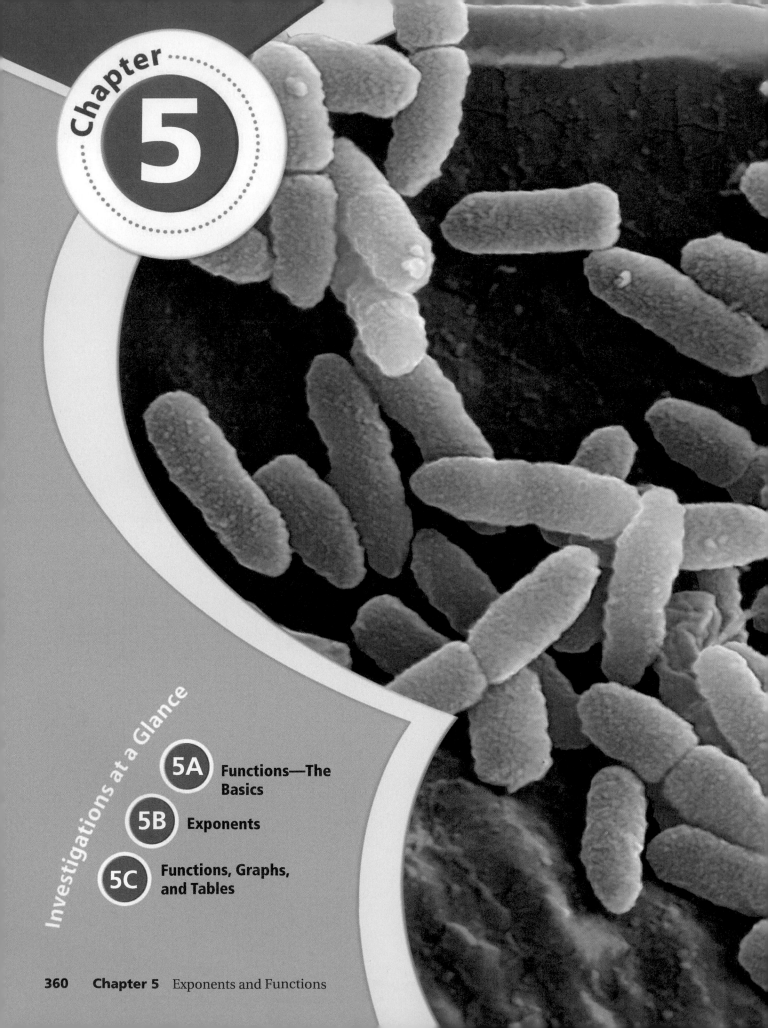

Chapter

5

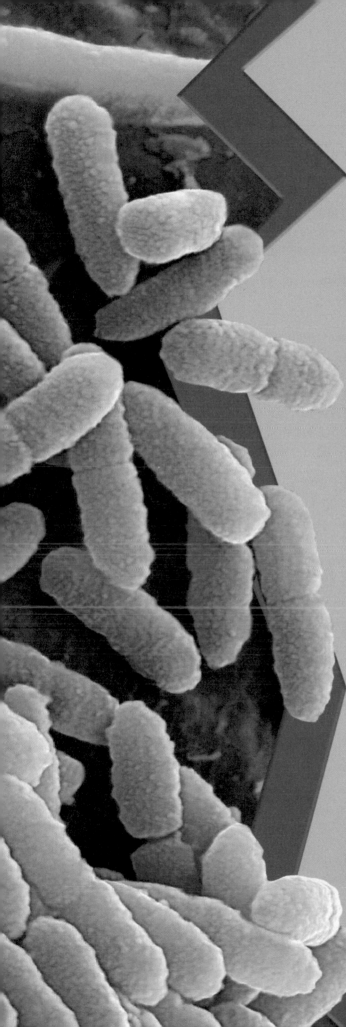

Exponents and Functions

Perhaps you first used exponents to find areas of squares using the formula $A = s^2$. You read s^2 as "s squared" or "the square of s." The *square of s* means the area of a square built with side s. Likewise, the *cube of s* (or s^3) means the volume of a cube built with side s.

Over time, the idea of exponents grew beyond the integers used for squaring and cubing. Mathematicians worked to keep a set of rules for exponents consistent for other types of exponents. The other types included negative integers and eventually all real numbers.

Exponential functions describe growth. The growth could be in your savings account or in a bacteria population. Computer viruses can also spread exponentially. Each of two infected computers can infect two more, each of which in turn infects two more, and so on. The number infected becomes quite large in a short time—a sign of exponential behavior.

In this chapter, you will explore some important features of functions, and then you will learn the rules for exponents. You will learn to "undo" exponents to solve equations. You will also work with exponential functions in which the variable is in the exponent.

Vocabulary and Notation

- base
- base case
- compositions
- compound interest
- consecutive outputs
- constant ratio
- cube
- domain
- exponent
- exponential decay
- exponential growth
- function
- graph of a function
- linear function
- negative exponent
- range
- recursive rule
- scientific notation
- square
- zero exponent

5A

Functions—The Basics

In *Functions—The Basics,* you will explore function rules. Functions are like machines. Functions take something in (input) and give something out (output) according to certain rules.

By the end of this investigation, you will be able to answer questions like these.

1. What is a function?

2. What is the relationship between a table and a function?

3. What is the domain of $f(x) = \dfrac{\sqrt{x}}{x - 9}$?

You will learn how to

- build a function from a word problem

- determine whether a relationship is a function based on its description or graph

- make input-output tables

- find the domain of a function

- graph a function

You will develop these habits and skills:

- Find a function rule using the guess-check-generalize strategy.

- Look for patterns in input-output tables.

- Recognize different ways to define and express a function.

- Compare graphs of functions and equations.

- Simplify and compare rules to find whether they are equivalent.

- Build functions and generate graphs on your calculator.

Like a function, a camera takes input—the image of your face, for example— and gives output—a photo.

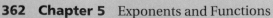

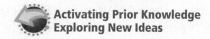

In many functions, there is a pattern that relates the input to the output. You can write a function rule to represent this relationship.

For You to Explore

In Problems 1 and 2, you will play the Guess My Rule game. You need two players, a Rule Maker and a Rule Breaker.

1. **Round 1** Your teacher gives the Rule Maker a function rule.
   - The Rule Breaker gives an input value to the Rule Maker.
   - The Rule Maker calculates the output. Do not let the Rule Breaker know the calculations! The Rule Maker gives the output value.
   - The Rule Breaker continues to give the Rule Maker an input value and receives the output value until the Rule Breaker guesses the rule.
   - The goal is to guess the rule by making the fewest possible guesses about the input values.

2. **Round 2** Switch roles with your partner. The Rule Maker writes the function rule in Round 2.

> For example, when the rule is Add 2 to the input, and the Rule Breaker inputs the value 4, the Rule Maker says, "6."

In Problems 3–5, Tony and Sasha play the Guess My Rule game.

3. In Round 1, Sasha is the Rule Maker.

Tony's Input	Sasha's Response
1	1 produces 5.
2	2 produces 3.
3	3 produces 25.
1	1 produces 11.

Tony says, "That rule's not fair!" What makes Tony say that?

4. In the next game, Tony is the Rule Maker. For a few of the inputs, Tony responds with a letter instead of a number.

Sasha's Input	Tony's Response
1	1 returns a.
2	2 returns 7.
5	5 returns 11.
1	1 returns b.
2	2 returns c.

> Tony uses the word *returns* instead of *produces* just for variety.

a. When Tony uses a fair rule, what is the value of c?

b. How are the variables a and b related?

c. Do you have enough information to find the value of a? Explain.

5. Sasha uses the rule "After each input, I flip a coin. When it shows heads, I write, 'x produces $x + 2$.' When it shows tails, I write, 'x produces $x + 3$.'" Sasha's responses are left blank below.

Tony's Input	Sasha's Response
1	1 produces ▪.
3	3 produces ▪.
−3	−3 produces ▪.
7	7 produces ▪.
1	1 produces ▪.

a. Can you know for certain Sasha's responses? Explain.

b. Will Tony complain that Sasha's rule isn't fair? Explain.

Exercises *Practicing Habits of Mind*

On Your Own

6. Tony and Sasha play the Guess My Rule game. What is Sasha's rule?

Tony's Input	Sasha's Response
0	0 returns 3.
2	2 returns 5.
3	3 returns 6.
8	8 returns 11.

7. Sasha uses the rule "x produces $x^2 + 1$." Use this rule to fill in the blanks.

Tony's Input	Sasha's Response
1	1 produces ▪.
▪	▪ produces 5.
5	5 produces ▪.
▪	▪ produces 2.
▪	▪ produces 1.

a. Is there more than one correct value that you can use to fill in any one of the blanks? Explain.

b. Using Sasha's rule, how many input values produce the output value 2? How many output values does the input value 2 produce?

8. Tony and Sasha play the game with a new rule. Based on Sasha's responses below, what is the output for the input $\frac{1}{2}$? For the input $\frac{3}{5}$? For Tony's input of 0, explain why Sasha does not respond. Is Sasha's rule fair?

Tony's Input	Sasha's Response
5	5 produces $\frac{1}{5}$.
2	2 produces $\frac{1}{2}$.
-3	-3 produces $-\frac{1}{3}$.
113	113 produces $\frac{1}{113}$.
0	0 produces . . .

9. Tony and Derman guess a new rule of Sasha's. Tony says, "The rule is 'x produces $3 - x$.'" Derman replies, "No, the rule is 'x produces $|x - 3|$.'" Is there any number that will help determine the correct rule? Explain.

Tony and Derman's Input	Sasha's Response
0	0 produces 3.
1	1 produces 2.
2	2 produces 1.
3	3 produces 0.

10. Tony and Derman guess another new rule. Tony says, "The rule is to multiply x by itself and then add x." Derman replies, "No, the rule is to multiply x by $x + 1$." Is there any number that will help decide the correct rule? Explain.

Tony and Derman's Input	Sasha's Response
0	0 produces 0.
1	1 produces 2.
2	2 produces 6.
3	3 produces 12.

Maintain Your Skills

Sasha and Tony play the game. Sasha's rule is pick a number, add $\frac{1}{2}$, double your answer, subtract 3, and find half of the result.

11. For each of Tony's inputs below, what output does Sasha's rule produce?
    a. 4   b. 5   c. 6   d. -4 e. -5
    f. -6 g. $\frac{1}{4}$ h. $\frac{3}{4}$ i. $6\frac{1}{4}$

12. For each of Sasha's responses below, what input did Tony give?
    a. 4   b. 5   c. 6   d. -4 e. -5
    f. -6 g. $\frac{1}{4}$ h. $\frac{3}{4}$ i. $6\frac{1}{4}$

Go Online
Video Tutor
www.successnetplus.com

13. Find a simpler rule that does the same thing as Sasha's rule.

5.02 Building Functions

You can build a function to calculate total cost.

Minds in Action

Sasha and Tony look at the deals on CDs at a music store Web site.

Sasha   Look, at the bottom of the page are all these CDs for 28% off.

Tony   Yes, but by the time you add in sales tax and shipping, you'd be better off going to the mall to get them.

Sasha   Are you sure? We'd better try pricing some. I'll choose a bunch, but I won't order them until we see how much they really cost.

> Businesses charge sales tax at the mall, too. What is Tony's logic here?

They pick out six CDs and add them to the shopping cart. Then they click on the checkout button.

For You to Do

Sasha and Tony's checkout page looks like this table.

Items to Purchase Now

Item	Price Original	Price Discounted	Tax (5%)	Shipping Cost	Total Cost
Ultimate Broadway	$12.98	■	■	$2.00	■
Greatest Movie Songs	$14.99	■	■	$2.00	■
Patriotic Medley	$11.98	■	■	$2.00	■
Top Country Hits	$16.98	■	■	$2.00	■
A History of Soul	$18.98	■	■	$2.00	■
90s Favorites	$ 5.89	■	■	$2.00	■

1. Copy and complete the table.

> ### Habits of Mind
>
> **Establish a process.** As you calculate the costs, keep track of your steps. Find and repeat the pattern in your steps. For example, multiply, subtract, multiply, add, and add again.

Sasha and Tony check some of the prices in the table.

Sasha   Let's try the first price, $12.98. To get the discount, I multiply the price by 0.28 to get 3.6344, or just $3.63. Then I subtract that from $12.98 to get the total cost. That gives $9.35.

Tony   Now let's figure the tax and shipping.

Sasha   A 5% tax on $9.35 equals 0.05 × 9.35, or 0.4675. Round that to $.47. Now we're back up to $9.82.

Tony   And shipping adds $2.00, so the total cost will be $11.82.

Sasha and Tony look at the checkout page, and the totals agree with their calculations.

Sasha   It's pretty mechanical. Look, for the next one, I write this.

Sasha writes on a piece of paper.

$$14.99 \times 0.28 = 4.1972$$
$$14.99 - 4.1972 = 10.7928$$
$$10.7928 \times 0.05 = 0.53964$$
$$10.7928 + 0.53964 = 11.33244$$
$$11.33244 + 2 = 13.33244$$

So, the total cost is $13.33. And that's what it is in the table!

Tony   Look, the calculations are even more mechanical if you keep track of the steps. They go this way. Suppose the cost is some number C.

Now Tony writes on a piece of paper.

$0.28C$	Discount
$C - 0.28C$	
$(C - 0.28C) \times 0.05$	Tax
$(C - 0.28C) + (C - 0.28C) \times 0.05$	Cost with tax
$(C - 0.28C) + (C - 0.28C) \times 0.05 + 2$	Total cost

Sasha   Good job! The last line is like a machine that does it all.

$$(C - 0.28C) + (C - 0.28C) \times 0.05 + 2$$

This rule calculates the total cost of any CD during the sale.

For You to Do

2. Use Sasha and Tony's machine to calculate the total cost of each CD in their list. Check your results against the total costs that you found on the checkout page.

Developing Habits of Mind

Establish a process. Sasha and Tony build a function machine that calculates the total cost of a CD given its list price. The rule they use is

$$(C - 0.28C) + (C - 0.28C) \times 0.05 + 2$$

Other people may write different rules to do the same thing.

When you establish a process for repeated calculations, you can find a general rule that works for any input x. You can use the rule to program your calculator, so that it becomes a function machine that does the calculations.

List Price of CD

Total Cost of CD

For You to Do

Use Sasha and Tony's rule from the preceding page. Find the total costs of CDs priced between $15 and $20. Use price increments of $1.

3. Describe any patterns in the table.

4. Find a simpler rule than Tony and Sasha's rule that agrees with the table.

5. Tony and Sasha pay 5% tax whether they buy CDs at the mall or the music store Web site. Assume that the nondiscounted price of each CD is exactly the same at the mall and at the music store Web site.

    a. At what price is it a better deal to buy a CD at the music store Web site? At the mall? (*Hint:* Make a table comparing final costs.)

    b. At what price is the final cost of a CD the same at the music store Web site and at the mall?

For Discussion

Function machines are all around you. Some examples include a(n)

- toaster   • TV remote control   • light switch   • ice maker

Each device takes an input (from you or a machine) and produces an output (toast, for example) in a predictable way.

6. What are the inputs and outputs for each function?

7. Describe the inputs and outputs of other devices that are functions.

> Each machine calculates the output from the input using a rule such as Tony and Sasha's CD rule. Often, only the people who built the machine know the rule.

Exercises *Practicing Habits of Mind*

Check Your Understanding

Changing units of time is sometimes necessary. To find miles traveled in an hour, you may need to change minutes to hours. To find time needed to stop a car quickly, you may need to change minutes to seconds.

1. Convert minutes to seconds.

    a. 9 min   **b.** 3.5 min   **c.** 4.1 min   **d.** 1.35 min   **e.** 2.43 min

    f. Find a rule for converting minutes to seconds.

2. Convert minutes to hours.

    a. 9 min   **b.** 35 min   **c.** 41 min   **d.** 135 min   **e.** 243 min

    f. Find a rule for converting minutes to hours.

3. For lunch at Steve's Diner, Alan has a hamburger and iced tea. Lou has a Caesar salad, a cup of chili, and a cola. Katie has a grilled cheese sandwich, French fries, and a ginger ale. The waiter hands them the check.

    a. Calculate the total amount each person owes including a 5% tax and an 18% tip on the pretax total.

    b. Write a rule that gives the total amount each person owes when you know the pretax cost of each person's food.

4. Antonio signs up for a charity run. His sponsors can donate either a fixed amount or an amount of money based on the number of miles that he runs. The table shows the amount that each of Antonio's sponsors will donate.

Steve's Diner

Item	Cost
Hamburger	$4.95
Caesar salad	$6.95
Cup of chili	$1.96
Grilled cheese	$4.50
French fries	$1.75
Cola	$.99
Iced tea	$.99
Ginger ale	$.99
Subtotal	$23.08
Tax (5%)	$1.15
Total	**$24.23**

Sponsors

	Fixed Donation	Donation per Mile
Mom	$ 0	$3.50
Uncle	$ 0	$2.75
Teacher	$10	$0
Coach	$ 0	$2.50
Agustina	$ 5	$0

To calculate how much money he will raise, Antonio makes this table.

Charity Run Donations

Number of Miles	Mom	Uncle	Teacher	Coach	Agustina	Total Donation
1	▪	▪	$10.00	▪	$5.00	▪
2	▪	▪	$10.00	▪	$5.00	▪
3	▪	▪	$10.00	▪	$5.00	▪
4	▪	▪	$10.00	▪	$5.00	▪
5	▪	▪	$10.00	▪	$5.00	▪

    a. Copy and complete the table.

    b. Write a rule that tells the total amount of money Antonio will raise based on how many miles he will run.

    c. If he runs 7 miles, how much money will Antonio make?

    d. How many miles must Antonio run to raise $50? To raise $100? Round up your answer to the nearest mile.

Show the total on a spreadsheet. See the TI-Nspire™ Handbook, p. 788.

5. Antonio's brother, Carlos, agrees to donate $1.50 for each mile. His grandmother agrees to donate $7.75 no matter how far Antonio runs. How does the rule in Exercise 4 change?

On Your Own

Exercises 6 and 7 are similar to Exercises 1 and 2. Your formulas will convert time measurements from larger to smaller units.

6. Convert hours to minutes. Round each answer to the nearest tenth of a minute.

   a. 3 h   **b.** 3.05 h   **c.** 4.1 h   **d.** 1.35 h   **e.** 2.43 h

   f. Find a rule for converting hours to minutes.

7. Convert seconds to minutes.

   a. 9 s   **b.** 37 s   **c.** 71 s   **d.** 105 s   **e.** 279 s

   f. Find a rule for converting seconds to minutes.

8. Filmmakers photograph movies on very long pieces of 35-mm film. Movie projectors play film at the rate of 90 feet per minute. A one-minute movie is 90 feet long. This list shows the running times of some popular movies.

   - *Finding Nemo*   1 hour, 41 minutes
   - *The Fellowship of the Ring*   2 hours, 58 minutes
   - *Beauty and the Beast*   1 hour, 24 minutes
   - *Field of Dreams*   1 hour, 46 minutes

   a. Calculate how many feet of film you need for each movie.

   b. A movie is *m* minutes long. Find a rule to calculate how many feet of film you need for the movie.

   c. How many feet of film do you need for a movie that is 4 hours long?

9. Sofia's car gets an average of 24 miles per gallon. Gas costs $2.11 per gallon.

   a. How much does it cost to travel 200 miles? To travel 400 miles?

   b. Write a rule that gives the cost of the trip when you know how many miles the trip is.

Gas prices change often. This price may not be realistic.

10. Suppose that the price of gasoline drops to $1.95. How does the price drop change the rule? Using the new price of gasoline, how far can Sofia travel for $20.00?

Go Online
www.successnetplus.com

11. Jody saves her money to buy a used car. The price of the car is $4000. The car dealer reduces the price by $125 for each month that the car remains unsold. Jody has $2500 in savings. She can save an additional $250 each month.

   a. Write an algebraic expression to represent each of the following.

   - price of the car in n months

   - amount of money Jody has saved after n months

   b. Determine the number of months until Jody can purchase the car. Show your work.

12. **Standardized Test Prep** Kai's car uses a gallon of gas to travel 28 to 32 miles. Gas prices range from $2.80 to $3.10 per gallon. Which amount is the best estimate of how much Kai spends on gas for a 1200-mile road trip?

   A. $91

   B. $105

   C. $119

   D. $133

13. **Take It Further** Everyone in a room shakes hands with everyone else exactly once.

   a. How many handshakes occur among 6 people? Among n people?

   b. Find a rule that computes the number of handshakes that occur.

Suppose your car gets 28 to 32 miles per gallon of gas. What value would *you* use to estimate how far your car will go on a full tank?

Maintain Your Skills

14. A store offers a holiday discount of 10% on everything in the store. The state sales tax is 5%, and the city tax is 3%. You apply each tax to the actual cost of items after the discount. What does it cost Derman to buy the following items when he applies the discount?

   a. A coat costs $49.99, and a belt costs $12.95.

   b. A CD player costs $49.99, and a CD costs $12.95.

   c. An air conditioner costs $499.90, and a fan costs $129.50.

Go Online
Video Tutor
www.successnetplus.com

5.03 Is It a Function?

The diagram illustrates how a function is like a machine. You supply the machine with an input. Then the machine follows a rule and gives back an output.

Input

The function is the machine.

The rule is what the machine does to the input to get the output.

Output

For example, Add 2 to the input is a rule that defines a function.

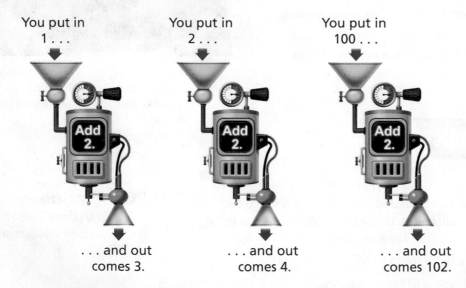

You put in 1 . . .

You put in 2 . . .

You put in 100 . . .

. . . and out comes 3.

. . . and out comes 4.

. . . and out comes 102.

There are many examples of rules that define functions. For example,

- Multiply the input by 3.
- Square the input.
- Take the number's absolute value and then add 5.

Only special kinds of rules, however, define functions.

In Lesson 5.01, Tony complains that some of Sasha's rules are illegal when the function gives two different outputs for the same input. One of Sasha's illegal rules is "x produces $x + 2$ or $x + 3$," depending on a coin flip.

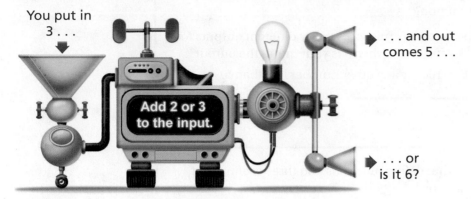

You put in 3 . . .

Add 2 or 3 to the input.

. . . and out comes 5 . . .

. . . or is it 6?

Mathematicians define functions as "predictable rules." In other words, each input must produce the same output every time it goes through the machine.

Definition

A **function** is a rule that assigns each element from the set of inputs to exactly one element from the set of outputs.

Sasha's illegal rule does not define a function, because the rule does not always give the same output. When 3 is the input, there are two possible outputs, 5 and 6.

Example

Problem Does the rule "Add 4 to the input and square the result" define a function?

Solution Yes, because each input gives precisely one output.

$$1 \text{ returns } (1 + 4)^2 = 5^2 = 25.$$
$$2 \text{ returns } (2 + 4)^2 = 6^2 = 36.$$
$$-1 \text{ returns } (-1 + 4)^2 = 3^2 = 9.$$
$$x \text{ returns } (x + 4)^2.$$

There are other rules that look different from $(x + 4)^2$ that you can find in the example, but they define the same function. For example, for any real number x, you can apply the basic rules of arithmetic to write a rule that looks different.

$$(x + 4)^2 = x^2 + 8x + 16$$

In words, the rule tells you to square the input, add the result to 8 times the input, and then add 16.

Example

Problem Does the rule "Find a number that is less than the input" define a function?

Solution No, it does not, because this rule gives many different outputs for the same input. For instance, when 5 is your input, the output can be 3, 2, $\frac{3}{7}$, -6, -100, or any other number less than 5.

For Discussion

1. Give three examples of rules that define functions and three examples of rules that do not define functions.

What happens when you put a variable such as x into the function machine instead of a particular number?

You put in x . . .

Add 2.

. . . and out comes $x + 2$.

Functions are often expressions like the expressions in Chapter 2. You can define functions in other ways, also. For example, you can give a set of instructions like the instructions in the Guess My Rule game in this chapter.

For Discussion

2. Tony suggests that $x \mapsto 3$ is not a function of x, because the rule does not actually use x. Is he correct?

3. Sasha suggests that $x \mapsto x$ is not a function, because the rule does not transform its input. Is she correct?

You read the symbol $\mapsto$ as "maps to." For example, you can read $x \mapsto x + 2$ as "x maps to x plus 2." This means add 2 to the input to get the output.

Exercises *Practicing Habits of Mind*

Check Your Understanding

1. Determine whether each rule defines a function. If it does, make a table of output values. Use integer inputs from −3 to 3. If the rule is not a function, explain.

Go Online
www.successnetplus.com

   a. Multiply the input by 5 and then add 2.

   b. Square the input.

   c. When x is the input, the output is a fraction larger than x.

   d. Take the absolute value of the input and then subtract 7.

   e. $x \mapsto \pm x$

2. For each rule in Exercise 1 that is a function, write the rule in "$x \mapsto$" form.

3. You can link function machines to make more complex functions. The diagram illustrates an example.

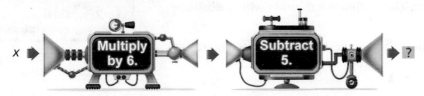

Make sure you can use what comes out of the first machine in the second machine.

   a. Copy the table at the right. Use this machine network to complete the table.

   b. What is the output when you put x into the network?

Input	Output
0	■
1	■
−2	■
5	■
■	7

4. When you switch the order of the two machines, you get another function.

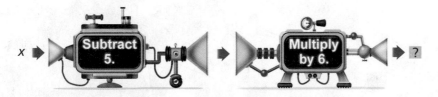

   a. Copy the table at the right. Use this machine network to complete the table.

   b. What is the output when you put x into the network?

   c. Is this function the same function you found in Exercise 3?

Input	Output
0	■
1	■
−2	■
5	■
■	7

On Your Own

5. Determine whether each rule defines a function. If it does, make a table of output values using integer inputs from 0 to 4. If it does not, explain.

   a. Take the opposite of the input and then add 2.

   b. Square the input and then subtract 4.

   c. $x \mapsto \dfrac{x^2 + 3x}{x - x}$

   d. x produces a number that is 4 units to the left of x on the number line.

   e. x produces a number that is 4 units away from x on the number line.

6. Modeling situations as functions is common. Decide whether each description represents a function. Explain.

   a. The input is a day of the year. The output is the average temperature in Barcelona on that day.

   b. The input is the speed of a car. The output is the time it takes for a car moving constantly at that speed to travel 100 miles.

   c. The input is a positive number. The output is a number whose absolute value is the input.

   d. The input is a year. The output is the population of the United States during that year.

Go Online
www.successnetplus.com

Population of the United States

1800s

Present Day

7. For each description in Exercise 6, reverse the descriptions for input and output. Which new descriptions result in functions? Explain.

8. **Write About It** Why do some people refer to the input of a function as the independent variable and the output as the dependent variable?

9. Dana's favorite number is 5. She invents five different rules shown below.

$$x \mapsto \frac{x}{5} + 4$$
$$x \mapsto 10(x - 5) + 5$$
$$x \mapsto 5^{x-4}$$
$$x \mapsto \frac{x^2}{5}$$
$$x \mapsto (x - 5)^2 + x$$

a. Show that each rule fixes 5. In other words, show that when the number 5 is the input, the number 5 is also the output.

b. Pick any whole number between 2 and 10 (except 5). Change Dana's rules so that the new rules fix the number you choose.

c. Show that your five new rules fix the number you choose.

10. **Standardized Test Prep** Which statement is true about the rule "Subtract 4 from the input and divide by 2"?

A. The rule is a function, because each input gives exactly one output.

B. The rule is not a function, because some inputs have fraction outputs.

C. The rule is a function, because each input gives a positive number output.

D. The rule is *not* a function, because the input 2 produces the values 1 and -1.

Maintain Your Skills

11. Tony plays with his calculator's square root key. He picks a large number such as 123 and finds its square root. Then he finds the square root of the result. Next he finds the square root of that result. He continues in this way 20 or 30 times. What does Tony get as a final output?

12. Try Tony's experiment in Exercise 11 with any integer greater than 1. Explain your results.

For Exercises 13–15, choose a value for x and apply the given rule. Use the output as the next input, and apply the rule again. Repeat the process several times. Explain your results.

13. $x \mapsto \frac{1}{x}$ **14.** $x \mapsto x^2$ **15.** $x \mapsto \frac{x + 3}{2}$

5.04 Naming Functions

Often you can more easily examine and ask questions about a function by giving it a name. You can often use a single letter, such as f, to name a function. You write the output of function f as $f(x)$ and say "f of x."

$$f(x) = 2x^3 - 1$$

> Computer programmers often use a term such as *cube* to name a function.

You can define a function using the "maps to" notation and name the function at the same time.

$$x \overset{f}{\mapsto} 2x^3 - 1 \text{ means the same as } f(x) = 2x^3 - 1.$$

Example

Problem The function f is defined by $x \overset{f}{\mapsto} x^2 - 2x + 1$.

What is each of the following?

$$f(1) \qquad\qquad f(3) \qquad\qquad f(\pi)$$
$$f(a + 7) \qquad f(a) + f(7)$$

What is $f(x)$?

Solution It often helps to say things in words. The notation $x \overset{f}{\mapsto} x^2 - 2x + 1$ means that f is a function with input x and output $x^2 - 2x + 1$.

$f(1)$ is the output of the function when $x = 1$. The notation looks like $1 \overset{f}{\mapsto} 1^2 - 2 \cdot 1 + 1 = 0$, or $f(1) = 0$.

Similarly, for each of the remaining inputs, replace x with the given input.

$$f(3) = (3)^2 - 2(3) + 1 = 4$$
$$f(\pi) = (\pi)^2 - 2(\pi) + 1$$
$$f(a + 7) = (a + 7)^2 - 2(a + 7) + 1$$
$$f(a) + f(7) = [(a)^2 - 2(a) + 1] + [(7)^2 - 2(7) + 1]$$

The function $f(x)$ is just $x^2 - 2x + 1$.

> Why is the following statement true?
> $f(a + 7) \neq f(a) + f(7)$?

Represent a function. You can write function notation in two ways. Each way emphasizes a different part of the function.

The $\mapsto$ notation highlights what the function does. The function $x \mapsto 7x^3 - 1$ transforms any input (x) into an output $(7x^3 - 1)$. The $f(\ )$ notation highlights the output of a function. When you write $f(x) = 7x^3 - 1$, x is the input, f is the function, and $7x^3 - 1$ is the output. In both cases, you define the function with the expression $7x^3 - 1$.

You name the function f. Its output for a given input x is $f(x)$.

You can give a function any name. Sometimes you use a letter such as g or h. On a calculator or a computer, you may name functions using a few letters.

Transformation Notation	Function Name	Function Notation
$x \mapsto 4x^2$	g	$g(x) = 4x^2$
$x \mapsto 3x - 7$	h	$h(x) = 3x - 7$
$x \mapsto \lvert x \rvert$	ABS	$\text{ABS}(x) = \lvert x \rvert$
$x \mapsto \sqrt{x}$	SQRT	$\text{SQRT}(x) = \sqrt{x}$

You can build combinations of function machines such as $\text{ABS}(g(x))$.

In goes x . . . out comes $g(x)$.　　　In goes $g(x)$ . . . out comes $\text{ABS}(g(x))$.

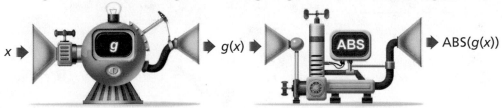

You usually call combinations of function machines such as $\text{ABS}(g(x))$ **compositions.**

For Discussion

1. Draw a function machine illustrating $x \mapsto \text{ABS}(h(x))$. Then draw a function machine illustrating $x \mapsto h(\text{ABS}(x))$.

2. Is $\text{ABS}(h(x)) = h(\text{ABS}(x))$?

3. What is the value of $\text{SQRT}(h(3))$? The value of $\text{SQRT}(h(1))$?

Use your calculator to discover the keys that are functions. Press each of the following keys.

4. ABS　　　　5. SIN　　　　6. RAND　　　　7. 10^x

Experiment with different inputs and make conjectures about which keys are functions. Record your observations. Then choose any other keys on the calculator. Which of these keys are functions?

Exercises *Practicing Habits of Mind*

Check Your Understanding

1. Copy the table. Use the function $f(x) = -2x + 5$ to complete the table.

Input, x	Output, $f(x)$
0	■
1	3
2	■
3	■
4	−3
5	■

2. Use the functions below for parts (a)–(e).

   $$\text{REC}(x) = \frac{1}{x}$$
   $$h(x) = x^2 + 4$$

   a. What is $h(2)$? REC(2)?

   b. Draw a function machine that illustrates REC($h(1)$). Then calculate REC($h(1)$).

   c. Draw a function machine that illustrates REC($h(x)$). Then calculate REC($h(5)$).

   d. Draw a function machine that illustrates $h(\text{REC}(x))$. Then calculate $h(\text{REC}(1))$ and $h(\text{REC}(5))$. Does $h(\text{REC}(x)) = \text{REC}(h(x))$?

   e. What result do you get when you calculate REC(0)?

3. Find two functions f and g such that $f(g(x)) = g(f(x))$.

4. Find at least two functions f such that $f(f(x)) = x$ for any value of x.

5. Some functions take multiple inputs, but these functions must always give back only one output. For instance, addition is a function that takes two inputs and gives back only one output.

$$ADD(a, b) = a + b$$

a b

Add.

$a + b$

Another way to write ADD(a, b) is
$(a, b) \mapsto a + b$.

Use each multi-input function for parts (a) and (b).

Addition $ADD(a, b) = a + b$
Multiplication $MULT(a, b) = ab$

a. What is the value of $ADD(1, 1)$? The value of $MULT(2, 3)$?

b. Is $ADD(a, b) = ADD(b, a)$?

c. What is the value of $MULT(a, ADD(b, c)) - ADD(MULT(a, b), MULT(a, c))$?

d. Is $MULT(3, ADD(x, 4)) = ADD(MULT(3, x), MULT(3, 4))$?

e. What is the value of $MULT(b, ADD(a, -a))$?

On Your Own

6. Use these four functions for parts (a) and (b).

$$f(x) = 3x + 1 \qquad\qquad x \overset{h}{\mapsto} x^2 + 1$$
$$x \overset{g}{\mapsto} 3x - 1 \qquad\qquad j(x) = 2x + 5$$

a. Hideki chooses one of these functions. When he uses the number 5 as the input, the output is 14. Can you tell which function he is using?

b. Hideki puts in a 0 and gets back a 1. Can you tell which function he is using?

c. Hideki says, "The input I chose this time gives the same output for function f and function j." What input did he choose?

d. What input(s), if any, give the same outputs for function g and for function j?

e. What input(s), if any, give the same outputs for function f and for function g?

For help defining functions, see the TI-Nspire Handbook, p. 788.

7. Suppose you drive on a straight road at 30 miles per hour. Model this situation using a function that converts driving time into distance traveled.

8. Dorothy describes the following number trick. Pick a number. Multiply it by 3. Add 5. Double it. Add 8. Divide by 6. Subtract the original number. Dorothy always tells your ending number.

   a. Choose at least 5 different numbers as inputs for Dorothy's function. Write the input-output pairs in a table.

   b. Input x into Dorothy's rule. Apply each step in Dorothy's rule to x and record each step. What is the final result?

> First, you multiply x by 3 to get $3x$. Then, use $3x$ as the input for the second step, adding 5, and so on.

9. Use the functions $g(x) = x^2 - 5$ and $h(x) = |3x + 1|$. Evaluate each function.

   a. $g(0)$, $g(1)$, and $g(-1)$

   b. $h(0)$, $h(1)$, and $h(-1)$

   c. $g(3) + 5$

   d. $g(4) + h(4)$

10. Let m represent a function that uses two points as inputs and gives back a number as an output. The two input points are $P(x_1, y_1)$ and $Q(x_2, y_2)$.

$$m(P, Q) = \frac{y_2 - y_1}{x_2 - x_1}$$

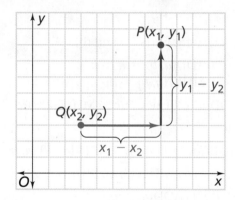

   a. What does the output $m(P, Q)$ represent?

   b. Calculate $m(P, Q)$ when P is $(-1, 2)$ and Q is $(2, 6)$.

11. **Standardized Test Prep** When t is 2.5, what is the value of $h(t)$ in the equation $h(t) = -16t^2 + 8t + 6$?

   A. -74 **B.** -54 **C.** -14 **D.** 126

Maintain Your Skills

12. Use these two functions to evaluate each function in parts (a)–(j).

$$f(x) = 3x + 1 \qquad g(x) = \frac{x - 1}{3}$$

   a. $f(2)$ b. $f(f(2))$ c. $f(f(f(2)))$

   d. $g(2)$ e. $g(g(2))$ f. $f(g(2))$

   g. $g(f(2))$ h. $f(g(f(2)))$ i. $g(f(g(f(2))))$

   j. $f(f(g(g(2))))$

The definition of a function describes mapping as a set of inputs corresponding to a set of outputs. Each set has a special name.

Definition

The set of inputs is called the **domain** of the function.

The set of outputs that a function produces is called the **range** of the function.

> The set of outputs is sometimes called the image of the function.

The definitions of function, domain, and range do not mention any numbers. You can design functions that use any kind of input, as long as each input always gives only one output. For example,

- A juicer is a function. The input is a piece of fruit. The output is the fruit juice.

- Your library's computer catalog system is a function. The input is the book's title. The output is the call number that tells you where to find the book.

> The call number is a function of the book.

For Discussion

Identify each domain and range.

1. The salary of a worker is a function of his or her skill level.

2. The price of an advertisement during a television show is a function of the number of viewers.

3. The magnitude of a sonic boom is a function of an airplane's weight and fuselage length.

Defining the domain of a function is just as important as writing the function rule. You can restrict the domain to a specific set of numbers even though your function rule works for other sets of numbers. For example, when your function maps time traveled against distance, you can define the domain values for time as the set of positive numbers.

Some functions break down with certain inputs. For example, a juicer can juice oranges, apples, and even carrots, but not shoes. Some function rules cannot use certain inputs either. You can exclude the numbers that do not work when you define the function domain.

For Discussion

4. What inputs do not work in the function $x \mapsto \frac{1}{x}$?

Example

Problem What is the domain of the function $x \mapsto \frac{1}{x - 7}$?

Solution This function takes numbers for input. You must decide what numbers make sense, or are valid, for the function.

Look at the function. Is there any number x for which $\frac{1}{x - 7}$ does not make sense? Since $x - 7$ is in the denominator, make sure that $x - 7$ never has the value of 0. To find when $x - 7$ equals 0, solve the equation below.

$$x - 7 = 0$$
$$x - 7 + 7 = 0 + 7$$
$$x = 7$$

When x equals 7, the function does not work. The domain is all real numbers except 7.

For You to Do

Find the domain of each function.

5. $x \mapsto \frac{1}{x + 2}$

6. $x \mapsto \frac{13x + 5}{2x + 1}$

7. $x \mapsto \frac{6x^2 + 52x - 37}{x^2 - 4}$

8. $x \mapsto x$th prime number

You can define some functions on a much smaller scale. For instance, the table at the right defines a perfectly good function. The domain of this function is {1, 2, 3, 4} and the range is {−3, 3, 4, 9}.

In the next investigation, you will look at tables in a different way. Tables provide a snapshot of a function with domain and range that are larger than what is in the table. Make sure you understand the context of any problem so you can decide whether the table is the entire function or just a snapshot.

Input	Output
1	3
2	4
3	9
4	−3

Exercises *Practicing Habits of Mind*

Check Your Understanding

1. **a.** What inputs, if any, are not valid for $x \mapsto \sqrt{x}$?

   b. What inputs, if any, are not valid for $x \mapsto \sqrt{|x|}$?

2. Determine the domain for each function.

   a. $g(x) = \sqrt{x - 2}$

   b. $x \mapsto x - 2$

   c. $x \mapsto \dfrac{1}{x - 2}$

   d. $h(x) = (x - 2)^2$

3. Use the functions $\text{REC}(x) = \dfrac{1}{x}$ and $h(x) = x^2 + 4$. Find the domain of each function given.

   a. $h(\text{REC}(x))$ **b.** $\text{REC}(h(x))$

4. Tables I–III show three sets of input-output values.

Table I	
Input	**Output**
2	4
9	8
−3	12
$\frac{1}{2}$	3
−1	4
100	7

Table II	
Input	**Output**
4	9
13	3
7	16
−2	−4
4	9
11	0

Table III	
Input	**Output**
−1	1
0	2
1	3
4	4
−3	5
−1	6

   a. Does each table define a function? Explain.

   b. For each table that defines a function, state the domain and range of the function.

5. **Take It Further** Find a function f such that, for all values of a and x, $f(ax) = a \cdot f(x)$.

6. **Take It Further** When $f(x + 2) = 5x - 4$, find each value.

   a. $f(3)$ **b.** $f(5)$ **c.** $f(7)$

7. What is the domain of $x \mapsto \dfrac{1}{x^2 - 25}$?

8. Use the function rule "Divide the input by 3 and write the remainder."

   a. Make an input-output table with integer inputs between 1 and 5.

   b. Is the value 0 a valid input? Is a negative integer a valid input? Explain.

9. Determine whether each description is a function.

   a. The input is a letter. The output is any word starting with that letter.

   b. The input is a person. The output is that person's age in years.

   c. The input is the name of a month. The output is the number of days in that month.

> Look at the outputs. For each valid input, there must be exactly one output.

10. **Standardized Test Prep** When $f(x) = x^4 - 5$, which of the four values is missing in the table?

x	f(x)
0	−5
−1	−4
■	11
3	76

   A. −4   **B.** −2   **C.** 4   **D.** 6

11. **Take It Further** Explore $x \mapsto \dfrac{1}{x - |x|}$ to determine what inputs, if any, are valid. What is the domain of $x \mapsto \dfrac{1}{x - |x|}$?

Go Online
www.successnetplus.com

12. Use the functions to find either a value or an expression in parts (a)–(o).

   $$f(x) = 3x + 2 \qquad x \overset{g}{\mapsto} \frac{x - 2}{3} \qquad h(x) = \frac{3}{x - 2}$$

   a. $f(7)$

   b. $g(7)$

   c. $h(7)$

   d. $f(g(5))$

   e. $g(f(5))$

   f. $h(g(5))$

   g. $h(6) \cdot g(6)$

   h. $h(-6) \cdot g(-6)$

   i. $h(x) \cdot g(x)$

   j. $f(a)$

   k. $f(a + 2)$

   l. $f(a + b)$

   m. $f(g(x))$

   n. $f(f(x))$

   o. $f\left(\dfrac{x - 2}{3}\right)$

Go Online
Video Tutor
www.successnetplus.com

5.06 Graphing Functions

You can represent functions in many ways. You have already used three ways: machines, expressions, and tables. Graphs provide another useful way to represent many functions.

Minds in Action

Tony plots outputs f(x) against inputs x.

Sasha Let's play the Guess My Rule game again.

Tony Okay, but please promise not to do any more crazy functions like $f(x) = \dfrac{3x^2 + 7x - 19}{x + 11}$.

Sasha Fine.

Sasha thinks for a moment and then writes $x \mapsto 4x - 3$.

Tony's Input	Sasha's Response
2	2 produces 5.
0	0 produces -3.
1	1 produces 1.
$\frac{1}{2}$	$\frac{1}{2}$ produces -1.

Tony I think your rule is "x produces $4x - 3$."

Sasha You're right! That was fast. What's your strategy?

Tony I turn your responses into a graph.

Sasha What do you mean?

Tony Each time you give me a response, I write my input and your response as a point. Then I plot that point. Since 2 produces 5, I plot (2, 5).

Sasha Okay. Since the value 0 produces -3, you plot (0, -3).

Tony Exactly. I do that for all points and look at the graph. It looks like all points fall on a line.

Sasha It does.

Tony I try to find an equation of a line that passes through these points.

First, I calculate the slope between (0, -3) and (1, 1).

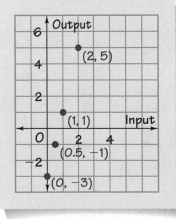

Tony plots outputs $f(x)$ against inputs x.

Tony scribbles some calculations on his paper.

Tony   The slope is 4. Then I write the equation as a point tester.

Sasha   How do you do that when there's no variable y?

Tony   It's just like before, except we use $f(x)$ instead of y. Since the number 4 is the slope, and (1, 1) is on the line, we can test any point $(x, f(x))$. The point is on the line when $\frac{f(x) - 1}{x - 1} = 4$.

Sasha   When you clean that up, you get $f(x) - 1 = 4(x - 1)$.

Tony   That simplifies to $f(x) - 1 = 4x - 4$.

Sasha   Or $f(x) = 4x - 3$. That was my rule!

For You to Do

1. Tony and Sasha play the Guess My Rule game.

Tony's Input	Sasha's Response
1	1 produces $-\frac{1}{6}$.
3	3 produces $2\frac{1}{2}$.
0	0 produces $-\frac{3}{2}$.
−1	−1 produces $-2\frac{5}{6}$.

Use Tony's graphing method described above to find Sasha's rule.

Definition

When g is a function, the **graph of g** is the graph of the equation $y = g(x)$.

Graphing the equation $y = g(x)$ is the same as graphing $g(x)$ against x.

For Discussion

2. The coordinate plane shows the graph of function f. Explain how to use this graph and the vertical line $x = -2$ to estimate $f(-2)$. Use the same method to estimate $f(0)$.

3. Give the approximate value(s) of x when $f(x) = 2$.

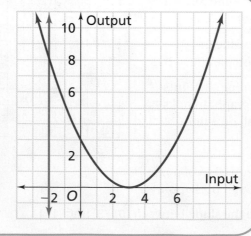

Tony and Sasha walk down a hall. Tony finds a sheet of paper on the ground. He picks it up and sees these drawings.

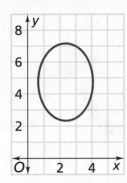 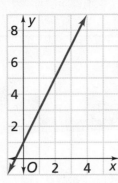 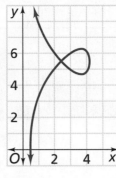 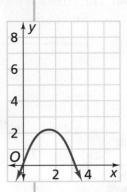

Tony   Look at this! Somebody is using my method for the Guess My Rule game.

Sasha looks at the drawings.

Sasha   I wouldn't get so excited, Tony. We're only allowed to use functions in the Guess My Rule game.

Tony   So?

Sasha   Some of those graphs aren't graphs of functions.

Tony   What do you mean?

Sasha   Well, suppose that the first graph is a graph of function $a(x)$. If I want to find the output for the function $a(3)$, I can do that by drawing a vertical line through 3. See, the vertical line hits the graph in 2 places!

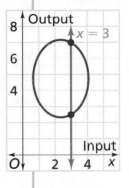

Tony   So what?

Sasha   In a function, each input always gives the same output.

Tony   Oh, right.

Sasha   In this graph, the input value 3 produces 2.5 or 7. The output values for $a(3)$ are 2.5 and 7 at the same time! That's an illegal rule!

Tony   I think I see. The vertical line $x = 3$ tells us the output when 3 is the input.

Sasha   Correct.

Tony   Since the vertical line hits two places on the graph, the input 3 gives two possible outputs.

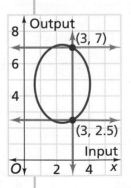

Sasha   So the graph isn't a function!

For Discussion

4. Use Sasha's method to determine whether each of the other three graphs Tony found is a graph of a function. Explain how to use Sasha's method for any graph. Then draw at least three new graphs of functions and three new graphs of nonfunctions.

Exercises *Practicing Habits of Mind*

Check Your Understanding

1. Find a function that produces each table. You can write your rule in $f(x)$ form, $x \mapsto$ form, or in words.

Habits of Mind

Visualize. Plot the points and see if you recognize the shape of the graph.

Table A

Input, n	Output
0	9
1	7
2	5
3	3
4	1

Table B

Input, s	Output
0	−1
1	0
2	3
3	8
4	15

Table C

Input, n	Output
1	2
2	$2\frac{1}{2}$
3	$3\frac{1}{3}$
4	$4\frac{1}{4}$
5	$5\frac{1}{5}$

Table D

Input, x	Output
0	12.875
1	13
2	13.125
3	13.25
4	13.375

2. Decide whether each graph is the graph of a function.

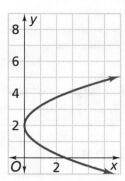 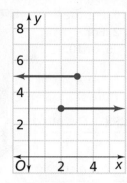 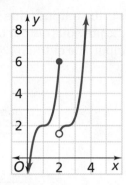 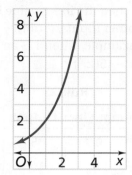

3. Suppose that you switch the axes in the coordinate planes in Exercise 2. In other words, let the *x*-axis represent the outputs and the *y*-axis represent the inputs. Which graphs are the graphs of functions in this case?

4. Tony and Sasha play the Guess My Rule game. After three inputs, Tony guesses the rule.

Tony says, "I think your rule is '$x \mapsto 2 - 5x$.'"

Sasha replies, "No, my rule is '$x \mapsto -5(x + 1) + 7$.'"

Tony says, "That's the same!"

a. Are the valid inputs for each rule the same?

b. Make an input-output table for each rule. Use at least five inputs. Are the tables the same?

c. Graph each rule. Are the graphs the same?

d. Are the rules the same? If not, explain when they are the same.

5. Travis compares two functions.

$$s(x) = (x - 1)^2 \qquad t(x) = x^2 - 1.99x + 1$$

Travis says, "When $x = 0$, both functions have an output value of 1. Then I graph them on a calculator. They look the same." Travis concludes that functions *s* and *t* are equal. Is Travis correct?

> For help graphing a function on the coordinate plane, see the TI-Nspire Handbook, p. 788.

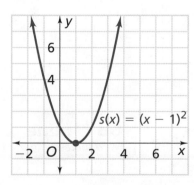 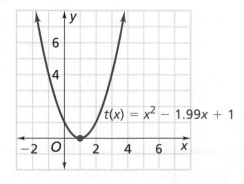

6. Copy the tables. Use rules C and D to complete the tables.

Rule C When the input value is 0, the output value is 5. For the other inputs, multiply the previous output by 2. For example, when 1 is an input, the output is 2×5, or 10.

Rule D $x \mapsto 5(2^x)$

Rule C

Input, *n*	Output
0	5
1	10
2	■
3	■
4	■
5	■

Rule D

Input, *x*	Output
0	5
1	10
2	■
3	■
4	■
5	■

> You can use the output for 0 to find the output for 1. The rule tells you to take the previous output and multiply that by 2. Notice that you cannot use this rule for inputs between 0 and 1, such as 0.5.

Look at the tables above. Consider both the set of valid inputs and the graph for each function. Compare and contrast the functions.

7. Function *v* uses positive integers for inputs and returns the number of positive factors that the input has.

Extend the table for whole number inputs up to 24. Make several conjectures about the function. Explain any shortcuts for calculating an output.

Input, *n*	Output, *v(n)*
1	1
2	2
3	2
4	3
5	2
6	4
7	2
8	4
9	3

On Your Own

8. Graph each function.

a. $x \mapsto 4x + 9$

b. $x \mapsto \dfrac{x^2}{5}$

c. $x \mapsto \dfrac{x}{2} + 4$

d. $x \mapsto x + 1$

Go Online
www.successnetplus.com

9. Which graph of a function has a maximum value of 10?

A.

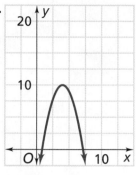

B.

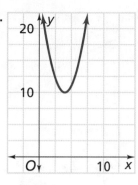

C.

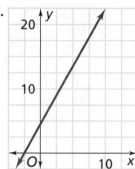

D.

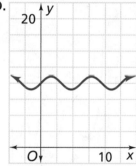

10. Elaine explains how she finds fixed inputs, or inputs that remain unchanged by a function. "Let's say you want to find a value fixed by the rule $x \mapsto 4x - 9$. First, graph $y = 4x - 9$. Then, graph $y = x$. The graphs intersect at (3, 3). See! The rule $x \mapsto 4x - 9$ fixes the value 3."

Use Elaine's method to find fixed inputs for each function in Exercise 8. Does her method work?

For other ways to graph on the coordinate plane, see the TI-Nspire Handbook, p. 788.

11. **Take It Further** The floor function takes any real number x as input and returns the greatest integer less than or equal to x. A common symbol for the floor function is $\lfloor \ \rfloor$.

a. Write a rule for $\lfloor x \rfloor$ on a number line.

b. Draw the graph of $x \mapsto \lfloor x \rfloor$.

12. Use the functions p and q given below.

$$p(x) = x - 2 \qquad q(x) = \frac{x^2 - 4}{x + 2}$$

x	$\lfloor x \rfloor$
3	3
3.5	3
3.9	3
3.99	3
4	4

a. Make an input-output table for each function. Use at least five inputs. Are the tables the same?

b. Are the valid inputs for each rule the same?

c. Graph each function. Illustrate your answers for parts (a) and (b) on your graphs.

13. Decide whether each graph is the graph of a function.

a.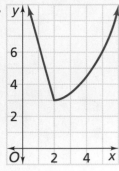

b.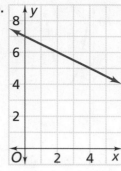

c.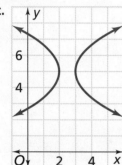

d.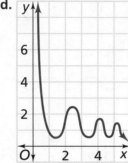

14. Use Rules 1 and 2 given below.

Rule 1 $x \mapsto 4x + 1$

Rule 2 $x \mapsto 4x + 1 + x(x - 1)(x - 2)$

a. Without calculating any values, determine whether the two rules define the same function.

b. Make an input-output table for each rule. Use whole-number inputs 0, 1, and 2. Are the tables the same?

c. Can you find an input value for which the outputs for the two rules differ?

15. Use the rules in Exercise 14 and Rules 3 and 4 given below.

Rule 3 $x \mapsto 4x + 1 + x(x - 1)(x - 2)(x - 3)(x - 4)$

Rule 4 $x \mapsto 4x + 1 + x(x - 1)(x - 2)(x - 3)(x - 4)(x - 5)$

a. Make an input-output table for Rules 1 and 3 using whole-number inputs from 0 to 4. Are the outputs the same?

b. Is Rule 3 the same function as Rule 1 or Rule 2? Explain.

c. Without calculating actual values, how do the outputs using Rule 1 and Rule 4 compare? Use whole-number inputs from 0 to 5. Explain.

d. Is it possible to write a rule that gives the same outputs as $x \mapsto 4x + 1$ and defines a different function? Use whole-number input values from 0 to 6. Then extend the input values to 100. Explain.

16. Standardized Test Prep Larissa selects mobile phone service. Each company charges a fixed monthly fee plus an additional charge for each minute in excess of the free time allowance.

Mobile Phone Service Plans

Company	Monthly Fee	Free Minutes per Month	Cost per Additional Minute
A	$35	300	$.08
B	$22	400	$.15

Larissa plans to use her mobile phone as her only phone. She predicts that she will use it between 600 and 900 minutes per month. To find t, the total monthly charge for each company based on m minutes of phone use, Larissa writes the equations below.

Company A $t = 35 + (m - 300)(0.08)$ when $m \geq 300$

Company B $t = 22 + (m - 400)(0.15)$ when $m \geq 400$

Which is the less expensive plan for 600 minutes of phone use per month?

A. Company A

B. Company B

C. Both plans cost the same amount for 600 minutes.

D. cannot be determined

> When Larissa talks for only 200 minutes per month, why don't her equations work?

Maintain Your Skills

Use the functions f and g for Exercises 17 and 18.

$$f(x) = 3x + 2 \qquad\qquad x \overset{g}{\mapsto} \frac{x - 2}{3}$$

17. Sketch the graph of each function.

  a. f

  b. $r(x) = f(x - 1)$

  c. $s(x) = f(x + 1)$

18. Sketch the graph of each function.

  a. g

  b. $t(x) = f(g(x))$

  c. $s(x) = g(f(x))$

Mathematical 5A Reflections

In this investigation, you learned how to write function rules, make input-output tables, and graph functions. These questions will help you summarize what you have learned.

1. Use $x \overset{f}{\mapsto} -2x + 3$ and $x \overset{g}{\mapsto} x^2 - 1$.

   a. Graph each function.

   b. Use your graphs to estimate $f(0.25)$ and $g(0.5)$.

   c. Use each function rule to find $f(0.25)$ and $g(0.5)$.

   d. Use your graph to approximate all values of x such that $g(x) = 2$.

2. Decide whether each statement defines a function. For each function, make a table using integer values from -2 to 2. Write the function in $x \mapsto$ form.

   a. Multiply the input by 2 and subtract 3.

   b. Multiply the input by a value that is one more than the input.

   c. When x is the input, the output is a value not equal to x.

   d. Take the opposite of the input and add 3. Then square the result.

3. Use $f(x) = 3x + 5$ and $g(x) = 3x^2$.

   a. $f(2)$

   b. $g(2)$

   c. $g(22)$

   d. $f(12)$

   e. $f(g(2))$

   f. $g(f(2))$

4. Determine the domain for each function.

    a. $f(x) = 2x - 7$

    b. $g(x) = x^2 + 1$

    c. $x \overset{h}{\mapsto} \sqrt{x - 1}$

    d. $A(x) = \dfrac{2}{x + 5}$

5. What is a function?

6. What is the relationship between a table and a function?

7. What is the domain of $f(x) = \dfrac{\sqrt{x}}{x - 9}$?

Vocabulary and Notation

In this investigation you learned these terms and symbols. Make sure you understand what each one means and how to use it.

The input could be two images and the output one photo.

- **composition**
- **domain**
- **function, $f(x)$**
- **graph of a function**
- **range**

Investigation 5B

Exponents

In *Exponents*, you will learn about integral (or integer) exponents. You will use the rules of exponents to make calculations. You will undo exponents to solve equations. You also will calculate using the zero exponent and negative exponents.

By the end of this investigation, you will be able to answer questions like these.

1. What are the basic rules of exponents?

2. Why is 2^0 equal to 1?

3. How can you write $\dfrac{2^3 \cdot 2^{-2} \cdot 2^7}{(2^5)^3 \cdot 2^{-2}}$ as a number without exponents?

You will learn how to

• make calculations involving integral exponents

• simplify expressions involving integral exponents

• explain and apply the basic rules of exponents

• calculate with the zero exponent and negative exponents

You will develop these habits and skills:

• Understand the meaning of exponential notation.

• Multiply, add, subtract, and divide with exponents.

• Extend concepts and patterns to build new mathematical knowledge.

A gecko has about 1×10^6 setae on its feet. Each seta branches into about 1×10^3 spatulae.

5.07 Getting Started

You may think of multiplication as repeated addition. The product $4 \cdot 3$ can mean "add 3 copies of 4 together."

$$4 \cdot 3 = \underbrace{4 + 4 + 4}$$

3 copies of 4

You may know that exponents work in a similar way. The expression 4^3 means "multiply 3 copies of 4 together."

$$4^3 = \underbrace{4 \cdot 4 \cdot 4}$$

3 copies of 4

In general, if n is a positive integer, a^n is the product of n factors of a. You read a^n as "a to the n."

$$a^n = \underbrace{a \cdot a \cdot a \cdot \cdots \cdot a}$$

n copies of a

> You call a the **base** and n the **exponent**.

What does a^1 mean? It may not look like a product, but it means that there is one factor of a.

$$a^1 = \underbrace{a}$$

1 copy of a

Here are some examples of expressions with exponents.

$$a^4 = a \cdot a \cdot a \cdot a$$
$$a^{10} = a \cdot a \cdot a \cdot a \cdot a \cdot a \cdot a \cdot a \cdot a \cdot a$$

Two exponents have special names. To **square** a number means to multiply the number by itself. The expression a^2 ("a squared") means $a \cdot a$. You can square any expression, including expressions with integers, fractions, and variables.

$$a^2 = a \cdot a \qquad\qquad 12^2 = 12 \cdot 12 = 144$$
$$\left(\frac{2}{5}\right)^2 = \frac{2}{5} \cdot \frac{2}{5} = \frac{2^2}{5^2} = \frac{4}{25} \qquad (4w)^2 = 4w \cdot 4w = 4^2 \cdot w^2 = 16w^2$$
$$(-3)^2 = (-3) \cdot (-3) = 9$$

Similarly, to **cube** a number means to multiply the number times the number times the number. In other words, you find the product of the number's square and the number. The expression a^3 ("a cubed") means $a \cdot a \cdot a$. You can cube any expression.

$$a^3 = a \cdot a \cdot a \qquad\qquad 12^3 = 12 \cdot 12 \cdot 12 = 1728$$
$$\left(\frac{2}{5}\right)^3 = \frac{2}{5} \cdot \frac{2}{5} \cdot \frac{2}{5} = \frac{2^3}{5^3} = \frac{8}{125} \qquad (4w)^3 = 4w \cdot 4w \cdot 4w = 4^3 \cdot w^3$$
$$= 64w^3$$
$$(-3)^3 = (-3) \cdot (-3) \cdot (-3) = -27$$

For You to Explore

1. There are 9 square feet in a square yard. There are 27 cubic feet in a cubic yard. Explain.

2. Here are some additional basic rules, but they are not all true. Substitute numbers for a, b, and c to check whether each equation is true. Decide whether each rule could be a basic rule. Use numerical examples as evidence. Write a convincing argument that summarizes your conclusions.

Group I

$a^b \overset{?}{=} (-a)^b$

$a^{b+c} \overset{?}{=} a^b + a^c$

$a^{b+c} \overset{?}{=} a^b \cdot a^c$

Group II

$a^b \overset{?}{=} b^a$

$a^b \cdot a^c \overset{?}{=} a^{bc}$

$(a^b)^c \overset{?}{=} a^{bc}$

Group III

$(a^b)^c \overset{?}{=} a^{(b^c)}$

$(a^b)^c \overset{?}{=} a^b \cdot b^c$

$\dfrac{a^b}{a^c} \overset{?}{=} a^{b-c}$

Group IV

$(ab)^c \overset{?}{=} a^c \cdot b^c$

$a^b \overset{?}{=} a(a^{b-1})$

$(ab)^c \overset{?}{=} a(b^c)$

3. Write each expression as a power of 6.

   a. $6^{51}6^{48}$ **b.** $(6^5)^7$ **c.** $6(6^{25}6^{14})$ **d.** $\dfrac{6^{95}}{6^{19}}$

> You will write each result using a base of 6 and an exponent. For example, 6^{14}.

4. Everyone who is born in the United States is eligible to receive a Social Security number that has nine digits. You can divide the digits into groups of three digits, two digits, and four digits. How many possible Social Security numbers are there?

Express your answer in two different ways.

   a. Find how many different nine-digit combinations are possible. Express this result as a power of 10.

   b. Think about dividing the nine digits into groups of three digits, two digits, and four digits. How many different combinations are possible for three digits? For two digits? For four digits? Can you use the number of combinations to find the total possible number of Social Security numbers?

Exercises *Practicing Habits of Mind*

On Your Own

5. Some states make license plates using combinations of three letters followed by three numbers. That is, you can have "ABC 123" on a license plate, but not "123 ABC." Using combinations of three letters followed by three numbers, how many license plates are possible?

6. Many garage door openers use a four-digit code, where each digit can be any number from 0 to 9. What is the total number of possible four-digit codes? Explain.

> In Exercises 6 and 7, express your answer as a power of 10.

7. If the code for a garage door opener is only two digits long, how many codes are possible? How many three-digit codes are possible? Explain.

8. Most credit card numbers are 16 digits long.

   a. If each digit can be any number from 0 to 9, how many different credit numbers are possible? Express your result in different ways. (*Hint:* Divide the 16 digits into smaller groups. Then, use your results from Exercises 6 and 7.)

   b. Some credit card numbers have special digits. Suppose a card's number must start with 37 followed by a nonzero digit. Then the 13 following digits can be any number from 0 to 9. How many different credit numbers are possible?

Maintain Your Skills

9. Rewrite each expression using exponents.

   a. $x \cdot x \cdot x \cdot 3 \cdot 3 \cdot y \cdot y$
   b. $a \cdot b \cdot b \cdot b \cdot 3 \cdot b \cdot a \cdot b \cdot a$
   c. $2 \cdot 3 \cdot m \cdot m \cdot m$
   d. $x \cdot x \cdot x \cdot x \cdot \frac{1}{x}$

Go Online
Video Tutor
www.successnetplus.com

5.08 Squares, Cubes, and Beyond—Some Basic Rules of Exponents

In Chapter 1, you explored the any-order, any-grouping properties (AOAG) for both addition and multiplication. In Lesson 5.07, you may have noticed that there is no AOAG property for exponents. For instance,

$$2^{20} = 1{,}048{,}576, \text{ but } 20^2 = 400.$$

In general, changing the order of exponents changes the outcome. This example shows that the any-order part of AOAG does not work.

> Most of the time, $a^b \neq b^a$. What are some examples where they are equal?

For Discussion

1. Check the any-grouping part of AOAG by comparing $(3^2)^4$ and $3^{(2^4)}$. Are they equal? Use a few other examples, such as $(2^3)^4$ and $2^{(3^4)}$. Does the any-grouping part of AOAG work for exponents?

> The convention for a^{b^c} is to consider it as $a^{(b^c)}$.

While there is no AOAG for exponentiation, there are some basic rules for exponents. In Lesson 5.07, you explored a collection of proposed basic rules. Group I explored one of these rules.

$$a^b \cdot a^c = a^{b+c}$$

Why is this rule true? Try it with numbers. For example, $(3^2)(3^5)$.

$$(3^2)(3^5) = \underbrace{(3 \cdot 3)}_{2 \text{ copies}} \cdot \underbrace{(3 \cdot 3 \cdot 3 \cdot 3 \cdot 3)}_{5 \text{ copies}} = \underbrace{(3 \cdot 3 \cdot 3 \cdot 3 \cdot 3 \cdot 3 \cdot 3)}_{2 + 5 = 7 \text{ copies}} = 3^7$$

When you multiply 3^2 and 3^5, there are a total of 7 factors of 3. You use the same process when you find the product $(3^b)(3^c)$.

$$(3^b)(3^c) = \underbrace{(3 \cdot 3 \cdot \ldots \cdot 3)}_{b \text{ copies}} \cdot \underbrace{(3 \cdot 3 \cdot \ldots \cdot 3)}_{c \text{ copies}} = \underbrace{(3 \cdot 3 \cdot \ldots \cdot 3)}_{b + c \text{ copies}} = 3^{b+c}$$

This argument works if the base is 2, -1, $\frac{1}{2}$, or even a variable, such as a. Now that you have an argument, or proof, you can write the theorem. This simple statement, the Law of Exponents, is very important to the discussion of exponents.

Theorem 5.1 *The Law of Exponents*

For any number a and positive integers b and c, $a^b \cdot a^c = a^{b+c}$.

You can only use Theorem 5.1 if the bases are the same. Consider the following.

$$7^3 \cdot 7^8 = 7^{3+8} = 7^{11} \qquad 6^3 \cdot 7^8 \neq (6 \cdot 7)^{3+8}$$

For You to Do

Simplify each expression.

2. $a^2 \cdot a^5$

3. $k^8 \cdot j^7 \cdot k^{13}$

4. $m^4(m^5)$

5. $r^3(s^7 + r^2)$

6. $4^3 \cdot x^2 \cdot 4 \cdot x^2$

7. $2^3 x^3 (2x)^2$

For Discussion

8. Use Theorem 5.1 and the basic rules for addition and multiplication to prove that $a^b \cdot a^c \cdot a^d = a^{b+c+d}$.

For You to Do

9. **What's Wrong Here?** Matt simplifies the expression $(4m)^3 - 2m - 2m(2m^2 - 1)$ as shown.

$$(4m)^3 - 2m - 2m(2m^2 - 1) = 4m^3 - 2m - 4m^3 + 2m$$
$$= 0$$

Emily simplifies the same expression in another way.

$$(4m)^3 - 2m - 2m(2m^2 - 1) = 64m^3 - 2m - 4m^3 + 2m$$
$$= 60m^3$$

Who is correct? Explain what one of the students did wrong.

Exercises *Practicing Habits of Mind*

Check Your Understanding

1. Without using a calculator, find which of the following expressions is equal to 2^{12}. Explain.

a. $2^{10} + 2^2$ **b.** $2^6 2^6$ **c.** $(2^{10})(2^2)$ **d.** $(2^4)(2^3)$

e. $(2^4)(2^4)(2^4)$ **f.** $2^9 + 2^3$ **g.** $2^{11} + 2^{11}$ **h.** $4(2^{10})$

2. **Write About It** If you write 10^6, 10^9, and 10^n in standard form, how many zeros are in each number? Explain.

3. **Take It Further** Suppose you expand $10^2 \cdot 5^3 \cdot 3^5 \cdot 2 \cdot 10^3 \cdot 8$ and write it as a single integer. Starting on the right, how many zeros are there from the units digit to the first nonzero digit?

4. Explain why the rule $(ab)^n = a^n b^n$ is true. It may help to draw diagrams similar to the diagrams at the beginning of this lesson.

> In Lesson 5.07, Group IV explored this rule.

5. Use the rule from Exercise 4 to simplify each expression.

   a. $5^3 2^3$ **b.** $4^6 25^6$ **c.** $9^{10}\left(\frac{1}{9}\right)^{10}$

   d. $20^4\left(\frac{1}{10}\right)^4$ **e.** $20^4 5^4$ **f.** $\left(\frac{4}{3}\right)^4\left(\frac{15}{2}\right)^4$

6. Use the 26 letters in the English alphabet.

   a. How many different combinations of three letters are possible? For example, NEK, KEN, and BBR are combinations.

   b. How many different combinations of n letters are possible?

   c. How many different three-letter combinations use all consonants?

   d. How many different three-letter combinations use all different letters?

> The vowels are A, E, I, O, and U. Consider the rest of the letters as consonants.

7. In one English dictionary, there are the following numbers of words.

   - 2 one-letter words
   - 96 two-letter words
   - 1238 three-letter words
   - 3391 four-letter words

   Only 2 out of the 26 possible one-letter sets are words.

   a. If you write a letter at random, what is the probability that you form a word? Write your result as a percent. Round to two decimal places.

   b. If you write two letters at random, what is the probability that you form a word? Write your result as a percent. Round to two decimal places.

   c. Which is more likely, forming a word using three random letters, or forming a word using four random letters?

8. A palindrome is a string of letters that is the same whether you read it backwards or forwards.

   a. How many different combinations of three letters are palindromes? An example is EVE.

   b. How many different combinations of four letters are palindromes? An example is OTTO.

   c. **Take It Further** How many different combinations of p letters are palindromes?

9. Rewrite each expression using exponents.

   a. $x \cdot y \cdot x \cdot y \cdot x \cdot y \cdot x$

   b. $m \cdot m^2 \cdot m^3 \cdot 3 \cdot 3 \cdot n \cdot n$

   c. $z \cdot z \cdot z^4 \cdot 5z$

   d. $(2x)^3 \cdot x \cdot x^3$

10. A National Football League field is $53\frac{1}{3}$ yards wide and 120 yards long including both end zones. How many square feet are in a football field?

11. **a.** If $2^x = 8$, what is the value of x?

    b. If $2^{y-1} = 16$, what is the value of y?

    c. If $2^{5z} = 64$, what is the value of z?

    d. If $(2^w)(2^w) = 64$, what is the value of w?

12. A craftsperson designs Russian nesting dolls so that each doll fits inside of the next larger doll. In a set of nesting dolls, the smallest doll, Doll 0, is 1 inch tall.

0   1   2

Note that these dolls are not drawn to scale.

Suppose each doll is twice as tall as the previous doll. How tall is each of the following dolls?

   a. Doll 1

   b. Doll 3

   c. Doll 8

   d. Doll n

Go Online
www.successnetplus.com

13. In a different set of Russian dolls, Doll 0 is only 0.75 inch tall. Suppose each doll is twice as tall as the previous doll. How tall is each of the following dolls?

a. Doll 1 **b.** Doll 3

c. Doll 8 **d.** Doll n

14. Standardized Test Prep What is the value of the expression $2 \cdot 2^2 \cdot 2^3$?

A. 20 **B.** 32

C. 64 **D.** 128

Maintain Your Skills

15. Simplify each expression.

a. 1

b. $1 + 10$

c. $1 + 10 + 10^2$

d. $1 + 10 + 10^2 + 10^3$

e. $1 + 10 + 10^2 + 10^3 + 10^4$

f. $1 + 10 + 10^2 + 10^3 + 10^4 + 10^5$

g. What is the pattern of the sums?

16. Simplify each expression.

a. $4 \cdot 1$

b. $4 \cdot 1 + 9 \cdot 10$

c. $4 \cdot 1 + 9 \cdot 10 + 5 \cdot 10^2$

d. $4 \cdot 1 + 9 \cdot 10 + 5 \cdot 10^2 + 2 \cdot 10^3$

e. $4 \cdot 1 + 9 \cdot 10 + 5 \cdot 10^2 + 2 \cdot 10^3 + 4 \cdot 10^4$

f. $4 \cdot 1 + 9 \cdot 10 + 5 \cdot 10^2 + 2 \cdot 10^3 + 4 \cdot 10^4 + 7 \cdot 10^5$

g. $4 \cdot 1 + 9 \cdot 10 + 5 \cdot 10^2 + 2 \cdot 10^3 + 4 \cdot 10^4 + 7 \cdot 10^5 + 2 \cdot 10^6$

h. What is the pattern of the sums?

Go Online
Video Tutor
www.successnetplus.com

17. Which of the following are identities?

a. $(-x)^1 \stackrel{?}{=} -x^1$

b. $(-x)^2 \stackrel{?}{=} -x^2$

c. $(-x)^3 \stackrel{?}{=} -x^3$

d. $(-x)^4 \stackrel{?}{=} -x^4$

e. $(-x)^5 \stackrel{?}{=} -x^5$

f. What is the pattern in the exponents?

> An identity is a statement that two expressions are equivalent under the basic rules of algebra.

This sand sculpture contains an estimated 10^{11} grains of sand.

Historical Perspective

A *googol* is a famous large number equal to 10^{100}. The mathematician Edward Kasner used this large number in a book he was writing in 1940. He asked his 9-year-old nephew, Milton Sirotta, for a name for the number. Milton replied, "Googol." The name stuck.

How large is a googol? Here is what it looks like.

10,000,000,000,000,000,000,000,000,000,000,000,000,000, 000,000,000,000,000,000,000,000,000,000,000,000,000,000, 000,000,000,000

A googol is much greater than the number of grains of sand on Earth or the number of known stars in the sky. In fact, some astronomers estimate that there are between 10^{72} and 10^{87} particles in the entire known universe. That is much less than a googol.

A googolplex is another number that is even greater than a googol. A googolplex looks like this.

$$10^{(10^{100})} \text{ or } 10^{\text{googol}}$$

You can write a googolplex with a 1 followed by a googol zeros. This number is so large that you cannot even write all the zeros. If you tried to write all the zeros of a googolplex in a book, the book would be larger than the entire universe!

Go Online
www.successnetplus.com

5.09 More Basic Rules of Exponents

There is a rule for dividing powers that have the same base.

For You to Do

1. Express $\frac{3^5}{3^3}$ as a power of 3.

2. Express $(2^4)^3$ as a power of 2.

3. Express $(xy)^4$ without using parentheses.

To divide two exponential expressions with the same base, such as 2^7 and 2^3, you can rewrite the exponents as repeated multiplication.

$$\frac{2^7}{2^3} = \frac{\overset{7 \text{ copies}}{\overbrace{2 \cdot 2 \cdot 2 \cdot 2 \cdot 2 \cdot 2 \cdot 2}}}{\underset{3 \text{ copies}}{\underbrace{2 \cdot 2 \cdot 2}}} = \frac{\overset{7-3 \text{ copies}}{\overbrace{2 \cdot 2 \cdot 2 \cdot 2 \cdot 2 \cdot 2 \cdot 2}}}{2 \cdot 2 \cdot 2} = 2^{7-3} = 2^4$$

You can cancel three copies of 2 in the numerator and three copies in the denominator. You are left with $7 - 3$, or 4, copies of 2 in the numerator.

For You to Do

4. Make a diagram like the one above to simplify $\frac{3^5}{3^3}$.

Theorem 5.2

For any number $a \neq 0$ and positive integers b and c where $b > c$,
$\frac{a^b}{a^c} = a^{b-c}$.

In this investigation, you will find a way to remove the restriction $b > c$.

For Discussion

5. Prove Theorem 5.2 by making a diagram like the one above to show that $\frac{a^b}{a^c} = a^{b-c}$. Assume that $b > c$ and $a \neq 0$.

6. How does your diagram change if $b < c$?

For You to Do

Compute each quotient, without a calculator.

7. $\dfrac{10^9}{10^8}$ **8.** $\dfrac{6^3 x^9}{3^3 2^2 x^5}$ **9.** $\dfrac{2^2}{2^5}$

To raise an exponent to another exponent, you can rewrite the exponents as repeated multiplication. For example, how many copies of 7 are in $(7^5)^3$?

$$(7^5)^3 = \underbrace{(7 \cdot 7 \cdot 7 \cdot 7 \cdot 7)}_{5 \text{ copies}} \cdot \underbrace{(7 \cdot 7 \cdot 7 \cdot 7 \cdot 7)}_{5 \text{ copies}} \cdot \underbrace{(7 \cdot 7 \cdot 7 \cdot 7 \cdot 7)}_{5 \text{ copies}} = 7^{5 \cdot 3} = 7^{15}$$

3 copies of 7^5

Each 7^5 includes five copies of 7. There are three copies of each 7^5, which gives a total of $5 \cdot 3$, or 15, copies of 7.

$$(7^5)^3 = 7^{5 \cdot 3} = 7^{15}$$

For You to Do

10. Make a diagram like the one above to simplify $(2^4)^3$.

These results lead to the third basic rule of exponents.

Theorem 5.3

For any number a and positive integers b and c, $(a^b)^c = a^{bc}$.

For You to Do

Expand each expression.

11. $(2^2)^3$ **12.** $(x^6)^7$

To write an expression, such as $(xy)^4$, without parentheses, multiply the expression by itself.

$$(xy)^4 = \underbrace{xy \cdot xy \cdot xy \cdot xy}_{4 \text{ copies}}$$

Remember that xy means $x \cdot y$. You can use AOAG to rearrange the factors. You can place all the x's together first, and then place all the y's together.

$$(xy)^4 = x \cdot y \cdot x \cdot y \cdot x \cdot y \cdot x \cdot y = \underbrace{x \cdot x \cdot x \cdot x}_{4 \text{ copies}} \cdot \underbrace{y \cdot y \cdot y \cdot y}_{4 \text{ copies}} = x^4 y^4$$

For You to Do

13. Make a diagram like the one above to simplify $\left(7a^2b\right)^3$.

Theorem 5.4

For any numbers a and b, and positive integer m, $(ab)^m = a^m b^m$.

Corollary 5.4.1

For any numbers a and b ($b \neq 0$) and positive integer m, $\left(\dfrac{a}{b}\right)^m = \dfrac{a^m}{b^m}$.

For Discussion

14. Prove Theorem 5.4 by making a diagram like the one above to show that $(ab)^m = a^m b^m$.

15. Prove Corollary 5.4.1 without making a diagram. (*Hint:* Use Theorem 5.4.)

For You to Do

Expand each expression.

16. $\left(10x^2\right)^3$ 17. $\left(a^3b\right)^{11}$ 18. $\left(\dfrac{4}{7}\right)^3$ 19. $\left(\dfrac{3x^3y^2}{wz^4}\right)^3$

Exercises Practicing Habits of Mind

Check Your Understanding

1. Suppose $A = c^3$ and $B = c^2$. Find two ways to write c^8 in terms of A and B.

2. Liz knows that 2^{10} is close to 1000. She estimates the value of 2^{21}. What do you suppose her estimate is?

3. Decide whether each expression equals 3^{15}, without using a calculator. Explain each result.

a. $(3^6)^9$

b. $(3^{10})(3^5)$

c. $(3^3)(3^5)$

d. $(3^{15})(3^1)$

e. $(3^5)(3^5)(3^5)$

f. $3^9 + 3^6$

g. $(3^5)^3$

h. $3^{14} + 3^{14} + 3^{14}$

i. $(3^3)^5$

j. $9(3^{13})$

k. $(3^5)^{10}$

l. $(3^1)^{15}$

4. Decide whether each expression equals 2^3, without using a calculator. Explain each result.

a. $\dfrac{2^6}{2^2}$

b. $\dfrac{2^6}{2^3}$

c. $(2^2)^1$

d. $\dfrac{(2^2)^5}{2^7}$

e. $\dfrac{2^9}{2^6}$

f. $\dfrac{2^9}{2^3}$

g. $\dfrac{2^7 2^8}{2^5}$

5. Use the fact that $2^8 = 256$. Find the units digit of 2^{16} and 2^{24}.

6. Find the units digit of $(19^3)^4$.

7. Find the units digit of $(2^5)^2 + (5^2)^2$.

On Your Own

8. In Lesson 5.08, you used a set of Russian nesting dolls. Recall that Doll 0 is 1 inch tall and that each doll is twice as tall as the doll before it. For example, Doll 1 is 2 inches tall, and Doll 2 is 4 inches tall. Now, consider two smaller dolls, Doll -1 and Doll -2.

-2 -1 0

a. How tall is Doll -1? How tall is Doll -2?

b. How tall is Doll -5?

9. **Standardized Test Prep** Simplify the expression $\dfrac{(2x^2y^3)^3}{4x^4y}$.

A. $\dfrac{1}{2}x^6y^6$

B. $2xy^5$

C. $\dfrac{1}{2}x^2y^8$

D. $2x^2y^8$

10. Decide whether each expression equals 5^6, without using a calculator. Explain each result.

Go Online
www.successnetplus.com

a. $5 \cdot 5 \cdot 5 \cdot 5 \cdot 5 \cdot 5$

b. $5^4 5^2$

c. $(5^3)(3^5)$

d. $\dfrac{5^{15}}{5^9}$

e. $\dfrac{(5^2)(5^2)(5^3)}{5}$

f. $5^5 + 5$

g. $\dfrac{5^{18}}{5^{12}}$

h. $(5^2)^3$

i. $(5^6)^1$

j. $(5^3)^3$

k. $\dfrac{(5^3)^3}{5^3}$

l. $5 + 5 + 5 + 5 + 5 + 5$

11. Use the fact that $4^6 = 4096$. Find the units digit of 4^7 and 4^{12}.

12. Write each expression as a single power of x.

a. $(x^2)^6$ b. $(x^2)^5$ c. $(x^3)^9$ d. $(x^{10})^{10}$

e. $\dfrac{x^8}{x^2}$ f. $\dfrac{x^9}{x^7}$ g. $\dfrac{1}{x^6}(x^{14})$

13. Simplify each expression.

a. $(7c)^2$

b. $(3x^2)^3$

c. $\left(\dfrac{2a}{3bc}\right)^4$

d. $\left(\dfrac{m^2 n^3}{p^4 q}\right)^{11}$

e. $\left(\dfrac{2v^3 w^2}{8v^2 w}\right)^3$

f. $4a^2\left(\dfrac{a^3}{2a^4}\right)^2$

A simplified expression has no parentheses and shows each base only once.

14. ZIP Codes in the United States are five-digit combinations of numbers, such as 48104 or 02134. How many possible five-digit ZIP Codes are there?

15. The United States Postal Service uses the ZIP + 4 Code that adds four extra digits at the end of a ZIP Code. If you live in ZIP Code 48104, your ZIP + 4 Code might be 48104-1126. How many possible nine-digit ZIP + 4 Codes are there? Can you find the result in two ways?

Maintain Your Skills

16. For each sequence, find a pattern. Use your pattern to write the next three terms in each sequence.

a. 256, 128, 64, 32, 16

b. 625, 125, 25

c. 27, 9, 3

d. $\dfrac{1}{8}$, $\dfrac{1}{4}$, $\dfrac{1}{2}$

e. 7^4, 7^3, 7^2

f. 3^3, 3^2, 3^1

g. $\left(\dfrac{1}{2}\right)^3$, $\left(\dfrac{1}{2}\right)^2$, $\left(\dfrac{1}{2}\right)^1$

THE WHITE
20500-0004
HOUSE

5.10 Zero and Negative Exponents

In Lessons 5.08 and 5.09, you learned the following three basic rules of exponents. For all numbers a and positive integers b and c,

Rule 1 $a^b \cdot a^c = a^{b+c}$

Rule 2 $\dfrac{a^b}{a^c} = a^{b-c}$, if $a \neq 0$ and $b > c$

Rule 3 $(a^b)^c = a^{bc}$

In each rule, there are annoying restrictions, such as b and c must always be positive integers. Also, for Rule 2, b must be greater than c.

The restrictions exist for the rules because there is no obvious way to describe how to calculate a zero or negative exponent. What does it mean to multiply a number by itself 0 times? What does it mean to multiply a number by itself -4 times?

Recall that in Chapter 1, you defined the meaning of a negative number by expanding an addition table. In Minds in Action below, Tony and Sasha explore the definition of a zero exponent. Their goal in developing the definition is to preserve the rules of exponents.

Minds in Action

Sasha and Tony are trying to find the value of 2^0.

Sasha $2^0 - 0$ makes sense to me. If 2^5 is five copies of 2, then 2^0 should be zero copies of 2, which is 0.

Tony   Yes, that makes some sense. Let's see whether it works with the first basic rule.

$$(a^b)(a^c) = a^{b+c}$$

Sasha   Alright. Using our example, we know that $(2^0)(2^5) = 2^{0+5}$.

Tony   We can use our definition that $2^0 = 0$ to calculate the value of the left side of the equation.

$$(2^0)(2^5) = (0)(32) = 0$$

Sasha   Finding the value of the right side is easy. $0 + 5 = 5$, so $2^{0+5} = 2^5 = 32$. Oh, no.

Tony   What?

Sasha   Well, now we have found that $0 = 32$, and that's obviously not right. I think we made a bad choice for our definition.

Tony   Hmm. We need another definition.

Sasha We want Theorem 5.1 to hold true, right? So, we want $(2^0)(2^5) = 2^{0+5}$.

2^{0+5} is just 2^5. So, we want $(2^0)(2^5) = (2^5)$.

Tony We have no choice. Divide each side of this equation by 2^5, and you have $2^0 = \dfrac{2^5}{2^5} = 1$.

Sasha So, 2^0 has to be 1. Otherwise, the rules we already know won't keep working.

> **Remember...**
>
> Theorem 5.1 says that if b and c are positive integers, then $a^b \cdot a^c = a^{b+c}$.

For Discussion

1. In the dialog, Sasha and Tony use the basic rule of multiplying exponents to find a definition of 2^0. Another way to find a definition of 2^0 is to use the basic rule for dividing exponents.

    $$\frac{a^b}{a^c} = a^{b-c}$$

    If you substitute $a = 2$, $b = 7$, and $c = 7$, you get the following equation.

    $$\frac{2^7}{2^7} = 2^{7-7}$$

    Explain why this approach produces the same definition that Sasha and Tony found, $2^0 = 1$.

Minds in Action

Tony and Sasha discuss possible definitions for 2^{-3}.

Tony Let's try to think this through instead of just guessing what 2^{-3} should be.

Sasha Alright. Well, we want our favorite rule to keep working.

$$(2^b)(2^c) = 2^{b+c}$$

Tony Well, what happens if we say $b = -3$ and $c = 3$?

Sasha I see where you're going. That's genius! Now we can say that $(2^{-3})(2^3) = 2^{-3+3} = 2^0$ since $-3 + 3 = 0$.

Tony Also, $2^0 = 1$, so we have $(2^{-3})(2^3) = 1$.

Sasha We can do what we did for 2^0. Solve for 2^{-3} as if it were an unknown.

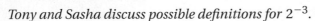
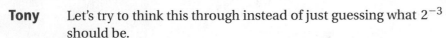

$$(2^{-3})(2^3) = 1$$
$$2^{-3} = \frac{1}{2^3}$$

So, $2^{-3} = \dfrac{1}{2^3}$.

Tony	That surprises me.
Sasha	I guess, but if 2^{-3} is going to satisfy the basic rules, that's the only definition that works.
Tony	That means $2^{-5} = \frac{1}{2^5}$, $2^{-6} = \frac{1}{2^6}$, and so on.
Sasha	So, a negative exponent is like dividing. If you have 2^{-3}, then you divide 1 by 3 factors of 2.
Tony	That makes sense. Exponentiation is just repeated multiplication and the opposite of multiplication is division.

For You to Do

2. How can you write $\frac{1}{2^{-3}}$ using only positive exponents?

You can formalize Tony and Sasha's work using these two definitions.

Definition

Zero exponent: If $a \neq 0$, then $a^0 = 1$.

Definition

Negative exponent: If $a \neq 0$, then $a^{-m} = \frac{1}{a^m}$.

> Do you understand why these statements are definitions rather than theorems? Are they the only possible definitions of zero and negative exponents?

For Discussion

3. Is the definition of negative exponents compatible with the definition of zero exponents? In other words, do the definitions satisfy the following equations?

- $2^0 = 2^{5+(-5)} = 2^5 \cdot 2^{-5}$
- $a^0 = a^{5+(-5)} = a^5 \cdot a^{-5}$
- $a^0 = a^{b+(-b)} = a^b \cdot a^{-b}$

For You to Do

Apply the basic rules to find the value of each variable. Check your results.

4. $2^5 \cdot 2^{-3} = 2^a$ 5. $2^5 \cdot 2^{-7} = 2^b$

6. $\frac{2^5}{2^7} = 2^c$ 7. $\frac{2^5}{2^{-7}} = 2^d$

8. $\frac{2^5}{2^c} = 2^8$

Exercises *Practicing Habits of Mind*

Check Your Understanding

A ratio table is similar to a difference table, except for the last column. A difference table has a Δ column that shows the difference between two consecutive rows. A ratio table has a $\div$ column that shows the ratio between two consecutive rows.

x	f(x)	$\div$
0	1	2
1	2	3
2	6	5
3	30	

For example, consider this ratio table. The 2 in the first row is the result of dividing the 2 in the second row by the 1 above it. Likewise, the 5 in the third row is the result of dividing 30 by 6. This table does not have constant ratios, since the numbers in the $\div$ column are not all the same.

For Exercises 1 and 2, copy and complete each table using the given function. Determine whether each table has a constant ratio.

1. $f(x) = 3^x$

x	3^x	$\div$
−3	■	■
−2	■	■
−1	■	■
0	■	■
1	■	■
2	■	■
3	■	

2. $g(x) = \left(\frac{1}{3}\right)^x$

x	$\left(\frac{1}{3}\right)^x$	$\div$
−3	■	■
−2	■	■
−1	■	■
0	■	■
1	■	■
2	■	■
3	■	

3. How are the tables in Exercises 1 and 2 related? Explain.

4. Dana says, "You can write any whole number as the sum of powers of 2 without ever repeating any of them."

Andrew replies, "Maybe. What about 13?"

Dana answers, "Let's see. 13 is $2^3 + 2^2 + 2^0$."

Andrew asks, "What about 17?"

Dana explains, "17 is $2^4 + 2^0$."

Is Dana correct? Write each number as a sum of the powers of 2.

a. 14 **b.** 15 **c.** 16 **d.** 31 **e.** 33

5. Take It Further Prove that Dana is correct for any positive integer n.

6. The multiplication table shows powers of ten, including 10^0, 10^1, 10^2, and so on along the axes. Each square in the table is the product of a number on the horizontal arrow and a number on the vertical arrow. For instance, the upper left corner contains 10^2, since $10^{-3} \cdot 10^5 = 10^{(-3)+5} = 10^2$. Copy and complete the table.

Multiplication Table

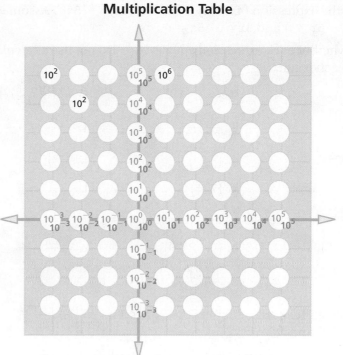

On Your Own

7. Write About It Compare your results in Exercise 6 to the following part of an addition table. How are the tables similar? Explain.

Addition Table

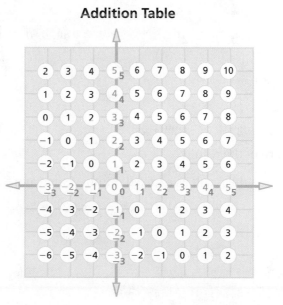

8. Simplify the expression $(4x + 5y - 6z)^0 + (3xy^2 - 5z)^0$. Assume that $4x + 5y - 6z \neq 0$ and $3xy^2 - 5z \neq 0$.

Go Online
www.successnetplus.com

9. Decide whether each expression equals 7^{-10}. Do not use a calculator. Explain each result.

   a. $\left(\frac{1}{7}\right)^{10}$ **b.** $7^{-4} \cdot 7^{-3}$ **c.** $(7^{13})(7^{-6})$

   d. $\frac{7^3}{7^{13}}$ **e.** $\frac{7^2}{7^3 7^4 7^4}$ **f.** $\frac{1}{7^{-10}}$

   g. $7^5 \cdot 7^{-2}$ **h.** $\left(\frac{1}{7^2}\right)^5$ **i.** $(7^5)^{-15}$

   j. $(7^5)^{-2}$ **k.** $(7^{-2})^5$ **l.** $\frac{1}{7^{10}}$

10. Write each expression as a single power of z.

   a. $(z^{-2})(z^4)$ **b.** $((z^3)^3)^{-3}$ **c.** $\frac{(z^2)(z^{-4})}{z^2}$

   d. $\frac{(z^0)^4}{z^{10}}$ **e.** $\frac{(z^7)^0}{(z^0)(z^{11})}$

11. Standardized Test Prep Simplify the expression $\dfrac{a^5 b^{-3}}{(a^2 b)^0} \cdot \dfrac{b^2}{a^{-4}}$, where $a \neq 0$ and $b \neq 0$.

   A. ab^{-1} **B.** $a^{-1}b^{-2}$ **C.** $a^9 b^{-1}$ **D.** $a^3 b$

Maintain Your Skills

12. Find each sum.

   a. 2^0 **b.** $2^0 + 2^1$ **c.** $2^0 + 2^1 + 2^2$

   d. $2^0 + 2^1 + 2^2 + 2^3$

   e. $2^0 + 2^1 + 2^2 + 2^3 + 2^4$

   f. $2^0 + 2^1 + 2^2 + 2^3 + 2^4 + 2^5$

   g. $2^0 + 2^1 + 2^2 + 2^3 + 2^4 + 2^5 + 2^6$

   h. What is the pattern of the results?

13. Find each sum. Express the result as a mixed number, such as $1\frac{2}{3}$.

   a. 2^0 **b.** $2^0 + 2^{-1}$ **c.** $2^0 + 2^{-1} + 2^{-2}$

   d. $2^0 + 2^{-1} + 2^{-2} + 2^{-3}$

   e. $2^0 + 2^{-1} + 2^{-2} + 2^{-3} + 2^{-4}$

   f. $2^0 + 2^{-1} + 2^{-2} + 2^{-3} + 2^{-4} + 2^{-5}$

   g. $2^0 + 2^{-1} + 2^{-2} + 2^{-3} + 2^{-4} + 2^{-5} + 2^{-6}$

   h. What is the pattern of the results?

Using large numbers can be difficult and confusing. For example, try comparing the masses of the sun and of Earth.

For Discussion

The mass of the sun is about 1,989,000,000,000,000,000,000,000,000,000 kilograms. The mass of Earth is about 5,973,700,000,000,000,000,000,000 kilograms.

1. Does the sun or Earth have the greater mass?

2. What methods did you use to compare the numbers to find the greater number?

To make this comparison much easier, you can use scientific notation to represent any real number uniquely.

Facts and Notation

A number written in scientific notation has the following form.

$$a \times 10^b, \text{ or } -a \times 10^b,$$

where $1 \leq a < 10$ and b is an integer.

The numbers 3.7×10^3 and -2.3×10^1 are written in scientific notation. The numbers -3700, 23, and 15×10^3 are not written in scientific notation.

> In algebra, you use · more often than × to represent multiplication. For example, $a \cdot b = a \times b$. Scientific notation is the exception. You write $a \times 10^3$, not $a \cdot 10^3$.

For You to Do

3. Why is 15×10^3 not written in scientific notation?

The restrictions on a may seem arbitrary, but they ensure that there is only one way to write any number in scientific notation.

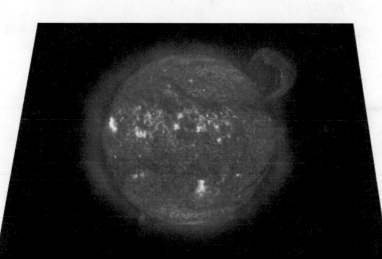

If the sun's circumference is about 2.7×10^6 mi, about how high did this solar flare reach?

Problem Write 47,000 and 0.0037 in scientific notation.

Solution To write a number in scienitific notation, you "pull out" multiples of 10 until you are left with a number between 1 and 10.

$$47{,}000 = 4700 \times 10$$
$$= 470 \times 10 \times 10$$
$$= 47 \times 10 \times 10 \times 10$$
$$= 4.7 \times 10 \times 10 \times 10 \times 10$$
$$= 4.7 \times 10^4$$

For numbers less than 1, you have to "put in" multiples of 10.

$$0.0037 = 0.037 \times \frac{1}{10}$$
$$= 0.37 \times \frac{1}{10} \times \frac{1}{10}$$
$$= 3.7 \times \frac{1}{10} \times \frac{1}{10} \times \frac{1}{10}$$
$$= 3.7 \times \left(\frac{1}{10}\right)^3$$
$$= 3.7 \times 10^{-3}$$

Exercises *Practicing Habits of Mind*

Check Your Understanding

1. Write each number in scientific notation.

   a. 1,340,000

   b. 0.00000609

   c. -3

   d. 0.9×10^5

   e. 379×10^5

   f. 602,000,000,000,000,000,000,000

   g. $(1.3 \times 10^5)(6 \times 10^7)$

   h. $(2.2 \times 10^2)(5 \times 10^4)$

2. Suppose there are approximately 6×10^9 usable telephone numbers in North America that are not assigned. If the government licenses 1×10^8 new telephone numbers each year, how many years will it take until North America runs out of telephone numbers?

3. Use the data from the beginning of this lesson.

    a. Write the masses of Earth and of the sun in scientific notation. Round each decimal to two decimal places. For example, you would write 1,234,567,890 as 1.23×10^9.

    b. How many times more massive is the sun than Earth?

4. Javan measures the length of his hair at the beginning and end of the month. He finds that his hair grows 1 inch per 30 days. How fast does his hair grow in miles per hour? Express your result in scientific notation.

5. Avogadro's number, 6.02×10^{23}, is an important number in chemistry. It represents the number of atoms (or molecules) in one mole of a substance. One mole of carbon weighs 12 grams. How many atoms of carbon do you have if you have 180 grams of carbon? Write your result in scientific notation.

On Your Own

6. Write each number in scientific notation.

    a. 10,000   **b.** 93,000

    c. 42,000,000   **d.** −86,500,000,000

    e. 0.073   **f.** 0.0000119

    g. $(3.5 \times 10^3)(2 \times 10^6)$ **h.** $(13 \times 10^2)(5 \times 10^8)$

    i. 13,100 + 2600   **j.** 400^3

7. Write each number in decimal notation.

    a. 1.86×10^6 **b.** 9.472×10^{10}

    c. 8.46×10^{-4} **d.** -3.77×10^{-10}

    e. 5.5×10^0 **f.** -4.09×10^{13}

8. Find the mean and median of the following numbers: 5×10^4, 5×10^3, 5×10^2, 5×10^1, 5. Which is easier to find, the mean or the median?

9. Write each number in scientific notation.

    a. 900×10^6

    b. 7300

    c. 0.8×10^9

    d. 50

    e. 110×10^2

    f. Find the median of the five numbers.

The Hubble Telescope sends about 120 gigabytes (giga $= 10^9$) of science data weekly.

10. **Standardized Test Prep** Simplify the expression
$$\frac{(4.5 \times 10^9)(7.0 \times 10^{-3})}{1.25 \times 10^2}.$$

A. 25,200

B. 36,000

C. 252,000

D. 31,500,000

In Exercises 11–13, you will find which quantity is greater:

• the number of stars in the universe

• the number of grains of sand on Earth

Which quantity do you think is greater?

11. Based on recent photographs from the Hubble Telescope, scientists estimate that there are 100 billion galaxies. The average galaxy contains 100 billion stars. About how many stars are in the universe? Write your result in scientific notation.

12. Use the following information to estimate the number of grains of sand on Earth.

• 8000 grains of sand are in 1 cubic centimeter of sand.

• 1 million cubic centimeters are in 1 cubic meter.

• 25 billion cubic meters of sand are on Earth.

About how many grains of sand are on Earth? Write your result in scientific notation.

13. Based on your estimates, which is greater, the number of stars in the universe or the number of grains of sand on Earth? By what factor is it greater?

There are 100 centimeters in a meter. Why are there 1,000,000 cubic centimeters in a cubic meter?

14. The planets are constantly in motion, so the distance between Earth and other astronomical objects is constantly changing. The table shows the average distance between Earth and a few astronomical objects.

Average Distance From Earth

Object	Distance (miles)
Moon	2.3×10^4
Mars	1.41×10^8
Neptune	2.7×10^9

SOURCE: United States National Aeronautics and Space Administration

A garden snail moves at the rate of about 3×10^{-2} miles per hour. If a garden snail could fly through space at that rate, how many hours would it take to reach the moon? To reach Mars? To reach Neptune?

15. Express each product in scientific notation.

   a. $(2 \times 10^5)^3$

   b. $(4 \times 10^7)^2$

   c. $(3 \times 10^2)^3$

   d. $(2.5 \times 10^4)^2$

   e. **Take It Further** How can you express the product $(a \times 10^b)^c$ in scientific notation?

16. Express each quotient in scientific notation.

   a. $\dfrac{9 \times 10^{10}}{3 \times 10^2}$

   b. $\dfrac{8 \times 10^8}{2 \times 10^2}$

   c. $\dfrac{6.4 \times 10^{12}}{4 \times 10^7}$

   d. $\dfrac{3.2 \times 10^{15}}{8 \times 10^5}$

17. Simplify each expression.

   a. 4×10^0

   b. $4 \times 10^0 + 9 \times 10^{-1}$

   c. $4 \times 10^0 + 9 \times 10^{-1} + 5 \times 10^{-2}$

   d. $4 \times 10^0 + 9 \times 10^{-1} + 5 \times 10^{-2} + 2 \times 10^{-3}$

   e. $4 \times 10^0 + 9 \times 10^{-1} + 5 \times 10^{-2} + 2 \times 10^{-3} + 4 \times 10^{-4}$

   f. $4 \times 10^0 + 9 \times 10^{-1} + 5 \times 10^{-2} + 2 \times 10^{-3} + 4 \times 10^{-4} + 7 \times 10^{-5}$

   g. $4 \times 10^0 + 9 \times 10^{-1} + 5 \times 10^{-2} + 2 \times 10^{-3} + 4 \times 10^{-4} + 7 \times 10^{-5} + 2 \times 10^{-6}$

   h. What is the pattern?

Go Online
Video Tutor
www.successnetplus.com

Mathematical 5B Reflections

In this investigation, you used the basic rules of exponents with positive, negative, and zero exponents. These questions will help you summarize what you have learned.

1. Some states in the United States make license plates by using combinations of two numbers, followed by two letters, and then two more numbers. 12AB34 is an example. Using this scheme, how many license plates are possible?

2. Simplify each expression without using a calculator.

   a. $x^2 \cdot x^3$

   b. $(3y)^2 \cdot y^5$

   c. $2^4 \cdot 5^4$

   d. $8^5 \cdot \left(\frac{1}{4}\right)^5$

   e. $a^8 \cdot b^5 \cdot a^{12}$

   f. $r \cdot r^2 \cdot (2t) \cdot r^3 \cdot (2t)^3$

3. Decide whether each expression equals 10^8 without using a calculator. Explain each result.

   a. $\left(10^2\right)^4$

   b. $10^5 \cdot 10^3$

   c. $10^5 + 10^3$

   d. $\left(10^4\right)^4$

   e. $2^8 \cdot 5^8$

   f. $10 \cdot 10^7$

   g. $\dfrac{10^{12}}{10^4}$

   h. $\dfrac{\left(10^2\right)^4}{10}$

The $(1 \times 10^6)(1 \times 10^3)$, or 1×10^9, spatulae on a gecko's feet allow it to climb up surfaces.

4. Write each expression as a single power of x.

   a. $(x^{-2})(x^5)$

   b. $\dfrac{x^4}{x^3}$

   c. $\dfrac{x^3}{x^4}$

   d. $\dfrac{(x^2)^{-3}}{x \cdot x^{-1}}$

   e. $\dfrac{(x^2)^0 \cdot (x^{-3})}{x^{-1}}$

5. Write each number in scientific notation.

   a. 82,000

   b. 0.00039

   c. $-28,000,000$

   d. 600×10^4

   e. 600×10^{-4}

   f. 0.031×10^5

6. What are the basic rules of exponents?

7. Why is 2^0 equal to 1?

8. How can you write $\dfrac{2^3 \cdot 2^{-2} \cdot 2^7}{(2^5)^3 \cdot 2^{-2}}$ as a number without exponents?

Vocabulary and Notation

In this investigation, you learned these terms and symbols.
Make sure that you understand what each one means
and how to use it.

- base
- cube of a number
- exponent
- negative exponent, $a^{\square m}$
- scientific notation
- square of a number
- zero exponent, a^0

Functions, Graphs, and Tables

In *Functions, Graphs, and Tables* you will learn to model a function using an equation, a graph, or a table. A function shows the relationship between input and output values. In a table you can see specific input and output values. A graph is a picture of the function.

By the end of this investigation, you will be able to answer questions like these.

1. How do you find a function that matches a table?

2. What is a recursive rule? How can you use recursion to define functions?

3. What is a recursive rule for the values in the table?

Input	Output
−1	6
0	5
1	4
2	3
3	2

You will learn how to

- determine whether a table represents a linear function

- fit a linear function to a table where possible

- calculate the outputs of a recursive rule

- describe a recursive rule

- find a recursive rule to match a table

You will develop these habits and skills:

- Use a Δ column to find whether a table represents a linear function.

- Use tables to answer questions involving recursive rules.

The position of the spring toy on each step depends on its position on the previous step.

Function tables can represent different types of functions. You can identify tables that represent linear functions by using an efficient method for finding the output values.

A **linear function** is a function with a graph that is a line. In For You to Explore, you will identify tables that represent linear functions.

For You to Explore

Determine whether each table represents a linear function. Plot the points on a graph to find collinear points.

1. Table A

x	A(x)
0	2
1	4
2	6
3	8
4	10

2. Table B

k	B(k)
0	1
1	4
2	7
3	10
4	13

3. Table C

a	C(a)
0	0
1	1
2	4
3	9
4	16

4. Table D

n	D(n)
0	−7
1	−4
2	−1
3	2
4	5

5. Table E

p	E(p)
0	−1
1	0
2	3
3	8
4	15

6. Table F

x	F(x)
0	4
1	2
2	1
3	$\frac{1}{2}$
4	$\frac{1}{4}$

7. Table G

x	G(x)
0	7
1	1
2	−5
3	−11
4	−17

8. Table H

n	H(n)
0	$\frac{4}{5}$
1	1
2	$1\frac{1}{5}$
3	$1\frac{2}{5}$
4	$1\frac{3}{5}$

9. Table I

x	I(x)
0	1
1	2
2	5
3	10
4	17

10. The table showing grain needed assumes that each person needs 323 kilograms of grain per year.

World Population

Year	Population (billions)
1975	4.08
1980	4.45
1985	4.86
1990	5.29
1995	5.72
2000	6.12

SOURCE: United Nations Secretariat

World Grain Production

Year	Grain Production (MMT)
1975	1237
1980	1429
1985	1647
1990	1768
1995	1708
2000	1842

SOURCE: United Nations Secretariat

Millet is a grain that farmers grow extensively in Africa and Asia. Farmers in India (photo below) use the wind to separate millet seeds from chaff.

World Grain Needed

Population (billions)	Grain Needed (MMT)
1	323
2	646
3	969
4	1292
5	1615

MMT stands for million metric tons. A metric ton is about 2205 pounds.

a. Use the tables to make predictions. Will there be enough grain to feed the world in 2020? In 2030?

b. What kinds of factors could change your predictions?

 **Exercises** *Practicing Habits of Mind*

On Your Own

11. Use Tables A and B.

Table A

Input	Output
0	2
1	4
2	6
3	8
4	10

Table B

Input	Output
0	$\frac{2}{3}$
1	2
2	6
3	18
4	54

a. Graph the data.

b. Based on your graphs, are the points collinear in Table A? In Table B?

12. You need to cut five 2 × 6's for the vertical roof supports shown in the diagram at the right. The boards are 16 inches apart. (The symbol " in the diagram stands for inches.) The length of the first board is 5 inches.

Roof Plan

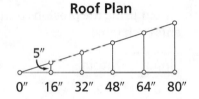

a. Calculate the lengths of the other four boards. Copy and complete the table.

Distance From End (in.)	Length of Board (in.)
16	5
32	■
48	■
64	■
80	■

b. How do you calculate the length at 32 inches? At 48 inches?

c. What pattern do you find in the table?

d. What is the slope of the roof?

13. **Standardized Test Prep** This table shows the water temperature in an industrial water heater. What is the rate of temperature increase in degrees per hour?

Industrial Water Heater

Time (h)	Water Temperature (°F)
0	72
3	87
6	102
9	117

A. 5 degrees per hour

B. 12.2 degrees per hour

C. 12.5 degrees per hour

D. 15 degrees per hour

Maintain Your Skills

Describe how to find each output using the previous output. Find a function that represents each table.

14.

Input	Output
0	0
1	3
2	6
3	9
4	12

15.

Input	Output
0	2
1	5
2	8
3	11
4	14

16.

Input	Output
0	−3
1	0
2	3
3	6
4	9

17.

Input	Output
0	−3
1	1
2	5
3	9
4	13

Go Online
Video Tutor
www.successnetplus.com

5.13 Constant Differences

When you make a table using a function, each input-output pair in the table represents a point on the graph of a function. For instance, the point (0, 1) is on the graph of the function that generates this table. The first row shows an input of 0 and an output of 1.

Input	Output	Δ
0	1	3
1	4	3
2	7	3
3	10	3
4	13	3
5	16	

> When you use integer inputs that increase by the same amount, you can spot patterns more easily.

To be certain that a table represents a linear function, you need to find the slope between all points in the table. That can take you a long time!

To make that work easier, you can add a third column to your table. Then you can keep track of the differences between **consecutive outputs** for evenly spaced inputs. You can record this difference in the Δ (delta) column in a table.

To find a Δ value, subtract the output in the given row from the output in the next row. For instance, in the highlighted portion of the table shown, 3 is in the Δ column next to 13, because 13 − 10 = 3.

For You to Do

1. Copy and complete the Δ column in each table.

Table A

Input	Output	Δ
0	0	■
1	1	■
2	4	5
3	9	■
4	16	■
5	25	

Table B

Input	Output	Δ
0	2	■
1	6	■
2	10	■
3	14	■
4	18	■
5	22	

In Table A, notice that the sum of the numbers highlighted in one row equals the number highlighted in the next row: 4 + 5 = 9. When the inputs are evenly spaced, this pattern occurs in every row of the table.

> This property is sometimes called the "up-and-over" property in tables with a Δ column.

In Lesson 5.12, you explored tables and their graphs. You learned that a table's graph lies on a line when the difference between consecutive outputs is the same.

Look for a pattern. Patterns can help you solve problems. In this table each output is 5 more than the previous output.

Input	Output	Δ
0	3	5
1	8	5
2	13	5
3	18	5
4	23	5
5	28	5
6	33	

Based on problems in Lesson 5.12, you might guess that the points with coordinates that are the input-output pairs in the table above are collinear. Graphing the points seems to confirm this fact.

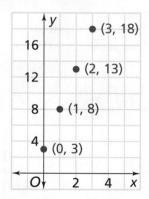

How do you know that the points in the graph fall on a line? The slope between any two points must be constant. To find the slope between the first two points (0, 3) and (1, 8), you can use the slope formula.

$$\text{slope} = \frac{y_2 - y_1}{x_2 - x_1} = \frac{8 - 3}{1 - 0} = \frac{5}{1} = 5$$

You can find the slope between the second and third points, (1, 8) and (2, 13), also.

$$\text{slope} = \frac{y_2 - y_1}{x_2 - x_1} = \frac{13 - 8}{2 - 1} = \frac{5}{1} = 5$$

The slopes are the same. You do not have to do all this work! The table has a difference column, so the value in the Δ column already shows the calculation for $y_2 - y_1$ for consecutive rows. The value equals 5. Since the input column increases by 1 from row to row, you know that $x_2 - x_1$ is always 1 for consecutive rows. The slope between any two points is 5.

What is the difference between rows that are not consecutive? Find the slope between (1, 8) and (4, 23). Explain.

To find a function that represents the values in the table below, look at how to find each output using the previous output. You can find the output 8 by adding 5 to the previous output, 3. The next output, 13, is the result of adding $8 + 5$, or $(3 + 5) + 5$. The calculations below show how to find the output 33.

Input	Output	Δ
0	3	5
1	8	5
2	13	5
3	18	5
4	23	5
5	28	5
6	33	

$$33 = 28 + 5$$
$$= (23 + 5) + 5 \qquad = 23 + 2 \cdot 5$$
$$= (18 + 5) + 2 \cdot 5 = 18 + 3 \cdot 5$$
$$= (13 + 5) + 3 \cdot 5 = 13 + 4 \cdot 5$$
$$= (8 + 5) + 4 \cdot 5 \quad = 8 + 5 \cdot 5$$
$$= (3 + 5) + 5 \cdot 5 \quad = 3 + 6 \cdot 5$$

In general, to find the output for input value n, start with 3 and add n 5's. The formula you write is $3 + 5n$. A function that agrees with the table is $f(n) = 3 + 5n$.

In fact, the graph of $f(n) = 3 + 5n$ is the same as the graph of $y = 3 + 5x$. They are both lines.

For You to Do

2. Explain how to find the number 28 in the table using the reasoning described above.

The tables below illustrate the "hockey stick method" for finding an output in any row. First, choose the row with the output you want to find. Next, add the first output and all Δ values in the rows above your chosen row. The sum equals the output for your chosen row.

Input	Output	Δ
0	1	3
1	4	3
2	7	3
3	10	3
4	13	3
5	16	

Input	Output	Δ
0	1	3
1	4	3
2	7	3
3	10	3
4	13	3
5	16	

Input	Output	Δ
0	1	3
1	4	3
2	7	3
3	10	3
4	13	3
5	16	

You can use the hockey stick method to find the output in a table. The output equals the sum of the numbers on the handle plus the number on the blade.

The number of times you add 3 to get the output is the same number as the input value.

Input	Output
2	$7 = 1 + 3 + 3 = 1 + 3(2)$
3	$10 = 1 + 3 + 3 + 3 = 1 + 3(3)$
4	$13 = 1 + 3 + 3 + 3 + 3 = 1 + 3(4)$
10	$1 + 3 + 3 + 3 + 3 + 3 + 3 + 3 + 3 + 3 + 3 = 1 + 3(10)$

In general, the output for input value n is $1 + 3n$, or $f(n) = 3n + 1$. The graph shows all the points on the same line, since the difference between outputs is 3. You can summarize these findings in a theorem.

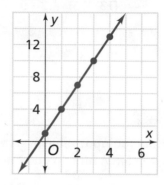

Theorem 5.5

When the differences between consecutive outputs in a table are the same, and the differences between consecutive inputs are the same, you can write a linear function for the table.

Habits of Mind

Detect patterns. When inputs increase by 1, the slope of the graph of the function is the same as the constant number in the difference column.

Exercises Practicing Habits of Mind

Check Your Understanding

1. Copy and complete the table for each rule.

   a. To find an output, multiply the input by 7. Then add 1.

   b. $x \mapsto x^2 - x - 4$

   c. $f(x) = -3x + 1$

   d. When 0 is the input, the output is 4. To find a new output, add 6 to the previous output.

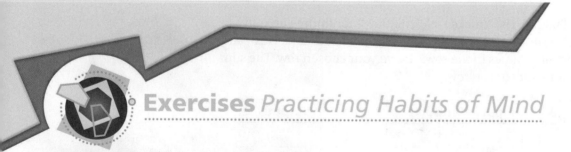

Input	Output	Δ
0	■	■
1	■	■
2	■	■
3	■	■
4	■	■
5	■	

2. Find a linear function that matches each table. If not possible, explain.

a.

Table L

Input, x	Output, $L(x)$
0	1
−1	−1
−2	−3
1	3
2	5

b.

Table M

Input, x	Output, $M(x)$
0	0
1	3
2	12
3	27
4	48

Habits of Mind

Look for relationships.
When a linear function such as $f(x) = ax + b$ matches a table, what is the relationship between a and b and the values in the table?

c.

Table N

Input, x	Output, $N(x)$
0	3
1	3
2	3
3	3
4	3

d.

Table O

Input, x	Output, $O(x)$
0	$-\frac{1}{3}$
1	0
2	$\frac{1}{3}$
3	$\frac{2}{3}$
4	1

3. In the table the variable a represents an arbitrary number.

Input	Output	Δ
0	3	a
1	■	a
2	■	a
3	■	a
4	$4a + 3$	a
5	■	

a. Copy and complete the table by finding the missing outputs in terms of a.

b. Find a linear function that matches the table.

How can you know that there is such a linear function?

4. In the table, variables a and b represent arbitrary numbers.

Input	Output	Δ
0	b	a
1	■	a
2	■	a
3	■	a
4	$4a + b$	a
5	■	■

a. Copy and complete the table in terms of a and b.

b. Find a linear function that matches the table.

c. You just proved Theorem 5.5 in parts (a) and (b). Explain.

5. Matt asks Emily for help in finding a function for Table P.

Matt says, "The difference between consecutive rows is always two, but I can't make any linear function work."

Emily replies, "That's because there is no linear function that works."

Table P

Input, n	Output, $P(n)$
0	1
1	-1
2	1
3	-1
4	1

a. Does this table represent a linear function? If so, what is it? If not, does this table of values contradict Theorem 5.5? Explain, using a graph or a diagram.

b. Describe the pattern in this table using words. Then write the pattern in $x \mapsto$ form.

On Your Own

6. **What's Wrong Here?** Matt decides whether a linear function generated Table D. Matt reasons, "Each output is two more than the previous output, so the function must be linear, but I can't make any rule work. For instance, $f(x) = 2x + 1$ works for the first few inputs, but it doesn't work for inputs 4 or 7."

Go Online
www.successnetplus.com

Table D

Input, x	Output, $f(x)$
0	1
1	3
2	5
4	7
7	9

a. What is Matt doing wrong? Explain.

b. Use plotted points or a diagram to show that the table does not match a linear function.

7. When a diver goes under water, the weight of the water exerts pressure on the diver. The table shows how the water pressure on the diver increases as the diver's depth increases.

Water Pressure on a Diver

Diver's Depth (ft)	Water Pressure (lb/in.²)
10	4.4
20	8.8
30	13.2
40	17.6
50	22.0

a. What is the water pressure on a diver at a depth of 60 feet? At a depth of 100 feet? Explain.

b. Write an equation describing the relationship between the depth D and the pressure P.

c. Use your equation in part (b) to determine the depth of the diver, assuming the water pressure on the diver is 46.2 pounds per square inch. Explain.

8. Copy and complete each table.

a.

Input	Output	Δ
0	■	6
1	■	6
2	■	6
3	■	6
4	13	6
5	■	

b.

Input	Output	Δ
0	1	■
1	3	■
2	9	■
3	27	■
4	81	■
5	243	

c.

Input	Output	Δ
0	−2	■
1	$-\frac{6}{5}$	■
2	$-\frac{2}{5}$	■
3	$\frac{2}{5}$	$\frac{4}{5}$
4	$\frac{6}{5}$	■
5	2	

d.

Input	Output	Δ
0	■	−2
1	■	−2
2	5	−2
3	■	−2
4	■	−2
5	■	

e. Which tables can you generate using a linear function?

f. Write a function for each table.

9. Emma cannot remember a linear function rule. She does remember that when 2 is the input, 3 is the output. When 4 is the input, 11 is the output. Does Emma remember enough to find a linear function rule? Explain.

10. Standardized Test Prep The table shows the annual salaries of company employees based on the number of years of employment. What is the annual salary of an employee who has just completed 10 years of service?

A. $46,500   B. $45,000

C. $43,500   D. $40,000

Annual Salary

Years of Employment	Salary
0	$30,000
1	$31,500
2	$33,000
3	$34,500
4	$36,000

11. Find a linear function for each situation.

a. Every even input gives an even output, and every odd input gives an odd output.

b. Every even input gives an odd output, and every odd input gives an even output.

c. Both even and odd inputs give odd outputs.

12. Without graphing, decide whether each table matches a linear function. For each table, graph the data and write a linear function, if possible.

a.

Table H

Input	Output
0	12
1	9
2	6
3	3
4	0

b.

Table I

Input	Output
0	11
1	3
2	2
3	1
4	−7

c.

Table J

Input	Output
0	12
1	6
2	3
3	$\frac{3}{2}$
4	$\frac{3}{4}$

d.

Table K

Input	Output
0	$\frac{1}{2}$
1	$1\frac{2}{3}$
2	$2\frac{5}{6}$
3	4
4	$5\frac{1}{6}$

Maintain Your Skills

13. Copy and complete each table. Find a linear function that gives the outputs.

a.

Input	Output	Δ
0	5	■
1	8	■
2	11	■
3	14	■
4	17	

b.

Input	Output	Δ
0	−7	■
1	−4	■
2	−1	■
3	2	■
4	5	

c.

Input	Output	Δ
0	12	■
1	9	■
2	6	■
3	3	■
4	0	

d.

Input	Output	Δ
0	r	s
1	■	s
2	■	s
3	■	s
4	■	

Go Online
Video Tutor
www.successnetplus.com

Recursive Rules

In Lesson 5.13 you used the hockey stick method to find a linear function, $x \mapsto 3 + 5x$, that matches this table.

Input	Output	Δ
0	3	5
1	8	5
2	13	5
3	18	5
4	23	5
5	28	5
6	33	

There is another way to describe this function rule. You can say, "The output for 0 is 3. For integer inputs that increase by 1, each output after the first one is 5 more than the previous output." This description of a function is an example of a **recursive rule,** an idea that is very useful in mathematics and science.

The first row in the table shows the starting number, or **base case,** 3. You can determine each row after the first row by looking at the row directly above it. Then follow the recursive rule of adding 5 to the previous output. The first several outputs are as follows.

> You can think of recursive rules as descriptions that tell how to get an output from previous outputs.

$$f(0) = 3$$
$$f(1) = f(0) + 5 = 3 + 5 = 8$$
$$f(2) = f(1) + 5 = 8 + 5 = 13$$

For You to Do

1. Describe a recursive rule that agrees with the table.

Input	Output
0	3
1	7
2	11
3	15
4	19
5	23
6	27

Find associations. Often you can associate what you learn in mathematics to things you see in everyday life. For example, a recursive rule produces patterns similar to patterns you see in nature.

Plants and trees often look as if they consist of smaller copies of themselves. A pine tree branch looks like the whole pine tree. A broccoli floret looks like a smaller version of the whole broccoli head. A recursive rule is similar, because the rule $f(n)$ contains a copy of itself, $f(n-1)$.

When you write a recursive rule, you tell how to get the next output from the previous output. For example, suppose you have a function f that matches the table shown. Instead of writing "The output for input 6 is the output for input 5 plus the difference 5," you can write the following equation.

$$f(6) = f(5) + 5$$

This reasoning works for other inputs, such as

$$f(5) = f(4) + 5$$
$$f(4) = f(3) + 5$$

n	$f(n)$	Δ
0	3	5
1	8	5
2	13	5
3	18	5
4	23	5
5	28	5
6	33	

The "backing up" method described here to find outputs does not work for the input 0. For 0, you need to find the output using the function equation. This statement of output is called the base case.

As the pattern continues, you get, for example,

$$f(127) = f(126) + 5$$

In general, $f(n) = f(n-1) + 5$. To calculate any output for function f, you need to use the function f itself. Suppose you have a function machine for f. If you open it, you would find another copy of the machine for function f.

To summarize the function using the recursive rule and base case, you write the following equation.

$$f(n) = \begin{cases} 3 & \text{if } n = 0 \\ f(n-1) + 5 & \text{if } n > 0 \end{cases}$$

For help defining a function recursively, see the TI-Nspire Handbook, p. 788.

For Discussion

2. Tony thinks that the recursive rule above defines a function that is the same as the linear function $x \mapsto 3 + 5x$. Is he correct? Test your answer with an input of $\frac{1}{2}$.

Example

Problem James saves $85. He wants to put it in a savings account so it will gain interest. Bank L makes the following offer: "If you keep your money with us, at the end of every year we'll give you $5." How much money will James have after 5 years if he invests in Bank L? Write a recursive rule that tells the amount of money James will have after *n* years.

Solution You can use a calculator to find the totals for the first few years. Enter the outputs in a table.

> For help showing the totals on a spreadsheet, see the TI-Nspire Handbook, p. 788.

Bank L

Year	James's Savings	Interest
0	$ 85	$5
1	$ 90	$5
2	$ 95	$5
3	$100	$5
4	$105	$5
5	$110	

At this point you can graph the results, or you can take a shortcut. Notice that the difference between consecutive outputs in the table is always $5. You can generate the table using a linear function. Since 5 is the value in the Δ column, you know that the graph has a slope of 5. Since the output for 0 is 85, $f(n) = 85 + 5n$.

For Discussion

3. Across the street from Bank L is Bank E. It offers James the following investment plan: "Every year, we'll add 5% of the money you had the previous year to your account." James sets up this table to explore Bank E's plan.

Copy and complete the table, rounding to the nearest cent. Which bank offers the greater return on James's money in the short run? In the long run?

Bank E

Year	James's Savings	Interest
0	$85	$4.25
1	▪	▪
2	▪	▪
3	▪	▪
4	▪	▪
5	▪	

> This rule is recursive, but it is different from the previous one. The resulting table does not have constant differences, so it cannot be matched with a linear function. However, can you still find a pattern?

Exercises *Practicing Habits of Mind*

Check Your Understanding

1. Copy and complete Table 1 using each of the following rules.

   a. To get a new output, add 4 to the previous output.

   b. To get a new output, multiply the previous output by 3.

   c. To get a new output, multiply the previous output by 2 and then add 2.

   d. To get a new output, multiply the input by 4 and then add 2.

Table 1

Input	Output
0	2
1	6
2	■
3	■
4	■
5	■

2. Which of the tables generates a linear function? Find a linear function for each table if possible.

   a. **Table 2**

Input	Output
0	8
1	4
2	2
3	1
4	$\frac{1}{2}$

   b. **Table 3**

Input	Output
0	5
1	7
2	9
3	11
4	13

   c. **Table 4**

Input	Output
0	−3
1	−1
2	1
3	3
4	5

   d. **Table 5**

Input	Output
0	3.4
1	34
2	340
3	3,400
4	34,000

3. Write a recursive rule for each table in Exercise 2.

4. Adam proposes that his mother changes his allowance according to the following rule: "The first week, you'll only give me $.02. Then each week after the first week, you'll pay twice what you paid the week before." He explains that even though this is less than the $5 per week he gets now, he will feel better because he will always get more than he got the previous week.

    a. If Adam's mother agrees with him, how much will Adam receive in the fifth week?

    b. How much will his allowance be in the tenth week? In the fifteenth week?

5. In Exercise 4, Adam tries to convince his mother to change his allowance. Adam's mother offers the following plan instead: "The first week you get $.16. Then each week after the first week you get $1.00 plus 75% of the previous week's allowance."

    a. Make a table that shows how much Adam will get for each of the first five weeks.

    b. How much will he get in the tenth week? In the fifteenth week?

    c. Is his mother's plan a better deal for Adam than his plan?

6. Adam makes a last attempt to outsmart his mother. He explains, "We'll use the same plan you proposed, except instead of starting with $.16, I'll start with $10."

Adam used to get $5 per week for allowance.

    a. Make a table that shows how much Adam will get each of the first five weeks.

    b. How much will he get in the tenth week? In the fifteenth week?

    c. Is Adam's new plan a good deal for Adam in the short run? In the long run?

7. Maria knows a mystery function g. She says, "First of all, $g(0) = 1$. Next, to get any output, multiply the input by the previous output. For example,

$$g(5) = 5 \cdot g(4)$$
$$g(6) = 6 \cdot g(5)$$
$$g(15) = 15 \cdot g(14)$$

and so on."

Make a table showing the first six entries for Maria's function. Can you find a simple rule that matches the table?

8. Do these two functions produce the same output for every nonnegative integer input? Make a table for each rule.

Go Online
www.successnetplus.com

$f: \quad x \mapsto \frac{x}{3} - \frac{2}{3}$

$g:$ When the input is 0, the output is $-\frac{2}{3}$. To get each new output, add $\frac{1}{3}$ to the previous output.

9. Dana's parents start saving money for her college education. They deposit $5000 in a fund that earns 10% interest at the end of each year. Write a recursive rule that describes how the amount of money increases over time. How much money will Dana's parents have after 3 years?

10. **Standardized Test Prep** Zack charges $2.50 per hour for baby-sitting one child. He charges $.75 per hour for each additional child. Which table shows Zack's hourly charges for baby-sitting?

A.

Number of Children	Hourly Charge
1	$2.50
2	$3.25
3	$3.25

B.

Number of Children	Hourly Charge
1	$3.25
2	$4.00
3	$4.75

C.

Number of Children	Hourly Charge
1	$2.50
2	$3.25
3	$4.00

D.

Number of Children	Hourly Charge
1	$3.25
2	$4.00
3	$4.00

11. Anna earns money by raking leaves. She buys a rake that costs $20. For each lawn she rakes, she earns $6.

a. Make a table using the number of lawns as the input. The amount of money she makes is the output. Calculate how much money Anna earns when she rakes 0 to 5 lawns.

Anna will lose money when she does not rake any lawns.

b. Describe the pattern in the output values. Can a linear function generate this table?

c. Anna wants to buy a video game that costs $54.99. How many lawns will she need to rake to earn that amount?

12. Dana's grandparents invest $5500 in an educational fund. The fund earns 6% interest at the end of each year. Write a recursive rule that describes how the amount of money will grow over time. How much money will Dana's grandparents have after 3 years? Round to the nearest penny.

13. You can make patterns of shapes by connecting matchsticks. Stage 1 is one square. You can obtain each consecutive stage by adding a square to the side of the previous stage. Draw a diagram showing Stages 4 and 5. Copy and complete the table. Write a recursive rule that describes this pattern.

Matchsticks Table

Stage	Number of Matchsticks
1	4
2	7
3	■
4	■
5	■

Maintain Your Skills

Make a table for each recursive rule. Use the integers 0 to 4 for input values. If possible, find a linear function that generates each table.

		Inputs	**Output**
14.	**a.** Rule A	$\begin{cases} 0 \\ 1 \text{ to } 4 \end{cases}$	3 6 more than the previous output
	b. Rule B	$\begin{cases} 0 \\ 1 \text{ to } 4 \end{cases}$	−4 6 more than the previous output
	c. Rule C	$\begin{cases} 0 \\ 1 \text{ to } 4 \end{cases}$	$\frac{1}{2}$ 6 more than the previous output
	d. Rule D	$\begin{cases} 0 \\ 1 \text{ to } 4 \end{cases}$	3 6 times the previous output

		Inputs	**Output**
15.	**a.** Rule 1	$\begin{cases} 0 \\ 1 \text{ to } 4 \end{cases}$	3 3 more than the previous output
	b. Rule 2	$\begin{cases} 0 \\ 1 \text{ to } 4 \end{cases}$	3 6 less than the previous output
	c. Rule 3	$\begin{cases} 0 \\ 1 \text{ to } 4 \end{cases}$	3 $\frac{1}{2}$ more than the previous output
	d. Rule 4	$\begin{cases} 0 \\ 1 \text{ to } 4 \end{cases}$	3 $\frac{1}{2}$ times the previous output

Go Online
Video Tutor
www.successnetplus.com

5.15 Constant Ratios

In Lesson 5.13, you learned that a table of consecutive outputs for a linear function has constant differences. This fact gives you an efficient way to identify tables that you can match with a linear function.

In this lesson, you will learn that consecutive outputs of exponential functions also reveal a pattern that can help you match a function to a function table.

In-Class Experiment

For each exponential function $f(x) = a \cdot b^x$, make an input-output table. Use whole-number inputs from 0 to 5.

1. $f(x) = 10(3)^x$ **2.** $g(x) = 4(3)^x$

3. $h(x) = 3(3)^x$ **4.** $j(x) = 10(6)^x$

5. $k(x) = 4(6)^x$ **6.** $m(x) = 3(6)^x$

7. $n(x) = 10(0.5)^x$ **8.** $p(x) = 4(0.5)^x$

9. $q(x) = 3(0.5)^x$

> You may want to use a calculator.

Make conjectures about the tables of exponential functions. Think about how to describe each table using a recursive rule. Where in the table do you find a and b?

> For example, in your first table, where do you find 10? Where do you find 3 in the table?

Minds in Action

Sasha and Tony try to match a function to this table.

Table 6

Input, x	Output, y
0	4
1	6
2	9
3	13.5
4	20.25

Tony   First, let's see whether the function could be linear. 6 – 4 is . . .

Tony scribbles some calculations on his paper.

Tony Look, this can't be matched with a linear function, because the Δ value isn't a constant.

Tony rewrites the table with the Δ column.

Input, x	Output, y	Δ
0	4	2
1	6	3
2	9	4.5
3	13.5	6.75
4	20.25	

Sasha That's right. Let's try dividing consecutive rows. $\frac{6}{4}$ is 1.5, and $\frac{9}{6}$ is also 1.5.

Tony Oh, yes, and $\frac{13.5}{9} = 1.5$. Also, $\frac{20.25}{13.5} = 1.5$.

Sasha So, the Δ value isn't a constant, but if I divide outputs instead of subtract them, I get a constant value in the division column.

Sasha makes a new table with a ÷ column.

Input, x	Output, y	÷
0	4	1.5
1	6	1.5
2	9	1.5
3	13.5	1.5
4	20.25	

Recall the up-and-over property from Lesson 5.13. In this table, everything is the product, instead of the sum, of the up-and-over values.

Tony The up-and-over property works here too, except everything is the product of the up-and-over values, instead of the sum.

$$6 = 4 \cdot 1.5$$

$$9 = 6 \cdot 1.5$$

$$13.5 = 9 \cdot 1.5$$

$$\vdots \quad \vdots \quad \vdots$$

Sasha   Well, since the up-and-over property works, so does the hockey stick method, except that you start with the number on the blade and multiply by the numbers on the handle.

Input, x	Output, y	÷
0	4	1.5
1	6	1.5
2	9	1.5
3	13.5	1.5
4	20.25	

To get the output for 3 using this method, you start with 4 and then multiply repeatedly by 1.5. The output for 3 is $4 \cdot (1.5)^3$.

Tony   The output for 4 is $4 \cdot (1.5)^4$, and . . .

Sasha   That's it! The rule $x \mapsto 4 \cdot (1.5)^x$ matches the table.

Tony and Sasha both check a few values of x.

Sasha   You know, finding exponential functions is a lot like finding linear functions. When I want to find a linear function, I subtract one output from the next output.

Tony   In exponential tables, though, the differences aren't constant, but the consecutive ratios always give the same number.

Sasha   Look, the constant ratio is the number that I raise "to the x" in the function.

Tony   It's kind of like we change addition to multiplication and multiplication to "power-raising." Instead of "4 plus 1.5 times x," we get something like "4 times 1.5 to the x."

Sasha   This needs more thought.

Tony and Sasha wander down the hall and ponder the situation.

> You can write this function recursively.
>
> $$f(x) = \begin{cases} 4 & \text{if } x = 0 \\ f(x-1) \cdot 1.5 & \text{if } x > 0 \end{cases}$$

> A ratio table shows a **constant ratio** if all the values in the ÷ column are equal.

For Discussion

10. In the dialog, Tony says, "The up-and-over property works here, too, except everything is the product of the up-and-over values, instead of the sum." How could Tony have reached that conclusion?

11. Sasha replies, "Well, since the up-and-over property works, so does the hockey stick method, except that you start with the number on the blade and multiply by the numbers on the handle." Why does the multiplication up-and-over property imply that the multiplication hockey stick method works?

12. Does Sasha's "4 times 1.5 to the x" work when $x = 0$?

For You to Do

13. Make a table for the function $g(x) = 5 \cdot \left(\frac{1}{2}\right)^x$. Use input values between 1 and 5. What is the constant ratio?

Exercises Practicing Habits of Mind

Check Your Understanding

1. Use Sasha's and other methods to determine whether you can match each table with a linear function, exponential function, or neither. Find the linear or exponential function that generates the table, if one exists.

> Model each function using your function modeling language.

a. Table 1

Input	Output
0	3.12
1	4.52
2	5.92
3	7.32
4	8.72

b. Table 2

Input	Output
0	19
1	40.09
2	84.59
3	178.48
4	379.6

c. Table 3

Input	Output
0	1
1	1
2	3
3	7
4	13

2. Find a linear, quadratic, or exponential function that matches each table.

a. Table 4

Input	Output
0	5
1	4
2	1
3	−4
4	−11

b. Table 5

Input	Output
0	3
1	6
2	12
3	24
4	48

c. Table 6

Input	Output
0	2
1	−1
2	−4
3	−7
4	−10

Go Online
www.successnetplus.com

d. Table 7

Input	Output
0	0
1	2
2	8
3	26
4	80

e. Table 8

Input	Output
0	$\frac{1}{3}$
1	$\frac{5}{6}$
2	$1\frac{1}{3}$
3	$1\frac{5}{6}$
4	$2\frac{1}{3}$

f. Table 9

Input	Output
0	1
1	3
2	9
3	19
4	33

3. This exercise is the same as Exercise 2, except that a and b can be any number. Find a function that matches each table.

a. Table 10

Input, x	Output, y
0	2
1	$2 + a$
2	$2 + 2a$
3	$2 + 3a$
4	$2 + 4a$

b. Table 11

Input, x	Output, y
0	a
1	ab
2	ab^2
3	ab^3
4	ab^4

4. In a TV show, the main character, Ian, had a bank account with a balance of only $.93. Ian was frozen for a thousand years. His balance of $.93 increased by 2.25% every year.

a. Write a recursive function that describes how much money Ian had after n years.

b. Use the function in part (a). How can you calculate the amount of money Ian had when he woke up? (*Hint:* Do not actually calculate the value unless you have all day!)

c. Explain why you can use the function $IAN(x) = 0.93(1.0225)^x$ to calculate how much money was in Ian's account after x years. (*Hint:* It may be useful to compare this function with the function you found in part (a).)

d. How much money did Ian have when he woke up?

5. Decide whether you can match each table with a linear function, exponential function, or neither. Find a linear or exponential function that generates the table, if one exists.

a. **Table D**

Input	Output
0	−2
1	1
2	4
3	7
4	10

b. **Table E**

Input	Output
0	5
1	4
2	1
3	−4
4	−11

c. **Table F**

Input	Output
0	8
1	5.5
2	3
3	0.5
4	−2

d. **Table G**

Input	Output
0	0.5
1	1
2	2
3	4
4	8

6. Find a rule that shows the relationship between x and y in the table at the right.

7. **Write About It** Is it possible to have an exponential rule in which every even input gives an even output and every odd input gives an odd output? If it is possible, find the rule. If not, explain.

8. Suppose Jon has 64 mg of caffeine in his bloodstream. After one hour, Jon has 48 mg of caffeine in his bloodstream.

   a. Find a linear relationship for the situation. Then find an exponential relationship for the situation.

   b. Use tables to show the linear and exponential relationships. For inputs, use 0 to 4 hours.

   c. Graph each relationship on the same coordinate plane.

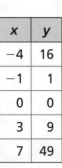

x	y
−4	16
−1	1
0	0
3	9
7	49

9. A recursive rule defines the first three stages of a sequence of shapes. The first shape is an upward-pointing triangle. To find the next shape, draw a downward-pointing triangle in the middle of every upward-pointing triangle.

Stage 1

Stage 2

Stage 3

Find a rule that gives the number of upward-pointing triangles at each stage. In Stage 1, there is only one larger triangle, and it is pointing upwards. In Stage 2, there are four smaller triangles, three of which are pointing upwards, and so on.

> Only count the smallest triangles at each stage.

a. Draw Stage 4 of this sequence. Using your drawing and the drawings above, copy and complete this table.

Stage	Number of Upward-Pointing Triangles
1	1
2	3
3	■
4	■

b. Find a function that matches the table in part (a).

c. **Take It Further** Find a function that has the number of downward-pointing triangles for each stage as its output.

10. Standardized Test Prep What is the first term in this exponential sequence that is an integer greater than 1? ■ , ■ , ■ , 64, 256, 1024, 4096, . . .

A. $\frac{1}{4}$

B. 1

C. 4

D. 16

11. Use these tables from Lesson 5.12 and the methods for finding linear and exponential functions in this lesson. Assume that the grain need per person is 323 kg per year.

World Population

Year	Population (billions)
1975	4.08
1980	4.45
1985	4.86
1990	5.29
1995	5.72
2000	6.12

SOURCE: United Nations Secretariat

World Grain Production

Year	Grain Production (MMT)
1975	1237
1980	1429
1985	1647
1990	1768
1995	1708
2000	1842

SOURCE: United States Department of Agriculture

World Grain Demand

Population (billions)	Grain Demand (MMT)
1	323
2	646
3	969
4	1292
5	1615

a. Are any of these tables linear, or almost linear? Are any of these tables exponential, or almost exponential?

b. If your results from part (a) suggest a linear or exponential pattern, extend the table according to the pattern. Add at least 5 values to each table.

c. Based on your approximations, will there be enough grain for the world in 2010? In 2025? Explain.

d. Do you think there will be more or less grain per person in 2050 than there is today? Explain.

For Exercises 12 and 13, let $f(x) = 2x + 10$ and $g(x) = 5x + 7$.

12. Find each value.

   a. $f(2)$

   b. $g(2)$

   c. $f\left(\frac{1}{2}\right)$

   d. $f(g(2))$

   e. $g(f(2))$

   f. $f\left(g\left(\frac{1}{2}\right)\right)$

13. Sketch each graph.

   a. f

   b. g

   c. $h(x) = f(g(x))$

   d. $j(x) = g(f(x))$

5.16 Compound Interest

Banks set a rate of growth for savings accounts, or the annual percentage rate (APR). They also set rules about how the account grows in value.

You can also call the APR the growth rate.

Minds in Action

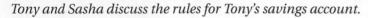

Tony and Sasha discuss the rules for Tony's savings account.

Tony It says here that I'll make 3% every year on the money in this savings account. The bank pays interest at the end of every year.

Sasha Is 3% a lot? It doesn't seem like much. How much did you put into the account?

Tony I invested $600.

Sasha Okay, so at the end of the year they'll give you 3% of $600, which is $18.

Tony That's not very much, but they say that the longer I leave the money in there, the more interest the account will earn.

Sasha So, you'll make $18 per year. That's not a big deal.

Tony No, I'll make more than $18 from then on. After one year, I won't have $600 anymore. I'll have $618. So, the next time you figure out my interest, you'll have to use $618, instead of $600, as your starting point.

Sasha Alright, at the end of the second year, they'll give you 3% of $618, which is $18.54.

Tony You could keep doing that over and over again. I can think of a recursive rule for this calculation. If I start a year with d dollars, at the end of the year they will pay me $d \cdot (0.03)$ in interest. That's a total of $d \cdot (1.03)$.

Sasha You start a year with d and end it with $d \cdot (1.03)$. That's just multiplying.

Tony Right, that makes the rule exponential. You are multiplying by 1.03 every year.

Sasha That's nice. So, the 1 in 1.03 represents the money you already had?

Tony Right, and the 0.03 is the interest the bank gives me for letting them use my money.

Sasha So, how would you figure out how much you have after 10 years?

You can write the rule like this.

$$b(t) = \begin{cases} 600 \text{ if } t = 0 \\ b(t-1) \cdot (1.03) \\ \quad \text{if } t > 0 \end{cases}$$

Tony   I take my $600 and keep multiplying by 1.03. Repeat this ten times using this equation.

$$600(1.03)^{10} = 806.35$$

Sasha   That's not bad. Still, it seems like a long time to put your money away for $200.

Tony   For every $3 I put in, I get about $1 back in interest after 10 years, no matter how much I put in. I've got $600 to invest now, but maybe I can invest a little more next year.

Sasha   I wonder how different the amount would be if the bank doubled the interest rate. If you make $200 at 3% interest, do you make $400 at 6% interest?

Most bank accounts, such as savings accounts and certificates of deposit (CDs), pay interest periodically. At the end of the period, the bank calculates the interest based on the current balance and adds the interest to the account.

For the next period, the bank calculates interest on the current balance, including the previously paid interest. Even interest earns interest! When you calculate interest this way, you earn **compound interest.** The interest grows at an exponential rate.

For Discussion

1. How much will Tony earn on a $600 investment after 10 years at 6% interest per year?

More Frequent Compounding

Generally, banks do not calculate compound interest annually. They may compound the interest every three months, monthly, daily, or even more frequently.

To calculate compound interest, you divide the annual percentage rate of interest into equal parts. The number of parts equals the number of times you calculate interest during the year. You use one of the parts to find the interest.

If two accounts have the same interest rate, the account that is compounded more frequently earns more money. For example, consider Tony's 3% APR account. If you compound it quarterly instead of annually, the growth rate is 0.75% per quarter (3% divided by 4 quarters).

Using Tony and Sasha's reasoning, you multiply the amount in Tony's savings account by 1.0075 each quarter. In 10 years, or 40 quarters, Tony will have $600(1.0075)^{40}$ dollars, or about $809. By choosing an account that is compounded quarterly, Tony will earn slightly more money.

Example 1

Problem Sasha reads an advertisement from BigBank that offers a 2.9% APR savings account compounded monthly. Over 10 years, how does this account compare to Tony's 3% APR account that is compounded annually?

Solution Determine how much money Sasha will have at the end of 10 years at BigBank. You can divide the APR of 2.9% into 12 equal parts, so that you multiply her total by $\frac{0.029}{12}$ each month. At the end of 10 years, her account will be compounded 120 times (10 · 12), so that her total will be the following.

$$600 \cdot \left(1 + \frac{0.029}{12}\right)^{120} \approx 801.58$$

This account earns only a few dollars less than the $806.35 that Tony's 3% APR account earns.

For Discussion

2. Which is better to have, an account at 6% APR compounded annually, or an account at 5.9% APR compounded monthly?

Example 2

Problem Tony invests $600 in a CD that earns 6% APR, compounded annually. How many years will it take for the money in his account to double?

Solution At the end of N years, Tony has $600(1.06)^N$ dollars.

You want to find the value of N, such that

$$1200 = 600 \cdot (1.06)^N$$

For now, you do not know a simple way to solve this equation for an exact value of N. But you can approximate a value for N by guessing, testing, and then refining your guess.

A CD is a certificate of deposit, which gives higher interest in exchange for a guarantee that you will not withdraw the money before a set date.

$1200 Goal

Guess, N (years)	Account Balance ($)	The actual N is . . .	The next guess should be . . .
5	802.94	higher	more than 5
20	1924.28	lower	between 5 and 20
10	1074.51	higher	between 10 and 20 (near 10)
11	1138.98	higher	between 11 and 20 (closing in)
12	1207.32	correct	

The value $N = 12$ is the solution. Even though there is a number N between 11 and 12 that solves the algebra equation, keep in mind that this bank account compounds annually, so there is no increase in the account value between 11 and 12 years. This graph shows the value in Tony's account each year for the first 20 years.

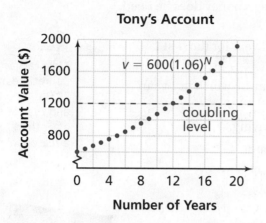

Tony's Account

With a calculator you can find that $N \approx 11.896$ solves the equation $1200 = 600 \cdot (1.06)^N$. However, that is not the correct answer for an actual bank account!

For Discussion

3. How long will it take for Tony's account to grow to $2400? To $4800? Explain.

Exercises *Practicing Habits of Mind*

Check Your Understanding

1. Jesse's savings account earns 2.5% APR compounded annually. His starting balance is $1200.

  a. How much money will Jesse have in the account after 1 year? After 2 years?

  b. Write a formula that gives Jesse's balance after N years.

  c. How much money will Jesse have in the account after 2 years and 9 months? Explain.

2. **Write About It** Tony earns about $200 in interest over 10 years using the savings account in the dialog. Will it take more or less time for Tony to earn the next $200 in interest? Explain.

3. Kevin saves money so that he will have $30,000 in 5 years. If his investment earns 6% interest, compounded annually, how much money does he need to invest today to have $30,000 in 5 years?

4. Suppose a car depreciates in value about 20% each year for the first 5 years.

   a. How much will a new car that costs $20,000 today be worth in 1 year? In 2 years?

   b. Write a rule for the car's value after N years of driving.

   c. Will the car ever be worth less than $1000? Explain.

Most cars actually depreciate more than 20% during the first year, and then less than 20% after that. About 20% is a reasonable average.

On Your Own

5. Use a calculator and sketch the graph of $y = 500(1.08)^x$ using the domain $0 \leq x \leq 20$. Describe a situation that this graph represents.

6. Ariela puts $500 in an investment account at 9% APR, compounded annually. After how many years will she be closest to doubling her starting investment?

7. Ariela wonders how the growth of her investment changes with higher or lower interest rates. Copy and complete the table below. For each interest rate, find the number of years after which Ariela will be closest to doubling her starting $500 investment.

Some cars eventually appreciate, or gain, in value.

Doubling Time

APR (%)	Number of Years Needed to Double Investment
3	▪
4	▪
5	▪
6	12
7	▪
8	▪
9	▪
10	▪
12	▪

Go Online
www.successnetplus.com

8. Many financial advisors use the Rule of 72 when offering advice about long-term investments.

The Rule of 72 To find the number of years it takes to double an investment's value, divide 72 by the interest rate. For example, the amount of time it takes to double an investment at 6% interest is about $\frac{72}{6}$, or 12 years.

a. How does the Rule of 72 compare to the results from Exercise 7?

b. According to the Rule of 72, how long will it take a credit card balance to double if its interest rate is 18% APR?

c. If Ariela invests $500 in an account at 9% APR for 40 years, how many times will her money double in value? How much money will she have after 40 years?

9. **Take It Further** Sketch or describe the graph of the following function.

$$y = (-1)^x$$

Include noninteger values of x in the domain, such as $\frac{1}{3}$. Notice that some values, such as $\frac{1}{2}$, cannot be in the domain.

10. **Standardized Test Prep** How much is a $100,000 investment worth after 3 years with 2.4% interest compounded annually? Round to the nearest dollar.

A. $102,400

B. $107,200

C. $107,374

D. $124,000

Maintain Your Skills

11. Suppose you invest $1000. Calculate the total value of each account.

a. 12 years, 2.5% APR compounded annually

b. 6 years, 5% APR compounded semiannually

c. 3 years, 10% APR compounded quarterly

12. Toni enters a contest with a $10,000 first prize. She will invest the winnings for 2 years. How much will she earn in 2 years in an account with each interest rate compounded annually?

a. 1% APR

b. 2% APR

c. 3% APR

d. 4% APR

e. 6% APR

f. 8% APR

Graphs of Exponential Functions

There are two types of exponential behavior, **exponential growth** and **exponential decay.**

Exponential growth

The amount of money in an interest-bearing bank account increases exponentially over time. In Lesson 5.16, you used a scatter plot for the amount of money in an account bearing 6% interest. If the value of N can be any positive number, you can draw this smooth graph.

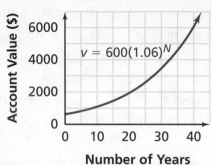

Exponential Growth

$v = 600(1.06)^N$

Exponential decay

Scientists use the carbon dating method to find the age of historic objects. The method uses a form of carbon that you find in plant or animal remains called carbon-14, or C-14. The C-14 decays exponentially by a natural process over time. The graph shows the percent of C-14 remaining after y years.

Notice that you write both exponential growth and exponential decay functions using the same general form $f(x) = a \cdot b^x$, where b is any positive real number. What does the graph of $C = 100 \cdot 2^{\frac{-y}{5700}}$ look like?

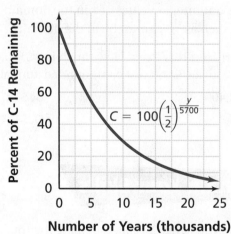

Exponential Decay

$C = 100\left(\frac{1}{2}\right)^{\frac{y}{5700}}$

For Discussion

1. What values of b lead to exponential growth? To exponential decay? Test some positive values of b and make a conjecture.

For help graphing exponential functions on the coordinate plane, see the TI-Nspire Handbook, p. 788.

You know that exponents can be positive, negative, or zero. In fact, exponential functions can take any real number as input. In some cases, depending on the situation that an exponential function represents, it may not make sense to allow negative numbers as input.

The graph shows the exponential function $f(x) = 3^x$. This function's domain is all real numbers. You may find it difficult to understand what $3^{\frac{1}{4}}$ or $3^{\sqrt{7}}$ means, but they are both real numbers.

The function increases continuously. As the input increases, the output increases. What is the result when you input negative numbers such as -500 or $-10,000,000$? Does the function ever cross the x-axis?

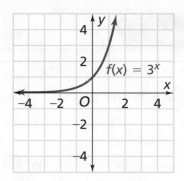

Developing Habits of Mind

Detect the key characteristics. According to the graph, $f(x) = 3^x$ appears positive no matter what value you use for x. Looks can be deceiving, but you can prove this fact. For positive values of x, you can develop a convincing argument from the fact that the function $f(x) = 3^x$ is always increasing.

Suppose x is a positive number. If it is an integer, then 3^x is definitely positive, since $3 \times 3 \times 3 \ldots$ must be positive for any number of 3's. If x is not an integer, then you can call r the rounded-down version of x. Then 3^r is definitely positive. Since x is larger than r, 3^x is larger than 3^r. Since 3^x is larger than a positive number, then it must be positive, too.

> For example, if $x = 3\frac{2}{3}$, then $r = 3$.

For negative values of x, the key to the proof is to think about reciprocals. Notice that if a number is positive, then its reciprocal is also positive. For example, both 83 and $\frac{1}{83}$ are positive.

If 3^a is positive, then $\frac{1}{3^a}$ must also be positive. From the definition of negative exponents, $\frac{1}{3^a} = 3^{-a}$. In short, if 3^a is positive, 3^{-a} is also positive. If x is negative, then $-x$ is positive. From the argument above, 3^{-x} must be positive, and then 3^x must be positive for negative values of x.

> Notice that $-x$ is not necessarily a negative number. The negative sign means to take the opposite of x. If x is negative, $-x$ is positive.

For Discussion

2. The argument is the same if the base is 4 or any number greater than 1. If the base is $\frac{1}{4}$, you can flip the argument. Since $\left(\frac{1}{4}\right)^x = 4^{-x}$, you can follow the same argument, replacing x with $-x$. Explain.

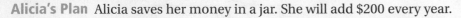

Example

Problem Alicia and Berta both save $2500.

Alicia's Plan Alicia saves her money in a jar. She will add $200 every year.

Bertha's Plan Berta saves her money in the bank, earning 6% interest each year compounded annually.

Who will save more money after 5 years? After 15 years?

Solution One way to determine who will save more money is to write a function to represent each savings plan. Then compare the graphs of the two functions. Alicia's plan has a constant difference of $200 per year, so after t years the following equation represents Alicia's savings.

$$a(t) = 2500 + 200t$$

Berta's plan earns interest at a rate of 6% per year. After 1 year, she has $2500(1.06)$. After 2 years, she has $2500(1.06)(1.06)$, or $2500(1.06)^2$. After t years, she has $2500(1.06)^t$. You can write Berta's balance as a function of t.

$$b(t) = 2500(1.06)^t$$

Graph both equations on the same axes.

The graphs show that Alicia will have more money after 5 years. Berta will have more money after 15 years. In fact, after about 11 years, Berta will have more money than Alicia.

For Discussion

3. How much more money than Berta does Alicia have after 5 years?

4. How can you find how many years it will take for Alicia's savings to double? For Berta's savings to double?

Exercises *Practicing Habits of Mind*

Check Your Understanding

Try this experiment with 40 coins, candies, or counters that have two distinguishable sides. Randomly toss them from a cup onto a table. Count the number of heads and return the heads to the cup. Remove the tails. Toss randomly the remaining coins, or "survivors," on the table. Repeat six times.

1. Copy and complete the table. Record the number of survivors.

Toss Number	Number of Survivors
0	40
1	■
2	■
3	■
4	■
5	■
6	■

2. Compare your results with the results from other groups. On average, how many survivors are there for the first toss? For the second toss?

3. **Write About It** Explain why about one fourth of the original number of coins survive the first two tosses.

4. Find a rule to calculate the average number of coins that survive t tosses.

On Your Own

5. Sketch each graph for $-3 \leq x \leq 3$.

   a. $y = 2^x$ **b.** $y = 1^x$ **c.** $y = 4^x$

   d. $y = \left(\frac{1}{2}\right)^x$ **e.** $y = 2^{-x}$ **f.** $y = \left(\frac{1}{10}\right)^x$

6. If b is any positive real number, for what values of b is the graph of $y = b^x$ increasing? For what values of b is the graph of $y = b^x$ decreasing?

> *Increasing* means that the value of y becomes greater as the value of x becomes greater.

7. A ball drops from 18 feet. On its first bounce, the ball rebounds to 12 feet. On its second bounce, it rebounds to 8 feet.

Bounce Height

Bounce, *b*	Height, *h* (ft)
0	18
1	12
2	8
3	■
4	■
5	■

a. Show that the ratio of the height of bounce 1 to the starting height is equal to the ratio of the height of bounce 2 to the height of bounce 1.

b. Copy and complete the table to show the height of bounces 3, 4, and 5.

c. Use the table. If *h* is the height of a certain bounce, write an expression that represents the height of the next bounce in terms of *h*.

d. Use the table. Write an equation that represents the relationship between height *h* and bounce *b*.

8. Standardized Test Prep What point do the graphs of $y = 2^x$, $y = 3^x$, $y = 5^x$, and $y = (\frac{1}{4})^x$ have in common?

A. $(-1, 0)$ **B.** $(0, 0)$ **C.** $(0, 1)$

D. The graphs have no common intersection point.

Go Online
www.successnetplus.com

Maintain Your Skills

9. Sketch each graph for $-3 \le x \le 3$.

a. $y = 5 \cdot 2^x$ **b.** $y = 5 \cdot 1.5^x$ **c.** $y = 5 \cdot 1.2^x$

d. $y = 5 \cdot 0.7^x$ **e.** $y = 5 \cdot 0.5^x$

f. Where does the graph of $y = 5 \cdot 0.001^x$ cross the *y*-axis?

10. Sketch each graph for $-3 \le x \le 3$ on the same coordinate plane.

a. $y = 2^x$ **b.** $(y - 1) = 2^x$ **c.** $(y + 1) = 2^x$

d. $(y - 2.5) = 2^x$ **e.** $(y + 1.5) = 2^x$

f. Without graphing, describe what the graph of $(y - 99) = 2^x$ looks like.

Mathematical 5C Reflections

In this Investigation, you explored linear functions and learned how to write recursive rules using data in a table. These questions will help you summarize what you have learned.

1. Copy and complete each table. Find a function that produces each table.

a.

Input	Output	Δ
0	▣	3
1	▣	3
2	▣	3
3	▣	3
4	14	3
5	▣	3

b.

Input	Output	Δ
0	5	▣
1	2	▣
2	−1	▣
3	−4	▣
4	−7	▣
5	−10	

2. Make a table for each recursive rule. Use the integer inputs from 0 to 5. Which tables can you generate using a linear function?

   a. If 0 is the input, the output is 3. To get a new output, take the previous output and subtract 2.

   b. If 0 is the input, the output is 8. To get a new output, multiply the previous output by $\frac{1}{2}$.

3. How do you find a function that matches a table?

4. What is a recursive rule? How can you use recursion to define functions?

5. What is a recursive rule for the values in the table?

Input	Output
−1	6
0	5
1	4
2	3
3	2

Vocabulary

In this investigation, you learned these terms. Make sure you understand what each one means and how to use it.

- base case
- compound interest
- consecutive outputs
- constant ratio
- exponential decay
- exponential growth
- linear function
- recursive rule

Recursion ends when there is no more input.

Project Using Mathematical Habits

Managing Money

Do you ever dream of going to college or buying a car? Usually, you save and borrow money for these large expenses. In this project, you will write a recursive rule to use in a spreadsheet and make decisions about managing money.

This project explores three ways to save and invest money: a certificate of deposit (CD), a savings account, and stock. In each case, you earn interest by lending your money. For each type of investment, the Annual Percentage Rate (APR) describes the investment's growth each year.

Materials

Paper, pencil, spreadsheet software

Earning Interest

1. Kara looks at three options for making her annual $600 rainy day investment.

   • savings account at 1.5% APR

   • certificate of deposit at 4.5% APR

   • stock investment at 10% APR

For each option, what is the amount of money that Kara earns if she invests for 3 years? For 10 years? For 30 years? Make a spreadsheet like the one below for each investment period.

2. Research the APR for savings and CD accounts at a local bank. Find the fees charged on minimum balances in various types of accounts. Which type of account is the best for investing a small amount? A large amount?

Comparing Payment Options

Make a spreadsheet showing the payment options for each situation below.

3. The Peña family finances a car for $8000. A car dealership offers a 7.9% APR loan for 4 years. Each month, the dealership charges interest on the balance of the loan. What is the monthly payment rounded to the nearest cent?

4. The Peñas need $32,000 in financing to buy their dream car. The loan is at 7.9% APR for 4 years.

   a. What is the family's monthly payment rounded to the nearest cent?

   b. How does this monthly payment compare to the monthly payment in Exercise 3?

5. The Peñas get a new finance offer for their dream car, a 5-year loan at 8.9% APR.

   a. How much does this reduce the family's monthly payment?

   b. How do the car payments in Exercises 4 and 5 compare?

	A	B	C	D	E
1	Year	Starting Balance	Interest	Deposit	Ending Balance
2	1	0	0	600	600
3					
4					

Would a $500 discount and 6.4% interest for 4 years be even better?

6. The car dealership makes its final offers on the dream car to the Peñas, a $1000 discount and 7.9% interest for 4 years, or no discount and 4.9% interest for 4 years. Which of these two offers should they take?

7. Nancy buys appliances for $1300 at Adequate Buy. She has two payment options. She can use a credit card that charges 10% APR, or she can use an Adequate Buy credit card that charges no interest for a year. Then she pays 15% APR after the first year.

Which card should Nancy use if she plans to make monthly payments of $110? Of $40?

8. The United States government offers college student loans that typically carry lower interest rates than car loans. Shannon graduates with a $12,000 student loan. The interest rate on her loan is 5% APR.

a. If Shannon pays off the loan in 10 years, find her monthly payment rounded to the nearest cent.

b. What percentage of Shannon's first payment is interest?

c. Suppose Shannon's student loan is $18,000 at 5% APR for 10 years. Estimate her monthly payment. Then find her monthly payment rounded to the nearest cent.

d. Suppose Shannon's loan is a bank loan of $12,000 at 8% APR for 10 years instead of a student loan of $12,000 at 5% APR for 10 years. How much more will her total payments be?

9. Take It Further Julie and Ben owe $215,354 on their existing mortgage. They have already paid for 3 years at 7% APR. A bank advertises a new 30-year loan at 6.5% APR. The bank charges $2500 in fees to issue the loan and adds the fee to the loan amount.

a. What is the monthly payment on Julie and Ben's existing mortgage?

b. If they choose to take a new loan, what will be the monthly payment?

c. How much money will they save, if any, by taking a new loan?

d. Experiment using a different bank rate or loan amount. Find how the monthly payment changes.

Go Online
www.successnetplus.com

Go Online
www.successnetplus.com

In **Investigation 5A,** you learned how to

- build a function from a word problem
- determine whether a relationship is a function based on its description or graph
- make input-output tables
- find the domain of a function
- graph a function

The following questions will help you check your understanding.

1. The diagram below shows two linked function machines.

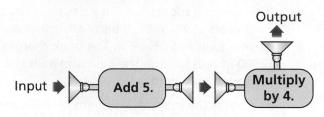

   a. Copy and complete the table for the function network.

Input	Output
0	▦
1	▦
−4	▦
6	▦
▦	28

   b. Form a new function by reversing the order of the two function machines.

   c. Are the outputs the same for the function networks in parts (a) and (b)? Explain.

2. Use $f(x) = 2(x - 5)$, $x \overset{g}{\mapsto} |x^2 - 3|$, and $h(x) = \sqrt{x - 1}$ to calculate the following.

   a. $f(0), f(1)$, and $f(-1)$

   b. $g(0), g(1)$, and $g(-1)$

   c. $h(0), h(1)$, and $h(-1)$

d. $f(g(3))$ and $g(h(5))$

e. Find the domains of functions f, g, and h.

3. Determine whether each description is a function. Explain.

   a. input: x, output: x^2

   b. input: x, output: $\pm\sqrt{x}$

In **Investigation 5B,** you learned how to

- make calculations involving integral exponents
- simplify expressions involving integral exponents
- explain and apply the basic rules of exponents
- calculate with positive, zero, and negative exponents

The following questions will help you check your understanding.

4. Simplify each expression.

   a. $x^4 \cdot x^3$ **b.** $2^6 \cdot 5^6$

   c. $(x^2)^4$ **d.** $\dfrac{x^{11}}{x^5}$

   e. $\dfrac{3^8}{3^6}$ **f.** $(12)^5 \cdot \left(\dfrac{1}{6}\right)^5$

5. Without a calculator, decide whether each expression equals 11^{-2}. Explain.

   a. $\dfrac{11^{10}}{11^8}$ **b.** $\dfrac{11^8}{11^{10}}$

   c. $\left(\dfrac{1}{11}\right)^2$ **d.** $11^0 \cdot 11^{-3} \cdot 11$

   e. $(11^3)^{-5}$ **f.** $\dfrac{1}{11^{-2}}$

6. Write each number in scientific notation.

   a. $5,000,000$ **b.** 0.00045

   c. 850×10^{-5} **d.** $(5.3 \times 10^2)(2 \times 10^{-4})$

   e. 300^2 **f.** $\dfrac{4.8 \times 10^6}{6 \times 10^{-2}}$

In **Investigation 5C,** you learned how to

- determine whether a table represents a linear function and fit a linear function to a table where possible
- calculate the outputs of a recursive rule
- describe a recursive rule and find one to match a table
- use exponential functions to calculate compound interest in a number of different schemes
- graph exponential functions and recognize important properties of exponential graphs
- match tables with constant ratios to exponential functions

The following questions will help you check your understanding.

7. Use Tables A and B for parts (a) and (b).

Table A

Input	Output
0	4
1	7
2	10
3	13
4	16

Table B

Input	Output
0	4
1	5
2	8
3	13
4	20

a. Draw a graph of each table of values. Does each graph appear to be linear?

b. Add a Δ column to each table and find the differences. Can you match each table with a linear function?

c. If you can match a table with a linear function, find a closed-form function that agrees with the table.

8. Copy and complete the table for each recursive rule.

Input	Output
1	■
2	■
3	■
4	■
5	■

a. To get a new output, add 6 to the previous output. When the input is 1, the output is −2.

b. To get a new output, multiply the previous output by 2 and add 3. When the input is 1, the output is −2.

9. Tony invests $10,000 in an account that pays 4.5% interest compounded semiannually.

a. How much money will be in the account after 5 years? After 10 years?

b. Suppose the interest on the account is compounded monthly. How much money will be in the account after 10 years? If the account is compounded monthly instead of semiannually, how much more interest will Tony's account earn?

10. Use the exponential equation $y = 2 \cdot 5^x$.

a. Copy and complete the table.

Input, x	Output, y	÷
0	■	■
1	10	■
2	■	■
3	■	■
4	■	

b. If $x = -1$, find the value of y.

c. Sketch a graph of the function.

d. If $2 \cdot 5^x = 100$, between what two integers is the value of x?

e. Find the value of x that solves the equation $2 \cdot 5^x = 100$ to the nearest hundredth.

11. Find an exponential rule $h(x)$ that matches the table below. Use the rule to calculate $h(-2)$ and $h(-5)$.

x	h(x)
0	3
1	12
2	48
3	192
4	768
5	3072

Go Online
www.successnetplus.com

Multiple Choice

For Exercises 1 and 2 use this function-machine network.

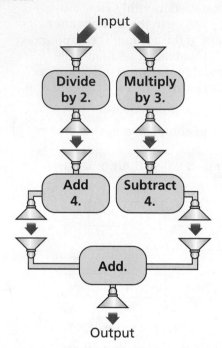

Input

Divide by 2.   Multiply by 3.

Add 4.   Subtract 4.

Add.

Output

1. If the input value to the network is −6, what is the output value?

A. 21   **B.** −7

C. −21   **D.** −30

2. If the output value from the network is 42, what is the input value?

A. 147   **B.** 21

C. 0   **D.** 12

3. Which recursive rule makes $f(3)$ equal 35?

A. $f(x) = \begin{cases} 25 & \text{if } x = 0 \\ f(x-1) + x & \text{if } x > 0 \end{cases}$

B. $f(x) = \begin{cases} 29 & \text{if } x = 0 \\ f(x-1) + 3 & \text{if } x > 0 \end{cases}$

C. $f(x) = \begin{cases} 29 & \text{if } x = 0 \\ 2 \cdot f(x-1) & \text{if } x > 0 \end{cases}$

D. $f(x) = \begin{cases} 41 & \text{if } x = 0 \\ f(x-1) - 2 & \text{if } x > 0 \end{cases}$

4. Which table cannot be described by a linear function?

A.

Input	Output
0	10
1	7
2	4
3	1
4	−2

B.

Input	Output
0	13
1	15
2	17
3	20
4	23

C.

Input	Output
0	−4
1	1
2	6
3	11
4	16

D.

Input	Output
0	2
1	1
2	0
3	−1
4	−2

5. What type of function is $h(x)$?

$$h(x) = \begin{cases} 11 & \text{if } x = 0 \\ 3 \cdot h(x-1) & \text{if } x > 0 \end{cases}$$

A. constant

B. linear

C. exponential

D. none of the above

6. Which rule gives the same outputs as the following recursive rule?

When the input is 0, the output is 3. To get outputs for integer inputs, add 2 to the previous output.

A. $x \mapsto 3(2^2)$

B. $x \mapsto 2x + 3$

C. $x \mapsto 3x + 2$

D. $x \mapsto 3x^2 + 3$

7. Simplify the expression $\dfrac{\sqrt{28}}{\sqrt{63}}$.

A. $\dfrac{4}{9}$

B. $\dfrac{2}{3}$

C. $\dfrac{2\sqrt{7}}{3}$

D. $\sqrt{7}$

Open Response

8. Juliana expects to work overtime this week. She will work 40 hours at her regular pay rate. Then she will work another 15 hours at $5 per hour more than her regular pay rate.

a. Draw a function-machine network whose input is Juliana's regular pay rate. The output is how much money she will make for the week (including overtime pay).

b. Juliana will make $735 this week (including overtime pay). What is her regular pay rate?

9. How long will it take your money to double if it is invested at 6% interest?

10. Jesse and Jamie both earn $500 during summer vacation. Jesse invests her $500 in an account that earns 3.5% interest compounded annually. Jamie invests his $500 in an account that earns 3.0% interest compounded quarterly. Whose investment will double first?

11. Copy and complete this table for the recursive rule $f(x)$.

$$f(x) = \begin{cases} 39 & \text{if } x = 0 \\ \frac{2}{3}f(x-1) + 4 & \text{if } x > 0 \end{cases}$$

Input	Output
0	39
1	■
2	■
3	■
4	■

12. Describe how to calculate the monthly payment on a 48-month car loan for $12,000 at 7.9% APR.

13. How do you know whether a table represents a linear function? Give at least three examples.

14. An exponential rule can generate the following table of values. Copy and complete the table. Then find a rule that you can use to generate the table.

x	y
−2	0.5
−1	■
0	■
1	13.5
2	■
3	121.5

Challenge Problem

15. A recursive rule B is defined as

$$B(m) = \begin{cases} C & \text{if } m = 0 \\ \frac{3}{4}B(m-1) + 4 & \text{if } m > 0 \end{cases}$$

where C is an unknown value that you find.

a. $B(5) = 259$. What is the value of C?

b. Find the value of $B(1,000,000)$ rounded to three decimal places.

Statistics and Fitting Lines

You might buy all of your cars with cash, but most people take out a loan when they buy a car. Shopping for the right car loan is a complicated process, full of choices. The techniques you will learn in this chapter will help you to compare your options.

To buy a car, you need to know how much you can afford as a down payment, what you can afford to pay per month on the loan, the interest rate, and the length of the loan. These variables can depend on the model of car you want to buy, the lender, and your credit rating. You can borrow the money through the car dealer, through a bank, or get a personal loan from a family member.

Sometimes car dealers have special promotional interest rates for certain models. Some dealers offer a rebate that you can use as all or part of your down payment. You are likely to have several different financing offers to consider. The financing might even influence your choice of car.

Vocabulary

- association
- balance point
- correlation coefficient
- dot plot
- fitting line
- independent
- line of best fit
- mean absolute error
- mean squared error
- negatively associated
- outlier
- positively associated
- standard error
- two-way frequency table

Investigation 6A

Statistical Data

In *Statistical Data,* you will explore ways to represent data that will help you find trends and patterns. Graphs and tables are powerful visual tools for summarizing and understanding large amounts of data.

By the end of this investigation, you will be able to answer questions like these.

1. How can you use graphs, charts, and tables to understand data?

2. How can you make informed conclusions about data?

3. Mr. Siddiqui tells his students about a correction for a test. He says, "It turns out that one problem didn't have a solution. To make up for my mistake, I gave everyone an extra 5 points credit for that problem. That changes the class average from 83 to 87 points." Is this possible? Explain.

You will learn how to

- determine the mean, median, and mode for a set of data, and decide how meaningful they are in specific situations

- interpret data lists, frequency tables, and stem-and-leaf displays

- determine the five-number summary for a set of data

- build data graphs such as histograms, box-and-whisker plots, and scatter plots

You will develop these habits and skills:

- Identify trends in data.

- Work with a variety of types of numbers in a variety of forms.

- Make and interpret visual and tabular representations of data.

- Identify limitations, or misuses, of visual representations of data.

Some visual information may not be what it seems. What you see depends on how you look at it.

You can use measures such as mean, median, and mode to interpret data such as test scores and sports averages. Workers in business, health care, and many other areas use these measures to help them make decisions.

For You to Explore

1. Work in pairs to gather data for this experiment. Each pair has a stopwatch.

   • The first person holds the stopwatch so that the second person cannot see it.

   • The first person says "Go" and starts the stopwatch.

   • The second person guesses when 30 seconds have elapsed and says "Stop."

   • The first person stops the watch.

   • The first person announces the actual time that elapsed and records that time. Round to the nearest second.

   • The first person times the second person once more. The first person reports and records the time for the second try.

   • The first and second person reverse roles. The second person has the stopwatch. The first person guesses when 30 seconds have elapsed.

   When you finish the experiment, you will have two recorded times for each person. What observations can you make about your data?

2. The table lists the ages of the winners of the Academy Awards Best Actor and Best Actress in a Leading Role awards, at the start of the year of their film achievements, from 1986 through 2006.

Winners Best Actor and Best Actress Awards

Year	Actor	Age	Actress	Age
1986	Paul Newman	61	Marlee Matlin	21
1987	Michael Douglas	43	Cher	41
1988	Dustin Hoffman	51	Jodie Foster	26
1989	Daniel Day-Lewis	32	Jessica Tandy	80
1990	Jeremy Irons	42	Kathy Bates	42
1991	Anthony Hopkins	54	Jodie Foster	29
1992	Al Pacino	52	Emma Thompson	33
1993	Tom Hanks	37	Holly Hunter	35
1994	Tom Hanks	38	Jessica Lange	45
1995	Nicolas Cage	31	Susan Sarandon	49
1996	Geoffrey Rush	45	Frances McDormand	39
1997	Jack Nicholson	60	Helen Hunt	34
1998	Roberto Benigni	46	Gwyneth Paltrow	26
1999	Kevin Spacey	40	Hilary Swank	25
2000	Russell Crowe	36	Julia Roberts	33
2001	Denzel Washington	47	Halle Berry	35
2002	Adrien Brody	29	Nicole Kidman	35
2003	Sean Penn	43	Charlize Theron	28
2004	Jamie Foxx	37	Hilary Swank	30
2005	Philip Seymour Hoffman	38	Reese Witherspoon	29
2006	Forest Whitaker	45	Helen Mirren	61

Source: Academy of Motion Picture Arts and Sciences

Sophia claims that the typical winner of the Best Actor award is much older than the typical winner of the Best Actress award. Make some arguments that support or oppose Sophia's claim.

Exercises *Practicing Habits of Mind*

On Your Own

Habits of Mind

Experiment. Try it with numbers! Calculate each measure using a set of seven scores.

3. Describe how to find each measure for seven test scores. What does each measure tell you?

   a. mean

   b. median

   c. mode

4. Milo sits next to a tollbooth and counts the number of people in each of 50 cars. He records his findings in the table. Then Milo calculates the mean number of people in each car.

Car Survey

Number of People in Car	Number of Cars
1	31
2	12
3	3
4	2
5	2

   a. What's Wrong Here? On his first try, Milo finds the mean of the five numbers, 31, 12, 3, 2, and 2, to be 10. Explain why this cannot be the mean number of people in each car.

   b. Find the correct mean number of people in each car.

5. **Write About It** Describe at least three situations in which you can use each measure.

   a. mean

   b. median

   c. mode

Find the total number of people Milo counted in 50 cars.

6. This table lists the salaries for the 25 players on a professional baseball team.

BASEBALL SALARIES
(thousands)

Position	Salary	Position	Salary
Pitcher	$380	Catcher	$850
Pitcher	$395	Catcher	$10,150
Pitcher	$430	First Base	$4,875
Pitcher	$600	First Base	$11,780
Pitcher	$850	Second Base	$3,750
Pitcher	$1,000	Shortstop	$520
Pitcher	$1,000	Shortstop	$7,950
Pitcher	$1,800	Third Base	$5,750
Pitcher	$2,100	Left Field	$4,875
Pitcher	$6,850	Center Field	$380
Pitcher	$7,150	Center Field	$520
Pitcher	$9,900	Right Field	$1,325
		Right Field	$12,800

  a. Calculate the mean salary and the median salary.

  b. Why is it not useful to calculate the mode?

7. A player representing the players' union argues that the players should make more money.

  a. Which measure, the mean or the median, supports more convincingly the case for raising salaries? Explain.

  b. What makes the mean and median so different for this data set?

  c. A salary cap limits the total amount a team can spend on players' salaries. If this team has reached its salary cap, what salary adjustments would increase the mean salary? The median salary?

Maintain Your Skills

8. Describe how you obtain the data set {22, 58, 47, 62, 79, 84, 34} from {20, 56, 45, 60, 77, 82, 32}. How do the mean and the median change?

6.02 Mean, Median, and Mode

Patterns in data may not be obvious. You have to see a regularity, search for a pattern, and then be able to describe and explain the pattern you find. Sometimes you may find and describe a pattern that gives no useful results.

The best techniques for studying data may not be obvious, either. Meanings that you find may depend as much on your choice of technique as on the data.

Suppose a student collects data through an online survey of United States residents using the survey question "What generic word do you use to describe a carbonated soft drink?"

A **frequency table** is a list of categories that classifies the number of occurrences in each category. The frequency table below shows soft-drink response data from four states. Each state represents a different region of the country.

What Do You Call Carbonated Drinks?

State	"Pop"	"Soda"	"Coke"	Other
Minnesota	4265	630	39	92
New York	3321	7364	262	200
Georgia	49	346	2196	149
Washington	2678	714	105	98

SOURCE: Alan McConchie's Survey

The other choices included cola, soda pop, tonic, and many more!

The table shows that 630 Minnesotans call soft drinks *soda* while 2678 people in Washington call soft drinks *pop*.

For Discussion

1. If someone asks you what a New Yorker most likely calls a carbonated soft drink, how would you decide?

Developing Habits of Mind

Represent an average. The word *average* has many meanings in everyday language. In statistics, there are three common ways to find an average.

Mean   Add the values and divide by the number of values.

Median   Arrange the values in order. Then, find the middle value. If there are two middle values, find the mean of the two middle values.

Mode   Find the data value that occurs most often.

The descriptions above tell you how to find each average. None of them tells you what each average is good for. The average you use depends on the situation. For example, the soft drink survey data are a collection of preferred words, not numbers. The only sensible average is the mode.

For You to Do

2. In the soft drink survey, what is the mode for each state? For all four states combined?

Example

A class of 20 students takes a 5-question multiple choice test. Each question is worth 20 points. The table shows the scores.

Test Scores

Score	Frequency
0	1
20	0
40	2
60	5
80	5
100	7

Notice that the sum of the frequencies, 20, is the number of students in the class.

Problem Find the mean, median, and mode.

Solution To find the mean, add the data values. Then divide by the number of values. To find the sum of the data, add the scores.

You can use the basic rules and calculate the mean using the table.

Test Scores

Score	Frequency
0	1
20	0
40	2
60	5
80	5
100	7

number of students	× score	= total of scores
1	× 0 =	0
0	× 20 =	0
2	× 40 =	80
5	× 60 =	300
5	× 80 =	400
7	× 100 =	700
		1480

The sum of the scores is $0 + 2(40) + 5(60) + 5(80) + 7(100) = 1480$.
The mean score is $1480 \div 20 = 74$.

To find the median, sort the data. Then find the middle value in the sorted list. Since there are 20 scores, the median breaks the scores into the top 10 scores and the bottom 10 scores. To find the median using the list below, start from the beginning of the list and count the number of scores until you count 10 scores.

$$\underbrace{0, 40, 40, 60, 60, 60, 60, 60, 80, 80,}_{\text{bottom 10}} \quad \underbrace{80, 80, 80, 100, 100, 100, 100, 100, 100, 100}_{\text{top 10}}$$

Again, you can use a frequency table to shorten your work when you find the median.

Test Scores

Score	Frequency
0	1
20	0
40	2
60	5
80	5
100	7

score	number of students
0	1
0–20	$1 + 0 = 1$
0–40	$1 + 0 + 2 = 3$
0–60	$1 + 0 + 2 + 5 = 8$
0–80	$1 + 0 + 2 + 5 + 5 = 13$
0–100	$1 + 0 + 2 + 5 + 5 + 7 = 20$

If there are 20 scores, the median is a number between the 10th score and the 11th score. You can add the number of students in each category in the table until you reach the median score. When you start with the lowest score and reach the 10th score and 11th score, you will find that they are both 80. So the median is 80.

> Can you find the median by starting with the highest score?

To find the mode, identify the score with the highest frequency. The mode is 100, since there are 7 scores of 100, more than any other score.

Just because you can calculate each average, you cannot assume that it has any significance. The next step, interpreting what the averages mean in relation to the data set, is more important.

> You can usually decide which values will be meaningful before calculating them.

Developing Habits of Mind

Represent an average in three ways. Here are some ways to interpret the statistical test results in the previous example.

- The mode tells you the most "popular" score. The mode is most meaningful when used with data from polls, such as one taken before an election or the soft drink poll. The mode tells you who or what item is most popular.

It is not clear what the mode tells you about the data in the Example, though. The most frequently occuring test score doesn't really mean much. You might think that a mode of 100 means that the class is doing well, but the mode gives you no idea about the other grades. The remaining scores might have been failing grades, and the mode might still be 100.

- The median shows the midpoint for the number of scores. A teacher might feel good about a class median test score of 80. At least half the students scored 80 or better.

Why does a teacher say "at least half"?

Similar to the mode, the median tells you where a particular score is. A set of data in which the first nine scores are 20 or below and the last 11 scores are 80 or above still has a median of 80. This respectable median masks the fact that too many students did not understand the test material.

- The mean gives a midpoint for the scores. If you subtract the mean from each number in the data set, and then add the differences, the sum is 0.

A mean of 74 may be a good performance on a test, but not necessarily. If 10 people score 48 and 10 people score 100, the mean is still 74.

Usually you cannot make informed decisions about data by looking at just one average. It may help to compare two averages, such as the mean and the median, to each other. You need to know more about the context of any statistics for them to be meaningful.

Exercises *Practicing Habits of Mind*

Check Your Understanding

1. Look at the lesson's Example about test scores. Verify that the mean is the balancing point by finding the sum of the differences between the scores and 74.

   a. How can you change these scores so that the mean score is 5 points higher?

   b. How can you change these scores so that the median score is 100?

2. **Standardized Test Prep** What statistical measure does a store manager use to determine the best-selling item in the store?

   A. mean   **B.** mode   **C.** range   **D.** median

If you have exactly two scores, the balancing point is at the midpoint of their graphs on the number line. Using 20 scores, the balancing point is harder to see.

3. Find the median of these five numbers.

$$3 \times 10^4 \qquad 5 \times 10^3 \qquad 6.02 \times 10^{23} \qquad 8.7 \times 10^5 \qquad 62$$

4. Describe how you obtain each data set below from the following data set. Then describe how the mean and median change.

{20, 56, 45, 60, 77, 82, 32}

a. {19, 55, 44, 59, 76, 81, 31}

b. {30, 66, 55, 70, 87, 92, 42}

On Your Own

5. Find the mean of each pair of numbers. Graph the numbers and the mean on a number line.

a. 5 and 15

b. −5 and 15

c. −5 and −15

d. 137 and 441

6. Standardized Test Prep Each of 50 people bowls one game in a charity event. The table shows the results of the games.

Bowlers' Scores

Score Range	Number of Bowlers
0–50	9
51–100	12
101–150	10
151–200	13
201–250	4
251–300	2

Based on the table, which statement about the bowlers' scores is true?

A. 6% of the bowlers score more than 200.

B. 52% of the bowlers score no more than 100.

C. The median score is between 51 and 100.

D. The median score is between 101 and 150.

Go Online
www.successnetplus.com

7. A spinner has eight zones. Each zone shows the number of coins you win for landing in that zone.

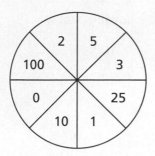

a. This game costs 4 coins for one spin. If each of the eight zones has the same probability of winning, is this a good game to play? Explain.

b. **Take It Further** A computer simulates the spinner and is programmed so that the eight zones are not equally likely. This table shows the probability of landing in each of the eight zones. What is the mean number of coins you expect to win in a single spin in this game?

Spinner Game

Zone	Probability (%)
0	17
1	40
2	15
3	10
5	10
10	5
25	2
100	1

c. **Take It Further** This game costs 4 coins for one spin, and you know the probabilities. Is this a good game to play? Explain.

Even though the balloons seem to fill the wall, the area for direct hits may be less than half the wall area.

8. Kay explains an unusual way of finding the mean of the data set {82, 68, 50, 100}.

She says, "First I guess a mean; say it's 80. Then I find that the differences from 80 of the data values are $+2$, -12, -30, and $+20$, or a total of -20. On average, the data values are $\frac{-20}{4}$, or -5, from my guess. That means that the real mean must be $80 - 5$, or 75. Check this out. It really works!"

   a. Use Kay's method to find the mean of the set {13, 29, 19, 15, 24, 26}.

   b. Take It Further Explain why Kay's method works.

   c. Can you use Kay's method to find the mean of the data in Exercise 4, Lesson 6.01? Explain.

9. Take It Further Use the basic rules of algebra to simplify each expression.

   a. $\left(\frac{a + b}{2} - a \right) + \left(\frac{a + b}{2} - b \right)$

   b. $\left(\frac{a + b + c}{3} - a \right) + \left(\frac{a + b + c}{3} - b \right) + \left(\frac{a + b + c}{3} - c \right)$

   c. How does this exercise relate to the topic of this lesson?

10. Derman looks at his five algebra test grades for the past two months.

Derman's Test Scores

Month	Test 1	Test 2	Test 3	Average Score
September	80	96	100	92
October	80	96		88

He says, "I can find my average test score for September and October by taking the average of 92 and 88." Is Derman correct?

11. Standardized Test Prep The mean of Ampara's first five quiz scores is 77. What score does she need on the sixth quiz to raise her average to 80?

   A. 80   **B.** 83   **C.** 92   **D.** 95

Maintain Your Skills

12. a. Find the mean and median of the data set {100, -25, 3, 7, 23, 17, 15}.

   b. Add six to each data value from part (a). Find the mean and median of the resulting data set.

   c. Double each data value from part (a). Find the mean and median of the resulting data set.

   d. How do the changes in the data set relate to the changes in the mean and median?

Go Online
Video Tutor
www.successnetplus.com

In Lesson 6.02 you learned some measures of the *center of data*, including the mean and median. Knowing the center of data is important, but it is part of a larger framework, including these questions:

- How widely *spread* are the data?

- What is the rough *shape* of the data?

- Are there individual *outliers*, elements of data that are not close to the rest of the data?

Visual representations of data make it easier to answer these important questions. One simple representation is the **dot plot**. Here is a dot plot for the ages of the 21 winners of Best Actor in a Leading Role from Lesson 6.01.

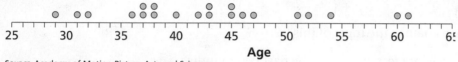

SOURCE: Academy of Motion Picture Arts and Sciences

Age

Each dot is one award winner, so two people won the Best Actor award at age 37 and no one won at age 57.

A dot plot can make some observations easier, especially gaps and outliers, and gives an overall sense of the data's center, spread, and shape.

For You to Do

1. Build a dot plot for the ages of the 21 winners of Best Actress in a Leading Role from Lesson 6.01.

2. Identify any significant gaps and outliers in the data.

A similar representation is the **histogram**, which shows frequencies as bars. Unlike dot plots, which display single values, the bars of a histogram (sometimes called *bins*) may have any fixed width. Here are two histograms for the Best Actor data:

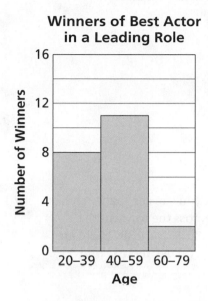

Winners of Best Actor in a Leading Role

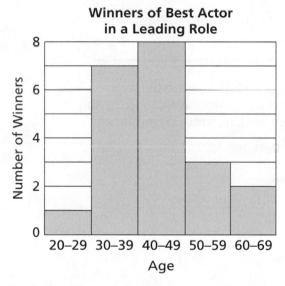

Winners of Best Actor in a Leading Role

> The bars of the histogram show intervals of data. The second bar tells you that seven people who won the Best Actor award were from 30 to 39 years old, since the next bar starts at 40.

Both histograms display the same data, but they have different shapes. The width of a histogram's bins can affect how well it shows the center, spread, shape, and outliers of the corresponding data. There is no single "correct" bin width for a histogram.

Go Online
www.successnetplus.com

For Discussion

3. For the Best Actor data, describe or draw a histogram with bin width 1.

4. How can you use a histogram to estimate the mean and median of data?

You can also use a stem-and-leaf display to show data that are divided into intervals. A **stem-and-leaf display** is a graph that organizes the leading digits of data as stems. The remaining digits become leaves. Each stem typically has more than one leaf. For example, here is an unordered stem-and-leaf display for the Best Actor data from Lesson 6.01.

Ages of Winners of Best Actor in a Leading Role

```
2 | 9
3 | 2 7 8 1 6 7 8
4 | 3 2 5 6 0 7 3 5
5 | 1 4 2
6 | 1 0
```

When you turn the stem-and-leaf display on its side, it looks similar to the histogram in this lesson with bin width 10.

Ages of Winners of Best Actor in a Leading Role

```
2 | 9
3 | 2 7 8 1 6 7 8
4 | 3 2 5 6 0 7 3 5
5 | 1 4 2
6 | 1 0
```

If you think of connecting the stem and the leaf, you can see that each leaf corresponds to a piece of data. When you read across the row where the stem is 3, you read the data values 32, 37, 38, 31, 36, 37, and 38. There are 7 data values corresponding to stem 3 in the interval between 30 and 39.

For You to Do

5. Use the stem-and-leaf display to find the ages of the winners of Best Actor in a Leading Role who were more than 50 years old.

The stem-and-leaf display above is unordered since the data in the leaves are not sorted. The ordered stem-and-leaf display shows the data sorted. An ordered stem-and-leaf display is useful when working with a large data set.

Ages of Winners of Best Actor in a Leading Role

```
2 | 9
3 | 1 2 6 7 7 8 8
4 | 0 2 3 3 5 5 6 7
5 | 1 2 4
6 | 0 1
```

For You to Do

6. Find the median age of the 21 Best Actor winners using an ordered stem-and-leaf display.

Exercises *Practicing Habits of Mind*

Check Your Understanding

1. Make a histogram for the Best Actor data in this lesson. Use bin widths of 5 years, such as 20–24 years, 25–29 years, and so on.

2. In 2001, the mean family income in the United States was $66,863. The median family income was $51,407. What could account for such a wide difference between these two measures?

3. The table lists how many prime numbers exist among the first 800 positive integers.

For help making a histogram, see the TI-Nspire™ Handbook, p. 788.

Prime Numbers

Interval	Number of Prime Numbers
1–100	25
101–200	21
201–300	16
301–400	16
401–500	17
501–600	14
601–700	16
701–800	14

Remember...

A prime number is a number with exactly two positive factors, 1 and itself. The number 1 is *not* prime, since it has only one positive factor.

a. Make a histogram for the data.

b. How does the number of primes change from the first interval to the last?

On Your Own

4. Use the dot plot you made of the ages of the Best Actress winners from the *For You To Do* on page 488.

a. Determine the median age for all Best Actress winners.

b. Estimate the mean age for all Best Actress winners.

c. Make an ordered stem-and-leaf display.

d. Make a histogram, and clearly mark the bin width you used.

If a stem between the least and the greatest values has no leaves, you still include the stem in the list of values.

5. Standardized Test Prep The stem-and-leaf display shows the ages of 50 teachers. Based on the stem-and-leaf display, which percent of the teachers are more than 50 years old?

A. 26%

B. 47%

C. 51%

D. 52%

Teachers' Ages

2	1 2 3 5 7
3	1 2 3 5 5 7 7 8
4	2 3 3 3 4 4 5 6 6 7 8
5	1 2 3 4 4 4 6 7 8 9 9 9
6	1 1 1 2 2 3 4 4 4 5 5 6 7 7

6. Draw a histogram for the teachers' ages in Exercise 5. Use five bins of width 10 years.

Use this stem-and-leaf display below for Exercises 7 and 8. To decide what items to stock, a store keeps track of the ages of customers who come into the store. This stem-and-leaf display shows the data for a 15-minute period.

Customers' Ages

0	6 7 8
1	0 1 1 1 2 2 3 4 4
2	5 8 8 8 8 8 9 9 9
3	3 4 8 9

7. a. Make a dot plot for the data.

    b. How many people enter the store during the 15-minute period?

    c. Using the dot plot, what do you notice as the most important feature of the data?

    d. What is the mode of the data? Explain how you can use the dot plot to find this information.

    e. The mean age in this group of customers is 21. Would you consider this a "typical" or "likely" age for a customer? Explain.

    f. How would you describe a "typical" or "likely" age for a customer in this group?

8. Plot the data in Exercise 7 using two different histograms. In one histogram, use bins of width 10 years: 0–9 years, 10–19 years, and so on. In the other histogram, use bins of width 10 years: 5–14 years, 15–24 years, and so on.

    a. What patterns of customers' ages do you find in your two histograms? What inference can you draw about the customers based on each pattern?

    b. Which of your histograms corresponds to the stem-and-leaf display?

    c. Is there anything you notice about the data that might help you decide which histogram better reflects the ages of the store's customers?

9. **Standardized Test Prep** The histogram shows a swim team's membership by age. How many swim team members are age 14 or older?

   A. 2

   B. 8

   C. 12

   D. 14

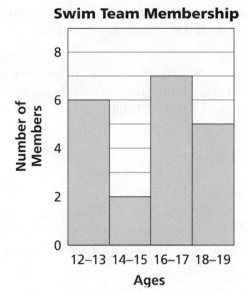

Swim Team Membership

10. Gather at least 20 pennies. Find the age of each penny.

   a. Make a dot plot of the data.

   b. Make a histogram of the data using 5-year bins.

11. A histogram of the salaries for players on a professional baseball team is displayed below. The mean salary and median salary are also marked.

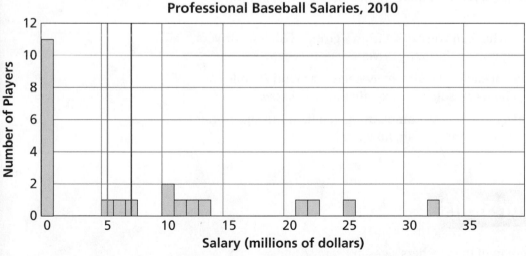

Professional Baseball Salaries, 2010

   a. Which marking is the median? Which one is the mean? How do you know?

   b. Based on the histogram, describe the overall shape of the data. Are the data clustered, symmetrical, or skewed?

   c. Identify any outliers in the data. Justify your reasoning.

   d. Explain the meaning of *median salary* to a person who doesn't understand the meaning of the term *median*.

   > What range of salaries is represented by the bin that starts at 0 and ends at 1?

12. Research the ages at inauguration of all U.S. Presidents and make a dot plot of the data. Then use the dot plot to make a histogram of the data using 5-year bins.

13. Two new cars, the Melody and the Harmony, are expected to get about 26 miles per gallon in city driving. The dot plots below show the miles per gallon for a sample of drivers of each car.

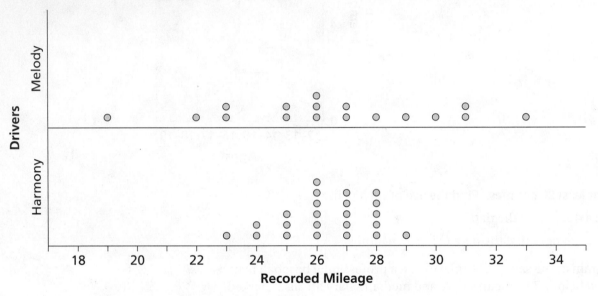

a. How does the spread of data compare for the Melody and Harmony drivers?

b. Based on the data, what can you expect from a group of Melody drivers that differs from a group of Harmony drivers?

c. The manufacturers of each car claim an average of around 26 miles per gallon. Are these claims reasonable? Explain how you know.

d. Which car will have more drivers complaining that their mileage is much less than 26 miles per gallon? Explain how you know.

Maintain Your Skills

14. a. Calculate the median of the teachers' ages in Exercise 5.

b. Where on the histogram do you find the median for the teachers' ages? What is the relationship between the median and the pattern of the data in the histogram?

Paired Comparisons— Box-and-Whisker Plots

The statistics you have learned can be very helpful when you work with two sets of comparable data. You might have sets of scores in two different classes, or the life expectancies of men and women. Paired comparisons give you powerful visual representations of data that you can use to make at-a-glance comparisons and interpretations of two data sets.

You can display and compare the results from two data sets using a **box-and-whisker plot.** Before you make the plot, you analyze the data using the five-number summary. The **five-number summary** is an overview of a sorted set of data that uses five numbers.

- The **minimum** is the least value.

- The **first quartile** is the data value that is greater than or equal to the lowest 25% of the data values.

- The **median** is the middle value of the sorted data set.

- The **third quartile** is the data value that is greater than or equal to the lowest 75% of the data values.

- The **maximum** is the greatest value.

These five numbers give the overall shape of a data set, since they split the data into four equal parts. Equal numbers of elements from the data set are in all of the four intervals between the summary numbers.

> Why do you think that you call this the third quartile? Is there a second quartile?

Developing Habits of Mind

Establish a process. To find the median, sort the data. The process depends on whether you have an odd or even number of elements.

- If an odd number of elements are in the data set, the median is the single value in the middle of the sorted list.

- If an even number of elements are in the data set, two elements are in the middle of the sorted list. The mean of those two numbers is the median.

The median splits the data set into two sets, the upper half and the lower half of the set. If the number of data points in the original set of data is odd, then the median is not in either set. In each data set, take the data above or below the median, even if some of the data points have the same value as the median. You can determine each quartile by finding the median of each of the two sets.

- To find the first quartile, find the median of the lower half of the data.

- To find the third quartile, find the median of the upper half of the data.

> **Remember...**
> You need to sort the data before calculating the median and quartiles!

Example

The table shows the life expectancies at birth for males and females in 14 countries having names that start with the letter A. Ages are rounded to the nearest year.

Life Expectancy at Birth

Country	Male	Female
Afghanistan	43	43
Albania	75	80
Algeria	72	75
American Samoa	72	80
Andorra	81	87
Angola	37	40
Anguilla	74	80
Antigua and Barbuda	70	75
Argentina	72	80
Armenia	68	76
Aruba	76	83
Australia	78	84
Austria	76	82
Azerbaijan	60	68

SOURCE: *The World Fact Book*, 2007

Problem Find the five-number summary for the life expectancy of females in these 14 countries.

Solution Sort the 14 data values from lowest to highest. The median is between the seventh and eighth values.

40, 43, 68, 75, 75, 76, 80, 80, 80, 80, 82, 83, 84, 87

Another way to find the two middle values is to cross out values at alternating ends of the list until only two are left.

40 43 68 75 75 76 80 80 80 80 82 83 84 87
40 43 68 75 75 76 80 80 80 80 82 83 84 87
⋮
40 43 68 75 75 76 80 80 80 80 82 83 84 87
40 43 68 75 75 76 80 80 80 80 82 83 84 87

The two middle numbers are 80 and 80. The median is their average, 80.

The first quartile is the middle value in the list below the median. The third quartile is the middle value in the list above the median.

40 43 68 75 75 76 80   80 80 80 82 83 84 87

The first quartile is 75. The third quartile is 82.

The maximum and minimum values are the first and last numbers in the sorted list. The five-number summary is below.

- minimum   40
- first quartile (Q_1)   75
- median   80
- third quartile (Q_3)   82
- maximum   87

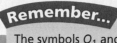
Remember...

The symbols Q_1 and Q_3 stand for the first and third quartiles.

For Discussion

1. Without calculating, can you tell whether the mean age for the 14 female life expectancies is greater than or less than 80? Explain.

You can find two basic measures of the spread of data using the five-number summary. One measure is the **range,** which is the difference between the maximum and minimum of the data. The other measure is the **interquartile range** (IQR), which is the difference between the third quartile (Q_3) and first quartile (Q_1). The range covers 100 percent of the data. The interquartile range covers the middle 50 percent.

You can present the five-number summary graphically using a box-and-whisker plot. This plot gives you some control over larger data sets. Here is a box-and-whisker plot for the data from the Example with directions for making the plot.

For help drawing a box-and-whisker plot, see the TI-Nspire Handbook, p. 788.

Female Life Expectancy

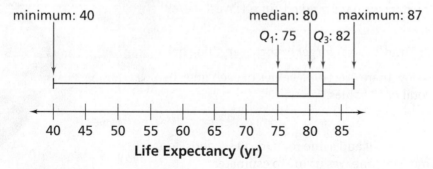

- Find the five-number summary.
- At each of the five numbers, draw a short vertical segment above a number line.
- Draw a box from the first to the third quartile representing the interquartile range. The vertical segment for the median is inside the box.
- Draw segments (whiskers) to connect the box to the minimum and maximum values.

A box-and-whisker plot gives additional information about the five-number summary. For example, the plot shows that there is a wide range of data between the minimum and the first quartile. The range of data is less between the first and third quartiles.

Sasha and Tony talk about the stopwatch experiment in Lesson 6.01.

Sasha So, we had 12 people try the experiment.

Tony Is there a table of how everyone did?

Sasha Sure, here are the two tries for each person.

Elapsed Time Estimates

Time 1	Time 2	Time 1	Time 2
28	36	29	31
26	35	24	27
7	27	23	32
24	28	29	26
26	37	31	34
14	30	24	31

Tony Wow, only one person hit 30 seconds exactly.

Sasha Right, it seems that most people counted 30 seconds too quickly the first time.

Tony Some counted way too quickly! Okay, I'll make a box-and-whisker plot for the data we have marked Time 1. We'll see what it looks like.

Sasha I'll do the same for Time 2. Don't forget to sort everything first.

Tony Sure thing. I also know there are 3 data values in each quartile, since there are a total of 12 values.

They work for awhile.

Sasha Okay, I think we're done. I'll add a line to mark 30 seconds, too, since that's the time everyone was trying to estimate.

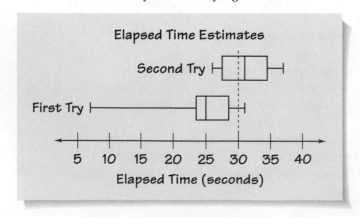

Why might it be difficult to tell how many seconds have elapsed with a 30-second timer?

Tony The plots really show the differences between the first try and the second try. Almost no one counted a full 30 seconds on the first try, but the median is more than 30 seconds on the second try!

Sasha I think it's interesting that the middle half of the data is still about as wide as it was before. I was expecting it to be more narrow.

Tony Yes, but overall, the spread is narrower. The second try doesn't show any crazy points that are far away from the rest.

Sasha That's true. In any case, putting the plots next to each other helps make these comparisons easy.

For Discussion

2. Using Sasha and Tony's box-and-whisker plot, which set of data has a wider interquartile range?

Since box-and-whisker plots provide a quick look at the shape of a data set, they are particularly well suited for paired comparison. Using these plots, you can quickly demonstrate that one data set is significantly different from another data set.

Exercises *Practicing Habits of Mind*

Check Your Understanding

1. **Standardized Test Prep** Which statement best interprets the data set {20, 15, 10, 20, 15, 10, 20, 20, 50}?

   A. Only the mean is 20.

   B. The range of the set of data is 20.

   C. The mean, median, and mode are all 20.

   D. The mode and median are not the same.

2. Using the data from the stopwatch experiment in Lesson 6.01, calculate the five-number summary for two data sets. The data sets are the first try and the second try at estimating 30 seconds.

3. Use the five-number summaries from Exercise 2 to make a paired box-and-whisker plot of the two data sets. Describe at least two differences between the data sets that the box-and-whisker plots show.

4. Each of two data sets has a median of 80. Set A has twice the interquartile range of Set B.

   a. Draw a possible paired box-and-whisker plot for Set A and Set B.

   b. Is it possible for the maximum value in Set A to be less than the maximum value in Set B, even though Set A has a greater interquartile range? Explain.

5. **Take It Further** The data set {61, 67, 70, 70, 76, 79, 80, 82, 84, 88, 91, 92, 95} has a median of 80.

   Describe a rule that makes a different data set that doubles the interquartile range but leaves the median, 80, unchanged.

> An example of a rule that makes a different data set: Add 5 to each data value and then double the sum.

On Your Own

6. Can you find each measure below using only a box-and-whisker plot? Explain.

   a. mean   **b.** median   **c.** mode   **d.** range

7. **Standardized Test Prep** The box-and-whisker plot below shows the heights of 20 players on a school soccer team.

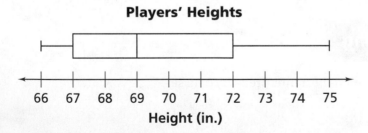

Players' Heights

Height (in.)

Based on the information in the box-and-whisker plot, which of the following statements must be true?

   A. The mean height of the team is 69 inches.

   B. Half of the players' heights are between 67 and 72 inches.

   C. The height of the shortest player on the team is 67 inches.

   D. The range of players' heights is 5 inches.

Go Online
www.successnetplus.com

8. Write About It Describe the steps you use to calculate the five-number summary for the 14 male life expectancies on page 496.

9. Here is the five-number summary for the 14 male life expectancies on page 496.

- Minimum   37
- First quartile (Q_1) 68
- Median   72
- Third quartile (Q_3) 76
- Maximum   81

Make paired box-and-whisker plots for the male and female life expectancies in the 14 countries. Describe what the plots show about the data sets.

The five-number summary for female life expectancies is on page 497.

10. Standardized Test Prep Felipe made this box-and-whisker plot using the heights of 40 baseball players.

Heights of Baseball Players

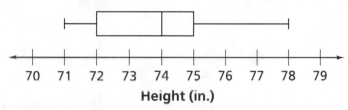

70   71   72   73   74   75   76   77   78   79

Height (in.)

Which of the following conclusions can you NOT draw from the box-and-whisker plot?

A. The range of players' heights is 7 inches.

B. At least 30 players are six feet tall or taller.

C. The mean height of the 40 players is 74 inches.

D. One quarter of the players are at least 6 feet 3 inches tall.

The median height of the nine players is the height of the fifth-tallest (or fifth-shortest) player.

11. **Write About It** The paired box-and-whisker plots show the test scores from two different classes on the same test.

Test Scores

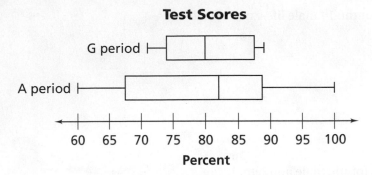

Based on the data, in which class would you prefer to be? Explain.

12. **Take It Further** Five numbers are in the data set $\{16, 4, 6, 2, x\}$. The mean and median are the same number. What are the possible values of x?

Maintain Your Skills

What is the mean of each data set?

13. $\{1, 2, 3\}$

14. $\{1, 2, 3, 4\}$

15. $\{1, 2, 3, 4, 5\}$

16. $\{1, 2, 3, 4, 5, \ldots, n\}$

17. $\{2, 4, 6, 8, 10, \ldots, 2n\}$

6.05 Categorical Data

So far, you have used number lines as tools to organize quantitative data, such as with dot plots and box-and-whisker plots. But *categorical data*, like yes-or-no answers to a survey, are not organized this way. In this lesson, you will learn some ways to deal with data organized into categories and some concepts that apply when more than one data variable is present.

In-Class Experiment

At a school, administrators are thinking about starting and ending the school day one hour later. A teacher was concerned that athletes may feel differently about this possibility than non-athletes. She conducted a survey of students in her class. She recorded whether or not they played a sport, and their response (*agree* or *disagree*) to the statement "Classes should start and end one hour later." Here are the responses from this study:

Study on School Start and End Times

Athlete or Non-Athlete?	Agree or Disagree?	Athlete or Non-Athlete?	Agree or Disagree?
Athlete	Agree	Athlete	Agree
Athlete	Disagree	Non-Athlete	Disagree
Non-Athlete	Agree	Athlete	Disagree
Non-Athlete	Disagree	Non-Athlete	Agree
Athlete	Agree	Non-Athlete	Agree
Athlete	Agree	Athlete	Agree
Non-Athlete	Disagree	Athlete	Disagree
Non-Athlete	Agree	Athlete	Disagree
Athlete	Disagree	Non-Athlete	Agree
Athlete	Disagree	Athlete	Disagree
Athlete	Agree	Non-Athlete	Disagree
Athlete	Agree	Athlete	Agree

1. Find a way to organize the responses numerically. Describe what you did.

2. Write a ratio of the number of athletes who agree with the statement to the total number of athletes.

3. Write a ratio of the number of athletes who agree with the statement to the total number of students who agree with the statement.

For the survey, there are two *categorical variables:*

• Are you an athlete or a non-athlete?

• Do you agree or disagree with the statement?

A **two-way frequency table** displays the distribution for two categorical variables. The frequency of responses for another group is displayed below.

	Athlete	Non-Athlete
Agree	10	5
Disagree	6	3

Each entry of this two-way table is the number (frequency) of students in a specific category for each variable. The table indicates that 10 of the 24 students in this group are athletes *and* agree with the statement.

Example

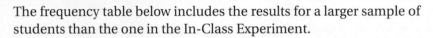

The frequency table below includes the results for a larger sample of students than the one in the In-Class Experiment.

	Athlete	Non-Athlete
Agree	31	23
Disagree	44	19

Problem

a. Write a ratio of the number of athletes who agree with the statement "Classes should start and end one hour later" to the total number of athletes.

b. Write a ratio of the number of students surveyed who agree with the statement to the total number of students surveyed.

Solution

a. 31 athletes agree, and 44 athletes disagree: there are 75 total athletes. The ratio of athletes who agree to all athletes is $\frac{31}{75}$, or about 41.3%.

b. For a complete count it makes sense to extend the table by adding totals.

	Athlete	Non-Athlete	Total
Agree	31	23	54
Disagree	44	19	63
Total	75	42	117

54 students agree, and 63 students disagree: there are 117 total responses. The ratio of students who agree to all students is $\frac{54}{117}$, or about 46.2%.

The 42 responses from non-athletes *do not matter* in this part of the problem.

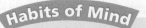

Habits of Mind

Read tables carefully. Sometimes, entries may be totaled in one direction but not the other.

For You to Do

4. What percent of non-athletes agreed with the statement?

5. What percent of those who agreed with the statement were non-athletes?

In the survey, non-athletes were more likely than athletes to agree with the statement. For this reason, you can say there is an **association** between the two types of students and their responses to the statement.

Association is also known as a *correlation*.

Often, variables have no association. If the percents of athletes and non-athletes who agreed with the statement were not significantly different, you could say the two variables are *not associated*, or **independent**.

To determine whether two categorical variables have an association, look at the distribution of one variable for each outcome of the second variable. Consider these two questions:

- What percent of athletes agree with the statement?
- What percent of non-athletes agree with the statement?

If the answers to these two questions are significantly different, then whether or not a student is an athlete is *associated* with whether or not the student agrees with the change. If the answers to these two questions are not significantly different, then the two categorical variables are independent. Two-way frequency tables help answer these questions quickly.

Habits of Mind

Use precise language. For now, there is no precise way to say what is a *significant* difference and what isn't. Essentially, a difference is significant if it is too rare to occur by chance. You'll revisit this concept in a later course, along with a more detailed definition of *independent*.

For Discussion

6. Think of two categorical variables you might expect to be independent. How would you determine if the variables are actually independent?

Developing Habits of Mind

Connect data and probability. Two-way frequency tables isolate data by category, and make it easier to answer *conditional* questions, such as "If you look only at athletes, what fraction agree with the statement?" Each row or column in a two-way frequency table is a *conditional distribution* made from a part of the original data.

The same concept also applies in probability. Consider a deck of cards, and the question "If a drawn card is not a jack, what is the probability that it is a face card?" A two-way frequency table can help you to analyze this question by listing the number of outcomes in each category:

	Jack	Not a Jack	Total
Face Card	4	8	12
Not a Face Card	0	40	40
Total	4	48	52

Remember...

There are 52 cards in a standard deck. The deck has 12 face cards: 4 jacks, 4 queens, 4 kings. The other 40 cards have 4 of each number from ace (one) through ten.

According to the two-way frequency table, there are 48 cards that are not jacks, and 8 of those are face cards. If a drawn card is not a jack, the probability that it is a face card is $\frac{8}{48}$, or $\frac{1}{6}$.

If a card *is* a jack, the probability that it is a face card is $\frac{4}{4} = 1$, a certainty. The probability of drawing a face card changes, depending on whether it is or isn't a jack. These conditional probabilities are different, and the two events (drawing a jack, drawing a face card) are not independent.

In this example, you can calculate exact probabilities, but a lot of data come from samples, studies, and surveys. The percentages reported by data can be used to estimate long-term probabilities. Keep in mind that estimates can change or improve with more data.

For You to Do

7. If a drawn card is a face card, what is the probability that it is a jack?

8. If a drawn card is *not* a face card, what is the probability that it is a jack?

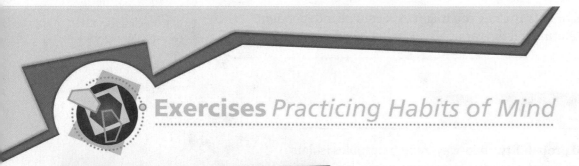

Exercises *Practicing Habits of Mind*

Check Your Understanding

1. Refer to the survey from the Example on page 504. What does each of the following fractions tell you in the context of the survey?

   a. $\frac{54}{117}$ b. $\frac{42}{117}$ c. $\frac{23}{42}$ d. $\frac{23}{54}$ e. $\frac{23}{117}$

2. Tess claims that athletes are more likely than non-athletes to agree with the statement from the Example on page 504.

   > *Tess:* 31 athletes agreed with the idea, but only 23 non-athletes agreed. It looks like athletes are more likely to agree, which surprises me.

   Give an argument supporting or rejecting Tess's claim. Are athletes actually more likely to agree than non-athletes?

3. A teacher recorded the gender of 100 students, and whether or not they were wearing a watch. This two-way frequency table shows the results.

Why is it not enough to say that more males wore watches?

	Wearing Watch	No Watch
Male	13	44
Female	9	34
Total	22	78

Which gender was more likely to wear a watch, males or females? Explain how you know.

4. In a study on a flu vaccine, of the 1000 people who received the flu vaccine, 149 still developed the flu. Of the 402 people who did not get the flu vaccine, 68 got the flu.

   a. Create a frequency table to summarize the results of this study.

   b. Do you think the vaccine helped reduce the occurrence of the flu? Provide evidence for your conclusions.

The two variables are the vaccine and the flu, and there are four possible situations.

5. Here is a two-way frequency table with variables where values should be:

	Left-Handed	Right-Handed
Male	a	c
Female	b	d

   a. Fill in the values of a, b, c, and d in a way that makes the two categorical variables independent. Explain how you know they are independent.

   b. In terms of the variables given, write a ratio of the number of left-handed people who are male to the number of males.

   c. In terms of the variables given, write a ratio of the number of right-handed people who are male to the number of males.

   d. In terms of the variables given, write a ratio of the number of males to the total number of people.

6. Take It Further For the two-way frequency table in Exercise 5, show that if the ratio of left-handed males to males equals the ratio of right-handed males to males, then the number of males who are left-handed equals the number of males who are right-handed.

7. Complete the two-way frequency table below for integers n from 1 to 100, and determine if the categorical variables are associated.

Remember...

1 is not a prime number, but 2 and 3 are. Prime numbers have exactly two factors.

	Prime	Not Prime
$1 \leq n < 25$	▪	▪
$25 \leq n \leq 100$	▪	▪

For Exercises 8–12, use the table below. It shows the results of a survey of students that was conducted to learn more about whether eye dominance is associated with other traits, such as handedness, gender, or being an athlete.

Most people are either left-eyed or right-eyed. You can find out which you are by holding your hands in front of you while looking at an object 10 to 15 feet away. Make a small space between your hands to see through to the object, and then close your right eye. If you can still see the object, you are left-eyed. If the object is hidden, open your right eye and close your left eye. If you can see the object now, you are right-eyed.

Survey Results

Name	Location	Eyedness	Handedness	Athlete	Gender
Elham Y	Connecticut	Right	Right	Yes	Female
Michael B	Connecticut	Right	Right	Yes	Male
Danielle S	L. A.	Right	Right	Yes	Female
Frederic P	Connecticut	Right	Left	Yes	Male
Jessica Y	L. A.	Left	Right	No	Female
Kaily W	Connecticut	Right	Left	Yes	Female
Anmol A	L. A.	Right	Right	Yes	Male
Aaron B	Connecticut	Right	Right	Yes	Male
Sahar B	L. A.	Right	Left	Yes	Female
Sam S	L. A.	Right	Right	No	Male
Alex S	L. A.	Right	Right	Yes	Male
Mitchell O	L. A.	Left	Right	Yes	Male
Alex L	L. A.	Left	Right	No	Male
Christian K	Connecticut	Left	Right	Yes	Male
Mariana B	L. A.	Right	Right	Yes	Female
Anna R	L. A.	Left	Right	No	Female
Nicolai S	L. A.	Right	Right	No	Male
Olivia A	Connecticut	Left	Right	Yes	Female
Matt W	L. A.	Left	Right	Yes	Male
Ben S	L. A.	Left	Right	Yes	Male
James C	Connecticut	Left	Left	No	Male
Susannah W	Connecticut	Right	Right	No	Female
Rae W	L. A.	Left	Left	Yes	Female
Will D	L. A.	Left	Right	Yes	Male

There are five categorical variables in this survey:

- Do you live in Los Angeles or Connecticut?
- Are you left-eyed or right-eyed?
- Are you left-handed or right-handed?
- Do you play a sport (yes or no)?
- Are you male or female?

8. Build a two-way frequency table to determine whether there is an association between location and eye dominance.

9. Build a two-way frequency table to determine whether there is an association between eye dominance and being an athlete.

10. Choose any two categorical variables and build a two-way frequency table to determine whether there is an association between them.

11. The following two-way frequency table came from a larger survey than the one on page 508.

	Athlete	Non-Athlete	Total
Left-Eyed	11	16	27
Right-Eyed	41	17	58
Total	52	33	85

a. In this survey, which group of students was more likely to be left-eyed: athletes or non-athletes? Describe the calculations you used.

b. Are the categorical variables of eye dominance and athletic status associated? Explain how you know.

12. Katrina noticed something unusual about the data.

> *Katrina:* It looks like there might be an association between being left-handed and being from Connecticut! That's very strange.

a. What fraction of students from Connecticut were left-handed?

b. What fraction of students from Los Angeles were left-handed?

c. **Reflect and Write** Do you think there is an association between handedness and location? What might you do to investigate this further?

13. Suggest two categorical variables you expect to be associated, and explain why you expect this.

14. Suggest two categorical variables you expect to be independent, and explain why you expect this.

15. Conduct a survey of at least 25 people on your categorical variables from Exercise 13 or 14. Then decide whether the categorical variables are associated or independent.

Maintain Your Skills

Exercises 16–18 use the life expectancy data from Lesson 6.04.

16. For the 14 countries, determine the mean life expectancy for:

   a. men

   b. women

17. Complete this two-way frequency table.

	Male Expectancy Below Mean	Male Expectancy Above Mean	Total
Female Expectancy Above Mean	■	■	■
Female Expectancy Below Mean	■	■	■
Total	■	■	■

18. Do you think there is an association between male and female life expectancy? Explain.

6.06 Two-Variable Data

In Lesson 6.04, Sasha and Tony made two box-and-whisker plots for the stopwatch experiment. Each plot represents a single set of data, either the times for the first try or the times for the second try.

You can think of the two times for each person as a coordinate pair: (time 1, time 2). Then, you can represent the two data sets together as a **scatter plot**, a graph showing each pair of related data as a point in the coordinate plane.

A scatter plot can be used to identify trends and *outliers*, data points that are significantly different from the rest of the data. An outlier could occur for many reasons, such as an inaccurate measurement or an unusual situation.

Minds in Action

Sasha and Tony continue talking about the stopwatch experiment in Lesson 6.01.

Sasha   Let's try a scatter plot. I'll draw a blank coordinate grid. We can draw a point for each person.

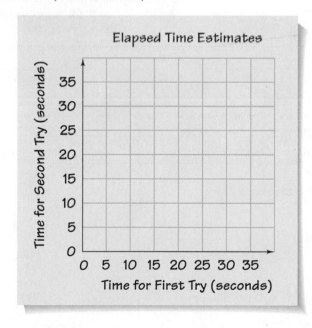

Tony   The data are positive for both variables, so we really only need the first quadrant.

Sasha   The first person estimates 28 seconds the first time and 36 seconds the second time. We'll draw the first point at (28, 36).

Tony   Does this look right?

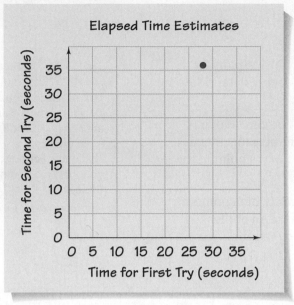

Sasha   Yes. Find 28 seconds on the horizontal axis and 36 seconds on the vertical axis. Let's do the rest to get the final scatter plot.

They plot all 12 points.

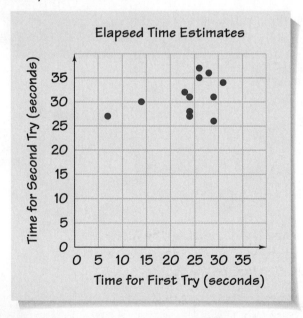

Sasha and Tony are plotting time on the second try against time on the first try. Should they connect the dots?

Tony   Most of the data seem clumped, and there are two points far to the left. I guess those are the outliers.

Sasha   I agree. Those two were way too fast their first time. Actually, I think almost everyone was faster on their first try.

Tony   Oh, and we could see that on the graph, by drawing a diagonal line through (0, 0) and (30, 30)!

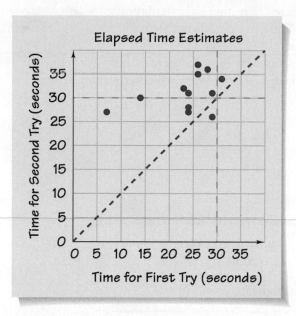

Elapsed Time Estimates

Sasha   Great job, Tony. Scatter plots seem pretty useful for analysis. And all we're doing is plotting one variable against another.

For You to Do

1. Build a scatter plot for the 14 countries' life expectancy data from Lesson 6.04. Each point's coordinates are the life expectancies for men and women in a particular country.

2. Describe any pattern you see in the scatter plot.

When you can see patterns in a scatter plot, there is an **association** between the two variables. Most associations can be described as *positive* or *negative*.

Definition

Two variables are **positively associated** when large values of the first variable tend to occur with large values of the second, and small values of the first variable tend to occur with small values of the second.

Two variables are **negatively associated** when large values of the first variable tend to occur with small values of the second, and small values of the first variable tend to occur with large values of the second.

For Discussion

3. Explain why there is a positive association for life expectancies for the 14 countries in the scatter plot from the *For You to Do*.

4. Consider the data for the stopwatch experiment. Is there a positive association between the two variables, a negative association, or neither? Explain how you know.

Associations can be strong or weak, and there are numerical calculations that measure the strength of associations. The most common calculation is the **correlation coefficient**, a calculation based on the data that returns a number between -1 and 1. Positive associations have positive correlation coefficients, and the correlation coefficient equals 1 or -1 only when the entire scatter plot lies on a straight line.

Some calculators can find the correlation coefficient for two variables.

| 1.0 | 0.8 | 0.4 | 0.0 | −0.4 | −0.8 | −1.0 |

For You to Do

5. One of these is the correlation coefficient for the male and female life expectancy data: -1, -0.99, -0.4, 0, 0.4, 0.99, 1. Which is it?

6. Estimate the correlation coefficient for the stopwatch experiment.

Developing Habits of Mind

Reason about calculations. Here are two common pitfalls to avoid when thinking about association and correlation:

• When the correlation coefficient is very close to 1 or –1, it suggests a strong linear association between the two variables. However, the correlation coefficient does not detect nonlinear associations. Consider the following data:

x	−3	−2	−1	0	1	2	3
y	9	4	1	0	1	4	9

Plotting these points shows a clear association: all the points make the equation $y = x^2$ true.

The correlation coefficient for these 7 data points is exactly zero! There is no *linear* association between these variables, but there is still an association.

• When two variables have an association, it does not mean that a change in one *causes* a change in the other. For example, life expectancies for men and women are positively associated, but this does not mean that male life expectancy is high *because* female life expectancy is high!

What are some possible causes of higher or lower life expectancy in different countries?

This is a very common fallacy in statistics. **Correlation does not imply causation.** For an example, see Exercise 6.

Some of the work in an advanced statistics class involves learning how to properly determine causation. It involves eliminating other possible causes for the association.

Exercises *Practicing Habits of Mind*

Check Your Understanding

1. Use the data from your stopwatch experiment in Lesson 6.01. Make a scatter plot similar to the plot shown in the Minds in Action box on pages 511–513..

For help drawing a scatter plot, see the TI-Nspire Handbook, p. 788.

2. Use the scatter plot in Exercise 1. Find the percent of students in your class who are too fast the first time and too slow the second time.

3. Here is a table showing the horsepower of several cars, as well as their fuel efficiency in miles per gallon.

Horsepower	110	255	198	173	292	197	155	202	209	210	332	210	194	200	266	170
Miles per Gallon	40	15	35	16	22	16	34	15	27	13	20	14	16	13	17	17

Make a scatter plot showing the horsepower on the horizontal axis and the fuel efficiency on the vertical axis.

a. Is there a positive association between these two variables? A negative association?

b. Estimate the correlation coefficient for these variables.

4. Here is a table of the results of the United States Census for the years 1900 through 1990.

a. Make a scatter plot. Show the years from 1900 to 2000 on the horizontal axis. Show the population from 0 to 300 million people on the vertical axis.

b. Based on the scatter plot, guess the U.S. population in the years 1890 and 2000.

United States Population

Year	Population (millions)
1900	76.2
1910	92.2
1920	106.0
1930	123.2
1940	132.2
1950	151.3
1960	179.3
1970	203.3
1980	226.5
1990	248.7

SOURCE: United States Census Bureau

The United States Census Bureau conducts a census every ten years, as required by the United States Constitution. The first census occurred in 1790.

5. A person's *arm span* is the distance between their fingertips when their arms are at their widest.

a. Estimate the correlation coefficient between *height* and *arm span*. Explain your estimate.

b. Measure the heights and arm spans of at least 10 people. Make a scatter plot showing the data.

c. Estimate the correlation coefficient for the data. How does this compare with your estimate from part (a)?

d. In your sample, which was more likely, being taller or shorter than your arm span? Explain how you know.

6. Here is a table of several countries' life expectancies, along with the number of televisions per 1000 people in those countries.

Country	Life Expectancy	TVs per 1000 People
Argentina	75.3	201.1
Australia	81.2	505.2
Bermuda	80.7	1009.7
Brazil	72.4	196.1
Canada	80.7	655.4
China	73.0	306.2
Egypt	71.3	99.3
Ethiopia	52.9	9.3
France	80.7	573.7
Germany	79.4	623.6
Hong Kong	82.2	266.7
Iceland	81.8	330.3
India	64.7	58.3
Italy	80.5	521.5
Japan	82.6	678.9
Malta	79.4	702.5
Mexico	76.2	241.0
Spain	80.9	401.6
Sweden	80.9	511.0
Switzerland	81.7	442.0
United Kingdom	79.4	504.6
United States	78.3	740.5

Make a scatter plot showing the life expectancy on the horizontal axis and the number of televisions per 1000 people on the vertical axis.

a. Is there a positive association between these two variables? A negative association?

b. **Write About It** Derman says the data make it clear that television helps people live longer. What would you say to him?

On Your Own

Another measure of association is called the Quadrant Count Ratio, or QCR. On a scatter plot, draw vertical and horizontal lines at the mean of each variable. This scatter plot shows the 14 countries' life expectancy data from Lesson 6.04, along with lines marking the means:

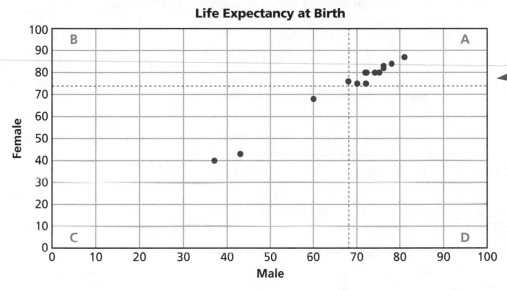

Life Expectancy at Birth

There are two points at (72, 80), but you can only see one.

The QCR counts the difference between the number of data points with positive and negative associations, and then divides by the total:

$$QCR = \frac{(\text{number of points in A and C}) - (\text{number of points in B and D})}{(\text{number of points})}$$

7. Determine the QCR for the life expectancy data.

8. **a.** What are the maximum and minimum possible values for QCR? Explain.

   b. Draw two scatter plots, one in which QCR is very close to zero, and one in which QCR is as negative as possible.

9. **a.** Copy and complete this two-way table for the data from Exercise 3:

	Horsepower Below Mean	Horsepower Above Mean
Miles per Gallon Above Mean	■	■
Miles per Gallon Below Mean	■	■

   b. Use the two-way table to compute the QCR for these variables.

> **Remember...**
> While the name of QCR includes *quadrant* because of the four zones, *quadrant* normally refers to the four parts of the coordinate plane.

> You will need to compute the mean of each variable. How does the two-way table compare to the scatter plot from Exercise 3?

10. Match each verbal statement with the value of QCR it best matches. Drawing sample scatter plots might help you decide.

   QCR values: −1   0   0.33   0.81   1

   a. Mrs. A: "Every student who was below average on test 1 was also below average on test 2. Every student who was above average on test 1 was also above average on test 2."

   b. Ms. B: "Most of the students who were below average on test 1 were below average on test 2. Similarly, most of the students scoring above average on test 1 were also above average on test 2. There were a few exceptions, but the trend was clear."

   c. Mr. C: "Wow, there was really no correlation between test 1 and test 2! Half the students who were below average on the first test were also below average on the second test, but half were above average! The same was true for the above average students!"

   d. Mr. D: "This is so weird. Every student who was below average on test 1 was above average on test 2, and vice versa."

   e. Mr. E: "Of those scoring above average on test 1, about 60% were above average on test 2, but 40% were below average."

11. **Standardized Test Prep** The scatter plot shows the women's winning times in the New York City Marathon and the Boston Marathon. Which of the following is true about the women's record time in either marathon?

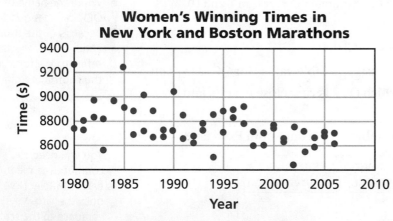

Women's Winning Times in New York and Boston Marathons

SOURCE: Boston Marathon official Web site and New York City Marathon official Web site

> In 1984, the winning times were only 2 seconds apart!

A. The women's record time occurred in 2002.

B. The women's record time occurred in 1985.

C. The women's record time occurred in 2006.

D. You cannot tell from the scatter plot in which year the women's record time occurred.

12. **Write About It** A class performed the stopwatch experiment from Lesson 6.01.

Elyse calculated the correlation coefficient between the first and second tries and found it was about −0.95. Does this mean that students' guesses got *worse* between their first and second tries? If not, what does a strong negative correlation mean?

13. **Take it Further**

 a. Consider the data set of points (1, 35), (2, 44), (3, 52), (4, 63), and (5, 71). Show that the mean $\bar{x}$ of the x-coordinates is 3 and the mean of the squares of the x-coordiantes $\overline{x^2}$ is 11.

 b. Find the values $\bar{y}$ and $\overline{y^2}$.

 c. To find the value of the expression $\overline{xy}$, find product of the coordinates for each point. Then find the mean of those products.

 d. Determine the two variables' correlation coefficient r by the following calculation.

$$r = \frac{\overline{xy} - \bar{x} \cdot \bar{y}}{\sqrt{\overline{x^2} - (\bar{x})^2} \cdot \sqrt{\overline{y^2} - (\bar{y})^2}}$$

Be careful! Each piece of this calculation is different.

Maintain Your Skills

Go Online
www.successnetplus.com

For Exercises 14 and 15, use the Best Actor and Best Actress age data in Lesson 6.01. Make each plot and describe your findings.

14. paired box-and-whisker plot

15. scatter plot

16. Find the mean of each data set.

 a. 4, 3, 9, 7, 7, 4, 8

 b. 14, 13, 19, 17, 17, 14, 18

 c. 1004, 1003, 1009, 1007, 1007, 1004, 1008

 d. $(n + 4)$, $(n + 3)$, $(n + 9)$, $(n + 7)$, $(n + 7)$, $(n + 4)$, $(n + 8)$

Mathematical Reflections 6A

In this investigation, you represented data using data lists, frequency tables, stem-and-leaf displays, histograms, box-and-whisker plots, and scatter plots. These questions will help you summarize what you have learned.

1. The list shows the number of glasses of lemonade Annette sold each day from July 13 to August 1.

   2   7   11   15   21   28   33   38   35   51   36   25   24   3   14
   16   20   22   31   26

   a. Use Annette's daily sales data to make a stem-and-leaf display.

   b. Make two histograms of Annette's sales data. On one histogram, use 5-unit intervals. On the other histogram, use 10-unit intervals.

   c. Based on the histograms, about how many glasses of lemonade did Annette sell on each day?

2. Which measure for average (mean, median, or mode) can you use to determine the winner of an election? Explain.

3. Make a box-and-whisker plot for the baseball salary information in Lesson 6.01.

4. How can you use graphs, charts, and tables to understand data?

5. How can you make informed conclusions about data?

6. Mr. Siddiqui tells his students about a correction for a test. He says, "It turns out that one problem didn't have a solution. To make up for my mistake, I gave everyone an extra 5 points credit for that problem. That changes the class average from 83 to 87 points." Is this possible? Explain.

What does this butterfly look like if you view it from the curb at the upper left?

Vocabulary

In this investigation, you learned these terms. Make sure you understand what each one means and how to use it.

- association
- box-and-whisker plot
- correlation coefficient
- dot plot
- first quartile
- five-number summary
- frequency table
- histogram
- independent
- interquartile range
- maximum
- mean
- median
- minimum
- mode
- negatively associated
- positively associated
- range
- scatter plot
- stem-and-leaf display
- third quartile
- two-way frequency table

Investigation 6B

Fitting and Data

In *Fitting and Data,* you will learn to analyze data. This includes real data that you quite likely cannot fit with a simple rule. For some types of real data, you will learn how to find a line that best fits the data. You will use the line of best fit to analyze the data and make predictions.

By the end of this investigation, you will be able to answer questions like these:

1. How do you find a line that fits a set of data?

2. What is the definition of the line of best fit?

3. What is the line of best fit for the data in the table at the right?

You will learn how to:

- decide whether a linear function reasonably represents a data set

- calculate the balance point of a data set

- estimate the slope of a fitting line

- calculate error, given a data set and a fitting function

- calculate the mean absolute error, mean squared error, and standard error

- use algebra to find the line of best fit for a set of data

Men's 1500-meter Olympic Gold Medal Times (seconds)					
Year	Time	Year	Time	Year	Time
1896	273.2	1932	231.2	1972	216.3
1900	246.2	1936	227.8	1976	219.2
1904	245.4	1948	229.8	1980	218.4
1908	243.4	1952	225.1	1984	212.5
1912	236.8	1956	221.2	1988	215.96
1920	241.8	1960	215.6	1992	220.12
1924	233.6	1964	218.1	1996	215.78
1928	233.2	1968	214.9	2000	212.07

SOURCE: *2007 ESPN Sports Almanac*

You will develop these habits and skills:

- Compare measures of error in data.

- Approximate scatter plots with graphs of simple functions.

- Graph linear equations.

- Evaluate the quality of a function's agreement with data.

- Use absolute value and square roots in calculations of error.

6.07 Getting Started

Activating Prior Knowledge
Exploring New Ideas

The problems in this lesson are about an experiment with a number cube. You will build a table that shows the number of rolls of the number cube and the cumulative total for all the rolls. For example, your table might look like the one below after 5 rolls.

Rolls	Total
0	0
1	5
2	10
3	14
4	16
5	22
⋮	⋮

> Why is the total zero after zero rolls, and not some other number?

For You to Explore

With a partner, roll a number cube 20 times.

1. Record the cumulative totals in a table like the one above. Then make a difference table for your results. It might look like the table below.

Rolls	Total	Δ
0	0	5
1	5	5
2	10	4
3	14	2
4	16	6
5	22	

> How do the numbers in the Δ column relate to the results of the rolls?

2. **Write About It** Look at the difference table you made in Problem 1. Is there a linear function that matches the table? Justify your answer.

3. Bethany rolls a number cube 100 times and records the total. Which of these totals is the most likely after 100 rolls? Explain.

   A. 98   **B.** 256

   C. 354   **D.** 412

4. Draw a scatter plot with the number of rolls r on the horizontal axis and the total T on the vertical axis. Here is a plot for the number cube example on the previous page.

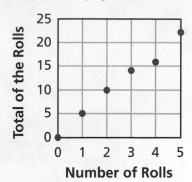

Your graph should go from 0 to 20 on the horizontal axis.

Describe your graph. How does your graph compare with the graphs of other groups?

5. On the same coordinate axes as your data, plot T against r for each of the functions below. Which function best fits the trends in your data? Which fits the worst?

   a. $T = r + 30$

   b. $T + 3r = 60$

   c. $T = 2.5r$

   d. $T = 3.5r$

   e. $T = 4.5r$

6. Think about a ruler with weights hanging from it.

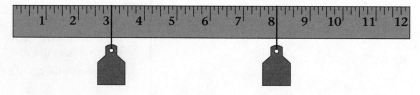

For the purpose of this exercise, assume the ruler is weightless and all the weights are equal.

   a. Suppose the ruler has two weights on it, at 3 inches and 8 inches. Where can you place the ruler on your finger to balance the weights?

   b. Suppose the two weights are at x inches and y inches. Write a rule that tells you where the ruler's balance point is.

   c. Suppose the ruler has three weights on it, at 1 inch, 3 inches, and 8 inches. Where is the ruler's balance point?

Exercises *Practicing Habits of Mind*

On Your Own

7. **Write About It** There were no Olympic Games held in 1916, 1940, or 1944, due to the two world wars. How can you make a guess about what the winning time would have been for the 1500-meter run in 1944? How can you make the same sort of predictions for Olympic Games in the future?

8. **a.** Lisa takes three tests. She gets scores of 85, 82, and 91. What is her average?

   b. A meter stick has three weights on it, at 85 cm, 82 cm, and 91 cm. Where is the ruler's balance point?

> Assume the ruler is weightless and all the weights are equal.

9. Every 10 years, the U.S. Census is taken. One of the reported calculations is the location in the United States that is the center of population. The report says,

   > The concept of the center of population as used by the U.S. Census Bureau is that of a balance point. That is, the center of population is the point at which [a map of the country] would balance if weights of identical size were placed on it so that each weight represented the location of one person.

   a. According to the Census Bureau, the population center of the U.S. has moved west in every census since its inception in 1790. Give some possible reasons why this has happened.

   b. A Census Bureau report explains how to calculate the center.

   > [T]he latitude of the center of population was determined by multiplying the population of each unit of area by the latitude of its population center, then adding all these products and dividing this total by the total population of the United States. The result is the latitude of the population center.

   What mathematical calculation is the Census Bureau describing?

> **Habits of Mind**
>
> **Look for relationships.** In geometry, you called balance points *centroids*. Is there a connection here?

10. The table below shows the coordinates of some points (x, y).

   a. How do you know that these points lie on a line?

   b. Find the equation of the line.

   c. Find the balance point for these five points by calculating the mean of the x-coordinates and the mean of the y-coordinates.

   d. Show that the balance point is on the line.

x	y
0	4
1	7
2	10
5	19
8	28

> Do not forget about the zero in the input list when calculating the mean of the five inputs.

11. The table below shows the coordinates of some points (x, y).

x	y
3	2
6	3
8	5
11	5
12	6

a. Plot the five points. How do you know that the points are not collinear?

b. These points follow a linear trend. Estimate the slope of a line that closely approximates the data.

c. Find the balance point for these five points.

d. Plot the balance point on the same graph as the five points. Explain why the balance point might be a good anchor for a line of best fit.

Habits of Mind

Communicate by context. Points are collinear if they lie on the same line. What do you think *linear trend* might mean?

Maintain Your Skills

The **balance point** $(\bar{x}, \bar{y})$ is the point with x-coordinate that is the average of the x-coordinates in the table and with y-coordinate that is the average of the y-coordinates in the table.

For Exercises 12–15, do the following steps.

Step 1: Compute the balance point $(\bar{x}, \bar{y})$.

Step 2: Build a new table by subtracting $\bar{x}$ from each x-value and subtracting $\bar{y}$ from each y-value.

Step 3: Compute the balance point for the new (x, y) values.

Step 4: Make and justify some conjectures about this process.

12.

x	y
0	4
1	7
2	10
5	19
8	28

$\longrightarrow$

$x - \bar{x}$	$y - \bar{y}$
■	■
■	■
■	■
■	■
■	■

13.

x	y
3	2
6	3
8	5
11	5
12	6

→

x − x̄	y − ȳ
■	■
■	■
■	■
■	■
■	■

14.

x	y
1900	246.2
1904	245.4
1908	243.4
1912	236.8
1920	241.8
1924	233.6
1928	233.2

→

x − x̄	y − ȳ
■	■
■	■
■	■
■	■
■	■
■	■
■	■

15.

x	y
73	6
22	66
16	54
60	18
6	9
73	13
10	82
6	85
8	73
33	57

→

x − x̄	y − ȳ
■	■
■	■
■	■
■	■
■	■
■	■
■	■
■	■
■	■
■	■

To slide along a grind rail, a skateboarder finds a balance point. How is a physical balance point related to the balance point of a data set?

Scientists perform experiments to collect data. Retailers keep track of sales figures and costs. Many professionals analyze data. They try to find patterns and relationships to make predictions.

There are many ways to represent data. You can use the scatter plot to spot trends in data.

These data points show a linear trend.

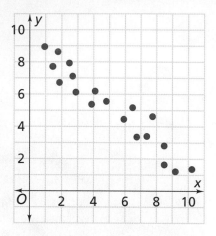

These data points do not show a linear trend.

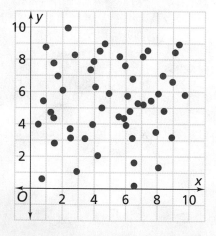

Bar codes and scanners simplify data gathering.

The trend of the data in the first scatter plot is linear. All the data points seem to follow a straight line. However, an entire set of data points is rarely collinear. You can find a **fitting line** that comes "close" to the data points. The equation of this fitting line helps you predict other data points.

Example

Problem Mark Green is the manager of concessions at Down the Chute Water Park. He wants to be able to estimate the amount of food he needs each day. Last summer, he collected data. He recorded the weather, the high temperature of the day, and the number of visitors to the park. This table shows the data for fourteen sunny days last summer.

Water Park Attendance

Temperature (°F)	Number of Visitors (thousands)	Temperature (°F)	Number of Visitors (thousands)
62	36.8	80	45.4
67	40.9	83	48.4
69	36.9	85	51.5
70	37.1	88	57.7
72	44.3	94	57.3
77	42.3	96	56.1
79	45.8	98	58.9

Write an equation that Mr. Green can use to estimate the number of visitors for any sunny day.

Solution Draw a scatter plot to see if there is a linear trend to the data.

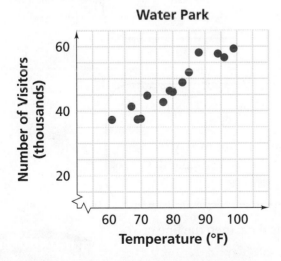

This scatter plot shows a general upward trend in data. You want to find the equation of a line that approximates the data. Remember, to find the equation of a line, you need a point on the line and the line's slope.

In Investigation 6A, you saw that the mean of a set of numerical data is the balance point of those numbers on a number line. Similarly, the mean of the data points is the balance point of those points on the coordinate plane. The x-coordinate of the balance point is the mean of the x-coordinates of the data, about 80°F. The mean of the y-coordinates is around 47,100 people. The fitting line should go through the point (80, 47.1).

You can write the balance point as $(\bar{x}, \bar{y})$.

Substitute these values into the general form of an equation.

$$y - 47.1 = m(x - 80)$$

What slope should you use? Make a guess at a reasonable slope. Draw a line that looks like it fits the data. Then determine the slope of that line. The slope is about $\frac{2}{3}$. The equation of a fitting line might be $y - 47.1 = \frac{2}{3}(x - 80)$.

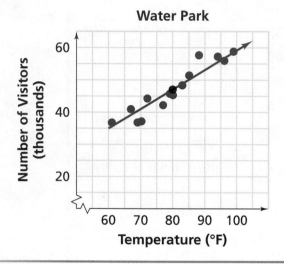

Water Park

Number of Visitors (thousands) vs. Temperature (°F)

For You to Do

1. The forecast is for sun, with a high of 75°F. Estimate how many people will visit the park.

2. Mr. Green knows that 57,500 people visited the park one sunny day. He forgot to write down the high temperature for that day. Estimate that day's temperature.

For any data set, if $(\bar{x}, \bar{y})$ is the balance point of the data, then the line of best fit is in the form $y - \bar{y} = m(x - \bar{x})$.

You might wonder how to decide whether one line is a better fit than another. Calculators use the balance point and a formula to find the best possible slope for the fitting line. This formula comes from minimizing the difference between the actual data and the results predicted by the fitting line.

Remember...

Note that ">" does not include equality.

Developing Habits of Mind

Check your work. When you find the equation of a fitting line, very few data points will actually satisfy the equation. You can determine how far off each data point is by comparing the actual data with the prediction.

Test Mr. Green's equation by plugging in each temperature to find the predicted number of visitors. Then compare the actual number of visitors to the predicted number according to the fitting-line equation.

Data vs. Line Fit

Temperature (°F)	Number of Visitors (thousands)		Error (Actual − Predicted)
$y - 47.1 = \frac{2}{3}(x - 80)$			
	Actual	Predicted	
62	36.8	35.1	1.7
67	40.9	38.4	2.5
69	36.9	39.8	−2.9
70	37.1	40.4	−3.3
72	44.3	41.8	2.5
77	42.3	45.1	−2.8
79	45.8	46.4	−0.6
80	45.4	47.1	−1.7
83	48.4	49.1	−0.7
85	51.5	50.4	1.1
88	57.7	52.4	5.3
94	57.3	56.4	0.9
96	56.1	57.8	−1.7
98	58.9	59.1	−0.2

The goal of finding the best fit is to make the numbers in the Error column as small as possible. Since some sets of data can contain hundreds of points, you need a single number that represents the error for the entire data set. Adding the individual errors does not really help. One prediction that is 10,000 too high offsets a prediction that is 10,000 too low.

What are the cutoff points for this inequality?

A **line of best fit** is the graph of the linear equation that shows the relationship between two sets of data most accurately.

Exercises *Practicing Habits of Mind*

Check Your Understanding

1. Your graphing calculator can find a linear regression of data. Consider the attendance data from Down the Chute Water Park. Enter the attendance data as thousands. Use 36.7 for 36,700 as in the table. The result is approximately $y = 0.678x - 7.1$.

   a. What do x and y represent in the calculator output?

   b. Plot the balance point (80, 47.1). Is it approximately on this line?

> The method for finding the line of best fit is **linear regression**. For help with linear regression, see the TI-Nspire Handbook, p. 788.

2. a. Where is the balance point on a ruler?

   b. Where is the balance point on a coin?

   c. **Write About It** Can an object have a balance point that is not part of the object? Explain and give an example.

3. Which equation best represents the data in the graph?

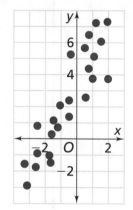

> The gymnast's balance point is along the vertical line that passes through her right hand.

   A. $y = 2x + 3$ **B.** $y = 2x - 3$

   C. $y = \frac{1}{2}x + 3$ **D.** $y = -2x + 3$

4. Use the table.

   a. Are all the points in the table on a line?

   b. Plot the data points. Is there a linear trend?

   c. Find and plot the balance point. Is the balance point along the trend?

United States Population

Year	Population (millions)
1900	76.0
1910	92.0
1920	105.7
1930	122.8
1940	131.7
1950	150.7
1960	179.3
1970	203.2
1980	226.5
1990	248.7
2000	281.4

Source: United States Census Bureau

On Your Own

5. Plot each data set. Is there is a linear trend to the data?

a. **Table 1**

Input	Output
1	2
2	4
3	7
4	9
5	12

b. **Table 2**

Input	Output
2	1
5	3
7	4
10	6
13	8

c. **Table 3**

Input	Output
2	0
3	6
4	8
5	6
6	0
7	−10

d. **Table 4**

Input	Output
1	−5
2	−1
2	2
3	4
4	9

Go Online
www.successnetplus.com

6. For each table in Exercise 5, calculate the balance point $(\bar{x}, \bar{y})$. Plot it along with the data.

7. For each table with a linear trend in Exercise 5, estimate the slope of the trend. Use the balance point you found in Exercise 6 to write a trend line equation. Graph each trend line on the same plot as your data.

8. These data follow a somewhat linear trend.

Input	Output
1	1.8
2	1.7
3	3.6
5	5.4
6	7.3
7	7.2

Plot the points. Then graph each line below on the same axes. Which line do you think fits the data best?

A. $y = x + 1$ **B.** $y = 0.5x + 2.5$

C. $y = 0.9x + 0.9$ **D.** $y = x + 0.5$

9. This table shows an analysis of the line with equation $y = x + 1$ from Exercise 8.

Data vs. Line Fit

Input, x	Actual, y	Predicted, $y = x + 1$	Error (Actual − Predicted)
1	1.8	2	−0.2
2	1.7	3	−1.3
3	3.6	4	−0.4
5	5.4	6	−0.6
6	7.3	7	0.3
7	7.2	8	−0.8

a. What do the negative values in the Error column suggest about this line as a line of best fit?

b. Perform the same analysis for the other lines in Exercise 8. Which line has the fewest errors? Which line has the smallest errors?

10. Standardized Test Prep The graph shows the total federal debt at the end of each year from 2001 through 2006. Use the line of best fit to predict the federal debt at the end of 2010.

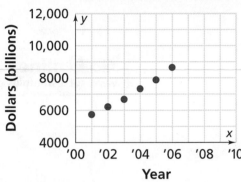

SOURCE: US Census Bureau

A. $570 billion

B. $9100 billion

C. $10,900 billion

D. $12,000 billion

Go Online
www.successnetplus.com

Maintain Your Skills

11. The balance point of the data from Exercise 8 is (4, 4.5). The line of best fit passes through that point. Consider these fitting lines.

$$y - 4.5 = x - 4$$
$$y - 4.5 = 2(x - 4)$$
$$y - 4.5 = 3(x - 4)$$

a. For each fitting line, make a table like the one in Exercise 9.

b. Add the values in the error column for each table. What pattern do the sums have?

c. What is the sum of the errors if the slope is $\frac{1}{2}$? If the slope is -18? If the slope is m? Explain.

> Notice that each line passes through the balance point (4, 4.5).

The table below shows the winning times for the men's 1500-meter run at each Olympics from 1896 until 2000.

Men's 1500-meter Olympic Gold Medal Times (seconds)					
Year	Time	Year	Time	Year	Time
1896	273.2	1932	231.2	1972	216.3
1900	246.2	1936	227.8	1976	219.2
1904	245.4	1948	229.8	1980	218.4
1908	243.4	1952	225.1	1984	212.5
1912	236.8	1956	221.2	1988	215.96
1920	241.8	1960	215.6	1992	220.12
1924	233.6	1964	218.1	1996	215.78
1928	233.2	1968	214.9	2000	212.07

Go Online
www.successnetplus.com

Here is a scatter plot for the data.

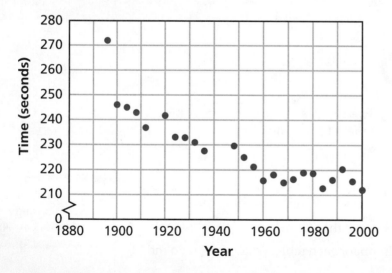

The data point for the 1896 Olympics is far away from the rest. Such a point is an **outlier**. Except for the 1896 data point, there is a general downward trend that seems to follow a straight path. It makes sense to approximate the data with a line.

On the other hand, the trend after 1960 seems to level out. You will investigate this idea in Exercise 6.

You have learned that a line with slope m through the point $(\bar{x}, \bar{y})$ has the following equation.

$$\bar{y} - k = m(\bar{x} - h)$$

In order to use this method for finding the equation of a fitting line, you need a point on the line and a slope.

When the data seem to follow a linear trend, a good anchor point for your fitting line is the balance point of the data. For the gold medal data, the balance point is (1949.8, 227.82). Throwing out the 1896 data point gives a slightly different balance point of (1952.2, 225.85).

Right now, you do not have a good definition of the best possible fitting line, so all you can do is approximate the slope of a fitting line that looks good to you. You will develop the definition of the line of best fit, and explore the reasons why that definition makes sense.

Remember...

The balance point (or centroid) has x-coordinate equal to the average of the x-coordinates of the data. Its y-coordinate is equal to the average of the y-coordinates of the data.

For You to Do

Copy the scatter plot of the gold medal data.

1. Use the balance point that excludes (1896, 273.2) and a slope that you estimate to draw a fitting line for the 1500-meter data. Find the equation of your line.

2. The Olympic Games were not held in 1944 because of World War II. Use your equation to estimate what a winning time in the 1944 Olympics might have been.

Developing Habits of Mind

Establish a process. Start thinking about how to decide whether one fitting line is better than another. Then you can develop the definition of the best-fit line.

Look at the table of gold medal times. When you plot the data, the vertical axis tells you the outcome of each race. The horizontal axis tells you when each outcome happened. If you want to use a line to predict future outcomes, you want the line's y-height at each year to be close to the y-height for the data point for that year. For example, you want the height of the line at 1920 to be close to 241.8.

You want a line that comes as close as possible to all the outcomes. So, you want to somehow minimize the overall differences between the data and the line's y-values.

The table below shows the calculation of the errors for one possible fitting line for the 1500-meter data. In the equation, x is the year and y is the time in seconds.

Data vs. Line Fit
$$y = -0.34x + 892.1$$

Year	Actual Time	Predicted Time	Error: Actual − Predicted
1900	246.2	246.1	0.1
1904	245.4	244.7	0.7
1908	243.4	243.4	0.0
1912	236.8	242.0	−5.2
1920	241.8	239.3	2.5
1924	233.6	237.9	−4.3
⋮	⋮	⋮	⋮
1992	220.12	214.8	5.32
1996	215.78	213.5	2.28
2000	212.07	212.1	−0.03

You often cannot make all the numbers in the error column small with one linear function. A line that makes one error small may make another error large. So you need some idea of overall error. Calculating the overall error is not as simple as just adding all the numbers in the error column, since negative and positive errors can cancel each other.

In fact, for any line that contains the balance point, the total sum of all the errors equals 0. See Exercise 8.

For Discussion

3. Think of a function you can apply to the numbers in the error column so you can add them together to get one measure of total error.

Developing Habits of Mind

Consider more than one strategy. You can always draw a line to approximate the data in a scatter plot. Sometimes, however, curves do a better job of minimizing error.

Even when lines do a good job of approximating the data, they often do it only locally. For example, you cannot use the line for $y = -0.34x + 892.1$ to predict 1500-meter times too far into the future. It would predict negative times. For what year does this first happen?

Exercises *Practicing Habits of Mind*

Check Your Understanding

1. a. Find the equations of three different lines that contain the point (3, 6).

   b. Find the equation of the one line that contains (3, 6) and (8, −1).

For Exercises 2 and 3, do parts (a)–(c).

   a. Draw a scatter plot for the points in the table.

   b. Calculate and plot the balance point.

   c. Explain whether it is reasonable to fit a line to the data.

2.

Time (seconds)	Distance (meters)
0	0
1	4.9
2	19.6
3	44.1
4	78.4

3.

Time (seconds)	$\sqrt{\text{Distance}}$ ($\sqrt{\text{meters}}$)
0	0
1	2.21
2	4.43
3	6.64
4	8.85

The numbers in the second column in Exercise 3 are the approximate square roots of the distances in Exercise 2.

4. Use the table of data at the right.

Plot the data points and the four lines given below on the same axes. Which line do you think fits the data best? Explain your choice.

   A. $y = x + 1$ **B.** $y = 0.5x + 2.5$

   C. $y = 0.9x + 0.9$ **D.** $y = x + 0.5$

Input	Output
1	1.8
2	1.7
3	3.6
5	5.4
6	7.3
7	7.2

5. On a coordinate plane, City A is at $(300, 20)$, City B is at $(700, 100)$, and City C is at $(1000, -400)$.

  a. If the three cities have about the same population, what is a good spot to call the "population center" for the cities?

  b. If City A has 100,000 people, City B has 200,000 people, and City C has 50,000 people, what is a good spot to call the population center for the cities?

6. Roger is looking at the gold medal data from the beginning of the lesson. He says, "I disagree with the claim that a single line fits the data. It seems to me, both from the table and the scatter plot, that there is a good fit to a line from 1900 to 1960, decreasing at about $\frac{1}{2}$ second per year. Then times were nearly static from 1960 to 2000."

Divide the data set into two parts. For each part, calculate the balance point and plot a good fitting line. Compare these two fits to the linear fit.

Part A: 1900–1960   **Part B:** 1960–2000

  a. Take It Further do these two fits suggest might have happened in the years when there were no Olympics?

  b. What does it predict for the year 2624?

On Your Own

7. In Exercise 4, there are four fitting lines suggested for a table of data.

  a. Build a table of errors for each of the other three lines listed in Exercise 4.

  b. Which line has the fewest errors?   **c.** Which line has the smallest errors?

Go Online
www.successnetplus.com

8. Use the data in Exercise 4.

  a. Find the equation of a line that contains the balance point.

  b. Show that the sum of the differences between the data and the corresponding points on your line is 0.

  c. Take It Further Show that the sum of the differences between the data and the corresponding points on any line that contains the balance point is 0.

For part (a), you get to pick the slope.

9. a. Where is the balance point of a ruler?

b. Where is the balance point of a coin?

c. Write About It Is it possible for an object to have a balance point that is not part of the object? Describe an example, or explain why it is impossible.

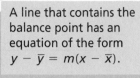

A line that contains the balance point has an equation of the form $y - \bar{y} = m(x - \bar{x})$.

10. Harvey rolls a number cube 85 times and writes down the outcomes. He counts 10 ones, 15 twos, 19 threes, 16 fours, and 11 fives.

a. How many sixes does Harvey roll?

b. Find the mean, median, and mode for Harvey's 85 rolls.

11. The table of data below comes from an experiment by Tor Carlson in 1913 on *Saccharomyces cerevisiae* (a type of yeast). The data show the number of hours elapsed and the number of yeast cells per square unit of area in a Petri dish.

Hours	Yeast Density
0	9.6
1	18.3
2	29.0
3	47.2
4	71.1
5	119.1
6	174.6
7	257.3

a. Draw a scatter plot for the eight data points.

b. Calculate and plot the balance point.

c. Is using a fitting line reasonable for these data? Explain your reasoning.

Where is the balance point of the forks and the blue toothpick?

12. **a.** For the table in Exercise 11, a graphing calculator gives the best-fit line $y = 33.4476x - 26.2917$. Copy and complete the table of errors.

Calculate the error as the actual value minus the predicted value.

Data vs. Line Fit: $y = 33.4476x - 26.2917$

Hours, x	Actual Yeast Density	Predicted Yeast Density, y	Error
0	9.6	■	■
1	18.3	■	■
2	29.0	■	■
3	47.2	■	■
4	71.1	■	■
5	119.1	■	■
6	174.6	■	■
7	257.3	■	■

b. Calculate the following numbers and arrange the list of numbers from least to greatest.

  I. the average of the absolute values of the errors

  II. the average of the errors

  III. the average of the squares of the errors

13. **Standardized Test Prep** Which line contains the point $(-1, 2)$ and has a slope of 4?

A. $y = 4x$

B. $y = 2x + 4$

C. $y = 2(2x - 1)$

D. $y = 4x + 6$

Maintain Your Skills

For Exercises 14–17, do parts (a)–(d).

a. Make a table of the function for integer inputs from 0 to 4.

b. Make a graph of the five input-output pairs in your table.

c. Find and plot the balance point of the five points in your table.

d. Decide whether the balance point is on the graph of the function.

Habits of Mind

Look for relationships. As usual, your job in these exercises is to practice calculations and to look for hidden theorems.

14. $f(x) = 3x + 1$

15. $x \mapsto 3x + 4$

16. $x \mapsto x^2$

17. $g(x) = x^2 + 3$

542 **Chapter 6** Statistics and Fitting Lines

6.10 The Line of Best Fit

Some calculators can find a *line of best fit* for any data set with two variables. In this lesson, you will learn more about what makes that line 'best' and how it is calculated.

The data table below shows the weight losses of ten people on the same diet and the number of months it took them to lose the weight.

Months	Pounds
5	18
2	2
15	54
10	39
18	65
8	25
5	12
13	41
23	72
11	46

The scatter plot below left suggests that a line might approximate the data well. To figure out the best line, you need to measure how good a line is. For example, the scatter plot below right shows the graph of $y = 3x - 1$ and the data.

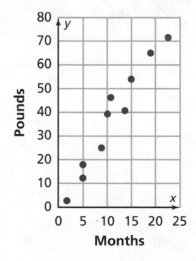

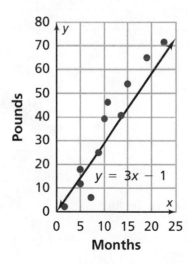

As you did in the previous lesson, you can calculate the errors from the approximating line.

Data vs. Line Fit: $y = 3x - 1$

Months	Pounds	Predicted	Error
5	18	14	4
2	2	5	−3
15	54	44	10
10	39	29	10
18	65	53	12
8	25	23	2
5	12	14	−2
13	41	38	3
23	72	68	4
11	46	32	14

You can show the error column of the table on the graph. Each error is the vertical distance between the actual data and the approximating line.

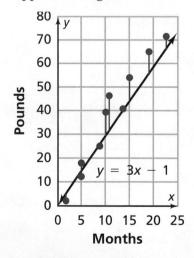

For example, the data point (15, 54) lies above the point (15, 45) on the line. The height of the "stick" from the data to the line is the error, which is 9.

Facts and Notation

One measure of overall error is the average length of the sticks. The lengths are the absolute values of the errors. Their average is the **mean absolute error**.

A calculator does something different to find the line of best fit. It sums the squares of the lengths of the sticks—the squares of the errors. The average of the squares of the errors is the **mean squared error**. The line of best fit minimizes the mean squared error.

Another useful measure of error is **standard error** or *root mean squared error*. It is just the square root of the mean squared error.

> Why do you take the square root? One reason is that it preserves units. For example, in the weight-loss data, the standard error is a measure of pounds, not pounds^2.

For You to Do

1. Calculate the mean squared error for the graph of $y = 3x - 1$ and the weight loss data. Can you find a line that has a smaller mean squared error?

In-Class Experiment

Here is a useful way to think about finding the line of best fit.

Suppose you have a moveable line on a scatter plot. You also have vertical sticks between the line and the data points. As you move the line, some sticks grow in length, while others shrink. If you keep track of the sums of the squares of the stick lengths, you can fine-tune the line position. You can adjust the line to make the overall error small.

2. You can turn this thought experiment into a real experiment. Use your dynamic geometry software and the data in the table at the beginning of this lesson.

Step 1 Make a scatter plot of the data.

Step 2 Construct a moveable line on the plot. Translating the line keeps the slope the same. Rotating the line changes the slope.

Step 3 Construct a vertical segment from each of the ten data points to the moveable line.

Step 4 Ask the system to calculate the sum of the squares of the vertical segment lengths.

Step 5 Adjust the line. Try to make it so that the sum in Step 4 is as small as possible.

> For more details, see the TI-Nspire Handbook, p. 788.

For Discussion

3. The mean squared error is the average of the squares of the errors. Why does making the sum of the squares of the errors as small as possible also minimize the mean squared error?

Exercises *Practicing Habits of Mind*

Check Your Understanding

1. Use the graph of data points at the right. Which line best fits the data in the graph?

    A. $y = 2x + 3$

    B. $y = \frac{1}{2}x + 3$

    C. $y = 2x - 3$

    D. $y = -2x + 3$

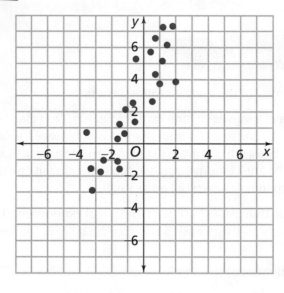

2. Use the table of data at the right.

   a. Which equation has a graph that best fits the data?

     A. $y = 3x - 1$ **B.** $y = -x + 8.4$

   b. For each equation in part (a), compare the following.

- the sum of the errors

- the mean absolute error

- the mean squared error

Input	Output
1	3
2	4.5
3	8.1
4	8

3. Tony looks at the data in Exercise 2 and wonders, "If I keep the slope at 3, which line will give me the smallest mean squared error?" Sasha says, "Every line with slope 3 has an equation $y = 3x + b$ for some number b. So, let's keep b variable and calculate the sum of the squares of the errors as a function of b."

   a. Copy and complete the following table for Tony and Sasha.

Data vs. Line Fit: $y = 3x + b$

Input	Output	Predicted	Error
1	3	$3 \cdot 1 + b = 3 + b$	$3 - (3 + b) = -b$
2	4.5	▩	▩
3	8.1	$3 \cdot 3 + b = 9 + b$	▩
4	8	▩	$-4 - b$

   b. What is the sum of the squares of the errors in terms of b?

   c. **Take It Further** What value of b minimizes the sum in part (b)?

   d. **Take It Further** What is the equation of the line that Tony wants?

Habits of Mind

Consider more than one strategy.
What is the balance point of the data?

4. Plot each data set below. Then use the plot to decide whether a line would be a good fit to the data.

Go Online
www.successnetplus.com

Table 1

Input	Output
1	2
2	4
3	7
4	9
5	12

Table 2

Input	Output
2	1
5	3
7	4
10	6
13	8

Table 3

Input	Output
2	0
3	6
4	8
5	6
6	0
7	−10

Table 4

Input	Output
1	−5
2	−1
2	2
3	4
4	9

5. For each table in Exercise 4, calculate the balance point $(\bar{x}, \bar{y})$. Plot it along with the data.

Remember...

$\bar{x}$ is the mean (average) of the x-values.

6. The data set at the right follows a linear trend. Find the mean absolute error for the graph of each equation.

   a. $y = x + 3$ **b.** $y = x + 2$
   c. $y = x + 4$ **d.** $y = 2x - 2$

7. Find the standard error for the first three lines in Exercise 7. According to standard error, which one is the best fit?

8. **Standardized Test Prep** What is the balance point of the data set below?

(5, 1), (6, 22), (14, 17), (23, 29), (34, 27), (38, 42)

   A. (6, 6)   **B.** (20, 23)   **C.** (120, 138)   **D.** (114, 132)

Input	Output
0	4
2	4
4	5
5	7
5	9
6	11
8	12
10	12

9. **Write About It** There is an old saying: The mean squared error downplays small errors and magnifies large ones.

   a. Explain what the statement means and why it is true. (*Hint:* What do you know about the squares of positive numbers less than 1 and greater than 1?)

   b. What are the advantages of a measure of error that downplays small errors and magnifies large ones?

10. **Take It Further** Use Tor Carlson's data from Lesson 6.09, shown below.

    a. Use a graphing calculator to find the best-fit quadratic function of the form $y = Ax^2 + Bx + C$.

    b. Find the best-fit exponential function of the form $y = A \cdot B^x$.

    c. Which function has the smaller standard error?

Hours	Yeast Density
0	9.6
1	18.3
2	29.0
3	47.2
4	71.1
5	119.1
6	174.6
7	257.3

For help, see the TI-Nspire Handbook, p. 788.

yeast cells magnified 2200 times

Maintain Your Skills

11. **a.** Find five numbers that have a mean of 23.

    b. Find five numbers that have a mean of 23 and a median of 25.

    c. **Take It Further** Find five numbers that have a mean of 23, a median of 25, and a mode of 27.

    d. **Take It Further** Find a different set of five numbers that also has a mean of 23, a median of 25, and a mode of 27.

12. Consider the five numbers you found in Exercise 14a.

    a. If you increase each number by 7, what is the new mean?

    b. If you double each number, what is the new mean?

    c. Use the five numbers to build a new set that has a mean of 1.

    d. Use the five numbers to build a new set that has a mean of 0.

13. Find the mean, median, and mode for each data set.

    a. 6, 6, 7, 7, 10, 10, 10   **b.** 4, 5, 6, 7, 10, 10, 14   **c.** −2, 3, 5, 7, 10, 10, 23

Remember...

The *median* is the middle number in a sorted list of the data. The *mode* is the most common data value.

Go Online
Video Tutor
www.successnetplus.com

In this investigation, you learned how linear functions can represent some data sets. You calculated the balance point for a data set and found the line of best fit. These questions will help you summarize what you have learned.

1. Find the line of best fit for the data in Table N.

Table N

Input	Output
−1	−2
2	88
5	48
6	58

2. How do you find a line that fits a set of data?

3. What is the definition of the line of best fit?

4. What is the line of best fit for data in the table below?

Men's 1500-meter Olympic Gold Medal Times (seconds)

Year	Time	Year	Time	Year	Time
1896	273.2	1932	231.2	1972	216.3
1900	246.2	1936	227.8	1976	219.2
1904	245.4	1948	229.8	1980	218.4
1908	243.4	1952	225.1	1984	212.5
1912	236.8	1956	221.2	1988	215.96
1920	241.8	1960	215.6	1992	220.12
1924	233.6	1964	218.1	1996	215.78
1928	233.2	1968	214.9	2000	212.07

SOURCE: *2007 ESPN Sports Almanac*

Vocabulary

In this investigation you learned these terms. Make sure you understand what each one means and how to use it.

• balance point
• mean absolute error
• mean squared error
• outlier
• standard error

In **Investigation 6A,** you learned how to

- determine the mean, median, and mode for a set of data and decide how meaningful they are in specific situations

- interpret data lists, frequency tables, and stem-and-leaf displays

- determine the five-number summary for a set of data

- build histograms, box-and-whisker plots, and scatter plots

The following questions will help you check your understanding.

For Exercises 1–3, use the stem-and-leaf display that shows the ages of the women's singles winners in the United States Open Tennis Championship.

**United States Open
Women's Singles
Tennis Championship
1993–2007**

```
1 | 6 7 9 9
2 | 0 0 1 1 2 2 2 4 5 6 7
```

1. Find the mean and mode.

2. Find the five-number summary.

3. Sketch a box-and-whisker plot.

In **Investigation 6B,** you learned how to

- decide whether a linear function can reasonably represent a data set

- calculate error measures for a given data set and fitting line

- find the balance point and line of best fit for a data set

The following questions will help you check your understanding.

4. Graph the data in the following data set.

 Find the balance point for the data set. Include it in your graph. Would a linear function be a good fit for the data?

x	y
0	11
0.5	8
1	6
2	4
4	2
5	1.5
6	1
7	0.5
10	0
12	0

5. Find the mean absolute error, mean squared error, and standard error for the data in the following table and the fitting line $y = 3x - 2$.

x	y
1	0.2
4	8.8
6	17
7	21.1

6. Calculate the line of best fit for the following data set.

x	y
1	−6
2	2
3	8
4	12

Multiple Choice

1. Which of the following lines best fits the data in the graph below?

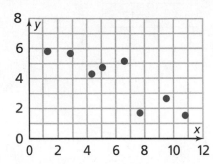

   A. $y = -\frac{1}{2}x - 2$ **B.** $y = -2x + 6$

   C. $y = -0.6x + 7$ **D.** $y = x - 3$

2. Which of the following statements about the line of best fit for a table of data is false?

   A. The line of best fit contains the centroid of the data.

   B. The line of best fit is the line with the least possible standard error.

   C. The line of best fit must contain at least two data points.

   D. The line of best fit may not have the least mean absolute error of any fitting line.

3. Which equation best represents the data in the graph?

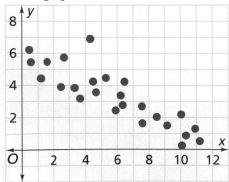

   A. $y = -x + 9$ **B.** $y = -\frac{1}{4}x + \frac{9}{2}$

   C. $y = -\frac{1}{2}x + 6$ **D.** $y = -\frac{1}{2}x + 5$

4. Based solely on this stem-and-leaf display of the ages of the 43 United States presidents at their first inauguration, which statement is true?

   Ages of United States Presidents at First Inauguration

4	3 6 6 6 7 8 9 9
5	0 1 1 1 2 2 2 2 4 4 4 4 4 5 5 5 6 6 6 6 7 7 7 7 8
6	1 1 1 2 4 4 4 5 8 9

   A. None of the presidents were inaugurated at age 58.

   B. The first quartile age at inauguration is 51 years.

   C. The range of ages is 42 years.

   D. The median age at inauguration is 54 years.

Open Response

Use Table R for Exercises 5 and 6.

Table R

Input	Output
−2.1	−8.2
1.3	−0.6
4	4.8
5.2	7.4

5. Calculate the mean absolute error, the mean squared error, and the standard error for the data in Table R and the fitting line $y = 2x - 3$.

6. Find the balance point for the data in Table R. Does the line with equation $y = 2x - 3$ pass through the balance point? Is $y = 2x - 3$ the line of best fit for the data?

7. Consider the following data table.

Input	Output
1	20
2	26
3	35
4	41
5	37
6	52
7	55

a. Find the balance point of the data.

b. For what value b does the graph of the line $y = 5x + b$ pass through the balance point of the data?

Input	Actual	Predicted	Error
1	20	■	■
2	26	■	■
3	35	■	■
4	41	■	■
5	37	■	■
6	52	■	■
7	55	■	■

8. Find a set of 10 numbers that has each property given.

a. median 85 and mean 80

b. mode 40 and median 78

c. mean 92 and mode 75

9. Find the mean, median, and range of the data set $\{-12, 30, 80, -30, 100, -80, -105, -100, 105, 12\}$.

Introduction to Geometry

A valuable geometry skill is being able to recognize what relationships between the parts or the measures of geometric figures stay the same while other elements associated with the figures change.

Here are some simple examples:
- The radius of a circle stays the same while you turn the circle about its center.
- The height of a triangle stays the same while you move a vertex of the triangle parallel to the triangle's base.
- The diagonals of a parallelogram bisect each other while you move the sides of the parallelogram.

Recognizing such constants is a mathematical *habit of mind*. There are many others. And they are a focus of this book. The ways you think about mathematics—your habits of mind—are among the invaluable life applications that you will take from this course.

Vocabulary and Notation

- altitude
- angle bisector
- congruent
- construction
- equidistant
- equilateral
- line of symmetry
- line segment
- median
- midline
- midpoint
- parallel lines
- parallel planes
- perpendicular bisector
- prism
- symmetric
- theorem
- $\angle ACB$ (angle *ACB*)

Investigation 7A

Picturing and Drawing

In *Picturing and Drawing*, you will learn the importance of pictures. Many problems are solved or made easier by drawing pictures. The pictures can be on paper, on a computer, or in your head. Even when your goal is to draw a picture on paper, mental pictures are important. Visualizing clear and detailed pictures in your head can help you draw better.

By the end of this investigation, you will be able to answer questions like these.

1. What is a line of symmetry?

2. What is a prism?

3. What should you keep in mind when you give traveling directions to someone or tell someone how to draw a figure or complete a task?

You will learn how to
- visualize mental images in order to analyze their parts

- analyze visual scenes in order to draw them

- develop clear language to describe shapes

You will develop these habits and skills:
- Write and follow careful directions.

- Identify and represent parallels.

- Use names, features, and algorithms to describe shapes accurately and precisely.

The roof of the Pantheon in Rome is a dome with a round opening (oculus) 29 ft in diameter. Describe the shadow cast by the roof of the Pantheon on the inside of the building.

For artists to draw realistic scenes, they must be able to draw shadows.

For You to Explore

1. Visualize a square casting a shadow on a floor or wall. Can the shadow be nonsquare? Nonrectangular? In other words, can the measures of the shadow's angles be other than 90°?

2. What kinds of shadows can an equilateral triangle cast? Can its shadow be circular?

Definition

When you can fold a figure in half so that the two halves fit exactly on top of each other, the shape is symmetric. The line that contains the fold is a line of symmetry.

For example, the vertical line through the first letter T below is a line of symmetry. The horizontal line through the second T is not a line of symmetry even though it divides the T into two identical parts. If you fold the T along the horizontal line, the two halves will not fit exactly on top of each other.

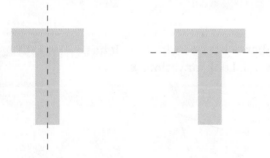

vertical line of symmetry

3. Which other letters are symmetric? Which letters are both horizontally symmetric and vertically symmetric?

4. Describe the lines of symmetry of a circle.

Exercises *Practicing Habits of Mind*

On Your Own

5. Which of the shapes below can cast a square shadow?
   Which ones cannot? Explain.

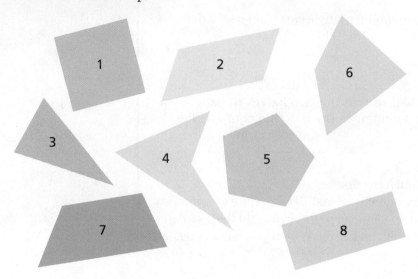

6. Classify each quadrilateral below by the number of lines of symmetry it has.
   Draw the lines of symmetry of each quadrilateral. Look for various kinds of
   lines of symmetry.

Go Online
Video Tutor
www.successnetplus.com

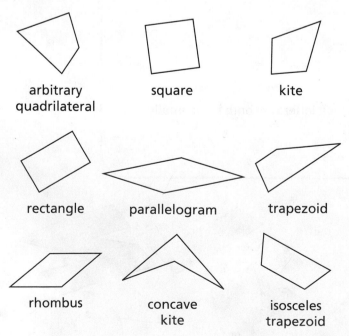

arbitrary
quadrilateral

square

kite

rectangle

parallelogram

trapezoid

rhombus

concave
kite

isosceles
trapezoid

Go Online
www.successnetplus.com

7. Suppose a light shines directly down on a triangle that is parallel to the ground. What properties of the triangle and its shadow are the same? What properties are different?

Maintain Your Skills

A grid polygon is a polygon that has all of its sides on the grid lines of graph paper. Three of the four figures below are grid polygons. Two of the grid polygons, B and D, are the same except for their positions.

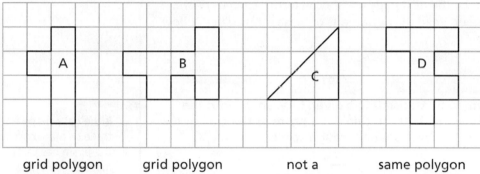

| grid polygon (encloses 5 grid squares) | grid polygon (encloses 7 grid squares) | not a grid polygon | same polygon as polygon B |

For Exercises 8–11, draw as many different grid polygons as you can that

- enclose the given number of grid squares
- have at least two lines of symmetry

Show all the lines of symmetry in each polygon.

8. 4 grid squares

9. 5 grid squares

10. 6 grid squares

11. 7 grid squares

7.02 Drawing 3-D Objects

Have you ever tried to write your name in letters that have a three-dimensional look?

You can use the recipe on the next page to turn "flat" letters like these

into "solid" letters like these

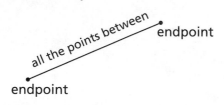

For You to Do

1. The steps of the recipe on the next page use special terms, such as *prism*, *parallel*, and *line segment*. Read the definitions of these terms. Then follow the steps of the recipe.

Definitions

A **prism** is a solid formed by translating a given base shape into the third dimension along a line. You can think of a prism as the trail of the base shape as you slide the base shape through space.

> If the base shape has three or more corners, the prism has three or more edges that are parallel.

A **line segment** is part of a line that contains two endpoints and all the points between the two endpoints.

Parallel lines are lines in the same plane that do not intersect.

Parallel planes are planes in space that do not intersect.

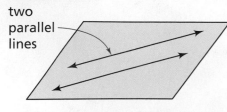

two parallel lines

two parallel planes

a plane (for example, a piece of paper)

> Unlike a piece of paper, a plane has no edges. A plane extends without end in the directions of the lines it contains.

Sample Recipe

Step 1 Choose a letter or other shape. Draw it in your notebook. This shape is the base of the prism that you will draw. The example at the right shows two bases. One is an L-shaped hexagon and the other is a house-shaped pentagon. If you like, you can rotate the base of your prism into the third dimension, as shown at the right.

Step 2 A prism needs two parallel bases, so draw a copy of your base shape near the first. Take care to make the line segments of the copy parallel to (and the same size as) the corresponding line segments of the first base. Note that the word *base* does not necessarily mean the bottom or the top of the solid. It can mean the front or the back, as shown at the right.

Step 3 Now connect the corresponding corners of the two bases. The result is called a wire-frame drawing.

Step 4 Wire-frame drawings can be visually confusing. Erasing the back lines may help the eye make sense of the picture. (It is usually easier to start with the wire-frame drawing and then erase the back lines, than it is to draw the correct view from scratch.) Go ahead and erase the appropriate lines in your picture.

Step 5 Shading can also help the eye make sense of the drawing. Shade all the visible parallel faces in your drawing. In general, you should shade the visible parallel faces in the same way.

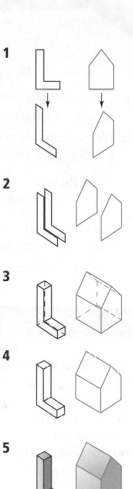

Now that the pentagonal prism looks like a house, the term *base* may be especially confusing. The *house's* base is the bottom rectangular face of the solid. The *prism's* bases are the front and back faces of the house.

Exercises *Practicing Habits of Mind*

Check Your Understanding

1. **Write About It** In each wire-frame drawing above, the segments that connect the two bases are parallel. Convince yourself that this is true. Then write a convincing argument to explain why.

2. **a.** In the block letters that you can draw by following the recipe in the lesson, which faces are parallel?

   b. Why would you normally shade parallel faces the same way? Under what conditions, if any, would you shade them differently?

3. Pictures that can be seen in more than one way can play tricks on the eye. Try to draw each figure at the right. What confuses you?

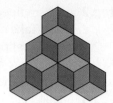

4. Choose a letter. Draw a 2-in. block version of it. Use the technique shown in this section. Shade a base of the prism. Explain why you chose this shape as the base.

On Your Own

5. Three-dimensional solids can also have symmetry. A *plane of symmetry* of a three-dimensional figure divides it into two identical pieces. If you think of replacing the plane with a mirror, the half of the figure that is reflected in the mirror looks the same as the half that is hidden behind the mirror. Find five different symmetrical objects around your house, such as tissue boxes, cans of soup, and so on. Describe the planes of symmetry of each. You may include drawings of your descriptions.

6. A plane is infinite. Any line in a plane divides the plane into two regions.

Remember...

What does the term *infinite* mean?

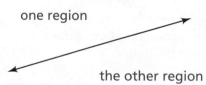

one region

the other region

Two lines may divide a plane into three or four regions, depending on how you place the lines.

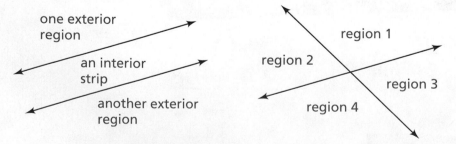

one exterior region

an interior strip

another exterior region

region 1

region 2

region 3

region 4

With five lines, what is the maximum number of regions into which you can divide a plane?

7. Take It Further Space is infinite. Any plane in space divides space into two regions. Two planes may divide space into three or four regions, depending on how you place the planes. Three planes divide space into as few as four or as many as eight regions. What is the maximum number of regions into which you can divide space with four planes? With five planes?

This is the three-dimensional version of Exercise 6, but it is hard to picture. Experienced mathematicians can puzzle for weeks over the questions asked here.

8. Standardized Test Prep The Soma Cube is a cube with side length three units. You can construct the cube 240 different ways from six shapes called tetracubes and one shape called a tricube. One of the tetracubes, shown at the right, is a branch or corner piece that is made of four cubes. One cube is hidden in the drawing at the right. (The Soma Cube was invented by Piet Hein. www.piethein.com)

How many planes of symmetry does this tetracube have?

A. 1   **B.** 2   **C.** 3   **D.** 4

Sometimes pictures help you visualize and understand quantities or relationships between quantities.

9. Write About It What does each picture below tell you about the multiplication of binomials? Give reasons for each answer.

$(a + b)^2 = a^2 + 2ab + b^2$ $(a + b)(c + d) = ac + ad + bc + bd$

10. Write About It The first figure above shows $(a + b)^2 = a^2 + 2ab + b^2$. Explain how the figure at the right shows a similar equation involving $(a + b)^2$.

11. Draw a picture that illustrates the equation $d(c + f) = dc + df$.

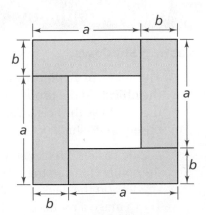

Maintain Your Skills

12. Make a list of all capital block letters that have lines of symmetry. Draw a three-dimensional representation of each capital letter. What kinds of symmetry do you see?

Go Online
www.successnetplus.com

It is often important to describe shape and other spatial information accurately with words.

You can describe shapes in many ways.

Names Some shapes have special names, such as *circle* or *square*. One name may be enough to describe a shape. When a shape looks like another shape that has a special name, you may use some extra words to describe the original shape. For instance, you may say, "like an upside-down L," "like a house lying on its side," or "saddle-shaped."

Features Often you may not know the shape of a figure or solid. You must determine the shape from some set of features. Scientists face this situation when they try to deduce the shape of a molecule from what they know about the atoms that form the molecule or from how the molecule scatters light or X-rays.

Recipes Sometimes, describing how a picture looks is not as helpful as describing how to draw it. For example, suppose you give someone traveling directions. You would more likely say to walk two blocks north, turn left, and walk another block than describe the path as an upside-down L. The recipes you use in mathematics are often called *algorithms* or *constructions*.

You will practice using each of these three ways to describe shapes. Then you will be better prepared to combine them in whatever manner best suits your purpose.

As you proceed, try to notice whether you use *names*, *features*, or *recipes* to describe pictures or to draw pictures from descriptions.

In-Class Experiment

Casting Shadows

The shape of an object's shadow usually depends on how light hits the object. In the problems below, you will think about solids and the shadows they cast. You will also deduce the properties of a solid based on its shadows.

1. A solid casts a circular shadow on the floor. When the solid is lit from the front, it casts a square shadow on the back wall. What solid might it be? Try to make a model out of clay, sponge, dough, or other material. Describe the solid in words as well as you can. Then try to draw a picture of it.

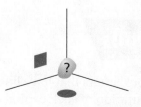

Objects under the midday sun on a clear day generally cast the most distinct and least-distorted shadows.

2. A solid casts a circular shadow on the floor. When the solid is lit from the left, it casts a triangular shadow on the right wall. What solid might it be? Try to make a model out of clay, sponge, dough, or other material. Describe the solid in words as well as you can. Then try to draw a picture of it.

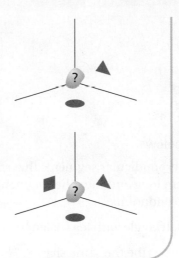

3. Suppose a solid casts a circular shadow on the floor, a triangular shadow when lit from the left, and a square shadow when lit from the front. What solid might it be? Try to make a model out of clay, sponge, dough, or other material. Describe the solid in words as well as you can. Then try to draw a picture of it.

Exercises *Practicing Habits of Mind*

Check Your Understanding

1. Suppose you follow these directions.

Face north. Walk four feet. Turn right. Walk six feet. Turn right again. Walk four feet. Turn right again and walk six feet. Turn right again.

a. What shape will your path form?

b. In what direction will you be facing when you finish?

c. The direction *turn right* does not specify how far to turn. Yet you probably made an assumption. What was your assumption? What makes it seem reasonable?

2. Pick a simple shape.

a. Describe it by name.

b. Describe it with a recipe that you can use to draw it.

3. Read the following recipe.

Draw two segments that are perpendicular at their midpoints. Connect the four endpoints in order.

a. Draw a shape that the recipe above describes.

b. Does the recipe describe only one shape? Explain.

4. Read the two recipes below.

   Recipe 1: Draw two perpendicular segments that share one endpoint. Make one segment 3 cm long and the other segment 6 cm long. Connect the other two endpoints.

   Recipe 2: Draw a right triangle with legs of length 3 cm and 6 cm.

   a. Do the two recipes describe the same shape?

   b. Draw the shapes that each recipe describes.

5. A quadrilateral has horizontal, vertical, and diagonal lines of symmetry.

   a. Draw a quadrilateral that fits this description.

   b. Is there only one quadrilateral that fits the description? Explain.

6. What three-dimensional solid has a circle as every cross section?

Maintain Your Skills

The exercises below use commands from Turtle Geometry. Turtle Geometry is a computer language that moves a cursor (the turtle) forward or backward. The programmer tells the cursor how many steps to move and in what direction. The command *FD 2* means "move forward 2 steps." *RT 90* means "turn to the right 90°." *Repeat 6* means "repeat the given command 6 times."

Follow the commands below. Use a computer or a pencil and protractor to trace out a path.

7. FD 2 RT 90, FD 2 RT 90, FD 2 RT 90, FD 2 RT 90

8. Repeat 6 [FD 2 RT 45]   9. Repeat 6 [FD 2 RT 60]

10. Repeat 8 [FD 2 RT 45]   11. Repeat 8 [FD 2 RT 30]

12. Repeat 12 [FD 2 RT 30]

13. **Standardized Test Prep** Amina entered the following commands into her Turtle Geometry program.

    RT 30 FD 20, RT 60 FD 30, RT 60 FD 20, RT 120 FD 50, RT 120 FD 20

    Which figure did the program draw for her?

    A. an irregular pentagon   **B.** an open figure

    C. a triangle   **D.** an isosceles trapezoid

Drawing From a Recipe—Reading and Writing Directions for Drawings

As you translate words into drawings and drawings into words, you will meet more geometry ideas. Many of them will be familiar to you. You may want to talk about others with classmates or your teacher. To talk about the new ideas, you will need to recall more terminology.

If you carefully follow the instructions in the recipe below, you will get a certain picture. Compare your picture to your classmates' pictures. Are they they same?

In-Class Experiment

Drawing From a Recipe

Step 1 Draw a horizontal line segment.

Step 2 Above the segment, draw two circles that are the same size and tangent to the segment. *Tangent* means "just touching." Leave some space between the two circles—a space roughly the size of the circles' diameter.

Step 3 Draw a line segment above the two circles and tangent to them. It should extend slightly beyond the two circles. Label this segment's left endpoint L and its right endpoint R.

Step 4 From L, draw a segment upward that is perpendicular to $\overline{LR}$ and about half the length of $\overline{LR}$. Label its top endpoint B. From R, draw another segment in the same way. Label its top endpoint F.

Step 5 Draw $\overline{BF}$.

Step 6 Use a pencil to lightly extend $\overline{BF}$ about two thirds of its length to the right. Label the endpoint of the new segment X.

Step 7 Use a pencil to lightly draw a segment downward from X that is perpendicular to $\overleftrightarrow{LR}$. This segment should be roughly the length of $\overline{FR}$. Find the midpoint of this new segment. Label it M.

Step 8 Draw $\overline{MR}$. Then erase the construction lines from Steps 6 and 7. What does your picture look like?

The two figures are tangent here, but not here.

Check Your Understanding

1. Use a pencil and straightedge to draw a large triangle. Find and label the midpoint of each side. Connect each midpoint to the opposite vertex. Label the points where these three segments intersect.

   Exercises 2–4 describe how to draw certain letters of the alphabet. Use the descriptions to draw the letters. The descriptions are fairly good, but you may have to guess what some parts of the descriptions mean. Check whether your results make sense.

2. Draw an equilateral triangle with 2-inch sides and a horizontal base. Find and connect the midpoints of the two nonhorizontal sides. Erase the base of the original triangle. What letter did you draw?

   > The prefix *equi-* means "equal." *Lateral* means "side." **Equilateral** means "sides with equal length."

3. Draw a circle with a $\frac{1}{2}$-inch radius. Draw a slightly larger circle directly below and tangent to the first circle. Draw the vertical segment that connects the centers of the circles. Draw the horizontal diameter of each circle. In the top circle, erase the bottom right 90° section of the circle. In the bottom circle, erase the top left 90° section of the circle. Then erase the vertical and horizontal segments that you sketched. What letter did you draw?

4. Draw a circle. Draw two diameters that are about 45° from vertical and are perpendicular to each other. Erase the 90° section of the circle on the right side of the circle. Then erase the diameters. What letter did you draw?

On Your Own

5. Write directions that describe how to draw your initials. Use precise language. Some letters are complicated to draw, so take advantage of any geometry terms that will make your directions more clear.

6. Write careful directions that describe how to walk from the door of your math classroom to the main office of your school.

7. Write directions that describe how to draw the figure at the right. Then have three classmates draw the figure following your directions. If any of the three pictures differs from the figure at the right, explain what you think caused the difference.

8. **Standardized Test Prep** Enrique has a system he uses to draw regular polygons inscribed in a circle.

Step 1 He draws a large circle. Then he draws a line tangent to the circle.

Step 2 For a polygon with m congruent sides, he divides 360° by $2m$ to get y.

Step 3 He then draws an angle with measure $y°$ such that the following statements are true.

- The point of tangency is the vertex of the angle.
- The tangent line is one side of the angle.
- The other side of the angle passes through the circle.

Step 4 Next, he draws a line segment from the point of tangency to the point where the other side of the angle intersects the circle.

Step 5 Finally, he uses a compass to construct $(m - 1)$ segments with endpoints on the circle such that the following are true:

- The $(m - 1)$ segments are congruent to the first segment.
- The m segments form a regular polygon.

If Enrique wants to draw a regular nonagon, or nine-sided polygon, inscribed in a circle, what number of degrees will he use for his angle with the tangent?

A. 10°   **B.** 20°   **C.** 40°   **D.** 80°

Where did I park the car?

The more difficult the task, the clearer the directions must be.

9. Carefully read and follow the recipe below.

Step 1 Draw a circle. Label the center of the circle point *A*.

Step 2 Draw a radius of the circle. Label its endpoint on the circle point *B*.

Step 3 Draw a segment that is tangent to the circle at *B*. The segment should be longer than the diameter of the circle.

Step 4 Draw a second radius of the circle that is perpendicular to $\overline{AB}$. Label the point where it touches the circle point *D*.

Step 5 Draw a segment that is tangent to the circle at *D*. The segment should intersect the other tangent segment.

Step 6 Label the intersection of the two tangent segments point *C*.

a. What kind of quadrilateral is *ABCD*?

b. Make a conjecture. In a circle, what is the measure of the angle formed by a radius and a line that is tangent to the circle at the endpoint of the radius?

Maintain Your Skills

Write directions that describe how to draw each figure.

10.
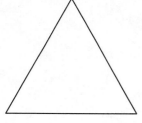

11.
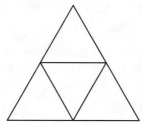

12.
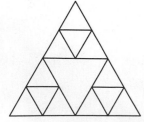

13.
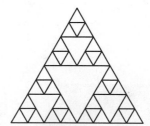

Go Online
www.successnetplus.com

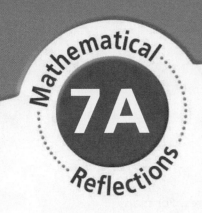

Mathematical 7A Reflections

In this investigation, you learned the importance of pictures. You found lines of symmetry. You also learned to draw three-dimensional solids. The following questions will help you summarize what you have learned.

1. Name three kinds of shapes that can cast a circular shadow. Name a shape that cannot cast a circular shadow. Explain your reasoning.

2. Draw a three-dimensional block version of the figure at right. Label the base. Shade any visible parallel faces.

3. How many lines of symmetry does a square have? How many lines of symmetry does a rectangle have? Can a rectangle ever have the same number of lines of symmetry as a square? Explain.

4. Read the following recipe.

   Draw two horizontal parallel segments that are the same length. Connect the two left endpoints. Connect the two right endpoints.

   a. Draw a shape described by this recipe.

   b. Does this recipe describe only one shape? Explain.

5. Write careful directions that describe how to draw the number 5. Use any geometry terms that might make your directions more clear.

6. What is a line of symmetry?

7. What is a prism?

8. What should you keep in mind when you give traveling directions to someone or tell someone how to draw a figure or complete a task?

Vocabulary

In this investigation, you learned these terms. Make sure you understand what each one means and how to use it.

- **equilateral**
- **line of symmetry**
- **line segment**
- **parallel lines**
- **parallel planes**
- **prism**
- **symmetric**

The shadow of the roof of the Pantheon covers the entire inside of the building except for one spot of sunlight.

Investigation 7B

Constructing

In *Constructing*, you will construct geometric figures. For many figures, you will have to deduce the recipes—how to construct each figure—on your own. Life often presents problems in this way. You know what you need, but not how to make it. Such problems have always inspired creative, inventive thinking. The solutions—the how-to parts—always depend on what tools are available.

By the end of this investigation, you will be able to answer questions like these.

1. What is the difference between drawing a figure and constructing a figure?

2. What is always true about the measures of the angles in a triangle?

3. How can you construct the perpendicular bisector of a segment?

You will learn

• to use hand construction tools

• that points on the perpendicular bisector of a line segment are equidistant from its endpoints

• about special segments that are associated with triangles

You will develop these habits and skills:

• Use hand construction tools.

• Choose the right tool for a construction (including paper folding).

• Identify values or relationships in geometric figures that stay the same when the figure changes.

Follow construction steps carefully and you get the desired result.

Measurements are approximations. However, very careful measurements can suggest exact relationships.

For You to Explore

For the problems below, use whatever tools seem best. Keep track of your answers, as well as *how* you solved each problem—what tools you used and how you used them.

Use these sets of lengths for Problems 1–4.

   3 in., 5 in., 7 in.   3 in., 5 in., 4 in.

   3 in., 8 in., 4 in.   2 in., 3 in., 3 in.

1. For each set of lengths given above, construct a triangle with those side lengths. If a triangle is not possible, explain why.

2. For each triangle you constructed in Problem 1, do the following.

   a. Measure the angles.

   b. Compare your triangle to someone else's triangle. Are the two triangles identical? Do the angles of the two triangles match exactly?

   c. Summarize and explain what you observe.

3. For each triangle you constructed in Problem 1, find the sum of the measures of its angles when the figure changes.

4. **a.** Do you believe that the property you noticed in Problem 3 holds for all triangles or only for some triangles? Explain.

   b. What would convince you that the sum of the measures of the angles of any triangle is always the same?

   Use these sets of angle measures for Problems 5 and 6.

   40°, 60°, 80°   60°, 70°, 80°   120°, 30°, 30°

   30°, 60°, 90°   90°, 90°, 90°

5. For each set of angle measures given above, construct a triangle with those angle measures. If a triangle is not possible, explain why.

6. For each triangle you constructed in Problem 5, do the following.

   a. Measure the lengths of the sides (in inches or centimeters, whichever is more convenient).

   b. Find the ratio of the longest side to the shortest side (divide the longest side by the shortest side).

   c. Compare your triangle to someone else's triangle. Are the two triangles identical? Are the ratios from part (b) equal?

   d. Summarize and explain what you observe.

Habits of Mind

Look for a relationship. In one of the triangles you constructed, exactly two sides are the same length. Why do you think this is true?

Exercises *Practicing Habits of Mind*

On Your Own

7. Choose a triangle you constructed for Problem 1. Without measuring, construct a new triangle with sides that are half the length of each side of your original triangle.

8. In Problems 1 and 5, some of the triangles were impossible to construct. Which ones were they? Explain what went wrong when you tried to construct each triangle.

9. In Problems 2 and 6, you used given side lengths and angle measures to construct triangles. Then you compared your results with those of classmates. Now compare the two experiments. In what ways, if any, are the results different?

After you completed Problems 1–3, you probably came to the following conclusion:

Conjecture 7.1 *Triangle Angle-Sum Conjecture*

The sum of the measures of the angles of a triangle is 180°.

You will prove this later.

10. Assume that the Triangle Angle-Sum Conjecture is true. Explain whether it is possible to construct a triangle with each of the given angle measures.

a. 50°, 50°, 50° **b.** 60°, 60°, 60°

c. 45°, 45°, 90° **d.** 72°, 72°, 36°

e. two 90° angles and a third angle

Maintain Your Skills

In each exercise below, construct three different triangles that meet the given condition.

11. one 30° angle and one 60° angle

12. one 40° angle and one 50° angle

13. one 20° angle and one 70° angle

Geometers distinguish between a drawing and a construction. You make a drawing to aid memory, thought, or communication. A rough sketch serves this purpose quite well. On the other hand, a **construction** is a guaranteed recipe. A construction shows how, in principle, to accurately draw a figure with a specified set of tools.

In your study of geometry you will probably use both hand construction tools and computer tools. The computer tools are introduced in the next investigation.

> Drawings are aids to problem solving. Constructions are solutions to problems.

Hand Construction Tools

Compass A compass is any device—even a knotted piece of string—that allows you to move a pencil a fixed distance around a certain point. A compass allows you to copy distances and to construct circles of any size that you can place anywhere.

Straightedge An object with a straight edge—even a piece of paper—helps you draw a segment to look straight. In general, a straightedge is unmarked and you cannot use it to measure distances. You can use a straightedge to draw a line through, or a segment between, two points. You can also use a straightedge to extend a drawing of a line.

Measuring devices Rulers and protractors are measuring devices. You can use a ruler to measure the length of a segment or the distance between two points. You can use a protractor to measure an angle.

Paper Paper is not just a surface on which to write and draw. You can use the symmetries formed by folding paper to construct geometric figures creatively. You can also use dissection—the process of cutting paper figures and rearranging their parts—as a powerful aid to reasoning.

String You can use string and tacks to build devices that you can use to construct circles, ellipses, spirals, and other curves.

> **Remember...**
> You use a ruler to draw straight segments and to measure distances. You can also use a ruler as a straightedge, ignoring its markings.

Minds in Action

Sasha and Tony are trying to draw a triangle with side lengths 3 in., 4 in., and 5 in.

Sasha I'm going to use three rulers to draw this triangle.

Tony Why *three* rulers?

Sasha Watch and learn, Tony. First, I'll draw a segment that is one of the given lengths, say the 5-inch segment. Then I'll use the other two rulers to represent the other two sides of the triangle and swing them toward each other until they meet. I'll connect the point where the two rulers meet to each end of the 5-inch segment. That gives me my triangle.

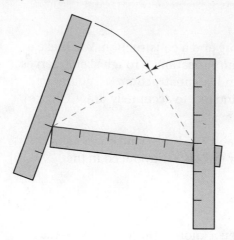

Tony Very nice, but I bet I can do the same thing with only one ruler.

Sasha Let's see!

Tony Okay. First I'll start just like you did and draw the 5-inch segment. Then I'll put the ruler at one end of the 5-inch segment, mark off 4 inches, and swing the ruler around with my pencil to sketch an arc.

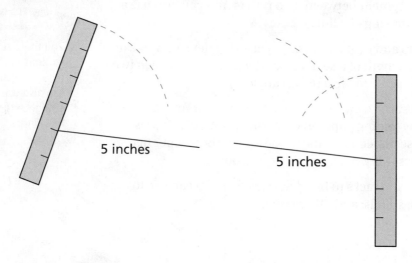

5 inches

5 inches

Then I'll put the ruler at the other end of the 5-inch segment, mark off the 3-inch side, and swing the ruler around to make another arc. And, voilà, there's my triangle!

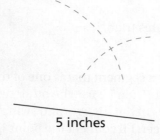

5 inches

For Discussion

1. Do you see Tony's triangle? Explain how you know his triangle has the correct side lengths.

2. The title of this lesson is *Compasses, Angles, and Circles*, but this lesson has not yet mentioned compasses, angles, and circles. How do Sasha's and Tony's ruler tricks both imitate a compass?

3. How can a compass make a geometric construction easier?

Example

Problem Draw a line segment. Without measuring, construct its midpoint. A **midpoint** is the point on a segment that is halfway between the two endpoints.

Solution The simplest approach is to use symmetry by folding. Fold the segment so that its endpoints lie on top of each other. This matches its two halves exactly. The point that separates the two halves is the midpoint.

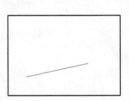 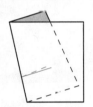 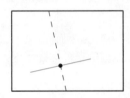

In fact, all points on the fold line are equidistant from the two endpoints of the segment. This is easier to see when the paper is folded. Any point on the fold is the same distance from each of the two original endpoints, because the endpoints are now at the same place.

> **Equidistant** means "the same distance."

The fold line is also perpendicular to the segment. You can show this by

- matching angles around the bisector to show they are congruent
- showing that the sum of the measures of the adjacent angles is 180°

Therefore, the fold line is the perpendicular bisector of the segment. The **perpendicular bisector** of a segment is a line that is perpendicular to a segment at the segment's midpoint.

Theorem 7.1 *Perpendicular Bisector Theorem*

Each point on the perpendicular bisector of a segment is equidistant from the two endpoints of the segment.

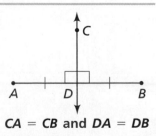

CA = CB and DA = DB

The converse of the Perpendicular Bisector Theorem is also true. Each point that is equidistant from the two endpoints of a segment is on the perpendicular bisector of the segment.

You can use the converse of the Perpendicular Bisector Theorem to find the midpoint of a segment using a compass and a straightedge. From each segment endpoint, swing an arc with radius *r*. Make sure that *r* is greater than half the length of the original segment.

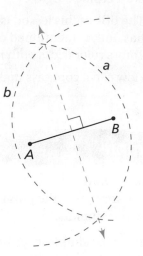

The two points of intersection of the arcs are both *r* units from each endpoint of the segment. The line through the two points is the perpendicular bisector of the segment. All points on the perpendicular bisector are equidistant from the endpoints of the segment. This includes the point of intersection of the perpendicular bisector and the segment, namely the midpoint of the segment.

To see this, fold the paper along the perpendicular bisector. You superimpose the two endpoints of the segment in this way. You also superimpose the two line segments from any point on the fold to each endpoint of the segment. This means that the distances from any point on the perpendicular bisector to the endpoints of the segment must be the same.

Exercises *Practicing Habits of Mind*

Check Your Understanding

For each construction described, do the construction and then tell how you did it. Use any hand construction tools *except* rulers, protractors, or other measurement tools. Do not forget paper folding. Some exercises are harder than others. If you have trouble with an exercise, skip it. Come back to it later. When you return to it, you will have more experience and knowledge.

1. Draw a line. Then construct a line with the given property.

   a. perpendicular to the given line

   b. parallel to the given line

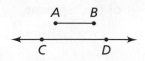

2. Start with a sheet of paper ($8\frac{1}{2}$ in. by 11 in.). Use paper folding and scissors to construct the largest square possible.

3. Start with the largest square you can construct from an $8\frac{1}{2}$ in.-by-11 in. sheet of paper (you may want to make a few of them). Then do the following:

   a. Construct a square with exactly one fourth the area of your original square.

   b. Construct a square with exactly one half the area of your original square.

4. Draw an angle. Then construct its bisector.

5. For each construction below, start with a new segment. Then use the segment to construct the given shape.

   a. an isosceles triangle with each congruent side also congruent to your segment

   b. an isosceles triangle with base congruent to your segment

   c. an equilateral triangle with each side congruent to your segment

   d. a square with each side congruent to your segment

6. Illustrate each definition below with a sketch. The first is done for you as an example.

An **angle bisector** is a ray that divides an angle exactly in half, making two congruent angles.

Definitions

   a. A triangle has three *altitudes*.

   An **altitude** is a perpendicular segment from a vertex of a triangle to the line that contains the opposite side.

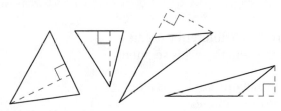

   b. A triangle has three medians.

   A **median** is a segment that connects a vertex of a triangle to the midpoint of the opposite side.

   c. A triangle has three *midlines*.

   A **midline** is a segment that connects the midpoints of two sides of a triangle.

7. Draw four triangles. Use one triangle for each construction below.

   a. Construct the three medians of the triangle.

   b. Construct the three midlines of the triangle.

   c. Construct the three angle bisectors of the triangle.

   d. **Take It Further** Construct the three altitudes of the triangle.

   e. Compare your constructions in parts (a)–(d) to other students' constructions. What are the similarities and differences? Write any conjectures you have.

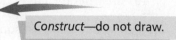

Construct—do not draw.

8. Start with a square. Construct its diagonals. Study the resulting figure. Write what you observe about the diagonals (lengths, angles formed, regions formed, and so on).

9. Start with an equilateral triangle. Construct a circle that passes through the three vertices of the triangle.

On Your Own

10. Copy this segment onto a sheet of paper.

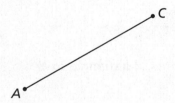

    Use a straightedge and a compass to construct two different isosceles triangles, each with two sides that are the same length as this segment.

11. Use a compass to construct two circles, such that one circle has a radius that is the same length as the diameter of the other circle.

12. Construct a quadrilateral with at least one 60° angle and all sides that are the same length.

13. Draw several different triangles. For each triangle, construct a circle that passes through all three vertices. For what kinds of triangles is the circle's center in the following locations?

    a. inside the triangle

    b. on the triangle

    c. outside the triangle

14. **Standardized Test Prep** Mr. Mendoza's geometry class came up with four conjectures about the medians and the altitudes of triangles. Which of the following conjectures is NOT correct?

   A. A median of a triangle divides the triangle into two smaller triangles of equal area.

   B. The intersection of the three medians of a triangle is always inside the triangle.

   C. In a right triangle, the altitudes intersect at the vertex of the largest angle.

   D. In an obtuse triangle, exactly one of the altitudes lies outside the triangle.

15. Salim planted three new saplings. He wants to install a rotating sprinkler to water the three saplings. Where should he install the sprinkler to make sure that all three saplings get the same amount of water?

   a. Trace the saplings onto your paper.

   b. Show where Salim should install the sprinkler.

   c. Explain your answer.

This is Salim's garden.

16. To reflect a point over a line, do the following:

   • Construct a perpendicular line from the given point A to the given line ℓ.

   • On the perpendicular, mark point A' on the other side of ℓ from A so that A' and A are the same distance from ℓ.

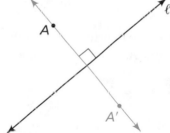

   a. On your own, draw a point and then draw a line that does not pass through that point.

   b. Follow the directions above to reflect the point over the line. Think of the line as a mirror. In the figure above, A' is the reflection of A in the mirror. A and A' are the same distance from and in the same position relative to the mirror.

Maintain Your Skills

17. Copy points A and B onto a sheet of paper. Then construct 15 different points that are equidistant from A and B.

A

B

Mathematical 7B Reflections

In this investigation, you learned the difference between a rough drawing or sketch and a geometric construction. The following questions will help you summarize what you have learned.

1. Describe each shape below using its features. Each description should be specific enough that no other shape can be confused with the given shape.

   a. isosceles trapezoid

   b. isosceles triangle

   c. rhombus

   d. regular octagon

2. Draw an angle and construct its bisector. Describe each step.

3. Copy $\overline{AC}$ at the right onto a sheet of paper. Then construct a square such that $\overline{AC}$ is one of its diagonals.

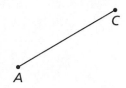

4. Write the steps that describe how to construct the circle that passes through points *A*, *B*, and *C* below.

   C

   A

   B

5. Is it possible to construct a triangle with angles that measure 30°, 60°, and 90°? If you think it is possible, construct such a triangle.

6. What is the difference between drawing a figure and constructing a figure?

7. What is always true about the measures of the angles in a triangle?

8. How can you construct the perpendicular bisector of a segment?

Vocabulary and Notation

In this investigation, you learned these terms and symbols. Make sure you understand what each one means and how to use it.

- **altitude**
- **angle bisector**
- **construction**
- **equidistant**
- **median**
- **midline**
- **midpoint**
- **perpendicular bisector**
- **theorem**

Different constructions give different results.

Geometry Software

In *Geometry Software*, you will make moving pictures of geometric figures. You will construct figures so that required features are built in. Then you will vary other features to experiment with the figures. For instance, you will build a square so that it will stay a square while you rotate it or resize it in any way you please.

By the end of this investigation, you will be able to answer questions like these.

1. How can you use geometry software to construct figures with specific features?

2. How can you use geometry software to discover properties of geometric figures?

3. How can you use geometry software to illustrate the difference between *drawing* a figure and *constructing* a figure?

You will learn how to
- use geometry software to construct figures

- explain the difference between a construction and a drawing

You will develop these habits and skills:
- Use geometry software to construct figures.

- Choose the right tool for a construction.

- Use geometry software to investigate familiar figures.

What changes when you drag any of the vertices *A*, *B*, or *C*?

Nine Point Circle

HYPOTHESIS:
1. Draw △ *ABC*.
2. Construct the midpoints *D*, *E*, and *F* of the sides of the triangle.
3. Construct the points *G*, *H*, *I*, where the altitudes intersect the sides of the triangle.
4. Label the intersection of the altitudes *O*. Construct the midpoints of $\overline{AO}$, $\overline{BO}$, and $\overline{CO}$.

CONCLUSION:
5. Points *D*, *E*, *F*, *G*, *H*, *I*, *J*, *K*, *L* are concyclic.

TO EXPLORE: manipulate the dynamic construction by dragging the points *A*, *B*, and *C*.

Every geometry software program has geometric construction tools, labeling tools, and movement tools.

For You to Explore

1. Use geometry software. Explore and ask questions until you can do the following.

   - Use line segments to draw a triangle.

   - Draw two circles. Connect them with a line segment. The segment's endpoints should be on the circles.

   - Move a point, segment, or circle in each of the first two drawings.

   - Draw a ray.

   - Draw a line.

   - Draw a point that travels *only* along a segment.

2. **a.** Use the point tool to place two points on your screen as shown below on the left. Then use only the circle tool to complete the picture below on the right. Make sure that your picture does not contain more than four points.

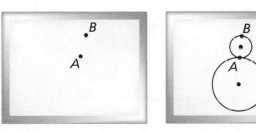

   b. Now move each point around and describe the effect on the drawing. It may help to label the points.

3. Construct a triangle with two vertices that can be moved about freely and one vertex that can only be moved on a circle.

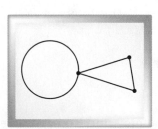

4. Draw two lines. Construct a triangle. Fix one vertex on one of the lines. Place the other vertices so that you can move both of them, but only along the other line.

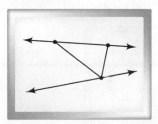

A bit of everything

For help constructing a ray or a line, see the TI-Nspire™ Handbook, p. 788.

On Your Own

5. **Write About It** Write directions for drawing the figures in Problems 2–4. Include directions for how to get a point to "stick" to a line or circle.

6. Buddy made the following sketch. He intended to fix one vertex on one line. He also wanted to place the other vertices so that he could move both of them, but only along the other line.

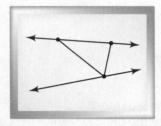

When the teacher checked Buddy's sketch, she selected a point and moved it to a new position, as shown below.

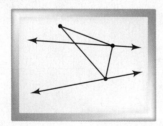

a. What mistake did Buddy make?

b. How can he fix his mistake?

7. If a line is perpendicular to $\overline{BC}$, must the line intersect $\overline{BC}$? Explain.

Maintain Your Skills

8. Use geometry software. Place two points *A* and *B* on your screen, as shown. Find positions for point *C* such that the measure of $\angle ACB$ is 90°.

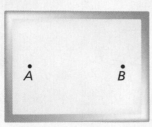

> The notation $\angle ACB$ ("angle *ACB*") means the angle formed by $\overline{CA}$ and $\overline{CB}$.

7.08 Drawings vs. Constructions

To construct a figure that stays the way you want when you move one of its parts, you must build in the required features. If a point must be on a line or circle, you cannot place the point first and then adjust it to look right. You must actually place the point *on* the line or *on* the circle.

When you build in the required properties with geometry software, you can move one part of a figure and all the other parts will adjust accordingly. For instance, parallel lines will remain parallel. The midpoint of a segment will remain the midpoint.

Example

Constructing a Windmill

Step 1 Open a new sketch page on your computer.

Step 2 Place point A on your screen. Then construct $\overline{BC}$. Your screen should now show four objects: three points, A, B, and C, and one segment, $\overline{BC}$.

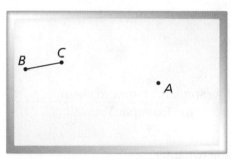

Due to software settings, labels for points may not appear automatically. Also, the labels for your points may be different from the labels shown here. Labels for points depend on the order in which you place the points. For help constructing a perpendicular or parallel line through a given point, see the TI-Nspire Handbook, p. 788.

Step 3 Use the appropriate tool to construct a line through A that is perpendicular to the line containing $\overline{BC}$. The line should stay perpendicular to $\overline{BC}$ no matter how you move A, B, or C.

Step 4 Construct a line through A that is parallel to $\overline{BC}$.

Step 5 Construct a circle centered at A with radius the same length as $\overline{BC}$. If you stretch or shrink $\overline{BC}$, the circle should stretch or shrink, accordingly. Again, you need a special tool for this construction. (Keep this sketch for Exercise 1.)

Radius of a circle usually refers to a segment from the circle's center to a point on the circle. *Radius of the circle* usually refers to the length of a radius.

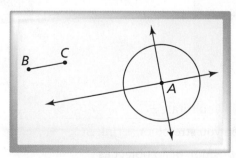

For Discussion

1. What happens when you use the selection tool to move *A*, *B*, and *C*?

Sometimes you need to use a line or a circle to construct a figure, but you may not want to see these construction lines in the finished product.

When you used construction lines to construct a figure by hand, you later erased them. When you use geometry software to construct a figure, you must not erase, or delete, the construction lines. You can, however, *hide* them. Find out how to use your software to hide parts of a construction.

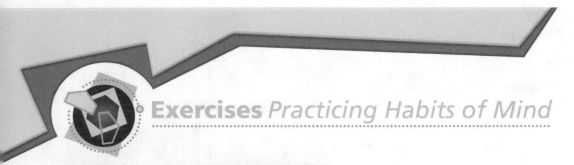

Exercises Practicing Habits of Mind

Check Your Understanding

In the Example you constructed a windmill. Follow Steps 1–3 below to clean up the construction. Refer to the diagram in Step 5 of the Example. You will use the windmill in Exercises 1 and 2.

Step 1 Place points where the circle intersects the two lines.

Step 2 Construct segments from the center of the circle to each intersection point.

Step 3 Hide (do not delete) the circle and the lines. Do not hide the segments.

> Sometimes you may want to hide a construction line or delete a mistake. See the TI-Nspire Handbook, p. 788.

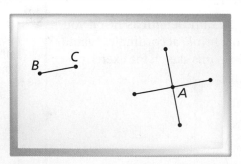

1. **a.** Describe what happens to the segments when you rotate $\overline{BC}$.

   b. Describe what happens to the segments when you stretch or shrink $\overline{BC}$.

2. Most geometry software allows you to trace the position of an object as you move it. Activate the Trace feature for the four points at the end of your windmill. Then move point *B* and watch what happens. Describe the effect.

3. Use geometry software to draw two intersecting segments. Move them until they look about the same length and perpendicular to each other at their midpoints. Move one of the endpoints. How is your sketch affected when you move this point, compared to how your construction is affected when you move point *B*?

On Your Own

4. **Write About It** Compare the tools used for hand constructions (paperfolding, compass, straightedge) to the basic tools of geometry software. How are they similar? How are they different? Do you think you can do more with one set of tools than with the other? Explain.

5. In Step 4 of the windmill construction (see the Example), why was it necessary to *construct* the line parallel to $\overline{BC}$ rather than *draw* it parallel to $\overline{BC}$?

6. Why did you need the circle to construct the windmill?

7. **Standardized Test Prep** Naima is frustrated. Her geometry software does not have a command that constructs a line tangent to a given circle. Which of the following methods can Naima use to construct a line that is tangent to a circle with center *O* so that point *P* on the circle is the point of tangency?

A. Construct the perpendicular bisector of $\overline{OP}$.

B. Construct the line that is perpendicular to $\overline{OP}$ at point *O*. Let *Q* be one point where this line intersects the circle. Construct $\overleftrightarrow{PQ}$.

C. Construct a line through *P* that is parallel to a diameter of the circle and that intersects the circle in two points.

D. Construct the line through *P* that is perpendicular to $\overline{OP}$.

Maintain Your Skills

Use geometry software.

8. **a.** Draw any triangle. Label it $\triangle ABC$.

   b. Construct *M*, the midpoint of $\overline{AB}$.

   c. Through *M*, construct a line parallel to $\overline{AC}$. Let *N* be the point where this line intersects $\overline{BC}$.

   d. Hide the line. Then draw $\overline{MN}$.

   e. Drag one of the vertices of $\triangle ABC$. Then compare the lengths of $\overline{MN}$ and $\overline{AC}$.

7.09 Drawing UnMessUpable Figures—Building Constructions

Here is one way to think about the difference between a construction and a drawing. Think about which properties of a figure remain unchanged when you move a point or other part of the figure.

If you *draw* (not *construct*) a square, you are guaranteed to have a quadrilateral at best. The figure may happen to look like a square at certain moments, but you can change it into a nonsquare quadrilateral by dragging a vertex or side. Its squareness is not guaranteed—it is not UnMessUpable, you could say.

Example

Problem Construct a square.

Solution Below are two possible solutions. Other solutions are possible as well.

Two adjacent congruent sides, four right angles Construct $\overline{AB}$. Construct a perpendicular to $\overline{AB}$ at each of points A and B. Construct the circle centered at A with radius $\overline{AB}$ to locate point C. Construct the line through C that is perpendicular to $\overline{AC}$ (or parallel to $\overline{AB}$) to locate point D. *ABDC* is the constructed square.

> **Congruent** sides are sides that are equal in length.

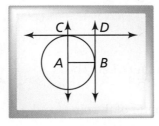

Three congruent sides with right angles between them Construct $\overline{AB}$. Construct a perpendicular to $\overline{AB}$ at each of points A and B. Construct two circles—one centered at A and one centered at B, each with radius $\overline{AB}$—to locate points C and D. *ABDC* is the constructed square.

> Measure the length of the segment and use it as the radius in constructing the circles. See the TI-Nspire Handbook, p. 788.

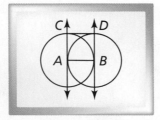

For Discussion

1. Describe other ways to construct a square.

Exercises *Practicing Habits of Mind*

Check Your Understanding

In the exercises below, your mission is to construct figures that are guaranteed UnMessUpable. No one should be able to change what is required for your figure by dragging a point or moving a segment. Work to construct the figure that is specified, not just a figure that looks like it.

1. Construct a parallelogram that will remain a parallelogram even if you move its vertices.

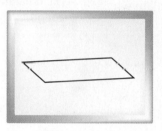
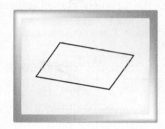

> A *parallelogram* is a quadrilateral with two pairs of parallel sides. Note that rectangles, rhombuses, and squares are all special types of parallelograms.

2. Construct two circles so that each circle passes through the center of the other circle. If you change the size of one circle, the size of the other circle should change with it.

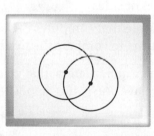

> For help constructing a circle with a given center through a given point, see the TI-Nspire Handbook, p. 788.

3. Construct three circles so that each circle passes through the centers of the other two circles. As you change the size of one circle, the sizes of the other two circles should also change.

> Why are the three points in this figure exactly the same distance from one another?

4. Construct an equilateral triangle that remains an equilateral triangle when you change its size and orientation.

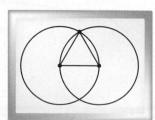

5. Construct the letter T with the following requirements. The top of the T is to remain perpendicular to and centered on the stem when you move points or segments of the T.

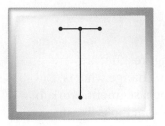

> Can you construct your T so it always stays upright?

6. Find two different ways to construct a guaranteed UnMessUpable rhombus with geometry software. Write clear directions for each construction. If either construction guarantees only a certain type of rhombus, explain why.

> A *rhombus* is a quadrilateral with four congruent sides.

7. a. Construct two rectangles that

- share one vertex
- have two sides lined up
- have one diagonal lined up, as shown, no matter how you move the vertices or sides

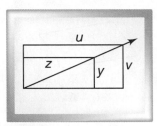

b. Your software has a feature that computes the ratio of the lengths of two segments. Use that feature to compare the two ratios $\frac{z}{y}$ and $\frac{u}{v}$.

8. Take It Further Construct a quadrilateral that you can distort in all sorts of ways but that will *always* have one pair of opposite sides equal in length.

9. **Take It Further** Use geometry software to construct a house in perspective. When you are done, your construction should have these features:

- You should be able to adjust the points on its near end so that the corresponding points on its far end adjust automatically.

- Your picture should include a *drag* point. Move the drag point to see what the house looks like from different perspectives.

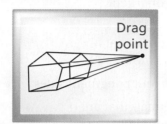

Drag the point to change the perspective. See the TI-Nspire Handbook, p. 788.

Developing Habits of Mind

Make a model. For the house you drew in Lesson 7.02, the following statements are true.

- Its two bases are identical.
- The segments that connect the bases are all parallel.
- The corresponding sides of the bases are parallel.

On the other hand, in the perspective construction of the house above, the following statements are true.

- The bases of the house are not identical (what mathematicians call "congruent"). They are, however, the same shape (what mathematicians call "similar").

- The segments that connect the bases are not parallel. Instead, they converge to a single point.

- The corresponding sides of the bases are parallel.

These facts suggest one way to construct a house in perspective. Sketch the near end of the house. Place a drag point (also called a vanishing point in both mathematics and art) on your screen. Connect the vertices of the house's near end to the vanishing point. Then construct the house's far end. Make sure each segment of the house's far end is parallel to the corresponding segment of the near end.

On Your Own

10. **Standardized Test Prep** The students in Ms. Lau's class used geometry software to construct a specific type of quadrilateral that keeps its required features if someone drags one of the vertices.

    - Jeremy's group constructed a parallelogram with congruent adjacent sides.

    - Amy's group constructed a quadrilateral with diagonals that bisect the quadrilateral's angles.

    - Alexandra's group constructed a quadrilateral with four congruent sides.

    - Sang's group constructed a quadrilateral with diagonals that are perpendicular and intersect each other at their midpoints.

    Which type of quadrilateral did each group construct?

    A. a rectangle **B.** a square **C.** a rhombus **D.** a trapezoid

11. **Write About It** As you learned to use geometry software, you probably also did some geometric thinking. List some geometric ideas, terminology, or techniques that you learned, relearned, polished up, or invented.

12. No geometry software allows you to construct a line that is perpendicular to another line or segment unless you first identify both a line (or a segment) *and* a point. Why is this a sensible restriction?

13. **Write About It** Select one of the UnMessUpable figures you constructed in Exercises 1–8. Write detailed directions that describe the construction process. To test your directions, switch with a partner. Do you both get the predicted results?

14. Look back at Exercise 4. How do you make sure that the triangle you construct is equilateral? Describe what features of the construction or the resulting figure guarantee that the triangle has three congruent sides.

Maintain Your Skills

Go Online
www.successnetplus.com

Use geometry software to construct the following figures. Describe required features that remain unchanged if you drag a vertex.

15.
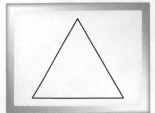

16.
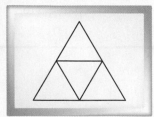

17.

In this investigation, you learned the difference between drawing and constructing with geometry software. You used software to construct figures that retained specific features no matter how you moved around their parts. The following questions will help you summarize what you have learned.

1. Tony had to construct a triangle inscribed in a circle. He drew the picture on the left. Sasha selected a vertex. She moved it and made the picture on the right. Explain Tony's mistake.

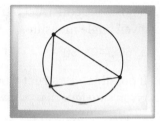 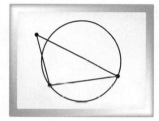

2. Construct an UnMessUpable square with a side length of 5 cm.

3. List steps that tell how to construct a rectangle with geometry software. The figure must remain a rectangle for any movement of its vertices.

4. Use geometry software to construct an equilateral triangle with side lengths that vary when you drag a point of the construction.

5. What feature do you have to make invariant in a parallelogram so that it is always a rhombus, no matter how you drag its vertices?

6. How can you use geometry software to construct figures with specific features?

7. How can you use geometry software to test for invariants?

8. How can you use geometry software to illustrate the difference between *drawing* a figure and *constructing* a figure?

Vocabulary and Notation

In this investigation, you learned this term and this symbol. Make sure you understand what each one means and how to use it.

- congruent
- ∠*ACB* (angle *ACB*)

Drag any of the vertices *A*, *B*, or *C*, and the points *D*, *E*, *F*, *G*, *H*, or *I* remain concyclic (on the same circle)!

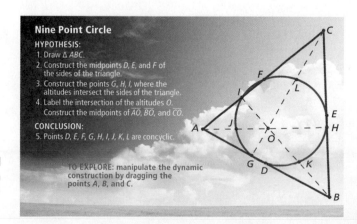

Nine Point Circle

HYPOTHESIS:
1. Draw △ *ABC*.
2. Construct the midpoints *D*, *E*, and *F* of the sides of the triangle.
3. Construct the points *G*, *H*, *I*, where the altitudes intersect the sides of the triangle.
4. Label the intersection of the altitudes *O*. Construct the midpoints of $\overline{AO}$, $\overline{BO}$, and $\overline{CO}$.

CONCLUSION:
5. Points *D*, *E*, *F*, *G*, *H*, *I*, *J*, *K*, *L* are concyclic.

TO EXPLORE: manipulate the dynamic construction by dragging the points *A*, *B*, and *C*.

Go Online
www.successnetplus.com

In **Investigation 7A** you learned how to

- visualize geometric objects well enough to draw them
- use clear language to describe shapes
- write and follow careful directions

The following questions will help you check your understanding.

1. Copy the figure. Draw all of its lines of symmetry.

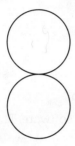

2. Write directions that describe how to draw this figure.

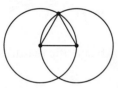

In **Investigation 7B** you learned how to

- distinguish between drawing a figure and constructing a figure
- use hand construction tools, including paper folding

The following questions will help you check your understanding.

3. If possible, construct a triangle with the given angle measures.

   a. 60°, 40°, 80°   **b.** 100°, 20°, 45°

4. If possible, construct a triangle with the given side lengths.

   a. 4 cm, 5 cm, 6 cm   **b.** 3 in., 2 in., 6 in.

5. What is always true about the measures of angles in a quadrilateral? About a polygon with *n* sides?

In **Investigation 7C** you learned how to

- use geometry software tools to construct UnMessUpable figures
- use geometry software to discover the properties of geometric figures

The following questions will help you check your understanding.

6. Construct an UnMessUpable square with side length 4 cm.

7. Use geometry software. Construct an UnMessUpable rectangle. What would you have to build into your rectangle to make the figure an UnMessUpable square?

8. The two lines below are parallel. If you choose any four points on the lines and connect them, will the result be a parallelogram? To get a parallelogram, which points can you choose randomly, and how do you have to choose the others?

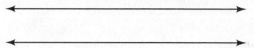

Multiple Choice

1. Which type of cross section can you NOT form by intersecting a plane and a right circular cone?

   A. an ellipse   **B.** a triangle

   C. a rectangle   **D.** a circle

2. Which figure has exactly two lines of symmetry?

   A. regular pentagon   **B.** circle

   C. square   **D.** rectangle

3. Which figure could be the intersection of two different planes?

   A. point   **B.** line

   C. line segment   **D.** plane

4. Which block letter has a vertical line of symmetry?

   A.   **B.**

   C.   **D.**

5. Which name best describes a parallelogram with four right angles?

   A. square   **B.** rectangle

   C. trapezoid   **D.** rhombus

6. Which method describes how to divide a segment into four congruent segments?

   A. Construct the midpoint of the segment.

   B. Construct the perpendicular bisector of the segment.

   C. Construct a square with each side congruent to the original segment.

   D. Construct the perpendicular bisector of the segment. Then construct the perpendicular bisector of each of the new segments.

7. The figures below show how to construct a type of segment associated with a triangle. What is constructed?

   A. altitude   **B.** median

   C. midline   **D.** angle bisector

8. Which method describes how to construct an altitude of a triangle?

   A. Construct the midpoint of one side of the triangle. Then construct the segment from that midpoint to the opposite vertex.

   B. Construct the perpendicular from a vertex to the opposite side.

   C. Construct the midpoint of two sides of the triangle. Then construct the segment connecting those two midpoints.

   D. Construct the angle bisector of one angle of the triangle.

Open Response

9. Draw a triangle on paper. Construct one of the triangle's altitudes and one of its medians..

10. Which of the figures below can you fold into a closed solid? For each one, name the solid or describe its features.

a.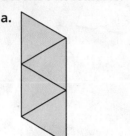

b.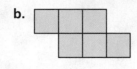

c.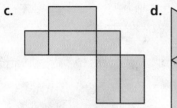

d.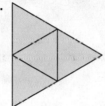

e.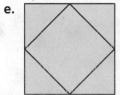

f.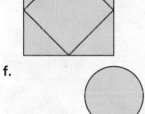

g.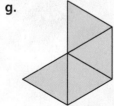

11. Use a compass and straightedge to construct an equilateral triangle. Describe how you completed this construction.

12. a. To construct a parallel line with geometry software, which two pieces of information do you need? Explain.

    b. To construct a circle with geometry software, which two pieces of information do you need? Explain.

Congruence and Transformations

Mathematics is at the core of computer graphics technology. Any drawing on a computer depends on analytic geometry, which assigns coordinates to every location in the plane (or in three-dimensional space). Analytic geometry also allows mathematical operations on those coordinates. Computers store drawings as a series of coordinates, along with functions that define relationships and connections between them.

You can draw curves on a computer with a vector pen. This tool allows you to select points and assign a vector to each point. The direction of the vector indicates the slope that the curve will have at that point. The size (or magnitude) of the vector indicates the degree to which that slope will affect surrounding points on the curve.

Computer animation depends heavily on the use of transformations. Transformations are functions on geometric objects. They produce images that are in new locations or orientations—reflections, rotations, and translations. You animate a figure by making a sequence of images under a set of transformations and dilations.

Vocabulary and Notation

- composition
- congruent
- fixed point
- image
- isometry
- line of reflection
- postulate
- preimage
- reflection
- rigid motion
- rotation
- transformation
- translation
- F' (F prime)
- F'' (F double prime)
- JK (length of JK)
- ⊥ (is perpendicular to)
- ≅ (is congruent to)

The Congruence Relationship

In *The Congruence Relationship*, you will study congruent figures—figures that are the same shape and the same size. To understand mathematics or the arts, history or psychology, science or social relationships, you look at how things differ and also at how they are the same. Mathematics looks at quantities, relationships in space, ways to classify items, and certain processes that are used. The focus of this investigation is shape and what it means when two shapes are the same.

By the end of this investigation, you will be able to answer questions like these.

1. What does it mean to say that two figures are congruent?

2. Why is it important to keep track of corresponding parts in congruent figures?

3. What are some ways to prove that two triangles are congruent?

You will learn how to
- define congruence

- interpret statements about congruent figures and use the correct notation to write statements

- test for congruence in triangles

You will develop these habits and skills:
- Name corresponding parts of congruent figures.

- Use triangle congruence postulates to show that two triangles are congruent.

- Make logical inferences to draw conclusions about congruence.

Some houses in master-planned developments are the same shape and size.

Mathematical language is clear and precise. Each word has exactly one meaning. Sometimes you invent new words. Sometimes you modify the meanings of familiar words. In either case, everyone must agree on which words to use and what those words mean.

For You to Explore

1. As a class, decide what you will mean by this statement: "These two figures are the same."

   To make a wise decision about the meaning of the statement, you might consider some specific cases. For example, look at the four figures below. Decide which figures you would call the same.

   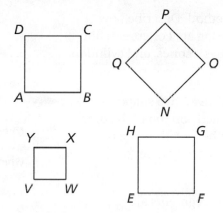

2. In some ways, all of the objects above are the same. Explain.

3. In some ways, they are all different. Explain.

   Mathematical language uses several words to describe two figures that are the same. For a start, we say that two figures are congruent if they have the same shape and the same size, regardless of location or orientation. But size and shape are not very precise terms, so we will develop a better definition.

   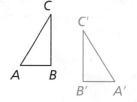

   > △ABC is congruent to △A'B'C', but they have different orientations. If you walk from A to B to C to A, you turn *left* twice. If you walk from A' to B' to C' to A', you turn *right* twice.

   Congruence is such an important mathematical relationship that it has its own symbol, ≅. In Problem 1 above, squares ABCD and EFGH are congruent. You write □ABCD ≅ □EFGH.

4. You can think of the congruence symbol as composed of two parts: = and ∼. What aspects of congruence might these two parts represent?

On Your Own

You can use *congruent* to describe figures in any number of dimensions. Here are some examples.

- 1 dimension: two line segments that are the same length
- 2 dimensions: two triangles that are the same shape and same size
- 3 dimensions: two spheres with the same radius, or
                 two tetrahedrons that are the same shape and same size

Go Online
Video Tutor
www.successnetplus.com

5. **Write About It** Assume you can use any tool or method. Describe how you can decide whether a pair of each of the following are congruent: line segments; angles; triangles; rectangular solids (boxes); cones; and cylinders.

One class chose the following test for congruence. Given two shapes drawn on paper, if you can cut out one and fit it exactly on top of the other shape (nothing hanging over above or sticking out below), then the two shapes are congruent. Or, two figures are congruent if they differ only in position.

The word *congruence* comes from the Latin word *congruens,* which means "to meet together." If you superimpose one figure on another and they meet edge to edge, then they are congruent.

6. Can you use this test to determine whether two line segments are congruent? Explain.

7. **Take It Further** How can you adapt the test so that you can use it to determine whether three-dimensional objects such as spheres or rectangular boxes are congruent?

Maintain Your Skills

Translate these congruence statements into English sentences.

8. $\triangle TRL \cong \triangle MTV$

9. $\overline{TO} \cong \overline{BE}$

10. $\square BARK \cong \square MEOW$

11. $\triangle LMO \cong \triangle L'M'O'$

12. $\angle ABC \cong \angle ABD$

Are these two gloves congruent?

Length, Measure, and Congruence

You can describe a single geometric object in more than one way. For example, you can refer to a line segment by its name or by its length. In the coordinate plane, you can also refer to a line segment by its slope. In geometry, it is important to make the distinction between a geometric object, such as a point or a segment or a circle, and a numerical value that describes it.

Symbols are designed to help make these distinctions. For example, the symbol $\overline{JK}$, with an overbar, represents the line segment with endpoints J and K. The symbol JK, without the overbar, represents the length of $\overline{JK}$.

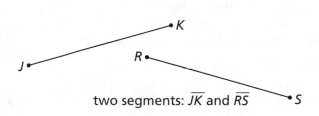

two segments: $\overline{JK}$ and $\overline{RS}$

You can compare two shapes to determine whether they are congruent. You can also compare two numbers to determine whether they are equal. You cannot, however, compare a shape to a number.

Minds in Action

Sasha and Tony discuss the seven statements below that seem to describe the two segments at the right.

- $JK \cong RS$
- $\overline{JK} \cong \overline{RS}$
- $JK = RS$
- $\overline{JK} = \overline{RS}$
- $JK = 1$ inch
- $\overline{JK} = 1$
- $\overline{JK} \cong 1$ inch

Sasha The sentence $JK \cong RS$ makes no sense!

Tony What do you mean?

Sasha Well, $\cong$ is the symbol for *congruent*, right?

Tony Yes.

Sasha So, when you use that symbol you're supposed to be comparing objects. Without the little line over them, JK and RS aren't segments. They're just lengths.

Tony That's being a little picky, don't you think?

Sasha No, not really. You have to make a distinction between things that are *equal*, like the lengths JK and RS, and things that are *congruent*, like $\overline{JK}$ and $\overline{RS}$.

Tony So, the statement $JK = RS$ is correct, right? Because it says that the two *measurements* are equal, and numbers can be equal.

Sasha Yes.

For Discussion

1. Determine whether each of the statements that Sasha and Tony discussed in the dialog is correct. If a statement is *not* correct, explain why.

2. If two segments are the same length, are they congruent? Explain.

3. If two segments are congruent, are they the same length? Explain.

The symbols for an angle and its measure are different from the symbols for a segment and its length, but the distinction is the same. An angle is a geometric object. Its measure is a number.

In the figure at the right, write $\angle NPQ$, $\angle QPN$, or $\angle P$ to refer to the first angle. Write $m\angle NPQ$ to refer to its measure.

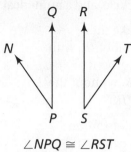

$\angle NPQ \cong \angle RST$
or
$m\angle NPQ = m\angle RST$

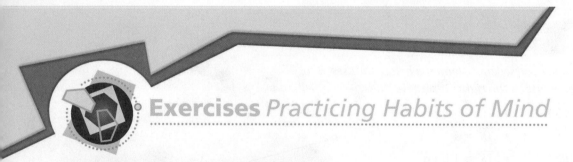

Exercises Practicing Habits of Mind

Check Your Understanding

1. Decide whether each statement below describes geometric objects or numbers. If a statement describes geometric objects, state whether points, segments, or other objects are explicitly mentioned.

   a. $JK = RS$ **b.** $\overline{JK} \cong \overline{RS}$

   c. $\overline{JK}$ and $\overline{RS}$ are the same length.

   d. The distance from J to K is the same as the distance from R to S.

2. **a.** Explain why the following statement is incorrect: $\angle NPQ = 56.6°$

   b. Write the following statement symbolically: Angle NPQ has a measure of 56.6 degrees.

3. If $m\angle NPQ = m\angle RST$, are the two angles congruent? Explain.

4. If $\angle NPQ \cong \angle RST$, are the measures of the two angles equal? Explain.

5. Explain whether the following statement is true or false: If two triangles are both congruent to the same triangle, then they are congruent to each other.

6. In △ABD at the right, $AD = BD$, $\overline{DC}$ is an altitude (that is, $\overline{DC} \perp \overline{AB}$), and *F* and *E* are midpoints. Decide whether each of the following statements is *true, false,* or *nonsensical.* Justify your answers. You may use measuring tools if you want.

Remember...

The symbol $\perp$ means "is perpendicular to."

a. $FD = DE$

b. $\overline{FD} = \overline{DE}$

c. $\overline{FD} = 1.5$ cm

d. $\angle ACD = 90°$

e. $\triangle DFB = \triangle DEA$

f. $\angle ACD$ is a right angle.

g. $\overline{FA} \cong \overline{BE}$

h. $\overline{FA} \cong \overline{BD}$

i. $\angle ADC = \angle BDC$

j. $m\angle ADC = m\angle BDC$

k. $m\angle DFB \cong m\angle DEA$

l. $\angle DFB \cong \angle DEA$

m. $\triangle DCA \cong \angle DCB$

n. $\triangle DCA \cong \overline{DC}$

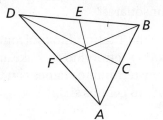

On Your Own

7. Define the following words or symbols.

a. congruent
b. $\cong$
c. $\perp$

8. **Standardized Test Prep** Anna has a simple rule for deciding which symbol to use.

Objects are congruent. Measurements of objects are equal.

Which of the following statements is NOT written correctly according to Anna's rule?

A. $\overline{DF} \cong \overline{RT}$

B. $m\angle CSD \cong m\angle BSL$

C. $\angle ADF \cong \angle WZM$

D. $AC = FH$

9. Are all equilateral triangles congruent? Explain.

Polyominoes are shapes that are made of squares. The sides of polyominoes meet edge to edge with no gaps or overlaps. The three shapes on the left are polyominoes. The three shapes on the right are not polyominoes, because the squares do not meet edge to edge.

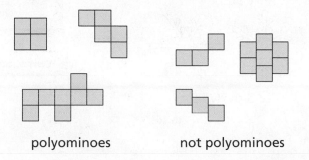

polyominoes

not polyominoes

Congruent polyominoes that have different orientations are not different polyominoes.

10. **Dominoes:** How many different polyominoes can you make with two squares?

11. **Trominoes:** How many different polyominoes can you make with three squares?

12. **Tetrominoes:** How many different polyominoes can you make with four squares?

13. Combine the T tetromino (polyomino with 4 squares) at the right with another tetromino to make an eight-square polyomino. How many tetromino shapes can you combine with the T tetromino to get this shape?

Maintain Your Skills

14. Assume you can use any tool or method. Describe how you can decide whether the figures in each pair are congruent.

a.
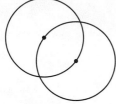

two circles

b.

two artists

c.
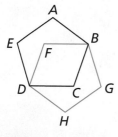

two pentagons,
ABCDE and *BGHDF*

d.

two bent arrows

e.

two stars

f.

two snowflakes

Go Online
www.successnetplus.com

610   Chapter 8   Congruence and Transformations

It is difficult to draw congruent figures by hand. It is also difficult to decide whether two given figures are congruent. You may not have the tools necessary. Or you may not want to take the time to use those tools. For these reasons, tick marks are very useful.

The picture below shows nine segments, with eight of the segments forming four angles. Like markings indicate which segments are congruent and which angles are congruent. For example, $\overline{ON} \cong \overline{BC}$ and $\angle GHI \cong \angle ABC$.

The small box that marks $\angle DEF$ indicates that $\angle DEF$ is a right angle.

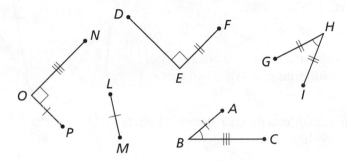

Habits of Mind

Compare. Are two segments that have different numbers of tick marks not congruent?

For You to Do

1. What other relationships are indicated in the above diagram?

A congruence statement communicates a large amount of information. The congruence statement $\triangle QRS \cong \triangle XYZ$ tells you that the two triangles are congruent. The orders in which the vertices are written also tells you that

$$\overline{QR} \cong \overline{XY}, \overline{RS} \cong \overline{YZ}, \text{ and } \overline{QS} \cong \overline{XZ},$$

and that

$$\angle Q \cong \angle X, \angle R \cong \angle Y, \text{ and } \angle S \cong \angle Z.$$

You can summarize this matching of parts in a congruence statement by saying that corresponding parts of congruent figures are congruent.

Remember...

For triangles, *parts* means "sides" and "angles".

The sails are congruent.
So are their corresponding parts.

Exercises *Practicing Habits of Mind*

Check Your Understanding

1. The two triangles at the right are congruent. Decide whether each
   congruence statement below is correct. Explain your reasoning.

   a. $\triangle DFA \cong \triangle GCE$ b. $\triangle DFA \cong \triangle EGC$

   c. $\triangle DFA \cong \triangle CEG$ d. $\triangle DFA \cong \triangle ECG$

   e. $\triangle DFA \cong \triangle GEC$ f. $\triangle DFA \cong \triangle CGE$

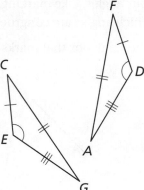

2. Even though only one of the statements above is correct, there are other
   correct congruence statements for these two triangles. Write two more
   triangle congruence statements.

3. **Write About It** Explain the meaning of the statement "corresponding parts
   of congruent figures are congruent." It may help to draw a picture.

4. On a single sheet of paper, draw and label two congruent triangles. Your
   triangles should be oriented differently. Use marks to indicate congruent
   segments and congruent angles. Exchange papers with a classmate. Write a
   congruence statement for your classmate's triangles.

On Your Own

5. Assume $\triangle CAT \cong \triangle DOG$. List all the corresponding parts.

6. **Standardized Test Prep** You are given that $\triangle DFG \cong \triangle CHK$. Which of the
   following statements is true by "corresponding parts of congruent figures
   are congruent"?

   A. $m\angle FGD = m\angle CKH$ B. $\overline{CH} \cong \overline{DG}$

   C. $DF = HK$ D. $\angle FGD \cong \angle KCH$

7. Use the figure below. Some pairs of triangles are *certainly not* congruent.
   List any pairs of triangles that appear to be congruent.

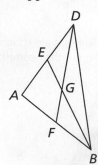

8. You can compare figures in many different ways. Congruence is a *shape* comparison. Area is a *quantitative* comparison. Use what you know about area to answer the following questions.

Similarity is another shape comparison. Perimeter is another quantitative comparison.

   a. If two polygons are congruent, must they have the same area? Explain.

   b. If two polygons have the same area, must they be congruent? Explain.

9. The figure below contains three congruent triangles.

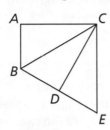

   a. Write a correct congruence statement for the three congruent triangles.

   b. On your own sketch, mark congruent corresponding parts.

   c. In quadrilateral *ABDC*, which triangle is congruent to △*ABC*?

   d. In △*BCE*, which triangle is congruent to △*ECD*?

10. The figure at the right is not drawn to scale. The markings indicate which pairs of segments and which pairs of angles are congruent. Segments that appear to be straight are meant to be.

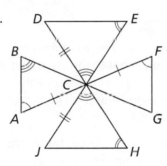

   a. Assume $m\angle F = 80°$, $m\angle H = 50°$, and $m\angle B = 40°$. What are the measures of $\angle A$, $\angle E$, and $\angle D$?

   b. Use a ruler and protractor to draw the figure to scale. Draw each angle with the correct angle measure. Draw congruent segments so that they are actually congruent.

Maintain Your Skills

11. Think about two congruent irregular pentagons. How many pairs of corresponding parts do they have? Draw and label your pentagons. Write a congruence statement. List all corresponding congruent parts.

8.04 Triangle Congruence

You know that corresponding parts of congruent figures are congruent. For triangles, you say that corresponding parts of congruent triangles are congruent. In other words, if two triangles are congruent, then their corresponding sides and corresponding angles are also congruent.

> You can abbreviate *corresponding parts of congruent triangles are congruent* as CPCTC.

The converse of this statement is also true. If the corresponding sides and corresponding angles of two triangles are congruent, then the triangles are congruent. This gives an exact method for proving triangles are congruent, but checking the six pairs of corresponding parts is a great deal of work.

For Discussion

1. Can you check fewer than six pairs of corresponding parts to determine whether two triangles are congruent? For instance, if the three angles in one triangle are congruent to the three angles in another triangle, are the two triangles congruent? Or if the three sides in one triangle are congruent to the three sides of another triangle, are the two triangles congruent?

2. Discuss the meaning of the following statement. *Information that is enough to specify one triangle is also enough to ensure that two triangles are congruent.* Is the statement true? Explain.

Classifying Your Information

You can *sometimes* determine whether two triangles are congruent when three parts of one triangle are congruent to three parts of another triangle. But not any three pairs of congruent parts guarantee that two triangles are congruent. For example, two triangles that have congruent corresponding angles are not necessarily congruent.

Which sets of three pairs of congruent parts guarantee that two triangles are congruent? To answer that question, first make a list of the possible combinations of three parts in one triangle. For example, $\triangle ABC$ has six parts: three sides and three angles.

three sides: $\overline{AB}$, $\overline{BC}$, and $\overline{AC}$
three angles: $\angle A$, $\angle B$, and $\angle C$

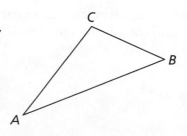

For You to Do

3. List the possible combinations of three parts of $\triangle ABC$. Here are two examples.

- $\angle A$, $\angle B$, $\angle C$
- $\overline{AB}$, $\angle A$, $\angle B$

You can classify your combinations in many ways. Here is a scheme that people have found useful. Note that this is *not* a list of ways to show two triangles are congruent.

Three Parts	Abbreviation Triplet	Meaning for a Triangle	Example for $\triangle ABC$
Three angles	AAA	Three angles of the triangle	$\angle A, \angle B, \angle C$
Two angles, one side	ASA	Two angles and the side between them	$\angle A, \overline{AB}, \angle B$
	AAS	Two angles and a side not between the angles	$\angle A, \angle B, \overline{BC}$
Two sides, one angle	SAS	Two sides and the angle between them	$\overline{AC}, \angle A, \overline{AB}$
	SSA	Two sides and an angle not between the sides	$\overline{AC}, \overline{AB}, \angle B$
Three sides	SSS	Three sides of the triangle	$\overline{AC}, AB, BC$

You read *ASA* as "angle-side-angle."

Order is important. SAS is not the same as SSA.

Which of these triplets can you use to prove that two triangles are congruent? You can investigate this question. Try to build two noncongruent triangles that share a given triplet. If you can, then the triplet does not guarantee triangle congruence. If you cannot, then there is a good chance that the triplet does guarantee congruence.

In-Class Experiment

Work with a partner or in a small group to determine which of the triplets below guarantee triangle congruence. For each triplet, try to build two noncongruent triangles with the given angle measures and side lengths.

4. **ASA** $m\angle A = 40°$, $AB = 2$ in., $m\angle B = 70°$

5. **AAS** $m\angle A = 40°$, $m\angle B = 70°$, $BC = 2$ in.

6. **SAS** $AC = 2$ in., $m\angle A = 60°$, $AB = 3$ in.

7. **SSA** $AC = 2$ in., $AB = 4$ in., $m\angle B = 20°$

8. **SSS** $AC = 2$ in., $AB = 3$ in., $BC = 4$ in.

The results of the In-Class Experiment suggest the following assumption.

Postulate 8.1 *The Triangle Congruence Postulates*

If two triangles share the following triplets of congruent corresponding parts, then the triangles are congruent.

- **ASA**
- **SAS**
- **SSS**

Remember...

Another word for assumption is *postulate*. A **postulate** is a statement that is accepted without proof.

What can you do with the AAS triplet? You can prove that this triplet guarantees triangle congruence if you assume that the other triangle congruence postulates are true. You also have to assume that the sum of the measures of the angles of a triangle is 180°.

And what can you do with the SSA triplet? In Exercise 7, you will show why this triplet does not guarantee triangle congruence.

Mathematicians like to make as few assumptions and to prove as many theorems as possible.

Exercises Practicing Habits of Mind

Check Your Understanding

For Exercises 1 and 2, do each of the following:

a. Construct △*ABC* with the given angle measures and given side lengths.

b. Compare results with a classmate. Are your triangles congruent?

c. If your triangles are not congruent, what additional information will guarantee that the triangles are congruent?

1. $m\angle A = 36°$, $m\angle B = 72°$, $m\angle C = 72°$

2. $m\angle A = 60°$, $AB = 8$ cm, $BC = 7$ cm

In Exercises 3 and 4, is △*ABC* ≅ △*ADC*? If the two triangles are congruent, state which triangle congruence postulate helped you decide.

3.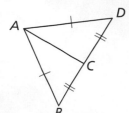

4.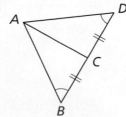

5. Show in two different ways that a diagonal of a square divides the square into two congruent triangles. Use a different triangle congruence postulate each time.

Remember...

A *square* is a quadrilateral with four congruent sides and four right angles.

6. You and a friend are making triangular pennants. Your friend says that each pennant should have a 30° angle, a 14-inch side, and an 8-inch side. Explain why this information does not guarantee that all the pennants will be congruent.

7. The diagram at the right proves, without words, that the SSA triplet does not guarantee triangle congruence. Explain the proof.

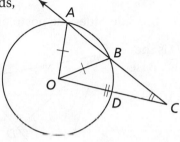

Note that point *O* is the center of the circle. Why use a circle in this proof without words?

On Your Own

For Exercises 8–12, do each of the following:

a. Tell whether the given information is enough to show that the triangles are congruent. The triangles are not necessarily drawn to scale.

b. If the given information is enough, list the pairs of corresponding vertices of the two triangles. Then state which triangle congruence postulate guarantees that the triangles are congruent.

8.

9.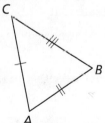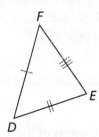

10.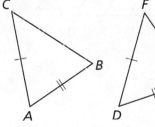

11.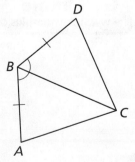

12.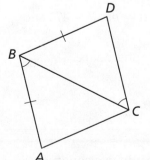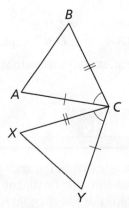

13. Standardized Test Prep In $\triangle ABC$, $\overline{CD}$ is the bisector of $\angle ACB$. Which of the following conjectures is true?

    A. There is not sufficient evidence to prove that $\triangle ACD \cong \triangle BCD$.

    B. $\triangle ACD \cong \triangle BCD$ is true by the Angle-Side-Angle postulate. In each triangle, the side between the two angles is $\overline{CD}$.

    C. $\triangle ACD \cong \triangle BCD$ is true by the Side-Angle-Side postulate. Angle ACD and $\angle BCD$ are the congruent angles that are between the two pairs of congruent sides.

    D. $\triangle ACD \cong \triangle BCD$ is true by the Side-Side-Side postulate.

14. In the figure at the right, $\overline{BD}$ is the perpendicular bisector of $\overline{AC}$. Based on this statement, which two triangles are congruent? Prove that they are congruent.

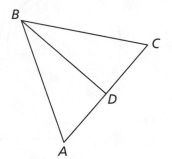

15. Take It Further In the figure at the right, $\overline{AD}$ is the perpendicular bisector of $\overline{BC}$. Based on this information, two triangles in the figure are congruent.

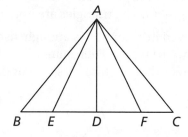

For each part, does the given piece of information help you determine that any additional triangles are congruent? If so, state the triangles and the congruence postulate that guarantees their congruence.

    a. $AB = AC$

    b. $\overline{AD}$ is the perpendicular bisector of $\overline{EF}$.

    c. $\angle EAD \cong \angle FAD$

16. Assume you know that the sum of the measures of the angles in a triangle is 180°.

    a. In $\triangle ABC$ and $\triangle DEF$, $m\angle A = m\angle D = 72°$, $m\angle B = m\angle E = 47°$, and $AC = DF = 10$ in. Is $\triangle ABC \cong \triangle DEF$? Explain.

    b. Explain why the AAS triplet guarantees triangle congruence.

Go Online
www.successnetplus.com

Maintain Your Skills

17. Does a diagonal of a rectangle divide the rectangle into two congruent triangles? Can you say the same for the diagonals of a parallelogram? For the diagonals of a trapezoid? For the diagonals of a kite? Explain.

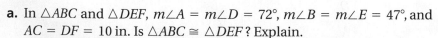

What are some good definitions for *rectangle, parallelogram, trapezoid,* and *kite*?

Mathematical 8A Reflections

In this investigation, you studied congruent figures—figures that are the same shape and size. You determined whether two figures were congruent based on relationships between their parts. You also learned postulates that you can use to prove two triangles are congruent.

1. **a.** Name the triangle congruence postulates.

    b. Explain what each one means.

    c. Draw a picture to illustrate each postulate.

2. Tell whether each statement below makes sense. If a statement does not make sense, explain why. Then rewrite the statement so that it does make sense.

    a. $MA \cong FL$

    b. $m\angle A = m\angle L$

    c. $MT = FO$

    d. $\overline{TA} \cong \overline{LO}$

    e. $\angle AMT = \angle LFO$

3. Triangle ABC and $\triangle DEF$ are isosceles. $\overline{AC} \cong \overline{BC}$ and $\overline{DF} \cong \overline{EF}$. If $\angle ACB \cong \angle DFE$ and $\overline{CB} \cong \overline{FD}$, can you determine whether the two triangles are congruent? Explain.

4. Draw $\triangle ABC$. Find the midpoint of $\overline{BC}$. Call it point O. Draw $\overrightarrow{AO}$. Mark point D on $\overrightarrow{AO}$ so that $\overline{OD} \cong \overline{OA}$. Draw BD and CD. Look for congruent triangles in your figure. (*Hint:* $\angle DOB \cong \angle AOC$ and $\angle AOB \cong \angle DOC$.) Explain why $\overline{BD} \cong \overline{AC}$. Explain why $\overline{CD} \cong \overline{AB}$.

5. In the figure at the right, $\overrightarrow{OD}$ is the angle bisector of $\angle AOB$. $\overline{OA} \cong \overline{OB}$. Explain why $\overline{AD} \cong \overline{BD}$.

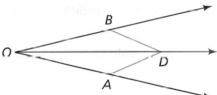

6. What does it mean to say that two figures are congruent?

7. Why is it important to keep track of corresponding parts in congruent figures?

8. What are some ways to prove that two triangles are congruent?

Vocabulary and Notation

In this investigation, you learned this term and these symbols. Make sure you understand what each one means, and how to use it.

- postulate
- $\cong$ (is congruent to)
- JK (length of $\overline{JK}$)
- $\perp$ (is perpendicular to)

These two houses are the same shape and size.

Transformations

In *Transformations*, you will explore reflections using paper folding or mirrors as well as the coordinate plane. You will also perform multiple reflections to make transformations called translations and rotations.

By the end of this investigation, you will be able to answer questions like these.

1. When you reflect an object over a line, what properties of the object are present in its image?

2. What happens when you compose two reflections? Three reflections? Four reflections?

3. $\triangle ABC$ has vertices $A(2, -1)$, $B(-2, -3)$, and $C(2, -3)$. When you reflect $\triangle ABC$ over the x-axis, what are the coordinates of its image $\triangle A'B'C'$?

You will learn how to

- model reflections using paper-folding techniques

- model compositions of reflections and classify the resulting transformation as a reflection, rotation, translation, or combination of transformations

- model rotations and translations in the plane, with and without coordinates

- understand properties of reflection, translation, and rotation in the plane

- identify fixed points for a given transformation or composition of transformations

You will develop these habits and skills:

- Use geometric properties of transformations in the coordinate plane.

- Recognize rules that map points onto other points and classify rules as particular transformations.

- Apply transformations to figures and to graphs of functions in the coordinate plane.

If a figure reflects onto itself o a line, then the line is a line of symmetry.

There are different types of **transformations** in a plane. A reflection suggests a mirror. But you can also experiment with reflections by folding paper.

In-Class Experiment

On a piece of plain paper, draw a capital letter F an inch or two high. Here is how to find the **image** of your letter F (the **preimage**) after reflection over a fold line.

- Fold the paper to cover the letter. The crease, or fold line, can be anywhere you like, but it should not intersect the letter.

- Trace the letter onto the back of the paper.

- Unfold the paper. Trace your tracing onto the front of the paper. Also, draw along the crease to show the fold line better.

This new picture is the image of your original picture after reflection over your fold line. Place a mirror along the fold line and look into the mirror from the side with the preimage. You will see this image in the mirror.

- Label the image with an uppercase letter different from F. Label the fold line with the corresponding lowercase letter.

- Choose some other lines of reflection and repeat this process using your original preimage F. You can have one or two fold lines intersect F.

- Visualize the process to avoid lines that will reflect the preimage off your paper and predict where the image will be on the paper. Check each prediction.

For You to Explore

1. On a plain piece of paper, use a ruler to draw a line segment $\overline{AB}$. Fold the paper by matching point A to point B. Call the fold line ℓ. Call the point where ℓ and $\overline{AB}$ intersect point X.

   a. Which segment has greater length, $\overline{AX}$ or $\overline{BX}$? Explain.

   b. Choose a point C on ℓ but not on $\overline{AB}$. What is the measure of $\angle AXC$?

   c. Describe $\triangle ABC$. Does it have any special characteristics?

   d. Describe the relationship between ℓ and $\overline{AB}$.

2. Look at a reflection you did in the In-Class Experiment. Mark several points on the preimage F. From each point, draw a segment to the corresponding point on the image. How do all these segments seem to relate to one another? How do they relate to the fold line?

3. Mark coordinate axes on a sheet of graph paper. Graph the rectangle *ABCD* with vertices $A(-3, 4)$, $B(-1, 4)$, $C(-1, 1)$, and $D(-3, 1)$.

Use rectangle *ABCD* as a preimage. Find the coordinates of its image after reflection over each of the following lines.

a. the *x*-axis (Label the image *EFGH*.)

b. the *y*-axis (Label the image *IJKL*.)

c. the line with equation $x = -1$ (Label the image *MNOP*.)

You can fold your paper to find image points or to check the correspondence. Also, redraw rectangle *ABCD* on new sections of graph paper as needed.

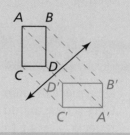

In this reflection, dotted lines are drawn between pairs of corresponding points.

Habits of Mind

Be systematic. In your answers to Exercise 3, list the points in order as they correspond to the points *A*, *B*, *C*, and *D* in the preimage.

4. Look at rectangle *ABCD* and its images from Exercise 3. For each rectangle listed below, describe the path from vertex to vertex, in alphabetical order, as either clockwise or counterclockwise looking at the front of the paper.

a. *ABCD*   **b.** *EFGH*   **c.** *IJKL*   **d.** *MNOP*

e. Do all the paths for the images go in the same direction? Does the path for the preimage go in the same direction?

5. Graph the points $U(-3, -4)$, $V(5, 0)$, and $W(2, 5)$. Find and graph their respective images U', V', and W' from reflection over the line $y = 2$. Then find the following distances.

a. *U* to U' **b.** *U* to the line $y = 2$ **c.** *V* to V'

d. *V* to the line $y = 2$ **e.** *W* to W' **f.** *W* to the line $y = 2$

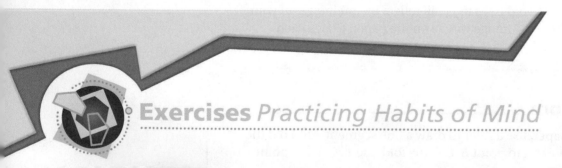

Exercises *Practicing Habits of Mind*

On Your Own

6. When you reflect a figure using the paper-folding method of the In-Class Experiment, is the image congruent to the original figure (the preimage)? Explain.

7. a. Graph quadrilateral *PQRS* with $P(1, 0)$, $Q(5, 4)$, $R(9, 2)$, and $S(5, -2)$. Find the slope of each side of *PQRS*. Show that *PQRS* is a parallelogram.

   b. Graph the image $P'Q'R'S'$ of *PQRS* after reflection over the line $y = -2$.

   c. Is $P'Q'R'S'$ also a parallelogram? Explain.

   d. Are the sides of the image $P'Q'R'S'$ parallel to the corresponding sides in the preimage *PQRS*? Explain.

8. a. Graph any quadrilateral and label it *ABCD*.

   b. Suppose you walk around your quadrilateral from *A* to *B* to *C* to *D* and then back to *A*. Will a person watching from above see your path as clockwise or counterclockwise?

   c. Reflect your quadrilateral over the line $x = -2$. Label the image *EFGH* so that $EFGH \cong ABCD$.

   d. Suppose you walk around this new quadrilateral from *E* to *F* to *G* to *H* and then back to *E*. Will a person watching from above see your path as clockwise or counterclockwise?

   e. Was the direction (clockwise or counterclockwise) the same for your preimage and for its image after reflection?

9. Plot $\overline{AB}$ on a coordinate plane, with endpoints $A(2, 5)$ and $B(4, 2)$. Reflect $\overline{AB}$ over the *x*-axis. Write the coordinates of A' and B', the images of *A* and *B*.

10. Graph the line with equation $2x + y = 6$. Write an equation for its image after a reflection over the *y*-axis.

Remember...

A parallelogram is a quadrilateral with two pairs of opposite sides. Slope is the ratio of the change in the *y*-coordinates to the change in the *x*-coordinates. If two lines have the same slope, then they are parallel.

Go **Online**
Video Tutor
www.successnetplus.com

For help graphing an equation, see the TI-Nspire™ Handbook, p. 788.

Maintain Your Skills

11. On a plain piece of paper, use a ruler to draw scalene $\triangle ABC$. Use the paper-folding method of the In-Class Experiment. Reflect $\triangle ABC$ over different lines of reflection. Describe where you fold the paper so that $\triangle ABC$ and its image have the following in common.

   a. no points   **b.** one point

   c. two points   **d.** one side

12. On a plain piece of paper, draw isosceles $\triangle DEF$ with $\overline{DE} \cong \overline{DF}$. Fold the paper to find the **line of reflection** for which $\triangle DEF$ and its image have all their points in common. Describe the position of this line of reflection.

Remember...

A **scalene triangle** has no sides that are the same length.

8.06 Reflections

In Lesson 8.05, you worked with reflections in the plane. You saw how you can map all the points of the plane to the points of the plane by reflecting over a line. You learned to find the images of points by folding paper, or by using the "mirror-image" technique.

Does every point map onto a point different from itself? For some reflections the points do, but for some they do not. Look at the following figure.

> In other words, every point is mapped somewhere by the reflection.

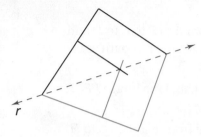

Definition

A point that is its own image after a transformation is a fixed point.

For Discussion

1. In the figure above, can you see points that are mapped onto themselves by reflection over *r*?

2. Draw a geometric object (such as a line, a triangle, or a circle) so that its image after the reflection over *r* is itself. Are all of its points fixed?

3. Describe all the fixed points for the reflection over line *r*.

You have seen what happens when you reflect a point over one line. What happens when you reflect a point over one line and then reflect the image of that point over a second line?

A figure that reflects onto itself over a line has line symmetry.

Use geometry software or paper and pencil.

4. Draw two parallel lines *r* and *s*. Also, draw a letter F like the one on the right.

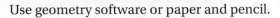

5. Reflect F over *r*. Refer to this image of F as F′.

6. Reflect F′ over *s*. Refer to this image of F′ as F″.

7. Are there any points in the plane that remained fixed through both reflections?

8. Compare F and F″. Is there a single transformation (not necessarily a reflection) that maps F onto F″? Explain.

9. Draw a different line for *s*. Make *s* intersect *r*. Construct F″ as before.

10. Are there any points in the plane that remained fixed after reflection over *r* and *s* for your new choice for *s*?

11. Compare F and F″. Is there a single transformation that maps F onto F″? Explain.

> For help reflecting an object over a line, see the TI-Nspire Handbook, p. 788.

> Read F″ as "F double prime."

For Discussion

Compare your results for the In-Class Experiment with the results of other students in your class. Discuss possible reasons for the differences and similarities you see.

12. What single transformation mapped F onto F″? Did this transformation map F onto F″ in both cases?

13. Did anyone have a different kind of single transformation?

14. When *r* and *s* intersected, what were the fixed points after reflection over *r* and then *s*? What were the fixed points when they were parallel?

15. What happens if *r* and *s* are the same line?

In Lesson 8.05, you folded paper and traced to produce a reflected image. You found that the fold line (which is the line of reflection) has a special property. It is the perpendicular bisector of every segment joining a point in the preimage to the corresponding point in the image.

You can use this special property to define *reflection*.

Definition

Suppose *P* is a point and ℓ is a line not containing *P*. A **reflection** over ℓ maps the point to *P′* such that ℓ is the perpendicular bisector of $\overline{PP'}$. If ℓ contains *P*, *P* is its own reflection image.

Exercises *Practicing Habits of Mind*

Check Your Understanding

1. Decide whether each statement is *always*, *sometimes*, or *never* true for reflection over a line. If a statement is always true or never true, prove it. If a statement is sometimes true and sometimes false, give an example of each case.

    a. A segment in a preimage must be the same length as the corresponding segment in the image.

    b. An angle in a preimage must have the same measure as the corresponding angle in the image.

    c. Collinear points in a preimage must have collinear image points.

    d. The slope of a segment in an image must be the same as the slope of the corresponding segment in the preimage.

    e. Segments in an image that correspond to segments that are parallel in the preimage must be parallel to each other.

    f. Segments in an image that correspond to segments that are perpendicular in the preimage must also be perpendicular.

2. **a.** Reflect $\overline{AB}$ with endpoints $A(2, 5)$ and $B(4, 2)$ over the line with equation $x = 4$. Write the coordinates of the endpoints of the image.

    b. Now reflect the image of $\overline{AB}$ over the line with equation $x = 8$. Write the coordinates of the endpoints of this new image.

    c. Describe a single transformation that maps $\overline{AB}$ onto the final image.

3. In the diagram below, P' is the image of P over ℓ. The points O and R are on ℓ. Prove $\angle POR \cong \angle P'OR$.

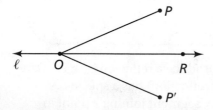

4. Prove that if a segment is parallel to a line of reflection, the image of the segment after reflection is also parallel to the line of reflection.

5. Complete parts (a) and (b) to show that the definition of reflection in the lesson describes a unique reflection image.

   a. Given a line ℓ and a point P not on ℓ, how many lines are there through P that are perpendicular to ℓ? Explain how you know.

   b. Given a line ℓ, a point P, and another line m through P and perpendicular to ℓ, explain how you can find a point P' on m such that ℓ is the perpendicular bisector of $\overline{PP'}$. Is there only one such point?

6. Use the definition of reflection to prove that a segment and its reflection image are congruent. In other words,

   Show that if ℓ is the perpendicular bisector of both $\overline{AA'}$ and $\overline{BB'}$, then $\overline{AB} \cong \overline{A'B'}$.

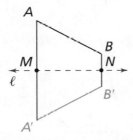

7. **a.** Reflect $\overline{AB}$ with endpoints $A(1, 2)$ and $B(3, 3)$ over the line $y = \frac{1}{2}$. Write the coordinates of the endpoints of the image.

   b. Now reflect the image of $\overline{AB}$ over the line $y = -1$. Write the coordinates of the endpoints of this new image.

   c. Describe a single transformation that maps $\overline{AB}$ onto the final image.

8. Reflect $\overline{AB}$ with endpoints $A(1, 2)$ and $B(3, 3)$ over the line $x = 4$. Now reflect the image over the line $y = -1$. Write the coordinates of the endpoints of the image of $\overline{AB}$ after these two reflections. Describe a single transformation that maps $\overline{AB}$ onto the final image.

9. Graph the line $x + 3y = 6$. Write an equation for its image after a reflection over the x-axis.

10. Standardized Test Prep Reflect point $R(2, -3)$ over the line $y = x$. What are the coordinates of the reflection image of point R?

A. $(-2, -3)$ **B.** $(-2, 3)$ **C.** $(-3, 2)$ **D.** $(2, 3)$

In Exercises 11–14, you are given an equation and its graph. Decide whether each graph has any lines of symmetry.

Remember...

If a figure maps onto itself after reflection over a line, then that line is a line of symmetry for the figure.

11. $y = |x|$

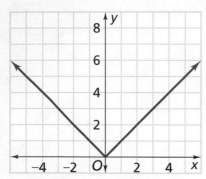

12. $y = x^2$

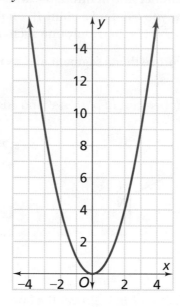

13. $y = x^2 + 2$

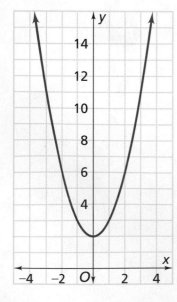

14. $y = x^2 + 2x + 1$

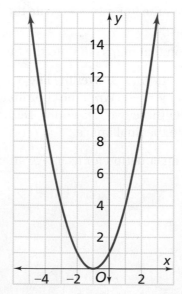

15. Trace the diagram below onto a sheet of plain paper. Use the letter F in this picture as a preimage.

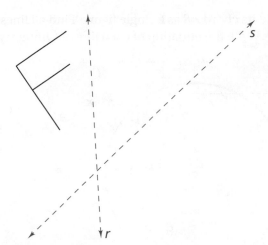

a. Reflect F over line *r*. Label this image *r*(F). Then reflect *r*(F) over line *s*. Label this image *s*(*r*(F)). Compare F and *s*(*r*(F)). Is there a single transformation that maps F onto *s*(*r*(F)) without using reflection?

b. Using the same diagram, draw two more lines. Call them *t* and *w*. Reflect *s*(*r*(F)) over *t* to obtain *t*(*s*(*r*(F))). Compare *F* and *t*(*s*(*r*(F))). Is there a single transformation that maps F onto *t*(*s*(*r*(F))) without using reflection?

c. Is there a single transformation that would map *r*(F) onto *t*(*s*(*r*(F))) without using reflection?

d. Compare F and *w*(*t*(*s*(*r*(F)))). Is there a single transformation that maps F onto *w*(*t*(*s*(*r*(F)))) without using reflection?

e. Find a pattern for your answers to parts (a)–(d).

Is this photograph upside down?

16. Think of the circle O and its chord AB as a single figure. Find all lines of symmetry for the figure. Write the equation of each line of symmetry.

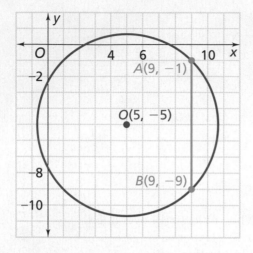

![Maintain Your Skills]

17. For the letters of the alphabet below, list those that appear to have each of the following.

ABCDEFGHI
JKLMNOPQR
STUVWXYZ

a. a vertical line of symmetry

b. a horizontal line of symmetry

c. both vertical and horizontal lines of symmetry

d. lines of symmetry that are neither horizontal nor vertical

e. rotational symmetry (other than full-turn rotational symmetry)

Having rotational symmetry means that, when you turn the paper, at some angle or angles the letter looks exactly as it did at the start.

8.07 Translations

In the In-Class Experiment of Lesson 8.06, you reflected the letter F over two parallel lines. Here are some conclusions you may have reached.

- The final image was congruent to the original F.
- You could obtain the final image from the original F by a single transformation—a "slide" with no spins or turns.
- No points on the plane were fixed.

This type of transformation is a **translation**. Any translation is a **composition** of two reflections, but you usually do not think of it that way.

In Exercise 6, you will prove that the composition of two reflections over parallel lines produces a translation.

For Discussion

1. How can you describe the transformation that maps *ABCD* onto *A′B′C′D′*?

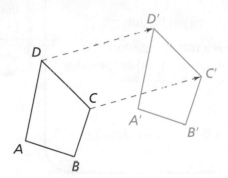

Try drawing more arrows to corresponding points. Some people call these arrows *vectors*.

How are the arrows related? Explain.

Digital artists use translations to make new arrangements of images.

Developing Habits of Mind

Write a description. The coordinate plane gives you an algebraic way to describe a translation. The diagram shows a translation of a quadrilateral.

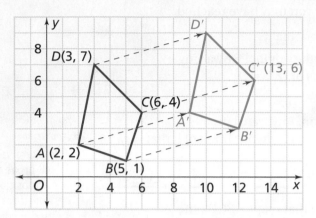

What are the coordinates of *A'*, *B'*, and *D'*?

Here, you "add" (7, 2) to each point of the preimage to get the image.

In general, a translation on the coordinate plane is a transformation that adds one value to every *x*-coordinate of the preimage and another (possibly the same) value to every *y*-coordinate of the preimage. In symbols,

$$(x, y) \mapsto (x + a, y + b)$$

where *a* and *b* are any real numbers. This notation describes a mapping. You say, "The translation (a, b) maps (x, y) to $(x + a, y + b)$."

Habits of Mind

Check your work. Verify your conjectures from Problem 1. Use numbers and the coordinate plane.

The relationships you described in Problem 1 are still true, but now you give such descriptions using numbers.

For You to Do

Graph a scalene right triangle. Find its image after applying each rule.

2. $(x, y) \mapsto (x + 8, y + 5)$

3. $(a, b) \mapsto (a - 8, b + 5)$

4. $(a, b) \mapsto (-a, b)$

5. $(x, y) \mapsto (x + 1, y + 2)$

6. $(x, y) \mapsto (x, -y)$

Which rules are translations? What are the other rules?

Minds in Action

Tony and Sasha want to translate the parabola $y = \frac{1}{2}x^2 + 1$ *by* $(2, -1)$.
They also want to write an equation for the image of the parabola after the translation.

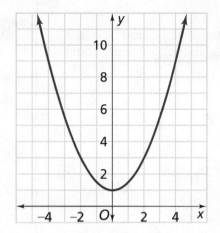

Tony This should be easy. I mean, we know that every point (x, y) maps to $(x + 2, y - 1)$. We can just plug those new expressions in for x and y. That should move everything 2 units to the right and 1 unit down.

Sasha That sounds reasonable enough.

Tony and Sasha graph $(y - 1) = \frac{1}{2}(x + 2)^2 + 1$.

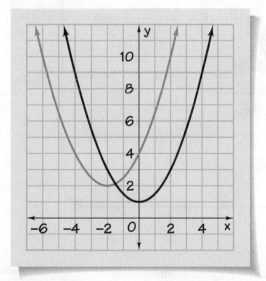

Tony Hey, that's out of order! The image parabola was translated in exactly the wrong direction! Where did we mess up?

Sasha Hmmm . . . wait a minute. The old equation was $y = \frac{1}{2}x^2 + 1$, right?

Tony Yes, so what?

Sasha That was written with the old x and the old y. We know that

$$y_{old} = \tfrac{1}{2}(x_{old})^2 + 1$$

But now we're talking about a different x and y.

$$x_{new} = x_{old} + 2$$
$$y_{new} = y_{old} - 1$$

Look, the only equation we have is in terms of x_{old} and y_{old}. We have to substitute something with x_{new} and y_{new} that are equal to x_{old} and y_{old}.

Tony Oh, I get it! Since

$$x_{old} = x_{new} - 2$$
$$y_{old} = y_{new} + 1$$

we have to plug in $x - 2$ for x and $y + 1$ for y.

Sasha Cross your fingers. Let's try it.

Tony and Sasha graph $(y + 1) = \tfrac{1}{2}(x - 2)^2 + 1$.

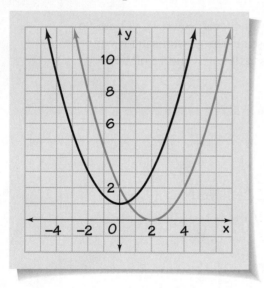

Tony Go, Sasha!

For You to Do

Translate the parabola with equation $y = \tfrac{1}{2}x^2 + 1$ by each translation below. Write an equation for the parabola's image after each translation.

7. $(0, -2)$

8. $(3, 0)$

9. $(1, 5)$

> For help translating an object by a given vector, see the TI-Nspire Handbook, p. 788.

Exercises *Practicing Habits of Mind*

Check Your Understanding

1. The diagram shows the transformation $AKLJ \rightarrow A'K'L'J'$.

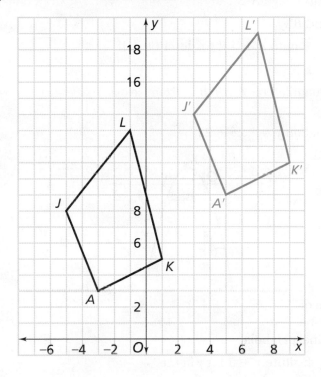

   a. How do you know that the transformation is a translation?

   b. Describe the translation.

   c. Describe what you have to do to the coordinates of the vertices of $AKLJ$ to get the coordinates of the vertices of $A'K'L'J'$.

2. Apply the rule $(x, y) \mapsto (x + 10, y + 6)$ to the vertices of a triangle. Then connect the three image points. What figure do you get? How is it related to your original triangle?

3. Find an equation of the image of line s with equation $2x + y = 3$ after the translation $(6, 7)$.

4. Graph $\overline{AB}$ with endpoints $A(1, 2)$ and $B(2, 5)$.

   a. Reflect $\overline{AB}$ over the line $x = 3$. Call its image $\overline{A'B'}$.

   b. Reflect $\overline{A'B'}$ over the line $x = 6$. Call its image $\overline{A''B''}$.

   c. Find the coordinates of A', B', A'', and B''.

   d. Is there a single mapping that sends $\overline{AB}$ onto $\overline{A''B''}$? If so, describe it. If not, explain why not.

5. Use coordinate methods to show that quadrilateral $AA''B''B$ in Exercise 4 is a parallelogram.

6. Here is a graph of the parabola with equation $y = -x^2 + 2x$.

   a. Substitute $x + 3$ for x in the equation of the parabola. Graph the result. Describe this result as a translation of the original parabola.

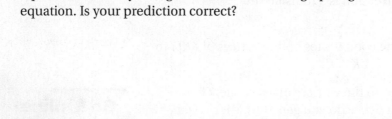

   b. Predict what graph will result if you substitute $x - 2$ for x in the equation. Check by doing the substitution and graphing. Is your prediction correct?

   c. Substitute $y - 2$ for y in the equation of the parabola. Graph the result. Describe this result as a translation of the original parabola.

   d. Predict what graph will result if you substitute $y + 3$ for y in the equation. Check by doing the substitution and graphing the new equation. Is your prediction correct?

7. Use this graph of the circle with equation $x^2 + y^2 = 4$.

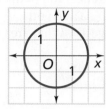

Find at least three points on the circle. Translate the circle by each translation below. Write an equation for the image of the circle after each translation.

a. $(0, -1)$

b. $(0, 1)$

c. $(6, 0)$

d. $(3, 4)$

8. Look at the circle with equation $x^2 + y^2 + 2x = 3$.

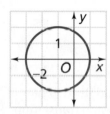

Find at least three points on the circle. Translate the circle by each translation below. Write an equation for the image of the circle after each translation.

a. $(0, -2)$

b. $(0, 2)$

c. $(3, 0)$

d. $(1, 4)$

> For help finding the coordinates of a point, see the TI-Nspire Handbook, p. 788.

9. **Standardized Test Prep** The transformation $(x, y) \rightarrow (x, 2a - y)$ defines a reflection over the line with equation $y = a$. Suppose you reflect the point $F(5, 3)$ over the line with equation $y = c$ to get the image F'. Then you reflect F' over the line with equation $y = d$ to get the image F''. What are the coordinates of F''?

   A. $(5, 2(c + d) - 3)$

   B. $(5, 2(d - c) - 3)$

   C. $(5, 2(c + d) + 3)$

   D. $(5, 2(d - c) + 3)$

Maintain Your Skills

10. This is an equation of the circle with radius 5 centered at the origin.

$$x^2 + y^2 = 25$$

    Find an equation for the circle with radius 5 centered at each point.

    a. $(4, 3)$

    b. $(-2, 6)$

    c. $(5, -1)$

11. What translation maps the graph of the equation you found in each part of Exercise 10 to an image centered at the origin? How does each translation transform the coordinates of a point (x, y)?

12. Show that the translations you described in Exercise 11 transform the respective equations you found in Exercise 10 into the equation $x^2 + y^2 = 25$.

Rotations

In the In-Class Experiment in Lesson 8.06, you saw what happened when you reflected the letter F over two lines that are not parallel.

Minds in Action

Derman is looking at his work from a recent In-Class Experiment.

Derman Hey Sasha, I've been thinking about the experiment we did in class for Lesson 8.06. I understand how you get a translation when you compose two reflections over parallel lines. But I have trouble understanding what happens when the lines aren't parallel.

Sasha Well, try to think how the final image was different from the original letter F you drew.

Derman Hmmm . . .

The original F and its final image were congruent.

I could have moved the final image and made it match up with the original F without flipping it.

But I couldn't have just translated it, because the transformation was different.

Sasha Right! The transformation involved some kind of a turn.

Derman Yes, and I also thought of another mysterious thing. You know how in a reflection, the line of reflection is fixed? Well, the first line is fixed for the first reflection. The second line is fixed for the second reflection. But the point of intersection is the only point fixed for both reflections! Doesn't that make it special?

Sasha I think there *is* something special about that point, but I don't think it's mysterious!

You can investigate this intersection point in the In-Class Experiment on the next page.

You will need geometry software, or paper, a ruler, a pencil, and a protractor.

Draw two lines, *r* and *s*, that intersect at *P* so that you can choose two points *R* and *S* on *r* and *s*, respectively, such that $m\angle RPS = 35°$. Choose at least 5 points *A*, *B*, *C*, *D*, *E* ... in the plane.

> You may choose some points on *r* or *s*, but make sure you choose some that are not on the lines, too.

1. Reflect your points once over *r* and then reflect their images over *s*. Use the following notation. Call *A'* the image of point *A* after the reflection over *r*. Call *A"* the image of *A'* after the reflection over *s*. Use the same notation for the other points *B*, *B'*, *B"*, and so on.

2. Compare $\angle APA"$, $\angle BPB"$, $\angle CPC"$, and so on. If you are using a protractor, your measurements may be inaccurate.

3. Compare $\angle RPS$ with the angles above.

4. What happens if you perform the reflections in the opposite order, that is, first over *s* and then over *r*?

The In-Class Experiment suggests another way to obtain the image of a point after reflections over two intersecting lines. This other transformation is a **rotation.**

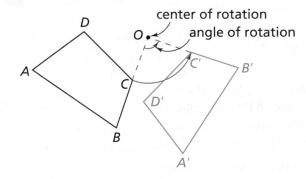

center of rotation
angle of rotation

In the figure above, *O* is the center of rotation. Arcs connecting corresponding points in the preimage and the image lie on concentric circles. If *P* is a point in the preimage and *P'* is the image of *P*, all angles of the form $\angle POP'$ are congruent. For example, in the figure above, $\angle DOD' \cong \angle AOA'$.

> **Remember...**
> Concentric circles have the same center. In this case, the center is *O*.

For Discussion

5. In the figure, $A'B'C'D'$ is the image of $ABCD$ after a rotation.

How can you find the center of rotation and the angle of rotation? Form a conjecture and prove it.

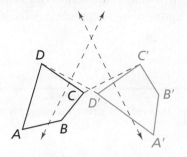

> What lines have been drawn in to help you?

Theorem 8.1

The composition of two reflections over intersecting lines produces a rotation. Its center is the intersection of the lines. The measure of the angle of rotation is equal to twice the measure of the smaller angle formed by the two lines.

Proof Begin with two lines ℓ and m, intersecting at O. Reflect a point P over line ℓ and call the image P'. Then reflect P' over m and call its image P''. Mark Q at the intersection of ℓ and $\overline{PP'}$ and R at the intersection of m and $\overline{P'P''}$. You want to show that a rotation about O through an angle twice the measure of the angle formed by ℓ and m will map P onto P''. You can break this proof down into two parts.

Part 1 Show that $m\angle POP''$ is twice the measure of the angle formed by lines ℓ and m. In other words, $m\angle POP'' = 2m\angle QOR$.

Part 2 Show that the rotation about O through $\angle POP''$ maps P to P''. In other words, show that $OP'' = OP$.

> Why does proving Parts 1 and 2 prove that if you rotate P about O through an angle of $2m\angle QOR$, you get P''?

For a proof of Part 1, you can use triangle congruencies you have already shown.

Since $\triangle PQO \cong \triangle P'QO$, the two angles labled α in the diagram are congruent. Since $\triangle P'RO \cong \triangle P''RO$, the two angles labled β are congruent. The angle of rotation, $\angle POP''$, has measure $2\alpha + 2\beta$ or $2(\alpha + \beta)$. The angle formed by lines ℓ and m, $\angle QOR$, has measure $\alpha + \beta$. So the angle of rotation is twice the measure of the angle formed by the intersecting lines of reflection.

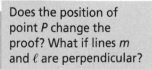

> Does the position of point P change the proof? What if lines m and ℓ are perpendicular?

For You to Do

6. Prove Part 2 in the proof of Theorem 8.1.

As you learned in Lesson 8.06, some geometric figures have a *line of symmetry*, a line where a figure maps to itself under reflection. The same can happen under rotation, with a specific center of rotation and angle of rotation. It is possible for a figure to be mapped onto itself in multiple ways.

Example

Problem Find all of the rotations and reflections that map rectangle *RECT* onto itself.

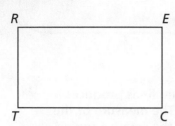

Solution Picture another copy of the rectangle placed on top of *RECT*. How could *RECT* be rotated to land exactly on itself? The center of rotation would have to be at the center of the rectangle, the intersection of its diagonals. Two rotations work. The first rotation is 180°, taking *R* onto *C* and *E* onto *T*:

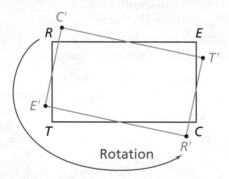

The second rotation is 360° (or 0°), leaving *RECT* in its starting orientation.

What about reflections? Look for lines of symmetry. A rectangle has two lines of symmetry, through the midpoints of opposite sides:

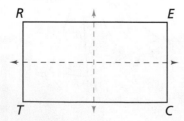

Through each of these lines of symmetry, the rectangle can be mapped onto itself. In total, there are 2 rotations and 2 reflections that map *RECT* onto itself.

Rotations larger than 360° are equivalent to a rotation less than 360°. If these are allowed, any figure has an infinite number of rotations that map the figure onto itself!

For You to Do

7. Draw what *RECT* would look like after each of its two possible reflections. Label the vertices of your images.

8. Draw what *RECT* would look like after performing *both* reflections, back-to-back. Label the vertices of your image.

Habits of Mind

Look for connections. Reflect *RECT* over one line, then reflect it over another line. What kind of transformation is that?

In-Class Experiment

For each figure in the table, answer the following questions.

9. How many lines of symmetry does the shape have?

10. If there is a line that the shape can be reflected over to map the shape onto itself, draw the line.

11. If a shape can be rotated so that it is mapped onto itself, describe the rotation.

12. Fill in the table with the information you found.

Shape	Number of Rotations	Number of Reflections	Total Ways to Map Figure Onto Itself
Non-Square Rectangle	2	2	4
Equilateral Triangle	■	■	■
Isosceles Triangle	■	■	■
Scalene Triangle	■	■	■
Parallelogram	■	■	■
Trapezoid	■	■	■

Remember...

A trapezoid is a quadrilateral with exactly one pair of parallel sides.

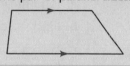

For Discussion

13. Do any special parallelograms or trapezoids have more possible rotations or reflections than others? Look for special cases.

Exercises *Practicing Habits of Mind*

Check Your Understanding

1. In the diagram, reflect quadrilateral *ABCD* over the *y*-axis to obtain *A'B'C'D'*. Reflect *A'B'C'D'* over the *x*-axis to obtain *A"B"C"D"*.

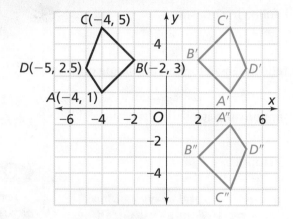

a. Find the coordinates of the vertices of *A'B'C'D'*.

b. Find the coordinates of the vertices of *A"B"C"D"*.

c. You can find a single rotation that maps *ABCD* onto *A"B"C"D"*. What tells you that such a rotation is possible?

d. Describe the rotation.

e. Compare the coordinates of the vertices of *ABCD* and of *A"B"C"D"*. What do you find?

2. a. For each regular polygon, draw all lines of symmetry and find all ways to rotate the regular polygon onto itself. Complete the table.

Shape	Number of Rotations	Number of Reflections	Total Ways to Map Figure Onto Itself
Equilateral Triangle	▪	▪	▪
Square	▪	▪	▪
Regular Pentagon	▪	▪	▪
Regular Hexagon	▪	▪	▪

b. Find a rule for the total number of ways to map a regular polygon onto itself.

c. Describe all the lines of symmetry for a regular polygon. Does the description change depending on the number of sides?

3. Use geometry software or a pencil and paper. Draw $\overline{AB}$ and a point O not on $\overline{AB}$. Find the image of $\overline{AB}$ after a counterclockwise rotation of 30° about O.

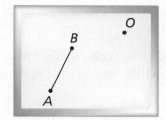

Habits of Mind

Experiment. What can you conclude if O is on $\overline{AB}$?

4. Think about the rotation that is the composition of reflections over r and then s.

Find the rotation image of $\overline{AB}$. Which point is the center of rotation? What is the angle of rotation? Could you have known either without finding the image of $\overline{AB}$?

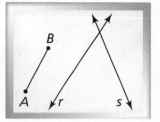

For help rotating an object, see the TI-Nspire Handbook, p. 788.

5. a. Draw a pentagon that has exactly one line of symmetry, or explain why it cannot be done.

   b. Take It Further Draw a pentagon that has exactly two lines of symmetry, or explain why it can't be done.

6. Square *SQRE* has four lines of symmetry.

   a. Reflect *SQRE* over any line of symmetry, and draw its new orientation. Label the vertices of your image.

   b. Reflect the new square over a *different* line of symmetry, and draw its new orientation. Label the vertices of your image.

   c. Describe a way to go directly from *SQRE* to the orientation found after the two reflections.

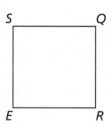

On Your Own

7. Draw $\triangle ABC$ and a point O. Find the image of $\triangle ABC$ after a counterclockwise rotation of 65° about O.

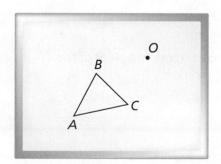

Try using your compass and protractor for this exercise.

8. Draw a quadrilateral and a point P. Find the image of the quadrilateral after a counterclockwise rotation of 90° with center P.

9. Explain why the vertex C of an isosceles triangle with $\overline{AB}$ as its base is a possible center of a rotation that maps A onto B. What is the angle of rotation?

10. Draw all of the lines of reflection that map a regular octagon onto itself.

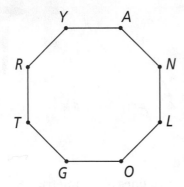

11. **Take It Further** Here $\triangle A'B'C'$ is the image of $\triangle ABC$ after a rotation about center O. (The label for B' is off of the screen.)

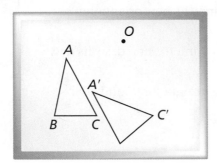

Find two lines over which a composition of reflections maps $\triangle ABC$ onto $\triangle A'B'C'$.

What angle will these two lines form?

12. **Standardized Test Prep** Rotate the letter W about a point P. Which of the following statements may NOT be true?

   A. The image letter is congruent to the original letter.

   B. The upper left point of the original W and the corresponding point of the image are the same distance from the point of rotation.

   C. The two angles at the bottom of the original W are congruent to the corresponding angles of the image.

   D. The original W and its image do not intersect.

13. You can obtain this figure by beginning with one of the F figures and repeatedly reflecting it over one and then over the other of the two lines.

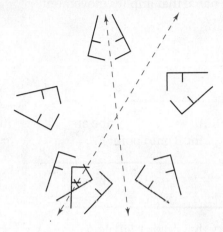

a. Which F might have been the first? How many could have been the first?

b. How might this figure continue?

c. Do you see any other repeated transformations?

d. Describe the patterns you see.

8.09 Congruence and Isometry

In this chapter, you have studied reflections, translations, and rotations. Each of these transformations map segments to segments of the same length, and angles to angles of the same measure. An **isometry** is any composition of reflections, translations, and rotations.

Another name for isometry is **rigid motion,** a name that implies movement without a change in shape or size.

> The name *isometry* comes from the Greek words *isos* (same) *métron* (measure).

For Discussion

1. Draw two segments $\overline{AB}$ and $\overline{DE}$ on paper with $AB = DE$. Describe an isometry that maps point A onto point D and point B onto point E.

> **Remember...**
>
> The isometry may involve more than one step, such as a translation followed by a rotation.

For You to Do

For each pair of triangles, describe an isometry that maps triangle ABC onto triangle DEF, or explain why no isometry exists. In each case, $\triangle ABC \cong \triangle DEF$.

2.

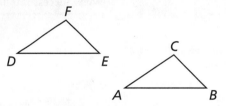

3.

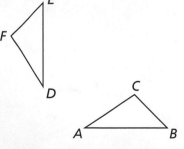

4.

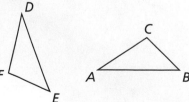

Given two congruent triangles, there is always an isometry that maps one onto the other. In fact, this is not restricted to triangles. In Investigation 8A, you learned an alternate definition for congruence: "Given two shapes drawn on paper, if you can cut one out and fit it exactly on top of the other, then the two shapes are congruent." This can be stated as a definition using the language of isometry:

Remember...

You first explored definitions of congruence in Lesson 8.01.

Definition (congruence)

Two shapes are **congruent** if there is an isometry that maps one shape onto the other.

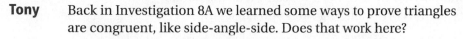

Tony looks back at Lesson 8.04 about triangle congruence.

Tony   Back in Investigation 8A we learned some ways to prove triangles are congruent, like side-angle-side. Does that work here?

Sasha   Sure! Whenever you use side-angle-side, the triangles are congruent.

Tony   That's not what I meant. I meant that if you only knew side-angle-side, could you make everything else line up right, and force the triangles to be congruent?

Sasha   Wow, that would be like *proving* SAS. Go on.

Tony   Imagine you start with two triangles *ABC* and *DEF*. You don't really know where they are. But you know $\overline{AB}$ and $\overline{DE}$ are congruent, $\overline{AC}$ and $\overline{DF}$ are congruent, and angle *A* is congruent to angle *D*.

Sasha   Wait, let me draw that.

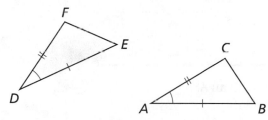

Tony   There's definitely a way to move $\overline{AB}$ without changing its size or shape so it lines up exactly with $\overline{DE}$. Put *A* on top of *D*. Then I can rotate triangle *ABC* to put *B* on top of *E*, since I know $\overline{AB}$ and $\overline{DE}$ have the same length. Now, if I can convince you that *C* has to be on top of *F*, then both triangles are in the same position, and we're done.

Sasha   Maybe. So you lined up one side. What about angle *A* and angle *D*?

Tony   It's beautiful! Since I put *A* on top of *D*, angle *A* and angle *D* have to be in the same place. They are on top of each other, so $\overline{AC}$ and $\overline{DF}$ line up.

Sasha   Wait, wait! That's not right. It could look like this:

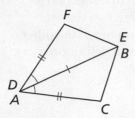

Tony   Oh, whoops. I need to say that triangle *ABC* is set up with *C* on the same side that *F* is. You can do that, since it's just a reflection.

Sasha   Really? That's okay? In that case, angle *A* and angle *D* do line up. I still don't see where you're going. You haven't proven point *C* is on top of point *F*.

Tony   Use the second side! $\overline{AC}$ and $\overline{DF}$ are congruent, so they have the same length. That means points *C* and *F* now have to share the same location, too! And we're done: if we can get all the points in the same spots, all the corresponding sides and angles are congruent.

Sasha   It's the same triangle now. I'm convinced.

For Discussion

5. In Investigation 8A, SAS was a postulate, a statement assumed to be true without proof. What, if any, new postulates allow Tony to prove SAS here?

There were three postulated triangle congruencies in Investigation 8A: SAS, ASA, and SSS. It is possible to prove all three using the properties of isometries.

Example 1

Problem   Use isometries to show that two triangles with an ASA (Angle-Side-Angle) correspondence are congruent.

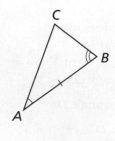 

Solution Start with two triangles *ABC* and *DEF* with $\overline{AB} \cong \overline{DE}$, $\angle A \cong \angle D$, and $\angle B \cong \angle E$. As with Tony's description for SAS, begin by aligning the matching sides: map *A* onto *D* and *B* onto *E*.

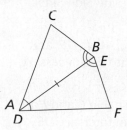

If necessary, reflect so that points *C* and *F* are on the same side of $\overline{DE}$. Now we must show that points *C* and *F* coincide.

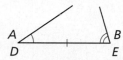

Angle *A* is in the same orientation and has the same measure as angle *D*. Therefore $\overline{AC}$ and $\overline{DF}$ must be in the same direction. Specifically, *C* must lie somewhere along $\overline{DF}$ or its extension. Angle *B* has the same relationship with angle *E*. Therefore *C* must also lie somewhere on $\overline{EF}$ or its extension. Since point *C* is on both of these lines, it must lie at the intersection of $\overline{DF}$ and $\overline{EF}$. The intersection is point *F*, so *C* and *F* coincide.

Once the correspondence of all three pairs of vertices is established, all sides and angles must be congruent. Because there is an isometry from one triangle to the other, any two triangles with an ASA correspondence must be congruent.

<table>
<tr><td>

We must show that points *C* and *F* will be in the same place.

</td></tr>
</table>

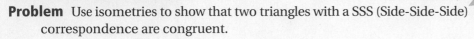

Example 2

Problem Use isometries to show that two triangles with a SSS (Side-Side-Side) correspondence are congruent.

Solution Start with two triangles ABC and DEF with $\overline{AB} \cong \overline{DE}$, $\overline{AC} \cong \overline{DF}$, and $\overline{BC} \cong \overline{EF}$. As before, begin by aligning A onto D and B onto E. If necessary, reflect so that points C and F are on the same side of $\overline{DE}$.

Now we must show that points C and F coincide. Suppose that C and F are *not* the same point. Then segment $\overline{CF}$ exists and does not intersect $\overleftrightarrow{DE}$, since C and F are on the same side of it.

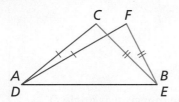

> **Habits of Mind**
>
> **Construct arguments.** The method used here is a *proof by contradiction*. The goal is to find an impossible consequence, a contradiction. If one is found, then C and F must be the same point.

Because the two triangles' sides are congruent, $DC = DF$ and $EC = EF$. By the converse of the Perpendicular Bisector Theorem, $\overleftrightarrow{DE}$ is the perpendicular bisector of $\overline{CF}$! This doesn't make sense, since $\overleftrightarrow{DE}$ doesn't even intersect $\overline{CF}$. This is a contradiction! Therefore, points C and F must be identical. Since there is an isometry that maps triangle ABC onto DEF, the triangles are congruent.

For Discussion

6. Why is there no need for a proof of AAS congruence here?

Exercises *Practicing Habits of Mind*

Check Your Understanding

1. Why can an isometry be considered a function? Explain.

2. If you know a certain transformation is an isometry, what other information do you need to know to determine where it maps a point? Explain.

3. Consider $\overline{AB}$ and a point P on the same plane, but not on $\overline{AB}$.

   a. If an isometry maps A onto P, describe all possible points the isometry could map B onto.

   b. What other information about the isometry would you need to know to determine exactly where point B is mapped?

4. Find some congruent figures from Chapter 2. For each pair of figures, describe an isometry that maps one figure onto the other figure.

5. The figures below show various transformations of the drawing at the right. Which figures represent isometries and which do not? Explain your answer.

a.

b.

c.

d.

e.

f.

6. Draw a triangle and consider an isometry made up of a translation and a reflection. Draw the vector of the translation and the axis of symmetry of the reflection. Construct the image of your triangle under the isometry. Is the image a triangle that is congruent to your original triangle? How do you know?

Try using dynamic geometry software for this problem.

On Your Own

7. Does an isometry exist that maps the circle with center O to the circle with center O' shown below? Explain why or why not.

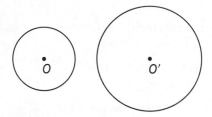

8. Consider the two triangles shown below with $\overline{AB} \cong \overline{A'B'}$, $\overline{BC} \cong \overline{B'C'}$, and $\overline{CA} \cong \overline{C'A'}$.

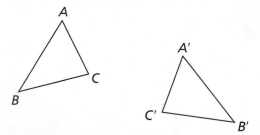

   a. Describe an isometry that maps $\triangle ABC$ onto $\triangle A'B'C'$.

   b. With dynamic geometry software, construct a third triangle A_1BC, as described in the SSS proof in Example 2. Triangle A_1BC is congruent to triangle $A'B'C'$, with $\overline{BC}$ congruent to $\overline{B'C'}$, and with A_1 lying on the same side of $\overline{BC}$ as A. Construct A_1 using the property that $\overline{BA_1}$ is congruent to $\overline{B'A'}$ and $\overline{CA_1}$ is congruent to $\overline{C'A'}$.

In this case $A'B'C'$ and A_1BC are congruent by SSS.

   c. Explain why, even if you do not use point A, your point A_1 always coincides with point A.

   d. Try using different properties to construct $\triangle A_1BC$ as a triangle congruent to $\triangle A'B'C'$ such that $\overline{BC}$ is congruent to $\overline{B'C'}$ and triangle A_1BC lies on the same side of $\overline{BC}$ as triangle ABC. For example, construct $\triangle A_1BC$ as congruent to $\triangle A'B'C'$ by SAS. Explain why, even if you do not use point A, your point A_1 always coincides with point A.

9. Use dynamic geometry software to construct two triangles with congruent sides. Do isometries exist that map one triangle onto the other? If so, describe one of these isometries.

10. Construct two triangles with congruent sides, given the first triangle and one of the sides of the second triangle, as shown below.

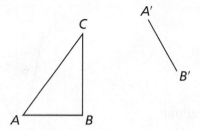

a. How many different triangles are possible to construct for the second triangle?

b. Describe an isometry that maps the first triangle onto the second one you constructed.

11. Construct two triangles with two respectively congruent sides and congruent included angles. You are given the first triangle and one congruent side and the congruent angle of the second triangle, as shown below.

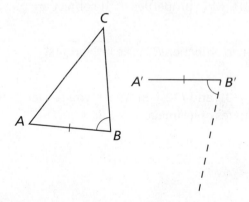

a. How many different triangles are possible to construct for the second triangle?

b. Describe an isometry that maps the first triangle onto the second one you constructed.

In this investigation, you learned how to reflect figures over a line, rotate figures in the plane, and apply transformations to figures and graphs of functions in the coordinate plane. These questions will help you summarize what you have learned.

1. Reflect $\overline{AB}$, with endpoints $A(-6,-2)$ and $B(1,5)$, over the line with equation $x = 3$. Write the coordinates of the endpoints of the image.

2. This parabola is a graph of the equation $y = 2x^2 + 3$.

   Translate the parabola by $(1, 2)$. Write an equation for the translated parabola.

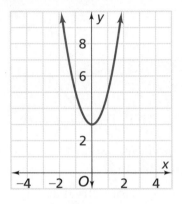

3. Find the coordinates of the endpoints $O(0, 0)$ and $P(3, 2)$ of $\overline{OP}$ after two reflections, the first over the line $y = 1$ and the second over the line $y = 5$. What transformation is the composition of these two reflections? Write a rule in the form $(x, y) \mapsto (\blacksquare, \blacksquare)$ to summarize this transformation.

4. Can you obtain a rotation by composing two other transformations? Explain with an example.

5. When you reflect an object over a line, what properties of the object are present in its image?

6. What happens when you compose two reflections? Three reflections? Four reflections?

7. $\triangle ABC$ has vertices $A(2, -1)$, $B(-2, -3)$, and $C(2, -3)$. When you reflect $\triangle ABC$ over the x-axis, what are the coordinates of its image $\triangle A'B'C'$?

Vocabulary and Notation

In this investigation, you learned these terms and symbols. Make sure you understand what each one means and how to use it.

- **composition**
- **congruent**
- **fixed point**
- **image**
- **isometry**
- **line of reflection**
- **preimage**
- **reflection**
- **rigid motion**
- **rotation**
- **transformation**
- **translation**
- *F′* (*F* **prime**)
- *F″* (*F* **double prime**)

Does the face have line symmetry?

Investigation 8C

Geometry in the Coordinate Plane

In *Geometry in the Coordinate Plane,* you will use coordinates in one and two dimensions. You will learn the Midpoint Formula and the Distance Formula, and you will use these formulas in a variety of proofs.

By the end of this investigation, you will be able to answer questions like these.

1. How can you tell by examining the coordinates of two points whether they lie on a horizontal line? On a vertical line?

2. How do you calculate the distance between two points?

3. A box has dimensions 3 in. by 5 in. by 4 in. What is the length of a diagonal?

You will learn how to

- calculate the distance between two points with given coordinates

- calculate the coordinates of the midpoint of a segment

- prove algebraically that three points are or are not collinear

- recognize when two lines are parallel or perpendicular

You will develop these habits and skills:

- Plot points with given coordinates in two dimensions.

- Describe the location of a point on a coordinate plane.

- Write equations of lines with given characteristics.

- Use subscript notation.

- Write proofs combining geometric and algebraic ideas.

The boxes are 11 in. by $8\frac{1}{2}$ in. by $5\frac{1}{2}$ in. and $13\frac{5}{8}$ in. by $11\frac{7}{8}$ in. by $3\frac{3}{8}$ in. What is the longest rose you could ship in one of these boxes?

The coordinate plane allows you to make connections between geometry and algebra.

You have been working with polygons and circles geometrically, proving results through logic and reasoning. Now you can use your algebra skills to investigate some of these geometric ideas in the coordinate plane.

For example, coordinates locate points, so they are helpful for locating special parts, such as the midpoint of a line segment. Since coordinates involve numbers, you can use them to calculate lengths and distances exactly rather than relying on approximate measurements.

For You to Explore

1. The coordinates of three vertices of a rectangle are given. Find the coordinates of the points described below.

   a. the fourth vertex

   b. four points that are inside the rectangle

   c. four points that are outside the rectangle

   d. four more points that lie on the rectangle

   e. How can you tell whether a point is inside the rectangle just by looking at its coordinates?

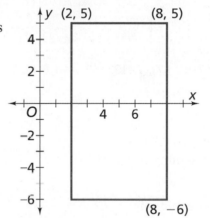

2. Suppose you have points $A(2, 5)$ and $B(2, 396)$.

   a. What is the distance between A and B?

   b. Find the coordinates of the midpoint of $\overline{AB}$.

3. **a.** How many vertical lines contain the point $(-1, 9)$?

   b. Name the coordinates of the intersection I of a horizontal line through $T(3, -5)$ and a vertical line through $R(-1, 9)$.

   c. Plot the points T, R, and I. Find the lengths of all three sides of $\triangle TRI$.

4. Suppose that $F(-1, 4)$ and $G(-3, -2)$.

   a. Find the coordinates of the midpoint of $\overline{FG}$.

   b. Find the length of $\overline{FG}$.

Go Online
Video Tutor
www.successnetplus.com

Exercises *Practicing Habits of Mind*

On Your Own

5. Find the coordinates of the midpoint of the segment below. Describe the method you used.

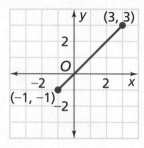

6. Suppose you have points $C(-5, -7)$, $D(12, -7)$, and $E(12, 3)$.

   a. Find the distance between C and D.

   b. Find the coordinates of the midpoint of $\overline{CD}$.

   c. Find the distance between D and E.

   d. Find the coordinates of the midpoint of $\overline{DE}$.

   e. Find the distance between C and E.

   f. Find the coordinates of the midpoint of $\overline{CE}$.

7. In the diagram, m is a vertical line. Find each of the following.

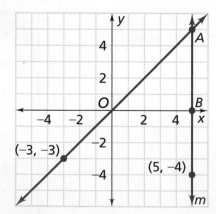

   a. the coordinates of A and B **b.** the length of $\overline{AB}$

   c. the coordinates of the midpoint of $\overline{AB}$ **d.** the area of $\triangle AOB$

   e. the length of $\overline{AO}$ **f.** the coordinates of the midpoint of $\overline{AO}$

8. List coordinates of points to make a connect-the-dots puzzle that draws your initials. Give it to a friend to try.

9. **Take It Further** How many quadrants in the coordinate plane does each line pass through?

   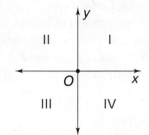

   a. a vertical line through the origin

   b. a vertical line not through the origin

   c. a nonvertical, nonhorizontal line through the origin

   d. a nonvertical, nonhorizontal line not through the origin

10. **Take It Further** Is it possible for a line to pass through only one quadrant? Is it possible for a line to pass through all four quadrants? Is there any slanting (nonvertical, nonhorizontal) line that passes through only two quadrants and does not contain the origin?

Maintain Your Skills

11. **a.** Copy and complete the table below.

A	B	C	D	E	F	G
(x, y)	$(x + 3, y)$	$(-x, y)$	$(x, -y)$	$(2x, 2y)$	$\left(\dfrac{x}{2}, \dfrac{y}{2}\right)$	$(-y, x)$
(2, 1)	■	■	■	■	$\left(1, \dfrac{1}{2}\right)$	■
(−4, 0)	(−1, 0)	■	■	■	■	■
(−5, 4)	■	(5, 4)	■	■	■	(−4, −5)

   b. On a piece of graph paper, plot the three points in Column A and connect them to form triangle A. Plot the three points in Column B and connect them to form a triangle B. Describe how the two triangles differ.

   c. On a new section of graph paper, draw triangles A and C. Describe how they differ.

   d. Use clean graph paper each time. Pair triangle A with each of triangles D, E, F, and G. Each time describe how the two triangles differ.

Habits of Mind

Look for patterns. List any conjectures you come up with.

Midpoint and Distance Formulas

Here is some very convenient notation.

When only a few points need names, you can call them A, B, C, and so on, and name their coordinates (a, b), (c, d), (e, f), and so on. If you have too many points, however, you can run out of letters. Since you can never run out of numbers, the convention is to use numbers as subscripts. For example, you could name the vertices of a decagon A_1, A_2, A_3, ..., A_{10}. You could name the vertices of an n-gon B_1, B_2, B_3, ..., B_n.

In-Class Experiment

Copy and complete the table below. Then answer the questions that follow.

Assume that point V_1 has coordinates (x_1, y_1), point V_2 has coordinates (x_2, y_2), and so on.

i	Coordinates of V_i	x_i	y_i
1	(■, ■)	■	■
2	(■, ■)	−2	■
3	(−4, −2)	−4	−2
4	(■, ■)	2	■

1. Here is a claim about the coordinates of the vertices of square $V_1V_2V_3V_4$.

   $$x_i = y_{i+1}$$

   Is the claim true when $i = 1$? That is, is it true that $x_1 = y_2$? Is the claim true when $i = 2$? When $i = 3$? When $i = 4$?

2. Here is another claim about the vertices of square $V_1V_2V_3V_4$.

   If V_i has coordinates (x_i, y_i), then V_{i+1} has coordinates $(-y_i, x_i)$.

   a. When $i = 2$, the claim says, "If V_2 has coordinates (x_2, y_2), then V_3 has coordinates $(-y_2, x_2)$." Look at the table and decide whether this is true.

   b. Find a value of i for which the statement does not make sense.

3. Name the vertices of the square for which it is true that $y_i = \frac{1}{2}x_i$.

4. Here is a rule for deriving a new set of points Q_i from the points V_1, V_2, V_3, and V_4.

   If $V_i = (x_i, y_i)$, then $Q_i = (x_i - 3, y_i + 4)$.

   a. The rule is written in algebraic symbols. Explain the rule in words.

   b. Find the new points Q_1, Q_2, Q_3, and Q_4 and plot them.

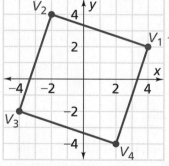

square $V_1V_2V_3V_4$

For example, is it true that $x_1 = y_{1+1} = y_2$?

5. If $P_1 = (x_1, y_1)$, and you know that P_2 is a second point on the same horizontal line, how can you write its coordinates?

6. Let $P_i = (x_i, y_i)$, $x_i = i + 3$, and $y_i = x_i - 4$. Plot P_i as i goes from 1 to 8. Describe the result.

Minds in Action

Sasha and Derman are trying to write a formula for finding the distance between two points. They are given

$$G = (x_1, y_1), \ H = (x_2, y_2)$$

Sasha Well, the distance between two points on a vertical or horizontal line is easy to find. Just subtract the unlike coordinates. If G is $(3, 4)$ and H is $(3, 90)$, then the distance between G and H is $90 - 4 = 86$.

Derman But we don't know that G and H are on a horizontal or vertical line. They're just *any* two points.

We used the Pythagorean Theorem to help us find the distance between two points that weren't on the same horizontal or vertical line before. Let's try that here.

Sasha Don't we need three points to make a triangle so we can use the Pythagorean Theorem?

Derman Watch! I'll make a third point:

Before you ask, I know that the third point is (x_1, y_2). In my picture I had to go over as far as the (x_1, y_1) point—that's where I got the x_1—and up as far as the (x_2, y_2) point—that's where I got the y_2.

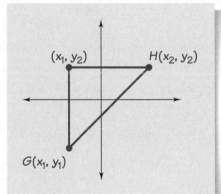

What are the lengths of the legs of this right triangle?

Sasha Great! Now let's use the Pythagorean Theorem to find the length of the hypotenuse of that triangle.

$$(x_2 - x_1)^2 + (y_2 - y_1)^2 = GH^2$$

So,

$$GH = \sqrt{(x_2 - x_1)^2 + (y_2 - y_1)^2}$$

Derman and Sasha's explanation is a proof of the following theorem.

Theorem 8.2 *Distance Formula*

The distance between two points (x_1, y_1) and (x_2, y_2) can be found using the Pythagorean Theorem. It is the square root of the sum of the square of the difference in the *x*-coordinates and the square of the difference in the *y*-coordinates.

Habits of Mind

Use facts you know. If you remember how you found it, you do not have to remember the Distance Formula. You can figure it out just by remembering the Pythagorean Theorem.

For You to Do

Find the distance between each pair of points.

7. $(1, 1)$ and $(-1, -1)$

8. $(1, 1)$ and $(4, 5)$

9. $(2, 4)$ and $(-4, -2)$

When you found the midpoint of a segment in Lesson 8.10, you may have used a method like this:

The *x*-coordinate is equal to the average of the *x*-coordinates of the endpoints. The *y*-coordinate is equal to the average of the *y*-coordinates of the endpoints.

Or, you can write it algebraically.

$$\left(\frac{x_1 + x_2}{2}, \frac{y_1 + y_2}{2} \right)$$

You can use Derman's diagram from Minds in Action to help justify this method for finding the midpoint.

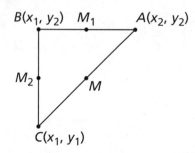

Theorem 8.3 *Midpoint Formula*

Each coordinate of the midpoint of a line segment is equal to the average of the corresponding coordinates of the endpoints of the line segment.

For You to Do

10. Find the midpoint of the segment with endpoints (1327, 94) and (−668, 17).

11. Find the midpoint of the segment with endpoints (1776, 13) and (2000, 50).

About halfway between Penzance and Land's End is the hamlet of Crows-an-wra. About how far, and in what direction, is the hamlet from this marker?

Exercises *Practicing Habits of Mind*

Check Your Understanding

1. Points A and B are endpoints of a diameter of a circle. Point C is the center of the circle. Find the coordinates of C given the following coordinates for A and B.

   a. $(-79, 687)$, $(13, 435)$

   b. $(x, 0)$, $(5x, y)$

2. The vertices of $\triangle ABC$ are $A(2, 1)$, $B(4, 8)$, and $C(6, -2)$.

   a. Find the lengths of the three sides of the triangle.

   b. Find the coordinates of the three midpoints of each side.

3. Consider the six points $A(5, 1)$, $B(10, -2)$, $C(8, 3)$, $A'(2, 3)$, $B'(7, 0)$, and $C'(5, 5)$. Show that $\triangle ABC \cong \triangle A'B'C'$.

4. **Write About It** Explain how to tell whether two triangles are congruent by doing calculations on the coordinates of their vertices.

5. Quadrilateral $STAR$ has vertices $S(-2, 8)$, $T(8, 2)$, $A(0, -4)$, and $R(-2, 0)$. Find the coordinates of the midpoints of the four sides of quadrilateral $STAR$. These points determine a new quadrilateral. Show that each pair of opposite sides of this new quadrilateral is parallel.

6. Pick any four points that form a quadrilateral in the coordinate plane. Find the midpoints of all four sides. Show that each pair of opposite sides of this new quadrilateral is parallel.

> One way to show that a quadrilateral is a parallelogram is to show that opposite sides are parallel. What is another way?

7. Take It Further Points A through G lie on a circle of radius 10, as shown in the figure. Find their missing coordinates.

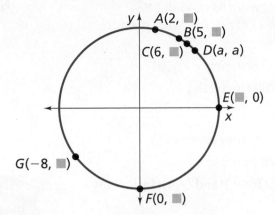

On Your Own

8. Three vertices of a square are $(-1, 5)$, $(5, 3)$, and $(3, -3)$.

   a. Find the center of the square.

   b. Find the fourth vertex.

9. Three vertices of a square are $(-114, 214)$, $(186, 114)$, and $(-214, -86)$.

   a. Find the center of the square.

   b. Find the fourth vertex.

10. $\overline{DE}$ has midpoint $F(4.5, 17)$ and one endpoint $D(2, 16)$. What are the coordinates of the other endpoint, E?

11. $\overline{AB}$ and $\overline{CD}$ bisect each other. Given the points $A(110, 15)$, $B(116, 23)$, and $C(110, 23)$, find E, the point of bisection. Also, find the coordinates of D.

12. A segment has length 25. Give possible coordinates for the endpoints of this segment in each case below.

   a. The segment is on a horizontal line.

   b. The segment is on a vertical line.

   c. The segment is neither horizontal nor vertical.

13. A segment has its midpoint at $(8, 10)$. List four possibilities for the coordinates of its endpoints.

14. A segment has one endpoint at $(-7, -2)$ and its midpoint at $(-2, 1.5)$. What are the coordinates of the other endpoint?

> **Remember...**
>
> Two segments bisect each other if they intersect at each other's midpoint.

15. Standardized Test Prep Julio is planning to swim across the lake at his summer camp. On a map, the coordinates of his starting point are $(-2\ cm, 3.5\ cm)$. The dock to which he will swim has coordinates $(14\ cm, -8.5\ cm)$. The scale on the map is 1 cm : 100 m. What distance will Julio have to swim?

A. 1200 meters   **B.** 1300 meters

C. 1600 meters   **D.** 2000 meters

16. Suppose you have points $P(5, 0)$ and $Q(15, 0)$.

a. Find six points that are just as far from P as they are from Q.

b. Find six points that are closer to P than they are to Q.

c. How can you tell if a point is equidistant from P and Q just by looking at its coordinates?

17. The endpoints of a line segment are the midpoints of two sides of a triangle. Show that the length of this segment is one half the length of the third side of that triangle. Show that this is true for any triangle. (Use subscript notation.)

Maintain Your Skills

Find the slope between each pair of points.

18. $(3, 85)$ and $(0, 124)$

19. $(0, 124)$ and $(4, 72)$

20. $(4, 72)$ and $(-111, 1567)$

21. $(-111, 1567)$ and $(2, 98)$

22. $(2, 98)$ and $(3, 85)$

Habits of Mind

Use a symbol. You could use d_s for the length of a side of the triangle. You must show that d_m, the distance between the midpoints, is $\frac{1}{2}d_s$. But think ahead. Would it be helpful to use $2d_s$ for the length of a side?

Remember...

You find slope by calculating the ratio between the change in y-coordinates and the change in x-coordinates.

Go Online
www.successnetplus.com

Parallel Lines and Collinear Points

This In-Class Experiment should help you remember what you might have learned about the equations of lines.

In-Class Experiment

1. Plot several points with y-coordinates that have each property.

   a. 1 more than the x-coordinate

   b. 2 more than the x-coordinate

   c. 1 less than the x-coordinate

   For each property, draw a picture that shows all the points with that property.

2. Plot several points with y-coordinates that have each property.

   a. twice the x-coordinate

   b. three times the x-coordinate

   c. four times the x-coordinate

   For each property, draw a picture that shows all the points with that property.

3. Some of the lines you drew have points with coordinates of the form $(x, x + \text{something})$.

   a. What do those lines have in common?

   b. Write the equations of those lines in the form $ax + by = c$.

   c. What do these equations have in common?

4. Some other lines you drew have points with coordinates of the form $(x, x \times \text{something})$.

   a. What do those lines have in common?

   b. Write the equations of those lines in the form $ax + by = c$.

   c. What do these equations have in common?

You may have proved the following theorem.

Theorem 8.4

Two nonvertical lines are parallel if and only if they have the same slope.

The proof of Theorem 8.4 depends on the following postulate.

Postulate 8.2

Let *A*, *B*, and *C* be three points, no two of which are in line vertically. Points *A*, *B*, and *C* are collinear if and only if the slope between *A* and *B*, *m(A, B)*, is the same as the slope between *B* and *C*, *m(B, C)*. In symbols:

A, *B*, and *C* are collinear $\Leftrightarrow$ *m(A, B) = m(B, C)*.

Developing Habits of Mind

Visualize. Here is another way to think about three collinear points, and this way has a bonus result! Think of points *A*, *B*, and *C* as vertices of a triangle. Also, think of *B* as moving continuously closer and closer to $\overline{AC}$.

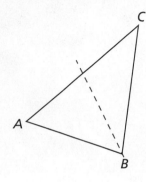
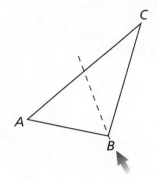
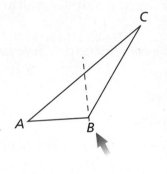

The Triangle Inequality says that *AB + BC > AC*. As *B* gets closer and closer to $\overline{AC}$, *AB + BC* gets closer and closer to *AC*. When *B* is on $\overline{AC}$, *AB + BC* is no longer greater than *AC*. In fact, *AB + BC = AC*.

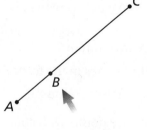

Now, suppose you are given three points, *A*, *B*, and *C*. Would knowing that *AC = AB + BC* be enough to prove that the three points are collinear?

Yes, it would be enough, because if *B* were not in line with *A* and *C*, then *A*, *B*, and *C* would be the vertices of a triangle. The three segment lengths would satisfy the Triangle Inequality. But the segment lengths do not satisfy the Triangle Inequality, so the points cannot be the vertices of a triangle. The points have to be collinear.

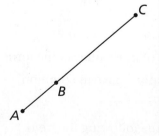

Problem Decide whether the following three points are collinear.

$A(1, 5)$ $B(-2,1)$ $C(7,13)$

Solution Use the Triangle Inequality.

$$AB = \sqrt{(1 - (-2))^2 + (5 - 1)^2} = \sqrt{9 + 16} = 5$$
$$BC = \sqrt{(7 - (-2))^2 + (13 - 1)^2} = \sqrt{81 + 144} = 15$$
$$AC = \sqrt{(7 - 1)^2 + (13 - 5)^2} = \sqrt{36 + 64} = 10$$

For the three lengths, $AC + AB = 10 + 5 = 15 = BC$. This means that A, B, and C are collinear, with A between B and C.

Habits of Mind

Check your work.
You can use another method—namely Postulate 8.2—to check the result in the Example.

For You to Do

Use the Triangle Inequality or Postulate 8.2 to decide whether the three points are collinear.

6. $A\left(\frac{2}{7}, 0\right)$ $B(0, 2)$ $C(1, 9)$

7. $A\left(\frac{1}{25}, 2\right)$ $B(1, 26)$ $C(7, 0)$

8. $A(2, 2)$ $B(3, 3)$ $C(5, 9)$

9. $A(2, 4)$ $B(0, 0)$ $C(3, 6)$

10. $A(-1, 3)$ $B(-2, 2)$ $C(2, 6)$

Exercises *Practicing Habits of Mind*

Check Your Understanding

1. Are the two lines with the given equations parallel? Explain.

   a. $2x + 3y = 0$ $2x + 3y = 4$

   b. $x + \frac{1}{3}y = 7$ $3x + y = 1$

   c. $x + \frac{1}{3}y = 7$ $3x + y = 21$

   d. $\sqrt{2}x + 4y = 0$ $2x + 4y = 0$

   e. $2\sqrt{2}x + 4y = 1$ $x + \sqrt{2}y = 3$

2. Find a point that is collinear with $A(5, 1)$ and $B(8, -3)$. Explain your method.

3. Give a set of instructions for finding points that are collinear with $A(5, 1)$ and $B(8, -3)$. Explain why your method works.

4. Is $P(-4, -14)$ collinear with $R(-40, -30)$ and $S(80, 20)$? Explain.

On Your Own

5. Two vertices of an equilateral triangle are at $(1, 0)$ and $(9, 0)$. Find coordinates for the third vertex.

6. For each possible pairing of lines, tell whether the lines

   - are parallel
   - intersect elsewhere
   - meet at the origin
   - are the same line

   > How many possible pairs are there to consider?

   ℓ: The y-coordinates are $\frac{1}{2}$ their x-coordinates.

   m: The y-coordinates are 3 more than their x-coordinates.

   n: The y-coordinates are 2 less than their x-coordinates.

   p: The y-coordinates are -2 times their x-coordinates.

   q: The y-coordinates are 5 times their x-coordinates.

   r: The y-coordinates are $\frac{1}{3}$ their x-coordinates.

7. Is $(110, 9)$ collinear with $(60, 10)$ and $(10, 11)$? Explain.

8. **Standardized Test Prep** The coordinates of point A are $(3, 4)$. The coordinates of point B are $(5, -1)$. Which point is NOT collinear with A and B?

   A. $(2, -5)$ **B.** $(1, 9)$ **C.** $(0, 11.5)$ **D.** $(4.6, 0)$

9. Draw two lines, a and b, with the following characteristics, on the coordinate plane.

   - Line a passes through $(0, 1)$ and $(1, 0)$.

   - Line b passes through the origin and makes a 45° angle with the axes as it enters Quadrant I.

   Find the coordinates of the point where lines a and b intersect.

Maintain Your Skills

10. Use the Triangle Inequality to test whether points lie on $\overline{RS}$ with endpoints $R(-40, -30)$ and $S(80, 20)$. Test some points that are collinear with R and S and some that are not.

11. **Take It Further** Now generalize your method. Suppose $R(r_1, r_2)$ and $S(s_1, s_2)$ are two points. Write an equation that has to be true if and only if a third point $P(p_1, p_2)$ lies on $\overleftrightarrow{RS}$. Simplify your equation until you come to a form like this.

$$(a - b) \cdot (c - d) = (e - f) \cdot (g - h)$$

(*Hint:* If an equation contains a square root, isolate it on one side and then square each side. You can repeat this step if necessary.)

Besides having the same slope, parallel lines are everywhere the same distance apart.

Habits of Mind

Establish a process. When you see that an expression becomes complex, take time to organize your work. This slows you down at first, but it will save you time in the end.

Go Online
www.successnetplus.com

8.13 Perpendicular Lines

The slopes of two perpendicular lines have a special relationship.

In-Class Experiment

Study the diagram.

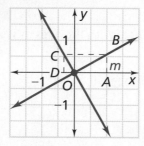

- $\overleftrightarrow{OB}$ and $\overleftrightarrow{OC}$ are perpendicular.
- Quadrilateral *ABCD* has sides $\overline{AB}$ and $\overline{CD}$ parallel to the *y*-axis.
- Its other sides $\overline{BC}$ and $\overline{AD}$ are parallel to the *x*-axis.
- $AB = m$ and $OA = 1$.

1. Find *CD* and *DO*.

2. What is the slope of $\overleftrightarrow{OB}$?

3. What is the slope of $\overleftrightarrow{OC}$?

4. What is the product of the two slopes you found in Problems 2 and 3?

You just proved part of a very important theorem.

Theorem 8.5

Two nonvertical lines are perpendicular if and only if the product of their slopes is −1.

Also, any horizontal line is perpendicular to any vertical line.

Tony wonders whether he has just seen a special case.

Tony   Hey Sasha, suppose the lines don't intersect at the origin. Is Theorem 8.5 still true?

Sasha   Well, Theorem 8.5 doesn't say anything about the lines having to intersect at the origin. But I agree that we have proved one direction of the theorem only for lines like that. Let's try to prove it for lines that could intersect anywhere.

Tony   Let's try to avoid a lot of work. Why don't we just try translating?

Sasha   That should work. The proof we came up with in the In-Class Experiment didn't really use the fact that the lines were through the origin. Look!

Sasha draws a diagram. She labels the rectangle like the one in the In-Class Experiment. She uses E instead of O for the intersection of the lines because it is no longer at the origin.

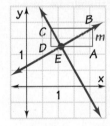

Tony   Wow, that's true! Everything is the same as before:

$$AB = CD = m$$

$$EA = 1$$

and

$$CB = DA = 1 + DE$$

Knowing that $\overleftrightarrow{EB}$ and $\overleftrightarrow{EC}$ are perpendicular and that $\angle EAB$ and $\angle EDC$ are right angles, we know that $\triangle EAB$ and $\triangle CDE$ are similar. So

$$\frac{CD}{EA} = \frac{DE}{AB}$$

This means that $DE = \frac{AB \cdot CD}{EA} = \frac{m^2}{1} = m^2$.

Sasha   Good, Tony! You really got it! So what are the slopes of $\overleftrightarrow{EB}$ and $\overleftrightarrow{EC}$?

Tony   That's easy! The slope of $\overleftrightarrow{EB}$ is m, just as before. The slope of $\overleftrightarrow{EC}$ is

$$-\frac{CD}{DE} = -\frac{m}{m^2} = -\frac{1}{m}$$

So the product of the slopes is $m \cdot -\frac{1}{m} = -1$.

For Discussion

Now prove the second part of Theorem 8.5: *If the product of the slopes of two lines is* −1, *then the lines are perpendicular.*

Look at the figure below, where $m \geq 0$.

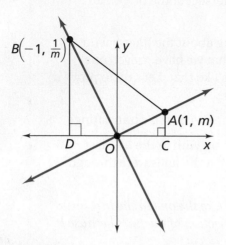

5. Find the slopes of $\overleftrightarrow{OA}$ and $\overleftrightarrow{OB}$. Show that the product of the slopes is −1.

6. Find BD, DO, OC, and AC.

7. Prove $\triangle BDO \sim \triangle OCA$.

8. Provide a justification for each step of the following proof.

Given $\triangle BDO \sim \triangle OCA$

Proof $m\angle DBO = m\angle COA$

$m\angle DBO + m\angle DOB = 90°$
$m\angle COA + m\angle DOB = 90°$
$m\angle BOA = 90°$

You can use Theorem 8.5 to find the distance between a point and a line.

For You to Do

9. Find an equation of the line through $P(3, 5)$ that is perpendicular to line ℓ with equation $2x + y = 9$.

10. Find the point of intersection Q of line ℓ and the perpendicular line you found.

11. What is the distance from P to ℓ?

Remember...

The distance from a point to a line is the length of the shortest segment from the point to the line. This segment is perpendicular to the line.

Exercises *Practicing Habits of Mind*

Check Your Understanding

1. Write equations for two different lines that are perpendicular to the line with equation $x + y = 3$. Are there other possibilities?

2. Write an equation of the line through point $(1, 0)$ and perpendicular to the line with equation $x + 2y = 4$.

3. Find the distance from P to s in the figure below.

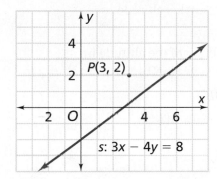

4. A circle has its center at the origin and radius 1. Find equations of two tangents to the circle through the point $(3, 0)$.

Remember...

What is the distance from a tangent to the center of the circle?

On Your Own

5. Write an equation for at least one line perpendicular to the line with each equation.

   a. $x + y = 2$ **b.** $x - y + 2 = 0$ **c.** $19x + 3y = 17$ **d.** $y = 3 + 4x$

6. Write an equation of the line through the given point and perpendicular to the line with the given equation.

   a. $(0, 0), 2x$ ~~2x3y~~ ~~7~~ ~~146~~ $= 0$ **b.** $(0, -3), y = -x + 2$

   c. $(-4, -3),$ **d.** $(1, 2), 2x - 3y + 1 = 0$

7. Find the distance from the given point to the given line.

   a. $(1, -2)$ to the line with equation $3x - y = -5$

   b. $(-1, 0)$ to the line with equation $y = 5x - 1$

   c. $(2, 2)$ to the line through points $(3, 1)$ and $(7, 4)$

   d. $(1, 2)$ to the line with equation $20x - 21y = 58$

8. Find the area of the triangle with the given vertices.

   a. $A(1, 1)$, $B(4, 5)$, $C(13, -4)$ **b.** $A(1, 1)$, $B(4, 2)$, $C(2, 3)$

9. Standardized Test Prep What is the equation of the line that is perpendicular at the point $(4, 1)$ to the line with equation $y = -\frac{1}{2}x + 3$?

   A. $y = \frac{1}{2}x - 1$ **B.** $y = 2x + 7$

   C. $-x + y = -3$ **D.** $2x - y = 7$

10. Graph quadrilateral $ABCD$ with vertices $A(\sqrt{2}, 4)$, $B(3, 3)$, $C(-\sqrt{2}, -4)$, and $D(-3, -3)$. How many right angles does it have? Prove your answer.

11. a. Draw $\triangle ABC$ on the coordinate plane, with vertices $A(1, 1)$, $B(5, 1)$, and $C(3, 6)$.

   b. Write an equation for the line containing the triangle's altitude relative to $\overline{AB}$.

   c. Find the coordinates of H, the point of intersection of the altitude in part (b) and the base $\overline{AB}$.

   d. Show algebraically that H is the midpoint of $\overline{AB}$.

12. a. Draw $\triangle ABC$ on the coordinate plane, with vertices $A(2, 3)$, $B(2, 7)$, and $C(8, 5)$.

   b. Find the coordinates of the midpoint M of $\overline{AB}$.

   c. Find an equation of the line through M and C.

   d. Show algebraically that the line through M and C is perpendicular to $\overline{AB}$.

To do this, you should write an equation for $\overleftrightarrow{AB}$.

Maintain Your Skills

13. Line r has equation $2x + 3y = 4$. Line s has equation $ax + by = c$.

   a. Find the distance of $(1, 2)$ from r.

   b. Find the distance of (x_P, y_P) from r as a function of x_p and y_p.

   c. Find the distance of $(1, 2)$ from s as a function of a, b, and c.

   d. Find the distance of (x_P, y_P) from s as a function of x_p, y_p, a, b, and c.

Go Online
www.successnetplus.com

A pier generally is built to be perpendicular to the shoreline. Why might this be so?

Mathematical

8C

Reflections

In this investigation, you learned how to calculate the midpoint and length of a segment, write equations of lines with given characteristics, and prove whether three points are collinear. These questions will help you summarize what you have learned.

1. For $A\left(-3, \frac{1}{2}\right)$ and $B\left(\frac{2}{3}, \frac{1}{4}\right)$, find the distance of A from the origin O and the distance from A to B.

2. Calculate the coordinates of the midpoint of $\overline{JK}$ with endpoints $J(0, 3)$ and $K(-4, -6)$.

3. Are the following points collinear? Explain.
$$\left(0, \frac{1}{2}\right), \left(-1, -\frac{5}{2}\right), \left(\frac{1}{2}, 2\right)$$

4. Write an equation for the line through the origin and perpendicular to the line with equation $2x + 3y = 0$.

5. How can you tell by examining the coordinates of two points whether they lie on a horizontal line? On a vertical line?

6. How do you calculate the distance between two points?

You can ship an 18-inch rose in the box that is $13\frac{5}{8}$ in. by $11\frac{7}{8}$ in. by $3\frac{3}{8}$ in.

Go Online
www.successnetplus.com

In **Investigation 8A** you learned how to

- define congruence
- test for congruence in triangles
- use the correct language and notation to read and write statements about congruent figures

The following questions will help you check your understanding.

1. Use $\triangle ABC$. Draw point D so that $\overline{BC}$ is the angle bisector of $\angle ACD$ and of $\angle ABD$. Prove that $\triangle ABC \cong \triangle DBC$.

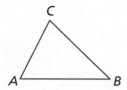

2. Use your drawing from Exercise 1. Choose a point P on $\overline{BC}$. Prove that $\overline{AP} \cong \overline{DP}$.

In **Investigation 8B** you learned how to

- use multiple methods for reflecting a figure over a line
- rotate a figure on the plane given a center and angle of rotation
- apply transformations to figures and the graphs of functions in the coordinate plane

The following questions will help you check your understanding.

3. Graph the line with equation $2x + y = 4$. Write an equation for its image after a reflection over the x-axis.

4. The point $Q'(-1, -3)$ is the reflection image of point $Q(3, 1)$. What is the reflection line? Explain how you know.

5. Copy the figure below. Draw its lines of symmetry.

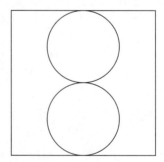

6. Copy the figure below. Draw the image of $\triangle ABC$ after a rotation of $70°$ around O in the counterclockwise direction.

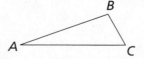

In **Investigation 8C** you learned how to

- plot points in two dimensions
- calculate the coordinates of the midpoint of a segment and find the length of a segment given the coordinates of its endpoints
- write equations of lines with given characteristics
- prove whether three points are collinear

The following questions will help you check your understanding.

7. $\overline{AB}$ has endpoints $A(-1, 1)$ and $B(3, 4)$. Find the length of $\overline{AB}$ and the coordinates of the midpoint of $\overline{AB}$.

8. Find the midpoint of the line segment with endpoints $(-2.5, 3.1)$ and $(6.7, -3.3)$.

9. Are the three points collinear?

  a. $\left(2, \frac{1}{2}\right), \left(0, \frac{3}{2}\right), (1, 1)$

  b. $(0, 5), (1, 12), (-1, 1)$

  c. $(-7, 20), (7, 6), (3, 10)$

10. Quadrilateral $ABCD$ has coordinates $A(-3, -3)$, $B(4, -1)$, $C(3, 7)$, and $D(-1, 1)$. Find the coordinates of the midpoints of each side of the quadrilateral. Prove that these four points form a parallelogram.

11. Are the lines with equations $4x - 6y = 24$ and $4x + 6y = 24$ parallel? Explain.

12. Write an equation of the line through $P(5, 6)$ and perpendicular to the line through $A(-3, 4)$ and $B(4, -2)$.

13. What is the slope of all lines perpendicular to the line with equation $3x + 7y = 42$?

Go Online
www.successnetplus.com

Multiple Choice

1. The line with equation $2x + y = -4$ is reflected over the y-axis. Which of these is an equation of the reflection?

A. $y = 2x - 4$

B. $y = -2x - 4$

C. $y = 2x + 4$

D. $y = -2x + 4$

2. $\overline{FG}$ has endpoints $F(-1, 0)$ and $G(2, 3)$. It is reflected first over the y-axis (as $\overline{F'G'}$) and then over the x-axis (as $\overline{F''G''}$). What are the coordinates of F'' and G''?

A. $F''(1, 0)$ and $G''(-2, 3)$

B. $F''(1, 0)$ and $G''(-2, -3)$

C. $F''(-1, 0)$ and $G''(2, -3)$

D. $F''(-1, 0)$ and $G''(-2, -3)$

3. Which rule translates $A(-2, 4)$ to $A'(-7, -3)$?

A. $(x, y) \mapsto (x - 5, y - 3)$

B. $(x, y) \mapsto (x - 5, y - 7)$

C. $(x, y) \mapsto (x + 5, y - 7)$

D. $(x, y) \mapsto (x + 5, y - 1)$

4. $\overline{XY}$ has endpoints $X(-4, -2)$ and $Y(2, 3)$. What are the coordinates of the midpoint of $\overline{XY}$?

A. $\left(-1, \dfrac{1}{2}\right)$

B. $\left(-1, \dfrac{3}{2}\right)$

C. $\left(3, -\dfrac{1}{2}\right)$

D. $\left(3, \dfrac{5}{2}\right)$

5. What is the approximate distance between $G(-3, 5)$ and $H(-1, -3)$?

A. 8.2

B. 4.4

C. 2.8

D. 2.4

6. If $\triangle DEF \cong \triangle LMN$, which of the following must be a correct congruence statement?

A. $\angle D \cong \angle N$ **B.** $\angle F \cong \angle L$

C. $\overline{EF} \cong \overline{MN}$ **D.** $\overline{DE} \cong \overline{NM}$

7. Which of these points is NOT collinear with $(15, 5)$ and $(60, 20)$?

A. $(-18, -6)$

B. $(-3, -1)$

C. $(0, 2)$

D. $(24, 8)$

Open Response

9. For each pair, decide whether the two figures are congruent. Explain your reasoning.

a.

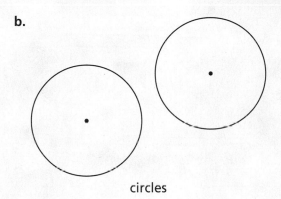

b.

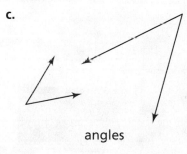

circles

c.

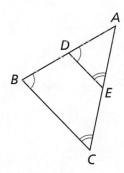

angles

9. Plot the points $A(1, 2)$ and $B(6, 8)$. Reflect $\overline{AB}$ over the x-axis. Write the coordinates of the images of its endpoints.

10. Here are equations of two lines.

$$s\colon 3x + 4y = 3 \qquad\qquad r\colon 16x - 12y = 28$$

Prove that $s \perp r$.

11. Quadrilateral *OACB* is a parallelogram with vertices $A(4, 5)$, $C(3, 6)$, and *O* the origin. What are the coordinates of *B*?

12. For $A(6, 12)$ and $B(-2, 8)$, find *C* if *B* is the midpoint of $\overline{AC}$.

13. For each diagram, use the given information. Determine whether the two triangles are congruent. If they are congruent, prove it using the triangle congruence postulates.

a. *ABCD* is a parallelogram. Is $\triangle ABC \cong \triangle CDA$?

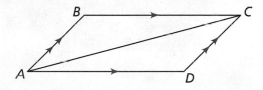

b. $\angle ADE \cong \angle B$ and $\angle AED \cong \angle C$. Is $\triangle ABC \cong \triangle ADE$?

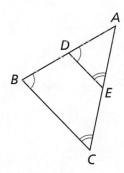

Honors Appendix

Honors Appendix

Vocabulary and Notation

- direction
- dot product
- equivalent vectors
- head
- identity matrix
- inverse
- linear combination
- matrix multiplication

- matrix transformation
- *n*-tuple
- parameter
- parametric equations
- scalar multiplication
- tail
- vector
- zero matrix, 0

Exploring Vectors

In *Exploring Vectors,* you will use points on the coordinate plane as algebraic objects. In other words, you will think of points as things that you can add or that you can multiply by any real number. Since points are also geometric objects, you will see the corresponding geometric consequences of these operations.

By the end of this investigation, you will be able to answer questions like these.

1. What are vectors?

2. How can you tell whether two vectors are equivalent?

3. Find the vector equation for the line through $A(1, 2)$ and $B(3, -4)$.

You will learn how to

- add points and multiply points by any real number and write the results both algebraically and geometrically

- work with vectors

- write a vector equation for any line on the coordinate plane

You will develop these habits and skills:

- See mathematical objects from a different perspective.

- Operate on points and vectors as algebraic objects.

- Use vectors to write equations of lines.

Geese stay in the V formation by flying with equivalent velocity vectors.

To help prepare for the study of vectors, you need to know how to multiply a point by a number and how to add two points. To multiply a point by a number (scale a point), you simply multiply each of its coordinates by that number. To add two points, you simply add the corresponding coordinates.

For You to Explore

1. Use one coordinate grid for parts (a)–(g). For each exercise, graph A and cA on the coordinate plane. How is the location of cA related to the location of A?

   > cA is the point you get when you *scale A* by *c*.

   a. $A(5, 1)$, $c = 2$

   b. $A(5, 1)$, $c = \frac{1}{2}$

   c. $A(3, 4)$, $c = 3$

   d. $A(3, 4)$, $c = \frac{1}{2}$

   e. $A(3, 4)$, $c = -1$

   f. $A(3, 4)$, $c = -2$

   g. $A(3, 4)$, $c = -\frac{1}{2}$

   What happens if, instead of scaling one point by many different numbers, you take many collinear points and scale them by the same number? The next few exercises ask you to look at that question.

2. Draw a picture of what you get if you scale each of the collinear points below by 2. Describe in words what you get.

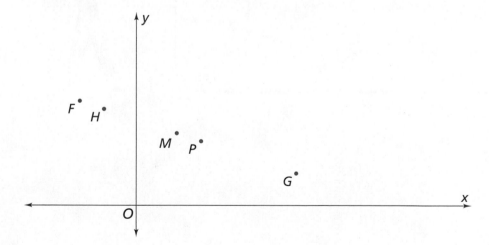

3. Think of a circle with radius 6 and center at the origin. What do you get if you scale all the points on the circle by 2? By $\frac{1}{2}$? By $-\frac{1}{2}$?

4. Use a separate coordinate grid for each part. On each grid, show O (the origin), A, B, and $A + B$.

   a. $A(5, 1)$ $B(3, 6)$

   b. $A(4, -2)$ $B(0, 6)$

   c. $A(4, -2)$ $B(-3, -5)$

   d. $A(4, -2)$ $B(-4, 2)$

   e. $A(4, -2)$ $B(-1, 4)$

   f. $A(3, 1)$ $B(6, 2)$

You may want to sketch a picture on graph paper.

Remember...

To add points, you add their corresponding coordinates. For example, $(-2, 7) + (4, 1) = (2, 8)$.

5. Suppose you have points $A(3, 5)$ and $B(6, -1)$.

   a. Plot B, $2B$, $0.5B$, $-1B$, $4B$, $-\frac{18}{5}B$, and three other multiples of B.

   b. What does the graph look like if you plot every possible multiple of B?

   c. Add A to each of the points you plotted in part (a). Plot the results on the same coordinate grid.

   d. What would your picture look like if you plotted the sum of A and each possible multiple of B?

6. Draw a polygon (like the one shown here if you like) on a coordinate grid. Apply each rule below to the vertices of the polygon. Draw the resulting polygon. Describe how each resulting polygon is related to the original.

   a. $(x, y) \mapsto (x + 8, y + 5)$

   b. $(x, y) \mapsto (x - 8, y + 5)$

   c. $(x, y) \mapsto (3x, 3y)$

   d. $(x, y) \mapsto \left(\frac{x}{2}, \frac{y}{2}\right)$

   e. $(x, y) \mapsto \left(\frac{x}{2} + 7, \frac{y}{2} + 10\right)$

   f. $(x, y) \mapsto (-x, y + 2)$

   g. $(x, y) \mapsto (2x, y + 2)$

Habits of Mind

Look for patterns. Can you make connections between the rules in Problem 6 and adding and scaling points?

On Your Own

7. **Write About It** Suppose *A* is a point and *c* is some real number. Describe geometrically how *cA* is related to *A*. How can you tell someone how to locate 2*A* if that person knows where point *A* is, but you do not? How are the coordinates of *cA* related algebraically to the coordinates of *A*?

8. **Write About It** Why is *scaling* a better term than *multiplying* when you refer to the operation that gives you *cA*?

9. Draw a picture of what you get if you scale each point shown by $\frac{1}{2}$. Describe what you get in words.

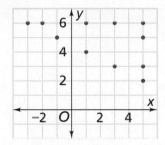

10. Draw what you get if you scale every point on the rectangle by   1. Then draw what you get if you scale each point by $\frac{5}{3}$.

11. Plot the sum of *P*(1, 4) and each point on the rectangle below.

> **Habits of Mind**
>
> **Visualize.** Of course, you cannot add *P* to every point of the rectangle, but what would you get if you could?

12. For each of the diagrams, write a rule that transforms the vertices of polygon *JKLM* to the vertices of polygon *J'K'L'M'*. (Use the ↦ notation.)

a.

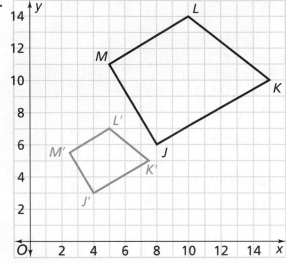

b.

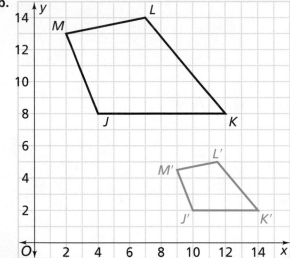

13. Jorge and Yutaka are both asked to transform $\triangle ABC$ with vertices $A(3, 6)$, $B(9, 6)$, and $C(9, 3)$. They are to scale it by $\frac{1}{4}$ and translate it 16 units to the right, but they are not told in which order to perform the transformations. Jorge chooses to scale the triangle first and then translate it. Yutaka translates first and then does the scaling.

a. Pick two vertices of $\triangle ABC$. Follow Jorge's and Yutaka's methods for each vertex. Write down where the images are.

b. Do both methods result in the same image triangle?

c. The two algebraic statements below describe Jorge's and Yutaka's methods. Which is Jorge's? Which is Yutaka's?

- $(x, y) \mapsto \frac{1}{4}(x, y) + (16, 0)$
- $(x, y) \mapsto \frac{1}{4}(x + 16, y)$

Maintain Your Skills

14. Here is a complicated rule.

$$(a, b) \mapsto \left(\tfrac{1}{2}(a - 3) + 5, \tfrac{1}{2}(b + 4) + 2 \right)$$

   a. Describe in words what this rule does.

   b. Simplify the algebra of the rule. Describe in words what your new (but equivalent) rule does.

15. Here is another complicated rule.

$$(x, z) \mapsto \left(\tfrac{1}{2}(2(x - 4) + 6), \tfrac{1}{2}(2(z + 3) - 4) \right)$$

   a. Describe in words what this rule does.

   b. Simplify the algebra of the rule. Describe in words what your new (but equivalent) rule does.

16. Compare $(x, y) \mapsto 2(x, y) + (2, 3)$ and $(x, y) \mapsto 2((x, y) + (1, 2))$. Do these rules give the same result?

17. Pick a point. Think about the following rule.

   Add $(2, 3)$.

   Scale by 3.

   Subtract $(1, 2)$.

   Now answer the following questions.

   a. If you start with $(4, 5)$, where do you end?

   b. If you start with $(-1, 3)$, where do you end?

   c. If you end with $(7, 1)$, where did you start?

   d. If you end with $(4, 6)$, where did you start?

   e. What simple rule is equivalent to the one above?

> **Habits of Mind**
>
> **Check your work.**
> Apply your rule to some points on a specific picture to check that your description is right.

Introduction to Vectors

In Lesson H.01, you saw some geometric effects of adding and scaling points. There is a very convenient language for using these concepts. It involves the notion of a vector.

In physics, people distinguish speed (such as 30 mi/h) from velocity. Velocity has a **direction** as well as a size, so that 30 mi/h northeast is different from 30 mi/h due south. You can model this idea on a coordinate system by thinking about line segments that have a direction.

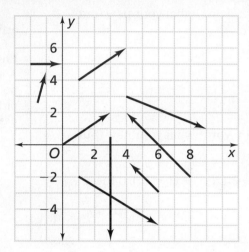

Each arrow in this figure can stand for a velocity. The length of the arrow is the speed. The direction of the arrow tells you which way the velocity is directed. The arrows are often called *vectors*. If *A* and *B* are points, the "vector from *A* to *B*" can be thought of as the arrow that starts at *A* and ends at *B*.

> For navigators, vectors might stand for trips or currents or wind velocities.

Definition

Given two points *A* and *B*, the vector from *A* to *B* is the ordered pair of points (*A*, *B*). Point *A* is the tail of the vector and point *B* is the head.

You can write the vector from *A* to *B* as $\overrightarrow{AB}$.

Minds in Action

Tony has seen vectors before and is a bit confused by this definition.

Tony   Hmm . . . I thought that two vectors with the same size and direction were the same, even with different heads and tails. According to this definition they aren't.

Sasha   If two vectors have the same size and direction, but different heads and tails, they are **equivalent vectors.**

For You to Do

Use the points $A(5, 1)$, $B(-2, 5)$, $C(9, -2)$, and $D(16, -6)$. On a coordinate system, draw each vector.

- $\overrightarrow{AB}$
- $\overrightarrow{CD}$
- $\overrightarrow{AC}$
- $\overrightarrow{BA}$
- $\overrightarrow{OA}$
- $\overrightarrow{OB}$
- $\overrightarrow{B(A + B)}$
- $\overrightarrow{A(A + B)}$
- $\overrightarrow{O(B + A)}$

$\overrightarrow{B(A + B)}$ means the vector with tail B and head $A + B$.

1. Which vectors that you drew have the same direction?

2. Which have opposite directions?

3. Which have the same size?

4. Which have the same head?

5. Which have the same tail?

In-Class Experiment

Suppose you are working on the coordinate plane.

6. For $A(5, 3)$ and $B(8, 7)$, find a vector with tail at the origin and the same size and direction as $\overrightarrow{AB}$.

7. For $A(3, 5)$ and $B(8, 1)$, find two points C and D (neither at the origin) such that the vector from A to B is equivalent to the vector from C to D. Find another point E such that the vector from the origin to E is equivalent to $\overrightarrow{AB}$ and $\overrightarrow{CD}$.

Equivalent vectors have the same size and direction.

8. Two vectors are shown below. Find a way to tell whether the two vectors are equivalent just by looking at their coordinates (and doing some calculations with them).

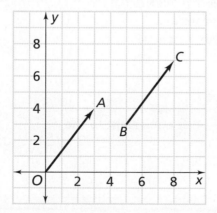

Here is a test you can use for deciding whether two vectors are equivalent.

Theorem H.1 *The Head-Minus-Tail Test*

Two vectors are equivalent if and only if head minus tail for one vector gives the same result as head minus tail for the other. In symbols: $\overrightarrow{AB}$ is equivalent to $\overrightarrow{CD}$ if and only if $B - A = D - C$.

Proof In general, you can write the coordinates of *A*, *B*, *C*, and *D* this way.

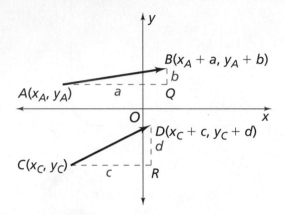

If $\overrightarrow{AB}$ and $\overrightarrow{CD}$ are equivalent, then $\overline{AB}$ is parallel to and congruent to $\overline{CD}$. Since the segments are parallel, the lines containing them have the same slope, so

$$\frac{b}{a} = \frac{d}{c}$$

This means that right $\triangle ABQ$ and right $\triangle CDR$ are similar. But the fact that $\overline{AB} \cong \overline{CD}$ implies that the two triangles are congruent. So, in particular, their corresponding legs are congruent.

$$(a, b) = (c, d), \text{ so } B - A = D - C$$

Conversely, if $B - A = D - C$, then $(a, b) = (c, d)$. So the legs of the two right triangles are congruent. This implies that $\overline{AB} \parallel \overline{CD}$ and that they have the same orientation. It also means that $AB = \sqrt{a^2 + b^2} = \sqrt{c^2 + d^2} = CD$. As a corollary, you have the following.

Corollary H.1.1

If *A* and *B* are points, the vector from *O* to $(B - A)$ is equivalent to the vector from *A* to *B*.

Look for relationships. To think about a class of equivalent objects, it is often enough to think of only one member of the class. Fractions provide a good example.

The fractions $\frac{1}{2}, \frac{2}{4}, \frac{3}{6}, \frac{4}{8}, \frac{5}{10} \ldots$, all belong to the same class. It is usually enough to let the simplified fraction $\frac{1}{2}$ represent the class.

Vectors provide another example. Because of Corollary H.1.1, any vector in the coordinate plane is equivalent to a vector with its tail at the origin. So, you can think of any vector with its tail at the origin as a representative of a whole class of equivalent vectors. If you think of it this way, the collection of all vectors with tails at the origin represents all the vectors in the coordinate plane!

Twenty-two vectors are shown here. How many classes of equivalent vectors are there?

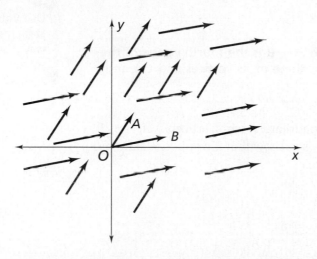

Corollary H.1.1 lets you identify any vector with a point in the coordinate plane. Think of point A as $\overrightarrow{OA}$, for example. To add vectors, you add points as you did in the Getting Started lesson. Vectors, however, give this addition a geometric flavor. If A and B are points (and vectors), how can you locate $A + B$ using geometry?

Vectors must have the same direction and magnitude to be equivalent.

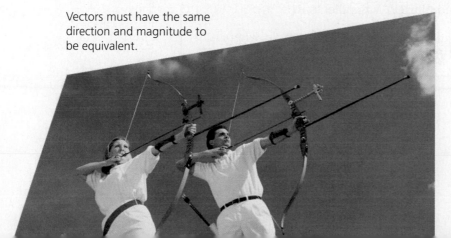

- For each pair of points A and B given below, plot the following four points: the origin O, A, B, and the sum $A + B$.

- Describe how $A + B$ is located with respect to the other three points.

- Draw segments connecting O to A and B. Draw segments connecting A and B to $A + B$. What kind of figure do you get in each case?

9. $A(-3, 5)$, $B(5, 1)$

10. $A(2, 3)$, $B(5, 1)$

11. $A(-2, -2)$, $B(0, 6)$

12. $A(-3, 3)$, $B(5, -5)$

13. $A(-3, 5)$, $B(10, 2)$

14. $A(-3, 5)$, $B\left(\frac{5}{2}, \frac{1}{2}\right)$

The In-Class Experiment suggests a theorem.

Theorem H.2

If $A = (a_1, a_2)$ and $B = (b_1, b_2)$, then $A + B$ is the fourth vertex of the parallelogram that has A, O, and B as three of its vertices and $\overline{OA}$ and $\overline{OB}$ as two of its sides.

Basically, you want to show that the quadrilateral with vertices O, A, $A + B$, and B is a parallelogram. One strategy is to show that the opposite sides are parallel.

Let $A = (a_1, a_2)$ and $B = (b_1, b_2)$.

Let $P = A + B = (a_1 + b_1, a_2 + b_2)$.

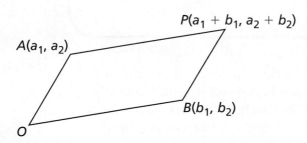

For You to Do

15. Prove that $\overline{OA}$ is parallel to $\overline{BP}$ and that $\overline{OB}$ is parallel to $\overline{AP}$.

16. Does Theorem H.2 hold if O, A, and B are collinear? For example, where is the parallelogram if $A(9, -1)$ and $B(18, -2)$?

Identifying vectors with points in the coordinate plane also gives the scaling of points a geometric flavor.

Theorem H.3

Suppose A is a point, c is a number greater than or equal to 1, and $B = cA$. Then,

- B is collinear with A and the origin.

- B is c times as far from the origin as A.

For $c > 1$, part 2 of the theorem implies that A is between O and B.

For You to Do

For each point A and value c given below, let $B = cA$. Then, show that the two statements in Theorem H.3 are true. That is, show

a. $OA + AB = OB$

b. $OB = cOA$

17. $A(3, 4)$, $c = 3$

18. $A(-5, 12)$, $c = 2$

19. $A(6, 8)$, $c = 1.5$

20. $A(3, 8)$, $c = 4$

Exercises *Practicing Habits of Mind*

Check Your Understanding

1. Use the points $A(5, 3)$ and $B(8, 7)$. Find a vector that starts at the origin, has the same direction as $\overrightarrow{AB}$, and is twice as long as $\overrightarrow{AB}$.

2. Use the points $R(7, 2)$ and $S(15, 6)$. Find the head of a vector that starts at $(4, -3)$ and is equivalent to the vector from R to S.

3. True or false: If A and B are any points, the vector from O to B is equivalent to the vector from A to $A + B$. Explain.

4. Use the points $A(8, 15)$, $B(-4, 3)$, and $P = A + B$. Draw a picture of O, A, B, and P. Show that $OA = BP$ and $OB = AP$.

5. Use the points $A(8, 6)$, $B(3, 1)$, and $P = A + B$. Draw a picture of O, A, B, and P. Show that $OA = BP$ and $OB = AP$.

6. For $A(3, 2)$ and $P(4, 5)$, locate each of the following.

   a. $P + A$ **b.** $P + 2A$ **c.** $P + 3A$ **d.** $P + 4A$

   e. $P + \frac{1}{2}A$ **f.** $P + \frac{1}{3}A$ **g.** $P + \frac{1}{4}A$

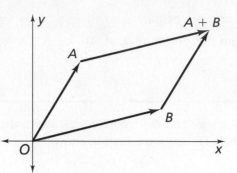

7. Here is a pair of fancy sentences: $\overrightarrow{A(A + B)}$ is equivalent to $\overrightarrow{OB}$, and $\overrightarrow{O(A + B)}$ is one diagonal of the parallelogram with vertices O, A, $A + B$, and B. Also, $\overrightarrow{OA}$ is equivalent to $\overrightarrow{B(A + B)}$.

Copy the figure shown here. Label the five vectors that are mentioned in the sentences above. Use $A(3, 5)$ and $B(8, 2)$ to show that $\overrightarrow{A(A + B)}$ is equivalent to $\overrightarrow{OB}$. Also, show that $\overrightarrow{OA}$ is equivalent to $\overrightarrow{B(A + B)}$. Use the head-minus-tail method.

8. Suppose T is the function that maps a point X to the point $X + (10, 5)$. Pick two points A and B. Draw the vectors from A to $T(A)$ and from B to $T(B)$. Show that these vectors are equivalent.

Remember...

This means that, for example, $T((4, 2))$ $= (4, 2) + (10, 5)$ $= (14, 7)$.

9. For $A(3, 4)$, $B(5, -12)$, and $P = A + B$, draw a picture of O, A, B, and P. Show that $OA = BP$ and $OB = AP$.

10. Let A, B, and C be any three points. Show that the quadrilateral with vertices B, C, $C + A$, and $B + A$ is a parallelogram by showing that opposite sides are congruent. Draw a picture.

Corollary H.1.1 says that $\overrightarrow{AB}$ is equivalent to the vector from O to $B - A$. Some people think of this as moving $\overrightarrow{AB}$ so its tail is at the origin. They say, "To move $\overrightarrow{AB}$ to the origin, just draw the vector from O to $B - A$."

Other people say it this way: "To move a vector to the origin, just subtract the tail from the head." The next exercises show you how you can apply this technique to the geometry of vectors.

11. Point A has coordinates $(1, 6)$. Point B has coordinates $(7, 8)$.

a. Calculate head minus tail for $\overrightarrow{AB}$. Draw a diagram that shows both $\overrightarrow{AB}$ and $\overrightarrow{O(B - A)}$. You have moved $\overrightarrow{AB}$ to the origin.

b. Now take the vector anchored at the origin. Move it to $P(3, -2)$ by adding P to the head and to the tail. Draw this new vector. What are the coordinates of its head and tail?

12. Prove the following theorem.

Theorem H.4

Adding the same point to the tail and to the head of a vector produces an equivalent vector.

Habits of Mind

Check the theorem. Use specific values to test this generalization. Draw a picture in the coordinate plane.

13. Show that if A and B are points, the midpoint of $\overline{AB}$ is $\frac{1}{2}(A + B)$.

14. Mathematical convention usually assigns

- capital-letter names to points
- lowercase names early in the alphabet to constants (numbers you know)
- lowercase names late in the alphabet to variables or unknowns (numbers you do not know yet, or numbers that can vary)

In the expressions below, A, B, C, M, X, Y, and Z are names of points. O is the name of a special point, the origin. The letters c, k, and x are names for numbers. Classify each expression as a *point*, a *number*, or just plain *meaningless*.

a. cB **b.** $c + A$ **c.** AB **d.** $c(AB)$ **e.** $k(OA)$

f. $A + B + C$ **g.** xX **h.** $(c + k)A$ **i.** $cA + B$ **j.** $A + B$

k. $c(A + B)$ **l.** $A(c + B)$ **m.** cZ **n.** $c(XY)$ **o.** $c(X + Y)$

p. $A(X + Y)$ **q.** AX **r.** $X + Y$ **s.** $M(C + X)$

15. Given two points A and B, how can you find a point that is on $\overleftrightarrow{AB}$ and one third of the way from A to B? Explain.

16. **Standardized Test Prep** Equivalent vectors have the same magnitude and direction. Which vector is equivalent to $\overrightarrow{EF}$? (Point O is the origin.)

A. $\overrightarrow{FE}$ **B.** $\frac{1}{2}\overrightarrow{O(E + F)}$ **C.** $\overrightarrow{O(E - F)}$ **D.** $\overrightarrow{O(F - E)}$

17. Suppose A, B, C, and D are the vertices of a quadrilateral.

a. Express the midpoints of the sides of the quadrilateral in terms of A, B, C, and D.

b. Show that the quadrilateral formed by joining the midpoints from part (a) is a parallelogram.

Maintain Your Skills

Go Online
Video Tutor
www.successnetplus.com

18. Use $\overrightarrow{AB}$ from Exercise 11. Find (and draw) vectors equivalent to $\overrightarrow{AB}$ with the following properties.

a. tail at $C(8, 3)$ **b.** tail at $J(-8, 3)$

c. tail at $K(0, 3)$ **d.** head at O

e. head at $C(8, 3)$ **f.** tail at B

Go Online
www.successnetplus.com

19. Suppose $A(3, 4)$, $B(9, 0)$, $C(-1, 2)$, and $D(5, -2)$. Show that $\overrightarrow{AB}$ is equivalent to $\overrightarrow{CD}$ by moving both vectors to the origin. Show also that $\overrightarrow{AC}$ is equivalent to $\overrightarrow{BD}$.

H.03 The Vector Equation of a Line

Theorem H.3 in the previous lesson describes points that are on the line containing the vector from the origin to a point *A*. You can generalize this theorem to describe the line through the origin and *A*.

Theorem H.5

If *A* is a point different from the origin, the set of all multiples of *A* is the line through the origin and *A*.

You might remember words such as *slope*, *y-intercept*, and *point-slope equation*. These terms had to do with equations of lines. In this lesson, you will revisit these terms and connect them with vectors.

Points $A(3, 1)$ and $B(8, -2)$ determine line $\overleftrightarrow{AB}$. How do you know if point $P(13, -5)$ or point $Q(13, -6)$ lies on $\overleftrightarrow{AB}$?

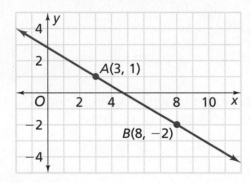

Minds in Action

Tony seems perplexed.

Tony   I guess we are going to have to use Theorem H.5, but I don't have the faintest idea how!

Sasha   Well, what would happen if *P* were on $\overleftrightarrow{AB}$? If we moved everything to the origin *O* by subtracting *A*, then $P - A$ would be on the line through *O* and $B - A$.

Tony   Stop! You're giving me a headache! Let me try to understand what you are saying with a picture. I calculated $B - A$ in my head, so . . .

Remember...

Sasha is using the technique from Exercise 11a in the previous lesson.

Tony draws a diagram showing his calculations.

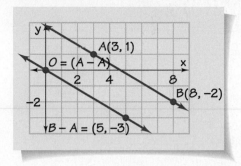

Sasha   Good! Do you see it now? $P - A = (10, -6)$. Thanks to Theorem H.5, we know that the point $P - A$ is on the line through $B - A$ and O only if $(10, -6)$ is a multiple of $(5, -3)$.

Tony   And it is! So now we can move everything back and know that P lies on $\overleftrightarrow{AB}$. Hurray!

Sasha   Okay, now it's your turn to see if Q is on $\overleftrightarrow{AB}$.

Tony $Q - A = (10, -7)$. I can't find any number k such that $(10, -7) = k(5, -3)$. It looks like Q isn't on $\overleftrightarrow{AB}$, because Theorem H.5 says that otherwise there would be such a number k.

Sasha   Good work, Tony!

So, in general, if a point X is on a line $\overleftrightarrow{AB}$, $X - A$ is a multiple of $B - A$. That is, there is a number k such that $X - A = k(B - A)$. So X lies on $\overleftrightarrow{AB}$ if

$$X = A + k(B - A)$$

This is a vector equation in X and k.

The converse is also true. If $X = A + k(B - A)$ for some number k, then X lies on $\overleftrightarrow{AB}$.

For You to Do

Find a vector equation of the line containing the two given points. Give three more points that satisfy each equation and three that do not.

1. $A(3, 5)$, $B(-1, -5)$

2. $P(8, -1)$, $Q(1, 7)$

3. $R(6, 7)$, $S(2, -3)$

4. $T(3, 5)$, $U(11, 11)$

You can describe parallel lines using vectors. This In-Class Experiment will help you gather ideas about parallel vectors.

In-Class Experiment

Here are some vectors.

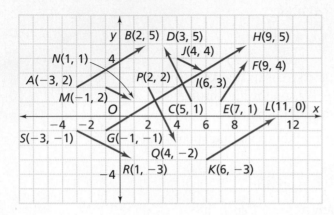

5. Which vectors are parallel?

6. Which are parallel in the same direction?

7. Which are parallel in opposite directions?

8. Which are equivalent?

9. Find a rule that uses head minus tail to tell you when two vectors are
- parallel in the same direction
- parallel in opposite directions

You can summarize the results of the In-Class Experiment in one general theorem.

Theorem H.6

Two vectors $\overrightarrow{AB}$ and $\overrightarrow{CD}$ are parallel if and only if there is a number k such that

$$B - A = k(D - C)$$

If $k > 0$, the vectors have the same direction. If $k < 0$, the vectors have opposite directions. If $k = 1$, the vectors are equivalent.

For Discussion

10. Write a proof for Theorem H.6.

For You to Do

11. Now prove the following theorem.

Theorem H.7

If *A* and *B* are points, then the segment from *O* to *B* − *A* is parallel and congruent to $\overline{AB}$.

$$\overline{O(B-A)} \parallel \overline{AB}$$

$$\overline{O(B-A)} \cong \overline{AB}$$

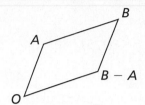

Exercises Practicing Habits of Mind

Check Your Understanding

1. Suppose you have points $A(4, 1)$, $B(9, 5)$, $C(3, -1)$, and $D(13, 7)$. Prove that $\overleftrightarrow{AB} \parallel \overleftrightarrow{CD}$.

2. Show that if *P* and *A* are points and *t* is a number, the segment from *P* to $P + tA$ is parallel to the segment from *O* to *A*.

For Exercise 2, refer to Exercise 6 from Lesson H.02.

3. For $A(4, 4)$ and $B(8, -4)$, look at $\triangle OAB$. Let *M* be the midpoint of $\overline{OA}$ and *N* be the midpoint of $\overline{OB}$. Show that $\overline{MN} \parallel \overline{AB}$ and $MN = \frac{1}{2}AB$.

4. Show that Theorem H.7 holds for $A(3, 5)$ and $B(7, 9)$.

Exercise 3 shows a special case of the Midline Theorem.

On Your Own

5. Use the points $A(-1, 3)$ and $B(2, 6)$. Find the head and tail of the vector that is equivalent to $\overrightarrow{AB}$, lies on $\overleftrightarrow{AB}$, and has its head on the line with each given equation.

    a. $y = 2$ **b.** $x = -3$

6. For $A(3, 2)$, $B(-4, 5)$, and $C(7, 4)$, show that $\triangle ABC \cong \triangle O(B-A)(C-A)$. Draw a picture.

7. Show that if A, B, and C are any three points, $\triangle ABC \cong \triangle O(B - A)(C - A)$.

8. The coordinates of P and A are given in the figure. Find a vector equation of the line through P and parallel to $\overrightarrow{OA}$.

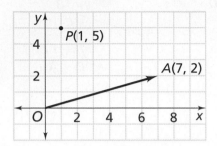

9. Show that the point $\frac{2}{3}A + \frac{1}{3}B$ is on $\overline{AB}$ $\frac{1}{3}$ of the way from A to B.

10. What point is on $\overline{AB}$ $\frac{1}{4}$ of the way from A to B?

11. For $A(3, 5)$ and $B(7, 1)$, find C if B is the midpoint of $\overline{AC}$.

12. **Standardized Test Prep** Points G and H have coordinates $(1, 3)$ and $(6, 5)$, respectively. Which point is NOT on $\overleftrightarrow{GH}$?

A. $J(-4, 1)$ **B.** $K(-9, -1)$

C. $L(0, 2.6)$ **D.** $M(-6, 0)$

13. Find vector equations of the three medians of $\triangle ABC$ with vertices $A(-1, 5)$, $B(5, -2)$, and $C(3, 5)$.

> What points of $\triangle ABC$ lie on its medians?

14. In the coordinate plane, draw $\triangle AOB$ with vertices $A(3, 6)$, $B(8, 1)$, and O, the origin. Find the midpoint M of $\overline{OA}$ and the midpoint N of $\overline{OB}$. Prove that $\overrightarrow{MN}$ is parallel to $\overrightarrow{AB}$ and that the size of $\overrightarrow{MN}$ is half the size of $\overrightarrow{AB}$.

Maintain Your Skills

15. Suppose A and B are points. Using vectors, explain how to locate each point.

a. $\frac{1}{3}A + \frac{2}{3}B$ **b.** $\frac{2}{3}A + \frac{1}{3}B$

c. $\frac{1}{4}A + \frac{3}{4}B$ **d.** $\frac{3}{4}A + \frac{1}{4}B$

e. $\frac{3}{5}A + \frac{2}{5}B$ **f.** $kA + (1 - k)B$ for $0 \le k \le 1$

16. The head of $\overrightarrow{OA}$ is $(1, 3)$. The head of $\overrightarrow{OB}$ is $(2, 0)$.

Find x and y such that $x\overrightarrow{OA} + y\overrightarrow{OB}$ has its head at each of the following points.

a. $(2, 1)$ **b.** $(4, 3)$ **c.** $(11, 1)$

d. $(5, 6)$ **e.** $(0, 8)$ **f.** $(1, -10)$

Go Online
www.successnetplus.com

Habits of Mind

Visualize. Draw the two vectors on graph paper. For each point, sketch how you could get from the origin to that point if you could travel only in the directions allowed by the two vectors.

704 Honors Appendix

H.04 Using the Vector Equation of a Line

In this lesson, you use vector equations of lines to find the point of intersection of two lines, when it exists. You also learn how to tell whether a point of intersection exists just by looking at the equations of the lines. Then you will see how to prove that the medians of a triangle are concurrent by using vector equations of lines.

In-Class Experiment

Use point $A(1, 2)$, point $B(-2, 6)$, and the origin O.

1. Plot line ℓ with equation $P = A + p(-3, 4)$ and line s with equation $Q = B + q(1, 1)$.

2. Explain how you can find the point of intersection of ℓ and s. Then find it.

3. Now plot the line r with equation $T = O + m(1, 1)$. Can you find the point of intersection for ℓ and r? The point of intersection for s and r?

4. Plot line t with equation $H = (3, 5) + v(4, 4)$. Can you find the point of intersection for ℓ and t? For s and t? For r and t? Make conjectures about when it is possible to find the point of intersection and when it is not. Can you tell by simply looking at the vector equation?

For Discussion

5. Discuss with your class your results to the In-Class Experiment above. Write a summary of what you discovered.

For You to Do

6. **What's Wrong Here?** Tony tried to solve the following problem, but got an inconsistent answer. Help him find his mistake.

Problem Write a vector equation of the line through $A(-1, 4)$ and $B(2, 6)$. Also, write a vector equation of the line through $C\left(\frac{1}{2}, 3\right)$ and $D(5, -1)$. Do the two lines intersect? If they do, find the point of intersection.

Solution Since $\overrightarrow{AB} = (2 - (-1), 6 - 4) = (3, 2)$, $\overrightarrow{CD} = \left(5 - \frac{1}{2}, -1 - 3\right) = \left(\frac{9}{2}, -4\right)$, and for any k

$$(3, 2) \neq k\left(\frac{9}{2}, -4\right)$$

you know the two lines intersect.

A vector equation for $\overleftrightarrow{AB}$ is

$$P = A + t(B - A)$$
$$P = (-1, 4) + t(3, 2)$$

A vector equation for $\overleftrightarrow{CD}$ is

$$Q = C + t(D - C)$$
$$Q = \left(\frac{1}{2}, 3\right) + t\left(\frac{9}{2}, -4\right)$$

So the value of t that gives the point of intersection can be found by solving the following system of equations.

$$-1 + 3t = \frac{1}{2} + \frac{9}{2}t$$
$$4 + 2t = 3 - 4t$$

The first equation has solution $t = -1$. The second equation has solution $t = -\frac{1}{6}$. This means the system has no solution. But the lines do intersect. What is wrong here?

There is a variation of the point-tester rule from Chapter 3 that works for vector equations of lines.

Example

Problem Does point $P(8, 9)$ lie on the line ℓ with vector equation $Q = (3, 5) + q(1, 2)$?

Solution If P lies on ℓ, then the following two equations would be satisfied for the same value of q.

$$8 = 3 + 1q$$
$$9 = 5 + 2q$$

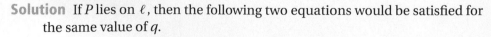

Why is this the case?

The first equation has solution $q = 5$, but the second equation has solution $q = 2$. Therefore, P does not lie on ℓ.

Exercises Practicing Habits of Mind

Check Your Understanding

In Chapter 6, you proved that the three medians of a triangle are concurrent and that the point of intersection is $\frac{2}{3}$ of the way from a vertex to the midpoint of the opposite side. You can use vector equations to check it out.

1. Plot points $A(3, 1)$, $B(5, 2)$, and $C(7, 7)$ on the coordinate plane and connect them to form $\triangle ABC$. Translate the triangle to the origin by subtracting A from each vertex. Call the new vertices $A_0 = O$, B_0, and C_0. Find the midpoints M, N, and K of sides $\overline{A_0B_0}$, $\overline{B_0C_0}$, and $\overline{C_0A_0}$, respectively.

> What does translating the triangle to the origin change in the results?

2. Use the figure you drew for Exercise 1 and write vector equations for $\overleftrightarrow{C_0M}$ and $\overleftrightarrow{B_0K}$. Do these lines intersect? Explain. If they do, find their point of intersection and label it G_0.

3. Refer to the figure you drew for Exercise 1 and write the vector equation of line $\overleftrightarrow{A_0N}$. Does G_0 lie on $\overleftrightarrow{A_0N}$?

4. Refer to Exercises 1–3. What are the values of the parameters in the vector equations of lines $\overleftrightarrow{A_0N}$, $\overleftrightarrow{B_0K}$, and $\overleftrightarrow{C_0M}$ that give point G_0? What does this result mean geometrically?

On Your Own

5. You are given point $A(-3, 4)$. How can you find the coordinates of a point B such that $\overrightarrow{OA}$ is perpendicular to $\overrightarrow{OB}$?

6. Find a vector equation of a line through $A(2, 4)$ and perpendicular to $\overrightarrow{OA}$.

7. Use vectors to show that the diagonals of a parallelogram bisect each other.

> **Habits of Mind**
>
> **Simplify the problem.** Assume that one vertex of the parallelogram is the origin O. If A, O, and B are consecutive vertices, the fourth vertex is $A + B$.

8. George has a way to find the population center for three cities of the same size. He puts the cities on a coordinate system, adds the coordinates of the three cities, and scales by $\frac{1}{3}$. In what sense is George's point the population center?

9. Martha extends George's method to allow for cities of different sizes. She first draws coordinates on the map and scales the coordinates of each city by its population. Next she adds the results, and then she divides the resulting point by the sum of the populations of all three cities. In what sense is Martha's point the population center?

10. Standardized Test Prep Which point is on the line with vector equation $F = (-2, 3) + r(1, -2)$?

A. $A(3, -7)$

B. $B(2, -3)$

C. $C(-3, 6)$

D. $D(1, 3)$

Maintain Your Skills

Exercises 11–13 will guide you through a proof of the fact that the three perpendicular bisectors of the sides of a triangle are concurrent. Use $\triangle OAB$, with $A(9, 2)$, $B(1, 8)$, and the origin O.

Go Online
www.successnetplus.com

11. Write vector equations for the lines $\overleftrightarrow{OA}$, $\overleftrightarrow{OB}$, and $\overleftrightarrow{AB}$. Find three vectors, each perpendicular to one of these lines.

12. Write vector equations for the line that contains the midpoint of $\overline{OA}$ and is perpendicular to $\overleftrightarrow{OA}$, the line that contains the midpoint of $\overline{OB}$ and is perpendicular to $\overleftrightarrow{OB}$, and the line that contains the midpoint of $\overline{AB}$ and is perpendicular to $\overleftrightarrow{AB}$. These lines contain the three perpendicular bisectors of the sides of the triangle.

13. Find the intersection point of the perpendicular bisector of $\overline{OA}$ and the perpendicular bisector of $\overline{OB}$. Check to see whether this point lies on the perpendicular bisector of $\overline{AB}$.

14. Write About It Think about how you proved that both the medians and the perpendicular bisectors of the sides of a triangle are concurrent.

a. Write general steps you can use to prove that three lines are concurrent.

b. Prove that the three altitudes of a triangle are concurrent. You can use $\triangle OAB$.

Go Online
www.successnetplus.com

Vector Equations of Lines

Here is one way to think of a straight line: start at a point P and change position in some fixed direction. You can write the point P as an ordered pair. If you write the direction as a vector, you can do the same with it. This way of thinking leads to a vector equation for lines.

Minds in Action

Tony and Sasha have been asked to figure out an equation for a typical point X on the line through point P with direction vector D.

Tony   Okay, we start at P and change position in direction D. That makes sense. Look at this picture.

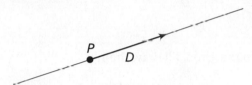

Sasha   So long as any amount can mean both positive and negative amounts. Otherwise we just get a ray.

Tony   We're supposed to write an equation for a typical point X on the line. Here it is.

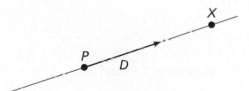

Sasha   Or it could be on the other side, like this

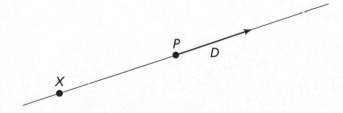

Tony   Or it could be in close, like this.

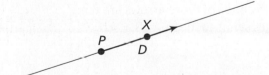

Sasha	Whatever. The vector D just has to be scaled to get all the way from P to X. So I think it's kD instead of D.
Tony	Hey, that's it, the part I was missing. From the last lesson, a point plus a vector is a point. You get from P to X by adding the vector kD. So $X = P + kD$. I think we're done!
Sasha	Maybe. You like that point plus vector stuff, but I don't think that way. I want it to be all vectors. Plus, I like vectors from the origin, not just left out there anywhere. And I think they should be named by their tails and heads.
Tony	Picky, picky. OK, let's see if we can do it that way. Maybe start with this?

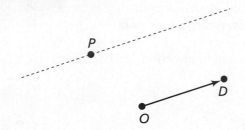

Sasha	Yeah, but get some multiples kD in there too. I'll draw them a little to the side so I can see them.

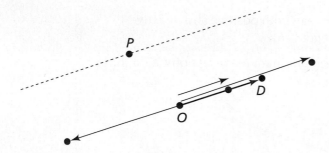

Tony	OK, now we've got to translate them to P, draw in $\overrightarrow{OP}$, and add head to tail.

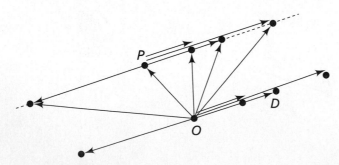

Sasha	Now we're cooking. The arrows between the two lines are the sums of P and kD. The points at the ends of those arrows are the points on the line. So now it makes sense to me, $X = P + kD$.

Tony Hey, what if we use your method, but add in the other order $kD + P$. Let's see, I think we get this.

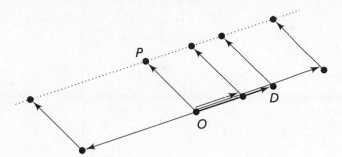

Sasha I like that. You haven't drawn in the sum vectors, but maybe it's clearer that way. You can see that you start with a line through the origin determined by the vector D. Then you translate the whole thing by vector P, getting a new line with the same direction but through the point P.

$X = P + kD$ is called a *vector equation of a line*, or the line expressed in vector form. You may replace the scalar k by the letter t, since t usually stands for a variable while k stands for a constant.

For You to Do

1. How would you write a vector equation of a line through two points P and Q? What direction vector would you use? Try out your idea, by finding a vector equation for the line through $P(-1, 4)$ and $Q(2, -2)$. Make sure both of these points satisfy your equation.

> What are good letters to use for real-number variables? The letters x and y are out since they are coordinates of X. So t is a good choice, as are s, u, and v.

Recall that equations are point-testers. This is true for vector equations of lines as well.

Example 1

Problem Consider the line with vector equation $X = (1, 3) + t(2, -3)$.

   a. Name two points on the line.

   b. Determine if $(4, -1)$ is on this line.

   c. Determine if $(-1, 6)$ is on this line.

Solution

   a. Pick t to be any real number. For example, the choice $t = 0$ gives the base point $P = (1, 3)$. The choice $t = 1$ yields $(1, 3) + (2, -3) = (3, 0)$.

   b. Substitute $(4, -1)$ for X to get the two real-number equations

$$4 = 1 + 2t$$
$$-1 = 3 - 3t$$

The first equation's solution is $t = \frac{3}{2}$. Substituting this t into the second equation does not work. So $(4, -1)$ fails the test. It is not on the line.

c. This time the two equations are

$$-1 = 1 + 2t$$
$$6 = 3 - 3t$$

The first yields $t = -1$, which does satisfy the second equation. So point $(-1, 6)$ passes the test. It is on the line.

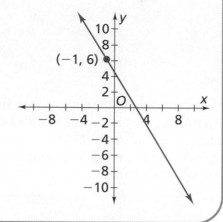

The vector form of a line has an extra variable, the t. This is called a **parameter.** It does not stand for a physical coordinate, the way x and y do. In mathematics, a parameter is a variable that does not appear in the picture but somehow determines what does appear.

So why is the vector form useful? Offhand, it seems that vector form only adds complication—the extra variable t.

The reason it is useful is that t can represent time and describe movement along the line.

> Vector equations for lines are sometimes called *parametric equations* for lines.

Example 2

Problem Two test cars start racing along straight lines in a flat desert. Suppose Car 1 starts at $(0, 0)$ and travels with constant velocity $(25, 40)$. That means, in each time unit, Car 1 travels $(25, 40)$ from where it was. (To make the speeds in this example somewhat realistic, let the units for distance be kilometers and the units for time be hours.) Suppose Car 2 starts at the same time at $(10, 25)$ and travels with velocity vector $(30, 45)$.

Do the paths of the cars intersect? Do the cars crash?

Solution At time t, Car 1 is at $(0, 0) + t(25, 40)$ and Car 2 is at $(10, 25) + t(30, 45)$.

To make sense of these equations, track Car 1's position for the first few hours. At $t = 0$, Car 1 is at $(0, 0)$. In one hour it moves along a vector equivalent to $(25, 40)$, so it reaches $(0, 0) + 1(25, 40)$. In 2 hours it has gone twice as far, so it reaches $(0, 0) + 2(25, 40)$. In general, after t hours it is at $(0, 0) + t(25, 40)$.

> t does not have to be an integer.

Set the locations of the two cars equal and solve.

$$(0, 0) + t(25, 40) = (10, 25) + t(30, 45)$$

If you write this out as two separate real-number equations, this is

$$0 + 25t = 10 + 30t$$
$$0 + 40t = 25 + 45t$$

which simplifies to

$$-5t = 10$$
$$-5t = 25$$

Clearly there is no solution that gives the same t for both equations.

But what does this mean? The two things you set equal are the positions of the cars at the same time t. No solution means there is no time t at which the cars are at the same place. So they do not crash.

How do you determine whether their paths intersect? Are there different times at which they pass through the same spot? In other words, is there a solution to

$$(0, 0) + t(25, 40) = (10, 25) + s(30, 45)$$

The expression on the left is the position of Car 1 at time t. The expression on the right is the position of Car 2 at time s. You do not know yet what these times are, or if there are times at which the location for both cars is the same, but you can solve and find out. Again, write out the real-number equations.

$$0 + 25t = 10 + 30s$$
$$0 + 40t = 25 + 45s$$

which simplifies to

$$-30s + 25t = 10$$
$$-45s + 40t = 25$$

Solve this system to give the solution $s = 3$, $t = 4$.

The paths intersect, but the cars pass through the intersection an hour apart—Car 2 at hour 3 and Car 1 at hour 4.

For You to Do

2. Find the intersection point for the cars' paths. Show that this point is on both lines according to their vector equations.

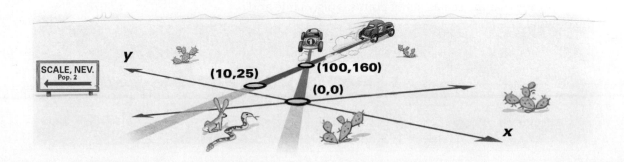

Exercises *Practicing Habits of Mind*

Check Your Understanding

1. Consider the line with vector equation $X = (1, 2) + t(3, 4)$. Test whether the points $(4, 6)$, $(-5, -5)$, and $(13, 18)$ are on the line.

2. Consider the line with parametric equation $X = (1, 0) + t(1, 2)$. Find a Cartesian equation of this line.

3. Find the slope of the line that is the graph of each of the following equations.

   a. $X = (1, 2) + t(3, 4)$ **b.** $X = (1, 2) + t(4, 3)$

   c. $X = (1, 2) + t(6, 8)$ **d.** $X = P + t(3, 4)$ for any point P

4. Find a vector equation for each of the following.

   a. the graph of $y = \frac{3}{2}x + 1$

   b. the graph of $(y - 3) = 4(x - 5)$

   c. the graph of $\frac{x}{2} + \frac{y}{3} = 1$

   d. the line through the points $(-2, 3)$ and $(3, 1)$

5. Let L be the line through $(2, 3)$ with direction vector $(3, -1)$. Find y such that $(-6, y)$ is on L.

6. Are there any lines in the plane that do not have a vector equation?

7. Give a general procedure for determining whether two vector equations

$$X = P + tD \quad \text{and} \quad X' = P' + tD'$$

describe the same line.

8. Consider the line with equation $X = (4, 3) + t(2, 1)$.

   a. Sketch the line.

   b. Now dilate all the points on the line by 2 with the origin as the center of the dilation. Sketch the result.

   c. Explain why this proves that the scaled set of points is also a line and is parallel to the original line.

9. Find a vector equation for the line through the points $(2, 3)$ and $(-1, 4)$.

10. A line has vector equation $X = P + tD$. Determine P and D if when $t = 0$, $X = (2, 3)$, and when $t = 1$, $X = (4, 5)$.

11. A line has vector equation $X = P + tD$. Determine P and D if when $t = 1$, $X = (2, -1)$, and when $t = 2$, $X = (4, 3)$.

12. **Take It Further** Consider the curve with vector equation $X = (1, 2) + t^3(2, -1)$.

    a. Find some points on this curve by using several values of t.

    b. Plot the curve. Describe the curve you graphed.

    c. Consider the curve given by the equation $X = (1, 2) + t^2(2, -1)$. Determine if this is the same set of points as $X = (1, 2) + t^3(2, -1)$.

13. Consider the two cars racing in the desert from the lesson. Recall that Car 1 starts at $(0, 0)$ and travels with velocity $(25, 40)$. That remains true in all the parts below, but the information on Car 2 changes.

    a. Suppose Car 2 starts at the same time at $(-10, -10)$ and travels with velocity vector $(30, 45)$. Determine if the paths of the cars intersect. Determine if the cars crash.

    b. Repeat part (a), except Car 2 starts at $(10, 10)$.

    c. Repeat part (a), except Car 2 has velocity $(30, 48)$.

    d. Repeat part (a), except Car 2 starts at $(30, 55)$ an hour later.

14. A vector equation of a line, $X = P + tD$, is unchanged in three dimensions. A line is still determined by a point and a direction but now X, P, D are triples. Let L' be the line through $(1, 2, 1)$ in the direction $(2, -1, 3)$. Find z such that $(5, 0, z)$ is on L'.

15. Two airplanes fly along straight lines. At time t airplane 1 is at $(75, 50, 25) + t(5, 10, 1)$ and airplane 2 is at $(60, 80, 34) + t(10, 5, -1)$.

    a. Determine if the airplanes collide.

    b. Determine if their flight paths intersect.

16. Which of the lines given by the following equations are the same? Explain.

    - $X = (1, -1) + t(3, 6)$
    - $X = (10, 17) + t(1, 3)$
    - $X = (10, 17) + s(1, 2)$

Go Online
www.successnetplus.com

The same is not true of Cartesian equations. Neither $y = mx + b$ nor $ax + by + cz = d$ is an equation of a line in three dimensions.

17. **Take It Further** You can think of a plane in three-space this way: You start at some base point P and move in each of two directions D_1 and D_2. Find a vector equation for a plane.

18. **Standardized Test Prep** Given U is the vector $(-3, 4)$ and V is the vector $(-1, 1)$. Which of the following points is on the line $U + tV$?

   A. $(0, 1)$ **B.** $(-3, -4)$ **C.** $(-4, -3)$ **D.** $(-1, 1)$

Maintain Your Skills

19. Consider the line with equation $X(t) = (1, 0) + t(-1, 1)$. Now consider X as a function of t.

   a. Explain why the graph of $X(t)$ is the line through $(1, 0)$ and $(0, 1)$.

   b. Using graph paper, plot the following points, labeling them with the names given here.

   $$X(0), X(1), X\left(\tfrac{1}{2}\right), X\left(\tfrac{1}{3}\right), X\left(\tfrac{2}{3}\right), X(2), X(3), X(-1)$$

> Writing *X(t)*, instead of just *X*, allows each point on the line to be identified with the value of the parameter for that point.

20. Consider the line with equation $Y(t) = (0, 1) + t(1, -1)$.

   a. Explain why this is the same line as in Exercise 19.

   b. Using graph paper, plot the following points, labeling them with the names given here.

   $$Y(0), Y(1), Y\left(\tfrac{1}{2}\right), Y\left(\tfrac{1}{3}\right), Y\left(\tfrac{2}{3}\right), Y(2), Y(3), Y(-1)$$

21. Let P and Q be two points in the plane. Explain where each of the following points is located relative to P and Q.

   a. $\tfrac{1}{2}P + \tfrac{1}{2}Q$ **b.** $\tfrac{1}{3}P + \tfrac{2}{3}Q$

   c. $\tfrac{2}{3}P + \tfrac{1}{3}Q$ **d.** $\tfrac{4}{5}P + \tfrac{1}{5}Q$

   e. $2P - Q$ **f.** $3P - 2Q$

> If you are having trouble, pick some sample points for *P* and *Q* and calculate the others.

Even though the cars' paths intersect, the cars arrived at different times, thus avoiding a collision.

In this investigation, you learned how to identify characteristics of vectors, add points and multiply them by any real number, and write a vector equation for any line on the coordinate plane. These questions will help you summarize what you have learned.

1. Use the points $A(-1, 5)$, $B(6, 2)$, and the origin O. What are the coordinates of M if $\overrightarrow{OM}$ is equivalent to $\overrightarrow{AB}$?

2. Use the points $A(-6, 8)$, $B(2, 7)$, $C(-3, 3.5)$, and $D(1, 3)$. Are $\overrightarrow{AB}$ and $\overrightarrow{CD}$ equivalent?

3. Use the points $A(-2, 1)$, $B(1, 6)$, $C(1, 1)$, and $D(7, 11)$. Compare $\overrightarrow{AB}$ and $\overrightarrow{CD}$.

4. Use the points $A(-1, -1)$ and $B(2, 3)$. Write coordinates for a point C such that $\overrightarrow{OC}$ is three times as long as $\overrightarrow{AB}$ and parallel to $\overrightarrow{AB}$.

5. Find a vector equation for the line through $A\left(\frac{2}{3}, 1\right)$ and $B(0, 4)$.

6. What are vectors?

7. How can you tell whether two vectors are equivalent?

8. Find a vector equation for the line through $A(1, 2)$ and $B(3, -4)$.

Vocabulary and Notation

In this investigation, you learned these terms and this symbol. Make sure you understand what each one means and how to use it.

• direction

• parametric equations

• parameter

By flying behind and slightly higher than another goose, a goose faces less wind resistance. In this way, it uses less energy to maintain its velocity vector.

Matrix Algebra

In *Matrix Algebra*, you will learn how to perform basic operations with matrices. You will explore and prove properties of matrix algebra. You will compare matrix properties to the properties of real numbers.

By the end of this investigation, you will be able to answer questions like these.

1. What is a dot product? How can you represent matrix multiplication using dot products?

2. What are some special cases in which $AB = BA$ is true for matrices A and B?

3. How can you solve this system of equations using matrix inverses? What is the solution?

$$x + 4y - z = -3$$
$$2x - 2y + z = 0$$
$$3x + y - 3z = -9$$

You will learn how to

- communicate and prove results about matrices, including the ideas of rows and columns and indices

- compute sums, differences, dot products, products, and inverses of matrices

- interpret and solve problems using matrix calculations

You will develop these habits and skills:

- Visualize an operation on a matrix as a product.

- Explore the algebraic structure of matrices and n-tuples.

- Reason deductively to prove properties about matrices or find counterexamples.

What is the sum of the different colors at each point on the cover?

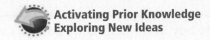

You can use tables to organize data.

For You to Explore

1. On the side of a box of cereal, there is a table that shows what percent of recommended daily food values are provided by 1 ounce of the cereal.

Daily Value

Carbohydrates	7%
Vitamin A	10%
Vitamin B$_{12}$	25%

Suppose for breakfast you eat 3 ounces of the cereal. Make your own personal table of the percent of your daily value you have met.

2. Cereal boxes usually give two columns in their daily percents table: one column for a standard serving of the cereal alone, and the other for the cereal and a standard amount of milk. Suppose the standard serving is 1 ounce of cereal, with or without one half cup of milk, and the table looks like this

	Cereal	Cereal With Milk
Carbohydrates	7%	9%
Vitamin A	10%	15%
Vitamin B$_{12}$	25%	35%

Make a bigger table with a column showing the percents for the one half cup of milk alone.

3. The weather bureau collects climate data for many U.S. cities. One set of data concerns cloudiness. Each day is classified as clear, partly cloudy, or cloudy. In an average year, Boston has 98 clear days and 164 cloudy days. On the other hand, Philadelphia has 93 clear days and 160 cloudy days, while San Francisco has 160 clear days and only 105 cloudy days.

Determine the average annual number of partly cloudy days in each of these cities. (Assume there are 365 days in a year.)

> Put the given information and the information you compute into a labeled table.

4. Return to the data in Problem 3. Suppose you want to determine the average number of clear, partly cloudy, and cloudy days for each of the three cities for

- two years
- the first half of the year (January to June)

Can you use the results of Problem 3 to calculate these numbers? If so, explain how. If not, explain why not.

5. The swim team buys swimsuits and goggles for its members. The team is going to buy 30 women's suits, 25 men's suits, and 55 pairs of goggles. The prices per item are $20 for a woman's suit, $15 for a man's, and $8 for a pair of goggles. You can display this information in a table.

	W	M	G
Number	30	25	55
Price ($)	20	15	8

What is the total amount the swim team will spend buying these things? Does the format of the table make it easy to describe the calculation?

6. The school cafeteria buys food wholesale. The following table shows a typical order.

	Beef	Pork	Chicken	Fish
Weight (lb)	200	50	250	100
Price ($/lb)	3.50	2.00	1.50	3.00

How much will the order cost?

Exercises *Practicing Habits of Mind*

On Your Own

7. The following table shows passenger car sales for various auto companies during a certain year.

Passenger Car Sales (millions of cars)

	Company A	Company B	Company C	Company D	Company E
Europe	0.4	0.2	0.2	0.2	1
United States	2	1.5	0.6	1	0.3
Asia	0.2	0.1	0.8	3.5	0.1

The table below shows the year's sales for other personal motor vehicles, including SUVs, vans, and light trucks.

Other Vehicle Sales (millions of vehicles)

	Company A	Company B	Company C	Company D	Company E
Europe	0.2	0.05	0.1	0.1	0.3
United States	2.6	1.8	0.8	1.2	0.1
Asia	0.1	0.05	0.5	1	0

Make a table of all personal motor vehicle sales for the year.

8. Here are tables of revenue (total money taken in) and expenditures (total money paid out) for the same auto companies during the same year.

Revenue (billions of dollars)

	Company A	Company B	Company C	Company D	Company E
Europe	18	7.5	9	10	38
United States	129	92.5	37	70	12
Asia	8	4.5	40	131	3

Expenditures (billions of dollars)

	Company A	Company B	Company C	Company D	Company E
Europe	17	7	9	9	32
United States	127	93	35	67	12
Asia	9	5	32	120	4

a. Make a table for profit (revenues minus expenditures).

b. For each company, calculate the total profit for all regions combined.

c. For each region of the world, calculate the total profit of all the companies combined.

Habits of Mind

Make strategic choices. For parts (b) and (c), what is a good way to display the results? In terms of the table, what are you doing?

9. Use the first set of data from Exercise 7.

   a. Suppose experts predict that sales of passenger cars will increase across the board by 5% in the following year. Make a table of predicted passenger car sales for the following year. How did you get it?

   b. Suppose it turns out that only Company D's sales increased by 5%. Company B's sales increased 3%, Company E's sales 2%, and the others had no change. Make a table for the actual sales. How did you get it?

   c. Suppose it turned out that growth is regional: All companies had 6% growth in Asia, but only 1% growth in the U.S., and a 1% decline in Europe. Make a table for the actual sales. How did you get it?

10. A local bakery has four trucks of different sizes. Their gas tanks hold different amounts of gas, and they get different miles per gallon, as shown in the table below.

	Trucks			
Tank Size (gal)	15	18	20	25
mi/gal	20	18	12	15

   If the bakery fills up all the tanks, how many miles of driving can it get from its fleet of trucks?

11. Return to the swim team from Problem 5. That table was just for the varsity squad. The team also buys suits and goggles for the JV squad at the same prices. These tables present the data a somewhat different way.

	W	M	G
Varsity Numbers	30	25	55
JV Numbers	25	22	47

20
15
8

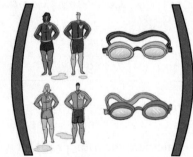

   a. What is the total amount the swim team will spend buying these things? Does the format of the tables make it easy to describe the calculation?

   b. There are at least two methods to calculate the answer to part (a). You can compute the cost for varsity and JV separately, or you can add the numbers in each category (women's suits, men's suits, goggles) first. Repeat part (a) using each method. Which method feels like less work? Explain.

For the matrices in Exercises 12 and 13, do parts (a)–(d).

a. Suppose you had to describe the matrix to a friend over the phone. How would you do it?

b. Write down or describe a 4×4 matrix that follows the same pattern as the given matrix.

c. Repeat part (b), but describe a 10×12 matrix.

d. You may have used many words to describe the general pattern in parts (a), (b), and (c). Can you think of a way to use symbols to be just as precise without as much explanation?

12. $M = \begin{pmatrix} 1 & 2 & 3 \\ 2 & 3 & 4 \\ 3 & 4 & 5 \end{pmatrix}$ **13.** $N = \begin{pmatrix} 1 & 1 & 1 \\ 2 & 4 & 8 \\ 3 & 9 & 27 \end{pmatrix}$

14. Consider the matrix below.

$$I = \begin{pmatrix} 1 & 0 & 0 \\ 0 & 1 & 0 \\ 0 & 0 & 1 \end{pmatrix}$$

This is the 3×3 identity matrix.

a. Suppose you had to describe this matrix to a friend over the phone. How would you do it?

b. Write down or describe a 6×6 matrix that follows the same pattern as the one you described for I.

c. If n is an unknown positive integer, how would you describe an $n \times n$ matrix with the same pattern?

15. Consider this 1×20 matrix.

$$A = (10 \quad 7 \quad 4 \quad 1 \quad -2 \quad -5 \quad \dots)$$

a. What might be the last entry in the matrix? Explain.

b. How would you describe this matrix to a friend without showing it? Can you do this with symbols?

c. **Take It Further** Now consider this 1×20 matrix.

$$B = (2 \quad 4 \quad 6 \quad 8 \quad \dots)$$

Suppose you wanted to combine these two matrices in the same way you combined the two rows in Problem 5. How would you describe to a friend what you need to do without showing the calculations? Can you do this with symbols?

Basic Matrix Operations— Addition, Subtraction, and Scalar Multiplication

You call the data displays in Lesson H.06 tables, or sometimes two-way tables, but to mathematicians they are just matrices with labels! Indeed, you can show such tables with all sorts of formatting.

Passenger Car Sales (millions of cars)

	Company A	Company B	Company C	Company D	Company E
Europe	0.4	0.2	0.2	0.2	1
United States	2	1.5	0.6	1	0.3
Asia	0.2	0.1	0.8	3.5	0.1

But the tables are still just matrices. So you can write them as such.

$$\begin{pmatrix} 0.4 & 0.2 & 0.2 & 0.2 & 1 \\ 2 & 1.5 & 0.6 & 1 & 0.3 \\ 0.2 & 0.1 & 0.8 & 3.5 & 0.1 \end{pmatrix}$$

Or, if it is helpful, you can keep the labels.

$$\begin{matrix} & A & B & C & D & E \\ \text{Europe} & \begin{pmatrix} 0.4 & 0.2 & 0.2 & 0.2 & 1 \\ \text{U.S.} & 2 & 1.5 & 0.6 & 1 & 0.3 \\ \text{Asia} & 0.2 & 0.1 & 0.8 & 3.5 & 0.1 \end{pmatrix} \end{matrix}$$

Developing Habits of Mind

Look for relationships. The tables help organize calculations people want to do. This means useful mathematical definitions are lurking! Try to identify the kinds of calculations that seem to be useful. See if you can define them for matrices independent of their particular use. Then you probably have concepts that will be useful in many places you have not yet imagined.

Consider Exercise 7 in Lesson H.06, where you combined tables of passenger car sales with other vehicle sales to get total sales of all personal motor vehicles. Abstractly, what did you do? You started with two matrices.

$$\begin{pmatrix} 0.4 & 0.2 & 0.2 & 0.2 & 1 \\ 2 & 1.5 & 0.6 & 1 & 0.3 \\ 0.2 & 0.1 & 0.8 & 3.5 & 0.1 \end{pmatrix} \text{ and } \begin{pmatrix} 0.2 & 0.05 & 0.1 & 0.1 & 0.3 \\ 2.6 & 1.8 & 0.8 & 1.2 & 0.1 \\ 0.1 & 0.05 & 0.5 & 1 & 0 \end{pmatrix}$$

You got the matrix below.

$$\begin{pmatrix} 0.6 & 0.25 & 0.3 & 0.3 & 1.3 \\ 4.6 & 3.3 & 1.4 & 2.2 & 0.4 \\ 0.3 & 0.15 & 1.3 & 4.5 & 0.1 \end{pmatrix}$$

So, mathematically, you took two matrices of the same size and added the corresponding entries. The result was another matrix of the same size.

To make an algebra out of this, you need to use symbols. The sum $A + B$ of matrices A and B is the matrix you get by adding the corresponding entries.

> The entries of a matrix are the numbers inside it.

For Discussion

1. Consider Exercise 8 from Lesson H.06. Define another matrix operation based on this exercise.

Exercise 9a in Lesson H.06 suggests another operation that takes one matrix and returns another matrix of the same size. You increase each entry by 5%. You can represent a percent increase as multiplication, in this case by 1.05. Since each entry of the matrix is multiplied by 1.05, the matrix is scaled. If you call the original matrix A, you can call the result $1.05A$. The process is **scalar multiplication.**

Scalar is another word for a number that you use when working with matrices. The product kA, where k is a number and A is a matrix, is another matrix you can get from A by multiplying each of its entries by k.

For You to Do

2. Use the matrices below.

$$A = \begin{pmatrix} 1 & 2 & 3 \\ 4 & 5 & 6 \end{pmatrix} \qquad B = \begin{pmatrix} 1 & 0 & 1 \\ 0 & -1 & 0 \end{pmatrix} \qquad C = \begin{pmatrix} 1 & 3 \\ 2 & 4 \end{pmatrix}$$

Compute $A + B$, $A - B$, $A + C$, $2A$, and $(-1)A$. Some of these expressions may be undefined.

Developing Habits of Mind

Detect the key characteristics. The definition of $A + B$ talks about "corresponding entries." In some cases, this may be clear. In other cases, such as in the definition of matrix multiplication, "corresponding entries" may not be clear. While it may be evident that you cannot add A and C in For You to Do Problem 2, shouldn't a good definition say something about that instead of leaving it for you to figure out? To address such clarity issues, you need more notation.

First, the size of matrix A is the number of its rows and its columns. Matrices A and B are the same size if they both have the same number of rows, m, and the same number of columns, n. More briefly, A and B are the same size if they are both $m \times n$. Two matrices must be the same size in order for you to add or subtract them.

Second, you need a way to talk about specific entries. Entries in a matrix need two coordinates—their row number and their column number. These numbers are listed as subscripts, called indices. So a 3×4 matrix A might be

The singular of *indices* is *index*.

$$A = \begin{pmatrix} a_{11} & a_{12} & a_{13} & a_{14} \\ a_{21} & a_{22} & a_{23} & a_{24} \\ a_{31} & a_{32} & a_{33} & a_{34} \end{pmatrix}$$

The first number in the subscript is the row number and the second is the column number. So, more generally, an $m \times n$ matrix could be

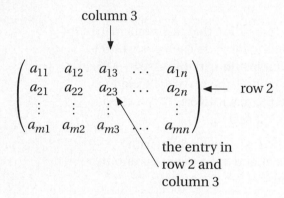

column 3

row 2

the entry in row 2 and column 3

For Discussion

3. Indices are like coordinates, in a way. How are they similar to coordinates? How are they different?

With this index notation comes a nice shorthand. You can write

Let $A = (a_{ij})$.

This notation tells us two things:

- The entries of A will all be a-something.

- For this matrix, i will be the index of the rows and j will be the index of the columns. That is, you will use i when referring to a typical row of A and j when referring to a typical column.

With this notation, you can indicate the size of A at the same time. You can write

Let A be the 3×5 matrix (a_{pq}).

or

Let $A = (a_{pq})$, $p = 1, 2, 3$, and $q = 1, 2, 3, 4, 5$.

You do not always have to use *i* and *j* as your indices. Sometimes there is a good reason not to.

For You to Do

4. Define $B = (b_{ij})$ to be the 3×2 matrix in which $b_{ij} = i^j$. Explain why this means that B is the matrix below.

$$B = \begin{pmatrix} 1 & 1 \\ 2 & 4 \\ 3 & 9 \end{pmatrix}$$

So what good is all this? The subscript notation is good for at least two reasons. First, it allows you to define matrices, even very big ones, without listing all the entries. Second, it allows you to give precise definitions of matrix operations such as sum and scalar product.

> For instance, with this notation you can feed large matrices into calculators and computers without a huge number of keystrokes.

Definition

If $A = (a_{ij})$ and $B = (b_{ij})$ are both $m \times n$ matrices, then their sum $A + B$ is defined to be the $m \times n$ matrix with ij entry $a_{ij} + b_{ij}$. In other words, if $C = A + B$, then $c_{ij} = a_{ij} + b_{ij}$.

In such definitions, it is understood that any statement about entry ij is true for every such entry, but you can also be explicit and say $c_{ij} = a_{ij} + b_{ij}$ for all i from 1 to m and all j from 1 to n.

$$c_{ij} = a_{ij} + b_{ij}, \; i = 1, 2, \ldots, m \text{ and } j = 1, 2, \ldots, n$$

For You to Do

5. Give similarly precise definitions for $A - B$ and kA.

Exercises Practicing Habits of Mind

Check Your Understanding

1. Identify each value for the matrix A.

$$A = (a_{ij}) = \begin{pmatrix} 1 & 2 & 3 \\ 4 & 5 & 6 \end{pmatrix}$$

a. the size of A **b.** a_{12} **c.** a_{21}

d. a_{23} **e.** a_{32}

2. Let $E = (e_{pq})$ with $e_{pq} = p^2 + 2^q$.

   a. Write out E if it is 4×1.   **b.** Write out E if it is 1×4.

3. Come up with formulas for the entries of each matrix.

   a. $A = \begin{pmatrix} 2 & 3 & 4 \\ 3 & 4 & 5 \end{pmatrix}$ **b.** $B = \begin{pmatrix} 1 & 2 & 3 \\ 3 & 4 & 5 \end{pmatrix}$ **c.** $C = \begin{pmatrix} 1 & 2 & 3 & 4 \\ 4 & 9 & 16 & 25 \end{pmatrix}$

4. Suppose you want to add single-row matrices such as $(1, 2, 3, 4, 5)$ and $(1, 4, 9, 16, 25)$. You do not need two indices to define addition.

   a. Give a definition of $A + B$ for single-row matrices.

   b. Give a definition of $A - B$ for single-row matrices.

   c. Give a definition of scalar multiplication for single-row matrices.

> Of course, the same approach works for single-column matrices.

5. On the side of a box of cereal, there is a table that shows what percent of recommended daily food values are provided by 1 ounce of the cereal.

      Carbohydrates 7%   Vitamin A 10%   Vitamin B_{12} 25%

If you eat 3 ounces, what percents do you get? What matrix and what matrix operation are involved in your calculation?

6. A mathematics teacher keeps a record of each student's points on homework and points on tests. For three students, here are the homework points and test points for the first and second marking periods.

> Of course, you can do this calculation without thinking about matrices. The point here is to illustrate that matrices are everywhere and, in some sense, you have been using them all your life.

First Marking Period Points

	Tony	Sasha	Derman
Homework	127	143	107
Tests	181	170	165

Second Marking Period Points

	Tony	Sasha	Derman
Homework	144	139	126
Tests	184	192	175

The teacher now wants to compute the homework points and test points for both marking periods combined. Help the teacher and do the computations. What matrix operation do you use?

7. Another mathematics teacher keeps records as percents. For three students, here are the homework percents and test percents for the first and second marking periods.

> Tony, Sasha, and Derman take more than one mathematics course.

First Marking Period Percents

	Sasha	Tony	Derman
Homework	94	98	85
Tests	95	91	83

Second Marking Period Percents

	Sasha	Tony	Derman
Homework	95	96	89
Tests	94	92	85

The teacher now wants to compute the homework percents and test percents for both marking periods combined. Can you compute this information from these tables? Explain.

On Your Own

8. Suppose $D = (d_{ij})$ is 3×3 and $d_{ij} = 2j$. Write out D.

9. Define the 2×4 matrix $C = (c_{jk})$ as $c_{jk} = k^j$. Write out C.

10. Define a matrix $M = (m_{ij})$ as $m_{ij} = \begin{cases} 1 & \text{if } i = j \\ 0 & \text{otherwise} \end{cases}$
    For each size, write out the matrix M.

    > This is your first example of a case statement defining a matrix. This type of definition is quite common.

    a. 4×4 **b.** 2×2 **c.** 4×3

11. **Standardized Test Prep** Define $D = (d_{jk})$ to be the 3×3 matrix in which $d_{jk} = (-j)^{(j+k)}$. Define $F = (f_{jk})$ to be the 3×3 matrix in which $f_{jk} = (2)^{(j-k)}$. If $G = D + F$, which is the entry in the second column of the third row of G?

    A. -241 **B.** -31.5 **C.** 85   **D.** 730

12. In Exercise 7 of Lesson H.06, you got one table about auto sales from two others. Viewing the tables as matrices, what matrix operation did you use?

13. In Exercise 8 of Lesson H.06, you got one table about auto industry finances from two others. Viewing the tables as matrices, what matrix operation did you use?

14. In Problem 4 of Lesson H.06, you got one table about weather from another. Viewing the tables as matrices, what matrix operation did you use?

Go Online
www.successnetplus.com

15. For three baseball players, Andre, Bobby, and Carlos, here are the RBIs and BAs for the first half and the second half of last season.

RBI is the total number of runs batted in. BA, or batting average, is the ratio $\frac{\text{total hits}}{\text{total at bats}}$.

First Half of Season

	A	B	C
RBI	31	37	42
BA	.263	.294	.283

Second Half of Season

	A	B	C
RBI	26	36	53
BA	.243	.291	.314

Suppose you want to know their RBIs and BAs for the entire season. Can you get them from these tables? Explain.

Maintain Your Skills

16. Suppose $z = 2y_1 + 5y_2$ and $\begin{aligned} y_1 &= 3x \\ y_2 &= -x \end{aligned}$

Express z in terms of x.

17. Suppose $z = 2y_1 + 5y_2 - 3y_3$ and $\begin{aligned} y_1 &= 3x \\ y_2 &= -x \\ y_3 &= 4x \end{aligned}$

Express z in terms of x. Is there a common pattern in this exercise and in Exercise 16? Explain.

18. Suppose again that $z = 2y_1 + 5y_2 - 3y_3$, but now $y_1 = 3$, $y_2 = -1$, and $y_3 = 4$. Evaluate z.

19. On a shopping spree in Europe, Bob spends 100 pounds in England, 150 euros in France, and 200 francs in Switzerland. At the time, a pound is worth \$1.80, a euro is worth \$1.25 and a Swiss franc is worth \$.75.

a. In dollars, how much does Bob spend?

b. How does this exercise connect to Exercises 16–18?

20. Suppose $z = a_1y_1 + a_2y_2 + a_3y_3$ and $\begin{aligned} y_1 &= b_1x \\ y_2 &= b_2x \\ y_3 &= b_3x \end{aligned}$

Express z in terms of x.

21. Suppose $\begin{aligned} z &= a_1y_1 + a_2y_2 + a_3y_3 \\ w &= b_1y_1 + b_2y_2 + b_3y_3 \end{aligned}$ and $\begin{aligned} y_1 &= c_1x \\ y_2 &= c_2x \\ y_3 &= c_3x \end{aligned}$

Express the matrix $\begin{pmatrix} z \\ w \end{pmatrix}$ in terms of x.

Habits of Mind

Look for relationships. Exercise 20 is meant to give you a general statement of something you have done several times already in this investigation. What is it?

H.08 Dot Products

The exercises in the Maintain Your Skills section in Lesson H.07 led to this general result in Exercise 20.

If

$$y_1 = b_1 x$$
$$z = a_1 y_1 + a_2 y_2 + b_3 y_3 \quad \text{and} \quad y_2 = b_2 x$$
$$y_3 = b_3 x$$

then

$$z = (a_1 b_1 + a_2 b_2 + a_3 b_3) x$$

When there are just two intermediate variables y_1 and y_2, the result is $z = (a_1 b_1 + a_2 b_2) x$. (This is the result in Exercise 16. What are the values of a_1, a_2, b_1, and b_2 there?)

If there are n intermediate variables y_1 through y_n, then the result is

$$z = (a_1 b_1 + a_2 b_2 + \cdots + a_{n-1} b_{n-1} + a_n b_n) x$$

So what should you make of all this? You can write some definitions!

First, a string of n numbers, say $(a_1, a_2, \ldots, a_n)$, is an **_n_-tuple**. Second, given two n-tuples $A = (a_1, a_2, \ldots, a_n)$ and $B = (b_1, b_2, \ldots, b_n)$, define their **dot product** $A \cdot B$ to be the number

$$a_1 b_1 + a_2 b_2 + \cdots + a_n b_n$$

This is exactly the expression you got for the coefficient of x in Exercise 20, with $n = 3$. Dot products have plenty of uses, as you will soon see. In fact, you have already seen dot products in some word problems, such as Exercise 19 in Lesson H.07.

For You to Do

Find each dot product, or explain why the calculation does not make sense.

1. $(1, 2) \cdot (-3, 4)$

2. $(2, 3) \cdot (-3, 2)$

3. $(1, 0, -1, 2) \cdot (3, 2, 1, x)$

4. $(1, 2) \cdot (2, -3, 4)$

Remember...

The most common name mathematicians use for an n-tuple is _vector_. The algebra of n-tuples is _vector algebra_. However, you are used to thinking of vectors as geometric objects—ordered pairs of points in a coordinate system.

Note that when $n = 2$, you have another geometric interpretation of n-tuples as points on the plane or as complex numbers represented as points on the complex plane. Also, when $n = 2$, you usually say "ordered pair" instead of "2-tuple."

You can view n-tuples as special thin matrices, either single rows or single columns, whichever seems more appropriate. For instance, the format of Exercise 20 suggests that you write the following.

$$\begin{pmatrix} y_1 \\ y_2 \\ y_3 \end{pmatrix} = \begin{pmatrix} b_1 \\ b_2 \\ b_3 \end{pmatrix} x$$

Do you see how viewing (y_1, y_2, y_3) as a matrix allows you to regard the x as a scalar and put it on the outside? In Exercise 20, if you regard $A = (a_1, a_2, a_3)$ as a row, then the expression $a_1b_1 + a_2b_2 + a_3b_3$ is the dot product of a row and a column. For dot products, it does not matter whether you think of the n-tuples as rows or as columns, so long as they both have the same number of elements.

When you multiply two n-tuples together, you do not get another n-tuple, you get a number. Usually, when you combine two things, you get the same sort of thing. For example, when you add two matrices, you get a matrix. When you multiply two complex numbers, you get a complex number. However, this is not the case for dot products.

> Not only do dot products show up in several places in this chapter, but they will show up in later math courses.

For You to Do

Do each set of computations. For each set, what is the relationship? How can you express the pattern?

5. $(1, 2, 3) \cdot (4, 5, 6)$ and $(4, 5, 6) \cdot (1, 2, 3)$

6. $(1, 0, 2) \cdot (x(1, -2, 2))$, $(x(1, 0, 2)) \cdot (1, -1, 2)$, and $x((1, 0, 2) \cdot (1, -1, 2))$

7. $(2, 3, 4) \cdot (c_1, c_2, c_3) + (3, 4, 5) \cdot (c_1, c_2, c_3)$ and $((2, 3, 4) + (3, 4, 5)) \cdot (c_1, c_2, c_3)$

Go back to the equations from Exercise 20 of Lesson H.07. You can think of this in terms of the following matrices.

$$A = (a_1, a_2, a_3)$$
$$B = (b_1, b_2, b_3)$$
$$Y = (y_1, y_2, y_3)$$

The exercise says

$$z = A \cdot Y, \ Y = Bx, \text{ and } z = A \cdot (Bx)$$

The solution to Exercise 20 is $z = (a_1 b_1 + a_2 b_2 + a_3 b_3)x$, which you can write as

$$z = (A \cdot B)x$$

So in this case, $A \cdot (Bx) = (A \cdot B)x$. A similar equality showed up in Problem 6 above.

> You can also write $x(A \cdot B)$. Since both x and $(A \cdot B)$ are numbers, they commute.

Is the following statement a rule about dot products?

$$(kA) \cdot B = A \cdot (kB) = (A \cdot B)k$$

Yes, this is a rule, or theorem, about dot products. And it is easy to remember because it looks similar to one of the basic rules of algebra. Although, if it is so familiar, what is left to prove? In the following dialog, Tony and Sasha grapple with some of these basic rules. In the exercises, you will discover and explain several other basic rules about n-tuples and dot products.

Tony and Sasha have been asked to justify, or find counterexamples to, two proposed rules for n-tuples.

$$(kA) \cdot B = k(A \cdot B) \text{ and } A + B = B + A$$

Tony Hey, Sasha, what's there to show? This is just basic algebra. Everybody knows that $(ka)b = k(ab)$ and $a + b = b + a$. These are just the basic rules of associativity and commutativity.

Sasha Yes, we already know them for real-number addition and multiplication, but here we have *n*-tuples and dot products.

Tony Ugh! If all the rules are the same and we know them, I don't see why we should have to show them again.

Sasha Well, they aren't really the same, because *n*-tuples aren't numbers, so their sum isn't quite a number sum. Maybe the rules aren't even true. Though I hope they are, because their form is so familiar— something we would want to use. So how should we start?

Tony I still don't get it. What do you mean that the sum isn't a number sum?

Sasha Well, when we say $a + b = b + a$ for numbers, we are saying $3 + 7 = 7 + 3$ and old stuff like that. But when we say $A + B = B + A$ for *n*-tuples, we are saying $(1, 2, 3) + (2, 4, 1) = (2, 4, 1) + (1, 2, 3)$ and new stuff like that. This is a new use of the plus sign, so we've got to think about whether it's right. So the first issue is, what does the plus sign mean for *n*-tuples? Our teacher never really told us.

Tony If they're just thin matrices, then it should be the same meaning as for matrices: Add corresponding entries.

Sasha So A and B would have to be the same size, say $1 \times n$, and we could write

$$A = (a_1, a_2, \ldots, a_n)$$
$$B = (b_1, b_2, \ldots, b_n)$$

Those old indices again, but only one at a time, thank goodness.

Tony $A + B$ is $(a_1 + b_1, a_2 + b_2, \ldots)$. Each entry is $a_i + b_i$.

Sasha Hey, each entry of $B + A$ is $b_i + a_i$. I think we're done, because $a_i + b_i = b_i + a_i$.

Tony No way! You're going in circles. You're saying that A and B commute because a_i and b_i commute.

Sasha   No, I'm not going in circles, because A and B are n-tuples and a_i and b_i are numbers. We already know that numbers commute. We've reduced it to the previous case!

Tony   Okay, I see what you mean. I guess they are different. It still feels like we're just doing the same thing, but let's go on to the other rule.

Sasha   Well, I see an important difference here. Both sides of $(kA) \cdot B = k(A \cdot B)$ are numbers. Both sides of $A + B = B + A$ are thin matrices.

Tony   Good news. To show that two matrices are equal, we had to show that they were equal entry by entry. Now we just have two numbers that have to be equal.

Sasha   Yeah, but each number is constructed in a complicated way. On the left, $(kA) \cdot B$, we start with A. Suppose $A = (a_1, a_2, a_3)$. Then we multiply by some number k. Then we dot with some other 3-tuple B. Let's say $B = (b_1, b_2, b_3)$.

Tony   Who says these vectors are 3-tuples?

Sasha   No one, but if we see what is going on for 3-tuples, maybe the general pattern won't be much different. Try it. You compute $(kA) \cdot B$.

Tony   All right. $kA = (ka_1, ka_2, ka_3)$, so then $(kA) \cdot B$ would be

$$(ka_1)b_1 + (ka_2)b_2 + (ka_3)b_3$$

Sasha   Thanks. Now the right side of the rule, $k(A \cdot B)$, is

$$k(a_1b_1 + a_2b_2 + a_3b_3)$$

So are the two sides the same or not?

Go Online
www.successnetplus.com

For Discussion

8. Are the two expressions that Tony and Sasha found actually the same?

Exercises *Practicing Habits of Mind*

Check Your Understanding

1. There were several dot-product exercises in Lesson H.06—you just did not know they were dot products. Which exercises involved dot products? Explain.

2. Find each dot product.

   a. $(1, 2, 3) \cdot (4, 5, 6)$

   b. $(4, 5, 6) \cdot (1, 2, 3)$

   c. $(1, 2, 3) \cdot \begin{pmatrix} 4 \\ 5 \\ 6 \end{pmatrix}$

   d. $\begin{pmatrix} 3 \\ 2 \\ 1 \end{pmatrix} \cdot \begin{pmatrix} 6 \\ 5 \\ 4 \end{pmatrix}$

   e. $\begin{pmatrix} 1 \\ 2 \\ 3 \end{pmatrix} \cdot (4, 5, 6)$

   f. $(1, 2) \cdot (3, 4, 5)$

3. Find each dot product.

   a. $(3, 4) \cdot (3, 4)$

   b. $(a, b) \cdot (a, b)$

   c. $(2, 3, 4) \cdot (2, 3, 4)$

4. Find an n-tuple Z that satisfies each equation.

   a. $(1, 2) + Z = (1, 2)$

   b. $(x, y) + Z = (x, y)$

   c. $(1, 2, -3, \pi) + Z = (1, 2, -3, \pi)$

5. Generalize from Exercise 4. Show that for each n-tuple X, there is another n-tuple Z such that $X + Z = X$.

6. **a.** Compute $(1, 0, 1) \cdot (x, y, z) + (0, 2, 1) \cdot (x, y, z) - (1, 2, 2) \cdot (x, y, z)$.

   b. Without actually computing any dot product, explain why the answer to part (a) has to be 0.

   > Not surprisingly, you call such a Z a zero.

7. The Distributive Property of dot products says

   $$A \cdot (B \pm C) = A \cdot B \pm A \cdot C$$

   and

   $$(A \pm B) \cdot C = A \cdot C \pm B \cdot C$$

   That is, the dot product distributes over n-tuple addition and subtraction. You worked out a specific example of this property in Problem 5 in the For You to Do section.

   Assuming this property, show that

   $$(A + B) \cdot (A + B) = A \cdot A + 2A \cdot B + B \cdot B$$

   > The sign $\pm$ means "plus or minus." When it appears more than once in an equation, you must make the same choice in every case. For instance, in the equation to the left, either use plus both times or use minus both times.

8. Again assuming the Distributive Property, show that

$$(A + B) \cdot (A - B) = A \cdot A - B \cdot B$$

9. Show that, for all n-tuples X (actually, for all matrices X), $(-1)X = -X$. While this should be true if matrix algebra is to behave properly, note that it is not automatically true, because the two sides mean entirely different things. The left side means the result of multiplying X by the scalar -1. The right side means whatever n-tuple W satisfies $X + W = (0, 0, \dots)$.

10. Use Exercise 9 to show that $A \cdot (-B) = -(A \cdot B) = (-A) \cdot B$ is a special case of the general rule $A \cdot (kB) = k(A \cdot B) = (kA) \cdot B$.

On Your Own

11. **Standardized Test Prep** Find the following dot product.

$$(3, -5, 4) \cdot (2, 6, 7)$$

A. $(5, 1, 11)$ **B.** $(6, -30, 28)$ **C.** 4 **D.** 17

12. Find each dot product.

     a. $(1, 0, 0) \cdot (x, y, z)$ **b.** $(0, 1, 0) \cdot (x, y, z)$ **c.** $(x, y, z) \cdot (0, 0, 1)$

13. Is there an associative property for dot products? That is, is the statement below true? Explain.

$$A \cdot (B \cdot C) = (A \cdot B) \cdot C$$

14. In parts (a)–(d), find each dot product.

     a. $(3, 4) \cdot (4, -3)$ **b.** $(3, 4) \cdot (-4, 3)$

     c. $(3, 4) \cdot (8, -6)$ **d.** $(a, b) \cdot (b, -a)$

15. **Take It Further** For parts (a)–(d) of Exercise 14, represent each ordered pair as a point on the plane and draw the vectors from the origin to those points. Do you notice anything? Pick some other pairs of ordered pairs, compute their dot products, and draw the associated vectors. Report on your findings.

16. **a.** Find A such that $A \cdot (1, 2) = 5$.

     b. Check that this same A satisfies $A \cdot (3, 6) = 15$.

     c. Find B such that $B \cdot (2, 4) = 10$.

     d. **Take It Further** Classify all A such that $A \cdot (1, 2) = 5$.

Go Online
www.successnetplus.com

17. The dot product satisfies the commutative property:

$$A \cdot B = B \cdot A$$

Explain why. Perhaps you can begin with $A = (a_1, a_2)$ and $B = (b_1, b_2)$ and work up to $A = (a_1, a_2, \ldots, a_n)$ and $B = (b_1, b_2, \ldots, b_n)$.

18. Find an n-tuple W that satisfies each equation.

a. $(1, 2) + W = (0, 0)$

b. $(x, y) + W = 0$

c. $(1, 2, -3, \pi) + W = 0$

19. Every number x has an additive inverse $-x$, which satisfies the property $x + (-x) = 0$. Generalize from Exercise 18 to define an additive inverse $-X$ for every n-tuple X. Show that $-X$ exists for every X. That is, for $X = (x_1, x_2, \ldots, x_n)$, find the coordinates of $-X$.

20. Show that the dot product distributes over n-tuple addition and subtraction.

$$A \cdot (B \pm C) = A \cdot B \pm A \cdot C$$

21. For real-number multiplication, there is an inverse, so you can solve $ax = b$ for x by multiplying both sides by a^{-1} to get $x = a^{-1}b$, assuming that $a \neq 0$, of course. Do n-tuples have dot-product inverses? That is, can you solve the equation $A \cdot X = b$ by taking the dot product with some n-tuple A^{-1}? Explain.

22. Write About It To what extent are dot-product rules the same as number rules? Is there a pattern to which rules are the same and which are not?

Maintain Your Skills

23. Consider the linear system below. Show how to represent z_1 and z_2 as a dot product using the vector $Y = (y_1, y_2, y_3)$.

$$z_1 = 2y_1 + 3y_2 + 4y_3$$
$$z_2 = 3y_1 - 2y_2 + 5y_3$$

24. Use the equations below.

$$z_1 = 2y_1 + 5y_2 - 3y_3 \qquad \text{and} \qquad \begin{aligned} y_1 &= 3x \\ y_2 &= -x \\ y_3 &= 4x \end{aligned}$$
$$z_2 = 3y_1 - y_2 + y_3$$

Express z_1 and z_2 in terms of x. What is the common pattern in this exercise and in Exercises 16 and 17 of Lesson H.07? Can you use dot products to do this exercise? Explain.

25. Suppose $a = 3p + 7q$ and $\begin{aligned} p &= 2x - 3y \\ q &= 5x + 4y \end{aligned}$

Express a in terms of x and y. Can you express your calculation using dot products? Explain.

26. Suppose $\begin{aligned} a &= 3p + 7q \\ b &= p - 2q \end{aligned}$ and $\begin{aligned} p &= 2x - 3y \\ q &= 5x + 4y \end{aligned}$

Express a and b in terms of x and y. Look for dot products again.

27. Exercise 24 gave you two sets of equations and asked you to find a third set by substitution. Suppose you represent each given set of equations with its matrix of coefficients. Putting the two matrices side by side, they are

$$\begin{pmatrix} 2 & 5 & -3 \\ 3 & -1 & 1 \end{pmatrix} \begin{pmatrix} 3 \\ -1 \\ 4 \end{pmatrix}$$

The solution to Exercise 24 is the set of equations

$$\begin{aligned} z_1 &= -11x \\ z_2 &= 14x \end{aligned}$$

You can represent this solution with the matrix

$$\begin{pmatrix} -11 \\ 14 \end{pmatrix}$$

Can you explain a method for getting the final matrix directly from the two given matrices?

28. Exercise 25 gave you two sets of equations and asked you to find another equation by substitution. Suppose you represent each given set of equations with its matrix of coefficients. Putting the two matrices side by side, they are

$$(3 \quad 7) \begin{pmatrix} 2 & -3 \\ 5 & 4 \end{pmatrix}$$

The resulting equation was $a = 41x + 19y$, so the resulting matrix is the row matrix (41 19). Can you explain a method for getting this row matrix directly from the two given matrices?

29. Exercise 26 gave you two sets of equations and asked you to find a third set by substitution. Suppose you represent each given set of equations with its matrix of coefficients. Putting the two matrices side by side, they are

$$\begin{pmatrix} 3 & 7 \\ 1 & -2 \end{pmatrix} \begin{pmatrix} 2 & -3 \\ 5 & 4 \end{pmatrix}$$

a. Write the matrix of coefficients of the resulting set of equations.

b. Can you explain a method for getting the final matrix directly from the two given matrices? Try to be as general as you can.

Matrix addition is defined by adding corresponding entries. It might make sense to define *matrix multiplication* the same way, entry-wise. It would be easy, but it is not done that way. Why not? A different, much less obvious definition turns out to be much more valuable. You will begin to see how valuable it is in this lesson, and you will see even more uses later as the chapter continues. Of course, historically it took time for mathematicians to realize which definition would be the most useful.

The "correct" definition grew out of the problem of linear substitutions. All the Maintain Your Skills exercises in the last two lessons were about linear substitutions. Consider Exercise 25 from Lesson H.08. The variables a and b are linear in p and q. That is, a and b are both sums of multiples of p and q. There are no squares, square roots, exponentials, or constant terms. Moreover, the variables p and q are linear in x and y. What are a and b when expressed directly in terms of x and y? In Exercise 25, you substituted the expressions for p and q into the equations for a and b and got the answer. In particular, a and b turned out to be linear in x and y as well. And the computation involved dot products. For instance, in Exercise 25, a turned out to equal $41x + 19y$, where

$$41 = (3, 7) \cdot (2, 5) \quad \text{and} \quad 19 = (3, 7) \cdot (-3, 4)$$

Another way to say this is to say a and b are **linear combinations** of p and q.

If linear substitutions occurred rarely, then each time you could do the work from scratch, as in Exercise 25. But, in fact, linear substitutions occur quite frequently in applications (see Example 2), so it is worth finding a time saver. Exercise 28 from Lesson H.08 suggests how. Just as you can speed up solving linear systems by writing matrices instead of equations, you can speed up substitutions by getting the final matrix directly from the two original matrices, as in Exercise 28. The method is to dot rows of the first matrix with columns of the second. This result is defined to be the matrix product.

For instance, continuing with Exercise 25, the matrices associated with the two sets of equations (a and b in terms of p and q and then p and q in terms of x and y) are

$$A = \begin{pmatrix} 3 & 7 \\ 1 & -2 \end{pmatrix} \quad \text{and} \quad B = \begin{pmatrix} 2 & -3 \\ 5 & 4 \end{pmatrix}$$

The matrix associated with the resulting set of equations (a and b in terms of x and y) is

$$C = \begin{pmatrix} 41 & 19 \\ -8 & -11 \end{pmatrix}$$

Note that the dot product of the first row of A with the first column of B is $(3, 7) \cdot (2, 5) = 41$, which is the coefficient of x in $a = 41x + 19y$ and the top left entry of C. Then note that $19 = (3, 7) \cdot (-3, 4)$, which is the dot product of the first row of A and the second column of B, and 19 is the top right entry of C. In all four cases, the dot product of the ith row of A and the jth column of B results in the ij entry of C. (Check this!) So taking the dot product of rows of the left matrix with columns of the right matrix does seem to be the thing to do.

Here is the definition of **matrix multiplication.**

Definition

Let A have as many columns as B has rows. Suppose A is $m \times n$ and B is $n \times p$. Let the rows of A be called $R_1, R_2, \ldots, R_m$. Let the columns of B be called $C_1, C_2, \ldots, C_p$. The product AB is defined to be the $m \times p$ matrix with an ij entry that is the number $R_i \cdot C_j$.

$$AB = \begin{pmatrix} R_1 \cdot C_1 & R_1 \cdot C_2 & \cdots & R_1 \cdot C_p \\ R_2 \cdot C_1 & R_2 \cdot C_2 & \cdots & R_2 \cdot C_p \\ \vdots & \vdots & \ddots & \vdots \\ R_m \cdot C_1 & R_m \cdot C_2 & \cdots & R_m \cdot C_p \end{pmatrix}$$

Example 1

Problem Let $A = \begin{pmatrix} 1 & 2 & 3 \\ 2 & 3 & 4 \end{pmatrix}$ and $B = \begin{pmatrix} 1 \\ -1 \\ 2 \end{pmatrix}$. Compute AB.

Solution A is 2×3 with rows $R_1 = (1, 2, 3)$ and $R_2 = (2, 3, 4)$.

B is 3×1 with the one column

$$C_1 = \begin{pmatrix} 1 \\ -1 \\ 2 \end{pmatrix}$$

So,

$$AB = \begin{pmatrix} R_1 \cdot C_1 \\ R_2 \cdot C_1 \end{pmatrix} = \begin{pmatrix} 5 \\ 7 \end{pmatrix}$$

In terms of the letters in the definition, $m = 2$, $n = 3$, and $p = 1$.

Go Online
www.successnetplus.com

For You to Do

Compute each product, or explain why it cannot be computed.

1. $\begin{pmatrix} 1 & 2 \\ 2 & 3 \\ 3 & 4 \end{pmatrix}\begin{pmatrix} 1 & -2 \\ -3 & 4 \end{pmatrix}$

2. $(1 \quad 2)\begin{pmatrix} 1 & -2 & 1 & 2 \\ 2 & 1 & -1 & 3 \end{pmatrix}$

3. $\begin{pmatrix} 1 & -2 & 1 & 2 \\ 2 & 1 & -1 & 3 \end{pmatrix}\begin{pmatrix} 1 & -2 \\ -3 & 4 \end{pmatrix}$

Visualize. Some people think about the matrix product AB as shown in the figure below. A is on the left and B is on top. The matrix that just fits on the bottom right between them is AB. The size is correct. To compute any entry in the product (represented by the large dot), you multiply the row in A directly to its left (represented by a segment) by the column in B directly above it. As usual, multiplying a row by a column means finding the dot product.

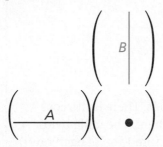

For Discussion

4. Why is A required to have as many columns as B has rows?

Mathematicians wrote the definition of a matrix product to mimic exactly what happens when you summarize the results of linear substitutions with matrices. So the following theorem should not be a surprise. In fact, the definition is constructed to make this theorem true!

Theorem H.8

Suppose matrix A represents a system where the z's are linear combinations of y's. Suppose matrix B represents a system where these y's are linear combinations of x's.

Then, by substitution, the z's are linear combinations of the x's, and the matrix that represents this system is the product AB.

Make sure you understand what it means to *represent* a linear system with a matrix. Write the system in the usual way in rows.

$$y_1 = 2x_1 + 3x_2 - 4x_3$$
$$y_2 = -5x_1 + x_2 + 8x_3$$

Then the matrix is $\begin{pmatrix} 2 & 3 & -4 \\ -5 & 1 & 8 \end{pmatrix}$.

You take the coefficients from the equations and arrange them in the matrix in the same order they appear, one row for each equation.

Example 2

Problem A steel company makes stainless steel and tempered steel. For either type, the raw ingredients are iron and coal, but in different amounts. The table below shows how many tons of iron and how many tons of coal the company needs to produce each ton of steel.

Tons of Raw Material per Ton of Steel

	Stainless Steel	Tempered Steel
Iron	1.1	1.3
Coal	0.5	0.3

In turn, there are costs associated with these raw goods. There is the cost of buying them, and there is also the cost of storing them. The table below shows the costs and the amount of space needed to store 1 ton of each raw good. The price is given in dollars and the space is given in cubic yards.

	Iron	Coal
Cost ($)	120	95
Space (yd³)	20	52

a. Turn the first table into a system of linear equations. Let s and t be the amounts in tons of stainless and tempered steel, respectively. The other two variables are i and c. What do they stand for?

b. Similarly, turn the second table into a linear system.

c. What the steel company would really like to know is the direct relationship among how much steel they produce, how much money they need to spend, and how much space they need. Figure this out. Express it as a table.

Solution

a. Let i be the number of tons of iron and c be the number of tons of coal. Then

$$i = 1.1s + 1.3t$$
$$c = 0.5s + 0.3t \tag{10}$$

Notice you can read these equations from the rows of the table.

b. Let p be the cost in dollars and q be the number of cubic yards of space needed. You get

$$p = 120i + 95c$$
$$q = 20i + 52c \tag{11}$$

c. To find the direct relationship between steel amounts and cost, you need to eliminate the intermediate variables i and c. As shown in parts (a) and (b), the dollar cost p and amount of space q are linear combinations of the amounts of iron i and coal c. Also, i and c are linear combinations of amounts of steel s and t. You could do the elimination by substitution, but Theorem H.8 says you can do it by matrix multiplication instead.

A real steel company would make many more types of steel and would use many more raw ingredients. But the form of the example is real. The main difference in actual practice is that the matrices are much bigger. Linear substitutions arise in real life whenever one set of things (here steel outputs) determines a second set (raw goods required) and that second set determines a third (costs).

The theorem says to compute AB, where A is the matrix of p and q in terms of i and c, and B is the matrix for i and c in terms of s and t. From system (11),

$$A = \begin{pmatrix} 120 & 95 \\ 20 & 52 \end{pmatrix}$$

From system (10),

$$B = \begin{pmatrix} 1.1 & 1.3 \\ 0.5 & 0.3 \end{pmatrix}$$

According to the definition of matrix multiplication,

$$AB = \begin{pmatrix} 120 \cdot 1.1 + 95 \cdot 0.5 & 120 \cdot 1.3 + 95 \cdot 0.3 \\ 20 \cdot 1.1 + 52 \cdot 0.5 & 20 \cdot 1.3 + 52 \cdot 0.3 \end{pmatrix} = \begin{pmatrix} 179.5 & 184.5 \\ 48 & 41.6 \end{pmatrix}$$

So

$$p = 179.5s + 184.5t$$
$$q = 48s + 41.6t$$

The table below shows the information the company wants to use.

	Stainless Steel	Tempered Steel
Cost ($)	179.5	184.5
Space (yd³)	48	41.6

Habits of Mind

Detect the key characteristics. Notice the order of multiplication is opposite from the order in which the data were introduced. It is natural to introduce the information top-down—you produced the final products from intermediate material, which you have to buy and store. But, once again, the order is reversed in terms of substituting equations.

For Discussion

5. Why is there such a fuss about which set of equations became matrix A on the left in the product? Is it true for matrices that $AB = BA$?

Developing Habits of Mind

Detect the key characteristics. To get the correct matrices when using Theorem H.8, you must write the equations in rows. But not every table translates to row equations. For instance, the steel company could have represented the original data about raw goods with this table.

Raw Materials per Ton of Steel

	Iron	Coal
Stainless Steel	1.1	0.5
Tempered Steel	1.3	0.3

If you then used the matrix $\begin{pmatrix} 1.1 & 0.5 \\ 1.3 & 0.3 \end{pmatrix}$, you would be in trouble! Always make sure you know which way the equations go before converting to matrices. If the equations correspond to the columns, as in the table above, you have to first flip them into rows.

Matrix Equations

So far in this investigation, you have used matrices to represent the coefficients of equations but not the equations themselves. But with matrix multiplication, you can also easily represent systems of equations.

$$4x - 5y = 3$$
$$3x + y = -1$$

becomes

$$\begin{pmatrix} 4 & -5 \\ 3 & 1 \end{pmatrix} \begin{pmatrix} x \\ y \end{pmatrix} = \begin{pmatrix} 3 \\ -1 \end{pmatrix}$$

$$z_1 = 2y_1 + 5y_2 - 3y_3$$
$$z_2 = 3y_1 - y_2 + y_3$$

becomes

$$\begin{pmatrix} z_1 \\ z_2 \end{pmatrix} = \begin{pmatrix} 2 & 5 & 3 \\ 3 & -1 & 1 \end{pmatrix} \begin{pmatrix} y_1 \\ y_2 \\ y_3 \end{pmatrix}$$

For Discussion

Go the other way: Translate each equation into a linear system. Were you more comfortable with one translation than the other? Explain.

6. $\begin{pmatrix} x \\ y \\ z \end{pmatrix} = \begin{pmatrix} 1 & 2 \\ 3 & 4 \\ 5 & 6 \end{pmatrix} \begin{pmatrix} u \\ v \end{pmatrix}$

7. $(x\ y\ z) \begin{pmatrix} 1 & 2 & 3 \\ 2 & 3 & 4 \\ -3 & -4 & -5 \end{pmatrix} = (3\ 5\ 7)$

> When equations have numbers on one side, you usually write the numbers on the right. When equations have single variables on one side, you usually write the variables on the left.

In short, if you allow yourself to put variables as well as constants into matrices and make use of single columns (or, less conveniently, single rows), you can express any linear system, no matter how big, as a single matrix equation. For instance, $Y = AX$.

It is cute, but does it really help? Time will tell.

And by the way, what happened to Gaussian Elimination? Matrices started out as a shorthand for solving linear systems, but solving systems has not played a role.

Matrix Operations on Calculators

Your calculator can do all the matrix and n-tuple operations discussed so far and more. See the TI-Nspire™ Handbook on p. 788 to find out how. Mathematicians and scientists routinely use calculators (or, more likely, computers) to do any matrix calculations bigger than about three rows or columns. For now, do all calculations by hand except where a calculator is requested. It takes a while to get a feel for all the things matrix multiplication can do, and the best way to get that feel is through hands-on practice.

Exercises Practicing Habits of Mind

The text has explained where matrix multiplication comes from. In this exercise set, you will begin to get a feel for all the things matrix multiplication can do. As always, look for patterns.

Check Your Understanding

1. Compute each product.

   a. $\begin{pmatrix} a & b \\ c & d \end{pmatrix}\begin{pmatrix} 1 & 0 \\ 0 & 1 \end{pmatrix}$

   b. $\begin{pmatrix} 1 & 0 \\ 0 & 1 \end{pmatrix}\begin{pmatrix} a & b \\ c & d \end{pmatrix}$

   c. $\begin{pmatrix} a & b \\ c & d \end{pmatrix}\begin{pmatrix} 2 & 0 \\ 0 & -3 \end{pmatrix}$

   d. $\begin{pmatrix} 2 & 0 \\ 0 & -3 \end{pmatrix}\begin{pmatrix} a & b \\ c & d \end{pmatrix}$

2. You can think of ordered pairs as representing points on the plane. Here you will begin to investigate what matrix multiplication does to points. You will return to this idea in Investigation HC.

   Throughout this exercise, let

   $$U - \begin{pmatrix} 1 \\ 0 \end{pmatrix}, \; V - \begin{pmatrix} 1 \\ 3 \end{pmatrix}, \; W - \begin{pmatrix} 2 \\ 6 \end{pmatrix}, \; X - \begin{pmatrix} -1 \\ -3 \end{pmatrix}, \; Y - \begin{pmatrix} 3 \\ 4 \end{pmatrix}, \text{ and } Z - \begin{pmatrix} -1 \\ 1 \end{pmatrix}.$$

   a. Plot $U, \ldots, Z$ as points on the plane.

   b. Let $A = \begin{pmatrix} 1 & 0 \\ 0 & -1 \end{pmatrix}$. Compute $AU, \ldots, AZ$.

   c. Plot the points in part (b) on the plane. Match the pairs U and AU, then V and AV, and so on. How is each point related to its match?

   d. Now let $B = \begin{pmatrix} 0 & -1 \\ 1 & 0 \end{pmatrix}$. Compute $BU, \ldots, BZ$. Plot the results on the plane.

   Match the pairs U and BU, then V and BV, and so on. How is each point related to its match?

3. Compute each product.

   a. $\begin{pmatrix} 1 & 2 & 3 \\ 4 & 5 & 6 \\ 5 & 3 & 1 \end{pmatrix}\begin{pmatrix} 0 \\ 1 \\ 0 \end{pmatrix}$

   b. $\begin{pmatrix} 1 & 2 & 3 \\ 4 & 5 & 6 \\ 5 & 3 & 1 \end{pmatrix}\begin{pmatrix} 1 \\ 1 \\ 1 \end{pmatrix}$

   c. $(0 \; 0 \; 1)\begin{pmatrix} 1 & 2 & 3 \\ 4 & 5 & 6 \\ 5 & 3 & 1 \end{pmatrix}$

   d. $(1 \; 0 \; -1)\begin{pmatrix} 1 & 2 & 3 \\ 4 & 5 & 6 \\ 5 & 3 & 1 \end{pmatrix}$

   e. $\begin{pmatrix} 1 & 2 \\ 4 & 5 \\ 5 & 3 \end{pmatrix}\begin{pmatrix} 0 & 0 \\ 0 & 0 \end{pmatrix}$

   f. $\begin{pmatrix} 0 & 0 \\ 0 & 0 \\ 0 & 0 \end{pmatrix}\begin{pmatrix} 3 & 5 \\ -2 & 6 \end{pmatrix}$

   Any matrix with all entries 0 is a **zero matrix**. You usually call it 0.

4. Translate each equation into a system of linear equations.

a. $\begin{pmatrix} p \\ q \end{pmatrix} = \begin{pmatrix} 1 & -1 \\ 3 & -2 \end{pmatrix} \begin{pmatrix} x \\ y \end{pmatrix}$

b. $\begin{pmatrix} 2 & 1 \\ 4 & 3 \\ 0 & 6 \end{pmatrix} \begin{pmatrix} a \\ b \end{pmatrix} = \begin{pmatrix} 3 \\ 5 \\ 7 \end{pmatrix}$

5. Translate each system into matrix form with the variables in a column.

a. $x = 2u - 3v + 4w$
$y = -u + 2v + \pi w$
$z = 7u - 4v - 2w$

b. $p = 2x + 3y - 4z$
$q = x - 3y$

c. $y_1 = 3x$
$y_2 = -x$
$y_3 = 4x$

6. Which of the following matrix operations are possible? Since only shape matters for this question, actual entries are not shown.

a. $\begin{pmatrix} \blacksquare & \blacksquare \\ \blacksquare & \blacksquare \\ \blacksquare & \blacksquare \end{pmatrix} + \begin{pmatrix} \blacksquare & \blacksquare \\ \blacksquare & \blacksquare \\ \blacksquare & \blacksquare \end{pmatrix}$

b. $\begin{pmatrix} \blacksquare \\ \blacksquare \\ \blacksquare \end{pmatrix} + \begin{pmatrix} \blacksquare & \blacksquare \\ \blacksquare & \blacksquare \end{pmatrix}$

c. $k \begin{pmatrix} \blacksquare & \blacksquare & \blacksquare \\ \blacksquare & \blacksquare & \blacksquare \end{pmatrix}$

d. $\begin{pmatrix} \blacksquare \\ \blacksquare \\ \blacksquare \end{pmatrix} \begin{pmatrix} \blacksquare & \blacksquare \\ \blacksquare & \blacksquare \end{pmatrix}$

e. $\begin{pmatrix} \blacksquare & \blacksquare \\ \blacksquare & \blacksquare \\ \blacksquare & \blacksquare \end{pmatrix} \begin{pmatrix} \blacksquare \\ \blacksquare \end{pmatrix}$

f. $\begin{pmatrix} \blacksquare & \blacksquare \\ \blacksquare & \blacksquare \end{pmatrix} \begin{pmatrix} \blacksquare & \blacksquare \end{pmatrix}$

g. $\begin{pmatrix} \blacksquare & \blacksquare \end{pmatrix} \begin{pmatrix} \blacksquare & \blacksquare \\ \blacksquare & \blacksquare \end{pmatrix}$

h. $\begin{pmatrix} \blacksquare & \blacksquare & \blacksquare \end{pmatrix} \begin{pmatrix} \blacksquare & \blacksquare \\ \blacksquare & \blacksquare \end{pmatrix}$

7. Your calculator knows how to multiply matrices. See the TI-Nspire™ Handbook on p. 788 for advice on doing matrix multiplication.

- Use your calculator to check your work on Exercise 3.

- Create a matrix multiplication problem that would be difficult to do by hand but that a calculator can handle. Do the multiplication with your calculator.

Anyone can make a mistake when entering a problem into a calculator. What are some ways you can check the calculator's result without doing the entire calculation by hand?

Sometimes dimensions are important.

8. Matrices A and B are *conformable* for multiplication in the order AB if the product AB is defined. Suppose $A = \begin{pmatrix} 1 & 3 & 5 \\ 2 & 4 & 6 \end{pmatrix}$.

 a. What size matrices B are conformable for multiplication with A in the order AB?

 b. What size matrices B are conformable for multiplication with A in the order BA?

 c. What size matrices B are conformable for multiplication with A in either order?

9. For what size matrix A is it true that whenever B is the same size as A, then AB exists?

10. For what size matrix A is it true that whenever B is the same size as A, then BA exists?

11. Consider the equations below.

$$z_1 = y_1 + 2y_2 \qquad y_1 = 2x_1 - x_2$$
$$z_2 = 3y_1 - 4y_2 \qquad y_2 = 3x_1 + x_2$$

 Use matrix multiplication (not direct substitution) to find formulas for z_1 and z_2 in terms of x_1 and x_2.

12. Return to Exercise 8 in Lesson H.07 and regard the profit table from part (a) as a matrix. How could you add down columns as in part (b) by matrix multiplication? How could you add across rows as in part (c) by matrix multiplication?

13. For fundraisers, Local High School has a car wash and a play. All students are encouraged to sell tickets at $5 for a car wash and $10 for the play. The bordered matrix below shows how many tickets each class has sold.

$$\begin{array}{c} \\ \text{Car} \\ \text{Play} \end{array} \begin{array}{ccc} \text{Sr} & \text{Jr} & \text{Soph} \\ \begin{pmatrix} 200 & 150 & 50 \\ 100 & 100 & 85 \end{pmatrix} \end{array}$$

 a. Copy and complete the following matrix. Use a matrix product to compute the entries.

$$\begin{array}{c} \\ \text{Revenue} \\ \text{Total tickets} \end{array} \begin{array}{ccc} \text{Sr} & \text{Jr} & \text{Soph} \\ \begin{pmatrix} \blacksquare & \blacksquare & \blacksquare \\ \blacksquare & \blacksquare & \blacksquare \end{pmatrix} \end{array}$$

 b. Use another matrix product to determine the total revenue and total ticket sales for all three classes together.

> You may be able to easily compute the entries in this matrix in your head, but the point is to recognize how you can use matrix multiplication in this situation.

14. Cereals A and B are multigrain cereals. The table below left shows how many ounces of certain grains are in one ounce of each cereal. The table on the right shows how many grams of vitamins X, Y and Z are in one ounce of those same grains.

	A	B
Wheat	0.3	0.5
Rice	0.3	0.2
Oats	0.3	0.3

	Wheat	Rice	Oats
Vitamin X	2	1	3
Vitamin Y	3	4	2
Vitamin Z	2	2	1

Use matrix multiplication to devise a table that shows how many grams of each vitamin is in one ounce of each cereal. That is, copy and complete the following table using matrix algebra.

	A	B
Vitamin X	■	■
Vitamin Y	■	■
Vitamin Z	■	■

On Your Own

For Exercises 15 and 16, compute each pair of matrix products.

Go Online
www.successnetplus.com

15. $\begin{pmatrix} a & b & c \\ d & e & f \\ g & h & i \end{pmatrix} \begin{pmatrix} 1 & 0 & 0 \\ 0 & 1 & 0 \\ 0 & 0 & 1 \end{pmatrix}$ and $\begin{pmatrix} 1 & 0 & 0 \\ 0 & 1 & 0 \\ 0 & 0 & 1 \end{pmatrix} \begin{pmatrix} a & b & c \\ d & e & f \\ g & h & i \end{pmatrix}$

16. $\begin{pmatrix} 1 & 0 & 0 \\ 0 & 1 & 0 \\ 0 & 0 & 1 \end{pmatrix} \begin{pmatrix} a_1 & a_2 \\ b_1 & b_2 \\ c_1 & c_2 \end{pmatrix}$ and $\begin{pmatrix} a_1 & a_2 \\ b_1 & b_2 \\ c_1 & c_2 \end{pmatrix} \begin{pmatrix} 1 & 0 \\ 0 & 1 \end{pmatrix}$

17. Standardized Test Prep Suppose A is a 3×2 matrix, B is a 2×4 matrix, and C is a 4×3 matrix. What are the dimensions of $B(CA)$?

A. 2×2 **B.** 3×3

C. 4×4 **D.** $B(CA)$ is not possible.

18. Use the matrices below. Compute AB and BA.

$$A = \begin{pmatrix} 3 & 4 \\ 1 & -2 \end{pmatrix} \quad B = \begin{pmatrix} 2 & -3 \\ 3 & 4 \end{pmatrix}$$

19. Use the matrices below.

$$A = \begin{pmatrix} 1 & 2 \\ 3 & 4 \end{pmatrix} \quad B = \begin{pmatrix} 2 \\ -1 \end{pmatrix} \quad C = \begin{pmatrix} 3 \\ 4 \end{pmatrix}$$

a. Compute $AB + AC$. Compute it exactly as it is written. Find AB first, then AC, and then add.

b. Compute $A(B + C)$. Again, do the computation exactly as written.

20. Use the matrices below.

$$A = \begin{pmatrix} 1 & 3 \\ 2 & 4 \end{pmatrix} \quad B = (2 \quad -1) \quad C = (3 \quad 4)$$

a. Compute $BA + CA$. Compute it exactly as it is written. Find BA first, then find CA, and then add.

b. Compute $(B + C)A$. Again, do the computation exactly as written.

21. Use the matrices below to compute each product.

$$A = \begin{pmatrix} 1 & 2 \\ 3 & 4 \end{pmatrix} \quad B = \begin{pmatrix} 2 & 3 \\ 4 & 5 \end{pmatrix} \quad C = \begin{pmatrix} 1 & 0 \\ -1 & -2 \end{pmatrix}$$

a. $A(BC)$

b. $(AB)C$

22. Do part (c) of the steel company example in this lesson again, but this time do it by substitution, not matrix multiplication. Which method do you prefer?

23. The following table shows the enrollments last year by gender at Local High School.

	Sophomores	Juniors	Seniors
Male	154	148	136
Female	162	155	150

a. Compute the total number of students per class. Show how you can express this computation as matrix multiplication.

b. Compute the total number of males and the total number of females in the high school. Show how you can express this computation as matrix multiplication.

c. Use parts (a) and (b) to compute the total enrollment two ways. Show how you can express each way as matrix multiplication.

Matrix multiplication is not necessarily the best way to do this calculation, but it is valuable to realize that you can use matrix multiplication to do it. You can use matrix multiplication for an amazing number of calculations.

24. Return to Exercise 9 in Lesson H.06 and regard the passenger car sales table as a matrix. Explain how to get each matrix for the following year by using matrix operations on the matrix for the original year.

25. Assume that the following table shows the number of grams of nutrients in one ounce of food indicated.

	Meat	Potato	Cabbage
Protein	5.5	0.5	3
Fat	5.5	0.03	0.02
Carbohydrates	0.1	6	1.5

a. If you eat a meal consisting of 9 ounces of meat, 20 ounces of potatoes, and 5 ounces of cabbage, how many grams of each nutrient do you get?

b. Why is this exercise in an investigation on matrices?

26. Continuing with the data from Exercise 25, suppose the military wants to use these same foods to feed new recruits a dinner providing 45 grams of protein, 35 grams of fat, and 100 grams of carbohydrates.

a. Write a system of equations, in traditional form, with a solution that would determine how much of each food the military should prepare for each recruit.

b. Rewrite your system of equations as a single matrix equation.

Do not solve the system right now. The calculations are messy. Later you will learn some methods for solving systems like this. See Exercise 9 in Lesson H.10.

27. Consider again Exercise 24 in Lesson H.08. Translate both sets of given equations into matrix equations. Translate the solution set of equations into a matrix equation.

28. Consider again Exercise 26 in Lesson H.08. Translate both sets of given equations into matrix equations. Translate the solution set of equations into a matrix equation.

29. **Take It Further** Suppose you have z's that equal linear expressions in y and y's that equal linear expressions in x. You know you can write the first linear system as $Z = AY$ and the second as $Y = BX$. Furthermore, you know from Theorem H.8 that the matrix for the z's in terms of the x's is AB. That is,

$$Z = (AB)X$$

But wait a minute. Now that you have matrix equations, you can just substitute $Y = BX$ into $Z = AY$. The result is

$$Z = A(BX)$$

Compare the two equations for Z in terms of A, B, and X. What do you conclude? Is this a proof of something?

30. Use the matrices below.

$$A = \begin{pmatrix} 1 & 2 & 1 \\ 2 & 5 & 1 \\ -1 & 1 & 2 \end{pmatrix} \qquad B = \begin{pmatrix} 1 & 0 & 0 \\ -2 & 1 & 0 \\ 1 & 0 & 1 \end{pmatrix} \qquad C = \begin{pmatrix} 1 & 0 & 0 \\ 0 & 1 & 0 \\ 0 & -3 & 1 \end{pmatrix}$$

a. Compute $D = BA$.

b. Compute $E = C(BA)$.

c. Compute $(CB)A$.

d. Do you recognize D and E? Explain.

Maintain Your Skills

31. Use matrix A below. Compute AB for each matrix B.

$$A = \begin{pmatrix} 1 & 2 & 3 \\ 4 & 5 & 6 \\ 7 & 8 & 9 \end{pmatrix}$$

a. $B = \begin{pmatrix} 0 \\ 1 \\ 0 \end{pmatrix}$
b. $B = \begin{pmatrix} 0 \\ 0 \\ -1 \end{pmatrix}$

c. $B = \begin{pmatrix} 0 & 0 & 0 \\ 0 & 0 & 1 \\ 0 & 0 & 0 \end{pmatrix}$
d. $B = \begin{pmatrix} 0 & 0 & 1 \\ 0 & 1 & 0 \\ 1 & 0 & 0 \end{pmatrix}$

Go Online
Video Tutor
www.successnetplus.com

32. Use the matrices below. Compute AB, AC, and AD.

$$A = \begin{pmatrix} 1 & 2 \\ 3 & 4 \\ 5 & 6 \end{pmatrix} \qquad B = \begin{pmatrix} 2 \\ -3 \end{pmatrix} \qquad C = \begin{pmatrix} 0 \\ 1 \end{pmatrix} \qquad D = \begin{pmatrix} 2 & 0 \\ -3 & 1 \end{pmatrix}$$

33. Use matrix A below. Compute CA for each matrix C.

$$A = \begin{pmatrix} 1 & 2 & 3 \\ 4 & 5 & 6 \\ 7 & 8 & 9 \end{pmatrix}$$

a. $C = (0 \quad 1 \quad 0)$
b. $C = (0 \quad 0 \quad -1)$

c. $C = \begin{pmatrix} 0 & 0 & 0 \\ 0 & 0 & 0 \\ 0 & 1 & 0 \end{pmatrix}$
d. $C = \begin{pmatrix} 0 & 0 & 1 \\ 0 & 1 & 0 \\ 1 & 0 & 0 \end{pmatrix}$

34. Use the matrices below. Compute EA, FA, and GA.

$$A = \begin{pmatrix} 1 & 2 \\ 3 & 4 \\ 5 & 6 \end{pmatrix} \qquad E = (1 \quad 0 \quad -1) \qquad F = (-1 \quad 2 \quad -1) \qquad G = \begin{pmatrix} 1 & 0 & -1 \\ -1 & 2 & -1 \end{pmatrix}$$

35. Compute each product.

a. $\begin{pmatrix} a & b \\ c & d \end{pmatrix}\begin{pmatrix} d & -b \\ -c & a \end{pmatrix}$

b. $\begin{pmatrix} d & -b \\ -c & a \end{pmatrix}\begin{pmatrix} a & b \\ c & d \end{pmatrix}$

36. Use the matrices below.

$$A = (a_1 \quad a_2 \quad a_3) \qquad B = \begin{pmatrix} b_1 \\ b_2 \\ b_3 \end{pmatrix}$$

a. Compute AB or explain why it does not exist.

b. Compute BA or explain why it does not exist.

37. Compute $\begin{pmatrix} 1 & 3 \\ 2 & 6 \end{pmatrix}\begin{pmatrix} 3 & -6 \\ -1 & 2 \end{pmatrix}$. Do you notice anything surprising about the result? Explain.

38. Check the following equation.

$$\begin{pmatrix} 1 & 3 \\ 2 & 6 \end{pmatrix}\begin{pmatrix} 2 \\ 3 \end{pmatrix} = \begin{pmatrix} 1 & 3 \\ 2 & 6 \end{pmatrix}\begin{pmatrix} 5 \\ 2 \end{pmatrix}$$

Do you notice anything surprising about this equation? Explain.

39. Use the matrices below.

$$A = \begin{pmatrix} 1 & 2 \\ 3 & 4 \end{pmatrix} \qquad B = \begin{pmatrix} -1 \\ 1 \end{pmatrix}$$

Compute $A(AB)$ and $(AA)B$. Are the answers the same? Was the amount of work the same?

Just as in real-number algebra, you can write AA as A^2.

40. Square each matrix.

a. $I = \begin{pmatrix} 1 & 0 \\ 0 & 1 \end{pmatrix}$

b. $B = \begin{pmatrix} 1 & 0 \\ 0 & -1 \end{pmatrix}$

c. $C = \begin{pmatrix} 0 & 1 \\ 1 & 0 \end{pmatrix}$

d. $D = \begin{pmatrix} \frac{\sqrt{2}}{2} & \frac{\sqrt{2}}{2} \\ \frac{\sqrt{2}}{2} & -\frac{\sqrt{2}}{2} \end{pmatrix}$

e. $E = \begin{pmatrix} \frac{1}{2} & \frac{\sqrt{3}}{2} \\ \frac{\sqrt{3}}{2} & -\frac{1}{2} \end{pmatrix}$

In this investigation, you learned how to compute sums, differences, dot products, products, and inverses of matrices. You also explored the properties of matrix algebra. These questions will help you summarize what you have learned.

1. Use the following matrices.

$$A = \begin{pmatrix} 3 & 1 \\ -1 & 0 \end{pmatrix} \quad B = (4 \quad 2) \quad C = \begin{pmatrix} 0 \\ -2 \end{pmatrix} \quad D = \begin{pmatrix} 5 & 0 \\ 1 & -2 \end{pmatrix}$$

For each part, either do the calculation or explain why it does not make sense.

a. $3D$ **b.** $A + B$ **c.** $A - D$ **d.** $B \cdot C$

e. $A \cdot C$ **f.** AB **g.** AC **h.** AD

2. Find a 3-tuple $E = (a \quad b \quad c)$ such that $E \cdot (-2 \quad 1 \quad 4) = 0$. Is the E you found the only possible answer? If so, explain why. If not, give another example.

3. For the following matrices, show that $F(G + H) = FG + FH$.

$$F = \begin{pmatrix} 1 & -1 \\ 2 & 0 \end{pmatrix} \quad G = \begin{pmatrix} -3 & 1 \\ 0 & 4 \end{pmatrix} \quad H = \begin{pmatrix} 0 & 1 \\ -2 & 0 \end{pmatrix}$$

4. Use the following matrices.

$$J = \begin{pmatrix} 1 & -1 \\ 0 & 2 \\ 3 & 1 \end{pmatrix} \quad K = \begin{pmatrix} 2 & -1 & 0 \\ 0 & -2 & 1 \end{pmatrix}$$

Is JK equal to KJ? Make a prediction and then find both products to check.

5. Give an example of a 2×2 matrix that does not have an inverse. Explain how you know.

6. What is a dot product? How can you represent matrix multiplication using dot products?

7. What are some special cases in which $AB = BA$ is true for matrices A and B?

8. How can you solve this system of equations using matrix inverses? What is the solution?

$$x + 4y - z = -3$$
$$2x - 2y + z = 0$$
$$3x + y - 3z = -9$$

Vocabulary and Notation

In this investigation, you learned these terms and symbols. Make sure you understand what each one means and how to use it.

- **dot product**
- **linear combination**
- **matrix multiplication**
- **n-tuple**
- **scalar multiplication**
- **zero matrix, 0**

Applications of Matrix Multiplication

In *Applications of Matrix Multiplication*, you will use matrices and matrix multiplication to model various situations, such as geometric transformations, transition problems, and probability problems.

By the end of this investigation, you will be able to answer questions like these.

1. Is it true that a matrix associated with a reflection must be its own inverse? If so, what are some relationships that must hold for the entries a, b, c, and d in a 2×2 reflection matrix $R = \begin{pmatrix} a & b \\ c & d \end{pmatrix}$?

2. What is an absorbing state, and what does such a state look like in a transition matrix?

3. A transition matrix for a fixed population of 150 is $\begin{pmatrix} 0.2 & 0.7 \\ 0.8 & 0.3 \end{pmatrix}$

   Does this matrix have a steady state? If so, what is it? If not, why not?

You will learn how to

- flexibly transition between systems of real-variable equations and matrices

- model the evolution of a system over time

- analyze sequences of repeated probabilities

You will develop these habits and skills:

- Reason about matrices as mathematical objects, like numbers, that you can compute with.

- Analyze a multistep process in several variables as a series of transition steps expressed as matrix multiplication.

- Visualize the result of matrix multiplication as a geometric transformation in the coordinate plane.

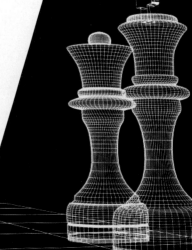

You can use matrices to record the coordinates of points in computer graphics.

Matrix notation gives you another way to solve systems of equations.

Minds in Action

Sasha is doing her matrix homework in the cafeteria when Xavier wanders up and looks over her shoulder. Xavier is taking first-year algebra.

Xavier   Hey Sasha, that looks pretty hard.

Sasha   That's what I thought. We're solving several equations at the same time, with several variables. But at least now we've learned a shorthand for writing it. We can write a system of equations of any size as simple as this: $AX = B$.

Xavier   I don't know anything about that several-equations stuff, but come on, $AX = B$ is easy.

Sasha   What do you mean?

Xavier   Just divide by A. We learned that in first-year algebra. So $X = \frac{B}{A}$.

Sasha   Nice try, Xavier, but you don't understand. We're not talking about $ax = b$ where a, b, and x are numbers. Why do you think I wrote capital letters? A and B are matrices.

Xavier   So what? Just do a basic move and divide by A.

Sasha   You can't divide by matrices. It hasn't been defined.

Xavier   Well, can you multiply by matrices, whatever they are?

Sasha   Yes.

Xavier   You can undo multiplication by using the inverse. Multiplying by 5 is undone by multiplying by $\frac{1}{5}$. So find the inverse A^{-1}.

Sasha   Who says there's an inverse matrix?

Xavier   Well, every number a has an inverse a^{-1}, where $a^{-1}a = 1$. So if you multiply both sides of $ax = b$ by a^{-1}, you get $1x = x = a^{-1}b$. Just do the same with your matrices, whatever they are—you still haven't told me.

> Well, 0 does not have a multiplicative inverse.

Sasha   Look, they're these two-way tables on my paper. They're not numbers and you can't multiply them to get numbers, so there's no way there's going to be some A^{-1} that you can multiply by A to get 1. You've got to do a lot more, like row reduce or add and subtract equations.

Xavier   Sorry! But it looked so simple, written $AX = B$.

Using good notation has several advantages. Yes, it makes complicated things easier to write, but it also suggests a way to think about an idea. The matrix equation notation made Xavier think about solving equations as in first-year algebra. As it turns out, he is right!

This was his argument: You solve $ax = b$ by multiplying both sides by a^{-1} to get $x = a^{-1}b$. Sasha objected because she thinks there is no matrix C such that $CA = 1$, so there cannot be a matrix that deserves to be called A^{-1}.

There is a matrix I such that $IX = X$. Such a matrix is an **identity matrix**, because multiplying by it gives you back what you start with identically.

What does I look like? Perhaps you know from earlier exercises. Consider the following equations.

$$\begin{pmatrix} 1 & 0 \\ 0 & 1 \end{pmatrix}\begin{pmatrix} x \\ y \end{pmatrix} = \begin{pmatrix} x \\ y \end{pmatrix} \qquad \begin{pmatrix} 1 & 0 & 0 \\ 0 & 1 & 0 \\ 0 & 0 & 1 \end{pmatrix}\begin{pmatrix} x \\ y \\ z \end{pmatrix} = \begin{pmatrix} x \\ y \\ z \end{pmatrix}$$

If X is $m \times 1$, then I is the $m \times m$ matrix with 0's everywhere except for 1's along the main diagonal. You denote all these matrices as I and call each one an identity matrix. If it is important to indicate the size, you can write I_2, I_3, etc.

So, Sasha was mistaken. You do not need the number 1. You need something that serves the same function as 1 in the matrix context. It exists: I.

If there is a matrix M such that $MA = I$, then M will serve the same role as a^{-1}, and Xavier's method for solving matrix equations will work. Starting with $AX = B$, multiply on the left by M, you get

$$X = IX = MAX = MB$$

Example

Problem See if Xavier's method works for the following system.

$$s + 2t = 5$$
$$3s + 4t = 6$$

Solution First, rewrite the system in matrix form.

$$\begin{pmatrix} 1 & 2 \\ 3 & 4 \end{pmatrix}\begin{pmatrix} s \\ t \end{pmatrix} = \begin{pmatrix} 5 \\ 6 \end{pmatrix} \qquad (12)$$

Now you need a 2×2 matrix M such that

$$M\begin{pmatrix} 1 & 2 \\ 3 & 4 \end{pmatrix} = \begin{pmatrix} 1 & 0 \\ 0 & 1 \end{pmatrix}$$

In Exercise 12, you will show that there is such a matrix.

$$M = \begin{pmatrix} -2 & 1 \\ \frac{3}{2} & -\frac{1}{2} \end{pmatrix}$$

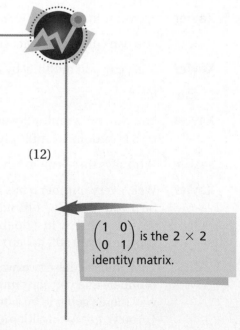

$\begin{pmatrix} 1 & 0 \\ 0 & 1 \end{pmatrix}$ is the 2×2 identity matrix.

Therefore, multiply both sides of (12) by M, just as you would to solve a real-number equation.

$$\begin{pmatrix} 1 & 2 \\ 3 & 4 \end{pmatrix}\begin{pmatrix} s \\ t \end{pmatrix} = \begin{pmatrix} 5 \\ 6 \end{pmatrix}$$

$$\begin{pmatrix} -2 & 1 \\ \frac{3}{2} & -\frac{1}{2} \end{pmatrix}\begin{pmatrix} 1 & 2 \\ 3 & 4 \end{pmatrix}\begin{pmatrix} s \\ t \end{pmatrix} = \begin{pmatrix} -2 & 1 \\ \frac{3}{2} & -\frac{1}{2} \end{pmatrix}\begin{pmatrix} 5 \\ 6 \end{pmatrix}$$

$$\begin{pmatrix} 1 & 0 \\ 0 & 1 \end{pmatrix}\begin{pmatrix} s \\ t \end{pmatrix} = \begin{pmatrix} -2 & 1 \\ \frac{3}{2} & -\frac{1}{2} \end{pmatrix}\begin{pmatrix} 5 \\ 6 \end{pmatrix} = \begin{pmatrix} -4 \\ \frac{9}{2} \end{pmatrix}$$

$$\begin{pmatrix} s \\ t \end{pmatrix} = \begin{pmatrix} -4 \\ \frac{9}{2} \end{pmatrix}$$

The solution is $s = -4$ and $t = 4\frac{1}{2}$.

For You to Do

1. It is often easier to check a possible solution than to find it. In the example above, check that M really is the inverse of $A = \begin{pmatrix} 1 & 2 \\ 3 & 4 \end{pmatrix}$ by computing MA. Then check that $\begin{pmatrix} s \\ t \end{pmatrix} = \begin{pmatrix} -4 \\ 4\frac{1}{2} \end{pmatrix}$ really does solve the original equations.

When a matrix A has a companion matrix M such that $MA = I$, this companion matrix is the **inverse** . You write it as A^{-1}.

Good news and bad news The good news is that your calculator knows how to find matrix inverses. Therefore, your calculator provides a quick way to solve the matrix system $AX = B$.

Step 1 Input A.

Step 2 Press one or more keys to get A^{-1}.

Step 3 Compute the product $A^{-1}B$.

The answer appears on your screen.

The bad news is that the inverse method does not always work, because A^{-1} does not always exist. The inverse never exists if A is not square, and it often does not exist even if A is square. This is quite different from the situation with real numbers, where only 0 has no multiplicative inverse. In contrast, Gaussian Elimination always works when solving the system $AX = B$ for any matrix A. It turns out A^{-1} exists precisely when the system $AX = B$ has a unique solution. Gaussian Elimination handles those systems, as well as systems with no solution or many solutions. On the other hand, in this course, you will mostly consider systems with unique solutions, so the inverse matrix method will generally work for you.

Habits of Mind

Check your definition. This is a working definition. As you will see in Exercise 5, you have to say a little more.

You can always press the exponent key ($\wedge$) followed by -1. On some calculators, there is an x^{-1} button that allows you to find inverses with a single keystroke. See the TI-Nspire Handbook, p. 788.

The 2 × 2 case In general, there is no simple formula for A^{-1} in terms of A, although there is a straightforward algorithm to determine whether A has an inverse and to find A^{-1} when it does—a variant of Gaussian Elimination! However, in the 2×2 case, there is a nice formula, which is worth knowing. Recall the result you discovered in Exercise 34 of Lesson H.9. If $A = \begin{pmatrix} a & b \\ c & d \end{pmatrix}$ and $B = \begin{pmatrix} d & -b \\ -c & a \end{pmatrix}$, then $BA = AB = (ad - bc)I$.
Therefore, as long as $ad - bc \neq 0$,

$$A^{-1} = \frac{1}{ad - bc} \begin{pmatrix} d & -b \\ -c & a \end{pmatrix}$$

What can you do if $ad - bc = 0$? It turns out there is never an inverse when $ad - bc = 0$, so the 2×2 case is completely resolved: A^{-1} exists if and only if $ad - bc \neq 0$, in which case you use the formula above for A^{-1}. See Exercise 14.

> **Habits of Mind**
>
> **Detect the key characteristics.**
> Here is one way to think about 2 × 2 inverses: To get A^{-1} you switch the entries on the main diagonal of A and switch the signs of the other two entries. Then you divide by the scalar $ad - bc$ This scalar shows up in many other contexts. It is the **determinant** of A.

Exercises *Practicing Habits of Mind*

Check Your Understanding

1. Return again to Sasha and Derman's favorite problem.

$$x + y + z = 2$$
$$2x - y + z = 5$$
$$x + 2y + 3z = 5$$

Solve this system using inverses.

2. Solve Exercise 21 from Lesson H.08 again, this time using the inverse.

3. Consider the system below.

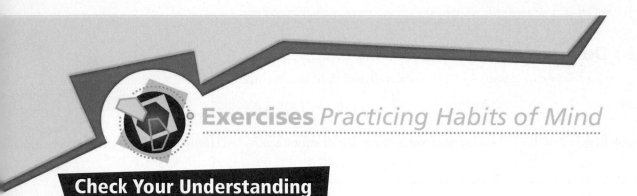

$$\begin{pmatrix} 1 & 2 \\ 2 & 4 \end{pmatrix}\begin{pmatrix} x \\ y \end{pmatrix} = \begin{pmatrix} 1 \\ 1 \end{pmatrix}$$

   a. Attempt to solve it geometrically, that is, by graphing the line corresponding to each equation. What happens?
   b. Attempt to solve it by Gaussian Elimination. What happens?
   c. Attempt to solve it by the inverse method. What happens?

> There is one matrix equation here, but there are two linear equations.

4. **Write About It** In proposing how to solve $AX = B$, Xavier initially wrote $\frac{1}{A}$ and put the A directly under the B, as in $\frac{B}{A}$. Why does the book only show the notation A^{-1}, and why always on the left, as in $A^{-1}B$, instead of BA^{-1} or $\frac{B}{A}$?

5. Let $A = \begin{pmatrix} 1 & 0 \\ 3 & 4 \\ 0 & 1 \end{pmatrix}$ and $M = \begin{pmatrix} 1 & 0 & 0 \\ 0 & 0 & 1 \end{pmatrix}$.

Check that $MA = I$ and $AM \neq I$. So M is only a one-sided inverse of A, something that does not happen with number multiplication.

6. In the example, you showed that $M = \begin{pmatrix} -2 & 1 \\ \frac{3}{2} & -\frac{1}{2} \end{pmatrix}$ is the inverse of

$A = \begin{pmatrix} 1 & 2 \\ 3 & 4 \end{pmatrix}$ in the sense that $MA = I$. Check whether $AM = I$.

7. Xavier said that every real number a has an inverse $\frac{1}{a}$. Is his statement true or false? Explain.

8. Consider the following equation: $\begin{pmatrix} 3 & -1 \\ -2 & 2 \end{pmatrix}\begin{pmatrix} 1 \\ 2 \end{pmatrix} = \begin{pmatrix} 1 \\ 2 \end{pmatrix}$

Does this mean that $\begin{pmatrix} 3 & -1 \\ -2 & 2 \end{pmatrix}$ is also an identity matrix? Explain.

> **Habits of Mind**
>
> **Detect the key characteristics.**
> As it turns out, the correct definition of an inverse for matrices is that M is an inverse of A if $MA = AM = I$. The working definition in the lesson was incomplete. The complete definition implies that only square matrices can have inverses, but a matrix being square is not sufficient.

On Your Own

9. Use inverses to solve the system of equations you set up for Exercise 26 of Lesson H.09.

10. Suppose in Exercise 26 of Lesson H.09 the military wants each meal to have 120 grams of carbohydrates instead of 100, but otherwise everything else stays the same. How many ounces of each food should the military now prepare for each recruit?

11. Show that the only matrix $\begin{pmatrix} a & b \\ c & d \end{pmatrix}$ that satisfies $\begin{pmatrix} a & b \\ c & d \end{pmatrix}\begin{pmatrix} x \\ y \end{pmatrix} = \begin{pmatrix} x \\ y \end{pmatrix}$ for all x and y is the 2×2 identity matrix $\begin{pmatrix} 1 & 0 \\ 0 & 1 \end{pmatrix}$.

Historical Perspective
Linear Equations and CAT Scans

When you get a CAT scan, the machine shoots X-rays through a slice of you from various angles. The strength of each beam when it comes out the other side reports the sum of the densities of matter along the ray. But your doctor is not interested in sums of densities. Your doctor wants to know the density at each point in the slice. The density indicates what sort of tissue, bone, or tumor is there. So, the software that creates the picture from the CAT scan essentially has to solve a system of summation equations similar to the one in Exercise 15, only much bigger.

12. Is there a matrix $\begin{pmatrix} x & y \\ z & w \end{pmatrix}$ that solves the following equation?

$$\begin{pmatrix} x & y \\ z & w \end{pmatrix}\begin{pmatrix} 1 & 2 \\ 3 & 4 \end{pmatrix} = \begin{pmatrix} 1 & 0 \\ 0 & 1 \end{pmatrix}$$

Write this single matrix equation as four ordinary equations. This gives you four linear equations in four unknowns. However, if you look at it carefully, you will see that this particular system is not hard to solve even by hand. Do it.

13. Is there a matrix $\begin{pmatrix} x & y \\ z & w \end{pmatrix}$ that solves the following equation?

$$\begin{pmatrix} 1 & 2 \\ 3 & 4 \end{pmatrix}\begin{pmatrix} x & y \\ z & w \end{pmatrix} = \begin{pmatrix} 1 & 0 \\ 0 & 1 \end{pmatrix}$$

Find out by converting this single matrix equation into four ordinary equations.

14. You already know that if $ad - bc \neq 0$, then $M = \begin{pmatrix} a & b \\ c & d \end{pmatrix}$ has the inverse $\frac{1}{ad - bc}\begin{pmatrix} d & -b \\ -c & a \end{pmatrix}$. Now show that you have not missed any matrices. Prove that M has an inverse only if $ad - bc \neq 0$.

15. Standardized Test Prep Suppose a_1 is the sum of x_1 and x_2, a_2 is the sum of x_2 and x_3, and a_3 is the sum of x_3 and x_1. If $(a_1, a_2, a_3) = (1, 2, 3)$, what are x_1, x_2, and x_3?

A. $(1, 2, 2)$ **B.** $(1, 2, 3)$ **C.** $(1, 0, 2)$ **D.** $(0, 1, 2)$

16. Take It Further Continuing with Exercise 15, forget all the work to find the individual x values. Is it possible to find the sum $x_1 + x_2 + x_3$ by adding the given equations? Explain.

17. Suppose b_1 is the sum of x_1 and x_2, b_2 is the sum of x_2 and x_3, b_3 is the sum of x_3 and x_4, and b_4 is the sum of x_4 and x_1. If $(b_1, b_2, b_3, b_4) = (1, 2, 3, 4)$, what are x_1, x_2, x_3, and x_4?

Go Online
www.successnetplus.com

Remember...

The system
$$ax + by = e$$
$$cx + dy = f$$
where a, b, c, d, e and f are known constants, has the unique solution $(x, y) = \left(\dfrac{de - bf}{ad - bc}, \dfrac{af - ce}{ad - bc}\right)$

Maintain Your Skills

18. Compute the inverse of each matrix.

a. $\begin{pmatrix} 1 & 0 & 0 \\ 0 & 2 & 0 \\ 0 & 0 & \frac{1}{3} \end{pmatrix}$ **b.** $\begin{pmatrix} 1 & 1 \\ 0 & 1 \end{pmatrix}$ **c.** $\begin{pmatrix} 1 & 2 & 3 \\ 0 & 4 & 5 \\ 0 & 0 & 6 \end{pmatrix}$ **d.** $\begin{pmatrix} 1 & 0 & 0 \\ 2 & 1 & 0 \\ 2 & 1 & 2 \end{pmatrix}$

e. $\begin{pmatrix} 1 & 2 & 0 & 0 \\ 3 & 4 & 0 & 0 \\ 0 & 0 & 1 & 2 \\ 0 & 0 & 3 & 4 \end{pmatrix}$ **f.** $\begin{pmatrix} 1 & \frac{1}{2} \\ \frac{1}{2} & \frac{1}{3} \end{pmatrix}$ **g.** $\begin{pmatrix} 1 & \frac{1}{2} & \frac{1}{3} \\ \frac{1}{2} & \frac{1}{3} & \frac{1}{4} \\ \frac{1}{3} & \frac{1}{4} & \frac{1}{5} \end{pmatrix}$

H.11 Matrix Properties

With addition and multiplication of matrices defined, there is a whole algebra of matrices. You can write expressions such as $(X + Y)^2$, equations such as $X^2 + 3X = B$, and even systems of matrix equations such as

$$AX + BY = C$$
$$DX + EY = F$$

Do the rules of ordinary algebra apply? For instance, are the following equations true?

$$(3X + 4Y) - 2(X - Y) = X + 6Y$$
$$(X + Y)^2 = X^2 + 2XY + Y^2$$

Also, does $AB = 0$ imply $A = 0$ or $B = 0$?

If the usual rules do apply, that would make it much easier to do matrix algebra.

The notation 0 stands for a matrix with all entries equaling zero.

Developing Habits of Mind

Make strategic choices. There are many moves you can make in ordinary algebra. Do you have to verify each of them from scratch to apply them to matrices? No, not necessarily. Instead, you can find a few basic rules and deduce the other valid rules from them. This deductive approach is one of the great achievements of mathematics. You have probably already used it in your first-year algebra course to prove properties of real numbers. First, you can identify some key properties as basic rules, for instance, the commutative properties of addition and multiplication and the Distributive Property.

$a + b = b + a$ and $ab = ba$ for all real numbers a and b

$a(b + c) = ab + ac$ for all real numbers a, b, and c

Then you can show that many other properties followed from the full set of basic rules. For instance, you can prove the expansion principle: To multiply two sums, multiply each term in the first sum by each term in the second sum and add the results.

$$(x + y + z)(a + b) = xa + xb + ya + yb + za + zb$$

Similarly, if all the same basic rules held for matrix algebra, then so would the expansion principle.

It turns out that most, but not all, of the basic rules for real numbers hold for matrices as well. You will see the consequences shortly.

Tony and Sasha have been asked to justify, or find counterexamples to, the matrix versions of the two commutative properties.

Tony   We're half done, because we have already seen in Exercise 17 from Lesson H.09 that $AB \neq BA$. So let's consider $A + B = B + A$. That's always been true in all the examples I've seen.

Sasha   But that's not a proof.

Tony   True, but I've caught on to how this is done. We already worked this out for *n*-tuples. Matrices $A + B$ and $B + A$ will be equal if the real numbers inside them are equal entry by entry. So consider a typical entry.

Sasha   I see. For the typical entry of $A + B$, you add the *A*-entry and the *B*-entry. For $B + A$, you add the *B*-entry and the *A*-entry. Since these entries are numbers, and we already know that number addition commutes, we're done.

Tony   It helps me to build an example. Let $A = \begin{pmatrix} 1 & 2 \\ 3 & 4 \end{pmatrix}$ and $B = \begin{pmatrix} 5 & 6 \\ 7 & 8 \end{pmatrix}$. The row-1, column-2 entry of $A + B$ is $2 + 6$. The row-1, column-2 entry of $B + A$ is $6 + 2$. But good old number addition commutes.

Sasha   I like that. And since there was nothing special about the row-1, column-2 entry, we've shown that corresponding entries agree in all cases, so $A + B$ and $B + A$ are equal.

Tony   Great! Now we're done, because we already know that matrix multiplication doesn't commute.

Sasha   Yes, we have a specific example where $AB \neq BA$, but I'm not happy with that.

Tony   Why not? A claim is false if there is even just one counterexample.

Sasha   Yes, but I don't think I understand yet why order matters for matrix multiplication. I don't know whether failure to commute is rare or common.

Tony   Let's look at the definition of matrix multiplication and see if it gives us any clues.

Sasha   I like to think about the definition with the dot product of rows and columns. So I think of the *ij* entry of *AB* this way.

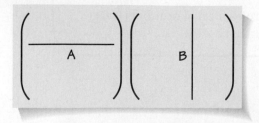

The horizontal and vertical lines I drew show how to compute a typical element of *A* times *B*: a dot product of the *i*th row of *A* and the *j*th column of *B*.

Tony Looks good.

Sasha Let's find the same entry of *B* times *A*.

Tony OK, now the picture looks like this.

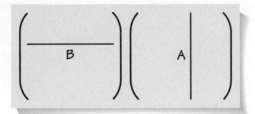

It looks about the same.

Sasha It only looks the same if you ignore that the matrices have been switched! See, the numbers that you multiply are all different. Here, let me draw in the row and column of numbers that we took the dot product of when the product was *AB*.

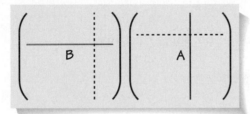

Look, they're almost completely different from the solid line entries that we used to compute *BA*. No wonder it is different!

Tony Hmm. Now I'm surprised that *AB* ever equals *BA* in any entry!

Sasha But we know it sometimes does, as in $AI = IA$ for an identity matrix. I guess those must be rare exceptions.

Tony I wonder if we can explain with your pictures why *I* commutes with other matrices.

You will give an explanation in Exercise 8.

For Discussion

1. While thinking about why $AB \neq BA$, Sasha drew a picture with square matrices. If you look at nonsquare matrices, you can argue just from the sizes and the products that you cannot have equality. Explain.

Facts and Notation

You can now summarize the properties of matrix algebra, as compared to the properties of real numbers.

Commutative Properties:

- $A + B = B + A$ **True**
- $AB = BA$ **False** (It is not true for all A and B.)

Associative Properties:

- $(A + B) + C = A + (B + C)$ **True**
- $(AB)C = A(BC)$ **True**

Distributive Property:

- $A(B + C) = AB + AC$ and $(B + C)A = BA + CA$ **True**

Because matrix algebra has both matrix multiplication and scalar multiplication, some of the basic rules of real numbers split into several matrix rules. Consider the Distributive Property. Along with the version above, there are also two scalar versions:

- $a(B + C) = aB + aC$ **True**
- $(a + b)C = aC + bC$ **True**

Again, because there are two types of multiplication, some rules may look like associative properties, but they are not.

- $a(BC) = (aB)C = B(aC)$ **True**
- $a(bC) = (ab)C = b(aC)$ **True**

Additive Identity:

- For each matrix A, there exists a matrix 0 of the same size such that $A + 0 = A$. The matrix 0 has the number 0 in every entry. **True**

Additive Inverse:

- For every matrix A there exists another matrix $-A$ of the same size such that $A + (-A) = 0$. In fact, if $A = (a_{ij})$, then $-A = (-a_{ij})$. **True**

Multiplicative Identity:

- For each square matrix A, there exists a matrix I such that $AI = IA = A$. If A is $m \times n$, and I_k is the $k \times k$ identity matrix, with 1's on the main diagonal and 0's elsewhere, then $I_m A = A I_n = A$. **True**

Multiplicative Inverses:

- For each matrix A, where $A \neq 0$, there exists a matrix A^{-1} such that $AA^{-1} = A^{-1}A = I$. **False**

When you consider a property with a sum like $A + B$ or a product like AB, you may assume that A and B are of the appropriate sizes for the operation.

Habits of Mind

Experiment. Where have you already seen examples for which the last rule is false?

Look for relationships. As Tony and Sasha noted, for those rules that are true, there are proofs. For those that are false, there are counterexamples and maybe some sort of intuitive way to see that there should be counterexamples.

But what do the proofs look like? The proof Tony and Sasha found for $A + B = B + A$ uses one standard matrix technique: Look at a typical entry (the *ij* entry). See whether the matrix identity reduces to a known numeric identity. In a similar way, proofs of facts about scalar multiplication often work out to be proofs about sums. See, for instance, Exercise 9.

Claims involving matrix multiplication are much more complicated to prove or disprove. This is because the formula for the typical entry of a product matrix is complicated.

Perhaps the most difficult basic rule to justify is the associative property of multiplication. Some earlier exercises illustrated instances of this property. They explained that the definition of matrix multiplication was tailored to make $A(BX) = (AB)X$ true, at least when X is a single column. You can accept the associative property of matrix multiplication as a working conjecture.

In particular, Exercise 26 in Lesson H.08

You will explore some of the multiplication rules in the exercises.

Beyond the Basics

Any matrix claim that just involves addition, subtraction, and scalar multiplication is correct if the basic algebra version of it is correct. But claims that involve matrix multiplication may be wrong.

For instance, the matrix equation

$$a(X + Y) - b(X + 2Y) = (a - b)X + (a - 2b)Y \qquad (13)$$

corresponds to the number equation

$$a(x + y) - b(x + 2y) = (a - b)x + (a - 2b)y \qquad (14)$$

Equation (13) uses just matrix addition and subtraction and scalar multiplication. Equation (14) is correct, therefore (13) is correct. Why is it? The basic rules for matrix addition, subtraction, and scalar multiplication are the same as the basic rules for number addition, subtraction, and multiplication. So however you justify (14) from the basic algebra rules, exactly the same justification works for (13) using the basic matrix rules.

However, the following matrix-product statement is false even though the corresponding statement for real numbers is true.

If $AB = 0$, then $A = 0$ or $B = 0$.

If $ab = 0$, then $a = 0$ or $b = 0$. (Zero Product Property)

Developing Habits of Mind

Consider more than one strategy. How can you determine whether a suspect claim is false? Sometimes you are lucky and you already have a counterexample that you discovered while doing something else. For instance, you discovered in Exercise 13 of Lesson H.08 that the Zero Product Property is false for dot products, and dot products are a special sort of matrix product. If you are not lucky, you should probably not start by trying random examples. If the first example or two shows the claim to be false, you have your answer, but you do not know why. On the other hand, if the claim works for the first five examples, were you lucky, or was this because the claim is true? There is no way to be sure.

A better approach is to try to prove the claim from the basic rules and any other known truths. Either you will succeed, in which case no search for counterexamples is necessary, or else you will discover how the proof breaks down. That will probably suggest how to find a counterexample.

A good navigation system will help you find what you are looking for.

How do you prove the Zero Product Property for real numbers? One proof goes this way.

Assume $ab = 0$. Either $a = 0$ or not. If it does, you are done. If it does not, multiply $ab = 0$ by $\frac{1}{a}$, getting $b = 0$. So, $a = 0$ or $b = 0$.

Aha! The proof uses the existence of a^{-1}, which works for numbers so long as $a \neq 0$. But it does not work for most matrices, so you might suspect that the Zero Product Property for matrices will fail when A is not invertible.

For You to Do

2. According to Exercise 14 in Lesson H.10, $A = \begin{pmatrix} 1 & 2 \\ 3 & 6 \end{pmatrix}$ is not invertible, because $1 \cdot 6 - 3 \cdot 2 = 0$. Find a nonzero 2×2 matrix B such that $AB = 0$.

The Zero Product Property is a property that eliminates a product. You go from a statement about ab to a statement about a or b. All such properties involve inverses somewhere, and all are suspect (and usually false) in matrix algebra. The following problem gives one more property that would be useful if it were true for matrices, but it is not.

For You to Do

3. One of the cancellation laws of number algebra is

   If $ab = ac$, then $b = c$ (unless $a = 0$).

   Show that the corresponding matrix statement is false.

   If $AB = AC$, then $B = C$ (unless $A = 0$).

   (*Hint:* Subtract AC from both sides and set up a zero product.)

> **Habits of Mind**
>
> **Make strategic choices.** The Zero Product Property will not necessarily fail for matrices. There might be a proof that does not use inverses and still works. But you should be very suspicious that the property will fail for matrices. It is now worth looking for a counterexample.

Exercises Practicing Habits of Mind

The exercises give some more examples of rules involving multiplication that break down. Be prepared for them to break down every time, except if special matrices like I are involved.

Check Your Understanding

1. Let $A = \begin{pmatrix} 1 & 2 & 3 \\ 4 & 5 & 6 \end{pmatrix}$.

   a. Find a matrix I such that $IA = A$.

   b. Find a matrix I such that $AI = A$.

   This exercise confirms the fact that a matrix can have different identities on the left and the right.

2. Show that every square matrix A commutes under multiplication with itself. Does A also commute with A^2? Explain.

3. You usually state the Distributive Property for number algebra in just one equation.
   $$a(b + c) = ab + ac$$
   Explain why the Distributive Property for matrices was stated in two equations.
   $$A(B + C) = AB + AC \text{ and } (B + C)A = BA + CA$$

4. Let $A = \begin{pmatrix} 1 & 2 \\ 3 & 6 \end{pmatrix}$.

   a. Find all 2×1 column matrices B such that $AB = 0$.

   b. Find all 2×2 matrices B such that $AB = 0$.

5. **What's Wrong Here?** In number algebra,
   $$(x + y)^2 = x^2 + 2xy + y^2$$

   Below is a proposed proof that the statement is also true for matrices. For each line that is correct, explain why. For each line that is wrong, explain why.
   $$(X + Y)^2 = (X + Y)(X + Y)$$
   $$= X(X + Y) + Y(X + Y)$$
   $$= (XX + XY) + (YX + YY)$$
   $$= X^2 + (XY + YX) + Y^2$$
   $$= X^2 + 2XY + Y^2$$

6. Does the expansion principle hold for matrix algebra?

7. Show that the following revised cancellation law is valid for matrix algebra:
   If A is invertible and $AB = AC$, then $B = C$.

   See the first Developing Habits of Mind section in this lesson for an explanation of the expansion principle.

8. Follow up on Tony's thought at the end of the dialog. Can you use Sasha's pictures to explain why AI is equal to IA? Explain.

> As Sasha did, assume that A is a square matrix.

On Your Own

9. Is $A + A = 2A$ true for all matrices? You can use the definitions of *sum* and *scalar multiple* for matrices. However, if you note that $1A = A$, then you can also use one of the basic rules for matrices.

10. Consider the special binomial expansion $(X + I)^2 = X^2 + 2X + I$. This is the matrix version of $(x + 1)^2 = x^2 + 2x + 1$. Is this special matrix binomial expansion correct for all square matrices? Explain.

> **Habits of Mind**
>
> **Detect the key characteristics.** Here, the matrix X must be square. Explain.

11. Show that $(X + Y)^2 = X^2 + 2XY + Y^2$ if and only if X and Y commute.

12. Explain why $A(B + C) = AB + AC$. That is, justify the Distributive Property for matrix algebra.

13. **a.** Show that the all-0's matrix Z never has a multiplicative inverse, no matter what its size.

    b. Show that there exist infinitely many 2×2 matrices A that do not have an inverse. In fact, show that there are infinitely many 2×2 matrices in which all four entries are nonzero and yet A^{-1} does not exist.

14. Consider again one of the basic rules of matrix algebra.

$$a(BC) = (aB)C = B(aC)$$

This rule says that three different computations give the same result. You can describe the first computation as, "First you multiply the two matrices and then you scale." Describe in your own words the three different computations.

15. Show that the claim $(X + bI)^2 = X^2 + 2bX + b^2I$ is correct for any square matrix X and scalar b.

16. **Write About It** What have you learned in this lesson about rules for matrix algebra?

17. **Standardized Test Prep** Suppose X is a 2×2 matrix. Cynthia has a system for constructing a 2×2 matrix Y such that $XY = YX$. She says if

$X = \begin{pmatrix} a & b \\ c & d \end{pmatrix}$, then $Y = \begin{pmatrix} f & kb \\ kc & f - k(a - d) \end{pmatrix}$.

Suppose $X = \begin{pmatrix} 5 & 2 \\ 1 & 4 \end{pmatrix}$, $y_{11} = 4$, and $y_{12} = 6$. What is YX?

A. $\begin{pmatrix} 4 & 6 \\ 3 & 1 \end{pmatrix}$ **B.** $\begin{pmatrix} 20 & 12 \\ 3 & 4 \end{pmatrix}$ **C.** $\begin{pmatrix} 26 & 32 \\ 16 & 10 \end{pmatrix}$ **D.** $\begin{pmatrix} 26 & 54 \\ 16 & 54 \end{pmatrix}$

> **Go Online**
> www.successnetplus.com

18. The multiplication formula for 1×1 matrices is especially simple. What is it? Are there any pairs of 1×1 matrices that do not commute?

19. Use the matrices A and D below.

$$A = \begin{pmatrix} a & 0 & 0 \\ 0 & b & 0 \\ 0 & 0 & c \end{pmatrix} \qquad D = \begin{pmatrix} d & 0 & 0 \\ 0 & e & 0 \\ 0 & 0 & f \end{pmatrix}$$

Compute AD and DA. What do you notice?

20. a. Find all matrices that commute under multiplication with $\begin{pmatrix} 0 & \\ & 1 \end{pmatrix}$.

  b. Find all matrices that commute under multiplication with $\begin{pmatrix} 0 & & \\ & 0 & \\ & & 1 \end{pmatrix}$.

  c. Expand $(X + I)^3$.

  d. Expand $(X + I)^4$.

  e. Expand $(X + Y)^3$. Compare this expansion with the expansion of $(X + Y)^2$ in Exercise 5. See if you can find a pattern.

  f. Expand $(X + Y + Z)^2$. Compare this expansion with the expansion of $(X + Y)^2$ in Exercise 5. See if you can find a pattern.

> The nonzero entries in A and D are on the main diagonal. Matrices with nonzero entries only along the main diagonal are *diagonal matrices*. You can display them with spaces instead of 0's to avoid visual clutter.
>
> $$A = \begin{pmatrix} a & & \\ & b & \\ & & c \end{pmatrix}$$

H.12 Getting Started

Look for patterns as you complete the following problems.

For You to Explore

1. Consider two sequences s and t, defined as follows.

   $$s(0) = t(0) = 1$$
   $$s(n) = s(n-1) + t(n-1) \qquad \text{for } n \geq 1 \qquad (15)$$
   $$t(n) = s(n-1) - t(n-1) \qquad \text{for } n \geq 1$$

   > A *sequence* is a function with a domain that is the nonnegative integers.

   a. Compute several terms of each sequence until you see a pattern. You might want to line up the two sequences this way.

   $$s(0) \quad s(1) \quad s(2) \quad s(3) \ldots$$
   $$t(0) \quad t(1) \quad t(2) \quad t(3) \ldots$$

   b. Since the equations that define the sequences are all linear, you can replace them with a single matrix equation. Let $S(n) = \begin{pmatrix} s(n) \\ t(n) \end{pmatrix}$ and $M = \begin{pmatrix} 1 & 1 \\ 1 & -1 \end{pmatrix}$.

   Verify that you can rewrite (15) as

   $$S(n) = \begin{cases} \begin{pmatrix} 1 \\ 1 \end{pmatrix} & \text{if } n = 0 \\ MS(n-1) & \text{if } n > 0 \end{cases}$$

   > Model the sequence S. See the TI-Nspire Handbook, p. 788.

   c. Note that $S(2) = MS(1) = M(MS(0)) = M^2 S(0)$, since matrix multiplication is associative. Explain why $S(n) = M^n S(0)$.

   d. Compute M, M^2, M^3, ... until you see a pattern. For as far as you computed powers of M, verify that $S(n) = M^n S(0)$.

2. Let $A = \begin{pmatrix} 1 & 1 \\ 0 & 1 \end{pmatrix}$. Compute powers of A until you can make a conjecture about a pattern.

3. Consider two sequences $u_0, u_1, \ldots$ and $v_0, v_1, \ldots$, defined as follows.

   $$u(0) = v(0) = 1$$
   $$u(n+1) = u(n) + v(n) \qquad \text{for } n \geq 0$$
   $$v(n+1) = v(n) \qquad \text{for } n \geq 0$$

   a. Compute several terms of each sequence until you see a pattern.

   b. You can replace the system of equations that defines these sequences with a single matrix equation. Define $U(n) = \begin{pmatrix} u(n) \\ v(n) \end{pmatrix}$ and find the matrix M such that $U(n+1) = MU(n)$.

   c. Compute M, M^2, M^3, ... until you see a pattern. For the powers n that you computed, verify that $U(n) = M^n U(0)$.

A geometric mapping is a function that maps points in the plane to other points in the plane in some organized way. One of the topics in this investigation is to understand what sorts of mappings of the plane you can describe with matrix multiplication.

For Exercises 4 and 5, let $M = \begin{pmatrix} -1 & 0 \\ 0 & 1 \end{pmatrix}$. If you think of $\begin{pmatrix} x \\ y \end{pmatrix}$ as a point in the plane, you can think of the following mapping as a geometric mapping.

$$X = \begin{pmatrix} x \\ y \end{pmatrix} \mapsto X' = M \begin{pmatrix} x \\ y \end{pmatrix} = \begin{pmatrix} -x \\ y \end{pmatrix}$$

You usually write points as horizontal ordered pairs (x, y). If you want to multiply them by a matrix on the left, then you must write them as columns. Doing so ensures that the matrix multiplication is defined.

4. One way to find out how a particular matrix M maps the plane is to choose several points X_1, X_2, ... that form a nice pattern and then see what patterns $X'_1 = MX_1$, $X'_2 = MX_2$, ... exhibit.

   Consider the following points. These are the integer points on the sides of a certain rectangle.

   $$\begin{pmatrix} 0 \\ 0 \end{pmatrix}, \begin{pmatrix} 1 \\ 0 \end{pmatrix}, \begin{pmatrix} 1 \\ 1 \end{pmatrix}, \begin{pmatrix} 1 \\ 2 \end{pmatrix}, \begin{pmatrix} 0 \\ 2 \end{pmatrix}, \begin{pmatrix} 0 \\ 1 \end{pmatrix}$$

   a. Plot each point.

   b. For each point X you plotted, compute and plot MX as well. Indicate which points pair up. You can draw an arrow from X to MX.

   c. What does the mapping seem to do to lines? To polygons?

   d. Describe what you think M does to the whole plane.

   e. Plot a few more points X that form a nice pattern. What do you think M will do to this pattern? Plot MX for your points and see if you are right.

5. If $X \mapsto MX$ maps the plane to itself, you can repeat the mapping.

   $$X \mapsto MX \mapsto M(MX) = M^2X \mapsto M(M^2X) = M^3X$$

   a. Consider M again. In Exercise 4, you probably decided that M reflects the plane over a certain line. If so, what should be the net effect if you repeat the mapping a second time?

   b. Compute M^2 and M^2X, where $X = \begin{pmatrix} x \\ y \end{pmatrix}$. Did you confirm your answer to part (a)?

6. Now consider the x-axis as a line and reflect points of the plane over that line.

   a. What are the images of the points $\begin{pmatrix} 2 \\ 1 \end{pmatrix}$, $\begin{pmatrix} -1 \\ -2 \end{pmatrix}$, and $\begin{pmatrix} 0 \\ 0 \end{pmatrix}$?

      What is the image of the generic point $\begin{pmatrix} x \\ y \end{pmatrix}$?

   b. Find a matrix M such that $X' = MX$ is the image of X after reflection over the x-axis for every point X.

   c. Determine, with and without matrices, the effect of doing this reflection twice.

Habits of Mind

Look for relationships. This repetition is the same function iteration that you have seen many times for numerical functions.

7. Now consider points in space and reflect them over the *xy*-plane.

    a. What are the images of the points (1, 2, 3), (1, 2, −3), (2, −1, 4), (0, 0, 0), and (*x, y, z*)?

    b. State how to express this reflection as a matrix multiplication. As usual, you will have to write points as columns. This time they are 3-tuple columns.

    c. Determine, with and without matrices, the effect of doing this reflection twice.

8. A certain car rental agency has two locations, one in Boston and one in Cambridge. All rentals are for one week, and the agency allows cars from both locations to be returned to either location. Experience shows that 80% of the cars rented in Boston return there, but only 50% of the cars rented in Cambridge return there. At the start of a certain month, the agency has 70 cars in each location. What will be the situation one week later? Two weeks later? Three weeks later? What happens many weeks into the future?

Model the rental car inventories problem. See the TI-Nspire Handbook, p. 788.

Exercises *Practicing Habits of Mind*

On Your Own

9. Let $M = \begin{pmatrix} 3 & 0 \\ 0 & 3 \end{pmatrix}$. Consider the mapping $X = \begin{pmatrix} x \\ y \end{pmatrix} \mapsto X' = M\begin{pmatrix} x \\ y \end{pmatrix} = \begin{pmatrix} 3x \\ 3y \end{pmatrix}$.

Think of $\begin{pmatrix} x \\ y \end{pmatrix}$ as a point in the plane and $X \mapsto MX$ as a geometric mapping.

As in Problem 4, consider the points $\begin{pmatrix} 0 \\ 0 \end{pmatrix}$, $\begin{pmatrix} 1 \\ 0 \end{pmatrix}$, $\begin{pmatrix} 1 \\ 1 \end{pmatrix}$, $\begin{pmatrix} 1 \\ 2 \end{pmatrix}$, $\begin{pmatrix} 0 \\ 2 \end{pmatrix}$, and $\begin{pmatrix} 0 \\ 1 \end{pmatrix}$.

    a. Plot each point.

    b. For each point *X* you plotted, compute and plot *MX* as well. Indicate which points pair up. You can draw an arrow from *X* to *MX*.

    c. What does the mapping seem to do to lines? To polygons?

    d. Describe what you think *M* does to the whole plane.

    e. Plot a few more points *X* that form a nice pattern. What do you think *M* will do to this pattern? Plot *MX* for your points and see if you are right.

    f. Explain why you might call this mapping $X \mapsto MX$ a scaling mapping with scale factor 3.

10. a. Consider again M from Exercise 9. What do you expect the net effect to be if you repeat the mapping a second time?

b. Compute M^2 and M^2X, where $X = \begin{pmatrix} x \\ y \end{pmatrix}$. Did you confirm your answer to part (a)?

c. What do you expect the net effect to be if you repeat the mapping a third time? Compute M^3 and then M^3X to confirm your answer.

11. Consider rotation of the plane by 180° counterclockwise around the origin.

a. What are the images of the points $\begin{pmatrix} 2 \\ 1 \end{pmatrix}$, $\begin{pmatrix} -1 \\ -2 \end{pmatrix}$, and $\begin{pmatrix} 0 \\ 0 \end{pmatrix}$?

What is the image of the generic point $\begin{pmatrix} x \\ y \end{pmatrix}$?

b. Find M such that this rotation is the mapping $X \mapsto MX$.

c. Determine, with and without matrices, the effect of doing this rotation twice.

12. Suppose there is a matrix M such that the mapping of the plane $X \mapsto MX$ is a 30° counterclockwise rotation around the origin. What would the mapping $X \mapsto M^2X$ accomplish?

> There is such a matrix, but do not worry for now what it is. This exercise is meant to be a thought experiment.

13. Suppose that in a certain developing country, 35% of the people in the countryside move to the cities each year, and only 5% of the people in the cities move to the countryside. Assume there are no births and deaths, and nobody moves to or from other countries. If there were 8 million people in the countryside and 4 million in the cities at the beginning of 2007, what will be the situation at the start of 2008? At the start of 2009? At the start of 2010? What will happen many years into the future?

> These assumptions are unreasonable, but it is always a good idea to start with a simple model and, once you understand that model, later build in more complications.

Maintain Your Skills

14. Use matrix M from For You to Explore Problem 1. Let $X(0) = \begin{pmatrix} 1 + \sqrt{2} \\ 1 \end{pmatrix}$, $X(1) = MX(0)$, $X(2) = MX(1)$, and so on.

  a. Compute $X(1)$, $X(2)$, $X(3)$, and $X(4)$.

  b. Now define $Y(0) = X(0)$, $Y(1) = \sqrt{2}Y(0)$, $Y(2) = \sqrt{2}Y(1)$, and so on. Compute $Y(1)$, $Y(2)$, $Y(3)$, and $Y(4)$.

  c. Now define $Z(0) = \begin{pmatrix} 1 - \sqrt{2} \\ 1 \end{pmatrix}$, $Z(1) = MZ(0)$, $Z(2) = MZ(1)$, and so on. Compute $Z(1)$, $Z(2)$, $Z(3)$, and $Z(4)$.

  d. Now define $W(0) = Z(0)$, $W(1) = -\sqrt{2}W(0)$, $W(2) = -\sqrt{2}W(1)$, and so on. Compute $W(1)$, $W(2)$, $W(3)$, $W(4)$.

15. Use the following matrices.

$$D = \begin{pmatrix} \frac{\sqrt{2}}{2} & -\frac{\sqrt{2}}{2} \\ \frac{\sqrt{2}}{2} & \frac{\sqrt{2}}{2} \end{pmatrix} \qquad P = \begin{pmatrix} 1 \\ 0 \end{pmatrix} \qquad Q = \begin{pmatrix} 2 \\ 1 \end{pmatrix}$$

Compute and plot $DP, D^2P, D^3P, \ldots$ and $DQ, D^2Q, D^3Q, \ldots$ until you see from your plot what is happening. What is the pattern?

16. Let $B = \begin{pmatrix} 1 & 1 \\ 1 & 0 \end{pmatrix}$.

  a. Compute B^2.

  b. Compute B^3.

  c. Compute several more powers. What patterns do you see?

  d. Define a sequence of column vectors $S(n) = \begin{pmatrix} s(n) \\ t(n) \end{pmatrix}$ as

$$S(n) = \begin{cases} \begin{pmatrix} 2 \\ 1 \end{pmatrix} & \text{if } n = 0 \\ BS(n-1) & \text{if } n > 0 \end{cases}$$

Compute several terms of the sequence. What patterns do you see?

  e. Find a system of nonmatrix equations for finding the next pair of values $s(n)$ and $t(n)$ from the previous values.

This is the reverse of For You to Explore Problem 1.

H.13 Geometric Transformations

In Lesson H.12, you studied geometric transformations, where each point in the plane gets mapped to another. For instance, the mapping $(x, y) \mapsto (x + 1, y)$ translates points in the plane (shifts everything over) one unit in the positive x-direction.

You can express many geometric transformations (mappings) with matrix multiplication. A transformation is a **matrix transformation** if you can express it in the form $X \mapsto AX$, where A is a 2×2 matrix and a point X is represented as a column vector $\begin{pmatrix} x \\ y \end{pmatrix}$. You use column vectors so that you can multiply them by matrices on the left. You say this mapping is associated with the matrix A.

In this lesson, you will get a feel for what matrices can do geometrically. The work will be exploratory. You will do examples, often by plotting many points.

> There are also geometric transformations of three-dimensional space, or even higher dimensions, using bigger matrices. Indeed, with the right methods, every matrix of any size can be analyzed geometrically!

Example 1

Problem Let $A = \begin{pmatrix} 2 & 0 \\ 0 & 2 \end{pmatrix}$. What does the map $X \mapsto AX$ do?

Solution Let $X = \begin{pmatrix} x \\ y \end{pmatrix}$. Then

$$AX = \begin{pmatrix} 2 & 0 \\ 0 & 2 \end{pmatrix} \begin{pmatrix} x \\ y \end{pmatrix} = \begin{pmatrix} 2x \\ 2y \end{pmatrix} = 2X$$

This map scales everything by the factor 2 with the dilation centered at the origin. Every point moves twice as far from the origin. As a consequence, every length doubles in size as well, since every length is a distance between points. For instance, look at the graph below. When you dilate all the points in the small triangle by 2, the result is the large triangle. The lower left vertex (2, 1) of the smaller triangle maps to (4, 2), which is the lower left vertex of the larger triangle. The point (4, 2) is twice as far as (2, 1) from the origin. Similarly, the small quarter circle maps to the larger quarter circle.

> Experimenting with transformations can help you understand the effects of mappings. See the TI-Nspire Handbook, p. 788.

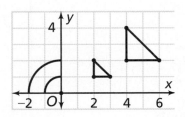

Experiment. Other matrix transformations in this lesson may be harder to interpret geometrically. How do you figure them out? Experiment! Start with several points in some sort of familiar shape. Plot them and plot all their images. You may need to use more than one figure and more than one shape.

For Discussion

1. Let $B = \begin{pmatrix} 1 & 0 \\ 0 & -1 \end{pmatrix}$. What does the map $X \mapsto BX$ do?

Example 2

Problem Let $R = \begin{pmatrix} 0 & -1 \\ 1 & 0 \end{pmatrix}$. What does the map $X \mapsto RX$ do?

Solution First, let $X = \begin{pmatrix} x \\ y \end{pmatrix}$. Then $RX = \begin{pmatrix} 0 & -1 \\ 1 & 0 \end{pmatrix} \begin{pmatrix} x \\ y \end{pmatrix} = \begin{pmatrix} -y \\ x \end{pmatrix}$.

You can rewrite the map $X \mapsto RX$ as $(x, y) \mapsto (-y, x)$. But it is still not so obvious what is going on. Plot some points and their images. Call the original points A, B, C, and D and their images A', B', C', and D'.

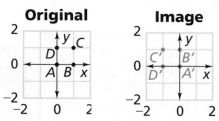

It seems the unit square has been rotated 90° counterclockwise around the origin $A = A'$. You could check this out with more points, for example, the points on the line with equation $x = 2$ or the points on the unit circle. Here is the result for the line with equation $x = 2$.

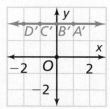

Indeed, the points on the line have been rotated, too.

However, you need a general argument to show that every point (x, y) is rotated 90° counterclockwise around the origin when it is mapped to $(-y, x)$. The next figure should help. What can you say about angles α, β, and γ?

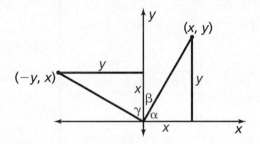

More on Reflections and Rotations

Any reflection over a line through the origin can be done by matrix multiplication. Any rotation around the origin can also be done by matrix multiplication. It is complicated to prove this with what you know, but the following examples illustrate it.

Example 3

Problem Use the matrix below.

$$M = \tfrac{1}{5}\begin{pmatrix} 3 & 4 \\ 4 & -3 \end{pmatrix} = \begin{pmatrix} \tfrac{3}{5} & \tfrac{4}{5} \\ \tfrac{4}{5} & -\tfrac{3}{5} \end{pmatrix}$$

It turns out that the mapping $X \mapsto MX$ is a reflection. Find the line of reflection.

Solution Any reflection in the plane has a line of reflection, also called the axis of reflection. You can visualize this by thinking of folding the plane along this line and mapping each point to the point it touches when you fold the plane. Another way to visualize it is by thinking of the line of reflection as a two-sided mirror. Then each point in the plane is mapped to its reflection in that mirror.

A reflection fixes a point if and only if the point is on the line of reflection. Assuming this mapping $X \mapsto MX$ is a reflection, a point $X = (x, y)$ is on the line of reflection if and only if $MX = X$. So write out this matrix equation as two real-number equations and solve them.

> If you fold a piece of paper, points on the fold do not touch other points. Only points not on the fold line will touch different points on the paper.

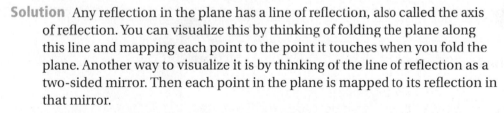

The bottom equation on the right is a multiple of the top equation. They are equivalent equations, so you can write them both as $y = \tfrac{1}{2}x$. This is the equation of the line of slope $\tfrac{1}{2}$ through the origin.

For You to Do

2. Let $N = \frac{1}{2}\begin{pmatrix} 1 & \sqrt{3} \\ -\sqrt{3} & 1 \end{pmatrix}$.

It turns out (though it is not obvious) that N is the matrix of a rotation around the origin. Plot some points to convince yourself it is a rotation and to discover the angle of rotation.

(*Hint:* Every point X will be rotated by the same angle, so you do not need to solve for X as in the last example. Instead, just pick some points X, compute NX, and see how much the original points are rotated.)

Example 2 suggests some points to pick, but you can also choose other points. You also need to check that NX is the same distance from the origin as X. Otherwise, the mapping is doing more than just rotating.

> In fact, you only need one point X, but just to confirm that this mapping really is a rotation, and to catch any arithmetic errors, use several points.

Other Matrix Transformations

Matrices can do much more than scaling, reflecting, and rotating. For example, they can do scaling by different factors in different directions.

For Discussion

3. Let $A = \begin{pmatrix} 3 & 0 \\ 0 & 2 \end{pmatrix}$. Predict what A does to the plane. Then show that you are right by computing what A does to the corners of the unit square. The unit square is the square with corners at $(0, 0)$, $(1, 0)$, $(1, 1)$ and $(0, 1)$.

Many matrices do this sort of multiple stretching, but not always in an obvious way.

Example 4

Problem Analyze the transformation $X \mapsto AX$, where

$$A = \begin{pmatrix} -2.7 & 1.4 \\ -2.1 & 2.2 \end{pmatrix}$$

Solution A few points may not make the pattern clear, but it gets clearer as you show more points. The graph on the left shows the original points and the graph on the right shows their images. Rather than label so many dots, a few of them are made different sizes. The biggest dot in the figure on the left maps to the biggest dot in the figure on the right.

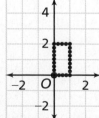
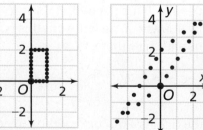

You can see that the segments of the rectangle get stretched, but the directions also get changed. For instance, in the left figure on the preceding page, take a sequence of points starting at the origin and moving along the positive *x*-axis. The images of these points in the right figure get flipped over and move down and left from the origin.

It turns out that the original shape does not clearly show what is happening. Look what happens to the parallelogram in the graph below. The parallelogram on the right is its image, using the same matrix *A*.

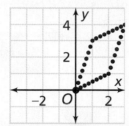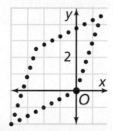

So the stretching is in a direction parallel to the sides of the parallelogram, with either a positive or negative scaling factor. For instance, the point (2, 1) on the left parallelogram gets mapped to $(-4, -2) = -2(2, 1)$ on the right. On the left side of the left parallelogram, the point (1, 3) gets mapped to $(1.5, 4.5) = \frac{3}{2}(1, 3)$ on the right.

How do you find these special directions, in which the map $X \mapsto AX$ just stretches? It turns out that most matrix transformations have them. You will be able to find them for many 2×2 matrices. See Exercises 10, 11, and 21.

> When $AX = kX$, *X* is an *eigenvector* for *A* and *k* is its *eigenvalue*. This is an important concept in more advanced matrix algebra. It is the basis on which you can give every matrix a geometric interpretation.

Matrices can do all sorts of things geometrically. You will explore this more in the exercises. Perhaps the important thing to remember is that you can use matrices to describe several key geometric transformations: scaling, reflection, and rotation.

What is common to all these transformations?

It is impressive, if confusing, that matrices can do all these different transformations. Fortunately, there are some common aspects to all the transformations $X \mapsto AX$. Have you noticed that, in all the matrix transformations so far, lines get mapped to lines and parallel lines get mapped to parallel lines? Some of the exercises address the reasons for this fact.

> Can matrices describe translations? Well, see below.

Another common aspect of all matrix transformations is that the origin gets mapped to the origin.

You can prove this with what you know. If $X \mapsto AX$, then substitute $\begin{pmatrix} 0 \\ 0 \end{pmatrix}$ for *X* and simply note that $A\begin{pmatrix} 0 \\ 0 \end{pmatrix} = \begin{pmatrix} 0 \\ 0 \end{pmatrix}$ for any 2×2 matrix *A*.

> The fact that lines map to lines can save you time when you are plotting points to see what a matrix transformation does. Just find the image of two distinct points. The image is the line through the two image points.

The fact that (0, 0) always gets mapped to itself is an important restriction. The first geometric transformation mentioned in this lesson, $(x, y) \mapsto (x + 1, y)$, is a translation, and it maps (0, 0) to (1, 0). So translations are not matrix transformations. In fact, neither are rotations if they are not centered at the origin. Think about it—in such a rotation, the origin will be rotated to somewhere else. Reflections are not matrix transformations either, unless the line of reflection goes through the origin.

So, are matrix methods in geometry only of limited use? No! You can fix this problem. One way is to shift coordinates so that a rotation, for instance, is centered at the origin. Another way avoids shifting coordinates by using 3×3 matrices.

See Exercise 23.

Exercises Practicing Habits of Mind

Check Your Understanding

1. Determine what each matrix does. That is, describe the geometric transformation associated with it.

   a. $A = \begin{pmatrix} -1 & 0 \\ 0 & 1 \end{pmatrix}$

   b. $B = \begin{pmatrix} 0 & 1 \\ 1 & 0 \end{pmatrix}$

2. Let $A = \begin{pmatrix} 2 & 0 \\ 0 & 2 \end{pmatrix}$. In Example 1, you showed that the mapping $X \mapsto AX$ scales every point by the factor 2. What do you think the mapping $X \mapsto A^{-1}X$ does? Confirm your conjecture by computing A^{-1} and then plotting a few pairs X and $A^{-1}X$.

3. Use matrix A from Exercise 2. What does the mapping $X \mapsto A^2X$ do? What does the mapping $X \mapsto A^{-2}X$ do? (As with numbers, A^{-2} means $(A^{-1})^2$.)

4. **Take It Further** Now think of each ordered pair $\begin{pmatrix} a \\ b \end{pmatrix}$ as representing a point $a + bi$ on the complex plane. Let $M = \begin{pmatrix} c & -d \\ d & c \end{pmatrix}$. Use your knowledge of complex plane geometry to describe geometrically what the mapping $X \mapsto MX$ does. Begin by computing $M\begin{pmatrix} a \\ b \end{pmatrix}$.

5. Example 3 claimed that $M = \frac{1}{5}\begin{pmatrix} 3 & 4 \\ 4 & -3 \end{pmatrix}$ is the matrix of a reflection over the line with equation $y = \frac{1}{2}x$. Plot this line and several points off the line. Pick points on either side of the line. For each of these points X, compute and plot MX. Are they reflections as claimed?

6. Continue with Example 3. If the mapping $X \mapsto MX$ reflects over the line with equation $y = \frac{1}{2}x$, what do you think the mapping $X \mapsto M^{-1}X$ does? How should M and M^{-1} be related? Confirm your conjectures by computing M^{-1}.

7. If $M = \frac{1}{5}\begin{pmatrix} 3 & 4 \\ 4 & -3 \end{pmatrix}$ is the matrix of a reflection, then it turns out there are points X such that $MX = -X$.

   a. Use the method of Example 3, where this matrix was introduced, to find all such points X. Plot several of them and their images MX.

   b. Let X be any one of the points you just plotted. Draw the vector to it from the origin.

      Let Y be any of the points on the line of reflection. Draw the vector to it from the origin. What is the angle between these two vectors? Why does this make sense?

   c. Take the dot product of your two points X and Y from part (b).

8. In light of Exercises 5 and 7, explain why reflections are examples of transformations that scale, but by different factors in different directions.

9. The text showed that you can represent a 90° rotation counterclockwise around the origin as

$$\begin{pmatrix} x' \\ y' \end{pmatrix} = \begin{pmatrix} 0 & -1 \\ 1 & 0 \end{pmatrix}\begin{pmatrix} x \\ y \end{pmatrix}$$

where (x, y) is the original point and (x', y') is the resulting point.

If you can rotate once, you can rotate twice. Call the original point X, the new point X', and the rotation matrix R. Then, to rotate twice, compute

$$X'' = RX' = R(RX) = (RR)X = R^2X$$

In this exercise, *rotate* always means counterclockwise around the origin.

   a. Without any use of matrices, determine the result if the point (x, y) is rotated by 90° twice.

   b. Confirm that you get the same answer as in part (a) using the matrix R^2.

   c. Without any use of matrices, determine the result if the point (x, y) is rotated by 90° three times.

   d. Determine how to do part (c) again with a power of R. Confirm that you get the same answer.

   e. Determine, with and without R, the result of rotating the point (x, y) by 90° four times.

10. This exercise shows, given a 2×2 matrix A, how to find scalars k and vectors X such that $AX = kX$. Use the matrix A below.

$$A = \begin{pmatrix} 1 & 1 \\ 2 & 0 \end{pmatrix}$$

  a. Write out the equation $AX = kX$ as two real-number equations and rewrite them so that both equations equal 0. Your equations will involve three unknowns, the unknown coordinates x and y and the unknown scalar k.

  b. In general, two linear equations in x and y equaling 0 will have only one solution $(x, y) = (0, 0)$. However, if the two equations turn out to be different equations for the same line, then there will be other solutions. When are two equations in the form below just different equations for the same line?

$$ax + by = 0$$
$$cx + dy = 0$$

  The first equation describes the line with equation $y = (-\frac{a}{b})x$ and the second equation describes the line with equation $y = (-\frac{c}{d})x$, so set $\frac{a}{b} = \frac{c}{d}$. Plug in the values of a, b, c, and d you found in part (a). Then solve the equation for k. The equation is quadratic, so you will get two solutions.

> Assume $b \neq 0$ and $d \neq 0$.

  c. Now, for each value of k, solve $AX = kX$ for x and y.

11. In Example 4, you were given the matrix below.

$$A = \begin{pmatrix} -2.7 & 1.4 \\ -2.1 & 2.2 \end{pmatrix}$$

The text made the claim that A stretches $(2, 1)$ by the factor -2 and stretches $(1, 3)$ by the factor 1.5 without any explanation. These claims were easy enough to check, but where did they come from? Using the method of Exercise 10, discover these facts for yourself.

12. Figure out the matrix that represents reflection over the line with equation $y = -x$.

  (*Hint:* Figure out what the reflection does to a few points that are easy to compute with, such as $\begin{pmatrix} 1 \\ 0 \end{pmatrix}$ and $\begin{pmatrix} 0 \\ 1 \end{pmatrix}$. Then find a matrix that accomplishes the same thing by multiplication.)

13. **Take It Further** The design at the right was made using $45°$ counterclockwise rotations. Figure out the matrix for $45°$ rotation counterclockwise around the origin.

14. **Take It Further** If the 2×2 matrix M is invertible, then the geometric mapping $X \mapsto MX$ maps lines to lines and parallel lines to parallel lines. (Even if M is not invertible, M generally maps lines to lines, but it maps some lines to points and some parallel lines to the same line or to a point.) It is easy to prove these facts once you describe lines in matrix form, but you have not done that yet. So here is the outline of a proof using what you know.

You know that a set of points (x, y) form a line if they are the solutions to an equation $ax + by = c$, where a and b are not both 0.

Now, if $\begin{pmatrix} x' \\ y' \end{pmatrix} = M\begin{pmatrix} x \\ y \end{pmatrix}$ is the typical point in the image set of the line and M is invertible, then $\begin{pmatrix} x \\ y \end{pmatrix} = M^{-1}\begin{pmatrix} x' \\ y' \end{pmatrix}$.

Also, M^{-1} is some matrix $\begin{pmatrix} p & q \\ r & s \end{pmatrix}$ and $\begin{aligned} x &= px' + qy' \\ y &= rx' + sy' \end{aligned}$

Substitute these expressions into $ax + by = c$ and regroup until you have something of the form $a'x' + b'y' = c'$. At that point, you have shown that the points (x', y') also form a line. (You also have to argue that a' and b' are not both 0.)

> And you also need to show that any point satisfying $a'x' + b'y' = c'$ is in the image set.

On Your Own

15. Let $A = \begin{pmatrix} 3 & 0 \\ 0 & 2 \end{pmatrix}$. In Problem 3, you showed that the mapping $X \mapsto AX$ stretches the plane by the factor 3 in the x-direction and by the factor 2 in the y-direction. What do you think the mapping $X \mapsto A^{-1}X$ does? Confirm your conjecture by computing A^{-1} and then plotting a few pairs X and $A^{-1}X$.

16. Continue with Example 2. If this mapping is indeed associated with rotation by 90° counterclockwise around the origin, then, for every point X, its image ought to be the same distance from the origin. Pick some points and compare the distances of X and AX from the origin.

17. Determine what each matrix does.

a. $B = \begin{pmatrix} 1 & 0 \\ 0 & 0 \end{pmatrix}$

b. $C = \begin{pmatrix} \frac{1}{2} & \frac{1}{2} \\ \frac{1}{2} & \frac{1}{2} \end{pmatrix}$

> These transformations are different from all those discussed in the text, because they are not one-to-one. That is, $X \mapsto AX$ maps many points to the same point.

18. Continue with the transformations associated with matrices B and C from Exercise 17. Also consider the lines with the following equations.

$$L_1: x = 1 \qquad L_2: x = 2 \qquad L_3: y = 1$$
$$L_4: y = -1 \qquad L_5: y = x \qquad L_6: y = x + 2$$

a. Find the image of each line under multiplication by B.

b. Find the image of each line under multiplication by C.

19. Suppose all you know about the matrix transformation $X \mapsto AX$ is that $(2, 1) \mapsto (-4, -2)$ and $(1, 3) \mapsto (1.5, 4.5)$. That is, you know only that

$$A\begin{pmatrix} 2 \\ 1 \end{pmatrix} = \begin{pmatrix} -4 \\ -2 \end{pmatrix} \quad \text{and} \quad A\begin{pmatrix} 1 \\ 3 \end{pmatrix} = \begin{pmatrix} 1.5 \\ 4.5 \end{pmatrix}$$

a. What does $(6, 3)$ map to? (*Hint:* What properties do you know about the matrix product $A(kB)$?)

b. What does $(2, 1) + (1, 3) = (3, 4)$ map to?

c. What does $(-1, 2)$ map to?

d. Explain why you can figure out what any point (x, y) maps to.

e. In fact, you know all about this matrix transformation. It is the mapping from Example 4 and $A = \begin{pmatrix} -2.7 & 1.4 \\ -2.1 & 2.2 \end{pmatrix}$. Confirm your answers to parts (a)–(c) by direct multiplication.

20. Take It Further Consider A from Exercise 19 again. Suppose there is another matrix B such that $B\begin{pmatrix} 2 \\ 1 \end{pmatrix} = \begin{pmatrix} -4 \\ -2 \end{pmatrix}$ and $B\begin{pmatrix} 1 \\ 3 \end{pmatrix} = \begin{pmatrix} 1.5 \\ 4.5 \end{pmatrix}$.
How are A and B related? Explain your reasoning.

21. Take It Further Let $R = \begin{pmatrix} 0 & -1 \\ 1 & 0 \end{pmatrix}$. This is the matrix from Example 2. Using the method of Exercise 10, find scalars k and points X such that $RX = kX$.

22. This lesson began with the mapping $(x, y) \mapsto (x + 1, y)$, which shifts everything over by one unit in the x-direction. It is not a matrix multiplication transformation because $(0, 0) \mapsto (1, 0)$. However, it is still a transformation that uses matrix algebra, because you can write it in the form $X \mapsto MX + B$, where $M = I$ and $B = \begin{pmatrix} 1 \\ 0 \end{pmatrix}$.

Show how to write the geometric transformation below in the form $X \mapsto MX + B$.

$$\begin{pmatrix} x \\ y \end{pmatrix} \mapsto \begin{pmatrix} x + 2y + 3 \\ 3x + 4 \end{pmatrix}$$

Go **O**nline
www.successnetplus.com

You may think that because the transformation associated with this matrix is a 90° rotation, there is no point X that is scaled by any scalar k. Do the algebra and see what happens.

23. You can often handle transformations that do not fix the origin with matrix multiplication methods by using the following method of adding a dimension. It works this way:

$$\begin{pmatrix} x \\ y \end{pmatrix} \rightarrow \begin{pmatrix} x \\ y \\ 1 \end{pmatrix} \rightarrow A\begin{pmatrix} x \\ y \\ 1 \end{pmatrix} = \begin{pmatrix} x' \\ y' \\ 1 \end{pmatrix} \rightarrow \begin{pmatrix} x' \\ y' \end{pmatrix}$$

You insert a third component in your starting point. Typically you insert 1. Then, you act on your new point with a 3×3 matrix A. Finally, you strip off the third component to get the final transformation.

Show that if you use this method on (x, y) with the matrix A below, then (x, y) maps to $(x, y) + (a, b)$. That is, show that the matrix A represents the translation by (a, b).

$$A = \begin{pmatrix} 1 & 0 & a \\ 0 & 1 & b \\ 0 & 0 & 1 \end{pmatrix}$$

> The method of adding a dimension is used in computer graphics routines. Computer graphics routines need to handle motions like translations and rotations around arbitrary points in space. So you can start with 3×3 matrices and add a dimension to get 4×4 matrices.

24. Imagine rotating the xy-plane 90° counterclockwise through the origin and then reflecting over the x-axis.

   a. Without any use of matrices, determine where the following points end up.

$$(1, 0), (0, 1), (1, 1), (-1, 1), (x, y)$$

   b. Find a matrix M such that the mapping $X \mapsto MX$ accomplishes what you did in part (a).

   c. Using your knowledge of matrices for rotations and reflections, find a matrix R for the rotation part of this exercise. Find another matrix R' for the reflection part.

   d. Verify that $M = R'R$. Explain why this makes sense.

   e. Express this transformation (the rotation followed by the reflection) as a single geometric action. It might be a rotation or a reflection.

25. Prove that if M is invertible (meaning the inverse M^{-1} exists), then the mapping of the plane $X \mapsto MX$ is one-to-one. That is, show that if $MX = MY$, then $X = Y$.

26. Prove the inverse of Exercise 25: If M is not invertible, then the mapping of the plane $X \mapsto MX$ is not one-to-one. (*Hint:* If $M = \begin{pmatrix} p & q \\ r & s \end{pmatrix}$ is not invertible, then you know that $ps - qr = 0$.)

27. Prove that, if M is invertible, then the mapping of the plane $X \mapsto MX$ is *onto*. A mapping is onto if for every X', there exists some X such that $MX = X'$. In other words, some point X is mapped to X'.

> A mapping is not one-to-one if you can find two points X_1 and X_2 such that $X_1 \neq X_2$ but $MX_1 = MX_2$.

28. Take It Further A set of points forms a line if and only if you can represent the points on the line in the form $X = P + tD$, with P any point on the line, D a nonzero ordered pair called the direction vector for the line, and t a parameter that can be any real number. Two lines are parallel (or the same line) if you can represent them in this form using the same D but different points P.

So if a set of points forms a line, then you can represent the set of images under M as the set with points that have the form $MX = M(P + tD)$.

But $P + tD$ is a matrix, so you can apply the Distributive Property, $MX = MP + t(MD)$. If M has an inverse, why does this identity prove that the set of image points MX forms a line?

For each line, P and D are fixed. This way of thinking about lines is *vector representation*. This representation works just as well in three dimensions, or in any number of dimensions.

29. Standardized Test Prep Which of the following statements is NOT true?

A. The sum of the squares of the elements of each row of a 2×2 matrix is 1 for a rotation with no dilation.

B. The square of a reflection matrix is the identity matrix. $(AA = I)$

C. Divide 360° by the angle of rotation. If the remainder is 0, then you must raise the transformation matrix to that quotient to get an identity matrix.

D. For a rotation, the inverse of a matrix must equal itself. $(M^{-1} = M)$

Maintain Your Skills

30. Use the following matrix descriptions.

$R =$ the matrix for rotation 90° counterclockwise around the origin
$F =$ the matrix for reflection over the x-axis
$S_{-1} =$ the matrix for dilating by $k = -1$ around the origin
$S_2 =$ the matrix for dilating by $k = 2$ around the origin

$(S_2R)X$ first rotates X by 90° and then scales by 2.

Describe a geometric transformation for each product matrix.

a. R^2 **b.** R^3 **c.** R^4 **d.** R^5 **e.** $(S_2)^2$

f. $S_{-1}S_2$ **g.** S_2S_{-1} **h.** $(S_{-1})^2$ **i.** F^2 **j.** S_2R

k. RS_2 **l.** FR **m.** RF

31. Many transformations of 3-dimensional space are matrix transformations. Points have the form $X = (x, y, z)$ and the matrices are 3×3. For each matrix M, figure out what the transformation $X \mapsto MX$ does.

a. $M = \begin{pmatrix} 2 & 0 & 0 \\ 0 & 2 & 0 \\ 0 & 0 & 2 \end{pmatrix}$ **b.** $M = \begin{pmatrix} 1 & 0 & 0 \\ 0 & 2 & 0 \\ 0 & 0 & 3 \end{pmatrix}$ **c.** $M = \begin{pmatrix} 1 & 0 & 0 \\ 0 & 1 & 0 \\ 0 & 0 & -1 \end{pmatrix}$

d. $M = \begin{pmatrix} 0 & -1 & 0 \\ 1 & 0 & 0 \\ 0 & 0 & 1 \end{pmatrix}$ **e.** $M = \begin{pmatrix} -1 & 0 & 0 \\ 0 & 1 & 0 \\ 0 & 0 & -1 \end{pmatrix}$ **f.** $M = \begin{pmatrix} 0 & 0 & 1 \\ 1 & 0 & 0 \\ 0 & 1 & 0 \end{pmatrix}$

Honors
Appendix
C

Mathematical Reflections

In this investigation, you used matrix multiplication to describe geometric transformations. You also used matrices and matrix multiplication to model situations that change over time. These exercises will help you summarize what you have learned.

1. Use the matrix transformation $X \to AX$ with the matrix $A = \begin{pmatrix} 0 & 1 \\ 1 & 0 \end{pmatrix}$.

   a. Graph the triangle with vertices (2, 1), (4, 1), and (2, 0). Find the image of this triangle after the transformation.

   b. Describe what this transformation does to any point (x, y) in the plane, both algebraically and geometrically.

2. Find a matrix B such that the mapping $X \to BX$ is a 90° clockwise rotation around the origin. Graph the three points from Exercise 1 both before and after this mapping to show the effect of your matrix.

3. Tori sets up a mountain bike rental business with stations at the north and south ends of the town forest. She starts with 50 bikes at each location. She notices that 90% of the bikes that start at the south end and 60% of the bikes that start at the north end are returned to the north station.

   a. Set up a transition matrix for this situation.

   b. How many bikes would you predict to be at each station after 2 weeks?

   c. How many bikes would you predict to be at each station after 4 weeks?

   d. Will this situation settle down in the long term? If so, what number of bikes will be at each station in the steady state?

4. A beetle passes through the life stages of egg, larva, and adult. In any one time period, an adult alive at the beginning of the time period will lay 100 eggs and die. 40% of eggs that are alive at the beginning of a time period will hatch into larvae. The rest will die. 10% of larvae alive at the beginning of a time period will survive to become adults. The rest will die.

   a. Set up a transition matrix for this beetle population.

   b. One adult beetle brings 10 larvae and 20 eggs and colonizes Derman's locker. After 6 time periods, what will Derman find when he opens his locker door?

Vocabulary

In this investigation, you learned these terms. Make sure you understand what each one means and how to use it.

- **identity matrix**
- **inverse**
- **matrix transformation**

······· TI-Nspire™ Technology Handbook ···········

Recognizing how to use technology to support your mathematics is an important habit of mind. Although the use of technology in this course is independent of any particular hardware or software, this handbook gives examples of how you can apply the TI-Nspire™ handheld technology.

Defining a Function, Lesson 5.04

1. Choose the **Define** option from the **Actions** menu (or type Ⓓ Ⓔ Ⓕ Ⓘ Ⓝ Ⓔ).

2. Type the function and press ◖enter◗.

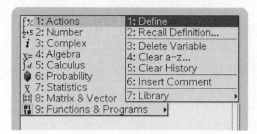

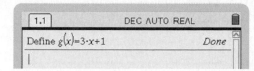

Defining a Function Recursively, Lessons 5.09, 5.12

1. Choose the **Define** option from the **Actions** menu. Name the function by typing Ⓑ ⟨ Ⓝ ⟩ ⟨=⟩. Press ◖ctrl◗ ◖X◗ to open the **Templates** palette. Choose 🔲 and press ◖enter◗.

2. Enter the function. Press ◖tab◗ to move from box to box. Press ◖enter◗ to complete the definition.

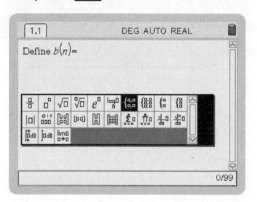

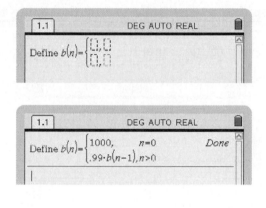

Graphing a Function, Lessons 4.06, 5.06, 6.08

1. Tab down to the entry line at the bottom of the screen. Type an expression in *x*.

2. Press ◖enter◗.

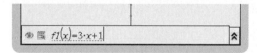

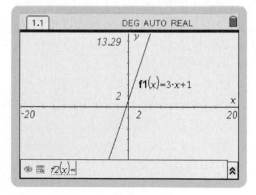

Graphing a User-Defined Function by Dragging It Onto the Axes, Lessons 5.06

1. Use the **Text** tool in the **Actions** menu. Type **Y** **=**, followed by the function. Press **enter**.

2. Position the cursor on the equation. Press **ctrl** **✱** to grab it. Drag the equation to the axes. Press **enter**.

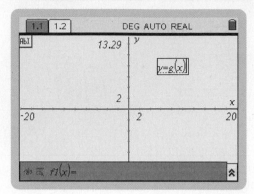
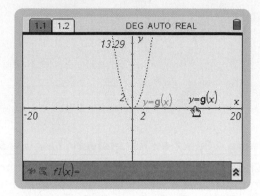

Graphing a User-Defined Function Using the Function Line, Lesson 5.06

1. Type the function into the function line. Press **enter** to graph it.

2. Redefine the function in the Calculator application.

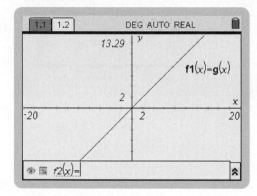
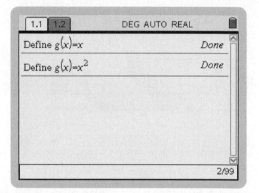

3. Switch to the Graphs & Geometry screen to see the updated graph.

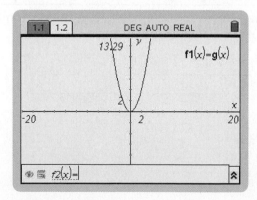

TI-Nspire™ Technology Handbook

Graphing a System of Inequalities, Lesson 4.07

1. Navigate to the function line using the **tab** key. Press **⬅** to delete the =. Type the inequality. (Use **ctrl** **<** for ≤ and **ctrl** **>** for ≥.)

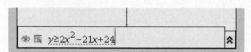

2. Press **enter** to graph the inequality.

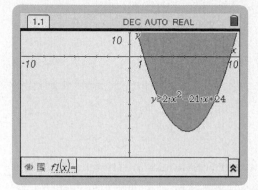

3. Enter the second inequality.

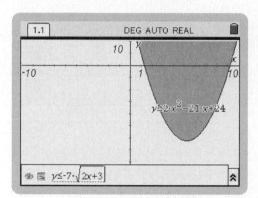

4. Press **enter** to graph the inequality.

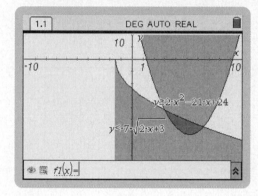

Finding the Intersection Point(s) of Two Graphs, Lessons 4.06

1. Choose the **Intersection Point(s)** option from the **Points & Lines** menu.

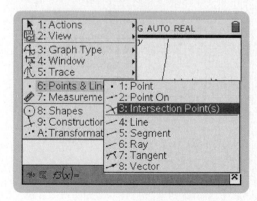

2. Position the pointer on the first graph. Press **enter**. Position the pointer on the second graph. Press **enter** to confirm.

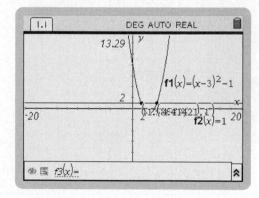

3. Position the pointer on one set of coordinates. Press **ctrl** **✲** to grab it. Drag the coordinates to the desired location and press **enter**.

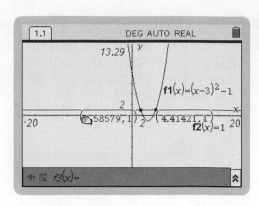

Using Spreadsheets, Lessons 5.09, 5.12

1. Press **⌂**. Choose **Lists & Spreadsheets**. Press **enter**.

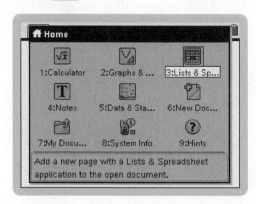

2. To label columns, navigate to the header cell. Type the column name. Press **enter**. Choose **Resize** from the **Actions** menu.

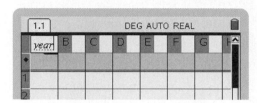

3. Press ◁ or ▷ until the column is the desired width. Press **enter**.

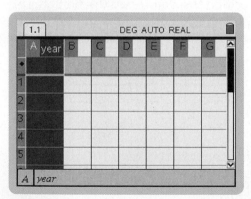

4. To enter data, navigate to the appropriate cell. Enter the data and press **enter**.

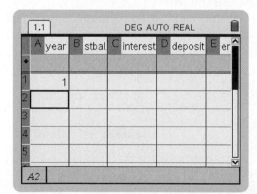

5. Type ⊜ Ⓐ ❶ ⊕ ❶ in cell A2.

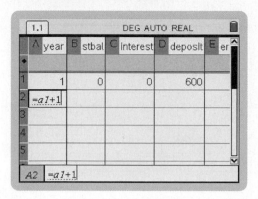

6. Press `enter`.

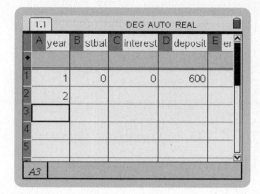

Using the Fill-Down Feature in a Spreadsheet, Lesson 5.12

1. Navigate to the cell you wish to fill down. Choose **Fill Down** from the **Data** menu.

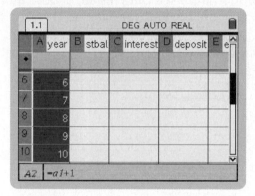

2. Press ▽ to highlight the desired range of cells. Press `enter`.

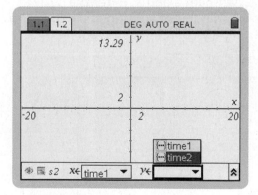

Generating a Scatter Plot, Lesson 7.06

1. Use existing data in a spreadsheet. Choose the **Scatter Plot** option in the **Graph Type** menu.

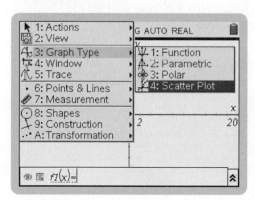

2. Select the desired variable from the *x*-value box. Press `enter`. Press `tab`. Do the same for the *y*-value box.

3. Choose **Zoom—Data** from the **Window** menu.

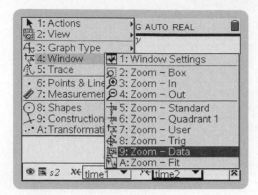 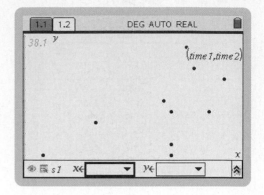

Making a Box-and-Whisker Plot, Lesson 7.03, 7.04

1. Navigate to the column with the data you wish to graph. Choose the **Quick Graph** option from the **Data** menu. Choose **Box Plot** from the **Plot Type** menu.

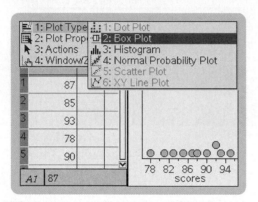 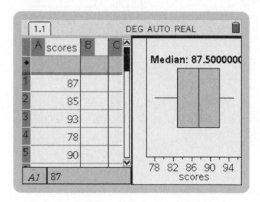

Finding the Line of Best Fit I, Lesson 7.10

1. Name the first two columns of a spreadsheet *a* and *b*. Enter the *x*-coordinates of your points in column *a* and the *y*-coordinates in column *b*.

2. Navigate to the Graphs & Geometry application. Choose **Scatter Plot** from the **Graph Type** menu.

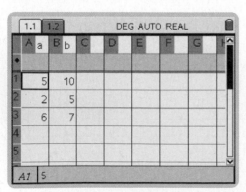 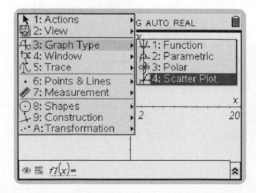

3. Press **enter** to select from among a list of possible *x*-values. Select *a*. Press **enter**.

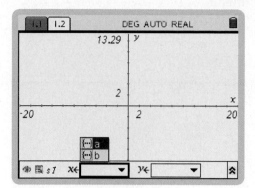

4. Press **tab** and then **enter** to select from among a list of possible *y*-values.

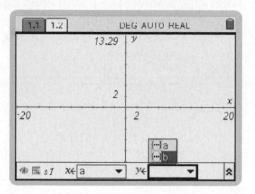

5. Select *b*. Press **enter** to view a scatter plot of the selected data.

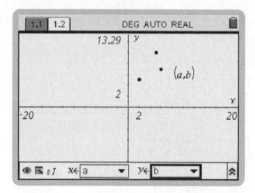

6. Choose **Function** from the **Graph Type** menu.

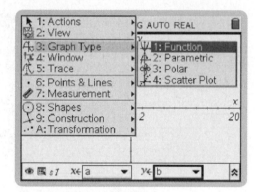

7. Graph any linear function. Here the function is $f(x) = 2$.

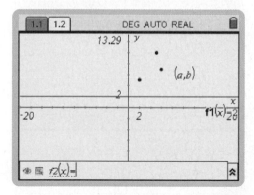

8. Choose **Parallel** from the **Constructions** menu.

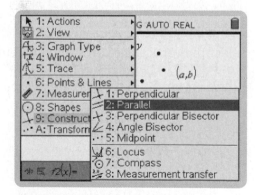

Finding the Line of Best Fit I, (continued)

9. Select a scatter-plot point with the cursor. Press **enter**. Select the *y*-axis. Press **enter** to construct a vertical line that passes through the point.

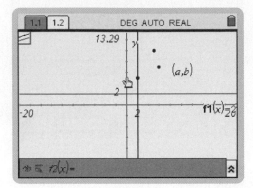

10. Choose **Segment** from the **Points & Lines** menu.

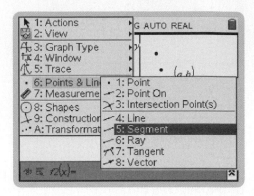

11. Select the point (Step 9) again. Press **enter**. Select the intersection point of its vertical line and the graph of the linear function. Press **enter** to construct a segment between the two points.

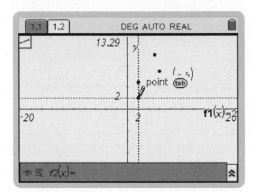

12. Choose **Hide/Show** from the **Actions** menu.

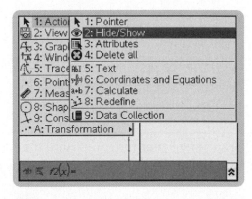

13. Select the vertical line (not the segment). Press **enter** to hide it. Press **esc** to exit the Hide/Show tool.

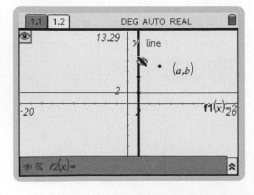

14. Repeat Steps 8–13 for the other points.

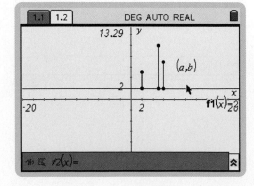

15. Choose **Length** from the **Measurement** menu.

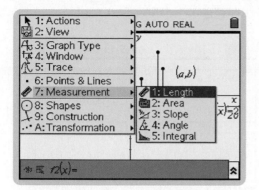

16. Select a segment. Press **enter**. Drag the measurement to the desired location on the screen. Press **enter** to anchor it.

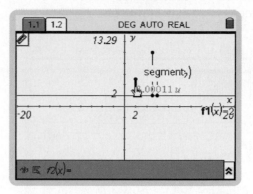

17. Repeat Step 16 for the other segments.

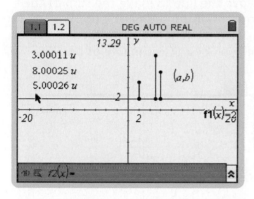

18. Choose **Text** from the **Actions** menu. Write $i^2 + k^2 + l^2$ on the screen.

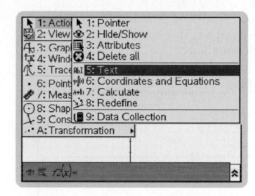

19. Choose **Calculate** from the **Actions** menu.

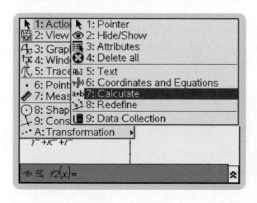

20. Position the cursor on $i^2 + k^2 + l^2$. Press **enter**.

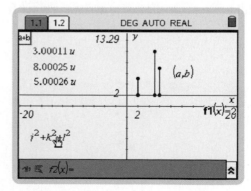

TI-Nspire™ Technology Handbook

21. Select a value for each variable. Position the cursor over the respective length measurements and press ⟨enter⟩ .

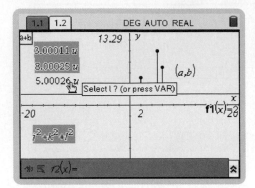

22. Drag the result of the calculation to the desired location. Press ⟨enter⟩ to anchor it. Press ⟨esc⟩ to exit the Text tool.

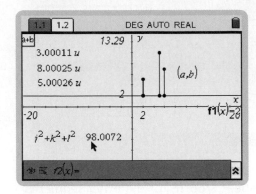

23. Use arrow keys to navigate to the horizontal line. Press ⟨ctrl⟩ ✪ to grab it. Drag the line to rotate and translate the line.

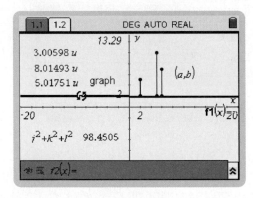

24. Move the line to make the sum of the squares of the segment lengths as small as possible. The line with the least value of $i^2 + k^2 + l^2$ is the line of best fit.

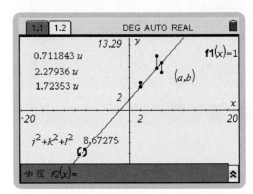

Finding the Line of Best Fit II, Lesson 7.10

1. Make a scatter plot of the data you wish to use.

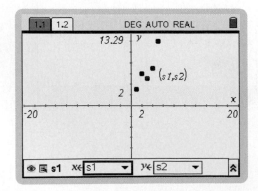

2. Navigate to the calculator application. Choose **Stat Calculations** from the **Statistics** menu. Choose **Linear Regression (mxb)**. Press ⟨enter⟩.

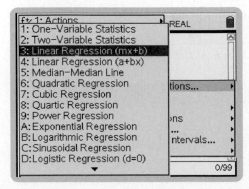

3. Select the data to use in the **X List** and **Y List** fields. Press (tab) to navigate between fields. Select a function name in the **Save RegEqn to** field.

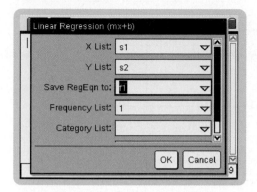

4. Press (enter) to show a summary of the linear regression.

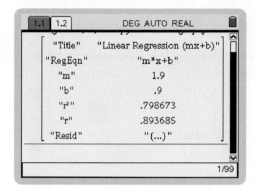

5. Navigate to the Graphs & Geometry application. Choose **Function** from the **Graph Type** menu.

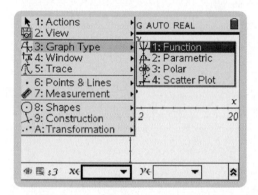

6. Press (tab) to navigate to the function entry line. Press △ to navigate to the linear regression function. Press (enter) to draw its graph.

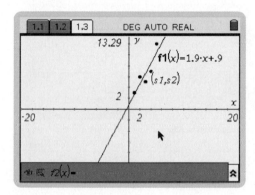

Finding the Quadratic Curve of Best Fit, Lesson 7.10

1. Navigate to the Calculator application. Choose **Stat Calculations** from the **Statistics** menu. Choose **Quadratic Regression**. Press (enter).

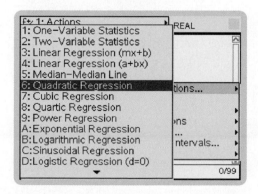

2. Select the data to use in the **X List** and **Y List** fields. Press (tab) to navigate between fields. Select a function name in the **Save RegEqn to** field.

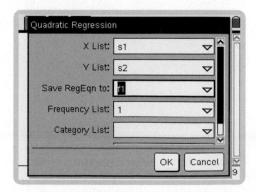

3. Press **enter** to show a summary of the quadratic regression. Navigate to the Graphs & Geometry application. Choose **Function** from the **Graph Type** menu.

4. Press **tab** to navigate to the function entry line. Press ⬆ to navigate to the quadratic regression function. Press **enter** to draw its graph.

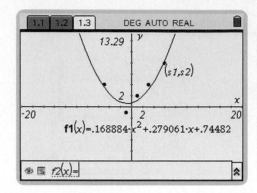

Constructing a Line Through Two Points, Lesson 8.07

1. Choose the **Line** option in the **Points & Lines** menu.

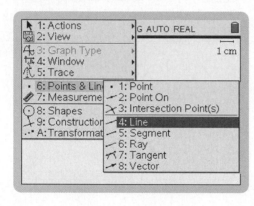

2. Position the pointer on a point. Press ✷. Position the pointer on the other point. Press ✷.

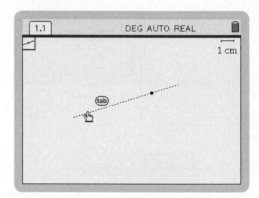

Constructing a Ray Through Two Points, Lesson 8.07

1. Choose the **Ray** option in the **Points & Lines** menu.

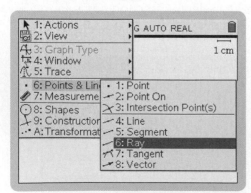

2. Position the pointer on the endpoint of the ray. Press ✷. Position the pointer on the other point and press ✷.

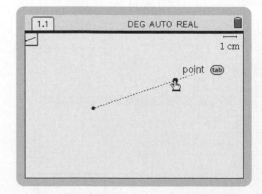

Dragging an Object, Lesson 8.09

1. Position the cursor on the object. Press ctrl (×).

2. Drag the object to the desired location. Press (×).

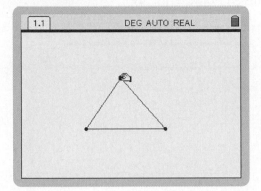

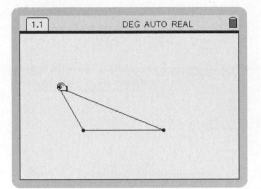

Hiding/Showing an Object, Lesson 8.08

1. Select **Hide/Show** from the **Actions** menu. Position the pointer on the object. Press (×) to hide the object.

2. Select **Hide/Show** from the **Actions** menu. Position the pointer on the hidden object. Press (×) to show the object.

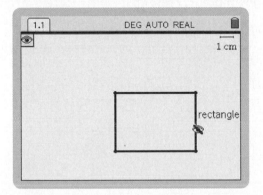

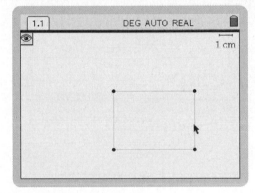

Deleting an Object, Lesson 8.08

1. Position the pointer anywhere on the object. Press (×) (⌫).

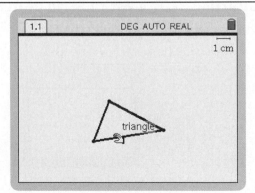

Constructing a Line Perpendicular to a Given Line Through a Given Point, Lessons 8.08

1. Choose the **Perpendicular** option in the **Construction** menu.

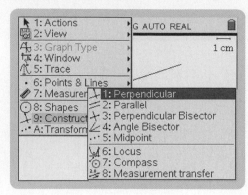

2. Position the pointer on the given line. Press ✺. Position the pointer on the given point. Press ✺.

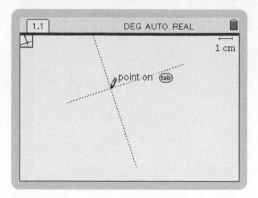

Constructing a Line Parallel to a Given Line Through a Given Point, Lessons 8.08

1. Choose the **Parallel** option in the **Construction** menu.

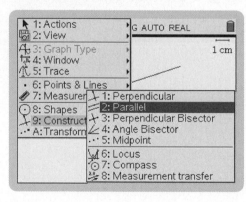

2. Position the pointer on the given line. Press ✺. Position the pointer on the given point. Press ✺.

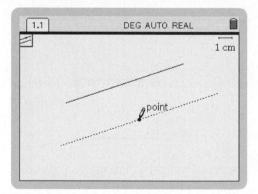

Constructing a Circle With a Given Center Through a Given Point, Lesson 8.09

1. Choose the **Circle** option in the **Shapes** menu.

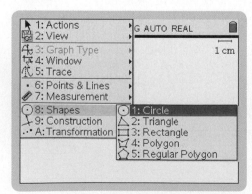

2. Position the pointer on the given center. Press ✺. Position the pointer on the given point. Press ✺.

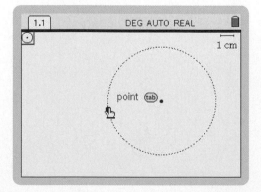

Constructing a Circle With a Given Center and Radius Length, Lesson 8.09

1. Use the **Text** tool in the **Actions** menu. Write the radius.

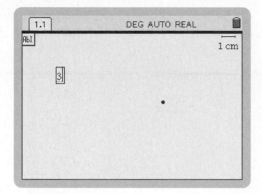

2. Choose the **Compass** option in the **Construction** menu.

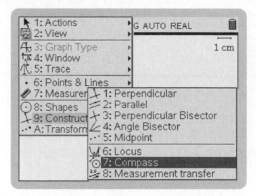

3. Position the pointer on the given center. Press ⊛.

4. Select the radius length on the screen. Press ⊛.

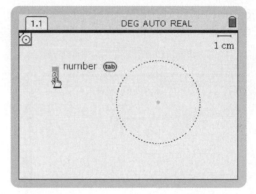

Measuring a Segment, Lesson 8.09

1. Choose the **Length** option in the **Measurement** menu. Position the pointer on the segment. Press ⊛.

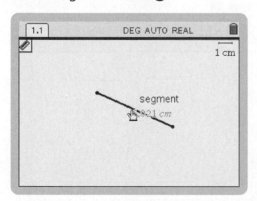

2. Move the pointer to drag the measurement. Press ⊛ to anchor it.

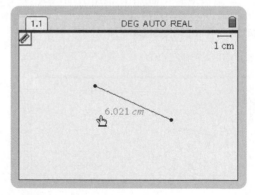

Translating an Object by a Given Vector, Lesson 9.11

1. Choose the **Translation** option in the **Transformation** menu.

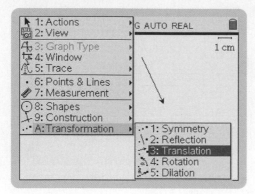

2. Position the pointer on the object. Press ⊛.

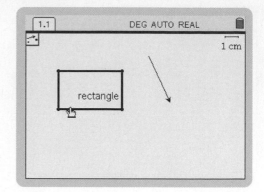

3. Position the pointer on the given vector. Press ⊛.

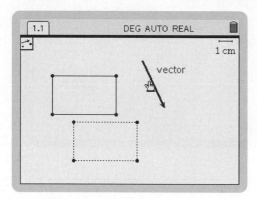

Reflecting an Object Over a Line, Lesson 9.10

1. Choose the **Reflection** option in the **Transformation** menu. Position the pointer on the line. Press ⊛.

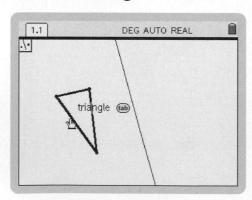

2. Position the pointer on the object. Press ⊛.

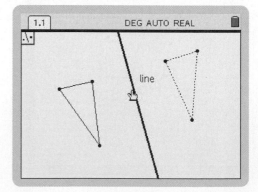

Rotating an Object About a Point by a Given Number of Degrees, Lesson 9.12

1. Check that the system settings show degree mode.

2. Use the **Text** tool in the **Tools** menu. Write the given number of degrees.

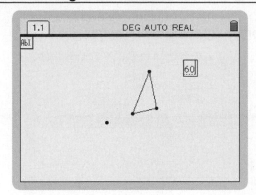

3. Choose the **Rotation** option in the **Transformation** menu.

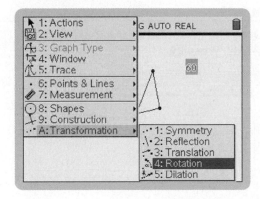

4. Place the pointer on the center of rotation. Press 🟤.

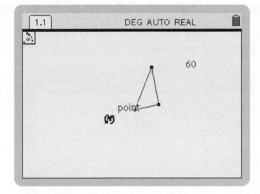

5. Place the pointer on the object. Press 🟤.

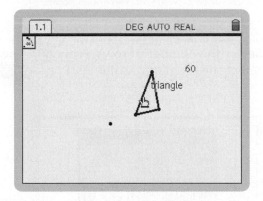

6. Select the angle of rotation on the screen. Press 🟤.

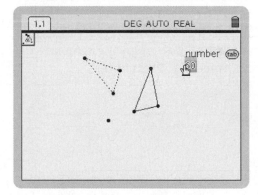

Finding the Coordinates of a Point (Graphing View Only), Lesson 9.11

1. Choose the **Coordinates and Equations** option in the **Actions** menu.

2. Position the pointer on the point. Press 🔘. Press 🔘 to anchor the label.

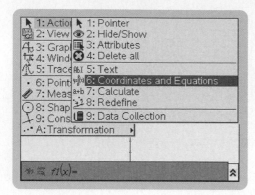

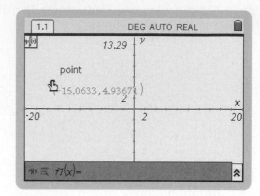

Graphing an Equation (Graphing View Only), Lesson 9.09

1. Use the **Text** tool in the **Actions** menu. Write the equation.

2. Drag the equation to the *x*-axis or the *y*-axis. Press 🔘.

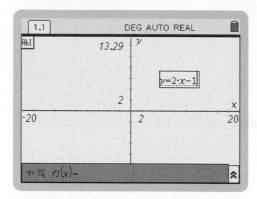

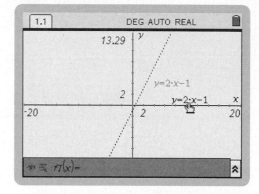

Entering a Matrix, Lesson H.09

1. Press **ctrl** **✕** to open the template palette. Select ▦. Press enter.

2. Select the number of rows. Press **tab**. Then select the number of columns. Press **enter**.

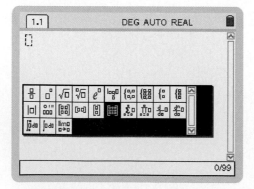

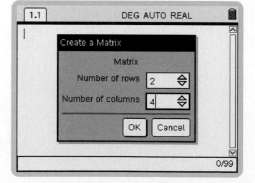

3. Type a value for each matrix element. Press **tab** or use the arrow keys to move from box to box.

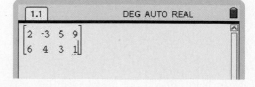

Multiplying Matrices, Lesson H.09

1. Enter a matrix. Press ⊗. Enter a second matrix. Press **enter**.

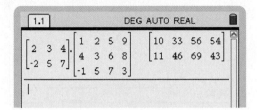

2. If the number of columns of the first matrix does not equal the number of rows of the second matrix, you see this image.

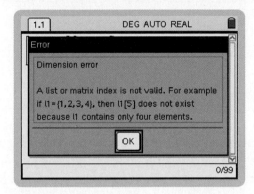

Finding the Inverse of a Matrix, Lesson H.10

1. Enter a square matrix. Press 🔼 ⊖ ↩ **enter**.

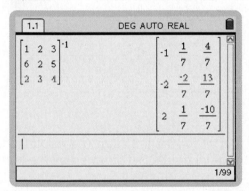

2. If the matrix has no inverse, you see this image.

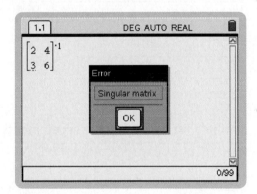

Using a Matrix to Transform Points, Lesson H.13

1. Define a 2-by-*n* matrix to model a set of *n* points. The first row consists of the *x*-coordinates, and the second row consists of the corresponding *y*-coordinates. Define lists of the *x*-coordinates and *y*-coordinates, in order.

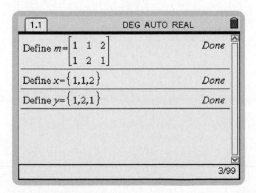

2. Navigate to the Graphs & Geometry application. Choose **Scatter Plot** from the **Graph Type** menu.

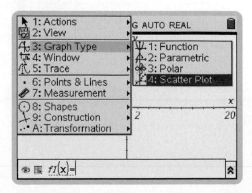

Using a Matrix to Transform Points (continued)

3. Select the data lists from Step 1 as the *x*- and *y*-values.

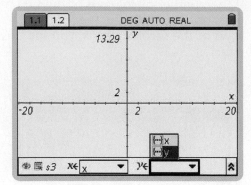

4. Press **enter** to see the points you will transform using a 2-by-2 matrix.

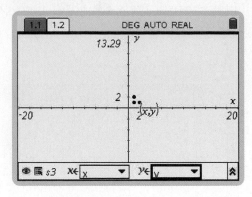

5. Define a transformation matrix *s*.

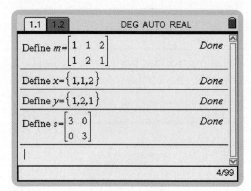

6. Define a list, *x*1. Name the list elements $(s \cdot m)[1,1]$, $(s \cdot m)[1,2]$, and so on.

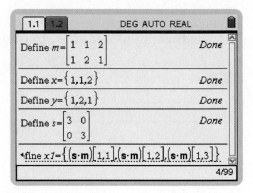

7. Define a list, *y*1. Name the list elements $(s \cdot m)[2,1]$, $(s \cdot m)[2,2]$, and so on.

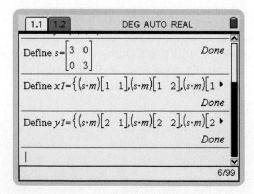

8. Make a scatter plot using *x*1 for the *x*-values and *y*1 for the *y*-values. The result is the original points transformed by the matrix *s*.

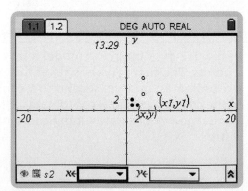

Using a Matrix to Transform Points (continued)

9. For a second transformation, press △ in the calculator screen until you highlight the definition of *s*. Press **enter** to copy it to the entry line.

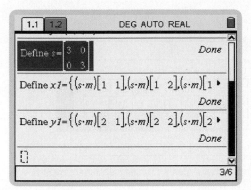

10. Use the arrow keys to change the values in *s*. Press **enter**.

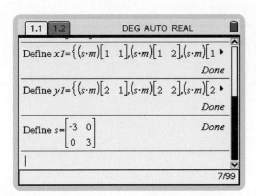

11. Press △ in the calculator screen until you highlight the definition of *x*1. Press **enter** to copy it to the entry line. Press **enter**.

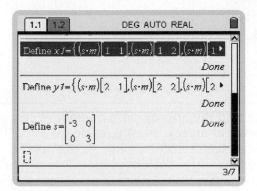

12. Repeat Step 11 with the definition of *y*1.

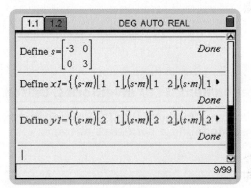

13. Navigate to the scatter plot from Step 8 to view the new transformation.

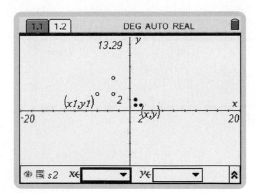

Modeling a Sequence, Lesson H.12

1. Choose **Define** from the **Actions** menu. Press Ⓜ ⊜. Enter the matrix shown. Press **enter**.

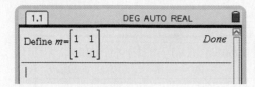

2. Choose **Define** from the **Actions** menu. Press Ⓢ ⊜. Press **ctrl** **✕** to open the template palette. Select 🔢. Press **enter**.

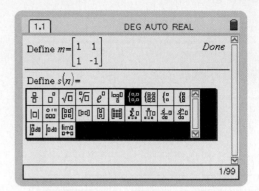

3. Enter the 2-by-1 matrix in the first box as shown. Complete the rest of the function. Press **enter**.

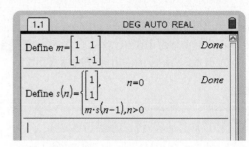

Modeling Rental Car Inventories, Lesson H.12

1. Define a recursive function $g(x)$ as shown. See **Modeling a Sequence** above.

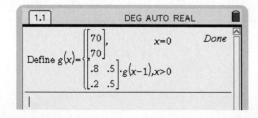

3. To find the approximate number of cars in each lot after n months, evaluate $g(n)$. The first element of the matrix is the number of cars in the Boston location. The second element is the number of cars in the Cambridge location.

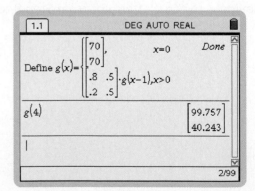

Tables

$\ldots$	and so on	$m\angle A$	measure of angle A
$=$	is equal to	$\circ$	degree(s)
$\approx$	is approximately equal to	$\triangle ABC$	triangle with vertices A, B, and C
$\neq$	is not equal to	$\square ABCD$	parallelogram with vertices A, B, C, and D
$>$	is greater than		
$\geq$	is greater than or equal to	n-gon	polygon with n sides
$<$	is less than	s	length of a side
$\leq$	is less than or equal to	b	base length
$\cdot, \times$	multiplication	h	height, length of an altitude
$+$	addition	a	apothem
$-$	subtraction	P	perimeter
$\pm$	plus or minus	A	area
$\mapsto$	maps to	B	area of a base
$|x - y|$	absolute value of $(x - y)$	V	volume
n^2	n squared	d	diameter
$\sqrt{x}$	nonnegative square root of x	r	radius
Δ	difference (delta)	C	circumference
$\Leftrightarrow$	if and only if	π	pi, the ratio of the circumference of a circle to its diameter
$\{\ \}, \varnothing$	empty set		
$\in$	is an element of	$\odot A$	circle with center A
A	point A	$\overset{\frown}{AB}$	arc with endpoints A and B
A'	image of A, A prime	$\overset{\frown}{ABC}$	arc with endpoints A and C and containing B
$\overleftrightarrow{AB}$	line through A and B		
$\overline{AB}$	segment with endpoints A and B	$m\overset{\frown}{AB}$	measure of $\overset{\frown}{AB}$
$\overrightarrow{AB}$	ray with endpoint A through B	$a : b, \frac{a}{b}$	ratio of a to b
AB	length of $\overline{AB}$	$\mathbb{Z}$	set of integers
$\parallel$	is parallel to	$\mathbb{Q}$	set of rational numbers
$\perp$	is perpendicular to	$\mathbb{R}$	set of real numbers
$\cong$	is congruent to		
$\sim$	is similar to		
$\angle A$	angle A		
$\angle ABC$	angle with sides $\overrightarrow{BA}$ and $\overrightarrow{BC}$		

Table 3 Measures

United States Customary	Metric

Length

12 inches (in.) = 1 foot (ft)	10 millimeters (mm) = 1 centimeter (cm)
36 in. = 1 yard (yd)	100 cm = 1 meter (m)
3 ft = 1 yard	1000 mm = 1 meter
5280 ft = 1 mile (mi)	1000 m = 1 kilometer (km)
1760 yd = 1 mile	

Area

144 square inches (in.^{2}) = 1 square foot (ft^2)	100 square millimeters (mm^2) = 1 square centimeter (cm^2)
9 ft^2 = 1 square yard (yd^2)	10,000 cm^2 = 1 square meter (m^2)
43,560 ft^2 = 1 acre (a)	10,000 m^2 = 1 hectare (ha)
4840 yd^2 = 1 acre	

Volume

1728 cubic inches (in.^{3}) = 1 cubic foot (ft^3)	1000 cubic millimeters (mm^3) = 1 cubic centimeter (cm^3)
27 ft^3 = 1 cubic yard (yd^3)	1,000,000 cm^3 = 1 cubic meter (m^3)

Liquid Capacity

8 fluid ounces (fl oz) = 1 cup (c)	1000 milliliters (mL) = 1 liter (L)
2 c = 1 pint (pt)	1000 L = 1 kiloliter (kL)
2 pt = 1 quart (qt)	
4 qt = 1 gallon (gal)	

Weight and Mass

16 ounces (oz) = 1 pound (lb)	1000 milligrams (mg) = 1 gram (g)
2000 pounds = 1 ton (t)	1000 g = 1 kilogram (kg)
	1000 kg = 1 metric ton

Temperature

32°F = freezing point of water	0°C = freezing point of water
98.6°F = normal body temperature	37°C = normal body temperature
212°F = boiling point of water	100°C = boiling point of water

Time

60 seconds (s) = 1 minute (min)	365 days = 1 year (yr)
60 minutes = 1 hour (h)	52 weeks (approx.) = 1 year
24 hours = 1 day (d)	12 months = 1 year
7 days = 1 week (wk)	10 years = 1 decade
4 weeks (approx.) = 1 month (mo)	100 years = 1 century

Tables

Table 3 Formulas From Geometry

You may need geometric formulas as you work through your algebra book. Here are some perimeter, area, and volume formulas.

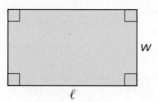

$P = 2\ell + 2w$
$A = \ell w$

Rectangle

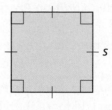

$P = 4s$
$A = s^2$

Square

$C = 2\pi r$ or $C = \pi d$
$A = \pi r^2$

Circle

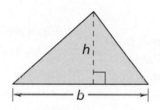

$A = \frac{1}{2}bh$

Triangle

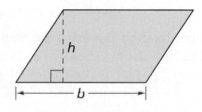

$A = bh$

Parallelogram

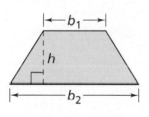

$A = \frac{1}{2}(b_1 + b_2)h$

Trapezoid

$V = Bh$
$V = \ell wh$

Rectangular Prism

$V = \frac{1}{3}Bh$

Regular Pyramid

$V = Bh$
$V = \pi r^2 h$

Right Cylinder

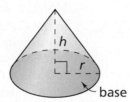

$V = \frac{1}{3}Bh$
$V = \frac{1}{3}\pi r^2 h$

Right Cone

$V = \frac{4}{3}\pi r^3$

Sphere

...Properties, Postulates, and Theorems...

Properties and Theorems

Theorem 3.1, p. 255

The slope between two points on a distance-time graph is the average speed of travel between those points.

Collinearity and Slope, p. 263

Three points A, B, and C, are collinear if and only if the slope between A and B is the same as the slope between B and C.

A, B, and C are collinear $\Leftrightarrow m(A, B) = m(B, C)$.

Chapter 4

Theorem 4.1, p. 279

The slope between any two points on a line is constant.

Theorem 4.2, p. 308

If two distinct lines have the same slope, then they are parallel.

Theorem 4.3, p. 309

If two lines have different slopes, then they must intersect in exactly one point.

Theorem 4.4
Additive Property of Equality, p. 313

If $X = A$ and $Y = B$, then $X + Y = A + B$, where A, B, X, and Y can be any mathematical expressions.

Theorem 4.5, p. 317

Given the system $ax + by = e$ and $cx + dy = f$, where a, b, c, d, e, and f are known constants, the unique solution is $(x, y) = \left(\frac{de - bf}{ad - bc}, \frac{af - ce}{ad - bc} \right)$ when $ad - bc \neq 0$. If $ad - bc = 0$, the graphs of the two equations have the same slope, so they are either parallel (the system has no solutions) or the same (the system has infinitely many solutions).

Theorem 4.6 p. 347

The solution to a linear inequality is a half-plane whose boundary is the graph of the corresponding equation. If the inequality uses < or >, the solution *does not* include the boundary line. If the inequality uses ≥ or ≤, the solution *does* include the boundary line.

Chapter 5

Theorem 5.1 *The Law of Exponents*, p. 402

For any number a and positive integers b and c, $a^b \cdot a^c = a^{b+c}$.

Theorem 5.2, p. 408

For any number $a \neq 0$ and positive integers b and c, where $b > c$, $\frac{a^b}{a^c} = a^{b-c}$.

Theorem 5.3, p. 409

For any number a and positive integers b and c, $(a^b)^c = a^{bc}$.

Theorem 5.4, p. 410

For any numbers a and b, and positive integer m, $(ab)^m = a^m b^m$.

Corollary 5.4.1, p. 410

For any numbers a and b ($b \neq 0$), and positive integer m, $\left(\frac{a}{b} \right)^m = \frac{a^m}{b^m}$.

Zero Exponent, p. 415

If $a \neq 0$, then $a^0 = 1$.

Negative Exponent, p. 415

If $a \neq 0$, then $a^{-m} = \frac{1}{a^m}$.

Scientific Notation, p. 419

A number written in scientific notation has the form $a \times 10^b$, or $-a \times 10^b$, where $1 \leq a < 10$ and b is an integer.

Theorem 5.5, p. 434

When the differences between consecutive outputs in a table are the same, and the differences between consecutive inputs are the same, you can write a linear function for the table.

Exponential Growth and Decay, p. 462

An exponential function has the form $f(x) = a \cdot b^x$, where b is any positive real number.

Chapter 7

Theorem 7.1
Perpendicular Bisector Theorem, pp. 579, 580

Each point on the perpendicular bisector of a segment is equidistant from the two endpoints of the segment.

Chapter 8

Postulate 8.1
The Triangle Congruence Postulates, p. 616

If two triangles share the following triplets of congruent corresponding parts, the triangles are congruent.

• ASA   • SAS   • SSS

Theorem 8.1, p. 641

The composition of two reflections over intersecting lines produces a rotation. Its center is the intersection of the lines. The measure of the angle of rotation is equal to twice the measure of the smaller angle formed by the two lines.

Properties and Theorems

Theorem 8.2 Distance Formula, p. 664

The distance between two points (x_1, y_1) and (x_2, y_2) can be found using the Pythagorean Theorem. It is the square root of the sum of the square of the difference in the x-coordinates and the square of difference in the y-coordinates.

Theorem 8.3 Midpoint Formula, p. 664

Each coordinate of the midpoint of a line segment is equal to the average of the corresponding coordinates of the endpoints of the line segment.

Theorem 8.4, p. 669

Two nonvertical lines are parallel if and only if they have the same slope.

Postulate 8.2, p. 670

Let A, B, and C be three points, no two of which are in line vertically. Points A, B, and C are collinear if and only if the slope between A and B, $m(A, B)$, is the same as the slope between B and C, $m(B, C)$.

Theorem 8.5, p. 674

Two nonvertical lines are perpendicular if and only if the product of their slopes is -1.

Honors Appendix

Theorem H.1 The Head-Minus-Tail Test, p. 694

Two vectors are equivalent if and only if head minus tail for one vector gives the same result as head minus tail for the other.

$\overrightarrow{AB}$ is equivalent to $\overrightarrow{CD}$ if and only if $B - A = D - C$.

Corollary H.1.1, p. 694

If A and B are points, the vector from O to $(B - A)$ is equivalent to the vector from A to B.

Theorem H.2, p. 696

If $A = (a_1, a_2)$ and $B = (b_1, b_2)$, then $A + B$ is the fourth vertex of the parallelogram that has A, O, and B as three of its vertices and $\overline{OA}$ and $\overline{OB}$ as two of its sides.

Theorem H.3, p. 697

Suppose A is a point, c is a number greater than or equal to 1, and $B = cA$. Then,
- B is collinear with A and the origin.
- B is c times as far from the origin as A.

Theorem H.4, p. 698

Adding the same point to the tail and to the head of a vector produces an equivalent vector.

Theorem H.5, p. 700

If A is a point different from the origin, the set of all multiples of A is the line through the origin and A.

Theorem H.6, p. 702

Two vectors $\overrightarrow{AB}$ and $\overrightarrow{CD}$ are parallel if and only if there is a number k such that $B - A = k(D - C)$. If $k > 0$, the vectors have the same direction. If $k < 0$, the vectors have opposite directions. If $k = 1$, the vectors are equivalent.

Theorem H.7, p. 703

If A and B are points, then the segment from O to $B - A$ is parallel and congruent to $\overline{AB}$.

Theorem H.8, p. 741

Suppose matrix A represents a system where the z's are linear combinations of y's. Suppose B represents a system where these y's are linear combinations of x's. Then, by substitution, the z's are linear combinations of the x's, and the matrix that represents this system is the product AB.

Glossary

A

additive identity (p. 30) The number 0 is the additive identity because when you add 0 to any number the result is the number itself.

additive inverse (p. 30) The additive inverse of a number is the number's opposite. The sum of a number and its additive inverse is 0.

algorithm (p. 61) An algorithm is a set of ordered steps for solving a problem.

altitude *See* **cone; cylinder; prism; pyramid; triangle.**

association (p. 505) An association is a dependent relationship between two variables.

axiom (p. 29) An axiom is a basic fact that does not require justification.

B

backtracking (p. 121) Backtracking is the process of solving an equation using, in reverse order, steps that undo the operations.

balance point (p. 526) The balance point is the point that represents the mean of data values.

base case (p. 440) The base case is the starting output in a table for a recursively defined function.

basic moves for solving equations (p. 144) The two basic moves for solving equations state that you can add the same number to each side of an equation or multiply each side of an equation by the same number without changing the solutions of the equation.

basic rules of arithmetic (p. 28) The basic rules of arithmetic govern how addition and multiplication work for the set of integers.

box-and-whisker plot (p. 495) A box-and-whisker plot is a data display that uses quartiles to form the center box and the maximum and minimum values to form the whiskers.

Players' Heights

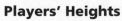
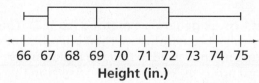

Height (in.)

C

collinear (p. 262) Collinear points are points that lie on the same line.

combining like terms (p. 104) Combining like terms is the process of grouping like terms to simplify an expression.

composition (p. 631) A composition of two transformations is a transformation that is equivalent to performing the first transformation and then performing the second transformation on the image of the first.

compound interest (p. 457) Compound interest is interest calculated on the current balance, including the previously paid interest.

congruent (p. 649) Two shapes are congruent if there is an isometry that maps one shape onto the other.

congruent figures (p. 649) Two figures are congruent if they have the same size and shape regardless of location or orientation.

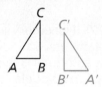

$\triangle ABC$ is congruent to $\triangle A'B'C'$.

correlation coefficient (p. 514) The correlation coefficient is a numerical calculation that measures the strength of associations.

cube (p. 399) To cube a number, you multiply the number times the number times the number.

cutoff point (p. 332) A cutoff point is an intersection point of two graphs used to help find the solution of an inequality in one variable. The x-coordinates of all the cutoff points divide the number line into regions to check.

D

decimal expansion (p. 41) The decimal expansion of a number gives the address of the number on a number line. The number is written as a sum of units, tenths, hundredths, and so on.

decimal representation (p. 42) The decimal representation of a number is the decimal form of the number. The decimal representation of a number can be used to approximate the value of, for example, a fraction or a square root.

direction *See* **vector.**

direct variation (p. 225) A direct variation is the relation of two variables that are in a constant ratio.

domain (p. 383) The domain of a function is the set of inputs of the function.

dot product (p. 731) The dot product is an operation over two n-tuples that returns a real number. If $A = (a_1, a_2, \ldots, a_n)$ and $B = (b_1, b_2, \ldots, b_n)$ then the dot product $A \cdot B$ is the real number $a_1b_1 + a_2b_2 + \ldots + a_nb_n$.

dot plot (p. 488) A dot plot is a graphical representation of a data set that shows data points on a simple scale.

E

elimination method (p. 314) The elimination method for solving a system of equations is adding or subtracting two equations to produce a new equation in which one of the variables is eliminated.

empty set (p. 127) The empty set (or null set) is a set with no elements. The solution set to an equation with no solutions is the empty set, also called the null set. In symbols, it is { } or ∅.

equation (p. 126) An equation is a mathematical sentence that states that two quantities are equal.

equivalent vectors (p. 692) Equivalent vectors are vectors that have the same size and direction, but different heads and tails.

expansion box (p. 72) An expansion box is a table in which numbers being multiplied are written in place-value parts along the top and down the side of the table. Each pair of place-value parts is multiplied and the products are added to give the final product.

exponential decay (p. 462) A situation modeled with a function of the form $y = ab^x$, where $a > 0$ and $0 < b < 1$.

exponential growth (p. 462) A situation modeled with a function of the form $y = ab^x$, where $a > 0$ and $b > 1$.

extension of a rule (p. 20) The extension of a rule extends a process from one group to a larger group. For example, you can extend the basic rules of arithmetic for whole numbers to integers.

F

first quartile See **five-number summary.**

fitting line (p. 495) A fitting line is a line that comes close to the data points in a scatter plot.

five-number summary (p. 495) A five-number summary is an overview of a sorted set of data that uses five key values.

- The *minimum* is the least value in the set.
- The *first quartile* is the data value that is greater than or equal to the lowest 25% of the data values.
- The *median* is the middle value of the set.
- The *third quartile* is the data value that is greater than or equal to the lowest 75% of the data.
- The *maximum* is the greatest value in the set.

fixed point (p. 624) A fixed point is an input that remains unchanged by a function.

frequency table (p. 481) A frequency table for a data set is a list of categories that classifies the number of data that occur in each category.

What Do You Call Carbonated Drinks?

State	"Pop"	"Soda"	"Coke"	Other
Minnesota	4265	630	39	92
New York	3321	7364	262	200
Georgia	49	346	2196	149
Washington	2678	714	105	98

Source: Alan McConchie's Survey

function (p. 373) A function is a rule that assigns each element from a set of inputs to exactly one element from a set of outputs.

G

graph of an equation (p. 196) The graph of an equation is the collection of all points with coordinates that make the equation true.

The coordinates of the points on the graph make $y = |x| - 1$ true.

graph of a function (p. 388) The graph of a function g is the graph of the equation $y = g(x)$.

guess-check-generalize method (p. 162) The guess-check-generalize method is a problem-solving method used to find the equation for a word problem. You guess the answer to the problem and keep track of the steps you use to check the guess. You repeat this process until you are able to generalize the steps with a variable and write the appropriate equation.

H

head *See* **vector.**

histogram (p. 489) A histogram is a graphical representation of a data set that shows frequencies of data as bars.

I

identity matrix (p. 756) An identity matrix is a square matrix with all entries 0 except for 1's along the main diagonal from the top left to the bottom right. Multiplying a matrix by an identity matrix will result in the original matrix.

image (p. 621) The image of a point is the matching point after a transformation.

independent (p. 505, 513) Two events A and B are independent if the result from one event has no effect on the other. If A and B are independent, then $P(A \text{ and } B) = P(A) \cdot P(B)$.

integer (p. 28) An integer is a number in the set $\mathbb{Z} = \{\cdots, -3, -2, -1, 0, 1, 2, 3, \cdots\}$

interquartile range (p. 497) The interquartile range of a data set is the difference between the third quartile and the first quartile.

intersection point (p. 215) An intersection point is a point where two or more graphs intersect.

inverse variation (p. 227) An inverse variation is the relation between two variables that have a constant product.

isometry (p. 648) An isometry, or rigid motion, is any composition of reflections, translations, and rotations.

L

least common denominator (p. 68) The least common denominator of two or more fractions is the least common multiple of their denominators.

like terms (p. 104) Like terms are terms in which the variable factors are exactly the same.

line of best fit (p. 531) A line of best fit is the graph of the linear equation that most accurately shows the relationship between two sets of data.

line of reflection *See* **reflection.**

line of symmetry (p. 559) The line of symmetry of a parabola acts as a mirror for a parabola and passes through the vertex.

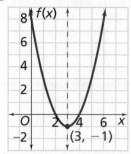

line segment (p. 562) A line segment is a part of a line consisting of two endpoints and all of the points between the two endpoints.

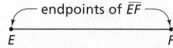

linear equation (p. 149) A linear equation is an equation in which the variable terms are not raised to a power. The graph of a linear equation is a line.

linear function (p. 427) A linear function is a function with a graph that is a line. For a linear function, the differences between consecutive outputs are the same, and the differences between consecutive inputs are the same.

lowest terms (p. 38) A fraction is in lowest terms when the numerator and denominator have no common factor other than 1.

M

matrix multiplication (p. 740) Let A have as many columns as B has rows. Say, A is $m \times n$ and B is $n \times p$. Let the rows of A be called $R_1, R_2, \ldots, R_m$. Let the columns of B be called $C_1, C_2, \ldots, C_p$. The product AB is defined to be the $m \times p$ matrix for which the entry ij is the dot product $R_i \cdot C_j$.

$$AB = \begin{pmatrix} R_1 \cdot C_1 & R_1 \cdot C_2 & \cdots & R_1 \cdot C_p \\ R_2 \cdot C_1 & R_2 \cdot C_2 & \cdots & R_2 \cdot C_p \\ \vdots & \vdots & \ddots & \vdots \\ R_m \cdot C_1 & R_m \cdot C_2 & \cdots & R_m \cdot C_p \end{pmatrix}$$

matrix transformation (p. 775) A transformation is called a matrix transformation if it can be expressed in the form $X \mapsto AX$, where A is a 2×2 matrix and points X are represented as column vectors $\begin{pmatrix} x \\ y \end{pmatrix}$ so that they can be multiplied by matrices on the left.

maximum (p. 495) The maximum of a graph is the highest value achieved on the vertical axis.

mean (p. 481) To find the mean of a set of numbers, divide the sum of the numbers by the number of values in the set.

mean absolute error (p. 545) The mean absolute error is the average of the absolute values of the differences between the line of best fit and the actual data points.

mean squared error (p. 545) The mean squared error is the average of the squares of the differences between the line of best fit and the actual data points.

median (p. 481, 495, 581) The median is the middle value in an ordered set of values. If there is an even number of values, the median is the mean of the two middle values. *See also* **five-number summary.**

midline (p. 581) A midline is a segment that connects the midpoints of two sides of a triangle. The midline is also known as a midsegment.

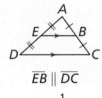

$$\overline{EB} \parallel \overline{DC}$$

$$EB = \tfrac{1}{2}DC$$

$\overline{EB}$ is a midline of $\triangle ACD$.

midpoint (p. 579) A midpoint is the point on a segment that is halfway between two endpoints. A midpoint on a coordinate grid is the average of the coordinates of the endpoints of the segment.

midpoint of $\overline{AB}$

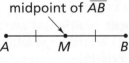

minimum (p. 495) The minimum of a graph is the lowest value achieved on the vertical axis.

mode (p. 481) The mode is the data value that occurs most often in a data set.

multiplicative identity (p. 30) The number 1 is the multiplicative identity because when you multiply any number by 1 the result is the number itself.

N

n-tuple (p. 731) An n-tuple is a string of n numbers.

negatively associated (p. 513) Two variables are negatively associated when large values of the first variable tend to occur with small values of the second, and small values of the first variable tend to occur with large values of the second.

negative exponent (a^{-m}) (p. 415) If $a = 0$, then $a^{-m} = \frac{1}{a^m}$.

negative number (p. 12) Negative numbers are the numbers less than zero.

null set *See* **empty set.**

number line (p. 12) A number line is a line that represents real numbers and continues forever in two directions.

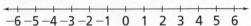

O

opposites (p. 13) Two numbers are opposites if they are equidistant from zero and on opposite sides of zero on a number line. The sum of opposites is zero.

outlier (p. 536) An outlier of a data set is a data point that is clearly separated from the rest of the data.

P

parallel lines (p. 562) Parallel lines are lines in the same plane that do not intersect.

parameter (p. 712) A parameter is an unknown coefficient.

perpendicular bisector (p. 579) The perpendicular bisector of a segment is a line that is perpendicular to the segment at the segment's midpoint.

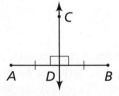

place-value part (p. 61) A place-value part is a number that has a single leading digit followed by some number of zeros.

point-tester (p. 196) A point-tester is an equation used to determine whether particular points are on a graph.

positively associated (p. 513) Two variables are positively associated when large values of the first variable tend to occur with large values of the second, and small values of the first variable tend to occur with small values of the second.

preimage (p. 621) The preimage is the original figure before a transformation.

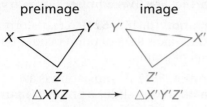

preimage   image

$\triangle XYZ \longrightarrow \triangle X'Y'Z'$

This transformation maps X to X', Y to Y' and Z to Z'.

prism (pp. 562) A prism is a polyhedron with two congruent and parallel *faces*, called the *bases*. The other faces, which are parallelograms, are the *lateral faces*. An *altitude* of a prism is a perpendicular segment that joins the planes of the bases. The *height* of the prism is the length of its altitude.

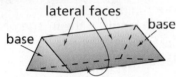

lateral faces

base   base

triangular prism

probability (p. 169) A probability is a fraction or decimal used to describe the likelihood that a specific event will happen.

Q

quadrant (p. 198) The *x*- and *y*-axes divide the coordinate plane into four quadrants.

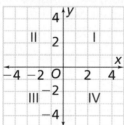

R

range (p. 497) The range of a function is the set of objects that are paired with objects from the domain. *See* **function**.

range of a function (p. 383) The range of a function is the set of outputs produced by the function.

reciprocal (p. 77) The reciprocal of a fraction is the result you get by exchanging the numerator and the denominator. When you multiply a number by its reciprocal, the product is 1.

recursive rule (p. 440) A recursive rule is a description that tells how to get an output from previous outputs.

reflection (p. 625) A reflection, or flip, is a transformation that maps a point in the plane to its mirror image using a *line of reflection* as a mirror.

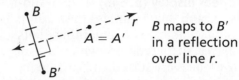

B maps to B' in a reflection over line *r*.

reversible operation (p. 120) An operation is reversible if there is a second operation that always brings you back to the situation before the first operation.

rigid motion *See* **isometry**.

rotation (p. 640) A rotation is a transformation that turns a figure about a fixed point, the *center of rotation*.

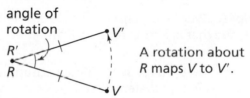

angle of rotation

A rotation about R maps V to V'.

S

scalar multiplication (p. 725) Multiplying a matrix by a number (called a scalar) is scalar multiplication.

scatter plot (p. 511) A scatter plot is a graph that shows each pair of related data as a point in the coordinate plane.

scientific notation (p. 419) A number in scientific notation is in the form $a \times 10^b$ or $-a \times 10^b$, where $1 \le a < 10$ and b is an integer.

slope (p. 249, 279) The slope between two points with different *x*-coordinates is the change in the *y*-coordinates divided by the change in the *x*-coordinates of the points.

solution (p. 126) A solution is a value of a variable that makes an equation true.

solution set (p. 127) A solution set is the collection of all solutions of an equation or inequality.

speed (p. 253) Speed is the rate at which distance traveled changes.

square (p. 399) To square a number, you multiply the number times itself.

standard error (p. 55) The standard error is a measure of error involving the square root of the mean squared error.

stem-and-leaf display (p. 545) A stem-and-leaf display is a graph that organizes the leading digits of data as stems. The remaining digits become leaves. In an ordered stem-and-leaf display, the leaves are sorted and written in ascending order.

Ages of Winners of Best Actor in a Leading Role

```
2 | 9
3 | 2 7 8 1 6 7 8
4 | 3 2 5 6 0 7 3 5
5 | 1 4 2
6 | 1 0
Key: 2 | 9 means 29 years
```

subscript (p. 249) The subscripts "1" and "2" indicate that x_1 and x_2 represent different variables.

substitution method (p. 301) The substitution method for solving a system of equations is solving one equation for one of its variables and then replacing that variable in the other equation with the resulting expression.

symmetric (p. 559) A figure is symmetric if you can fold it in half so that the two halves fit exactly on top of each other.

system of equations (p. 304) A system of equations is a group of equations with the same variables. A solution of the system is a set of values of the variables that make all the equations true.

T

third quartile See **five-number summary.**

transformation (p. 189, 621) A transformation is a rule that takes a set of points and produces another set of points.

translation (p. 631) A translation is a transformation that slides a graph or figure horizontally, vertically, or both without changing the size or shape of the graph. A translation on a coordinate plane is a transformation that adds a numeric value to each coordinate of the image.

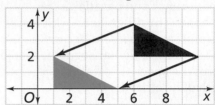

The blue triangle is the image of the black triangle under the translation $(-5, -2)$.

two-way frequency table (p. 504) A two-way frequency table displays the distribution for two categorical variables.

V

variable (p. 93) A variable is a placeholder for an unknown number.

vector (p. 692) A vector is an arrow that starts at one point, the *tail*, and points to a second point, the *head*. Given two points A and B, the vector from A to B is the ordered pair of points (A, B).

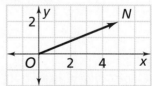

Vector *ON* has initial point *O* (tail) and terminal point *N* (head). The ordered pair notation for the vector is (5, 2).

Z

zero exponent (a^0) (p. 415) If $a \neq 0$, then $a^0 = 1$.

Selected Answers

Chapter 1

Lesson 1.01
On Your Own

6. It increases by 2; moving up is the same as adding 1, and moving right is the same as adding 1.

Lesson 1.02
Check Your Understanding

1. a. on 6/18, with check number 003 **b.** More than $160 **c.** Answers may vary. Sample: He could deposit more money into his account. **2. a.** 36°F **b.** −11°F **3. a.** 3 **b.** 14 **c.** −3 **d.** −1 **e.** Subtract 9. **f.** 5

On Your Own

4. a. 3 **c.** 15 **e.** Subtract 7.

Lesson 1.03
Check Your Understanding

1. a–d. Explanations may vary. Samples are given. **a.** True; sums of two positive integers are in the upper right quadrant of the extended addition table, where all entries are positive numbers. **b.** True; sums of two negative integers are in the lower left quadrant of the extended addition table, where all entries are negative numbers. **c.** False; for example, $-5 + 7 = 2$. **d.** False; for example, $-7 + 5 = -2$. **2.** $3 + (-11) = (-4) + (-4)$ $(-23) + 13 = 1 + (-11)$ $20 + (-10) = 2 + 8$ $32 + (-18) = 16 + (-2)$ **3.** Answers may vary. Sample: Find the answer to the addition problem $11 + (-5)$. **4.** Answers may vary. Sample: To evaluate $a - b$, locate a in the addition table, and move down b entries. **5.** a, c, e **6.** 143 will show up in every column. The 143's form a diagonal, down and to the right.

On Your Own

7. a. 6 **c.** −7 **e.** 0 **9. a.** 0 **11.** The positive numbers are located above the "0 diagonal" from Exercise 10; a large triangle in the upper right part of the table.

Lesson 1.04
Check Your Understanding

1. a. 1444 **b.** −1444 **c.** −1444 **d.** 1444 **e.** −1444 **f.** 1444 **2. a.** 4 **b.** 4 **c.** −4 **d.** −4 **e.** $\frac{1}{4}$ **f.** $-\frac{1}{4}$ **3.** 9 and 9 **4. a.** Answers may vary. Sample: $4 \cdot (3) = 12$. Moving down 1 entry subtracts 4, so moving down 6 entries to −3 subtracts 24. Therefore $4 \cdot (-3) = -12$. **b.** Answers may vary. Sample: $4 \cdot (-3) = -12$. Moving left

1 entry adds 3, so moving left 8 entries adds 24. Therefore $-4 \cdot (-3) = 12$. **5.** 8 times; $10 \cdot 1 = 10$, $5 \cdot 2 = 10$, $2 \cdot 5 = 10$, $1 \cdot 10 = 10$, $(-10) \cdot (-1) = 10$, $(-5) \cdot (-2) = 10$, $(-2) \cdot (-5) = 10$, $(-1) \cdot (-10) = 10$ **6.** 72 **7. a.** 0 **b.** 1

On Your Own

8. b, d. Examples may vary. Samples are given. **b.** False; for example, $(-2)(-3) = 6$ and $(-2)(-5) = 10$. **d.** True; for example, $(-2)(3) = -6$ and $(2)(-5) = -10$. **9.** 4 and 4 **12.** in the upper right quadrant and the lower left quadrant; large squares in the upper right and lower left quadrants

14. Answers may vary. Sample: As you move up the diagonal, the differences between each entry and the previous one are successive even numbers, starting with 4.

Lesson 1.05
Check Your Understanding

1. Answers may vary. Sample: The table is symmetric about the diagonal along the perfect squares; therefore, the order of the multiplication does not matter. **2.** Answers may vary. Sample: The numbers in the 1 column of the multiplication table are identical to the numbers directly to the right in the vertical axis, and the numbers in the 1 row of the multiplication table are identical to the numbers directly below in the vertical axis. **3.** 5; $5 + (-5) = 0$ **4.** all but inverses of addition

On Your Own

5. Answers may vary. Samples are given. **a.** $10 \cdot 473$ **c.** $42 \cdot (200 + 3)$ **6. a.** 39 **e.** −18

Lesson 1.06
On Your Own

5. a–d.

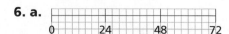

6. a.

Lesson 1.07
Check Your Understanding

1. $\frac{1}{7}, \frac{3}{7}, \frac{4}{7}, \frac{6}{7}, \frac{9}{7}, \frac{10}{7}$ **2.** $\frac{0}{6}$ or 0, $\frac{1}{6}, \frac{4}{6}$ or $\frac{2}{3}, \frac{5}{6}, \frac{6}{6}$ or 1 **3.** $\frac{0}{3}$ or 0, $\frac{1}{3}, \frac{2}{3}, \frac{4}{3}$ or $1\frac{1}{3}, \frac{5}{3}$ or $1\frac{2}{3}$
4. a. 8 **b.** 25 **c.** 9 **d.** 14 **e.** 51 **f.** 6 **g.** $2\frac{1}{2}$ **h.** 6

i. 33 **5.** The numbers are not in order.

6.

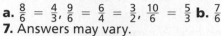

a. $\frac{8}{6} = \frac{4}{3}$, $\frac{9}{6} = \frac{6}{4} = \frac{3}{2}$, $\frac{10}{6} = \frac{5}{3}$ **b.** $\frac{7}{6}$

7. Answers may vary.

Sample:

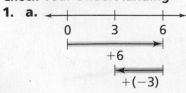

On Your Own
8. Answers may vary. Sample: $\frac{7}{3}$, $\frac{-7}{-3}$, $\frac{14}{6}$, $\frac{-42}{-24}$
11. a. Q **e.** R **14. a.** 2 **c.** 5

Lesson 1.08
Check Your Understanding
1. a. 0.4 **b.** 0.66666 . . . , repeating decimal
c. 0.875 **d.** 2.25 **e.** 0.55555 . . . , repeating
decimal **f.** 0.63636 . . . , repeating decimal
2. a. $\frac{12}{25}$ **b.** $\frac{247}{100}$ **c.** $\frac{1}{5}$ **d.** $\frac{3333}{1000}$ **e.** $\frac{19}{5}$ **f.** $-\frac{1369}{1000}$
g. $\frac{8}{9}$ **h.** $\frac{41}{99}$ **3.** Yes, and yes; explanations
may vary. Sample: The mean of two numbers
always exists and is always between the two
numbers.   **4. a–c.** Answers may vary. Samples
are given. **a.** 0.991, 0.992 **b.** 0.99991, 0.99992
c. 0.9999991, 0.9999992 **d.** Yes; explanations
may vary. Sample: You can divide the segment
between the two points on a number line into
thirds. The points of division are two numbers
between the original two.

5.

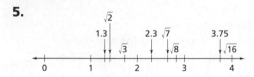

6. a. The scale is way off. **b.** Either 3 will be
indistinguishable from 0, or the number line
will be extremely long.

On Your Own
7. 0.06, 0.09, 0.12, 0.18, 0.21, 0.24, 0.27
9. a. $\frac{163}{100}$ **e.** $-\frac{1}{8}$ **12.** 3.009, 3.08, 3.18, 3.5999, 3.7
Lesson 1.09
Check Your Understanding
1. **a.**

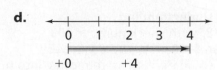

b.

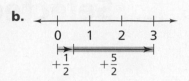

c.

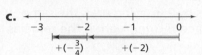

d.

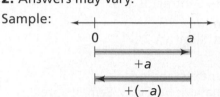

2. Answers may vary.
Sample:

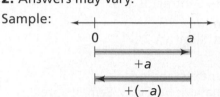

3. a. Q **b.** S **c.** P **d.** R **4.** Tony lined up the tips
of the arrows.   **5. a.** $\frac{8}{3}$ **b.** $\frac{1}{2}$ **c.** $\frac{1}{3}$ **d.** $\frac{5}{77}$ **e.** 0
6. a. 1, $\frac{3}{2}$, 2, $\frac{5}{2}$, 3 **b.** $\frac{1}{4}$, $\frac{3}{4}$, 1, $\frac{5}{4}$, $\frac{3}{2}$ **c.** $\frac{1}{8}$, $\frac{3}{8}$, $\frac{1}{2}$, $\frac{5}{8}$, $\frac{3}{4}$
d. $\frac{1}{9}$, $\frac{2}{9}$, $\frac{1}{3}$, $\frac{4}{9}$, $\frac{5}{9}$

On Your Own
9. a. 0.4, 0.6, 0.8, 1, 1.2
c. 1.1, 3.3, 4.4, 5.5, 6.6   **10. a.** 0 **d.** 8
Lesson 1.10
Check Your Understanding
1. a. 8 **b.** 7 **c.** 12 **d.** 5   **2.** Moving the negative
sign rotates the rectangle, but the area
remains the same.   **3.** If 0 had an inverse, the
product of the inverse and zero would be 1.
But the product of any number and 0 is always

0.   **4. a.** V **b.** Y **c.** U **d.** X **5. a.** $\frac{1}{4}$ **b.** 2 **c.** 4
d. $\frac{1}{2}$ **e.** $-\frac{1}{9}$ **f.** $-\frac{1}{3}$ **g.** Answers may vary. Sample:
First find the number that must equal the
quantity in the parentheses in order to make
the equation true. Then find the number to fill
in the blank that would make the sum inside
the parentheses equal the number you got in
the first step.

On Your Own
6. a. 6 **d.** $\frac{8}{15}$ **8. a.** V **c.** Y
Lesson 1.11
On Your Own
3. $A = 2$, $B = 3$, $C = 9$ **5. a.** $94.97

Lesson 1.12
Check Your Understanding

1–7. Answers may vary. Samples are given.
1. This algorithm uses the any-order, any-grouping property of addition. It works best with summands that are close to round numbers.   **2.** This algorithm uses the any-order property of addition. It works best with a sum featuring several summands, where certain pairs of them add to place-value parts.   **3.** This algorithm uses the any-order, any-grouping property of addition since borrowing expresses a number as a sum of two summands, one of which you then add to a neighboring number in the subtraction problem. This algorithm will work well in nearly any situation, though others may work better in some cases.   **4.** This algorithm relies on the any-grouping property of addition along with the property that subtraction is the same as adding the opposite. It works best when the difference between the two numbers is less than either of them.
5. This algorithm uses the any-order property of addition, since it does not matter which place values you add first. This algorithm is convenient for adding numbers in your head.
6. This operation works because addition and subtraction are inverse operations. This algorithm is convenient for adding numbers in your head.   **7.** This algorithm uses the any-order property of addition. It only works with consecutive integers.

On Your Own

10. 8795   **13.** $98\frac{1}{3}$ yd or 295 ft   **14. a.** No; the units are not the same. **c.** $5333\frac{1}{3}$ yd^2

Lesson 1.13
Check Your Understanding

1. 1   **2. a.** 15; 15 **b.** 16; 56; 60 **c.** when they have no common factor **d.** No; the product of two denominators is always a common denominator, and therefore a greater common denominator cannot be the *least* common denominator.   **3. a.** $\frac{23}{44}$ **b.** $\frac{4}{5}$ **c.** Answers may vary. Sample: Jill's method works because each summand is being multiplied by 1, and therefore does not change. **d.** yes

On Your Own

4. 21   **5. a.** $\frac{1}{11}$ **c.** $\frac{1}{4}$ **9. a.** $\frac{5}{3}$ **c.** $\frac{3}{4}$

Lesson 1.14
Check Your Understanding

1. a. Multiply each of the place-value parts of one number by the other number. Add the results. **b.** Multiplying a number by the sum of the place-value parts of another number is the same as adding the products of that number and each place-value part of the other number. **c.** This algorithm is almost always useful, though it can sometimes be hard to do in your head.   **2. a.** Multiplying by $\frac{1}{2}$ and then multiplying by 10 is the same as multiplying by $\frac{10}{2}$, or 5, by the any-grouping principle of multiplication. **b.** This algorithm is most useful when it is easy to calculate half of a number. **c.** Take a quarter of a number and then multiply by 100.   **3. a.** This algorithm is based on the Distributive Property since
$8 \cdot 99 = 8 \cdot (100 - 1) = 800 - 8 = 792$
b. This algorithm works only when multiplying by 99, and works best when the resulting subtraction is easy to calculate. **c.** Multiply by 100 and then subtract twice the starting number.   **4. a.** To see how this algorithm works, consider an example. To multiply 29 and 24, you can write 29 as a sum of 1 and powers of 2. So 29×24
$= (16 + 8 + 4 + 1) \times 24$
$= (2^4 + 2^3 + 2^2 + 1)$
$= (2^4 \times 24) + (2^3 \times 24)$
$\quad + (2^2 \times 24) + (1 \times 24)$
Notice that this process exactly mimics the way you find the sum of the starred entries in the double column in the table. **b.** This algorithm is not useful in most cases.   **5. a.** This algorithm works because multiplication is repeated addition. As the slanted line goes up each vertical unit, it also goes across the number of units given by the product of the factor that comes from the dashed horizontal line and the factor that comes from the intersection of the slanted line and the bold horizontal line. **b.** This algorithm is mainly useful as a visualization tool.

c.

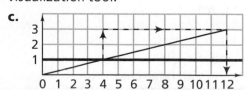

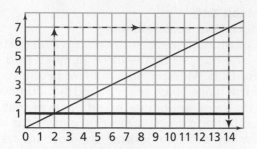

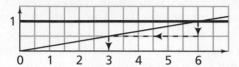

d. To divide a number by 2, for instance, draw a slanted multiplication line that crosses the horizontal line at 2. Start at the number you want to divide by 2 and move up until you reach the multiplication line. Then move to the left until you reach the vertical line. The number you reach is the quotient.

On Your Own
6. c. 12 days **8. a.** 3738 **c.** 73,593 **9.** $A = 4$, $B = 2$, $C = 8$, $D = 5$, $E = 7$

Lesson 1.15
Check Your Understanding
1. Answers may vary. Sample: To transport 17 people in cars that seat 4 per car, you need 5 cars. **2.** Answers may vary. Sample: If a restaurant bill is $17 for four people, the cost per person is $4.25. **3. a.** $\frac{7}{10}$ **b.** 3 **c.** 1 **d.** $\frac{3}{2}$ **e.** because of the any-order, any-grouping properties **4. a.** $\frac{5}{6}$ **b.** 2 **c.** Answers may vary. Sample: Multiplying by the denominator is the same as multiplying by the numerator of the reciprocal, and vice versa. **5. a.** 21 **b.** 46 **c.** 22 **d.** 25 **e.** $\frac{7}{4}$

On Your Own
8. a. 80 **c.** 75 **10. a.** $\frac{1}{5}$

Chapter 2
Lesson 2.01
On Your Own
4. Yes, it will always work. **5.** You get twice your number every time. **7.** 10

Lesson 2.02
Check Your Understanding
1. a. 10 **b.** 6 **c.** 52 **d.** 64 **e.** $m - 1$ **f.** $n + 1$
2. a. doctors **b.** gallons of water **c.** medical kits **d.** pillows **e.** blankets **3. a.** II **b.** IV **c.** I **d.** III **e.** V **4. a.** Choose a number. Multiply by 2 and then add 1. **b.** Choose a number, subtract 1, and then multiply by −2. **c.** Choose a

number, add 2, multiply by 5, and then subtract 2. **d.** Choose a number, add 1, multiply by 3, subtract 2, multiply by 7, and then subtract 9. **5.** $2 \cdot ((x + 5) - 11) + 3$

On Your Own
6. b. 16 **7. b.** III **10. a.** ℓw **b.** $2\ell + 2w$
11. a. $\frac{x}{2}$

Lesson 2.03
Check Your Understanding
1. 610 beds, 2700 pounds of food, 5000 gallons of water; 1310 beds, 5600 pounds of food, 10,500 gallons of water **2. a.** 10 **b.** 10 **c.** 10 **d.** 10 **3. a.** $3(n - 1) + 5$ **b.** 35 **c.** 5
4. a. $5(3n - 2)$ **b.** 50 **c.** 10 **5. a.** 24 **b.** $\frac{35}{2}$
c. $\frac{7}{4}$ **d.** $\frac{7}{4}$ **6. a.** $3 \cdot (7 + 3) = 30$
b. $(-3 + 3) \cdot 5 + 11 = 11$
c. $-3 + 3 \cdot (5 + 11) = 45$
d. $25 - (5 + 4 \cdot 5) = 0$
e. $25 - (5 + 4) \cdot 5 = -20$

On Your Own
7. a. 2 cubic meters **9. a.** 14 **e.** −28 **10. a.** 32
e. 60 **11. a.** 2.5 meters per second

Lesson 2.04
Check Your Understanding
1. The trick results in 6 every time; yes;
$\frac{(2x + 7) \cdot 5 + 25}{10} - x = 6$ **2.** Add 35.
3. a. Subtract 3. **b.** Subtract your starting number. **4. a.** 15 **b.** 15 **c.** 15 **d.** 15 **e.** 15 **f.** 15 **g.** 15
h. $\frac{x + 2x + 3x + 4x + 5x}{x} =$
$\frac{1}{x}(x + 2x + 3x + 4x + 5x) =$
$\frac{x}{x} + \frac{2x}{x} + \frac{3x}{x} + \frac{4x}{x} + \frac{5x}{x} =$
$1 + 2 + 3 + 4 + 5 = 15$
5. a. $12x + 6$; $8x + 10$ **b.** $7x - 28$; $2x + 6$
c. $3x - 4$; $12x - 15$ **d.** $90 - 18x$; $38 - 4x$

On Your Own
6. a. yes **c.** No; by way of a counterexample, let $x = 1$ and $y = 0$. Then $6xy = 0$, but $4x + 2y = 4$. **7. a.** $10x + 18$; $10x + 22$
9. e. $\frac{4}{3}$ **12. b.** 35

Lesson 2.05
Check Your Understanding
1. a. $\frac{a}{b} = a \cdot \frac{1}{b}$ **b.** $c - d = c + (-d)$
c. $ab = (-a) \cdot (-b)$ **d.** If $a \cdot b = 1$, then $a = \frac{1}{b}$ and $b = \frac{1}{a}$. **2. a.** If "$a = 0$" is true, then "$a = 0$ or $b = 0$" is true **b.** Every nonzero number has a reciprocal. **c.** The left side becomes b and the right side becomes 0.
d. It shows that either a or b has to be 0. That is, if $a \neq 0$, then $b = 0$.

On Your Own
3. a. $4♥6 = 3(4) + 6 = 18$ **b.** 22 **c.** no
5. a. $x + 2$ **d.** $4x + 8$ **6. a.** $4x + 19$
7. c. $6x - 23$ **8. a.** $x \rightarrow x + 6 \rightarrow 3x + 18 \rightarrow$
$3x + 8 \rightarrow 6x + 16 \rightarrow 6x + 66 \rightarrow x + 11$

Lesson 2.06
On Your Own
8. a. 9 **d.** Impossible; any number other than
0 divided by itself equals 1. **9. a.** 5 times
f. unable to determine

Lesson 2.07
Check Your Understanding
1. Unbuckle the seat belt, open the door, stand
up, and close the door. The steps are reversed
and then performed in the opposite order.
2. Answers may vary. Sample: $2 \rightarrow 2 + 6 = 8$
$\rightarrow 8 \div 4 = 2 \rightarrow 2 \times 8 = 16 \rightarrow 16 + 7 = 23$
$\rightarrow 23 \times 10 = 230$ Undo by dividing by 10,
subtracting 7, dividing by 8, multiplying by 4,
and subtracting 6. **3. a.** Add 13; subtract 13.
b. Divide by -2; multiply by -2. **c.** Multiply
by 5, subtract 12 and then multiply by 3; Divide
by 3, add 12, and then divide by 5. **d.** Multiply
by 15 and then subtract 36; add 36 and then
divide by 15. **4.** 10 **5.** $\frac{1}{3}$

6. a.

Input, x	Output, x^2
-4	16
-3	9
-2	4
-1	1
0	0
1	1
2	4
3	9
4	16

b. There is more than one input for certain
outputs.

c.

Input, x	Output, x^3
-4	-64
-3	-27
-2	-8
-1	-1
0	0
1	1
2	8
3	27
4	64

yes

d.

Input, x	Output, x^4
-4	256
-3	81
-2	16
-1	1
0	0
1	1
2	16
3	81
4	256

Input, x	Output, x^5
-4	-1024
-3	-243
-2	-32
-1	-1
0	0
1	1
2	32
3	243
4	1024

Input, x	Output, x^6
-4	4096
-3	729
-2	64
-1	1
0	0
1	1
2	64
3	729
4	4096

Input, x	Output, x^7
-4	$-16,384$
-3	-2187
-2	-128
-1	-1
0	0
1	1
2	128
3	2187
4	16,384

All odd powers are reversible.

e. The product of an even number of negative
numbers is positive. All odd powers of -3 are
negative.

On Your Own
7. a. Square a number and then add 6; not
reversible. **b.** Multiply by 3 and then subtract
28; add 28 and then divide by 3.
8. -2 **11.** Tables B and D **14. a.** 5 **d.** -6

Lesson 2.08
Check Your Understanding

1. -4 **2.** $\frac{117}{2}$ **3.** 120 **4.** -8 **5.** 55

6. $\frac{39}{5}$ **7. a.** 7 **b.** 1 **c.**

a	b
0	$\frac{25}{2}$
1	12
2	$\frac{23}{2}$
3	11
4	$\frac{21}{2}$
5	10

d. $b = \frac{75 - 3a}{6}$ **8. a.** $1^3 + 26(1) = 27 =$
$11(1)^2 + 16$; $8^3 + 26(8) = 720 = 11(8)^2 + 16$
b. Answers may vary. Sample: 0 and 3 (any
number other than 1, 2, or 8 is not a solution).
c. 2

On Your Own

10. a. Add 2, multiply by 3, and then subtract 1. **11. a.** 4 **d.** $-\frac{5}{3}$

Lesson 2.09

On Your Own

10. a. 6 **13. a.** no **b.** yes **14. a.** yes **c.** no **15. a.** 42

Lesson 2.10

Check Your Understanding

1. $\ell = 15$ **2.** $j = 5$ **3.** $n = \frac{3}{2}$ **4.** $x = \frac{8}{5}$
5. $x = -5$ **6.** $y = 8$ **7.** $a = 3$ **8.** $u = 7$
9. $m = 9$ **10. a–e.** Answers may vary. Samples are given. **a.** $x + 5$ **b.** $11 - x$ **c.** $5x + 15$ **d.** $6x - 12$ **e.** the value of the expression when $x = 3$ **11. a.** $r = 14$
b. $x = -2$ **c.** $a = -\frac{3}{20}$ **d.** $s = 50$

On Your Own

12. $r = 2$ **14.** $p = 12$ **15.** $x = 4$
16. a. $x = 7$ **e.** $x = 3$ **17. b.** $x + 2$
19. a. $x = 3$ **c.** $b = \frac{9}{5}$

Lesson 2.11

Check Your Understanding

1. a. $x = 9$ **b.** $x = -\frac{1}{6}$ **c.** $x = -\frac{1}{6}$
d. $a = 9$ **e.** $z = 9$ **f.** True for all values of n. **2.** Answers may vary. Sample: Subtract $48x$ from each side. Add 15 to each side. Divide by the coefficient of x, which is 25. **3.** The ending number will be 11. **4. a.** Subtract 6 from each side. **b.** Subtract t from each side. **c.** Add 100 to each side. **d.** Subtract $3t$ from each side. **e.** Subtract $5t$ from each side.

f. Multiply each side by 5. **5.** $x = \frac{7}{2}$ for all the equations in Exercise 4; since all the equations came about by applying the basic moves to the same equation, they all have the same solution. **6. a.** Subtract 13 from 27 to get 14. Divide 14 by 4 to get $\frac{7}{2}$. Add 7 to get $\frac{21}{2}$. **b.** $4(x - 7) + 13 = 27$
$4(x - 7) + 13 - 13 = 27 - 13 \quad 4(x - 7) = 14$
$\frac{4(x - 7)}{4} = \frac{14}{4} \quad x - 7 = \frac{7}{2} \quad x - 7 + 7 =$
$\frac{7}{2} + 7 \quad x = \frac{21}{2}$ **c.** Answers may vary. Sample: The two processes are similar in that the backtracking steps in part (a) are exactly the operations performed in part (b). They are different in that, when you use backtracking, you are only performing the operations on the number on the right side of the equation. When you use basic moves to solve, you must always perform the operation on each side of the equation. **7. a.** $4z + 2 = z - 4$; by the basic moves, $z = -2$. **b.** $2x + 2 = 2x + 7$;

after subtracting $2x$ from each side, you get $2 = 7$, which is false. **c.** $3s + 12 = 3(s + 3) + 3$; by the Distributive Property, $3(s + 3) + 3 = 3s + 9 + 3 = 3s + 12$.

On Your Own

8. $f = 20$ **11. a.** Subtract 4 from each side. **e.** Divide each side by 2.
13. a. $x \to 3x \to 3x + 5 \to 12x + 20 \to$ $12x + 36 \to x + 3 \to 3$ **b.** Yes; the ending number is always 3. **16. a.** all numbers

Lesson 2.12

Check Your Understanding

1. $r = 4$ **2.** $w = \frac{3}{4}$ **3.** no solution
4. $u = \frac{32}{7}$ **5.** $r = 4$ **6.** all real numbers
7. a–e. Answers may vary. Samples are given.
a. $2x + 1 = 7$ **b.** $3x + 4 = 2x + 9$
c. $7x - 10 = 4x - 5$ **d.** $14x + 21 = 8x - 45$
e. $x = x + 1$ **8. a.** Subtract 15 from each side.
b. Subtract $(6x + 2y)$ from each side.
c. Subtract $6x$ from each side. **d.** Subtract $6x$ from each side and then divide each side by 2. **9.** 19 **10. a.** 72 **b.** -15 **c.** 100
11. a. false **b.** true **c.** false **d.** may be true or false **e.** true **f.** true **g.** may be true or false **h.** true **i.** may be true or false

On Your Own

12. $a = -\frac{5}{2}$ **13.** all real numbers
15. a. $x = \frac{20}{3}$ **16. a.** true **b.** false

Lesson 2.13

Check Your Understanding

1. $x = \frac{9}{2}$ **2.** $j = 1$ **3.** $k = \frac{8}{3}$
4. $x = -10$ **5.** $s = -\frac{6}{5}$ **6.** $w = -4$
7. $q = \frac{5}{2}$ **8.** $e = \frac{9}{4}$ **9.** $x = 1$ **10.** $z = -\frac{1}{3}$
11. Answers may vary. Sample: If $a = b = 1$, then $(a + b)^2 = (1 + 1)^2 = 2^2 = 4$, but $a^2 + b^2 = 1 + 1 = 2$.

12.

13.

14.

On Your Own

15. $a = \frac{13}{2}$ **19.** $x = -\frac{1}{2}$ **22. a.** $24x - 84$ **f.** $-12x + 24$

828

Selected Answers

Lesson 2.14
On Your Own
5. a. sometimes true **c.** never true; $-3 \neq 3$
f. always true; $6 = 6$ **6.** \$15 per hour **7. a.** 3

Lesson 2.15
Check Your Understanding
1. a. Answers may vary. Sample: because one fourth of 4 is 1, which is an easy number to work with **b.** 5 **c.** 15; 12 is $4 \cdot 3$, and 15 is $5 \cdot 3$.
d. 168 **2. a.** no **b.** yes **c.** no
d. $8(35 + n) = 360$ **e.** $n = 10$ **3.** 5 **4. a.** yes
b. no **c.** yes **d.** \$103.53 **5.** 9 years old

On Your Own
6. 504 pages **7.** 51 years old **9. a.** not join
11. 98 **12.** \$12

Lesson 2.16
Check Your Understanding
1. a. The equation states that the ratio between price with discount and original price is 80%. **b.** Division by zero is undefined.
c. $d - 12 = \frac{8}{10}d$ **d.** $10d - 120 = 8d$
e. $d = 60$ **2. a.** $\frac{3}{10}$ **b.** $\frac{7}{10}$ **c.** 0.9 **d.** $1 - p$
3. 0.75 **4.** no **5. a.** 7.44; 8.0 **b.** no;
$\frac{6.4 + 8.0 + 8.1 + 6.5 + 8.2 + 7.6}{6} \approx 7.467$
c. Answers may vary. Sample:
8.0, $\frac{6.4 + 8.0 + 8.1 + 6.5 + 8.2 + 8.0}{6} \approx 7.533$
d. $\frac{37.2 + x}{6} = 7.5$ **e.** $x = 7.8$ **6. a.** 7.4
b. 7.7; 7.25

On Your Own
7. 141 **9.** 16 years old **10.** about 2545 miles

Lesson 2.17
Check Your Understanding
1. $y = -x - 13$ **2. a.** $y = \frac{13}{4}$ **b.** $y = \frac{33}{4}$
c. $x = -\frac{13}{2}$ **d.** No; replacing x with 20 and y with 13 yields $79 = 78$, which is false. **e.** No; since the equation in part (e) is equivalent to the equation in part (d), (20,13) is not a solution. **3. a.** $w = \frac{4}{3}h$ **b.** $h = \frac{3}{4}w$ **c.** $\frac{45}{4}$ in.
d. 28 in. **e.** 35 in. **4. a.** No; if you substitute 10 for x and 6 for y, you get $86 = 90$, which is false.
b. $y = \frac{15}{2}$; any other value for y makes the equation false. **c.** Answers may vary. Samples: (0, 15), (18, 0), (6, 10), (12, 5) **d.** The points fall on a straight line. **5. a.** between \$2524 and \$2674 **b.** \$4524 to \$4674
c. $p - 75 \leq g \leq p + 75$ **6. a.** Once you remove the border, the remaining space should

have the proportions of the photograph. So if you take away 4 from the width and 4 from the height, then these should be in a 4-to-3 ratio.
b. $w = \frac{4(h - 4)}{3} + 4$, or $\frac{4h - 4}{3}$ **c.** $\frac{44}{3}$ in.
d. $\frac{56}{3}$ in. **e.** $\frac{76}{3}$ in. **7. a.** No; 4 nickels and 8 dimes are \$1. **b.** No; 6 nickels and 4 dimes are \$.70. **c.** $0.05n + 0.1d = 0.9$ **d.** $d = 9 - 0.5n$
e. No; if Chi had an odd number of nickels, $9 - 0.5n$ would not be an integer.

On Your Own
8. a. not true; $5y = 10x + 20$ **d.** true
9. a. $2\ell + 2w$ **c.** $\ell = -5 + 3w$ **11. a.** no
12. a. $p = \frac{210 - 41\ell}{26}$

Chapter 3
Lesson 3.01
On Your Own
6.
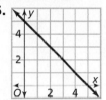
The graph is a line.
7.
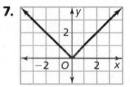
The graph is shaped like a V. **8. a.** Answers may vary. Sample: (0, 3), (1, 3), (2, 3), (3, 3), (4, 3), (5,3) **b.** Answers may vary. Sample: (3, 0), (3, 1), (3, 2), (3, 4), (3, 5), (3, 6) **c.** The y-coordinate is 3.

Lesson 3.02
Check Your Understanding
1. a. The point moves to the right. **b.** The point moves up. **c.** The point moves to the left. **2.**
a. The points, and the square, move 1 unit to the right. **b.** The points, and the square, move 5 units to the right and 2 units up. **c.** The points, and the square, move 2 units to the left and 1 unit up. **3. a.** Yes; answers may vary. Sample: $(x, y) \mapsto (x + 5, y + 4)$ **b.** Yes; answers may vary. Sample: $(x, y) \mapsto (x + 5, y - 2)$

4. a. The points move vertically to twice their original distance from the *x*-axis. The square is transformed into a rectangle twice as tall as it is wide, with twice the area. **b.** The points move horizontally to twice their original distance from the *y*-axis. The square is transformed into a rectangle twice as wide as it is tall, with twice the area. **c.** The points move horizontally and vertically to twice their original distances from both the *x*-axis and *y*-axis. The square remains a square, but with side lengths twice as long. **d.** Each point moves counterclockwise to the position of an adjacent corner of the square. The square remains unchanged.   **5.** Answers may vary. Samples: $(x, y) \mapsto (-x, y)$, $(x, y) \mapsto (y, x)$

6. a.

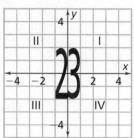

b.

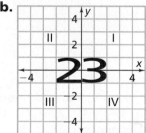

c.

7. Answers may vary. Sample: Any two quadrants must be either adjacent or opposite. If a line passes through only two opposite quadrants (and no other quadrants), it must also pass through the only point that the borders of the two quadrants have in common, namely the origin. For a line to pass through two adjacent quadrants, but not a third quadrant, it must be entirely on one side of one of the axes. This is possible only if the

line is parallel to that axis—that is, vertical or horizontal. Therefore it is not possible for a slanted line to pass through only two quadrants and not pass through the origin as well.

On Your Own
8. a. The new point is the same distance away from, but on the other side of, the *y*-axis.
10. c. yes; a rectangle; 27 square units

13.

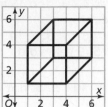 a cube

Lesson 3.03
Check Your Understanding
1. a. Answers may vary.
Sample: (0, 4), (1, 4), (2, 4), (−1, 4), (−2, 4), (1.2, 4)

b. The graph is a horizontal line passing through the point (0, 4).

2. a.

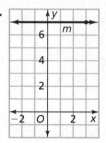

b. Answers may vary. Sample:
(0, 7), (1, 7), (−1, 7), (900, 7), (0.01, 7), (−7, 7)
c. Answers may vary. Sample: (0, 0), (1, −7), (−1, 1),(90, 1), (1, 90), (−7, 5)
d. A point is on *m* if its *y*-coordinate is 7.
e. $y = 7$

3. a.

b. Answers may vary. Sample: (3, 0), (3, 1), (3, −1), (3, 900), (3, 0.01), (3, −3) **c.** Answers may vary. Sample: (0, 0), (−3, 1), (1, −1), (0.01, 900), (900, 0.01), (5, −3) **d.** A point is on *ℓ* if its *x*-coordinate is 3. **e.** $x = 3$
4. a. (5, 0) and (−3, 4) are on the graph.

(−3, 0) is not on the graph. **b.** Answers may vary. Sample: (−5, 0), (0, 5), (3, 4), (3, −4)
5. a. Answers may vary. Sample: (0, 0), (1, 1), (17, 17), (−1, −1), (π, π)
b. Answers may vary. Sample: (0, 1), (1, 0), (3, 4), (−1, 1), (π, −π) **c.** The graph is a line that passes through the origin.

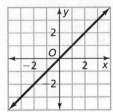

The x- and y-coordinates for each point on the line are equal.

6. a. Answers may vary. Sample:

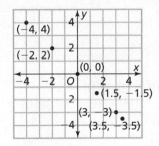

b. The graph is a line. **c.** D; the x- and y-coordinates for each point on the line are opposites.

On Your Own
7. a. $y = 4$ **8. a.** on neither **d.** on r
10. b. $y = 2$ **11. b.** $x = -4$

c.

Lesson 3.04
Check Your Understanding
1. The equation $2y + 3x = 4$ has a different graph from the other three. You can change the other three into each other using basic moves.   **2. a.** 5 **b.** $\frac{5}{2}$ **c.** $\frac{25}{2}$ **d.** $\frac{9}{2}$ **e.** $-\frac{5}{2}$ **f.** 15

a–f.
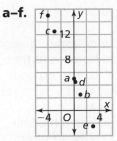

g.
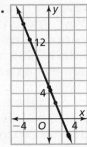

3. The first graph is the graph of $y - 3 = |x|$ and the second graph is the graph of $y = |x - 3|$. You can tell which graph is which by testing points from the graph in each equation.   **4.** From left to right and top to bottom, the graphs correspond to equations b, a, d, and c. You can tell which graph corresponds to which equation by plotting several points that satisfy each equation.

5. a. $h = 160 - 16t^2$ **b.** 160 ft **c.** 144 ft, 96 ft, 16 ft **d.** 3.2 s

e.
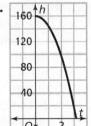

f.
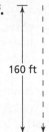

160 ft

6. a. $h = 320 - 16t^2$ **b.** 320 ft **c.** 304 ft, 256 ft, 176 ft, 64 ft **d.** No; the grape takes about 4.5 seconds to fall 320 feet.

e.
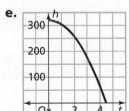

On Your Own
8. a. II; the graph of $y = -2$ is a horizontal line that passes through (0, −2).

9.
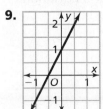

Lesson 3.05
Check Your Understanding
1. a–c. Answers may vary. Samples are given. **a.** Fred starts 8000 feet from home and then walks home at a steady rate. **b.** The number of people willing to buy a movie ticket decreases as the price of the ticket increases. **c.** Julie starts with 8 gallons of gas in her tank. She runs out after 200 miles. **2. a–b.** Answers may vary. Samples are given. **a.** George starts out slowly, then speeds up for 4.5 hours, then slows down for 0.5 hour, and then stops, 25 miles from home. **b.** Martha starts out faster than George, and travels at varying speeds for about 3.5 hours, at which time she is 30 miles from home. Then she turns around and takes another 5.5 hours driving home. **c.** Assuming they are taking the same route, George and Martha pass each other, going in opposite directions. **d.** George is not moving. **e.** 60 miles **f.** 25 miles **3.** The graph starts at the origin because, at time 0, the height of the water is 0. The height increases at a constant rate, which means that for every additional unit of time, the height increases by the same amount. **4.** (I)–B; (II)–A; (III)–D; (IV)–F; (V)–E; (VI)–C; buckets I and II have straight sides, so the water level rises at a constant rate. But since II is narrower than I, the graph for II is steeper. The water level in bucket III rises at a constant rate until the bucket becomes narrower, and then it rises at a faster constant rate. Bucket IV starts narrow, so it starts to fill quickly. It slows down, so the graph becomes less steep over time. When it is halfway filled, it begins to fill more quickly again, and the graph becomes steeper. Bucket V begins filling slowly since it has a wide base, so the graph starts relatively flat. Bucket V gets narrower, so the water level rises more quickly, and the graph gets steeper. Bucket VI is the opposite of bucket V, so its graph starts steep and becomes less steep over time.

On Your Own
5. b. He turns around and starts back home.
6. Answers may vary. Sample:

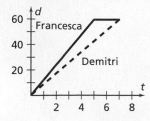

8. d. 5

Lesson 3.06
Check Your Understanding
1. a. (100, 25) satisfies neither equation. **b.** (−25, −25) does not satisfy the second equation. **c.** (1000, 1000) does not satisfy the second equation. **d.** (1000, 500) satisfies neither equation. **e.** (500, 500) satisfies both equations. **2.** Answers may vary. Sample: $x = 3$, $y = -1$ **3. a.** No; if the graphs intersect at a point (a, b), then

$b = 3a - 2 = 3a + 2$. But $3a - 2 = 3a + 2$ implies $-2 = 2$, which is false. Therefore, the two graphs do not intersect. **b.** You get a false statement. **4. a–b.** Answers may vary. Samples are given. **a.** $y = 0$, $y = 1$ **b.** The graphs never intersect because they are both horizontal lines. **5. a.** The equation $x^2 + y^2 = 25$ corresponds to the circle. The equation $16x^2 + 9y^2 = 288$ corresponds to the ellipse. **b.** The four intersection points are (3, 4), (−3, 4), (−3, −4) and (3, −4). The square of any number, positive or negative, is always positive.
$(\pm 3)^2 + (\pm 4)^2 = 9 + 16 = 25$
$16(\pm 3)^2 + 9(\pm 4)^2 = 16(9) + 9(16) = 144 + 144 = 288$

On Your Own
7. Answers may vary. Sample: $y = 4$; $x = -5$

Lesson 3.07
On Your Own
4. a. Answers may vary. Sample:
(−3, 9), (−2, 4), (−1, 1), (0, 0), (1, 1), (2, 4), (3, 9)
5. a.

6. c. shifted 3 units to the left **7. a.** yes
9. b. 39.2 m/s; 78.4 m/s; 156.8 m/s
c. v doubles **10. a.** 250 lawns

Lesson 3.08
Check Your Understanding
1. a. $200,000 **b.** 21 **c.** It is an inverse variation. If the number of winners doubles, then the prize for each winner is halved. **d.** $p = \frac{1{,}000{,}000}{w}$, where w is the number of winners and p is the prize per winner. **2. a.** Yes; since (8, 2) is on the graph, (2 · 8, 2 · 2) = (16, 4) is also on the graph. **b.** $c = \frac{1}{4}$ **c.** Answers may vary. Sample: A campground shower costs $.25 per minute. Here x is the length of the shower, and y is the cost of the shower in dollars.

3. a. no **b.** no **c.** yes **d.** yes **e.** no **f.** yes
4. a. no **b.** no **c.** yes **d.** yes **e.** yes **f.** no   **5.** The value of y decreases; y cannot equal 0.   **6.** The graph is symmetrical about the lines $y = x$ and $y = -x$ and symmetrical about the origin.
7. a. Answers may vary. Samples: $(12, -1)$, $(6, -2)$, $(4, -3)$, $(3, -4)$, $(2, -6)$, $(1, -12)$
b. Quadrants II and IV; for $xy = -12$ to be true, either x or y must be negative, while the other is positive.
c.

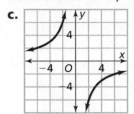

8. 0   **9. a.** $(-a)(-b) = (-1)(-1)(ab) = ab = 100$; $ba = ab = 100$ **b.** $(-b, -a)$

On Your Own
10. a. $25 **d.** Direct variation; when the number of cartons doubles, the total cost also doubles.   **12. a.** $y = 7x$ **16. a.** x cannot be 0. Division by 0 is undefined.

Lesson 3.09
Check Your Understanding
1. all of them   **2.** $y = x^2$ and $y = |x|$ **3.** none of them   **4. a.** I: $y = |x|$; II: $y = x^3$; III: $y = \frac{1}{x}$ **b.** I: $y = x^2$; II: $y = x$; III: $y = x^3$
5. a. $y = \sqrt{x}$ **b.** $y = x^3$ **c.** $y = |x|$ **d.** $y = x$
e. $y = x^2$ **f.** $y = \frac{1}{x}$ **g.** $y = x^3$ **h.** $y = \sqrt{x}$
6. $\frac{1}{x}$, $\sqrt{x}$, $|x|$, x^2, x^3

7. a. **b.**

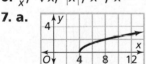

$x \geq 4$ and $y \geq 0$ $x \leq 0$ and $y \geq 0$

On Your Own
9. $\frac{1}{x}$, x, x^3, x^2, $|x|$ **12. a.** 2   **14. c.** The value of d quadruples.

Lesson 3.10
On Your Own
7. a. 3 ft   **8. a.** $x = 5$ **9. a.** The three points are collinear because they are on the same line.   **10.** 8 mi/h

Lesson 3.11
Check Your Understanding
1. a. $\frac{7}{4}$ **b.** $\frac{7}{4}$ **c.** $-\frac{8}{9}$ **d.** $-\frac{8}{9}$ **e.** $-\frac{8}{9}$ **f.** $-\frac{5}{4}$ **g.** $\frac{4}{5}$
h. $-\frac{5}{4}$ **i.** 0 **j.** 0 **k.** 1 **l.** undefined
2. a–d. Answers may vary. Samples are given.
a. $(0, 6)$ **b.** $(1, 4.5)$ **c.** $(2, -6)$ **d.** $(3, -1)$ **e.** The

points are collinear.   **3. a–b.** Answers may vary. Samples are given. **a.** $A(0, 0)$, $B(2, 2)$
b. $C(0, 0)$, $D(-2, 2)$ **c.** $F(2, 3)$, $G(-2, 3)$
d. $K(7, 2)$, $L(7, -2)$ **4.** Answers may vary. Sample: The graphs that have constant slope involve only x and y multiplied by constant coefficients, with no exponentiation.

4. a.

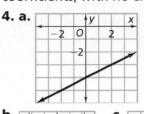

b. **c.**

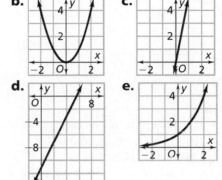

d. **e.**

f.

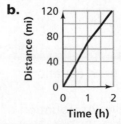

5. Answers may vary. Sample: Ski slopes, hiking trails, and roller coaster tracks all vary in steepness.   **6.** $r = 2$

On Your Own
7. a. $-\frac{2}{3}$ **d.** undefined   **8. a.** Answers may vary. Sample: $(4, 0)$ **9. a.** One point is above and to the right of the other point.   **10. a.** $-\frac{4}{3}$

Lesson 3.12
Check Your Understanding
1. a. 75 mi/h **b.** 0 mi/h **c.** Answers may vary. Sample: If you have points $D(0.5, 37.5)$ and $E(1.25, 75)$, then $m(D, E) = 50$.   **2. a.** $6
b. About 57 mi/h; no, he will not get fined.
3. a. $6 **b.** about 67 mi/h; yes **c.** about 3 hours, 5 minutes   **4. a.** at most $59\frac{1}{11}$ mi/h
b.

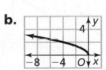

5. a. 280 mi; 4 h **b.** Answers may vary. Sample:

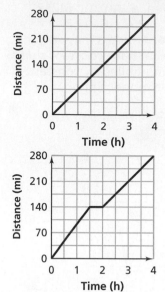

On Your Own
6. a. Car A: Hybrid car; Car B: Sedan; Car C: SUV **7. a.** About 41 s **8. a.** miles per hour **10. a.** 1,150 yd **b.** about 26 s
13. a. between *O* and *P*, *Q* and *S*, and *S* and *U* **b.** between *Q* and *S*

Lesson 3.13
Check Your Understanding
1. a. yes **b.** yes **c.** yes **d.** no **2.** points *A*, *B*, and *D*; $m(A, B) = m(B, D) = 1$ **3.** Answers may vary. Sample: It is sufficient to compare just two of the slopes to test collinearity. If you know two of the slopes are equal, then the third must be equal to the other two.
4. a–c. Answers may vary. Samples are given.
a. $(1, -4)$ **b.** $(-4, 0)$ **c.** $(2, 4)$ **5.** Answers may vary. Sample: $\frac{y-3}{x-2} = -\frac{7}{10}$

On Your Own
6. a. Answers may vary. Sample: $(0, -3)$, $(2, 5)$, $(4, 13)$; yes **8. a.** Not on ℓ; the slope between $R(-2, 4)$ and $(1, 3)$ is $-\frac{1}{3}$. **9. a.** $a = \frac{11}{4}$

Chapter 4
Lesson 4.01
On Your Own
7. a. 9000 ft **8. c.** 42,000 ft; yes
11. a. $\frac{y}{x-5} = \frac{1}{2}$ **12. e.** $y = 2x - 5$

Lesson 4.02
Check Your Understanding
1. $y - 2 = -\frac{1}{4}(x - 6)$; yes; both equations simplify to $y = -\frac{1}{4}x + \frac{7}{2}$.
2. Answers may vary. Sample: An equation of the line through the points $(5, 6)$ and $(3, 2)$ is

$y - 2 = 2(x - 3)$; $(1, -2)$ is on the line because $-2 - 2 = 2(1 - 3)$ simplifies to the true statement $-4 = -4$, and $(6, 6)$ is not on the line because $6 - 2 = 2(6 - 3)$ simplifies to the false statement $4 = 6$. **3. a.** $y - 7 = -1(x - 6)$
b. $y - 4 = x - 5$ **c.** $y = \frac{1}{3}x$ **d.** $y = \frac{1}{3}x + 10$
e. $y = -x$ **4. a.** $y = 7$ **b.** $x = 5$ **c.** $y = x$
d. $y = 0$ **5. a.** yes; $\frac{3}{4}$, $(4, 0)$, $(0, -3)$ **b.** no **c.** yes; $\frac{3}{4}$, $(4, 0)$, $(0, -3)$ **d.** yes; 5, $\left(\frac{7}{5}, 0\right)$, $(0, -7)$
e. yes; $\frac{3}{4}$, $(4, 0)$, $(0, -3)$ **f.** yes; $-\frac{5}{3}$, $\left(-\frac{27}{5}, 0\right)$, $(0, -9)$ **g.** no **h.** yes; $\frac{3}{4}$, $(3, 0)$, $\left(0, -\frac{9}{4}\right)$
i. yes; $-\frac{5}{3}$, $\left(\frac{24}{5}, 0\right)$, $(0, 8)$ **6.** Choose two points *A* and *B* on the line with *x*-coordinates *a* and *b*, respectively (where $a \neq b$). Then $A = (a, 3a - 7)$, $B = (b, 3b - 7)$, and $m(A, B) = \frac{(3b - 7) - (3a - 7)}{b - a} = \frac{3b - 3a}{b - a} = \frac{3(b - a)}{b - a} = 3.$

On Your Own
9. a. -5 **11. b.** 42.50

Lesson 4.03
Check Your Understanding
1. a. $y - 3 = -1(x - 4)$ **b.** $y - 5 = \frac{1}{3}(x + 2)$
c. $y + 3 = \frac{4}{5}(x - 7)$ **d.** $y + 5 = -\frac{11}{7}(x + 1)$
e. $y + \frac{1}{2} = 2\left(x + \frac{3}{2}\right)$ **f.** $y + 9.8 = -4.38(x - 14.6)$ **g.** $y = \frac{5}{6}x + 12$
h. $y = -\frac{2}{3}x - 3$ **i.** $y = \frac{5}{16}x - \frac{8}{5}$ **j.** $y = \frac{21}{13}x + 5$
k. $y = 9$ **l.** $x = -8$

2. a.
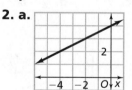
b.
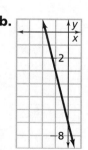

c.
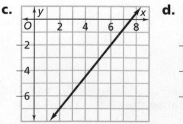
d.
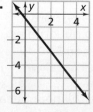

e.
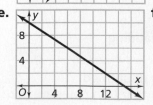
f.
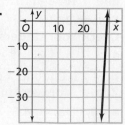

g.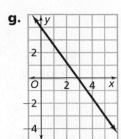

h.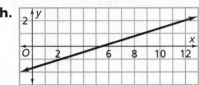

3. a. 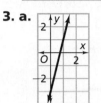 **b.**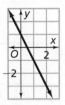

c. 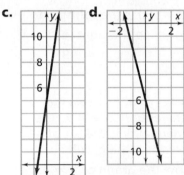 **d.**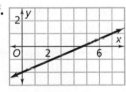

e. 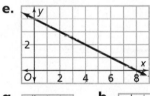 **f.**

g. 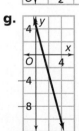 **h.**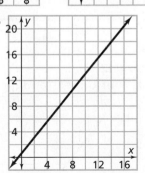

On Your Own

4. $\frac{389}{3}$ **8.** $y + 5 = 4(x + 3)$ **19.** $y = \frac{5}{4}x - \frac{1}{2}$
40. $y = 6x - 1$

Lesson 4.04
Check Your Understanding
1. a. Yakov **b.** at 2 s **c.** 20 ft **d.** Yakov's speed is 20 ft/s; Demitri's speed is 10 ft/s. **e.** $y = 20x$

f. $y = 10x + 20$ **g.** $20x = 10x + 20$; $x = 2$
2. a. They run at the same speed. **b.** Yakov does not overtake Demitri. **c.** Both speeds are 10 ft/s. **d.** $y = 20x$ **e.** $y = 20x + 20$ **f.** Yakov does not overtake Demitri. **3. a.** Yakov is ahead of and stays ahead of Demitri.
b. No; the graphs keep getting farther and farther apart. **c.** $(-2, -20)$ **d.** no

On Your Own
5. Derman **7.** yes; in about 45 seconds

Lesson 4.05
On Your Own
7. a. A and C are on neither; B is on both.
8. b. Answers may vary. Sample: $(0, 0)$; $(5, 5)$ is on p but not on q; $(0, 2)$. **9.** Answers may vary. Sample: $x + y = -2$ and $2x + y = 0$

Lesson 4.06
Check Your Understanding
1. $1.29 **2.** $v = 1.29$; $a = 0.89$ **3. a.** BigPhone costs $.57; LittlePhone costs $.67.

b. 3.5 min **c.** BigPhone **4. a.** $\left(-\frac{1}{4}, -8\frac{1}{2}\right)$
b. $\left(3, \frac{3}{4}\right)$ **c.** $(-4, -12)$ **d.** $(-2, 5)$ **e.** no solution
f. $\left(\frac{1}{2}, 2\right)$ **5. a.** Walton: $2.82; Newtham: $2.25 **b.** Walton: $4.15; Newtham: $4.00
c. Walton: $t = 2.25 + 0.19m$; Newtham: $t = 1.50 + 0.25m$

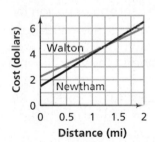

d. 1.25 mi **e.** Walton **f.** when the distance is greater than 1.25 mi **6. a.** $\left(\frac{1}{8}, \frac{15}{8}\right)$ **b.** $\left(\frac{14}{3}, 3\right)$
c. $\left(\frac{100}{19}, \frac{100}{19}\right)$ **7.** Answers may vary. Sample: comparing the costs of two phone service plans based on the number of minutes used
8. Answers may vary. Sample: comparing the costs of three phone service plans based on the number of minutes used

On Your Own
9. a. Just Plumbing **13. a.** $(84, 1482)$ **b.** No solution; the slopes are the same.

Lesson 4.07
Check Your Understanding
1. a. parallel **b.** intersecting **c.** parallel **d.** identical
e. intersecting **f.** intersecting **2.** Tony is right.
3. Answers may vary. Sample: BiggerPhone plan costs $.39 for a connection and $.04 per minute.

The line $y = 0.04x + 0.39$ is parallel to and above the line $y = 0.03x + 0.39$ for all values of x.
4. The two equations are equivalent.

On Your Own
5. $y - 15 = -\frac{1}{5}(x - 10)$ **8.** $y = ax$
9. a. $y = -3$

Lesson 4.08
Check Your Understanding
1. a. $x = 18$, $y = 12$ **b.** $a = \frac{1}{2}$, $b = 5$ **c.** $x = 2$, $y = 0$ **d.** no solution **e.** $w = -3$, $z = 0$
f. $x = 2$, $y = 15$ **2.** The cost of one granola bar is \$.50. The cost of one drink is \$1.25.
3. Multiply each side of the second equation by -2. Add the equations. Solve for y. Substitute 8 for y in one of the original equations. Solve for x. Check the solution by substituting both values into each equation. **4. a.** $y = 1$
b. $x = 6$ **c.** The line $5x + 3y = 33$ also passes through $(6, 1)$. **5.** $x = 6$, $y = 3$, $z = -2$
6. Answers may vary. Sample: Multiply each side of the second equation by $-\frac{a}{c}$. This yields $-ax - \frac{ady}{c} = -\frac{af}{c}$. Add this equation to the first equation in the system. The resulting equation is $by - \frac{ady}{c} = e - \frac{af}{c}$, or $\frac{bcy - ady}{c} = \frac{ce - af}{c}$. Solve for y to get $y = \frac{ec - af}{bc - ad} = \frac{af - ec}{ad - bc}$. To find x, multiply each side of the second equation by $-\frac{b}{d}$ and follow a similar line of reasoning.

On Your Own
7. a. Answers may vary. Sample: $y = 3x + 3$, $y = 3x - 7$
8. c. \$8.25 **10. a.** $(7, -5)$ **11. d.** no solution

Lesson 4.09
On Your Own
10. a. 3 **b.** $(0, 0)$, $(2, 2)$, $(-2, -2)$ **c.** $x = 0$, $x = -2$, or $x = 2$ **d.** $x < -2$ or $0 < x < 2$
11. a. $a > 13$

Lesson 4.10
Check Your Understanding
1. a. 2 **b.** 1 **c.** 0 **2. a.** 1 **b.** 0 **c.** 0 **d.** 2 **e.** 1 **f.** 1
3. a. horizontal line containing $(0, 0)$; the x-axis **b.** -5 and 2 **c.** $-5 < x < 2$ **4.** b, d, e, f **5.** $x^2 + Bx + C$ has solutions if $B^2 \geq 4C$.

On Your Own
7. a. $x = \pm 4$ **10. a.** true **b.** false

Lesson 4.11
Check Your Understanding
1. a.
  b.
  c.

d.
2. a. $x > \frac{73}{7}$ **b.** $1 < x < 7$ **c.** $x < -11$ or $x > 5$
d. $2.9 \leq x \leq 3.1$ **e.** No solution. The inequality is never true. **f.** $x > \frac{73}{7}$ **g.** $x \leq -1$ or $x = 0$ or $x \geq 1$ **3. a.** $x < 5$ **b.** Answers may vary. Sample: The image on the graphing calculator does not give any useful information about the intersection of the lines, since the two lines are so close together. You could adjust the graphing calculator's window to find the intersection, but it is easier to solve the inequality with algebra. **4. a.** $x > \frac{11}{3}$
b. Subtract $2x$ from each side, add 17 to each side, and divide each side by 3. **c.** $x > \frac{20}{3}$
d.

The solution to part (c) is the solution to part (a) translated 3 units to the right. **e.** $x > \frac{44}{3}$
f. $x > -\frac{13}{3}$ **5.** $x \neq 4$ **6a.** $x = -3$
b. $x = -11$**c.**

d. $x \leq -11$ or $x > -3$ **e.** Answers may vary. Sample: Graph the equation $y = 2$. The solution to the inequality is the set of all x-coordinates for which the graph of $y = \frac{x - 5}{x + 3}$ is below the graph of $y = 2$.

On Your Own
9. $-1 < x < 0$ or $x > 1$

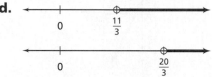

10. b. true

11. a.

14. a. always true

Lesson 4.12
Check Your Understanding
1. a.

b.

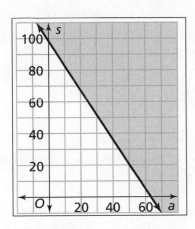

2.

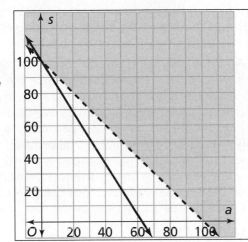

yes

3. a.

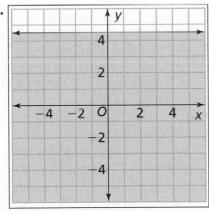

b.

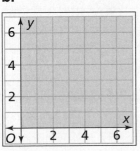

c.

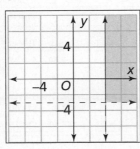

d.

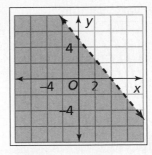

e.

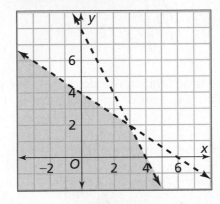

f.

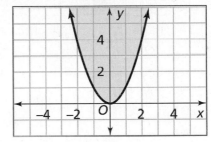

g.

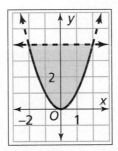

h. no solution

4. a. If $x = 3$, the denominator $= 0$ and division by 0 is undefined.

b–c.

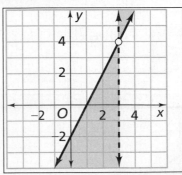

5. a. Answers may vary. Sample:

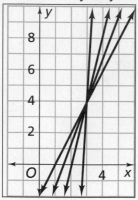

b. There is no limit to the slope. Yes. See part (c). **c.** This is the set of lines bounded by the line $(y - 4) = 2(x - 3)$, or $y = 2x - 2$, and the vertical line $x = 3$.

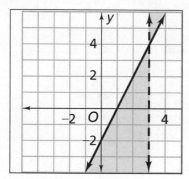

On Your Own
7. (3, 2) **8. b.** (6, 2) **d.** (11, 2)

Lesson 4.13
Check Your Understanding
1. a

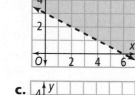

b.

c.

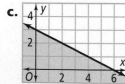

d.

2. a.

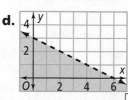

b.

c.

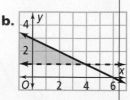

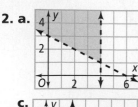

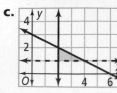

3. $\begin{cases} x < 0 \\ x < 0 \end{cases}$
On Your Own
9. D
10.

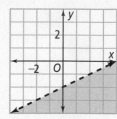

Answers may vary. Sample: Points that Jacob has shaded should not be shaded, since they do not make the inequality true. For example, Jacob has shaded (0, 0), but substituting (0, 0) into the inequality gives   which is false.

11. Answers may vary. Sample: Step 1: Graph the line   Make this line dashed since the inequality has a less than sign, not a less than or equal to sign. Select a point above or below the line. Substitute it into the inequality and see if it makes the inequality true or false. If it makes the inequality true, shade all points on the same side of the line as the test point. If it makes the inequality false, shade all points on the opposite side of the line as the test point.

Chapter 5
Lesson 5.01
On Your Own
6. Sasha's rule is "x returns $x + 3$,'' or "Add 3 to the input,'' or anything equivalent. **7. a.** Yes, you can fill in the second line with 2 or −2 and the fourth line with 1 or −1. **9.** any number greater than 3, because these inputs will give different outputs

Lesson 5.02
Check Your Understanding
1. a. 540 s **b.** 210 s **c.** 246 s **d.** 81 s **e.** 145.8 s
f. $S = 60M$ **2. a.** 0.15 h **b.** 0.583 h **c.** 0.683 h

d. 2.25 h **e.** 4.05 h **f.** $H = \frac{M}{60}$ **3. a.** Alan: $7.31, Lou: $12.18, Katie: $8.91
b. $c + 0.05c + 0.18c = 1.23c$
4. a.

Charity Run Donations						
Number of Miles	Mom	Uncle	Teacher	Coach	Agustina	Total
1	$ 3.50	$ 2.75	$10.00	$ 2.50	$5.00	$23.75
2	$ 7.00	$ 5.50	$10.00	$ 5.00	$5.00	$32.50
3	$10.50	$ 8.25	$10.00	$ 7.50	$5.00	$41.25
4	$14.00	$11.00	$10.00	$10.00	$5.00	$50.00
5	$17.50	$13.75	$10.00	$12.50	$5.00	$58.75

b. $3.50d + 2.75d + 10 + 2.50d + 5 =$ $15 + 8.75d$, where d is the distance Antonio runs in miles. **c.** \$76.25 **d.** 4 mi; 10 mi **5.** The new rule would be that if Antonio runs d miles, he will raise $22.75 + 10.25d$ dollars.

On Your Own
6. a. 180 min **8. c.** 21,600 ft **10.** $1.95\left(\frac{M}{24}\right)$; 246.2 mi

Lesson 5.03
Check Your Understanding
1. a. a function; Output column: $-13, -8, -3,$ $2, 7, 12, 17$ **b.** a function; Output column: $9, 4, 1, 0, 1, 4, 9$ **c.** Not a function; for input -3, there are many outputs, $\frac{1}{2}, \frac{1}{4}$, etc. **d.** a function; Output column: $-4, -5, -6, -7,$ $-6, -5, -4$ **e.** Not a function; for input -3, there are two outputs, -3 and 3.
2. a. $x \mapsto 5x + 2$ **b.** $x \mapsto x^2$ **d.** $X \mapsto |x| - 7$
3. a. The missing output values are $-5, 1,$ $-17, 25$; the missing input value is 7. **b.** $6x - 5$ **4. a.** The missing output values are $-30, -24, -42, 0$; the missing input value is $\frac{37}{6}$. **b.** $6(x - 5)$ **c.** no

On Your Own
5. a. a function; Output column: $2, 1, 0,$ $-1, -2$ **6. a.** A function; for each day, there is one average temperature. **7. a.** Not a function; for some average temperatures, there is not exactly one day of the year with that average temperature.

Lesson 5.04
Check Your Understanding
1. Output column: $5, 3, 1, -1, -3, -5$ **2. a.** $8; \frac{1}{2}$

b. $1 \rightarrow \boxed{x^2 + 4} \rightarrow 5 \rightarrow \boxed{\frac{1}{x}} \rightarrow \frac{1}{5}; \frac{1}{5}.$

c. $x \rightarrow \boxed{x^2 + 4} \rightarrow x^2 + 4 \rightarrow \boxed{\frac{1}{x}} \rightarrow \frac{1}{x^2 + 4}; \frac{1}{29}$

d. $x \rightarrow \boxed{\frac{1}{x}} \rightarrow \frac{1}{x} \rightarrow \boxed{x^2 + 4} \rightarrow \left(\frac{1}{x}\right)^2 + 4;$

$h(\text{REC}(1)) = 5$; $h(\text{REC}(5)) = 4\frac{1}{25}$; no
e. Division by 0 is undefined. **3.** Answers may vary. Sample: Choose f and g to be the same function. **4.** $f(x) = x$ and $f(x) = -x$
5. a. 2; 6 **b.** yes **c.** 0 **d.** yes **e.** 0

On Your Own
6. a. Yes; only g maps 5 to 14. **e.** There are none. **7.** $d = 30t$, where t is time in hours and d is distance in miles. **9. c.** 9

Lesson 5.05
Check Your Understanding
1. a. all negative real numbers **b.** no invalid inputs **2. a.** all real numbers ≥ 2 **b.** all real numbers **c.** all real numbers except 2 **d.** all real

numbers **3. a.** all real numbers except 0 **b.** all real numbers **4. a.** No; Tables I and II both define functions; Table III does not, as input -1 has two outputs. **b.** Table I: domain—$-3, -1, \frac{1}{2}, 2, 9, 100$; range—$3,$ $4, 7, 8, 12$; Table II: domain—$-2, 4, 7, 11,$ 13; range—$-4, 0, 3, 9, 16$ **5.** Answers may vary. Sample: $f(x) = x$, $a = 3$, and $f(3x) = 3 \cdot f(x)$ **6. a.** 1 **b.** 11 **c.** 21

On Your Own
7. all real numbers except 5 and -5 **8. b.** Yes; yes; if the remainder is defined so that it must be 0, 1, or 2, then you can divide 0 and negative numbers by 3 and get a remainder.

Lesson 5.06
Check Your Understanding
1. $A(n) = -2n + 9$; $B(s) = s^2 - 1$; $C(n) = n + \frac{1}{n}$; $D(x) = 0.125x + 12.875$
2. no; no; yes; yes **3.** the first and fourth graphs **4. a.** yes **b.** Answers may vary. Sample:

x	$2 - 5x$
0	2
1	-3
2	-8
3	-13
4	-18

x	$-5(x + 1) + 7$
0	2
1	-3
2	-8
3	-13
4	-18

yes

c. The graphs are the same. **d.** yes **5.** No; answers may vary. Sample: $s(1) = 0$ and $t(1) = 0.01$ **6.** Rule C: Output column: 5, 10, 20, 40, 80, 160 Rule D: The tables are the same for identical inputs. Rule C inputs are nonnegative integers. Rule D inputs are all real numbers. **7.** Output column: 4, 2, 6, 2, 4, 4, 5, 2, 6, 2, 6, 4, 4, 2, 8; conjectures may vary. Sample: Square numbers have an odd number of factors, and all numbers except for 1 have at least two factors; explanations may vary. Sample: Prime numbers only have two factors.

On Your Own
8. a. $4x + 9$

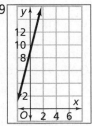

12. a. Answers may vary. Sample:

x	p(x)
−2	−4
−1	−3
0	−2
1	−1
2	0

x	g(x)
−2	undef.
−1	−3
0	−2
1	−1
2	0

no

13. a. yes **c.** no **14. a.** not the same function

Lesson 5.07
On Your Own
5. $26^3 \cdot 10^3 = 17{,}576{,}000$ **6.** 10^4; there are ten choices for each digit, and four digits.
8. a. 10^{16}

Lesson 5.08
Check Your Understanding
1. a. $2^{10} + 2^2 \neq 2^{12}$; $2^{10} + 2^2 = 2^2(2^8 + 1)$ This number is divisible by an odd number $(2^8 + 1)$, but 2^{12} is divisible only by even powers of 2, which are all even.
b. $2^6 \cdot 2^6 = 2^{12}$; this follows from Theorem 6.1.
c. $(2^{10})(2^2) = 2^{12}$; this follows from Theorem 6.1. **d.** $(2^4)(2^3) \neq 2^{12}$; by Theorem 6.1, $(2^4)(2^3) = 2^7$.
e. $(2^4)(2^4)(2^4) = 2^{12}$; this follows from For Discussion Problem 8.
f. $2^9 + 2^3 \neq 2^{12}$; $2^9 + 2^3 = 2^3(2^6 + 1)$. This number is divisible by an odd number $(2^6 + 1)$, but 2^{12} is divisible only by even powers of 2, which are all even. **g.** $2^{11} + 2^{11} = 2^{12}$; $2^{11} + 2^{11} = 2 \cdot 2^{11} = 2^1 \cdot 2^{11} = 2^{1+11} = 2^{12}$ **h.** $4(2^{10}) = 2^{12}$; $4(2^{10}) = 2^2(2^{10}) = 2^{2+10} = 2^{12}$
2. 10^6, 10^9, and 10^n have 6 zeros, 9 zeros, and n zeros respectively; when you multiply a number by 10, it has the effect of adding one zero to the end of the number. **3.** 8
4. Answers may vary. Sample: in the product $(ab)(ab)(ab)\ldots$ (where (ab) is multiplied n times), there are n instances of a, and n instances of b. By AOAG, the product equals $(aaa\ldots)(bbb\ldots) = a^n b^n$. **5. a.** 10^3 **b.** 100^6
c. 1 **d.** 2^4 **e.** 100^4 **f.** 10^4 **6. a.** 26^3 **b.** 26^n
c. 21^3 **d.** $26 \cdot 25 \cdot 24 = 15{,}600$ **7. a.** 7.69%
b. 14.20% **c.** The three-letter word is more likely. **8. a.** 26^2 **b.** 26^2 **c.** If p is even, there are $26^{\frac{p}{2}}$. If p is odd, there are $26^{\frac{(p+1)}{2}}$.

On Your Own
9. a. $x^4 y^3$ **11. a.** 3 **12. c.** 256 in.
13. c. 192 in.

Lesson 5.09
Check Your Understanding
1. Answers may vary. Sample: A^2B; B^4
2. 2,000,000 **3a.** No; $(3^6)^9 = 3^{6\cdot9} = 3^{54}$
b. Yes; the result holds due to Theorem 6.1. **c.** no; $(3^3)(3^5) = 3^{3+5} = 3^8$ **d.** no; $(3^{15})(3^1) = 3^{15+1} = 3^{16}$ **e.** Yes; the result holds due to For Discussion Problem 8.
f. no; $3^9 + 3^6 = (3^6)(3^3 + 1) = (3^6)(28)$ This product is even while 3^{15} is odd. **g.** Yes; the result holds due to Theorem 6.4. **h.** yes; $3^{14} + 3^{14} + 3^{14} = 3 \cdot 3^{14} = 3^1 \cdot 3^{14} = 3^{1+14} = 3^{15}$ **i.** Yes; the result holds due to Theorem 6.4. **j.** yes; $9(3^{13}) = (3^2)(3^{13}) = 3^{2+13} = 3^{15}$ **k.** no; $(3^5)^{10} = 3^{5\cdot10} = 3^{50}$
l. Yes; the result holds due to Theorem 6.4. **4a.** no; $\frac{2^6}{2^2} = 2^{6-2} = 2^4$ **b.** yes; $\frac{2^6}{2^3} = 2^{6-3} = 2^3$ **c.** no; $(2^2)^1 = 2^{2\cdot1} = 2^2$ **d.** yes; $\frac{(2^2)^5}{2^7} = \frac{2^{10}}{2^7} = 2^{10-7} = 2^3$ **e.** yes; $\frac{2^9}{2^6} = 2^{9-6} = 2^3$ **f.** no; $\frac{2^9}{2^3} = 2^{9-3} = 2^6$ **g.** no; $\frac{2^7 2^8}{2^5} = \frac{2^{15}}{2^5} = 2^{15-5} = 2^{10}$ **5.** 6; 6 **6.** 1 **7.** 9

On Your Own
8. a. $\frac{1}{2}$ in.; $\frac{1}{4}$ in. **10. a.** Yes; this is the definition of 5^6, five multiplied by itself six times. **11.** 4; 6 **12. a.** x^{12} **13. a.** $49c^2$

Lesson 5.10
Check Your Understanding
1.

x	3^x	÷
−3	$\frac{1}{27}$	3
−2	$\frac{1}{9}$	3
−1	$\frac{1}{3}$	3
0	1	3
1	3	3
2	9	3
3	27	

2.

x	$\left(\frac{1}{3}\right)^x$	÷
−3	27	$\frac{1}{3}$
−2	9	$\frac{1}{3}$
−1	3	$\frac{1}{3}$
0	1	$\frac{1}{3}$
1	$\frac{1}{3}$	$\frac{1}{3}$
2	$\frac{1}{9}$	$\frac{1}{3}$
3	$\frac{1}{27}$	

3. The outputs are reciprocals.
4. a. $2^3 + 2^2 + 2^1$ **b.** $2^3 + 2^2 + 2^1 + 2^0$
c. 2^4 **d.** $2^4 + 2^3 + 2^2 + 2^1 + 2^0$
e. $2^5 + 2^0$ **5.** Answers may vary. Sample: if n is a power of 2, you are done. Suppose n is not

a power of 2. Then $2^a < n < 2^{a+1}$ for some integer a. Therefore $n = 2^a + k$ for some integer k less than 2^a. If k is a power of 2, you are done. If not, then $2^b < k < 2^{b+1}$ for some integer $b < a$. Therefore $k = 2^b + m$ for some integer m less than 2^b. Continue with this process. Eventually it will end, because you started with a finite positive integer.

6.

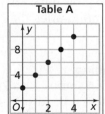

On Your Own

8. 2 **10. a.** z^2

Lesson 5.11
Check Your Understanding
1. a. 1.34×10^6 **b.** 6.09×10^{-6} **c.** -3×10^0
d. 9×10^4 **e.** 3.79×10^7 **f.** 6.02×10^7
g. 7.8×10^{12} **h.** 1.1×10^7 **2.** 60 years
3. a. 1.99×10^{30}; 5.97×10^{24} **b.** about
330,000 **4.** 2.192×10^{-8} mi/h
5. 9.03×10^{24}

On Your Own
6. b. 9.3×10^4 **7. b.** 94,720,000,000
d. -0.000000000377 **11.** 1×10^{22}

Lesson 5.12
On Your Own
11. a.

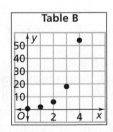

b. yes; no **12. b.** Answers may vary. Sample:
32 is twice 16, so support length must be twice
5, or 10. 48 is 3 times 16, so support length
must be three times 5, or 15.

Lesson 5.13

Check Your Understanding
1. a.

Input	Output	Δ
0	1	7
1	8	7
2	15	7
3	22	7
4	29	7
5	36	

b.

Input	Output	Δ
0	−4	0
1	−4	2
2	−2	4
3	2	6
4	8	8
5	16	

c.

Input	Output	Δ
0	1	−3
1	−2	−3
2	−5	−3
3	−8	−3
4	−11	−3
5	−14	

d.

Input	Output	Δ
0	4	6
1	10	6
2	16	6
3	22	6
4	28	6
5	34	

2. a. $L(x) = 2x + 1$ **b.** Not possible;
consecutive output differences are not the
same. **c.** $N(x) = 3$ **d.** $O(x) = \frac{1}{3}x - \frac{1}{3}$
3. a. Output column: 3, $a + 3$, $2a + 3$, $3a + 3$,
$4a + 3$, $5a + 3$ **b.** $f(x) = ax + 3$ **4. a.** Output
column: b, $a + b$, $2a + b$, $3a + b$, $4a + b$,
$5a + b$ **b.** $f(x) = ax + b$ **c.** Explanations may
vary. Sample: This table represents any table
that has constant differences a and an output
b for input 0. It shows that any input x has
output $ax + b$, which is a linear function.
5. a. No; the differences in the Δ column are
not constant. Instead, they alternate between
-2 and 2. **b.** Output for 0 is 1. Subsequent
values alternate between 1 and -1. $x \mapsto (-1)^x$

On Your Own
6. a. Matt has not noticed that the differences
between consecutive inputs are not the
same. **8. f.** a. $f(x) = 6x - 11$ b. $f(x) = 3^x$
c. $f(x) = \frac{4}{5}x - 2$ d. $f(x) = -2x + 9$ **9.** Yes;
for input 2, output is 3. For input 4, output is
11. For consecutive inputs 2, 3, and 4 to have
constant-difference outputs, the output for 3
has to be halfway between 3 and 11, or 7. The
constant difference is 4. The linear function is
$E(x) = 4x - 5$.

Lesson 5.14
Check Your Understanding
1. a. Output column: 2, 6, 10, 14, 18, 22
b. Output column: 2, 6, 18, 54, 162, 486
c. Output column: 2, 6, 14, 30, 62, 126
d. Output column: 2, 6, 10, 14, 18, 22
2. a. no linear function **b.** $x \mapsto 2x + 5$
c. $x \mapsto 2x - 3$ **d.** no linear function

3. **a.** $f(n) = \begin{cases} 8 & \text{if } n = 0 \\ \dfrac{f(n-1)}{2} & \text{if } n > 0 \end{cases}$

b. $f(n) = \begin{cases} 5 & \text{if } n = 0 \\ f(n-1) + 2 & \text{if } n > 0 \end{cases}$

c. $f(n) = \begin{cases} -3 & \text{if } n = 0 \\ f(n-1) + 2 & \text{if } n > 0 \end{cases}$

d. $f(n) = \begin{cases} 3.4 & \text{if } n = 0 \\ 10f(n-1) & \text{if } n > 0 \end{cases}$

4. a. \$.32 **b.** \$10.24; \$327.68

5. a.

Week	Allowance
1	\$ .16
2	\$1.12
3	\$1.84
4	\$2.38
5	\$2.79

b. \$3.72; \$3.93 **c.** no

6. a.

Week	Allowance
1	\$10.00
2	\$8.50
3	\$7.38
4	\$6.54
5	\$5.91

b. \$4.45; \$4.11 **c.** yes; no **7.** Input column: 0, 1, 2, 3, 4, 5, Output column: 1, 2, 6, 24, 120; Rule: g maps 0 to 1, 1 to 1, and any other positive integer n to the product of all positive integers less than or equal to n; $g(n) = 1 \cdot 2 \cdot 3 \cdot \ldots \cdot (n-1) \cdot n$.

On Your Own
9. For input 0, the output is \$5000; for other inputs, multiply the previous output by 1.1; \$6655. **11. c.** 13 lawns

Lesson 5.15
Check Your Understanding
1. a. $f(x) = 1.4x + 3.12$ **b.** None exists.
c. None exists. **2. a.** $f(x) = 5 - x^2$
b. $f(x) = 3(2)^x$ **c.** $f(x) = 2 - 3x$
d. $f(x) = 3^x - 1$ **e.** $k(x) = \frac{1}{3} + \frac{x}{2}$
f. $f(x) = 2x^2 + 1$ **3. a.** $y = 2 + ax$
b. $y = a(b)^x$

4. a. $m(n) = \begin{cases} 0.93 & \text{if } n = 0 \\ m(n-1) \cdot 1.0225 & \text{if } n > 0 \end{cases}$

b. Multiply 0.93 by 1.0225 once for the first year, then again for the second year, then

again for the third year, and so on, 1000 times.
c. Multiplying 0.93 by 1.0225 n times is the same as evaluating $0.93 \cdot 1.0225^n$.
d. \$4,283,508,450

On Your Own
5. a. $D(x) = -2 + 3x$ **6.** Answers may vary. Sample: $y = x^2$ **8. a.** $y = 64 - 16x$; $y = 64\left(\frac{3}{4}\right)^x$ **9. b.** $f(n) = 3^{n-1}$

Lesson 5.16
Check Your Understanding
1. a. \$1230; \$1260.75 **b.** $J = 1200(1.025)^N$, where J is the amount of money Jesse has.
c. \$1260.75; the interest is paid annually, only at the end of the year. **2.** Less time; at the end of the first year, Tony's balance is greater than at the beginning of the first year. As a result, he earns more interest in the second year than in the first. **3.** \$22,417.75
4. a. \$16,000; \$12,800 **b.** $V = 20,000(1 - 0.2)^N$
c. Yes; the value of the car will be less than \$1000 after 14 years.

On Your Own
6. 8 years **8. a.** The rule of 72 is very close to the results in Exercise 7.

Lesson 5.17
Check Your Understanding
1. Answers may vary. **2.** Answers may vary. Sample: about 20; about 10 **3.** Half of $\frac{1}{2}$ is $\frac{1}{4}$.

Chapter 6
Lesson 6.01
On Your Own
3. a. Add the test scores and divide by 7. *Mean* is what people most often think of as the average. **b.** Put the test scores in numerical order. The median is the fourth test score. The median tells the middle point of a data set.
c. Find the test score that occurs most often. The mode tells the value or values that occur most often in a data set. **4. b.** 1.64 **6. b.** There are five modes for this data set. **7. b.** There are a few very high salaries that skew the mean.

Lesson 6.02
Check Your Understanding
1. a. Answers may vary. Sample: Add 20 points to five different test scores. **b.** Answers may vary. Sample: Change the top 11 scores to 100. **2.** B **3.** 3×10^4 **4. a.** Subtract 1 from every element in the set. The mean and the median will also be 1 less. **b.** Add 10 to every element in the set. The mean and the median will also be 10 more.

On Your Own

5. b.
$$\overset{\bullet}{\underset{-5 \quad 0 \quad 5 \quad 10 \quad 15}{\longleftrightarrow}}$$

7. a. Yes; the average winning per play is 18.25 coins, while the cost per play is only 4 coins.   **8. a.** 21   **10.** no

Lesson 6.03
Check Your Understanding

1.

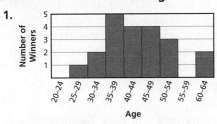

2. Answers may vary. Sample: There may be relatively few families with very high incomes, and many more with lower incomes.

3. a.

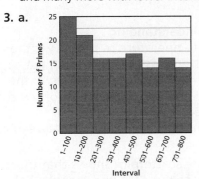

b. They decrease.

On Your Own

4. a. 34

b. about 37

c.

2	1 5 6 6 8 9 9
3	0 3 3 4 5 5 5 9
4	1 2 5 9
5	
6	1
7	
8	0

Key: 2 | 1 means 21 years

Lesson 6.04
Check Your Understanding

1. a. Answers may vary. Sample: Add 20 points to five different test scores. **b.** Answers may vary. Sample: Change the top 11 scores to 100. **2.** B **3.** 3×10^4 **4. a.** Subtract 1 from every element in the set. The mean and the median will also be 1 less. **b.** Add 10 to every element in the set. The mean and the median will also be 10 more.

On Your Own

5. b.
$$\overset{\bullet}{\underset{-5 \quad 0 \quad 5 \quad 10 \quad 15}{\longleftrightarrow}}$$

7. a. Yes; the average winning per play is 18.25 coins, while the cost per play is only 4 coins.   **8. a.** 21   **10.** no

Lesson 6.05
Check Your Understanding

1. a. $\frac{54}{117}$ is the ratio of students who agree that school should end one hour later to all students.

b. $\frac{42}{117}$ is the ratio of non-athletes who participated in the survey to all students who participated in the survey.

x. $\frac{23}{42}$ is the ratio of those who agree that school should end one hour later to non-athletes.

d. $\frac{23}{54}$ is the ratio of non-athletes to those who agree that school should end one hour later.

e. . $\frac{23}{117}$ is the ratio of students surveyed who are non-athletes and agree that school should end one hour later to all students surveyed.

2. No, athletes are not more likely to agree than non-athletes. Tess is paying attention only to the numbers of athletes and non-athletes who agree with the idea of extending the school day. She should be looking at the percentage of athletes and non-athletes that agree. $\frac{31}{75}$, or about 41.3% of athletes agree, but $\frac{23}{42}$, or about 54.7% of non-athletes agree.

3. Males; About 22.8% of males surveyed were wearing a watch, and about 20.9% of females surveyed were wearing a watch.

On Your Own

8.

	Right-Eye Dominance	Left-Eye Dominance
Connecticut	6	3
L. A.	7	8

About 46.2% $\left(\frac{6}{13}\right)$ of people with right-eye dominance live in Connecticut, but only about 27.3% $\left(\frac{3}{11}\right)$ of people with left-eye dominance live in Connecticut, so these variables seem to be associated.

9.

	Athlete	Non-Athlete
Right Eye Dominance	10	3
Left Eye Dominance	7	4

About 58.9% $\left(\frac{10}{17}\right)$ of athletes are right-eye dominant, but only about 42.9% $\left(\frac{3}{7}\right)$ of non-athletes are right-eye dominant, so these variables seem to be associated.

10 Check students' work.

11a. Non-athletes; about 48.4% of non-athletes $\left(\frac{16}{33}\right)$ are left-eye dominant, but only 21.1% $\left(\frac{11}{52}\right)$ of athletes are left-eye dominant.

b. Yes; The variables of eye dominance and athletic status are associated, since the difference in the percentages is significant.

Lesson 6.06
Check Your Understanding

3.
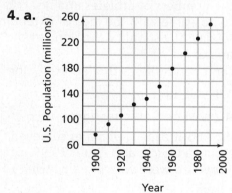

a. The data are negatively associated. Greater horsepower tends to correspond to fewer miles per gallon.

b. Answers will vary.

4. a.
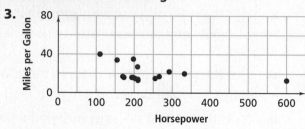

On Your Own

7. $\frac{6}{7}$

8. a. The maximum possible value for QCR is +1 and the minimum possible is −1. All of the data points could fall in regions A and C (leading to a QCR of +1) or all of the data points could fall in regions B and D (leading to a QCR of −1).

b. Answers may vary. A scatter plot with a QCR close to zero will have an approximately even distribution of points in each of the four quadrants. A scatter plot where the QCR is as negative as possible will have all the points in regions B and D.

8. a. The maximum possible value for QCR is +1 and the minimum possible is −1. All of the data points could fall in regions A and C (leading to a QCR of +1) or all of the data points could fall in regions B and D (leading to a QCR of −1).

b. Answers may vary. A scatter plot with a QCR close to zero will have an approximately even distribution of points in each of the four quadrants. A scatter plot where the QCR is as negative as possible will have all the points in regions B and D.

Lesson 6.07
On Your Own

8a. 86 **9a.** Answers will vary. Sample: More people are living in the western regions of the country. **10a.** For each pair of points the slope is 3, so the points lie on a line. **b.** $y = 3x + 4$.

Lesson 6.08
Check Your Understanding

1. a. x is the temperature in °F and y is the number of attendees in thousands.

b. yes, $47.1 \approx 0.678(80) - 7.1$ **2. a.** at the center of the ruler **b.** at the center of the coin **c.** Yes; answers may vary. Sample: A boomerang has its balance point between its arms. **3.** A

4. a. no **b.** The scatterplot shows that there is a linear trend to the data and that the balance point is along this linear trend.

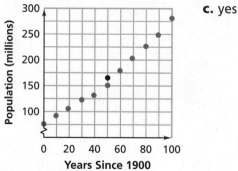

c. yes

On Your Own

5. a.
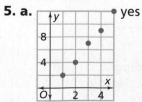 yes

9. a. The predicted values are too high.

844

Lesson 6.09
Check Your Understanding
1a. Answers may vary. Samples:
$y = 2x$, $y = x + 3$, $y = 6$ **b.** $7x + 5y = 51$
2a–b.

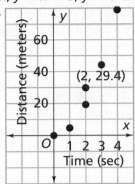

b. (2, 29.4) **c.** No; the points seem to lie on a curve, not a line.
3a–b.

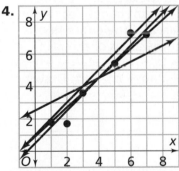

b. (2, 4.426) **c.** Yes, the points seem to lie on a line.

4.

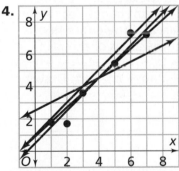

Lines (c) and (d) seem to fit the data.
5a. (667, −93) **b.** (629, 6) **6.** For 1900–1960: (1929, 233.2); a linear function is $f(x) = -0.5(x - 1929) + 233.3$. For 1960–2000: (1980, 216); a linear function is $f(x) = 216$. The two functions fit the data better than the

single function $f(x) = -0.34x + 892.1$.
a. Using $f(x) = -0.5(x - 1929) + 233.3$ for the dates prior to 1960, $f(1916) \approx 240$, $f(1940) \approx 228$, $f(1944) \approx 226$.
b. Using $f(x) = 216$ for dates after 1960, $f(2623) = 216$.

On Your Own
8a. The balance point is (4, 4.5); an equation is $y = x + 0.5$ or $y = 0.9x + 0.9$. **b.** For line (c), the sum of the errors is 0 and for line (d) the sum of the errors is 0. **10a.** 14 sixes **b.** mean: 3.5; median: 3; mode: 3 **12a.** Data vs. Line Fit: $y = 333.4476x - 26.2917$

Hours, x	Actual Yeast Density, y	Predicted Yeast Density, y	Error
0	9.6	−26.3	35.9
1	18.3	7.2	11.1
2	29.0	40.6	−11.6
3	47.2	74.1	−26.9
4	71.1	107.5	−36.4
5	119.1	141.0	21.9
6	174.6	174.4	0.2
7	257.3	207.8	49.5

Lesson 6.10
Check Your Understanding
1. A **2a.** A **b.** For $y - 3x - 1$: sum of errors is −2.4; mean absolute error is 1.15; mean squared error is 2.565. For $y = -x + 8.4$: sum of errors is 1; mean absolute error is 2.9; mean squared error is 8.855.
3a.

Input	Output	Predicted	Error
1	3	$3 \cdot 1 + b = 3 + b$	$3 - (3 + b) = -b$
2	4.5	$3 \cdot 2 + b = 6 + b$	$4.5 - (6 + b) = -1.5 - b$
3	8.1	$3 \cdot 3 + b = 9 + b$	$8.1 - (9 + b) = -0.9 - b$
4	8	$3 \cdot 4 + b = 12 + b$	$8 - (12 + b) = -4 - b$

b. $4b^2 + 12.8b + 19.06$ **c.** −1.6
d. $y = 3x - 1.6$ **4a.** $y = x + 3.4$
b. $y = 2x + 0.9$ **c.** $y = 5.9$

On Your Own
4. Table 1.

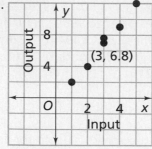

Table 2.

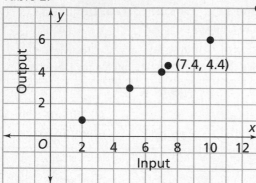

Table 3.

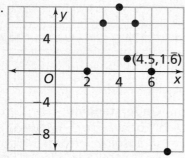

Table 4.

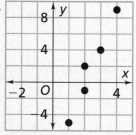

Tables 1, 2, and 4 show a linear trend.
5a. (3, 6.8) **6a.** 1.25 **7a.** 1.32

Chapter 7
Lesson 7.01
On Your Own
6. 1 line of symmetry:

2 lines of symmetry:

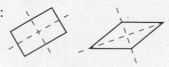

4 lines of symmetry:

All others have no lines of symmetry.
7. The triangle and its shadow have the same shape, but the shadow is larger.

Lesson 7.02
Check Your Understanding
1. Answers may vary. Sample: Since the two bases are the same distance apart at all points, the connecting lines appear to be the same length. Since the points on the second base are translated in the same direction from the corresponding points on the first base, the connecting segments take on the same slope. This makes them parallel. **2a.** Faces with corresponding edges parallel in the block letter should be parallel. **b.** Light hits parallel faces at the same angle; answers may vary. Sample: Different shading on parallel faces would be necessary if other objects affect the light that the parallel faces receive. **3.** Answers may vary. Sample: The darkest regions sometimes appear to be upper parts of a three-dimensional figure. Then they suddenly switch to be right-hand parts of a different figure. **4.** Drawings may vary. The letter shape is the base of the prism.
On Your Own
6. 16 **10.** The area of the entire figure is $(a + b)^2$. The length of each side of the white square is $a - b$, so the area of the white square is $(a - b)^2$. Each shaded rectangle has area ab. The area of the entire figure equals the sum of the areas of the parts, so $(a + b)^2 = 4ab + (a - b)^2 = 4ab + a^2 - 2ab + b^2$, or $a^2 + 2ab + b^2$. **11.** Drawings may vary. Sample:

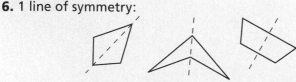

Lesson 7.03
Check Your Understanding
1a. a rectangle **b.** north **c.** The assumption is that the right turn is a 90° right turn. This is reasonable because 90° turns are common in everyday experience. **2a–b.** Answers may vary. Samples are given. **a.** a square **b.** Draw a segment. At each endpoint of this segment, draw another segment. The two new segments should be perpendicular to the first, should each be the same length, and should be on the same side of the original segment. Connect the other two endpoints of the two new segments to form a closed figure. **3a.** Answers may vary. Your

figures should be rhombuses or squares. **b.** No; although the shape will have to be a rhombus, it can be a square if the segments drawn have the same length.

On Your Own

5a.

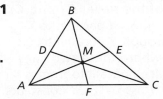

b. Yes; the figure must be a square, though the size of the square can vary. Squares are the only quadrilateral with horizontal, vertical, and diagonal lines of symmetry. **6.** a sphere

Lesson 7.04

Check Your Understanding

1

2. A **3.** S **4.** C

On Your Own

9a. square **b.** a right angle

Lesson 7.05

On Your Own

8. The 3 in.-8 in.-4 in. triangle in Problem 1 is impossible to construct because $3 + 4 < 8$. The 60°-70°-80° and 90°-90°-90° triangles in Problem 5 are impossible to construct because their angle sums would be greater than 180°. **9.** Comparing the results from Problem 6 shows that equal angle measures yield triangles that have the same shape, though the triangles may be different sizes. Comparing results from Problem 2 shows that equal side lengths yield triangles that are both the same shape and the same size. **10.** Triangles are possible for parts (b), (c), and (d) since the angle measures have a sum of 180°. No triangles are possible for parts (a) and (e) because the angle measures do not have a sum of 180°.

Lesson 7.06

Check Your Understanding

1a. Mark two points, A and B, on the given line. Construct the perpendicular bisector of $\overline{AB}$. **b.** Use the procedure from part (a) to construct a line perpendicular to the perpendicular bisector from part (a). **2.** Make a diagonal fold and crease the paper so that one corner of the sheet falls on the opposite long edge. Cut off the narrow rectangular strip of excess paper. **3a.** Fold the square to make the left side match the right side. Fold the resulting rectangle so that the top

side matches the bottom side. **b.** Open the folded sheet from part (a). Fold the corners of the large square inward to meet at the point of intersection of the crease lines. The new crease lines form a square with half the area of the large square. **4.** Answers may vary. To construct the bisector of an angle, fold through the vertex so that the sides of the angle coincide. **5a.** Answers may vary. Sample: Construct a circle centered at one endpoint of the segment and having the segment as a radius. Draw another radius, not collinear with the first. Draw the segment that connects the endpoints on the circle. **b.** Answers may vary. Sample: Fold the segment in half so that its endpoints coincide. Mark a point on the crease line (but not the midpoint of the original segment), and draw segments from that point to the endpoints of the segment. **c.** Answers may vary. Sample: Open the compass to the length of the segment. Use that radius and construct the two circles that have centers at the endpoints of the segment. Select a point where the circles intersect and draw segments from that point to the endpoints of the segment. **d.** Answers may vary. Sample: Construct perpendicular lines through the endpoints of the given segment. Construct a circle, with one of the endpoints as its center, that passes through the other endpoint. Construct a line parallel to the original segment through one of the points of intersection of the circle and the line perpendicular to the original segment.

6b.   **c.**

7a–c. Midpoints (the key to the constructions in parts (a) and (b) in the exercise) and angle bisectors have been constructed in earlier exercises. **d.** Answers may vary. Sample: Let the triangle be $\triangle ABC$. Construct a circle with center A that passes through B. If $\overline{BC}$ intersects the circle at another point, call this point D. If it does not, extend $\overline{BC}$ until it intersects the circle at D. Construct the midpoint of $\overline{BD}$ and call it E. The segment $\overline{AE}$ is an altitude of $\triangle ABC$. Construct the other two altitudes in a similar way. **e.** Answers may vary. **8.** Answers may vary. Sample: The diagonals of a square have the same length; each diagonal divides the square in half; the diagonals intersect at right angles;

the diagonals cut the square into four right triangles that are the same size and shape.
9. Answers may vary. Sample: Construct the perpendicular bisectors of two sides of the equilateral $\triangle ABC$. The perpendicular bisectors intersect at a point X. Construct the circle that has center X and radius XA.

On Your Own
13a. acute triangles **b.** right triangles
c. obtuse triangles   **15a.** Sketches may vary.
b. Construct the perpendicular bisectors of two of the sides of the triangle that has the bases of the saplings as vertices. Place the sprinkler at the point of intersection of the perpendicular bisectors. **c.** Answers may vary. Sample: The point of intersection of the perpendicular bisectors of the triangle that the three saplings form is the center of the circle that passes through the three saplings. If you place the sprinkler at this point of intersection, the sprinkler is equidistant from the three saplings.

Lesson 7.07
On Your Own
5. Answers may vary. Sample: To construct the figure in Exercise 2, use the circle tool to construct a circle centered at A that passes through B. Then construct a circle with an arbitrary center that passes through a point on the first circle. To construct the figure in Exercise 3, draw a circle first using the circle tool. Place a point on the circle and construct a triangle with the segment tool using this point as one of the vertices. To construct the figure in Exercise 4, draw two lines and then place one point on one line and two points on the other line, using the point tool. Connect all three points using the segment tool.   **7.** No; a line and a segment do not need to touch to be perpendicular. If the segment can be extended to intersect the line at a right angle, then the line and the segment are perpendicular.

Lesson 7.08
Check Your Understanding
1a. The other two segments rotate. One of them remains perpendicular to $\overline{BC}$ and the other parallel to $\overline{BC}$. The position of point A does not change. **b.** The segments that intersect at A also stretch or shrink. Their lengths are equal to BC.   **2.** The four points trace paths that result in a figure that has rotational symmetry.   **3.** Because the two segments have no constructed relationship to each other, they move independently. When

you stretch or shrink one, the other does not change at all.
On Your Own
5. Drawing the line parallel to $\overline{BC}$ fails to link the behavior of the line to changes in $\overline{BC}$. As a result, the segments that intersect at A will not act like arms of a windmill.   **6.** The circle keeps the arms of the windmill the same length as $\overline{BC}$.

Lesson 7.09
Check Your Understanding
1–5. Constructions may vary.   **6.** Answers may vary. Sample: Method 1—Construct a circle with center C. Construct two noncollinear radii of the circle, $\overline{CX}$ and $\overline{CY}$. Construct a line through X parallel to $\overline{CY}$. Construct a line through Y parallel to $\overline{CX}$. Let P be the point where these two lines intersect. The required parallelogram is $CXPY$. Method 2—Construct $\overline{AB}$. Construct the perpendicular bisector of $\overline{AB}$. Construct a circle with its center at the midpoint of $\overline{AB}$. Mark the points D and E where the perpendicular bisector intersects the circle. The required parallelogram is $ADBE$.
7a. Answers may vary. **b.** The ratios are equal.
8–9. Constructions may vary.
On Your Own
12. There are infinitely many lines perpendicular to any given line or segment. Specifying a point makes it possible to tell the software which of these infinitely many lines you want.

Chapter 8
Lesson 8.01
On Your Own
6. Yes; if two segments have the same length, one will fit exactly on top of the other. You can ignore the widths of the segments because a line segment represents a one-dimensional object.   **7.** Answers may vary. Sample: For spheres, cut through their centers with a straight slice and then compare the radii of the cross sections. For rectangular boxes, make a net that wraps perfectly around each box.

Lesson 8.02
Check Your Understanding
1a. numbers **b.** segments **c.** segments and numbers **d.** points and numbers   **2a.** $\angle NPQ$ is a geometric object, and $56.6°$ is a numerical measure. **b.** $m\angle NPQ = 56.6°$ **3.** Yes; if two angles have equal measures, then you can place one angle on top of the other so that

they fit exactly.   **4.** Yes; if you can put one angle on top of another to get a perfect match, then the protractor positions can also be matched exactly when you measure them. **5.** Yes; if two triangles are congruent to the same triangle, then they can all be superimposed onto one another so that they fit exactly.   **6a.** True; F and E are midpoints of segments that have the same length, so halves of those segments have the same length. **b.** Nonsensical; two segments cannot be equal. They can only be congruent. **c.** Nonsensical; a segment cannot equal a length. **d.** Nonsensical; an angle cannot equal a length. **e.** Nonsensical; triangles cannot be equal. They can only be congruent. **f.** True; $\overline{DC} \perp \overline{AB}$ and perpendicular segments form right angles. **g.** True; by part (a), $FA = BE$, therefore $\overline{FA} \cong \overline{BE}$. **h.** False; $FA = \frac{1}{2}DA = \frac{1}{2}BD$. **i.** Nonsensical; two angles cannot be equal. They can only have the same measure. **j.** True; if you fold along $\overrightarrow{DC}$, then $\overrightarrow{DA}$ and $\overrightarrow{DB}$ will coincide. **k.** Nonsensical; two measurements cannot be congruent. **l.** True; if you fold along $\overline{DC}$, the angles match perfectly. **m.** Nonsensical; a triangle cannot be congruent to an angle. **n.** Nonsensical; a triangle cannot be congruent to a segment.

On Your Own

9. No; equilateral triangles are not congruent if their side lengths are different.   **11.** two

Lesson 8.03
Check Your Understanding

1. Explanations may vary. Samples are given. **a.** No; $\overline{DF} \cong \overline{EC}$, not $\overline{GC}$. **b.** No; $\overline{DF} \cong \overline{EC}$, not $\overline{EG}$. **c.** No; $\angle D \cong \angle E$, not $\angle C$. **d.** Yes; $\angle D \cong \angle E$, $\overline{DF} \cong \overline{EC}$, $\overline{FA} \cong \overline{CG}$, $\overline{DA} \cong \overline{EG}$. **e.** No; $\angle D \cong \angle E$, not $\angle G$. **f.** No; $\angle D \cong \angle E$, not $\angle C$.   **2.** Answers may vary. Sample: $\triangle DAF \cong \triangle EGC$, $\triangle ADF \cong \triangle GEC$ **3.** Answers may vary. Sample: If you can place one figure on top of another so that they match perfectly, then the figures are congruent and the parts that match are the corresponding parts that are congruent. **4.** Answers may vary.

On Your Own

5. $\angle C \cong \angle D$, $\angle A \cong \angle O$, $\angle T \cong \angle G$, $\overline{CA} \cong \overline{DO}$, $\overline{AT} \cong \overline{OG}$, and $\overline{CT} \cong \overline{DG}$ **7.** $\triangle AFD \cong \triangle AEB$, $\triangle FBD \cong \triangle EDB$, $\triangle EGD \cong \triangle FGB$ **8a.** Yes; if two polygons are congruent, then one can be made to fit exactly on top of the other. What is inside the polygons will match, too, and area is a numerical measure of the inside. **b.** No; for example, a 4 in.-by-4 in. square has the same

area as a 2 in.-by-8 in. rectangle, but they are not congruent.

Lesson 8.04
Check Your Understanding

1a. Constructions may vary. **b.** not necessarily **c.** one of the side lengths   **2a.** Constructions may vary. **b.** not necessarily **c.** Answers may vary. Sample: the length of the third side **3.** yes; SSS   **4.** yes, though you would need to first deduce that $\overline{AB} \cong \overline{AD}$; SAS   **5.** Let the square be $ABCD$, and choose the diagonal $\overline{BD}$. All sides of a square are congruent, and all angles of a square are right angles and hence congruent. The sides $\overline{BA}$ and $\overline{DA}$ and their included right angle in $\triangle BAD$ are congruent, respectively, to sides $\overline{BC}$ and $\overline{DC}$ and their included right angle in $\triangle BCD$. So $\triangle BAD \cong \triangle BCD$ by SAS. Also, $\overline{BD} \cong \overline{BD}$, so $\triangle BAD \cong \triangle BCD$ by SSS. **6.** Answers may vary. Sample: SSA is not a valid test for congruence.   **7.** Answers may vary. Sample: If SSA were a valid way to prove congruence, then $\triangle COA \cong \triangle COB$, implying that $m\angle COA = m\angle COB$. But $\angle COB$ is entirely contained within $\angle COA$, so these two angles cannot be equal in measure.

On Your Own

9a. yes **b.** $\triangle ABC \cong \triangle DEF$; SSS   **11.** no **14.** $\triangle ABD$ and $\triangle CBD$; since $\overline{BD}$ is the perpendicular bisector of $\overline{AC}$, $\overline{AD} \cong \overline{CD}$ and $\angle ADB \cong \angle CDB$. $\overline{BD}$ is common to the two triangles. Therefore, $\triangle ABD \cong \triangle CBD$ by SAS.

Lesson 8.05

7a. $\overline{PQ}$: 1, $\overline{QR}$: $-\frac{1}{2}$, $\overline{RS}$: 1, $\overline{SP}$: $-\frac{1}{2}$; the slopes of opposite sides of $PQRS$ are equal. Hence $PQRS$ has its opposite sides parallel. Therefore, $PQRS$ is a parallelogram.   **9.** $A(2, -5)$, $B(4, -2)$ **10.** $-2x + y = 6$

Lesson 8.06
Check Your Understanding

1a. Always; if you fold along the line of reflection, a segment in the preimage will coincide with the corresponding segment in the image. **b.** Always; if you fold along the line of reflection, an angle in the preimage will coincide with the corresponding angle in the image. **c.** Always; if you fold along the line of reflection, the image of a line is a line. **d.** Sometimes; answers may vary. Sample: Suppose the line of reflection is $y = x$. For $A(2, 4)$ and $B(5, 7)$, the image of $\overline{AB}$ is $\overline{A'B'}$ with $A'(4, 2)$ and $B'(7, 5)$. Both segments have slope 1. For $C(5, 9)$ and $C'(9, 5)$, the image of $\overline{AC}$ is $\overline{A'C'}$, but $\overline{AC}$ has slope $\frac{5}{3}$, and $\overline{A'C'}$ has slope $\frac{3}{5}$. **e.** Always; answers may vary. Sample:

A transversal of two parallel segments in the preimage will form congruent corresponding angles with the segments. The angle measures will, by part (b), be preserved in the image. So the segments in the image will be parallel. **f.** Always; answers may vary. Sample: By part (b), angle measures are preserved. **2a.** $A' = (6, 5)$, $B' = (4, 2)$ **b.** $A'' = (10, 5)$, $B'' = (12, 2)$ **c.** a translation 8 units to the right (that is, in the positive direction, parallel to the x-axis) **3.** Draw $\overline{PP'}$. Label point S where PP' and ℓ intersect. Since P' is the reflection of P over ℓ, ℓ is the perpendicular bisector of PP'. $\overline{PS} \cong \overline{P'S}$ by definition of bisector. $\overline{OS} \cong \overline{OS}$ by the reflexive property. $\triangle OSP$ and $\triangle OSP'$ are right triangles. $\triangle OSP \cong \triangle OSP'$ by LL. $\angle POR \cong \angle P'OR$ by CPCTC. **4.** Suppose $\overline{AB} \parallel \ell$, and let $\overline{A'B'}$ be the image of $\overline{AB}$ for reflection over ℓ. Then ℓ is the perpendicular bisector of $\overline{AA'}$ and $\overline{BB'}$. If M is the midpoint of $\overline{AA'}$ and N is the midpoint of $\overline{BB'}$, then $ABNM$ and $A'B'NM$ are rectangles. It follows that $\overline{A'B'} \parallel \overline{MN}$ and hence that $\overline{A'B'} \parallel \ell$.
On Your Own
7a. $A'(1, -1)$, $B'(3, -2)$ **b.** $A''(1, -1)$, $B''(3, 0)$ **c.** a translation down 3 units **9.** $x - 3y = 6$
12. Yes, the y-axis; the point at $(0, 0)$ is on the graph and on the y-axis. All other points of the graph are above the x-axis. For each $b > 0$, the line with equation $y = b$ intersects the graph of $y = x^2$ at $\left(-\sqrt{b}, b\right)$ and $\left(\sqrt{b}, b\right)$. These correspond to the endpoints of a segment whose midpoint is $(0, b)$. **15a.** yes **b.** no **c.** yes **d.** yes **e.** Answers may vary. Sample: If a figure is reflected over a line, the image over a second line, and so on, and if the number of reflections performed is even, then the final image can be obtained from the original figure by using a single rotation or a single translation.

Lesson 8.07
Check Your Understanding
1a. Answers may vary. Sample: You can slide the original figure straight from the original to the new position and all vertices will match. **b.** Answers may vary. Sample: It is the translation accomplished by sliding $AKLJ$ to the right 8 units and up 6 units.
c. $(x, y) \mapsto (x + 8, y + 6)$ **2.** A triangle; the image is congruent to the original and is obtained by translating the original to the right 10 units and up 6 units. **3.** $2x + y = 22$
On Your Own
5. Answers may vary. Sample: $\overline{AA''}$ and $\overline{BB''}$ have slope 0 and hence are parallel. Also $AA'' = BB'' = 6$. Since $AA''B''B$ has a pair of

opposite sides that are parallel and congruent, it is a parallelogram. **8.** Answers may vary. Sample: $(-3, 0)$, $(-1, 2)$, and $(1, 0)$
a. $(x + 1)^2 + (y + 2)^2 = 4$
b. $(x + 1)^2 + (y - 2)^2 = 4$
c. $(x - 2)^2 + y^2 = 4$
d. $x^2 + (y - 4)^2 = 4$

Lesson 8.08
Check Your Understanding
1. **a.** $A'(4, 1)$, $B'(2, 3)$, $C'(4, 5)$, $D'(5, 2.5)$
b. $A''(4, -1)$, $B''(2, -3)$, $C''(4, -5)$, $D''(5, -2.5)$
c. Theorem 7.1 states that the composition of two reflections about intersecting lines produces a rotation. Its center is the intersection of the lines. The angle of rotation is equal to twice the measure of the angle formed by two lines.
d. a rotation of 180° around the origin
e. If (x, y) are the coordinates of a point of $ABCD$, then the corresponding point of $A''B''C''D''$ has coordinates $(-x, -y)$.
On Your Own
7.

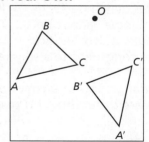

8. Check students' work.
9. $CA = CB$, so A and B are on the circle with center C and radius CA; the measure of the angle of rotation is the same as $m\angle ACB$.
10.

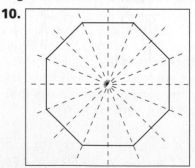

11. Answers may vary. Sample: Draw $\overleftrightarrow{OA}$ and $\overleftrightarrow{OA'}$. Construct the line k that bisects $\angle AOA'$. If you reflect $\triangle ABC$ over $\overleftrightarrow{OA}$ and then reflect the image over k, you get $\triangle A'B'C'$.
12. D

Lesson 8.09
Check Your Understanding

1. An isometry can be thought of as a function that maps points in the plane to points in the plane. Formally, an isometry is a function from $\mathbb{R}^2$ to $\mathbb{R}^2$.

2. Answers may vary. Sample: You would need a description or ordered list of the transformations that make up the isometry.

3. a. any point on the circle with center P and radius AB

b. Answers may vary. Sample: a description of the transformations that make up the isometry, including the order they were performed in

4. Answers may very. Check students' work.

5. a. Isometry; the composition of a reflection and a translation is an isometry.

b. Not an isometry; the transformation scales the figure, which does not preserve length.

c. Not an isometry; the transformation stretches the figure, which does not preserve length.

d. Isometry; the transformation is a translation.

e. Isometry; the transformation is a translation.

f. Not an isometry; the transformation scales the figure, which does not preserve length.

On Your Own

7. No; a transformation that takes one circle to the other does not preserve length.

8. a. Answers may vary. Sample: Rotate $\triangle ABC$ until $\overline{BC}$ is parallel to $\overline{B'C'}$. Then translate $\triangle ABC$ until point C is concurrent with point C'. Then reflect so that point B is concurrent with point B'.

b. Answers may vary.

c. Point A is a fixed distance from point B and a fixed distance from point C. Point A_1 is the same distance from point B and the same distance from point C as point A. Therefore, point A_1 coincides with point A.

d. Answers may vary.

Lesson 8.10
On Your Own

6a. 17 **b.** $(3.5, -7)$ **c.** 10 **d.** $(12, -2)$ **e.** $\sqrt{389}$ **f.** $(3.5, -2)$ **7a.** $A(5, 5), B(5, 0)$ **b.** 5 **c.** $(5, 2.5)$ **d.** 12.5 **e.** $5\sqrt{2}$ **f.** $(2.5, 2.5)$ **9a.** 0 **b.** 2 **c.** 2 **d.** 3

Lesson 8.11
Check Your Understanding

1a. $(-33, 561)$ **b.** $\left(3x, \dfrac{y}{2}\right)$ **2a.** $AB = \sqrt{53}$, $BC = 2\sqrt{26}$, $AC = 5$ **b.** length of median from $A = \sqrt{13}$, length of median from $B = 8.5$, length of median from $C = \dfrac{\sqrt{205}}{2}$

3. $AB = A'B' = \sqrt{34}$, $BC = B'C' = \sqrt{29}$, $AC = A'C' = \sqrt{13}$, so $\triangle ABC \cong \triangle A'B'C'$ by SSS. **4.** Answers may vary. Sample: Use the Distance Formula to calculate the side lengths of each triangle. If the side lengths for the two triangles are the same, then the triangles are congruent by SSS. **5.** Answers may vary. Sample: Starting with $\overline{ST}$ and going clockwise, let the midpoints of the sides of $STAR$ be P, Q, V, and W. Use the Midpoint Formula to show that these are the points $P(3, 5)$, $Q(4, 1)$, $V(-1, -2)$, and $W(-2, 4)$. Use the Distance Formula to show that $PW = VQ = \sqrt{26}$ and $PQ = WV = \sqrt{37}$. Since the opposite sides of $PQVW$ are congruent, $PQVW$ is a parallelogram. **6.** Answers may vary. Sample: Quadrilateral $ABCD$ has vertices $A(3, 1)$, $B(4,7)$, $C(11, 3)$, and $D(8, -5)$. The midpoint of $\overline{AB}$ is $E(3.5, 4)$, of $\overline{BC}$ is $F(7.5, 5)$, of $\overline{CD}$ is $G(9.5, -1)$, and of $\overline{DA}$ is $H(5.5, -2)$. $EFGH$ is a parallelogram because the opposite sides are the same length. $EF = GH = \sqrt{17}$ and $EH = FG + 2\sqrt{10}$ **7.** $A(2, 4\sqrt{6})$, $B(5, 5\sqrt{3})$, $C(6, 8)$, $D(5\sqrt{2}, 5\sqrt{2})$, $E(10, 0)$, $F(0, -10)$, $G(-8, -6)$.

On Your Own

11a. $(-14, 14)$ **b.** $(86, -186)$ **13.** $E(113, 19)$, $D(116, 15)$ **16.** $(3, 5)$

Lesson 8.12
Check Your Understanding

1a. Parallel; the graphs of the lines are different and the ratios of corresponding coefficients are equal. **b.** Parallel; the graphs of the lines are different and the ratios of corresponding coefficients are equal. **c.** Not parallel; the lines are the same. **d.** Not parallel; the ratios of corresponding coefficients are not equal. **e.** Parallel; the graphs of the lines are different and the ratios of corresponding coefficients are equal. **2.** Answers may vary. Sample: $C(6.5, -1)$; find the coordinates of the midpoint of $\overline{AB}$. **3.** Answers may vary. Sample: Start with $B(8, -3)$. Add 3 to the x-coordinate and subtract 4 from the y-coordinate to get $(11, -7)$, the coordinates

of a new point on $\overleftrightarrow{AB}$. Do the same with the new point, and continue in this fashion to get still more points.; the slope of $\overleftrightarrow{AB}$ is $\frac{-4}{3}$, and the procedure gives new points that are collinear with A and B by Theorem 7.5
4. No; answers may vary. Sample: The slope of $\overline{PR}$ is $\frac{4}{9}$, but the slope of $\overline{RS}$ is $\frac{5}{12}$. By Theorem 7.5, the points are not collinear.

On Your Own
5a. By the Midpoint Formula, the midpoint of each diagonal has coordinates (5.5, 1).
b. By Theorem 2.8, $ABCD$ is a parallelogram.
8. Yes; the segments joining two points at these locations all have slope $-\frac{1}{50}$. By Theorem 7.5, the points are collinear.

Lesson 8.13
Check Your Understanding
1. Answers may vary. Sample: $y = x$, $y = x + 1$; yes, infinitely many **2.** Answers may vary. Sample: $2x - y = 2$ **3.** $\frac{7}{5}$
4. Answers may vary. Sample:
$(\sqrt{2})x + 4y = 3\sqrt{2}$ and $(\sqrt{2})x - 4y = 3\sqrt{2}$
On Your Own
6. a–d. Answers may vary. Samples are given.
a. $3x + 2y = 0$ **b.** $x - y = 3$
c. $x - 2y = 2$ **d.** $3x + 2y = 7$ **7a.** $\sqrt{10}$
b. $\frac{3\sqrt{26}}{13}$ **c.** $\frac{7}{5}$ **d.** $\frac{80}{29}$ **10.** Four; slope $\overline{AB} =$

$\frac{1}{-3 + \sqrt{2}}$, slope $\overline{BC} = \frac{7}{3 + \sqrt{2}}$, slope $\overline{CD} =$
$\frac{1}{-3 + \sqrt{2}}$, and slope $\overline{DA} = \frac{7}{3 + \sqrt{2}}$. Since
opposite sides of $ABCD$ have equal slopes, they are parallel. Hence $ABCD$ is a parallelogram. (slope $\overline{AB}$) $\cdot$ (slope $\overline{BC}$) $= -1$, so $\overline{AB}$ and $\overline{BC}$ are perpendicular. Hence $\angle B$ is a right angle. Therefore $ABCD$ is a rectangle and hence has four right angles.

Honors Appendix
Lesson H.01
On Your Own
9.

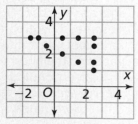

The original figure has been dilated with respect to the origin by a factor of $\frac{1}{2}$.
13a. Jorge: $A'(16.75, 1.5)$, $B'(18.25, 1.5)$, $C'(18.25, 0.75)$; Yutaka: $A'(4.75, 1.5)$, $B'(6.25, 1.5)$, $C'(6.25, 0.75)$ **b.** no **c.** Jorge used $(x, y) \mapsto \frac{1}{4}(x, y) + (16, 0)$, and Yutaka used $(x, y) \mapsto \frac{1}{4}(x + 16, y)$.

Lesson H.02
Check Your Understanding
1. $\overrightarrow{OA}$, with $O = (0, 0)$ and $A = (6, 8)$ **2.** (12, 1)
3. True; if $A = (a_1, a_2)$ and $B = (b_1, b_2)$, then $B - O = (b_1, b_2)$ and $(A + B) - A = (a_1 + b_1, a_2 + b_2) - (a_1, a_2) = (b_1, b_2)$. Since $B - O = (A + B) - A$, it follows from Theorem 7.7 that the vector from O to B is equivalent to the vector from A to $A + B$.
4.

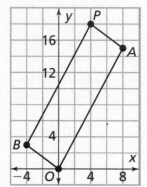

By the Distance Formula, $OA = 17$, $BP = 17$, $OB = 5$, and $AP = 5$. So $OA = BP$ and $OB = AP$.
5.

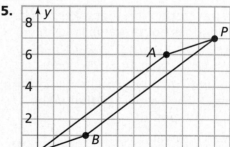

By the Distance Formula, $OA = 10$, $BP = 10$, $OB = \sqrt{10}$, and $AP = \sqrt{10}$. So $OA = BP$ and $OB = AP$. **6a.** (7, 7) **b.** (10, 9) **c.** (13, 11)
d. (16, 13) **e.** $\left(\frac{11}{2}, 6\right)$ **f.** $\left(5, \frac{17}{3}\right)$ **g.** $\left(\frac{19}{4}, \frac{11}{2}\right)$
On Your Own
7. For $\overrightarrow{A(A + B)}$, $(A + B) - A = (11, 7) - (3, 5) = (8, 2)$. For $\overrightarrow{OB}$, $B - O = (8, 2) - (0, 0) = (8, 2)$. So

$\overrightarrow{A(A + B)}$ is equivalent to $\overrightarrow{OB}$. For $\overrightarrow{OA}$, $A - O = (3, 5) - (0, 0) = (3, 5)$. For $\overrightarrow{B(A + B)}$, $(A + B) - B = (11, 7) - (8, 2) = (3, 5)$. So $\overrightarrow{OA}$ is equivalent to $\overrightarrow{B(A + B)}$. **15.** $\frac{1}{3}B + \frac{2}{3}A$; the point $\frac{1}{3}$ of the way from A to B is $A + \frac{1}{3}(B - A)$. Simplify $A + \frac{1}{3}(B - A)$ to obtain $\frac{1}{3}B + \frac{2}{3}A$.

Lesson H.03

Check Your Understanding

1. Answers may vary. Sample: $B - A = (5, 4)$ and $D - C = (10, 8)$. Hence $D - C = 2(B - A)$. $\overrightarrow{AB}$ and $\overrightarrow{CD}$ are not collinear. It follows from Theorem 7.12 that $\overrightarrow{AB}$ and $\overrightarrow{CD}$ have the same direction and that $\overleftrightarrow{AB}$ and $\overleftrightarrow{CD}$ are parallel.
2. Assume $A \neq O$, $t \neq 0$, and O, A, and P are not collinear. By Theorems 7.8 and 7.11, it follows that O, P, tA, and $P + tA$ are the vertices of a parallelogram. $\overrightarrow{O(tA)}$ and $\overrightarrow{P(P + tA)}$ are opposite sides of the parallelogram and hence are parallel. Since $\overline{OA}$ and $\overline{O(tA)}$ are collinear, it follows that $\overline{OA}$ and $\overrightarrow{P(P + tA)}$ are parallel. **3.** The midpoint M of $\overline{OA}$ is $\frac{1}{2}(O + A) = (2, 2)$. The midpoint N of $\overline{OB}$ is $\frac{1}{2}(O + B) = (4, -2)$. The vectors $\overrightarrow{MN}$ and $\overrightarrow{AB}$ are noncollinear and $N - M = (2, -4) = \frac{1}{2}(B - A)$. By Theorem 7.12, it follows that $\overline{MN} \parallel \overline{AB}$. By the Distance Formula, $MN = 2\sqrt{5}$ and $AB = 4\sqrt{5}$. So $MN = \frac{1}{2}AB$. **4.** $B - A = (4, 4)$, so the segment from O to $B - A$ has slope 1 and length $4\sqrt{2}$. The segment from A to B also has slope 1 and length $4\sqrt{2}$. So $\overline{O(B - A)}$ is parallel to and congruent to $\overline{AB}$.

On Your Own

8. $X = (1, 5) + t(7, 2)$ **10.** $\frac{1}{4}B + \frac{3}{4}A$

Lesson H.04

2. For $\overleftrightarrow{C_0M}$, an equation is $P = (4, 6) + t\left(-3, -\frac{11}{2}\right)$. For $\overleftrightarrow{B_0K}$, an equation is $Q = (2, 1) + k(0, 2)$. You can see from the equations that $\overleftrightarrow{C_0M}$ is not vertical, that $\overleftrightarrow{B_0K}$ is vertical, and hence that the lines must intersect. The point of intersection is $\left(2, \frac{7}{3}\right)$.
3. $F = (0, 0) + q\left(3, \frac{7}{2}\right)$; yes **4.** $t = \frac{2}{3}$, $k = \frac{2}{3}$, $q = \frac{2}{3}$; the point of intersection of the medians is two thirds of the way from each vertex to the corresponding midpoint.

On Your Own

5. Answers may vary. Sample: Interchange the coordinates of $(-3, 4)$ to get $(4, -3)$ and

then change the sign of the second coordinate of $(4, -3)$ to get $(4, 3)$. Use $(4, 3)$ for B.
8. To define the "center of population," think of the cities as weights at three points. If each person (in each city) is a weight of the same size, the center of gravity lies at the point George describes.

Lesson H.05

Check Your Understanding

1. $(4, 6)$: **yes**; $(-5, -5)$: **no**; $(13, 18)$: **yes**
2. $y = 2x - 2$ **3. a.** $\frac{4}{3}$ **b.** $\frac{3}{4}$ **c.** $\frac{4}{3}$ **d.** $\frac{4}{3}$
4. a–d. Answers may vary. Samples are given.
a. $X = (0, 1) + t(2, 3)$ **b.** $X = (5, 3) + t(1, 4)$
c. $X = (0, 3) + t(2, -3)$ **d.** $X = (-2, 3) + t(5, -2)$ or $X = (3, 1) + t(5, -2)$ are two equations.
5. $y = \frac{17}{3}$ **6.** no **7.** For the lines to be the same, it is necessary that D' be a scalar multiple of D (i.e., the lines are parallel). Once it is known that the lines are parallel, then check to see if P' is on the first line. If that turns out to be true, the lines are identical, since a line is uniquely determined by a point and a slope.

8. a.

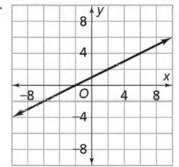

b.

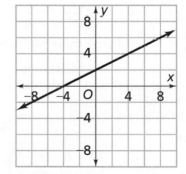

c. The direction vector is scaled, but the direction is not changed. Since the two lines have the same direction vector, they must be parallel.

On Your Own

9. Answers may vary. Sample:
$X = (2, 3) + t(-3, 1)$

13. a. The paths intersect and these cars crash.

14. $z = 7$

Lesson H.06

On Your Own

7.

	A	B	C	D	E
EUR	0.6	0.25	0.3	0.3	1.3
US	4.6	3.3	1.4	2.2	0.4
ASIA	0.3	0.15	1.3	4.5	0.1

8a.

	A	B	C	D	E
EUR	1	0.5	0	1	6
US	2	−0.5	2	3	0
ASIA	−1	−0.5	8	11	−1

b.

A	B	C	D	E
2	−0.5	10	15	5

c. EUR 8.5
US 6.5
ASIA 16.5

10. 1239 mi

Lesson H.07

Check Your Understanding

1a. 2×3 **b.** 2 **c.** 4 **d.** 6 **e.** There is no 3rd row.

2a. $\begin{pmatrix} 3 \\ 6 \\ 11 \\ 18 \end{pmatrix}$ **b.** $(3 \quad 5 \quad 9 \quad 17)$ **3a.** $a_{ij} = i + j$

b. $b_{ij} = 2(i − 1) + j$ **c.** $c_{ij} = (i + j − 1)^i$

4a. $A + B = (c_{ij})$, where $c_{ij} = a_{ij} + b_{ij}$.

b. $A − B = (c_{ij})$, where $c_{ij} = a_{ij} − b_{ij}$.

c. $k \cdot A = (c_{ij})$, where $c_{ij} = k \cdot a_{ij}$.

5. $3 \cdot \begin{pmatrix} 6 \\ 8 \\ 10 \end{pmatrix} = \begin{pmatrix} 18 \\ 24 \\ 30 \end{pmatrix}$ or

$3 \cdot (6 \quad 8 \quad 10) = (18 \quad 24 \quad 30)$

6. $\begin{pmatrix} 271 & 282 & 233 \\ 365 & 362 & 340 \end{pmatrix}$ This is matrix addition.

7. The matrices cannot be added term-by-term; the teacher could change the percent information to point information, then find the means of the entries in the matrices.

On Your Own

9. $\begin{pmatrix} 1 & 2 & 3 & 4 \\ 1 & 4 & 9 & 16 \end{pmatrix}$ **10a.** $\begin{pmatrix} 1 & 0 & 0 & 0 \\ 0 & 1 & 0 & 0 \\ 0 & 0 & 1 & 0 \\ 0 & 0 & 0 & 1 \end{pmatrix}$

12. matrix addition

Lesson H.08

Check Your Understanding

1. In Lesson 4.4, Exercises 5, 6, 10, and 11 were dot products. **2a.** 32 **b.** 32 **c.** 32 **d.** 32 **e.** 32 **f.** The dot product is not defined. **3a.** 25

b. $a^2 + b^2$ **c.** 29 **4a.** (0, 0) **b.** (0, 0) **c.** (0, 0, 0, 0)

5. For any n-tuple X, there is a unique n-tuple $Z = (0, 0, \ldots, 0)$ such that $X + Z = X$.

6a. 0 **b.** Answers may vary. Sample: Rewrite the expression as $(1 + 0 − 1, 0 + 2 − 2, 1 + 1 − 2) \cdot (x, y, z) = (0, 0, 0) \cdot (x, y, z) = 0$.

7. $(A + B) \cdot (A + B)$
$= (A + B) \cdot A + (A + B) \cdot B$
$= A \cdot A + B \cdot A + A \cdot B + B \cdot B$
$= A \cdot A + A \cdot B + A \cdot B + B \cdot B$
$= A \cdot A + 2A \cdot B + B \cdot B$

8. $(A + B) \cdot (A − B)$
$= A \cdot (A − B) + B \cdot (A − B)$
$= A \cdot A − A \cdot B + B \cdot A − B \cdot B$
$= A \cdot A − A \cdot B + A \cdot B − B \cdot B$
$= A \cdot A − B \cdot B$

9. If X is the n-tuple $(x_1, x_2, \ldots, x_n)$, then $(−1)X = (−1)(x_1, x_2, \ldots, x_n) = (−x_1, −x_2, \ldots, −x_n)$. Then $X + (−1)X = (0, 0, \ldots, 0)$ so $−1(X) = −X$.

10. We know that $A \cdot (kB) = k(A \cdot B) = (kA) \cdot B$, so $A \cdot ((−1)B) = A \cdot (−B)$ by Exercise 9, and $A \cdot (−B) = −(A \cdot B) = (−A) \cdot B$.

On Your Own

13. No **14a.** 0 **b.** 0 **c.** 0 **d.** 0 The Zero Product Property, that if a product is zero then at least one of the factors is zero, does not hold for dot products. **18a.** (−1, −2) **b.** (−x, −y) **c.** (−1, −2, 3, −π)

Lesson H.09

Check Your Understanding

1a. $\begin{pmatrix} a & b \\ c & d \end{pmatrix}$ **b.** $\begin{pmatrix} a & b \\ c & d \end{pmatrix}$ **c.** $\begin{pmatrix} 2a & −3b \\ 2c & −3d \end{pmatrix}$

d. $\begin{pmatrix} 2a & 2b \\ −3b & −3d \end{pmatrix}$

2a.

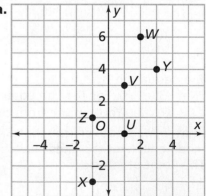

b. $AU = \begin{pmatrix} 1 \\ 0 \end{pmatrix}$, $AV = \begin{pmatrix} 1 \\ −3 \end{pmatrix}$, $AW = \begin{pmatrix} 2 \\ −6 \end{pmatrix}$,

$AX = \begin{pmatrix} −1 \\ 3 \end{pmatrix}$, $AY = \begin{pmatrix} 3 \\ −4 \end{pmatrix}$, $AZ = \begin{pmatrix} −1 \\ −1 \end{pmatrix}$

c.

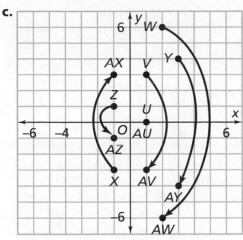

Corresponding points are reflections of each other over the *x*-axis.

d. $BU = \begin{pmatrix} 0 \\ 1 \end{pmatrix}$, $BV = \begin{pmatrix} -3 \\ 1 \end{pmatrix}$, $BW = \begin{pmatrix} -6 \\ 2 \end{pmatrix}$,

$BX = \begin{pmatrix} 3 \\ -1 \end{pmatrix}$, $BY = \begin{pmatrix} -4 \\ 3 \end{pmatrix}$, $BZ = \begin{pmatrix} -1 \\ -1 \end{pmatrix}$

Each point in part (d) is a rotation of the original point by 90° counterclockwise.

3a. $\begin{pmatrix} 2 \\ 5 \\ 3 \end{pmatrix}$ **b.** $\begin{pmatrix} 6 \\ 15 \\ 9 \end{pmatrix}$ **c.** $(5 \quad 3 \quad 1)$ **d.** $(-4 \quad -1 \quad 2)$

e. $\begin{pmatrix} 0 & 0 \\ 0 & 0 \\ 0 & 0 \end{pmatrix}$ **f.** $\begin{pmatrix} 0 & 0 \\ 0 & 0 \\ 0 & 0 \end{pmatrix}$ **4a.** $p = x - y$,

$q = 3x - 2y$ **b.** $2a + b = 3$, $4a + 3b = 5$, $6b = 7$

5a. $\begin{pmatrix} x \\ y \\ z \end{pmatrix} = \begin{pmatrix} 2 & -3 & 4 \\ -1 & 2 & \pi \\ 7 & -4 & -2 \end{pmatrix} \begin{pmatrix} u \\ v \\ w \end{pmatrix}$

b. $\begin{pmatrix} p \\ q \end{pmatrix} = \begin{pmatrix} 2 & 3 & -4 \\ 1 & -3 & 0 \end{pmatrix} \begin{pmatrix} x \\ y \\ z \end{pmatrix}$ **c.** $\begin{pmatrix} y_1 \\ y_2 \\ y_3 \end{pmatrix} = x \begin{pmatrix} 3 \\ -1 \\ 4 \end{pmatrix}$

6a. possible **b.** not possible **c.** possible **d.** not possible **e.** possible **f.** not possible **g.** possible **h.** not possible **7.** Answers may vary.
8a. Matrix *B* must have 3 rows. **b.** Matrix *B* must have 2 columns. **c.** Matrix *B* must have 3 rows and 2 columns. **9.** any square matrix
10. any square matrix
11. $z_1 = 8x_1 + x_2$, $z_2 = -6x_1 - 7x_2$
12. To add down the columns, you can multiply on the left by a 1×3 matrix of 1's. To add across columns, you can multiply on the right by a 5×1 matrix of 1's.

13a. $\begin{pmatrix} 5 & 10 \\ 1 & 1 \end{pmatrix} \begin{pmatrix} 200 & 150 & 50 \\ 100 & 100 & 85 \end{pmatrix} =$
$\begin{pmatrix} 2000 & 1750 & 1100 \\ 300 & 250 & 135 \end{pmatrix}$

b. $\begin{pmatrix} 2000 & 1750 & 1100 \\ 300 & 250 & 135 \end{pmatrix} \begin{pmatrix} 1 \\ 1 \\ 1 \end{pmatrix} = \begin{pmatrix} 3850 \\ 685 \end{pmatrix}$

14. $BA = \begin{pmatrix} 2 & 1 & 3 \\ 3 & 4 & 2 \\ 2 & 2 & 1 \end{pmatrix} \begin{pmatrix} 0.3 & 0.5 \\ 0.3 & 0.2 \\ 0.3 & 0.3 \end{pmatrix} = \begin{pmatrix} 1.8 & 2.1 \\ 2.7 & 2.9 \\ 1.5 & 1.7 \end{pmatrix}$

On Your Own

15. $\begin{pmatrix} a & b & c \\ d & e & f \\ g & h & i \end{pmatrix}, \begin{pmatrix} a & b & c \\ d & e & f \\ g & h & i \end{pmatrix}$

19a. $AB + AC = \begin{pmatrix} 0 \\ 2 \end{pmatrix} + \begin{pmatrix} 11 \\ 25 \end{pmatrix} = \begin{pmatrix} 11 \\ 27 \end{pmatrix}$

b. $A(B + C) = \begin{pmatrix} 1 & 2 \\ 3 & 4 \end{pmatrix} \begin{pmatrix} 5 \\ 3 \end{pmatrix} = \begin{pmatrix} 11 \\ 27 \end{pmatrix}$

21a. $\begin{pmatrix} -3 & -26 \\ -7 & -58 \end{pmatrix}$ **b.** $\begin{pmatrix} -3 & -26 \\ -7 & -58 \end{pmatrix}$

25a. 74.5 g protein, 50.2 g fat, 128.4 g carbohydrates **b.** The problem (and solution) can be written as
$\begin{pmatrix} 5.5 & 0.5 & 3 \\ 5.5 & 0.03 & 0.02 \\ 0.1 & 6 & 1.5 \end{pmatrix} \begin{pmatrix} 9 \\ 20 \\ 5 \end{pmatrix} = \begin{pmatrix} 74.5 \\ 50.2 \\ 128.4 \end{pmatrix}$.

Lesson H.10
Check Your Understanding

1. $\begin{pmatrix} x \\ y \\ z \end{pmatrix} = \begin{pmatrix} 1 \\ -1 \\ 2 \end{pmatrix}$

2. $\begin{pmatrix} a \\ b \\ c \\ d \end{pmatrix} = \begin{pmatrix} 0 \\ \frac{1}{2} \\ \frac{1}{2} \\ 0 \end{pmatrix}$

3a. The two lines $x + 2y = 1$ and $2x + 4y = 1$ are parallel, so the system has no solution.

b. Gaussian Elimination results in $\left(\begin{array}{cc|c} 1 & 2 & 1 \\ 0 & 0 & -1 \end{array} \right)$,
and the second row indicates that the system has no solution. **c.** The inverse does not exist $(ad - bc = 0)$. **4.** Answers may vary. Sample: To solve $AX = B$, find A^{-1} and write $A^{-1}AX = A^{-1}B$ or $X = A^{-1}B$.

5. $MA = \begin{pmatrix} 1 & 0 & 0 \\ 0 & 0 & 1 \end{pmatrix} \begin{pmatrix} 1 & 0 \\ 3 & 4 \\ 0 & 1 \end{pmatrix} = \begin{pmatrix} 1 & 0 \\ 0 & 1 \end{pmatrix}$ and

$AM = \begin{pmatrix} 1 & 0 \\ 3 & 4 \\ 0 & 1 \end{pmatrix} \begin{pmatrix} 1 & 0 & 0 \\ 0 & 0 & 1 \end{pmatrix} = \begin{pmatrix} 1 & 0 \\ 3 & 4 \\ 0 & 1 \end{pmatrix}$, so

$MA \neq AM$.

6. $AM = \begin{pmatrix} 1 & 2 \\ 3 & 4 \end{pmatrix} \begin{pmatrix} -2 & 1 \\ \frac{3}{2} & -\frac{1}{2} \end{pmatrix} =$

$\begin{pmatrix} -2+3 & 1-1 \\ -6+6 & 3-2 \end{pmatrix} = \begin{pmatrix} 1 & 0 \\ 0 & 1 \end{pmatrix} = I$

7. No, zero is a real number but it does not have an inverse.

8. No; for example, $\begin{pmatrix} 3 & -1 \\ -2 & 2 \end{pmatrix} \begin{pmatrix} 1 \\ 1 \end{pmatrix} = \begin{pmatrix} 2 \\ 0 \end{pmatrix}$ and $\begin{pmatrix} 1 \\ 1 \end{pmatrix} \neq \begin{pmatrix} 2 \\ 0 \end{pmatrix}$.

On Your Own

10. Using $M = \begin{pmatrix} 5.5 & 0.5 & 3 \\ 5.5 & 0.03 & 0.02 \\ 0.1 & 6 & 1.5 \end{pmatrix}$, the system is

$M \begin{pmatrix} m \\ p \\ c \end{pmatrix} = \begin{pmatrix} 45 \\ 35 \\ 120 \end{pmatrix}$. Then $\begin{pmatrix} m \\ p \\ c \end{pmatrix} = M^{-1} \begin{pmatrix} 45 \\ 35 \\ 120 \end{pmatrix}$

$\approx \begin{pmatrix} 6.3 \\ 19.8 \\ 0.2 \end{pmatrix}$. 6.3 oz meat, 19.8 oz potatoes,

0.2 oz cabbage

11. If $\begin{pmatrix} a & b \\ c & d \end{pmatrix} \begin{pmatrix} x \\ y \end{pmatrix} = \begin{pmatrix} x \\ y \end{pmatrix}$, then $ax + by = x$

and $cx + dy = y$. The only values of a, b, c, and d that satisfy both equations simultaneously are

$a = 1$, $b = 0$, $c = 0$, and $d = 1$ or $\begin{pmatrix} 1 & 0 \\ 0 & 1 \end{pmatrix}$.

12. $\begin{pmatrix} x & y \\ z & w \end{pmatrix} = \begin{pmatrix} -2 & 1 \\ \frac{3}{2} & -\frac{1}{2} \end{pmatrix}$

Lesson H.11
Check Your Understanding

1a. $I = \begin{pmatrix} 1 & 0 \\ 0 & 1 \end{pmatrix}$ **b.** $I = \begin{pmatrix} 1 & 0 & 0 \\ 0 & 1 & 0 \\ 0 & 0 & 1 \end{pmatrix}$

2. If $A = B$, then by substitution $AB = AA = BA$, so square matrices commute with themselves under multiplication. Also, $AA^2 = AAA = A^2A$ because matrix multiplication is associative.
3. Answers may vary. Sample: Matrix multiplication is not always commutative, so

$A(B + C) \neq (B + C)A$. Therefore we need a distributive property for $A(B + C)$ and another distributive property for $(B + C)A$.

4a. $B = \begin{pmatrix} -2c \\ c \end{pmatrix}$ for any value of c.

b. $B = \begin{pmatrix} -2c & -2d \\ c & d \end{pmatrix}$ for any values of c and d.
5. Line 1: OK, by the definition of squaring; Line 2: OK; distribute the second factor $(X + Y)$ over the two terms of the first factor; Line 3: OK; distributive property; Line 4: OK, by the definition of squaring; Line 5: wrong because $XY \neq YX$. The last line should be $X^2 + XY + YX + Y^2$. **6.** yes **7.** Since A^{-1} exists and $AB = AC$, $A^{-1}(AB) = A^{-1}(AC)$. Then $(A^{-1}A)B = (A^{-1}A)C$ or $B = C$. **8.** Answers may vary. Sample: When you multiply a square matrix M by its appropriate identity matrix, there is only one element in each row of M that results in a nonzero term, and that is the same whether the identity is to the left or to the right of M.

On Your Own

9. Answers may vary. Sample: $A + A = 1A + 1A = (1 + 1)A = 2A$ **10.** Answers may vary. Sample: From Exercise 5, $(X + Y)^2 = X^2 + XY + YX + Y^2$. Substituting I for Y gives us $(X + I)^2 = X^2 + XI + IX + I^2 = X^2 + 2X + I$. **13a.** For a zero matrix Z and another matrix B, $ZB = Z$. Since $ZB \neq I$ for any B, matrix Z cannot have an inverse.

Lesson H.12
On Your Own
9b.

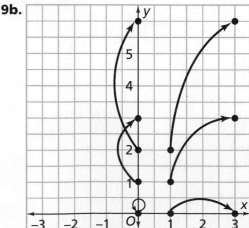

c. The mapping dilates line and polygons by a factor of 3, with the origin as the centre of the dilation.

11a. The images are $\begin{pmatrix} -2 \\ -1 \end{pmatrix}$, $\begin{pmatrix} 1 \\ 2 \end{pmatrix}$, $\begin{pmatrix} 0 \\ 0 \end{pmatrix}$, and $\begin{pmatrix} -x \\ -y \end{pmatrix}$, respectively. **b.** $M = \begin{pmatrix} -1 & 0 \\ 0 & -1 \end{pmatrix}$

Lesson H.13
Check Your Understanding

1a. $(x, y) \mapsto (-x, y)$, which is a reflection over the y-axis. **b.** $(x, y) \mapsto (y, x)$, which is a reflection over the line $y = x$.

2. $A^{-1} = \begin{pmatrix} \frac{1}{2} & 0 \\ 0 & \frac{1}{2} \end{pmatrix}$; $A^{-1}\begin{pmatrix} x \\ y \end{pmatrix} = \begin{pmatrix} \frac{1}{2} & 0 \\ 0 & \frac{1}{2} \end{pmatrix}$

$\begin{pmatrix} x \\ y \end{pmatrix} = \begin{pmatrix} \frac{1}{2}x \\ \frac{1}{2}y \end{pmatrix}$

3. $A^2 = \begin{pmatrix} 4 & 0 \\ 0 & 4 \end{pmatrix}$, so $A^2\begin{pmatrix} x \\ y \end{pmatrix} = \begin{pmatrix} 4x \\ 4y \end{pmatrix}$;

$A^{-2} = \begin{pmatrix} \frac{1}{4} & 0 \\ 0 & \frac{1}{4} \end{pmatrix}$, so $A^{-2}\begin{pmatrix} x \\ y \end{pmatrix} = \begin{pmatrix} \frac{1}{4}x \\ \frac{1}{4}y \end{pmatrix}$.

4. $M\begin{pmatrix} a \\ b \end{pmatrix} = \begin{pmatrix} c & -d \\ d & c \end{pmatrix}\begin{pmatrix} a \\ b \end{pmatrix} = \begin{pmatrix} ac - bd \\ ad + bc \end{pmatrix}$, or M maps the point $a + bi$ to $ac - bd + (ad + bc)i = (a + bi)(c + di)$. **5.** The result of the matrix is to reflect each point over the line $y = \frac{1}{2}x$.

6. The mapping $X \mapsto M^{-1}X$ reflects a preimage over the line $y = \frac{1}{2}x$; $M^{-1} = \begin{pmatrix} \frac{3}{5} & \frac{4}{5} \\ \frac{4}{5} & -\frac{3}{5} \end{pmatrix}$ so

$M^{-1} = M$. **7a.** If a point is on the line $y = -2x$, then its image is also on that line. **b.** $90°$
c. $(2t)s + t(-2s) = 0$ **8.** A reflection scales by 1 in the direction of the line of reflection (points on this line are not moved) and scales by -1 in the perpendicular direction identified in exercise 7. **9a.** $180°$ (counterclockwise) rotation
b. $R^2 = \begin{pmatrix} -1 & 0 \\ 0 & -1 \end{pmatrix}$, so $R^2\begin{pmatrix} x \\ y \end{pmatrix} = \begin{pmatrix} -x \\ -y \end{pmatrix}$.

c. $270°$ counterclockwise rotation

d. $R^3 = \begin{pmatrix} 0 & 1 \\ -1 & 0 \end{pmatrix}$, so $R^3\begin{pmatrix} x \\ y \end{pmatrix} = \begin{pmatrix} y \\ -x \end{pmatrix}$.

e. $R^4 = \begin{pmatrix} 1 & 0 \\ 0 & 1 \end{pmatrix}$, which is the same as a (clockwise) rotation of $360°$ **10a.** $x + y = kx$, $2x = ky$; $(1 - k)x + y = 0$, $2x - ky = 0$
b. $k = 2$, $k = -1$ **c.** If $k = 2$, the equations are $-x + y = 0$ and $2x - 2y = 0$; the solution to that system is any point on the line $y = x$. If $k = -1$, the equations are $2x + y = 0$ and $2x + y = 0$; the solution to that system is any point on the line $y = -2x$. **11.** Answers may vary. Sample: Using the technique from Exercise 10 results in the proportion $\frac{-2.7 - k}{-1.4} = \frac{2.1}{2.2 - k}$; solving that proportion gives $k = -2$ or $k = \frac{3}{2}$. The value $k = -2$ results in a system of equations with a solution of all points on the line $y = \frac{1}{2}x$. The value $k = \frac{3}{2}$ results in a system of equations with a solution of all points on the line $y = 3x$.

12. $M = \begin{pmatrix} 0 & -1 \\ -1 & 0 \end{pmatrix}$ **13.** $M = \begin{pmatrix} \frac{\sqrt{2}}{2} & -\frac{\sqrt{2}}{2} \\ \frac{\sqrt{2}}{2} & \frac{\sqrt{2}}{2} \end{pmatrix}$

14. Answers may vary.
On Your Own

15. $X \mapsto A^{-1}X$ dilates the plane by a factor of $\frac{1}{3}$ horizontally and by a factor of $\frac{1}{2}$ vertically;

$A^{-1} = \begin{pmatrix} \frac{1}{3} & 0 \\ 0 & \frac{1}{2} \end{pmatrix}$. **16.** Answers may vary.

Sample: Using the general point $\begin{pmatrix} x \\ y \end{pmatrix}$,

$\begin{pmatrix} 0 & -1 \\ 1 & 0 \end{pmatrix}\begin{pmatrix} x \\ y \end{pmatrix} = \begin{pmatrix} -y \\ x \end{pmatrix}$, and the distance from the origin to $\begin{pmatrix} x \\ y \end{pmatrix}$ or to $\begin{pmatrix} -y \\ x \end{pmatrix}$ is $\sqrt{x^2 + y^2}$.

19a. $(-12, -6)$ **b.** $(-2.5, 2.5)$
24a. The images are $(0, -1)$, $(-1, 0)$, $(-1, -1)$, $(-1, 1)$, $(-y, -x)$. **b.** $\begin{pmatrix} 0 & -1 \\ -1 & 0 \end{pmatrix}$

Index

Index

coordinate plane, 190, 196, 198, 201, 207, 215, 217, 233, 342, 352, 357, 388, 393, 540, 607, 704
  geometry in, 658–79
coordinates, 187, 698
  corresponding, 688
  of intersection points, 323
  x-coordinate, 208, 249, 338, 526
  y-coordinate, 208, 249, 338, 526, 623
corollary, 694, 695
correlation, 505
correlation coefficient, 514
corresponding coordinates, 688
corresponding parts, 611–13
cubes, 221, 361, 378, 399
cubic growth, 235
cutoff points, 332, 334, 531

D

data
  categorical, 503–10
  center of, 488
  displays, 488–94
  fitting and, 522–51
  fitting lines to, 536–42
  linear trends in, 528–35
  points, 357, 544
  probability and, 505–6
  statistical, 476–521
  tables, 719–20
  two-variable, 511–19
decimal expansion, 41
decimal representation, 42
decimals
  breaking into place-value parts, 62
  conversion to fractions, 43
  notation, 421
  on number line, 41–45
  repeating, 43
denominator, 38
  least common, 68, 69
determinant, 758
Developing Habits of Mind, 20, 29–30, 38, 42, 47, 52, 72, 77, 105, 122, 153–54, 173, 197, 202, 216, 226, 230, 236, 248, 255–56, 304, 326, 332, 350, 367, 379, 432, 441, 463, 481–82, 483–84, 495, 505–6, 514, 531, 538, 594, 632, 670, 695, 724, 725–26, 741, 743, 761, 765, 766, 776
diagonal matrix, 769
diagrams, 212, 409, 410

diameter, 570
direction, 692
direct variation, 225–30
  defined, 225
  lightning and, 232
  representing, 226
displays, data, 488–94
  box-and-whisker plots, 495–502, 519
  dot plot, 488, 492, 493
  histograms, 489, 491, 492, 493
  scatter plot, 511, 516, 518, 529, 543
  stem-and-leaf display, 490, 491
distance formulas, 662–68
distance-time graphs, 244, 254, 258, 356
  slope and, 289–93
distinct lines, 308
distribution, conditional, 505
distributive property, 30, 52, 53, 54, 72, 104, 105, 111, 112, 153–54, 180, 735, 761, 764
division
  of fractions, 77–78
  ladder, 82
  line, 74
  long, 82–83
  using subtraction, 82–83
  traditional, 82
domain, 383, 384, 386
dominoes, 610
dot plot, 488, 492, 493
dot products, 731–38
drag point, 594
drawings
  arrows, 631
  constructions *versus,* 589–91
  picturing and, 558–73
  from recipes, 569–72
  shapes, 566–68
  3-D objects, 562–65
  UnMessUpable figures, 592–96

E

Eigenvalue, 779
Eigenvector, 779
elapsed time, 498, 511–13
elimination method
  Gaussian, 757
  solving systems with, 313–18
ellipse, 217
empty set, 127
endpoints, 626, 627, 636, 667
equality
  additive property of, 313
  on number line, 138

equations, 116–32
  backtracking to solve, 117, 118, 121, 122, 126–28, 128–29, 137
  basic moves for solving, 143–45
  building, 162–63
  Cartesian, 715
  defined, 126
  equivalent, 284
  false, 322, 334
  graph of, defined, 196
  graphs and, 186–219
  guess-check-generalize method, 162, 167, 168
  identical, 310
  intersecting, 310
  linear, 134–57, 274–318
  of lines, 279–81
  matrix, 744, 758, 760
  with more than one variable, 172–73
  parallel, 310
  parametric, 712
  parentheses in, 302
  point-slope, 700
  as point-testers, 195–97, 199, 236, 264, 277, 279, 311, 351
  reversing operations in, 120–22
  solutions of, 126
  substitution, 300–304
  systems of, 300–304
  true, 322, 334
equidistant, 579
equilateral triangles, 570, 581
equivalent equations, 284
equivalent fractions, 37, 67
equivalent vectors, 692, 693
errors
  mean absolute, 545, 553, 554
  mean squared, 545, 553, 554
  standard, 545, 554
evaluation, of expressions, 98–99
expansion box, 72, 75, 76, 85, 155
exponential decay, 462
exponential functions, 447
  graphs of, 462–66
exponential growth, 462
exponents, 398–425
  basic rules of, 408–10
  negative, 413–15
  rules of, 402–3
  scientific notation, 419–23
  zero, 413–15

Index

inputs, 431
   nonnegative, 226, 445
   on number line, 37
intercepts
   x-intercept, 284
   y-intercept, 284
interest
   compound, 456–61
   earning, 468
interquartile range (IQR), 497
intersection, 296, 349, 350
   of graphs, 215–18, 244
   points, 215, 270, 300, 302–3,
      304, 306, 307, 308–9, 323,
      331, 580
intervals, testing, 333
**invariance under translation
   theorem,** 546
inverses
   additive, 30, 111, 764
   defined, 757
   matrix, 755–60
   multiplicative, 111, 755, 764
inverse variation, 225–30
   defined, 227
   representing, 230
isometry, 653–54
   congruence and, 648–55
   defined, 648
isosceles triangles, 581

J

jiffy graphs, 284–85

K

Kelvin, 132
kites, 618

L

ladder division, 82
Law of Exponents, 402
least common denominator,
   68, 69
length, congruence and,
   607–10
like terms, 104
   combining, 104
linear combinations, 739
linear equations
   CAT scans and, 759
   defined, 149
   failure of backtracking in,
      138–39
   graphs and, 274–318
   pair of, 299
   solutions of, 148–49
   solving, 134–57
linear functions, 436, 437, 452
   defined, 427

linear inequalities
   graphing, 345–50
   solution of, 347
linear regression, 532
linear trends, in data, 528–35
line of best fit, 531, 543–49
lines, 273–359
   applications of, 320–55
   distinct, 308
   division, 74
   equations of, 279–81
   fitting, 528
   fitting data to, 536–42
   horizontal, 262, 281, 316
   jiffy graphs, 284–85
   multiplication, 74
   parallel, 281, 308–10, 562,
      601, 669–73
   perpendicular, 674–78
   of reflection, 623
   of symmetry, 558, 561, 598,
      600, 628, 642, 680
   vector equation of, 700–704,
      705–8
   vertical, 389, 660
line segments, 35, 562, 569,
   582, 607
long division, 82–83
lowest terms, 38

M

magnitude, 230
matching corner, 194
matrix
   conformable, 747
   diagonal, 769
   equations, 744, 758, 760
   identity, 723, 756
   inverses, 755–60
   nonzero, 769
   notation, 761
   operations, 724–30
   operations on calculators,
      744
   properties, 761–69
   scalar multiplication, 725
   transformation, 775
   zero, 745
matrix algebra, 718–53
   dot products, 731–38
   operations, 724–30
matrix multiplication, 739–52
   applications of, 754–87
maximum value, 495, 517
mean, 421, 481, 484, 487, 499,
   519, 548, 698
mean absolute error, 545, 553,
   554
mean squared error, 545, 553,
   554

**measurement, congruence
   and,** 607–10
median, 421, 481, 483–84, 487,
   490, 491, 494, 495, 499,
   500, 501, 549, 704
   of triangles, 581
midline, of triangles, 581
midpoints, 484, 579, 591, 609,
   659, 660, 708
   formulas for, 662–68
minimum value, 495, 517
mode, 481, 499, 549
money, managing, 468–69
moving steadily graph, 255
multiplication
   algorithms, 71–72
   associative property of, 111
   commutative property of,
      28, 52, 111
   of fractions, 77–78
   line, 74
   matrix, 739–52
   number line, 51–55
   of positive numbers, 51
   scalar, 725
   visualizing, 52
multiplication table, 9, 84, 87,
   417
   extending, 23–24
multiplicative identity, 30,
   111, 764
multiplicative inverse, 111,
   755, 764

N

negative exponents, 413–15
   defined, 415
negatively associated, 513
negative numbers, 12–13, 240,
   463
   addition of, 17, 33
   bookkeeping and, 12, 14
nonnegative integers, 226, 445
notation, 174, 330, 378
   angle, 588
   decimal, 421
   matrix, 761
   scientific, 419–20
   standard, 580
n-tupelo, 731, 732, 736
null set, 127
number line, 12, 34–57, 334
   addition, 46–50
   decimals on, 41–45
   equality on, 138
   fractions on, 37–38
   horizontal, 39
   inequalities on, 330
   integers on, 37
   labeling, 57

Index

Index

Index

Acknowledgments

Staff Credits

The Pearson people on the CME Project team—representing design, editorial, editorial services, digital product development, publishing services, and technical operations—are listed below. Bold type denotes the core team members.

Ernest Albanese, Scott Andrews, Carolyn Artin, Michael Avidon, Margaret Banker, Suzanne Biron, Beth Blumberg, Stacie Cartwright, Carolyn Chappo, Casey Clark, Bob Craton, Jason Cuoco, Sheila DeFazio, Patty Fagan, **Frederick Fellows**, **Patti Fromkin**, Paul J. Gagnon, Cynthia Harvey, Gillian Kahn, Jonathan Kier, Jennifer King, Elizabeth Krieble, Sara Levendusky, Lisa Lin, Carolyn Lock, Clay Martin, **Carolyn McGuire**, Rich McMahon, Eve Melnechuk, Cynthia Metallides, **Hope Morley**, Jen Paley, Linda Punskovsky, Mairead Reddin, Marcy Rose, Rashid Ross, Carol Roy, Jewel Simmons, Ted Smykal, Laura Smyth, Kara Stokes, Richard Sullivan, Tiffany Taylor-Sullivan, Catherine Terwilliger, Mark Tricca, Lauren Van Wart, Paula Vergith, **Joe Will**, **Kristin Winters**, Allison Wyss

Additional Credits

Niki Birbilis, Gina Choe, Cynthia Metallides, Christine Nevola, Jill A. Ort, Lillian Pelaggi, Deborah Savona

Cover Design 9 Surf Studios

Cover Photography Mike Chew/Corbis; Ajosch/AFP/Getty Images

Illustration Kerry Cashman, Rich McMahon, Jen Paley, Rashid Ross, Deborah Savona, Ted Smykal

Photography

Chapter 1: Pages 2–3, Randy Faris/Corbis; 8, Jason Hawkes/Corbis; 12, Thom Lang/Corbis; 25, Kyodo News; 29, Javier Pierini/Digital Vision/GettyImages; 33, Atlanpic/Alamy; 34, Clement McCarthy/Alamy; 39, Robert Estall photo agency/Alamy; 56 Inset, Rubberball/Royalty Free; 56 BR, Clement McCarthy/Alamy; 71 BR, Pablo San Juan/Corbis; 71 inset, Mike McQueen/Corbis; 74, AP Photo/Charlie Riedel; 83, AP Photo/Austin Daily Herald, Eric Johnson.

Chapter 2: Pages 88–89, Darrin Zammit Lupi /Reuters/Corbis; 90l, JUPITERIMAGE/Brand X/Alamy; 90r, JUPITERIMAGE/Brand X/Alamy; 98, Larry Williams/Corbis; 101, Beth Perkins/Getty Images; 108, Robert Fried Photography; 115, Ariel Skelley/Corbis; 116, Anthony West/Corbis; 124, Handout/Reuters/Corbis; 129, Design Pics Inc./Alamy; 131, Mary Evans Picture Library/Alamy; 132, Stefan Schuetz/zefa/Corbis; 134, Bob Elsdale/Getty Images; 136, William Manning/Corbis; 155, Paul A. Souders/Corbis; 157, Bob Elsdale/Getty Images; 158, Jim McIsaac/Getty Images; 160, David Young-Wolff/Photo Edit; 170, John Eder/Getty Images; 172, Gene Blevins/LA Daily News/Corbis; 178, VALDRIN XHEMAJ/epa/Corbis.

Chapter 3: Pages 184–185, Lester Lefkowitz/Getty Images; 186, Ausloeser/zefa/Corbis; 189, Kelly-Mooney Photography/Corbis; 198, Bibliothèque Nationale, Paris, France, Lauros / Giraudon / The Bridgeman Art Library; 199, Sam Jordash/Getty Images; 204, Ken Welsh/Alamy; 206, Joseph Sohm/Visions of America/Corbis; 210, Mark Harmel/Getty Images; 215, TIMLI/Photonica/Getty Images, Inc.; 217, Victor Habbick Visions/Photo Researchers, Inc.; 219, Varie/Alt/Corbis; 220, James L. Amos/Corbis; 223, PhotoAlto/SuperStock; 230, Hulton Archive/Getty Images; 232, Ralph H. Wetmore II/Getty Images, Inc.; 234, Jim West/Alamy; 239, Jeff Greenberg/Photo Edit; 241, James L. Amos/Corbis; 242, David R. Frazier Photolibrary, Inc./Alamy; 243tl, Dennis Hallinan/Alamy; 243tr, JG Photography/Alamy; 243bl, Wes Thompson/Corbis; 243br, Reino Hanninen/Alamy; 250, Craig Lovell/Corbis; 260, Michael Steele/Getty Images; 266, Kara Stokes; 267, David R. Frazier Photolibrary, Inc./Alamy.

Chapter 4: Pages 272–273, Team Russell/ImageState/International Stock Photography Ltd.; 272–273 background, Craig Tuttle/Corbis; 274, Kay Nietfeld/epa/Corbis; 276, Jeff Greenberg/Photo Edit 295, John Kelly/Getty Images; 296, Brian Bahr/Getty Images, Inc.; 305, Grant Faint/The Image Bank/Getty Images, Inc.; 308, tom viggars/Alamy; 317, Simon Marcus/Corbis; 319, AP Photo/Sue Ogrocki; 320, Gunter Marx Photography/Corbis; 355, Gunter Marx Photography/Corbis.

Chapter 5: Pages 360–361, Juergen Berger/Science Photo Library; 362, Digital Vision Ltd; 371, Ingram Publishing/Alamy; 397, Digital Vision Ltd; 398, Dr. Dennis Kunkel/Visuals Unlimited/Getty Images; 407, Roger Bamber/Alamy; 412, Rudy Sulgan/Corbis; 419, Planetary Photojournal; 422 tr, Editorial/Getty Images; 422 inset, AP Images/NASA; 424, Peter Weber/Getty Images; 426, Kara Stokes; 428tr, Getty Images, Inc.; 428bl, Joe McDonald/Corbis; 437, Buzz Pictures/Alamy; 460, Car Culture/Corbis; 467, Kara Stokes.

Chapter 6: Pages 474–475, Corbis/Don Mason/RM; 476–477, Edgar Mueller; 486, Paul Wood/Alamy; 498, Matthias Kulka/zefa/Corbis; 501, Elsa/Getty Images; 520, Edgar Mueller; 527, Super Stock; 528, Ted Horowitz/Corbis; 532, AP Photo/Glodow Nead Communications, George Nikitin; 541, Carolyn Chappo; 549, Jupiter Images/Manfred Kage.

Chapter 7: Pages 556–557, Randy Faris/Corbis; 558, Jason Hawkes/Corbis; 571, Thom Lang/Corbis; 573, Kyodo News; 574, Javier Pierini/Digital Vision/Getty Images, Inc.; 585, Atlanpic/Alamy.

Chapter 8: Pages 602–603, David Parmenter/www.daveparm.com; 604, Chris Daniels/Corbis; 606, Lew Robertson/Corbis; 611, Roger Ressmeyer/Corbis; 619, Chris Daniels/Corbis; 620, image100/Alamy; 624, image100/Alamy; 629, Craig Tuttle/Corbis; 657, image100/Alamy; 658, Heather Wright; 665, Adam Woolfitt/Corbis; 673, Joel Day/Alamy; 678, Bob Krist/Corbis; 679, Frank Krahmer/zefa/Corbis.

Honors Appendix: Pages 684–685, Peter Arnold/Jochen Tack; 686, Redmond Durrell/Alamy; 695, Comstock/Corbis; 716, Frank Krahmer/Getty Images; 717, Frank Krahmer/zefa/Corbis; 718, Alamy/RubberBall; 746, Corbis/George Shelley; 754, istockphoto.com/Sharon Shimoni; 759 both, AP Images/Dave Bowman; 766, Getty Images/Christian Lagereek.

Grateful acknowledgment is made to the following for copyrighted material: 6, "Dodge Ball" excerpted from The Heart of Mathematics, 2nd Edition by Edward Burger and Michael Starbird. Copyright © 2005 by Key College Publishing, Emeryville, California. Used by permission; 454, "United Nations Population Estimates" from www.un.org. Copyright © 2000–2007 by The United Nations; 522, 536, 550, "Gold Medal Times (in seconds) from the Men's 1500-Meter Run" from Sports Illustrated 2007 Almanac. Copyright © 2006 Time Inc. Home Entertainment.

Note: Every effort has been made to locate the copyright owner of the material reprinted in this book. Omissions brought to our attention will be corrected in subsequent editions.

Additional Credits

Chapter 1: Whole chapter taken from Chapter 1 of *CME Project: Algebra 1*.

Chapter 2: Whole chapter taken from Chapter 2 of *CME Project: Algebra 1*.

Chapter 3: Investigations 3A, 3B, and 3C taken from *CME Project: Algebra 1* Investigations 3B, 3D, and 4A, respectively.

Chapter 4: Investigations 4A and 4B taken from *CME Project: Algebra 1* Investigations 4B. and 4C, respectively. Lessons 4.9, 4.10, 4.11, and 4.12 taken from *CME Project: Algebra 1* Lessons 4.13, 8.10, 4.14, and 8.11, respectively. Lesson 4.13 taken from *CME Project: Algebra 1* Common Core Additional Lessons.

Chapter 5: Investigations 5A and 5B taken from *CME Project: Algebra 1* Investigations 5A and 6A, respectively. Lessons 5.12, 5.13, and 5.14 taken from *CME Project: Algebra 1* Lessons 5.7, 5.8, and 5.9, respec-

tively. Lessons 5.15, 5.16, and 5.17 taken from *CME Project: Algebra 1* Lessons 6.15, 6.13, and 6.14, respectively.

Chapter 6: Lessons 6.1, 6.2, 6.4, and 6.8 taken from *CME Project: Algebra 1* Lessons 3.5, 3.6, 3.8, and 4.15, respectively. Lessons 6.3, 6.5, and 6.6 taken from *CME Project: Algebra 1 Common Core Additional Lessons*. Lessons 6.7, 6.9, and 6.10 taken from *CME Project: Algebra 2* Lessons 1.6, 1.7, and 1.8, respectively.

Chapter 7: Whole chapter taken from *CME Project: Geometry* Investigations 1A, 1B, and 1C.

Chapter 8: Investigations 8A and 8C taken from *CME Project: Geometry* Investigations 2A and 7B, respectively. Lessons 8.5, 8.6, and 8.7 taken from *CME Project: Geometry* Lessons 7.1, 7.2, and 7.3, respectively. Lessons 8.8 and 8.9 taken from *CME Project: Geometry Common Core Additional Lessons*.

Honors Appendix: Lessons H.01, H.02, H.03, and H.04 taken from *CME Project: Geometry* Lessons 7.10, 7.11, 7.12, 7.13, respectively. Lesson H.05 taken from *CME Project: Precalculus* Lesson 6.12. Investigations B and C taken from *CME Project Algebra 1* Investigations 4B and 4C, respectively.